INTREPID AVIATORS

★ ★ ★ ★ ★

THE AMERICAN FLYERS WHO SANK

JAPAN'S GREATEST BATTLESHIP

GREGORY G. FLETCHER

NAL
CALIBER

NAL CALIBER
Published by the Penguin Group
Penguin Group (USA) Inc., 375 Hudson Street,
New York, New York 10014, USA

USA | Canada | UK | Ireland | Australia | New Zealand | India | South Africa | China
Penguin Books Ltd., Registered Offices: 80 Strand, London WC2R 0RL, England
For more information about the Penguin Group visit penguin.com.

Published by NAL Caliber, a division of Penguin Group (USA) Inc. Previously published in an NAL
Caliber hardcover edition.

First NAL Caliber Trade Paperback Printing, July 2013

NAL Caliber Trade Paperback ISBN: 978-0-451-23991-4

The Library of Congress has catalogued the hardcover edition of this title as follows:
Fletcher, Gregory G.
    Intrepid aviators: the true story of USS Intrepid's Torpedo Squadron 18 and its epic clash with the
superbattleship Musashi/Gregory G. Fletcher.
        p. cm.
    Includes bibliographical references and index.
    ISBN 978-0-451-23696-8
1. United States. Navy. Torpedo Squadron Eighteen.   2. Intrepid Aircraft (carrier)—History.
3. Musashi (Battleship)—History.   4. World War, 1939–1945—Campaigns—Philippines.   5. Leyte
Gulf, Battle of, Philippines, 1944.   6. World War, 1939–1945—Aerial operations, American.
7. World War, 1939–1945—Naval operations, American.   I. Title.   II. Title: True story of USS
Intrepid's Torpedo Squadron 18 and its epic clash with the superbattleship Musashi.
    D790.37818th .F54 2012
    940.54'25995—dc23   2012001025

Printed in the United States of America
10 9 8 7 6 5 4 3 2 1

Set in Adobe Garamond Pro
Designed by Elke Sigal

PUBLISHER'S NOTE
While the author has made every effort to provide accurate telephone numbers, Internet addresses and
other contact information at the time of publication, neither the publisher nor the author assumes any
responsibility for errors, or for changes that occur after publication. Further, publisher does not have any
control over and does not assume any responsibility for author or third-party Web sites or their content.

ALWAYS LEARNING   PEARSON

To my father, who lived it, and his shipmates

★

CONTENTS

Chapter One: In the Philippine Sea 1

Chapter Two: In California 53

Chapter Three: In Hawaii 80

Chapter Four: In Lingga Roads 123

Chapter Five: In the Middle Latitudes 145

Chapter Six: In the Visayas 171

Chapter Seven: Over Luzon 185

Chapter Eight: Over Formosa 207

Chapter Nine: In the Sibuyan Sea 227

Chapter Ten: On Strike 2 Able 238

Chapter Eleven: On Strike 2 Baker 259

Chapter Twelve: On Strike 2 Charlie 265

Chapter Thirteen: Off Banton and Cape Engano 279

Chapter Fourteen: Off Banton and Luzon   303

Chapter Fifteen: On Panay   326

Epilogue   366

Acknowledgments   370

Appendix of Awards   372

Bibliography   377

Source Notes   385

Index   410

MAPS AND LINE DRAWINGS

Plate One: Western Pacific Area   x

Plate Two: Philippine Islands Area and Palaus   149

Plate Three: Air Group 18 Strikes of 24 October Against *Musashi*   281

Plate Four: The Sinking of *Musashi*   282

Plate Five: USAFFE Guerrilla Districts on Panay   330

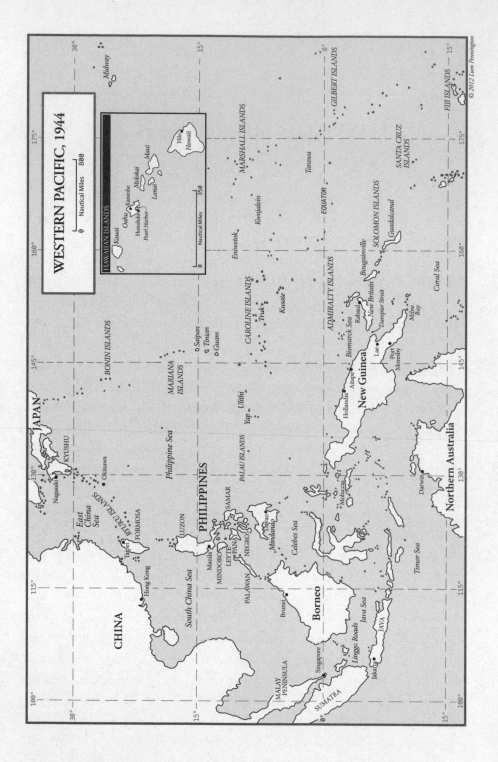

WESTERN PACIFIC, 1944

Nautical Miles
0   800

HAWAIIAN ISLANDS

Kauai
Oahu Kaneohe
Honolulu Molokai
Pearl Harbor Lanai Maui

Hilo
Hawaii

Nautical Miles
0   350

Midway

JAPAN
KYUSHU
Nagasaki
Okinawa
RYUKYU ISLANDS
East China Sea
FORMOSA
Taipei
Hong Kong

CHINA

MARSHALL ISLANDS

GILBERT ISLANDS

FIJI ISLANDS

SANTA CRUZ ISLANDS

BONIN ISLANDS

Tarawa

EQUATOR

SOLOMON ISLANDS

Guadalcanal

MARIANA ISLANDS
Saipan
Tinian
Guam

CAROLINE ISLANDS
Truk
Kusaie

Eniwetok

Kwajalein

ADMIRALITY ISLANDS

Bougainville

New Britain
Rabaul
Dampier Strait

Bismarck Sea

Coral Sea

PHILIPPINES
SAMAR
LUZON
Manila
MINDORO
PANAY
LEYTE
NEGROS
PALAWAN
Cebu
Mindanao
Davao

Ulithi
Yap
PALAU ISLANDS

Philippine Sea

New Guinea
Hollandia
Aitape
Lae
Port Moresby
Milne Bay

Celebes Sea

Moluccas

Timor Sea

Darwin

Northern Australia

South China Sea

Borneo

Brunei

Java Sea

Celebes Sea

MALAY PENINSULA
Singapore

Lingga Roads

JAVA
Jakarta

SUMATRA

30°
175°
160°
145°
130°
115°
100°

15°
175°
160°
145°
130°
115°
100°

0°

15°

30°

© 2012 Lum Pennington

CHAPTER ONE

IN THE PHILIPPINE SEA

★　★　★　★　★

The staccato notes of reveille, played on a bugle, blared from a loudspeaker in the passageway outside the junior officers' bunkroom. Inside, behind a flame-proof curtain that served as a door, Ensign Willard M. Fletcher, United States Naval Reserve, rolled up on one elbow and squinted groggily at the luminescent dial of his wristwatch. It was four a.m. He had been keeping a running count of the days since leaving Pearl Harbor in August 1944; today was October 24, 1944, his seventy-fifth consecutive day at sea.

Ensign Fletcher—his family called him Will and his buddies called him Fletch—was a naval aviator assigned to Torpedo 18, an attack squadron stationed aboard the aircraft carrier *Intrepid*. Though not scheduled to fly today, he was required to report at five a.m. to his squadron ready room for flight quarters, a mandatory muster of all pilots and aircrew.

Intrepid was steaming through the middle Pacific latitudes, roughly fifteen degrees above the equator, when reveille sounded. The junior officers' bunkroom, a shipboard dormitory known as "Boys Town," was warm from the tropical heat, the air heavy with humidity and the musky odor of many men sleeping in close quarters. An electric fan bolted to the bulkhead droned back and forth in desultory time but did little to cool the room. Will had drifted off to sleep listening to the purr of the fan, but he had slept only fitfully. He could not get comfortable in the heat. His skin was clammy and his bedsheet damp with perspiration. He kicked aside his cover sheet and swung his legs over the bunk rail. He consoled himself with the notion that he might be able to nap for a few minutes in his ready room chair before attending to his collateral duty as assistant squadron maintenance officer.

Will had joined the United States Navy in August 1942 as an aviation cadet. Like all new enlistees, he had been introduced to the navy's peculiar vocabulary and learned new words for everyday objects. He had learned, for example, that his bed was called a "rack" in navy lingo. In civilian life, he had associated the word "rack" with a medieval instrument of torture and, as a new cadet, he had wondered naively why anyone would use such a gruesome term to describe a bed. Two years later, on his maiden voyage aboard a navy ship, he discovered the answer. Ordered to the Naval Air Station Barbers Point, Hawaii, in May 1944, he had embarked as a passenger aboard an escort carrier making the five-day run from San Fransico to Pearl Harbor. On his first night at sea, he had slept (or tried to) on a standard enlisted man's rack, which was essentially a metal frame with a canvas bottom, suspended from the overhead by chains and covered with a thin, flameproof mattress. The rack had swung like a pendulum, exaggerating the movement of the ship as it pitched and rolled through steep Pacifc swells. For the better part of two days, Will had lain awake in his rack, seasick beyond cure or caring. Although his officer's rack aboard *Intrepid* did not sway as much as an enlisted man's rack—it was a narrow bunk bed affixed solidly to the wall (which is called a "bulkhead" in navy jargon)—it wasn't any more slumber-inducing. A navy rack, he was fond of saying afterward, looked and slept like one.

Will had learned to smoke after he joined the navy—nearly everyone smoked—and now he craved a morning cigarette. His flight suit, which was a cotton khaki coverall similar to those worn by garage mechanics, hung from a hook by his rack. He fished a pack of Lucky Strikes and a Zippo lighter from the breast pocket of the flight suit, grabbed his shaving kit, and shuffled off in his skivvies to the officers' washroom (called the "head") to grab a smoke and prepare himself for the day. He hoped the smoking lamp (the official signal that smoking was permitted aboard ship) was lit.

If you had met Will Fletcher before the war, say on the main street of his hometown of Edwardsville, Illinois, when he was in the fullness of his senior year in high school, you would have thought him an ordinary young man, though perhaps better-looking than most. His sky blue eyes were handsomely set beneath a high forehead. He had a straight, well-proportioned nose, and his teeth were remarkably large, white, and even. He smiled easily. His hair was chestnut brown and naturally wavy. As a student, Will had trimmed his hair short at the temples and allowed it to grow long on top. In the fashion of the day, he had slicked his hair back over his head with pomade, except for an unruly lock that he allowed to droop above his right eye. Girls found this attractive. He was five feet, ten inches tall, but the thinness of his frame made him seem taller than he was, an impression heightened by his adolescent manner of standing with his hands in his pockets and his shoulders drawn up in a perpetual shrug. The navy had made him cut his hair short and stand up straight. He had endured eighteen months of navy flight training, the rigors of which had matured him greatly, survived three months of sea duty aboard *Intrepid*, and accumulated nearly eighty hours of carrier combat flying in fair weather and foul. Since leaving Edwardsville, Will Fletcher had become an exceptionally self-confident young man. Some would say cocky.

As Will awoke on the morning of October 24, *Intrepid* zigzagged through the Philippine Sea at fourteen knots, roughly half her maximum speed. An *Essex*-class aircraft carrier commissioned in April 1943, *Intrepid* was part of Task Group 38.2, a collection of twenty-three warships that also included the light carrier *Cabot*, the battleships *New Jersey* and *Iowa*, three light cruisers—*Vincennes*, *Biloxi*, and *Miami*—and sixteen fast destroyers of the *Fletcher* class. The *Fletcher* class of ships had been named after the uncle of Rear Admiral Frank Jack "Black Jack" Fletcher, a nonaviator who had served with distinction as the carrier task force commander at the Battle of the Coral Sea in May 1942, and again the next month at the Battle of Midway. Young sailors often asked Will whether he was related to old Black Jack; he wasn't.

On October 24, *Intrepid* and her companion ships were "standing by in strategic support" of the American invasion of the Philippine Islands. Six days earlier, an enormous American invasion armada consisting of more than seven hundred warships, including troop transports, cargo vessels, and landing craft, had steamed under cover of darkness into Leyte Gulf, the ocean area south of Samar island and east of Leyte. At daybreak on October 20, American battleships, cruisers, and destroyers of the United States 7th Fleet had bombarded the landing area within San Pedro Bay, a thumb-shaped bulge in the northwest corner of Leyte Gulf. At about nine forty-five a.m., waves of amphibious assault vehicles and landing craft carrying soldiers of the United States Sixth Army had crossed the line of departure and headed toward the beaches near the towns of Dulag, San Jose, and Tacloban on Leyte's eastern shore. Initial Japanese resistance on Leyte had been disorganized and ineffectual. By nightfall on October 21, 132,000 American troops had waded ashore, including their leader, General Douglas MacArthur, supreme commander of the Southwest Pacific Area.

The amphibious landings in Leyte Gulf were the opening phase of the Allied effort to liberate the Philippine archipelago and wrest control of the islands from the Imperial Japanese Army, an occupation force of over 350,000 men. For General MacArthur, the Leyte Gulf invasion was also the defining moment in a crusade of personal and professional redemption.

MacArthur had retired from the United States Army in 1937 to serve as military adviser to the government of the Philippine Commonwealth, the first popularly elected Philippine government in the nation's postcolonial history. Awarded the title of field marshal by President Manuel Quezon, MacArthur organized and trained the fledgling Philippine Army, an army mentored by United States Army and Navy officers but comprised entirely of Filipino conscripts. In July 1941, as diplomatic relations between the United States and Japan steadily deteriorated, President Roosevelt had recalled MacArthur to active duty as a lieutenant general in the United States Army and given him command of the new "Philippine Division," a force comprised of both Filipino and American military units.

War had come suddenly to the United States on December 7, 1941, with the Japanese carrier strike on Pearl Harbor. On December 22, two divisions of the emperor's Fourteenth Army, more than sixty thousand men, had landed in Lingayen Gulf in northern Luzon. As the Japanese marched rapidly southward toward Manila, the Philippine Division had attempted a defense on the central plain of Luzon, but the Japanese had landed more troops at Lamon Bay on the eastern coast of Luzon on the twenty-fourth, and threatened to trap MacArthur's forces in a pincer movement. MacArthur had ordered a retreat, and, within two weeks of the initial Japanese invasion, most of MacArthur's overmatched troops had withdrawn to the Bataan Peninsula west of Manila Bay. MacArthur, his wife and son, his headquarters staff, and the principal members of the Philippine government had taken refuge on Corregidor, an island fortress in the mouth of Manila Bay. The inability of the United States government to reinforce or resupply MacArthur's troops on Bataan had decided the issue of who would control the Philippines. Without reinforcements and resupply, the Philippine Division had no hope of defeating the Japanese. In late February 1942, President Roosevelt had ordered MacArthur to abandon Corregidor and proceed to Australia, there to take command of all United States troops in the southwest Pacific region. At dusk on March 11, the general, his family, and selected members of his staff had escaped Corregidor, making their way by U.S. Navy patrol boat six hundred miles south to Mindanao and then by B-17 bomber to Australia. Arriving in Adelaide, MacArthur had made his famous promise to the Filipino people: "I shall return."

The general had left behind 80,000 troops of the Philippine Division on Bataan: 67,500 Filipinos and 12,500 Americans. In May 1942, these beleaguered troops had surrendered to the Japanese. The victors had marched their prisoners northward to squalid camps in the interior of Luzon. The Japanese had brutalized their captives along the way, depriving them of water, food, rest, and medical attention, and wantonly executing many by bayoneting and beheading. The Japanese army's barbaric treatment of the prisoners of Bataan had become widely known among the Allies; they referred to the infamous episode as the Bataan Death March.

After nearly three years of war, after fierce sea and air battles fought in the equatorial Pacific by the U.S. Navy, after bloody jungle fighting in New Guinea, and after deadly amphibious campaigns waged by American soldiers and marines on exotically named Pacific islands in the Solomons, Gilberts, Marshalls, Marianas, and Carolines, the United States had made good on General MacArthur's promise. Ashore at Leyte, the general had wasted no time rallying the native people to his cause, including former Filipino soldiers who had refused to surrender to the Japanese and had fled into the mountains to become guerrillas. Broadcasting from a mobile radio unit on the landing beaches south of Tacloban, MacArthur had proclaimed, "People of the Philippines, I have returned. By the grace of Almighty God, our forces stand again on Philippine soil—soil consecrated in the blood of our two peoples. The hour of your redemption is here. . . . Rally to me. Let the indomitable spirit of Bataan and Corregidor lead on. As the lines of battle roll forward to bring you within the zone of operations, rise and strike. Strike at every favorable opportunity. For your homes and hearths, strike! For future generations of your sons and daughters, strike! In the names of your sacred dead, strike!"

With *Intrepid* and *Cabot* at its core, Task Group 38.2 was one of three fast carrier task groups stationed off the eastern Philippines on October 24. Together, these three task groups comprised part of Task Force 38, a fast carrier striking force under the command of Vice Admiral Marc A. Mitscher and, ultimately, of Admiral William F. Halsey, commander of the United States 3rd Fleet. The ships of Task Force 38 had not participated in the Leyte landings; naval support of the landing force had been the job of the United States 7th Fleet. The strategic role of Task Force 38 was to destroy enemy naval and air forces threatening the Leyte area on and after October 21. So far, no Japanese warships had challenged the American landings at Leyte, and only a few land-based enemy airplanes had appeared over the beachhead.

Shaved, showered, and dressed in his flight suit, Will Fletcher sat down in *Intrepid*'s wardroom for a breakfast of scrambled eggs and a side of fried bologna. The eggs had been reconstituted from powder and lay on the plate in a puddle of yellow water. Will pushed them aside, a decision he later regretted. The steward, a young black man in heat-wilted blue dungarees, offered him black coffee, but Will declined. He hadn't acquired a taste for navy coffee, which was normally thick and viscous as tar. He had been raised among a household of English immigrants who drank nothing but tea. Will had packed a tin of tea into his footlocker before he reported aboard ship, because he feared the wardroom mess wouldn't offer any. His buddies had teased him about his fondness for tea, calling him a crazy Limey, but Will ignored them. He ordered hot water from the steward and dipped one of his precious tea bags into a heavy porcelain cup.

Other sleepy-eyed pilots drifted into the wardroom. Lieutenant Junior Grade Raymond J. Skelly, a lanky, long-faced Minnesotan with jet-black hair, pulled up a chair and sat beside Will at the breakfast table. Ray Skelly had been among the first pilots assigned to Torpedo 18 when the squadron was commissioned at Alameda, California, in July 1943. Skelly, twenty-three years old, was two years older than Will. When Will joined the squadron at Kaneohe, Hawaii, in June 1944, Skelly had taken the young pilot under his wing like a fraternity brother adopts a pledge. Skelly had offered him tips on flying techniques and helped him adjust to squadron politics. The two pilots frequently flew together in the same division, Division 2, led by Lieutenant John G. "Bud" Williams, the squadron executive officer. Skelly and Will had bonded as friends, perhaps because they both had been raised in rural Midwestern towns, but they were different men temperamentally. Skelly had a fondness for all-night drinking bouts and high-dollar poker games; Will didn't drink much and he couldn't afford to lose money at poker. But Skelly and Will both shared a passion for acey-deucey, and they played the game constantly.

Acey-deucey is a pastime favored by naval aviators, perhaps because it is a game of chance and skill, like flying itself. Players throw dice from a cup and take turns moving checkers around a backgammon board in whatever combinations the dice allow. The object is to block your opponent's path and move your own checkers around the game board before your opponent does. The first player to shift his checkers around the board and remove them entirely wins the game. Skelly had taught Will how to play, but Will had caught on quickly and surpassed his teacher, defeating Skelly handily game after game. Although losing to his protégé irked Skelly, he always cheerfully accepted Will's invitations to play, figuring the dice had to roll in his favor sometime.

Lieutenant Junior Grade Kenneth P. Barden bustled into the wardroom and signaled the steward for a cup of hot coffee. Kenny, as his family and friends called him, hailed from Pocahontas, Arkansas. He had played football and baseball at Arkansas Polytechnic College before the war and had maintained the wiry, athletic build of a shortstop, despite a prodigious appetite for beer. Like Skelly, Barden had been one of the original pilots assigned to Torpedo 18 and he and Skelly had become inseparable drinking companions and liberty mates during their training days in California. Possessed of a mathematical mind well suited to poker, bridge, cribbage, acey-deucey, and virtually any other endeavor involving numbers, Barden served as the squadron's flight officer, which meant he had the collateral duty of scheduling pilots for combat missions and antisubmarine patrols. Because of his status as flight officer, and his friendship with the squadron's air combat intelligence officer, Lieutenant Commander Ernest Allen, Barden was usually one of the first pilots to know what was going on.

Barden cradled his coffee cup and confided to Skelly and Will that some-thing big was happening. *Intrepid* had moved closer to the Philippines over-night, and Commander William E. "Wild Bill" Ellis, the commander of Carrier Air Group 18 (Air Group 18), had ordered a long-range search mission to be launched at first light. Twenty-four warplanes, sixteen fighters and eight dive-bombers, would scour the western reaches of the Sibuyan Sea, the island-speckled ocean that lies at the heart of the Philippine archipelago, looking for a large formation of Japanese warships reportedly approaching the Philippines from the southwest. Lieutenant Commander Lloyd Van Antwerp, the com-manding officer of Torpedo 18, had instructed Barden to notify all torpedo plane pilots who were on standby status—the squadron had nine or ten torpedo plane pilots on standby status at any one time—that they might be launched as early as an hour or two after sunrise.

Skelly and Will were not surprised. They had learned the night before that a significant number of Japanese warships were on the move. In the dark early-morning hours of October 23, two American submarines, *Darter* and *Dace*, had sighted columns of enemy surface ships off Palawan Island, which lies several hundred miles to the southwest of Leyte, and had attacked the lead elements. The submarine commanders reported by radio that they had sunk two Japanese cruisers and damaged a third, but the submariners had dived deep to evade coun-terattacks by Japanese destroyers and had lost contact with the enemy formation. The balance of at least eleven enemy warships, including three large battleships, had steamed on undeterred. No one on the American side knew precisely how many Japanese warships there were in this group or where they were headed, and American intelligence officers were greatly concerned. Were the enemy ships dis-covered by *Darter* and *Dace* merely a raiding force, or were they part of a major fleet movement? Skelly and Fletcher had retired to their racks that night knowing a confrontation of some kind was possible the next morning. Now, sitting at the breakfast table, Kenny Barden confidently predicted Commander Ellis's search-ers would locate the Japanese surface force within two hours, and that Air Group 18 would launch air strikes against the enemy fleet by midmorning.

Air Group 18 was *Intrepid*'s aerial striking force, her main offensive weapon, her reason for being. The group consisted of three squadrons: Torpedo 18, offi-cially abbreviated VT-18, Fighting 18 (VF-18), and Bombing 18 (VB-18). In U.S. Navy nomenclature, the abbreviation "V" indicated a squadron of heavier-than-air aircraft (as opposed to a patrol squadron of lighter-than-air dirigibles, which carried the letter designation "Z"). The second letter of the abbreviation identified the type of warplane with which the squadron was equipped. Thus, the letter "T" designated a squadron of torpedo bombers, "F" indicated a squadron of fighters, and "B" indicated a squadron of dive-bombers. A squadron's number always corresponded with the official number of the air group to which the squadron was assigned, and each air group in the fleet was assigned a distinct number.

Air Group 18's aircraft were all single-engine, propeller-driven warplanes designed to operate from an aircraft carrier. The pilots of VT-18 flew torpedo bombers known as TBM-1C Avengers, each of which was crewed by one pilot, a radioman, and a turret gunner. VT-18 had a complement of twenty-eight pilots, a roster of nearly seventy aircrewmen, and an inventory of eighteen Avengers. The pilots of VF-18 flew high-performance, single-seat fighters known as F6F Hellcats. VF-18 had a complement of fifty pilots and an inventory of forty-three Hellcats, thirty-eight of which were the newest 5-series, while five were older 3-series models that had been adapted for night flying. The pilots of VB-18 flew SB2C-3 Helldivers, a warplane designed for steep, near-vertical bombing attacks on the target. Helldivers were crewed by one pilot and a radar operator who doubled as a tail gunner. VB-18 had a complement of thirty-eight pilots, about forty-five aircrewmen, and an inventory of twenty-eight Helldivers.

Will and most of his fellow pilots would have been content if the intelligence officers' fears about major Japanese fleet movements proved unfounded. The men of Air Group 18 and *Intrepid* were tired. Since early September 1944, *Intrepid* had launched more than sixty air strikes and innumerable patrols as part of Task Force 38's fast carrier raids throughout the western Pacific. *Intrepid*'s Air Group 18 had bombed enemy airfields in the Palau Islands, attacked enemy ports and air bases in the Central Visayas, bombed enemy airfields on Luzon, and sunk enemy freighters near Coron Bay and Subic Bay. The aircraft carrier had ridden out a heavy typhoon off Ulithi, raided Okinawa, and fought a three-day running battle over Formosa that had cost her air group dearly. The men of Air Group 18 and *Intrepid*'s ship's company—the sailors who crewed the carrier—had been in a state of constant combat readiness for nearly three months. They had worked eight-hour days and stood four-hour watches, punctuated by high-tempo flight operations and constant alarms and drills at all hours of the day and night. The men were drained.

Fletcher, Skelly, and Barden finished their breakfast in the officers' wardroom—Will never touched his scrambled eggs—and headed topside to VT-18's pilot ready room. They first climbed the steel ladders (stairs are called ladders in the navy), which took them from the second deck, where the wardroom was located, to the main deck, which was where *Intrepid*'s main aircraft storage and repair facility, or hangar bay, was located.

The hangar bay was a cavernous space that ran nearly the entire length of the carrier and had the look of a high-ceilinged assembly plant. Maintenance crews worked in the hangar bay twenty-four hours a day, breaking airplanes apart and putting them back together again. Mechanics thought nothing of making major repairs—changing out a wing or an engine—within the space of a single eight-hour shift. The hangar bay resounded constantly with factory noises: the whine of electric motors, the hum of air compressors, the musical clang of dropped tools, the rumble of ventilation fans, the burp of air hammers, and the shouts of men. The air smelled of aerosols and solvents, of oil, gasoline, hydraulic fluid, and paint. At night, rows of incandescent lamps in the overhead illuminated the hangar bay as brightly as a high school football field, while heavy, fireproof blackout curtains kept the lights from becoming a beacon for enemy submarines.

The hangar bay was crammed with airplanes, most of which had been stowed with their wings folded and their landing gear lashed to the deck with tie-down ropes or chains. The wings of all carrier-based warplanes were designed to fold at a hinge point near the fuselage, thereby conserving space aboard ship and facilitating the movement of aircraft from the hangar bay to the flight deck and back again. To Will, who had spent a few summers digging potatoes on a farm in southern Illinois, the airplanes squatting in the hangar bay with folded wings reminded him of fat hens nesting cheek by jowl in a chicken coop.

The three torpedo plane pilots walked across the hangar bay from the starboard side of the ship to the port side. They picked their way between the parked warplanes, stepping over tie-down ropes and giving way to busy mechanics. The pilots noticed a squad of plane handlers shoving a dive-bomber toward *Intrepid*'s elevator number two, the deck-edge lift on the port side of the ship. An enlisted plane captain sat in the cockpit and operated the airplane's wheel brakes while ten or twelve plane handlers pushed the heavy craft onto the elevator platform. Mechanics and plane handlers were assigned to *Intrepid*'s air department; these were men of the ship's company responsible for repairing, fueling, arming, launching, and recovering Air Group 18's warplanes and for moving them about the ship. Plane handlers constantly repositioned airplanes, shifting them from the flight deck to the hangar deck for repair and stowage, and back again to the flight deck for launch. To shift aircraft between decks, they used three powerful hydraulic elevators, each of which boasted a platform area of about twenty-five hundred square feet, the size of a modest three-bedroom house. Plane handlers also moved airplanes from the rear of the flight deck forward during aircraft recovery (carrier planes normally landed in the rear one-third of the flight deck) and then moved them aft again for launching. It was standard practice whenever the carrier was cruising in a combat zone for plane handlers working the mid and morning watches (the period between four a.m. and eight a.m.) to position a mix of torpedo bombers, dive-bombers, and fighters on the flight deck in sufficient numbers for a first strike at dawn.

Reaching the port side of the hangar bay, the pilots jogged up the switchback ladders that led topside to VT-18's ready room. Ready rooms were the primary battle stations for all flying personnel and air group staff. They served as prestrike briefing rooms, poststrike debriefing rooms, classrooms, clubhouses, smoking lounges, and game rooms all rolled into one. There were seven ready rooms aboard *Intrepid*, all clustered together port-side amidships on *Intrepid*'s gallery deck, a partial deck that was sandwiched below the flight deck and above the hangar bay. Each squadron in the air group was assigned a ready room for its pilots' exclusive use. Enlisted airmen in the dive-bombing and torpedo squadrons also had ready rooms separate from those of their officer-pilots, although aircrews sometimes briefed toegther. Commander Ellis, the air group commander, was assigned his own ready room for staff briefings and briefings of squadron flight leaders and intelligence officers.

Will, Ray, and Kenny reached the gallery deck shortly before five a.m. The passageway outside VT-18's ready room was jammed with officers and men reporting to flight quarters. The pilots and aircrew among them were easily distinguishable. All were lean young men, clean shaven, with neatly trimmed hair. None of them wore eyeglasses. Nearly all of the pilots, like Will, wore baggy khaki-colored summer flying suits, and some, like Will, wore regular uniform shoes instead of their ankle-high flying boots in an attempt to stay cool in the Pacific heat. Boots were required flying equipment, but Will figured he'd get away with shoes for muster, because he wasn't on the morning flight schedule.

Several nonflying officers mingled with pilots in the passageway; these were primarily administrative, intelligence, and gunnery officers attached to one of the three squadrons. They wore short-sleeved, open-necked khaki shirts and khaki cotton trousers, all rumpled from the heat. The few enlisted men loitering in the passageway, primarily aviation yeomen (clerks) and messengers, stood out; enlisted men wore pale blue chambray shirts and dark blue bell-bottom trousers.

By tradition, and out of respect for rank, enlisted men gave way to an officer in a ship's passageway, and a junior officer gave way to a more senior officer. Will glimpsed an enlisted man trying to navigate his way through the passageway past a knot of officers. He was an air group messenger, identifiable by the tin box he carried under one arm. Placing secret papers in a locked metal box and then entrusting the container to a messenger for hand delivery to the right persons were the customary means of distributing confidential information aboard ship. This messenger was in a hurry. He hustled toward VF-18's ready room, dancing left and right down the passageway like a broken-field runner. Will guessed the messenger carried last-minute instructions for the search mission.

The three torpedo plane pilots filed into VT-18's pilot ready room and took their assigned seats. The room filled quickly, and by four fifty-five a.m. most of the squadron's twenty-eight Avenger pilots were in their chairs.

Like many of the interior spaces aboard *Intrepid*, VT-18's pilot ready room was a steel-walled compartment with a doorway, or hatch, at one end. About fifteen feet wide and forty feet long, with a low overhead only about nine feet high, the room had an unfinished, industrial look. Uncovered pipes and electrical cables were attached to the bulkheads, and overhead beams were exposed, like I-beams in a warehouse. A single ventilation duct that blew both hot air and cold hung from the overhead. *Intrepid*'s ready rooms were among the few spaces aboard the carrier that were air-cooled, a creature comfort that made ready rooms popular places for napping and socializing whenever the ship was cruising in the middle latitudes. Reading lights, bowl-shaped fixtures that resembled street lamps (they were called lamps in navy jargon), and emergency battle lanterns encased in red glass and wire baskets also hung from the overhead. U.S. Army–style helmets, looking like hams curing in a barn, dangled from overhead on hooks; pilots were expected to don these helmets for protection from shrapnel if *Intrepid* were under attack. There were thirty briefing chairs in the ready room, one for each pilot. Each briefing chair was a leather recliner fitted with a small writing table that folded across one arm like a school desk. The chairs faced the narrow end of the room opposite the entrance, where large chalkboards hung on the bulkhead. The chalkboards, painted with white lines, boxes, and grids, served as strike status and bulletin boards. Adjacent to the chalkboards sat a gray yeoman's desk, a telephone, and a Teletype. A loudspeaker wired to the ship's communications system, the 1MC, hung in one corner.

The senior pilots sat in front, closest to the chalkboard, while the junior pilots took seats in the rear of the room. The torpedo plane pilots waited patiently for morning muster by the VT-18's administrative officer, Lieutenant Frank Scrano, and the daily situation briefing by VT-18's air combat intelligence officer, Lieutenant Commander Ernest Allen. Pilots dozed as they waited for Allen, or sipped coffee, flipped through old magazines, reread letters from home, or swapped the latest scuttlebutt. A few discussed in low voices the sightings by *Darter* and *Dace* and wondered whether a big fleet battle might be looming.

As was naval custom when a senior officer entered a room, someone barked, "Attention on deck," and the pilots jumped to their feet. Lieutenant Commander Allen and Lieutenant Scrano walked down the aisle between the rows of seated pilots to the front of the ready room. Allen put the men at ease with, "Seats," and the pilots dropped back into their chairs.

Allen, thirty-seven years of age, was a square-jawed New Yorker with a thin-lipped smile. Born in Greenville, South Carolina (the youngest of seven children), Allen had attended Furman College and then obtained a master's degree in English literature from Columbia. In 1929, he was hired by Central Hanover Bank and Trust Company, notwithstanding the financial clouds that were gathering over Wall Street at the time. In July 1942, he gave up the comfortable life of a New York banker and accepted a reserve commission in the navy, ultimately attending the navy's air combat information school. He listed a Park Avenue address in Manhattan, two blocks east of the Central Park Reservoir, as his home of record.

As the highest-ranking officer in the squadron after Lieutenant Commander Van Antwerp, Allen served as a member of *Intrepid*'s so-called "brain trust," the cadre of senior officers who bore operational responsibility for planning and executing the carrier's offensive missions and for evaluating the results. The brain trust included Rear Admiral Gerald F. Bogan, the commander of Task Group 38.2 who flew his flag aboard *Intrepid*; Captain Joseph P. Bolger, the commanding officer of *Intrepid*; the air officer who ran *Intrepid*'s air department; Commander Ellis, the commander of Air Group 18; the commanders of the three squadrons embarked aboard *Intrepid*: VF-18, VB-18, and VT-18; two or three intelligence officers assigned to the air group; and three squadron intelligence officers, including Lieutenant Commander Allen. Ernie Allen was always a man in the know. For the young pilots in the squadron, most of whom had been reared in small towns, Allen was a father figure from a far more sophisticated world, and he carried the same Olympian aura of authority as Ellis or Van Antwerp.

Scrano took muster, mostly by looking around the room to verify that the pilots were in their customary seats, and Allen began his briefing. Confirming Kenny Barden's scuttlebutt that VF-18 and VB-18 would launch a reconnaissance mission at dawn to search for a large Japanese task force that had been sighted by American submarines off Palawan Island, he added some new details. Commander Ellis had formed six search teams, Allen reported, each comprised of three Hellcats and one radar-equipped Helldiver. Each search team would explore a ten-degree sector west of *Intrepid* to a distance of three hundred nautical miles. Collectively, the six search teams, numbered clockwise Sector One through Sector Six, would blanket the area between 230 and 290 degrees true, a wedge-shaped area encompassing the Sibuyan Sea between Mindoro island in the south and Manila Bay in the north. To communicate with *Intrepid* across the distance, Ellis would station two fighters 150 miles out, halfway between the aircraft carrier and the search perimeter, to relay any sightings of the enemy ships to *Intrepid* by radio. A seventh search team of four fighters would fly as far west as Palawan Island itself.

Allen then announced—to no one's surprise—that the brain trust had been working through the night on a battle plan. In anticipation of locating the enemy task force later that morning, Commander Ellis and the air officer had ordered preparations for a full-blown first strike, Strike 2 Able. (The numeral 2 referenced a strike by *Intrepid*; the code letter Able referenced the first strike of the day.) The striking force would be comprised of at least thirty-one aircraft from *Intrepid*—eight VT-18 Avengers, twelve VB-18 dive-bombers, and eleven VF-18 fighters—and perhaps aircraft from other carriers in the task group. Allen acknowledged that no one was quite sure where the Japanese were headed or how large this enemy naval force really was. Japanese warships might enter the Sibuyan Sea south of Mindoro island, or they might remain west of Mindoro and proceed toward Manila or Japanese home waters. If they entered the Sibuyan Sea, they would pose a serious threat to the American ships supporting the Leyte Gulf landings. Regardless of their destination, if the enemy came within range of *Intrepid*'s carrier planes, Commander Ellis intended to attack. Allen concluded by reporting that *Intrepid* would set readiness condition one, general quarters, at five thirty a.m., and that the reconnaissance force would begin taking off at six a.m.

Until Ellis's search planes located the enemy task force, there would be little for VT-18's torpedo plane pilots to do but stand by in the ready room and wait for further instructions. But if *Intrepid* launched Strike 2 Able, VT-18's torpedo plane pilots would play a pivotal role. They would have the job of sinking or disabling the enemy warships with heavy torpedoes.

Torpedo attack was a unique form of aerial attack for which VT-18's pilots had been specially trained. VT-18's Avengers, the largest carrier-borne warplanes of the period, were each capable of carrying in their bellies a single Mark 13 2A aerial torpedo specifically designed to be dropped from an airplane. Fourteen feet in length and twenty-two inches in diameter, the Mark 13 2A weighed twenty-two hundred pounds and mounted in its warhead six hundred pounds of Torpex, a substance with nearly twice the explosive power of TNT. On a torpedo run, an Avenger pilot would approach his target at high speed and low altitude, flying only a few hundred feet above the water. The pilot would weave from side to side, or "jink," to evade enemy antiaircraft fire. When he had closed to within fifteen hundred yards of his target, the pilot would release his torpedo and bank away, hugging the water until he had escaped out of range of the enemy's guns. The Mark 13 2A would arm itself on striking the water and race toward the target at thirty-four knots and at a depth of eight to twelve feet. (The running depth could be adjusted to the size and draft of the target.) If the torpedo ran straight and true, it would penetrate the armor plate of the enemy warship and detonate with devastating results.

Allen concluded his briefing, and at five thirty a.m. the morning call to general quarters sounded over *Intrepid*'s 1MC, the carrier's internal public address system. An alarm bell clanged throughout the ship, and *Intrepid*'s chief boatswain's mate intoned over the 1MC, "General quarters, General quarters. All hands man your battle stations and set material condition Zebra."

General quarters was a mandatory call to action that no sailor, officer or enlisted, could ignore whether he was on duty or off. When the bell rang, ship's company and air group personnel dropped whatever they were doing—bolting from their racks if they were sleeping and abandoning their meals in place if they were eating—and dashed off to their assigned battle stations. They manned all main and secondary gun batteries, fire control and damage control stations, communications and combat information centers, critical engineering spaces, and flight deck stations, and they did so with practiced alacrity. To expedite the flow of the men to their battle stations, sailors were instructed to descend using ladders on *Intrepid*'s port side and to ascend using ladders on her starboard side. Sailors sometimes ignored this convention like schoolchildren ascending the down staircase, but they did so at risk of physical injury. The ship's executive officer recorded the elapsed time between the sounding of the alarm and the moment when all stations reported manned and ready. Woe to sailors who lagged behind.

The directive "set material condition Zebra" instructed crewmen to close watertight doors and hatches, but to keep open certain designated hatches to permit ventilation, distribution of food, and attending to calls of nature. Sailors stood by the open hatches, ready to seal them if ordered. Because VT-18's pilots were already at their battle stations in the ready room when general quarters sounded, they remained where they were.

At five fifty-five a.m., as the sun broke above the eastern horizon, *Intrepid* changed course to 060 degrees and accelerated into the wind. Her huge engine screws churned the water at 174 r.p.m., and the big ship rattled and hummed. Ten minutes later, the first of Commander Ellis's search planes, a VF-18 Hellcat, rolled down *Intepid*'s flight deck; the last search plane, a VB-18 Helldiver, lifted off the flight deck at six twenty-seven a.m. The snarl and rumble of the departing aircraft filtered into VT-18's ready room. When the flight deck grew silent, Will Fletcher glanced at his wristwatch. *Intrepid* had launched twenty-four airplanes in twenty-two minutes. Not bad, but probably slower than Commander Ellis preferred. Will estimated the search planes would arrive over the western Sibuyan Sea in ninety minutes.

At six thirty-two a.m., the chief boatswain's mate sounded his pipe over *Intrepid*'s 1MC—the boatswain's pipe emitted a piercing whistle—and announced, "Secure from general quarters; set readiness condition three and material condition Yoke." These orders placed *Intrepid* in a lower state of readiness, a "cruising readiness condition" where the danger of surprise air attack still existed, but the risk of surprise attack by enemy surface forces was remote. Under condition Yoke, sailors opened watertight doors and hatches, and most returned to their daily routines. Two thirds of the ship's antiaircraft gunners secured their weapons, while one-third remained at their gun mounts with ammunition ready as a precaution against air attack from Japanese airplanes based on Luzon or Samar.

VT-18's torpedo plane pilots remained in their ready room, waiting for Ellis's reconnaissance planes to report. No combat strike would be launched without a good fix on the whereabouts of the enemy task force and its composition. Normally, *Intrepid* and Air Group 18 launched three and sometimes four strikes a day when enemy targets presented themselves, and VT-18 normally contributed six to eight Avengers to each strike. On any given day, some of VT-18's torpedo plane pilots were more likely to fly than others; some might fly more than once, while some might not fly at all. Lieutenant Commander Van Antwerp had divided his squadron of twenty-eight pilots into three standing divisions of eight pilots each, and he had designated four pilots to act as spares or reserves to be assigned to the various divisions as necessary. Will and Ray Skelly most often flew as members of Division 2, which was usually the second division of torpedo bombers to be launched in any series of strikes. Lieutenant Commander Van Antwerp himself led Division 1, which was normally the first torpedo bomber division launched in any series.

Will wagered Skelly a soft drink that Division 2 wouldn't fly for several hours, if it flew at all that day. He challenged Skelly to a few games of acey-deucey to pass the time, and the two friends settled comfortably into their ready room chairs with the game board open between them.

Puzzling over Japanese intentions, the brain trust had decided that the collection of enemy warships attacked by *Darter* and *Dace*, the true size and composition of which were still unknown, might enter the western Sibuyan Sea through Tablas Strait, irrespective of whether the Japanese were bound for Leyte Gulf or Luzon. Confident that Ellis's search groups would discover something worthwhile to attack, the brain trust updated the task group's battle plans and set tentative launch times. *Intrepid* would launch not one but three consecutive strikes against the enemy, the trust decided. All thirty-one warplanes of the first strike, Strike 2 Able—fueled, armed, manned, and ready for immediate launch—would be positioned on *Intrepid*'s flight deck for takeoff no later than eight thirty a.m. Air group 18 would be prepared to launch a second strike, Strike 2 Baker, on the heels of Strike 2 Able at about ten thirty a.m. When Commander Ellis's search planes returned to the carrier, the air department would quickly refuel and rearm the returning dive-bombers and fighters and supplement them with as many serviceable Avengers as were available for a possible third strike, Strike 2 Charlie.

Commander Ellis wanted to attack the enemy beyond three hundred nautical miles if at all possible; the farther from Leyte Gulf the enemy warships were sunk or turned away, the better. But a long-distance air strike presented Ellis with a serious practical problem: Would his strike group have sufficient fuel to locate the enemy, execute its attacks, and return safely to the carrier? The problem was especially acute for VT-18's Avengers. When carrying a twenty-two hundred pound aerial torpedo, an Avenger's combat radius was limited to 225 nautical miles; if launched at a target more than 225 miles away, VT-18's Avengers would have insufficient gas to return to *Intrepid*, and their crews would likely conclude their mission with a swim. To enable his torpedo planes to reach the enemy warships and have a fighting chance of returning safely, Commander Ellis and *Intrepid*'s air officer decided to equip the eight Avengers assigned to Strike 2 Able with range-extending, wing-mounted external drop tanks. Drop tanks, two for each airplane, would add 125 gallons of gasoline to the torpedo bomber's normal internal fuel load of 335 gallons and extend its combat radius to 340 nautical miles. In all likelihood, the Avengers dispatched on *Intrepid*'s subsequent strikes, Strikes 2 Baker and Charlie, would not require drop tanks; if the Japanese surface force turned east toward Leyte, the enemy himself would obligingly close the range.

Taking off with two external drop tanks and a heavy Mark 13 torpedo posed extraordinary risks for the Avengers' aircrew. An Avenger carrying three crewmen of average heft, a Mark 13 torpedo, a full load of gas internally in its main fuselage and wing tanks, and two external drop tanks filled to capacity would weigh about 17,800 pounds, or nearly nine tons. An Avenger so loaded would tip the scales far in excess of its maximum gross takeoff weight of 17,650 pounds and be too heavy to catapult safely. The pilot's only takeoff option would be a free deck launch, in which he ran his engine up to maximum power and accelerated down the length of the flight deck as if taking off from a runway.

Although this was the normal method of launching a torpedo bomber from a carrier, the deck launch of an Avenger at its maximum gross weight of 17,650 required a takeoff run of at least five hundred feet, more than half the length of *Intrepid*'s flight deck. The question was: How much deck would an overweight Avenger require? There was also a serious aerodynamic issue: The bulky drop tanks, which looked like bulbous-nosed trash cans, added considerable aerodynamic drag. These two powerful forces in combination, weight and drag, would resist the airplane's efforts to get airborne. Complicating matters further, a deck launch at 17,650 pounds was aerodynamically possible only if *Intrepid* could generate a minimum of thirty-five knots of relative wind over her flight deck. Any less wind over the flight deck would necessitate a longer takeoff run. The big unknown was whether VT-18's overweight torpedo bombers would achieve flying speed before they reached the end of the deck.

None of VT-18's pilots had any prior experience with overweight carrier takeoffs. Aeronautical engineers at Grumman Aircraft Engineering Corporation had carefully calculated the maximum takeoff weight for an Avenger and set the limit for sound aeronautical reasons—above 17,650 pounds, the engine might not generate sufficient thrust to get the airplane airborne, and the wings might not generate adequate lift to keep the airplane aloft and climbing. Under normal circumstances, no prudent pilot would ever knowingly attempt an overweight takeoff; the maneuver was simply too problematic and dangerous to rehearse. Grumman engineers had neither prescribed a standard procedure for executing an overweight takeoff in an Avenger, nor offered any reliable intelligence on how the torpedo bomber would perform if someone was reckless enough to try one. Insofar as Commander Ellis and Lieutenant Commander Van Antwerp knew, no Avenger squadron in the entire United States Navy had ever attempted a torpedo-and-drop-tank takeoff from an aircraft carrier. Not only would the torpedo-plane pilots on Strike 2 Able be compelled to fly a long-distance combat mission over enemy-held territory and press home the attack, an inherently risky undertaking by itself, but they would be required to perform an aeronautical experiment normally reserved for navy test pilots: They would fly their airplanes under conditions that were unknown or "off the performance chart."

For Commander Ellis, the immediate military opportunity and necessity justified the risks. Ellis had no doubt his search planes would find the enemy fleet. The sightings by *Darter* and *Dace* presaged a major air-sea engagement, a battle in which powerful Japanese warships would be the primary object of Air Group 18's attentions. To inflict maximum damage on the enemy, Ellis needed his torpedo bombers with him in the vanguard of the attack. VT-18's Avengers and their heavy Mark 13 torpedoes were his most potent offensive weapons. Bombs, rockets, or even bullets might sink a plodding Japanese merchantman, but sinking or disabling a well-armored Japanese warship required torpedoes. The sightings by *Darter* and *Dace* had offered Ellis a golden opportunity to carry out one of the primary offensive missions for which he had trained his air group—the destruction of enemy fleet units—and he intended to make the most of it despite the risks to his Avenger crews during takeoff.

VT-18's skipper concurred fully in Ellis's decision to equip his Avengers with drop tanks. Lieutenant Commander Van Antwerp—called "Van" by his friends—was an ambitious officer with a can-do attitude. He had played football at Michigan State University (until he sustained a career-ending shoulder injury), entered the army's ROTC program, and graduated from college as a second lieutenant with a degree in engineering. Deciding he wanted to fly rather than lead troops on the ground, Van Antwerp had given up his army commission and enrolled as a naval aviation cadet. On graduating from flight training in 1938, he had received a regular commission in the navy, as opposed to a reserve commission. His rise to command was no small accomplishment in a tradition-bound service where the Navy Department normally awarded coveted "flag-path" positions, such as skipper of a combat squadron aboard a fleet carrier like *Intrepid*, to Naval Academy graduates.

Van Antwerp had been VT-18's first permanent skipper—he had "stood up the squadron," in navy jargon—and taken seriously his responsibility for training his pilots and aircrew for carrier operations and combat. Van was an aggressive flier himself, and he pushed his pilots to perform well around the ship. He demanded VT-18's pilots fly tight formation and achieve the shortest launch and recovery times (the time between engine start and takeoff, and the interval between landings, measured in minutes). Some of the younger pilots resented his prodding and regarded the skipper as something of a showboat, but Van Antwerp had led his 1st Division personally in every series of air strikes VT-18 had launched to date, and his insistence on tight-formation flying had saved lives over Formosa a few weeks earlier. He had promoted the idea among his men from the very beginning that Avenger pilots were a special breed of naval aviator. He constantly reminded them that VT-18's torpedo planes came in low and fast and delivered the heaviest offensive punch in carrier aviation. The men of VT-18 were "torpeckers" and should be damned proud of it.

At about eight a.m., Van Antwerp, trailed closely by Ernie Allen, strode into VT-18's ready room, and the assembled torpedo-plane pilots jumped to their feet. Van Antwerp ordered his men to take their seats, put away their cards and checker games, and listen up. *Intrepid's* Sector Three search team had sighted "many Jap ships" eight miles south of Mindoro, he announced, course 030, speed ten to twelve knots. Further reports on the composition of the Japanese formation were expected momentarily. Allen switched the 1MC in the ready room to the tactical radio frequency used by Ellis's search teams. The pilots leaned forward in their seats and riveted their attention on the 1MC speaker box, straining to hear the search teams' transmissions over the static. Within minutes, Sector Three's amplified emergency contact message crackled over *Intrepid's* 1MC with details on the Japanese flotilla: "Thirteen DD [destroyers], 4 BB [battleships], 8 CA [cruisers] off southern tip of Mindoro. Course 050, speed ten to twelve knots. No train or transports."

The torpedo-plane pilots looked at one another in astonishment. This was a formidable enemy task force indeed, far larger than *Darter* and *Dace* had reported or 3rd Fleet's intelligence officers had anticipated. Twenty-five big-gunned surface warships, roughly three hundred nautical miles away, steaming through the southern entrance to the Sibuyan Sea. But no enemy aircraft carriers. Where were they?

No one who knew Admiral Bogan or Wild Bill Ellis doubted they would order VT-18 to attack the Japanese task force within the hour. If things held true to form, VT-18's Division 1 would launch first as part of Strike 2 Able, followed ninety minutes later by Division 2 as part of Strike 2 Baker, and then by Division 3 as part of Strike 2 Charlie. Bogan and Ellis might even try to launch a fourth strike, cobbled together from returning pilots and standby pilots. To a man, VT-18's torpedo plane pilots realized that the day of the Big Fleet Battle, the long-anticipated clash between the United States 3rd Fleet and the Imperial Japanese Navy, had finally arrived. The opening phases of the Big Fleet Battle were also going to be a naval aviators' show exclusively, a knock-down fight between American carrier-based fighters, dive-bombers, and torpedo planes in one corner and big-gunned Japanese surface warships in the other. VT-18's torpedo plane pilots, fighting beside their brethren from VF-18 and VB-18, would be among the first to enter the fray. The battleships, cruisers, and destroyers of Task Force 38 and Task Group 38.2 were far too distant from the enemy to lend any weight or support.

I've lost my bet with Skelly, Will realized soberly.

The pilot who had relayed Sector Three's detailed contact message to *Intrepid* was Lieutenant Junior Grade W. H. Millar of VB-18. The excitement in Millar's voice had been unmistakable, his enthusiasm contagious. Millar's report inspired most of the torpedo-plane pilots in VT-18's ready room with the thrill of the hunt, though some of them absorbed the news with a measure of unspoken dread. VT-18 had been in combat for a long time. The odds had to turn against a few of them at some point. Who would be the unlucky ones today?

Lieutenant Commander Allen switched the 1MC back to the ship's communication circuit, and Van Antwerp demanded his men's full attention. Addressing his pilots from the front of the ready room like a schoolteacher lecturing his class, Van Antwerp confirmed what everyone now knew for certain: Strike 2 Able would launch within the hour, probably sooner. Then, quite unexpectedly, the skipper announced that Division 1 would not fly Strike 2 Able, as was customary. Van Antwerp had modified the usual rotation: Lieutenant Bud Williams's Division 2 would fly Strike 2 Able, not Division 1. While this scheduling change registered among his pilots, the skipper informed everyone that all of the Avengers assigned to Strike 2 Able had been equipped with drop tanks for the long flight into the Sibuyan Sea.

The latter announcement provoked a few low whistles of surprise and even a few murmurs of protest and disbelief. Van Antwerp held up his hand. He acknowledged that Strike 2 Able's Avengers would exceed their maximum takeoff weight by a few hundred pounds, but he insisted there was no alternative. Strike 2 Able's torpedo bombers couldn't reach the enemy warships without the additional fuel, he explained, and he had confidence his torpeckers could execute the overweight takeoff safely in any event.

Skelly, who had lost two out of three acey-deucey games to Will, leaned across the still-open game board and muttered, "Jesus, every time I play with you, shit like this happens."

Van Antwerp didn't offer any reason for assigning Division 2 to Strike Able.

The change obviously meant that Division 1—the skipper's own division—would not be making the first overweight torpedo-and-drop-tank takeoff in Avenger history. Ensign Bernard J. "Ben" St. John, a young torpedo-plane pilot who found the skipper's old-school, gung ho personality annoying at times, suspected Van Antwerp was apprehensive about attempting the overweight takeoff himself and had substituted Division 2 accordingly. In truth, Commander Ellis probably ordered Van Antwerp to make the change. Ellis had asked his squadron commanders on previous occasions to assign specific divisions, even specific pilots, to specific strikes. Bud Williams's division had demonstrated superior proficiency in torpedo attack and posted a pretty good record so far. In September, Williams's division had attacked several Japanese freighters and tankers with torpedoes near Subic Bay in western Luzon and scored six torpedo hits out of eight drops. Commander Ellis likely wanted Williams's torpeckers in the first wave of the attack on the Japanese warships. Furthermore, Admiral Bogan had selected Ellis to lead Strike 2 Able and act as the target coordinator for a combined strike group comprised of warplanes from *Intrepid* and the light carrier *Cabot*, the only other aircraft carrier operating with Task Group 38.2 on the morning of October 24. If Ellis led Strike 2 Able himself, a senior squadron commander would be required to lead *Intrepid*'s second strike of the day, and Van Antwerp was the logical choice to lead it.

Changing the order of battle from Division 1 to Division 2 was a simple procedure. Earlier that morning, yeomen had entered the names of the pilots and crewmen regularly assigned to Division 1 on the ready room status board. They had also chalked in the bureau and side numbers of the Avengers assigned to Strike 2 Able, together with *Intrepid*'s position and course, winds aloft, codes, times, and radio frequencies. When Van Antwerp announced the change, Kenny Barden, whose collateral duty as flight officer was to manage the flight schedule and match VT-18's aircraft with their aircrew, erased the names of the Division 1 pilots from the status board and scribbled in new names. Barden hand-lettered "Fletcher" in one of the pilot grids painted on the status board, and "Skelly" in another, thus confirming that both Will and Ray would participate in Strike 2 Able as members of Bud Williams's Division 2. The eight torpedo bombers and the standby plane listed on the status board would remain the same; the Avengers assigned to Strike 2 Able were fungible and could be flown by any of the pilots in the squadron.

Will noted that he would have his usual aircrew flying with him. Aviation Radioman Third Class (ARM3C) Robert G. Westmoreland would be Will's radioman, and Aviation Machinist Mate Second Class (AMM2C) George E. Christman Jr. would be his turret gunner. Will had flown with these two enlisted men regularly since VT-18 first went aboard *Intrepid* in August 1944; the three men had become a good team. Will also learned he would be the fourth Avenger to launch, and that he would fly off the right wing of Lieutenant Junior Grade Elmer B. Vaughn.

Vaughn was a bantam rooster of a man, much shorter than the average naval aviator. Vaughn's friends called him "Squatty," a nickname Vaughn much preferred over his given name of Elmer. He was twenty-seven years of age and claimed Bartlett, Tennessee, just north of Memphis, as his home. He spoke in a lazy, country-boy drawl that masked his intelligence and intensity, and had a puckish sense of humor and a gregarious nature. On the ground, Vaughn loved to pull practical jokes; in the air, he was all business, and he excelled at formation flying and glide bombing. Like Skelly, Vaughn had taken a liking to Will and treated him like a kid brother. Will loved Vaughn for his easy Southern affability, and he admired and trusted Vaughn as a section leader.

Van Antwerp ordered the newly assigned pilots to "suit up" on the double and take their seats in the ready room for Lieutenant Commander Allen's final prestrike briefing. Admiral Bogan and Commander Ellis wanted all Strike 2 Able crews sitting in their cockpits, ready to start engines no later than eight thirty a.m.

Will, Skelly, Vaughn, and the other pilots who suddenly found their names on Barden's status board quickly donned their flight gear, most of which hung from hooks on the ready room bulkheads. Each of Air Group 18's pilots had been issued a .38-caliber revolver and a six-inch survival knife. Will slipped a bandolier of ammunition over his right shoulder and buckled his holster belt around his waist. The holster fit snugly beneath his left arm, and his survival knife dangled from the belt in a leather sheath.

VT-18's pilots and aircrew had also been issued bright yellow inflatable life preservers called Mae Wests. Will placed his Mae West over his head and shoulders, wrapped the leg straps around his thighs, and buckled the straps at his chest. In an emergency, a crewman could inflate his life preserver by discharging carbon dioxide capsules into the chest and neck bladders or by blowing through mouth tubes. Survival gear was clipped to the front of a Mae West within easy reach, including a battery-powered strobe light, a whistle, and packets of dye marker that, when released into the sea, stained the ocean a bilious green and made a downed pilot more visible to a search plane.

Next, Will slipped his parachute harness over his shoulders and buckled its canvas straps across his chest and around each leg. The parachute pack itself was stowed in the cockpit seat of Will's assigned Avenger; he would attach the pack to his harness when he was airborne. The pilot's survival kit was also stowed in the cockpit seat; the survival kit, which Will would buckle to his harness when he entered the cockpit, contained a one-man inflatable raft, a tin flask of fresh water, zinc oxide cream to block the sun, more packs of dye marker, Benzedrine pep pills to keep the pilot awake, Atabrine tablets to combat malaria if he landed in the jungle, Halazone tablets for purifying drinking water, sealed packages of hard candy, fishing hooks, line, and another whistle. The pilot's parachute pack and survival kit served double duty in an Avenger as his seat cushion. Avenger radiomen and turret gunners were not issued individual rafts or survival kits; they depended on their Mae Wests and a large three-man lift raft stowed in the Avenger's fuselage abaft the pilot's cockpit station.

Will opened the drawer beneath the seat of his ready room chair and extracted his flying cap, goggles, and gloves. Though called a "helmet," his summer flying cap was made of khaki-colored canvas and looked like a ladies' swim cap with earphones attached. His Plexiglas flying goggles were wide and thick and resembled the eyewear of a downhill skier. His gloves, sewn from calfskin, were brown and sweat-stained. Last, Will picked up his plotting board, a portable writing tray on which he would record times, headings, speeds, distances, navigational fixes, radio frequencies and observations. His plotting board also mounted a plastic compass rose, a tool that would help him track his course across a trackless sea. Will glanced down anxiously at his shiny uniform shoes. There would be no time to change into his sturdier flying boots. He took his seat, ready to hear what Allen had to say.

Lieutenant Commander Allen launched into his final situation briefing, speaking in his rapid-fire South Carolinian–*cum*–NewYorker accent. He summarized the objective of Strike 2 Able, which was simply to "seek out and destroy [the] Japanese task force." He repeated the essence of Sector Three's report—a very large enemy surface force was rounding the southern tip of Mindoro and entering Tablas Strait, which is the southern entrance to the Sibuyan Sea—and quickly outlined the tactical situation. Although the enemy formation had been heading north when it was discovered, it might turn east. The Japanese warships could easily traverse the Sibuyan Sea in a single day, and the enemy armada might attempt to pass through San Bernardino Strait south of Luzon into the Philippine Sea. If the enemy task force reached Leyte Gulf in force, they could obliterate the scores of thin-hulled American transports and supply ships anchored there in support of the invasion. The big-gunned warships could destroy supply dumps on the beaches, leaving American troops ashore without ammunition or food. The American invasion of the Philippines might become a disaster. This enemy task force had to be stopped.

Allen then disclosed a sobering detail from Sector Three's report: Among the four battleships in the Japanese armada were two massive warships, possibly superbattleships of the *Yamato* class. These were mythical vessels, never before committed by the Imperial Japanese Navy to a major offensive (although American intelligence officers knew that at least one of these superbattleships had been on the periphery of the action at Midway and the Marianas). The only Americans ever to have beheld a *Yamato*-class battleship were a few submariners. American intelligence had estimated the displacement of the *Yamato* class at forty-five thousand tons, larger than *Intrepid* by about a third. The *Yamato*s were also reputed to mount monster eighteen-inch naval guns, much bigger than the sixteen-inch naval guns carried by the newest American battleships of the *Iowa* class. But the most unsettling fact about the *Yamato* class of battleships was that no American flier had ever engaged one in combat before. No one in American air intelligence had an accurate picture of the number or type of antiaircraft guns that these massive enemy battleships mounted for self-defense.

Allen confirmed that Admiral Bogan had strengthened Air Group 18's striking force with ten Hellcats and four Avengers from *Cabot*'s Air Group 29, which was also under Bogan's authority as task group commander, and that Commander Ellis would serve as group leader for the combined strike group. But Allen emphasized that Air Group 18 would otherwise be all alone on this first mission. *Intrepid* and *Cabot* were the closest aircraft carriers to the enemy, and the only carriers within range of striking the Japanese formation. Task Group 38.3 was too far to the north to be of assistance until later in the day, and Task Group 38.4 was too far south.

Bud Williams rose next to speak briefly as division leader. Williams was a well-muscled man with a baby face and a balding pate. Despite his cherubic features, Williams had a commanding presence and a forceful personality. He treated his men with even-tempered tough love, like a good high school principal. Williams could be fussy about small things—nitpicking was a universal complaint about squadron executive officers, whose duty it was to keep people in line—but he cared deeply about his men and they knew it. Lieutenant Williams was twenty-nine, six or seven years older than most of the pilots in his squadron, and eight years older than Will Fletcher. His pilots called him Granny.

Williams had been briefed earlier in the morning by Ellis and Van Antwerp. Williams confirmed that Air Groups 18 and 29 would execute a standard coordinated attack against the enemy fleet. VF-18 and VF-29 would fly air cover for Strike 2 Able and engage any enemy fighters that might rise up from island airfields in defense of the Japanese task force. VB-18's Helldivers would attack the enemy formation first, nosing over into their dive-bombing runs from twelve thousand feet. The dive-bombers would approach and attack the enemy warships along their longitudinal axis. The fighters would go in next from ten thousand feet, strafing the targets to divert enemy antiaircraft fire from the approaching torpedo planes. VT-18 and VT-29 would go in last and execute low-level torpedo attacks. Destruction of the enemy's huge capital ships—probably the *Yamatos*—would be the principal objective of Strike 2 Able. Commander Ellis would assign targets over the tactical radio frequency.

At this point in their flying careers, VT-18's torpedo-plane pilots could execute the standard carrier departure and rendezvous maneuver blindfolded, but Williams dutifully reminded his pilots of the procedures. Fighters would launch first, followed by dive-bombers and torpedo planes in that order. When their turn came, Williams's eight Avengers would launch one after another in rapid sequence, ideally at no more than thirty-second intervals. Williams would take off first and climb straight ahead for four minutes, after which all eight Avengers should be airborne. After four minutes, Williams would begin a shallow left turn back toward *Intrepid* at fifteen hundred feet, gradually reversing course and passing a thousand yards abeam the carrier on her port side in the opposite direction. The Avenger pilots flying behind Williams would cut across his radius of turn and join up with him in the same sequence in which each had launched. Each pilot would glide into the standard wingman position beside his section leader. Williams would fly at the point of the formation with three Avengers arrayed off his right wing and four arrayed off his left. (This was called an unbalanced "vee" formation.) When Williams had collected all of his Avengers after takeoff, he would lead his formation upward in a slow climb to nine thousand feet. Commander Ellis, flying a Hellcat, would be orbiting above the aircraft carrier waiting for them, along with the fighters of VF-18 and the dive-bombers of VB-18. When *Cabot's* contingent of warplanes joined Strike 2 Able, Ellis would turn his combined strike group west toward the enemy.

Lieutenant Williams cautioned his pilots to use extreme care during their overweight takeoff with drop tanks. *Intrepid* would generate at least thirty knots of wind over her flight deck, and the high relative wind would help reduce the airplane's takeoff roll. But the pilots must pay close attention to airspeed and not overrotate the airplane's nose on takeoff. The Avengers' usual tendency to settle off the bow would be exacerbated by the additional weight and drag of the drop tanks. Williams counseled everyone to maintain airspeed and not to retract their wing flaps until they were at a safe altitude and airspeed.

Van Antwerp predicted that Commander Ellis would concentrate the Avengers' torpedo attacks on one or two of the larger warships, rather than weaken the division's punch by scattering airplanes among many different targets. The division would likely execute a standard "hammer and anvil" attack on one of the big battleships. To execute the hammer and anvil, Williams's Avenger division would split into two groups of four airplanes; the two groups would approach the target simultaneously but on opposite flanks. No matter which direction the enemy ship turned to evade the attack, she would expose one of her steel sides to a torpedo broadside. Although Admiral Bogan and Commander Ellis had not yet received final authorization to launch Strike 2 Able from Vice Admiral Marc A. Mitscher, the task force commander, Van Antwerp expected the order could come at any minute.

At about eight twenty a.m., the familiar command, "Now hear this. Now hear this. All pilots man your airplanes," buzzed across the 1MC speaker. The order jolted VT-18's ready room to action. The pilots of Division 2 jumped to their feet, pulled their flying caps over their heads, snatched up their goggles and gloves, tucked their plotting boards under their arms, and jostled toward the ready room door. The pilots of Divisions 1 and 3, whose turn would come soon enough, offered the departing torpeckers backslaps and handshakes of encouragement and spoke the customary parting words: "Go get 'em, boys. Good luck and good hunting."

In the passageway outside VT-18's ready room, Williams's torpeckers mingled with eleven fighter pilots from VF-18 and twelve dive-bomber pilots from VB-18, all of whom who were headed for the port-side, deck-edge ladder that led from *Intrepid*'s gallery deck to her flight deck. The lanky Commander Ellis, taller than most of the pilots in his air group, was conspicuous among them. The enlisted airmen who had been assigned to fly Strike 2 Able's Helldivers and the Avengers were not far behind. Twelve VB-18 rear-seat men, eight VT-18 turret gunners, and eight VT-18 radiomen merged into the passageway behind the pilots, and the entire assemblage of aviators, fifty-nine officers and men in all, streamed purposefully toward the deck-edge ladder.

After seven months of joint training in Hawaii and three months at sea, the 250 officers and men of Air Group 18 had come to know one another, just as students at a high school or small college come to know the members of their class. Despite the functional divisions and natural rivalries among the three squadrons, every aviator in the air group had friends and acquaintances who were members of other squadrons; men had card-playing buddies, basketball buddies, buddies from flight training, drinking buddies, even buddies from the same hometown in other squadrons. Normally, these pilots and airmen would have been conversational, even jocular. But the aviators assigned to Strike 2 Able said little to one another as they walked toward the flight deck. Strike 2 Able was going to be very different from any of the combat sorties these men had flown before, and the mood of most of them was subdued.

There were good reasons for reflection. Although Air Group 18 had attacked dozens of Japanese merchant vessels and sampans on previous missions, none of its aviators had ever before executed an attack on a Japanese warship more potent than a minesweeper or a patrol boat. Today's target was going to be an armada of powerful Japanese warships, more than twenty-five of them, all heavily gunned. At least one and maybe two of the warships were reputed to be among the largest battleships in the world. Although Air Group 18 had endured episodes of intense enemy antiaircraft fire on earlier bombing missions over the Philippines and Formosa, none of its aviators had ever before attacked a highly mobile formation of enemy warships, a flotilla that would no doubt maneuver evasively and concentrate its counterfire to greatest effect. None of Air Group 18's aviators had yet faced first-line Japanese naval gunners, who were renowned for their accuracy and tenacity. The uncertainty of what lay ahead weighed heavily on Strike 2 Able's pilots and aircrew. Will Fletcher, still adjusting to the idea that he would have to get his Avenger airborne with a torpedo and two drop tanks, tried not to think too much about the targets. He concentrated instead on his immediate tasks ahead, which were to get his airplane started, get safely off the carrier, and join up with his squadron mates and Ellis's strike group.

To reach the flight deck, Strike 2 Able's flyers filed through a hatch and climbed up an exterior ladder. The day was warm already, though the tropical sun was still far from its zenith. Heat radiated from the steel ladder treads and handrails. The airmen blinked and squinted in the morning sunlight. Moving from a cool, dark ready room to the open-air flight deck was like emerging from a cave onto a bright sunny beach. The pilots clasped their plotting boards close to their sides to prevent their charts from being blown overboard and fanned out across the flight deck in groups of two and three, trotting toward their airplanes like atheletes taking the field.

Intrepid's flight deck, slightly more than 840 feet in length and 109 feet wide at the widest, covered an area of nearly two acres, the equivalent of one and a half football fields. The flight deck was constructed largely of wood, like a heavy-duty hardwood floor. Hundreds of fir planks, each about the width of a railroad tie, were bolted to thin underplates of steel and separated every few feet by aircraft tie-down beams made of steel. Functionally, the flight deck was divided into three separate areas from the rear of the ship forward: the aircraft landing area farthest aft; the run-up area amidships (also known as the barrier area); and the takeoff area forward (also known as the catapult area).

The landing area extended forward from *Intrepid*'s stern about four hundred feet, encompassing nearly half of the carrier's overall length. Thirteen arresting gear cables stretched across the landing area at intervals of about twenty feet and were elevated slightly off the flight deck by chafing plates and lifts. All carrier-based aircraft were fitted with a tail hook that was designed to engage an arresting gear cable on touchdown. Each arresting gear cable was connected to a hydraulic braking engine located beneath the flight deck; when an airplane "caught a wire," the arresting gear cable dragged a piston through a cylinder filled with hydraulic fluid. This counterforce resisted the pull of the airplane and brought it to an abrupt stop.

The engine run-up area was the place where carrier pilots ran up their engines to maximum power just before releasing their brakes for takeoff. This area was located adjacent to *Intrepid*'s "island," a multideck superstructure that towered above *Intrepid*'s flight deck amidships on her starboard side. The island housed the aircraft carrier's primary flight control station, or "pri-fly" (the function of which was similar to an aircraft control tower at a civilian airport); the ship's pilothouse, navigation, and flag bridges (the flag bridge was used for signaling); and other spaces devoted to air defense and ship handling. *Intrepid*'s run-up area contained five collapsible wire fences, or barriers, that could be strung across the flight deck during landing operations like cattle fences. The barriers protected the forward areas of the flight deck from airplanes that failed to engage an arresting wire on touchdown. Deck crews raised the barriers whenever an airplane was on final approach, and collapsed them as soon as the airplane had landed safely and hooked a wire; during takeoff operations, deck crews collapsed the barriers or removed them completely.

The takeoff or catapult area extended forward from the run-up area to *Intrepid*'s bow, a distance of about 450 feet. This was the "runway" area, where carrier pilots made their final takeoff runs into the wind at full power. The flight deck catapults—*Intrepid* had two of them, one on her port side and the other on her starboard—brought an airplane quickly up to flying speed by slingshotting it off the bow. But catapults were not used to launch aircraft on a major strike. The catapult mechanism was hydraulically actuated and could not be recycled with sufficient speed or reliability to launch thirty or forty warplanes within the space of fifteen or twenty minutes, which was the desired launch rate. Catapults were used primarily to launch smaller groups of airplanes on combat air patrols and search missions, when winds were light, or when the flight deck was too constrained for a deck launch. In most cases, carrier pilots made a "free deck launch" from the ship unaided by the catapults.

The warplanes assigned to Strike 2 Able, all thirty-one of them, were tied down four abreast in the landing area with their wings folded. The Avengers, each armed with a torpedo set to run at a depth of eight feet, were parked farthest aft. The heavy torpedo bombers would require the longest takeoff roll and be the last to launch. Three rows of Helldivers were parked next in line. Each of the dive-bombers was armed with a single thousand-pound bomb; eight of the twelve carried armor-piercing bombs designed to penetrate the armor plate of a warship before detonating. Three rows of Hellcats were parked farthest forward; the fighters were armed with .50-caliber machine gun ammunition but no bombs.

Air Group 18's Avengers and Helldivers were painted in the same tricolor scheme: deep blue-gray (called sea blue) on the upper surfaces, lighter blue (intermediate blue) along the sides of the fuselage, and flat white (nonspecular white, in navy jargon) on the undersurfaces. Hellcats were painted glossy sea blue overall. None of the airplanes had nose art or decoration; their paint scheme was strictly functional. The wings and fuselage of each airplane were marked with a recognition insignia that identified the plane as American. The American navy design consisted of a dark blue circle, three or four feet in diameter, with a white star in the center and a blue-bordered white stripe behind it. The tips of the warplanes' propellers were painted yellow so the men on the flight deck could see the arc of a spinning propeller and stand clear. The side number of each warplane was stenciled on its vertical stabilizer and engine cowling, and a white cross, or plus sign, was stenciled on the tail above the side number. The plus sign was the distinguishing mark of an Air Group 18 airplane; no other air group in the navy had the same mark.

Scores of flight deck personnel stood among the parked airplanes and waited patiently for the aviators to come to them. Strike 2 Able could not be launched without the coordinated efforts of specialized flight deck crews, the members of which wore distinctively colored cloth helmets or slipover jerseys that identified each man's role in the launch process. There were chock men in purple jerseys who stood ready to remove the wooden wheel chocks that prevented the airplanes from rolling off the flight deck. There were fuel service crews wearing red caps, who had pumped high-octane aviation gasoline from deck-edge fueling stations into the airplanes' gas tanks. Hook men wearing green jerseys stood ready to operate the arresting gear if an airplane was forced to return to the carrier after takeoff. Plane directors, or taxi men, in yellow shirts were prepared to orchestrate the movement of airplanes from the parking area to the engine run-up and takeoff areas. There were "talkers" in brown shirts, who provided a voice communication link between the air officer in pri-fly and supervisors on deck. Firefighters in red helmets and jerseys, and "hot papas" clad in heavy asbestos suits waited on standby to suppress fires and rescue aircrew from burning aircraft. There were plane captains, one for each airplane, wearing their ordinary blue chambray shirts; they had conducted preflight inspections of the airplanes selected for the strike and stood ready to assist the pilots in starting their engines.

Although *Intrepid* was steaming through the Philippine Sea on a southwesterly course at sixteen knots, the flight deck was relatively calm. The prevailing sea breeze, blowing steadily from the east at fourteen knots, largely offset the wind generated by the carrier's own motion and reduced the air moving across the deck to a light zephyr. The flight deck was hot and quiet, except for the omnipresent drone of exhaust from the ship's eight oil-fired boilers that vented through uptake pipes (the "stack") in *Intrepid*'s island. The escaping stack gas sounded like a one-note bagpipe and carried a pungent burned odor, like the chemical effluvium of a diesel refinery.

Will and Ray Skelly wove their way through the rows of Hellcats and Helldivers and searched for the side numbers of their Avengers. Will located his assigned torpedo bomber in the front row of Avengers on the starboard side. He hadn't flown this particular airplane before. She was Bureau of Aeronautics Number 73202, with the side number "7" painted on her tail and engine cowling. The Avenger's plane captain greeted Will beneath the propeller hub, and the two of them began a quick walk around.

The pilot handbook for the TBM Avenger describes it as a "single-engine, midwing, all-metal monoplane of semi-monocoque construction." This latter phrase meant that the airplane drew much of its structural strength from the metal skin attached to its frame. The TBM was the largest carrier-borne warplane in the navy's inventory, with a fuselage forty feet long and five feet wide at its widest. When fully extended, its wings spanned fifty-four feet, a distance nearly half the width of *Intrepid*'s flight deck. The wings stood six feet above the deck at their root (the place where they attach to the fuselage) and angled upward to ten feet above the flight deck at their tips. An air-cooled Wright Cyclone R-2600-20 engine powered the Avenger. The "R" stood for radial, meaning that the engine's cylinders were arranged circumferentially around the propeller shaft; the R-2600-20 boasted fourteen cylinders in two rows of seven. The engine generated seventeen hundred horsepower and spun a variable-pitch, three-bladed propeller that measured thirteen feet from tip to tip. The pilot's flight station, covered by a Plexiglas "greenhouse" canopy, sat atop the fuselage. The gunner's egg-shaped ball turret sat abaft the pilot's flight station and mounted a .50-caliber machine gun. The radioman's flight station was located inside the fuselage aft of the main wing; his compartment housed a small .30-caliber machine gun for shooting at targets below the airplane. Despite the handbook's description, the Avenger was not constructed entirely of metal. To conserve weight, the Avenger's control surfaces (her ailerons, elevators, and rudder) were covered with varnished fabric instead of aluminum.

Number seven's plane captain, a young man about Will's age, followed Will around like a proud father as Will inspected the Avenger for any obvious defects that would render it unairworthy. The plane captain reported that number seven had a full bag of gas, two full drop tanks, thirty gallons of engine oil, and no discrepancies. Will paused to study the bulbous drop tanks that were fastened under each wing near the main landing gear strut, inboard of the wing hinge, shaking them gently to check their integrity. He also peered into the Avenger's open bomb bay to ensure his torpedo was nestled securely against its braces and properly wired. The torpedo, round and thick as a tree trunk, hung menacingly in its shackles.

In making his preflight rounds, Ray Skelly passed Lieutenant Junior Grade John F. Forsyth, a dive-bomber pilot whose Helldiver was parked in the row immediately ahead of Skelly's torpedo bomber. Forsyth shouted at Ray, "You torpedoes are going to have it rough today."

Skelly didn't hear Forsyth correctly. "The hell you say," Skelly yelled back. "We're going to get it today."

An oval hatch on the Avenger's starboard side permitted crew access to the interior of the fuselage. After completing his preflight, Will joined his two crewmen, Westmoreland and Christman, at the hatch. He shook hands with both men and wished them luck. The two crewmen, clad in khaki coveralls and flight gear nearly identical to Will's, climbed through the hole to reach their flight stations. Will hauled himself up on the airplane's right wing and, gripping his plotting board, inched forward along the wing root toward the cockpit.

The plane captain had clambered up the Avenger's port wing and opened the canopy side panels, thereby exposing the cockpit to the sky. He now stood on the wing root beside the cockpit waiting for Will to board, like a squire attending his knight. Will lowered himself onto the pilot's seat, stowed his plotting board beneath the main instrument panel, and adjusted his parachute pack and survival pack beneath his buttocks. He didn't buckle his parachute to his torso harness yet. In VT-18, it was standard practice for the pilot to take off without his parachute attached to his torso harness because of the difficulty of escaping the Avenger's cockpit in the event of a water landing. Westmoreland and Christman would not wear a parachute for takeoff either; their flight stations were too confining. Chest parachutes were available in the radioman's compartment near the fuselage hatch; if a crewman had to jump, he would buckle one of these to his harness.

The plane captain leaned into the cockpit as Will settled into his seat. He handed Will his shoulder straps and connected the cords of the young pilot's earphones. Will slipped his fingers into his leather flying gloves and quickly ran his eyes around the cockpit. The Avenger's primary flight instruments and engine gauges were arrayed directly in front of him in the upper instrument panel. The Avenger's control column, the "stick" that controls the airplane's pitch and roll, stood between his knees. The rudder pedals, which control the airplane's yaw, lay beneath the balls of his feet on either side of a center console of secondary instruments. The Avenger's engine control quadrant lay within easy reach of Will's left hand; the engine control quadrant held three levers by which the pilot adjusted the engine's manifold pressure, fuel mixture, and supercharger. Rows of silver-headed toggle switches lay at Will's right hand; these controlled the airplane's electrical and armament circuits and its communication and navigation radios. Each of VT-18's Avengers was identically equipped, and everything in the cockpit of number seven seemed to be in order.

The plane captain scampered down from the Avenger's wing and grabbed a fire extinguisher. Having a fire bottle in hand would enable him to quickly douse an engine fire on start, which was a common occurrence when cranking a big radial engine. He positioned himself to the left of the Avenger's nose, which was the plane captain's appointed place for engine start, and made eye contact with Will. Plane captain and pilot made sure each could see the other clearly.

Will completed the prescribed prestart checklist. He touched the engine controls and switches in the recommended sequence, muttering to himself the name of each item on the list. Ignition and accessory switches off; mixture idle cutoff; supercharger low; propeller pitch low; cowl flaps open; throttle cracked open. Will had logged over 290 flight hours in Avengers and was thoroughly familiar with his airplane, but he followed his checklists diligently nevertheless. The process of completing the checklists ordered his thoughts, calmed his nerves, and gave him confidence. But more important, the Avenger's big radial engine was temperamental and difficult to start. The last thing Will wanted to do was screw up the start sequence and be scrubbed ignominiously from the mission. When he finished his checklist, Will placed his hands on the airplane's canopy bow. This was the signal to his plane captain that he was ready. There was nothing for either of them to do now except wait patiently for the order to start engines.

The launch sequence would involve four distinct phases: engine start, taxi, engine run-up, and takeoff. *Intrepid*'s air officer, called the air boss, controlled each phase of the launch from his pri-fly command post on the island. From his cockpit perch, Will had a clear view forward of *Intrepid*'s pri-fly station and her flag bridge one deck below it; his lines of sight left and right were largely blocked by his Avenger's folded wing panels, which acted like blinders on a horse. Will fixed his attention on pri-fly and the flag bridge; the earliest sign the air boss was ready to get things rolling would come from the flag bridge.

While Strike 2 Able's aviators were manning their planes, signalmen on *Intrepid*'s flag bridge hoisted identical sets of signals up the carrier's port and starboard halyards and then lowered them halfway. Each set of signals consisted of a Fox flag (a bloodred diamond on a white field), a black canvas ball about the size of a medicine ball, and five or six brightly colored numerical pennants. The Fox flags and black balls alerted the battleships, cruisers, and destroyers of *Intrepid*'s screening force that she was about to commence flight operations and launch aircraft; the numerical pennants advised the screening force of the aircraft carrier's "impending course and speed" for launch, or "Fox Corpen." When *Intrepid* turned into the wind to launch Strike 2 Able, the ships of the screen would maneuver in synchrony to the same Fox Corpen. Hoisting the Fox flags and black balls up the halyard and lowering them halfway, called "hoisting at the dip," was a "prepare to execute" signal; hoisting the signals rapidly from the dip to the top of the carrier's yardarm, called "two-blocking," was an "execute" signal, the order to conform to the carrier's movements.

The signals hung limp at the dip, and Will glimpsed at the heavens while he waited. The azure sky was as blue and deep as the ocean beneath it. Thin streaks of cirrus, far higher than Will's Avenger would ever fly, caught the morning sun, and a few cumulus clouds with incandescent white tops and blue-gray bottoms drifted lazily past *Intrepid* at two thousand feet like fat balloons. Otherwise, the air was clear with good visibility, eight miles or more.

The weather was much too good, Will observed glumly. Sunny skies and unlimited visibility, normally a happy combination for aviators, were a grave disadvantage for an Avenger pilot on a torpedo run. In fine weather, enemy antiaircraft gunners could detect an approaching torpedo plane at far greater range and keep them within their sights for far longer periods. Will figured he would need all the luck the Fates allowed him today. Though not a superstitious man, he took some comfort in the fact that Kenny Barden had assigned him Avenger number seven for this mission.

Earlier that morning, Rear Admiral Bogan had alerted Admiral Halsey, 3rd Fleet commander, that *Intrepid* and *Cabot* would be ready to launch a first strike against the Japanese task force by eight thirty a.m. Admiral Halsey flew his flag aboard the battleship *New Jersey*, which, on the morning of October 24, was steaming only twenty-five hundred yards off *Intrepid*'s starboard beam as a unit of Task Group 38.2 and serving as the task group guide. Halsey had learned the precise location of the Japanese armada in Tablas Strait at about eight twenty a.m., and Japanese intentions were now clear to him. The Imperial Japanese Navy had decided to contest the American invasion of the Philippines and had committed a powerful naval force to the effort, including its prized *Yamatos*. The Japanese obviously wanted to provoke a showdown with 3rd Fleet, and Halsey was happy to oblige. He viewed the appearance of the Japanese fleet in the Sibuyan Sea as an opportunity to deliver a crushing blow to the enemy. He had briefly considered sending Task Force 38, battleships and all, west through the San Bernardino Strait to confront the oncoming Japanese in the Sibuyan Sea, but the danger of enemy minefields had persuaded Halsey to rely instead on concentrated air strikes.

At eight twenty-seven a.m., Halsey issued the order authorizing Bogan to attack, bypassing altogether the commander of Task Force 38, Vice Admiral Marc Mitscher. Halsey's signal to Bogan read, "Strike! Repeat strike! Good luck."

Halsey's order filtered down through the chain of command. At eight forty-six a.m., Will watched as blue-shirted sailors on *Intrepid*'s flag bridge heaved on the lines that hoisted the black balls and Fox flags to the top of the carrier's yardarms. This was the signal to execute the course change. Seconds later, *Intrepid* sounded her horn—she loosed a prolonged basso profundo blast that carried for miles around the ship—and began a turn to her Fox Corpen of 070 degrees, a heading that would take her directly into the prevailing wind. The carrier heeled slowly into the turn, and Will felt the deck tip beneath him. *Intrepid*'s four large brass screws churned the water at 199 r.p.m., and the big ship, quivering to her core, accelerated ponderously to her launch speed of twenty-five knots.

The ship's horn was a call to action for every sailor on *Intrepid*'s flight deck, whether sitting in the cockpit of an airplane or standing on deck. Everyone tensed, anticipating the next series of commands the air boss would issue in rapid succession over *Intrepid*'s flight deck loudspeakers. The air boss's first command, "Stand by to start engines," crackled through the loudspeaker as soon as the sound of the ship's horn faded.

Will immediately initiated his engine start sequence. He set his throttle at twelve hundred r.p.m., selected the center main tank for his supply fuel, and energized the airplane's battery. The batteries of a few Avengers and Helldivers proved too weak to energize their electric starter motors, and the plane captains of these invalids had to hand-crank a mechanical generator for electrical power. Will's plane captain had assured him he wouldn't need a manual start, and Will hoped the boy was right.

"Stand clear of propellers," sounded next from the flight deck loudspeaker.

Will's plane captain flashed him a thumbs-up, a confirmation that the arc of his propeller was clear of chock men, fire bottles, and other obstructions. Will engaged the electric primer, which injected fuel into the engine's cylinders.

The command, "Start engines," arrived a beat later. To alert anyone on deck who may not have heard the verbal order above the wind, *Intrepid*'s air boss sounded an air whistle. At the shriek of the whistle, plane captains and chock men reflexively stepped back, double-checking that they were clear of the deadly propeller arcs.

Three elements—fuel, air, and electricity—are necessary to start a gasoline motor, and these three elements must be mixed in exactly the right proportions. Achieving the right balance in an Avenger's R-2600-20 engine was not easy. The plane captain must have properly prepared the engine for start (usually by pulling the propeller by hand through a few rotations), and the pilot must manipulate the engine controls deftly. Will moved his starter switch to the MESH position, which engaged the Avenger's electric starting motor. He heard the motor's reassuring whine and, slowly, his propeller began to move, like the blades of a windmill in a stiffening breeze. Will counted six blades passing his nose and flipped his ignition switch to "both," thereby energizing the airplane's double-wired ignition system. The torpedo bomber coughed and shuddered, and puffs of gray smoke belched from its engine exhausts. As the Avenger's propeller began to spin more rapidly—the R-2600-20 ran initially on priming fuel and emitted a low *plump, plump, plump, plump*—Will moved his mixture control to automatic rich and decreased the flow of priming fuel. To Will's relief, his R-2600-20 roared to life on the first attempt. More important, his sometimes cranky radial engine didn't falter or fade but settled quickly into a throaty rumble. Will eyed his engine oil and temperature gauges for any sign of trouble and found none. The Avenger's big propeller whirled smoothly in front of his nose, inscribing a blurry yellow circle. Will tested his propeller control by altering the propeller's pitch; the propeller made a deep fluttering noise as it changed blade angles, like a flock of quail flushed from the brush.

The fighter pilots started their Hellcats' big Pratt & Whitney radial engines by firing shotgun shell–style starter cartridges; the gas from the cartridge spun an impeller that rotated the engine crankshaft. The *pop, pop, pop* of the fighters' starter cartridges sounded like a ragged fusillade of gunfire; as the Pratt & Whitney engines caught, the tom-tom beat of combustion rose steadily. Less than one minute after the air boss's start command, all thirty-one warplanes had boomed to life. The voices of their engines merged into an earsplitting chorus, a steady crescendo of thunder like an army of percussionists pounding on kettledrums fortissimo and presto. Sitting near the rear of the pack, Will felt the brunt of the noise; the sound rattled his chest and the air was acrid with the smell of engine exhaust.

By eight fifty a.m., *Intrepid* and her consorts had completed a sweeping turn to the Fox Corpen of 070 degrees, and Task Group 38.2 was slicing through the Philippine Sea at twenty-five knots. The prevailing sea breeze blew from 080 degrees at sixteen knots, producing in combination with the carrier's velocity through the water nearly forty knots of wind down the center of *Intrepid*'s flight deck. This was a class-eight wind on the Beaufort Scale, a gale force gust sufficient to set whole trees in motion and snap branches. The wind buffeted the men still standing on deck, such as chock men and yellow-shirts, whipping the fabric of their clothing and diluting their voices. Speech became impossible and walking difficult. The Fox flags and signal pennants streamed aft in carnival display.

Commander Ellis in his Hellcat was the first pilot to launch. Chock men removed all wheel chocks from beneath the idling airplanes and dashed to the deck edge, carrying the heavy wooden chocks like suitcases. Following the hand signals of a yellow-shirt, Ellis eased his fighter out of its parking space and taxied forward to the run-up area adjacent to *Intrepid*'s island. As Ellis exited the parking row, he extended his Hellcat's wings and locked them. The flight deck director, called Fly I, stood at the engine run-up point; his job was to control the takeoff sequence and time each airplane's takeoff run with the pitch of the ship. On Fly I's signal, Ellis ran up his engine, released his brakes, and rolled down the deck for takeoff.

Commander Ellis's Hellcat lifted off the flight deck at eight fifty-three a.m., followed by ten more Hellcats at roughly thirty-five-second intervals. VB-18's fourteen dive-bombers, including the Helldiver piloted by Lieutenant Junior Grade John Forsyth, took off within the space of seven or eight minutes. By nine-oh-seven a.m. it was the Avengers' turn.

A yellow-shirt beckoned Lieutenant Bud Williams's Avenger out of its parking row. Williams, as division leader, would be the first of VT-18's Avenger pilots to launch on Strike 2 Able, and the first-ever Avenger pilot to attempt an overweight carrier takeoff and climb-out with drop tanks. Squatty Vaughn, Ray Skelly, Will Fletcher, and the four torpedo-plane pilots idling in the back row would follow Williams in that order.

Will was vitally interested in observing Bud Williams's takeoff run, but so were many others. Word had spread quickly throughout the ship that Strike 2 Able's torpeckers were going to deck-launch with drop tanks and torpedoes, something never tried before. The catwalks on *Intrepid*'s island, called Vultures' Row, were crammed with curious onlookers. These included Ensign Ben St. John and other VT-18 pilots who were scheduled to fly later in the day, eager and anxious to see how well their buddies and their heavily laden Avengers performed. The question on everyone's mind was whether Williams's torpedo bomber would reach flying speed before it arrived at the end of *Intrepid*'s flight deck. Men debated whether it would fly, but there was no disagreement about the consequences if it didn't. If Williams's Avenger couldn't get airborne and splashed down in front of the carrier, *Intrepid* could not turn aside or stop in time. Displacing thirty-five thousand tons and steaming at twenty-five knots, the carrier would simply run over Bud and his hapless crew.

Fly I ordered Williams to run up his engine to full power and release his brakes. Bud's torpedo bomber crept forward on its initial takeoff roll, its engine hammering. Bright ribbons of water vapor corkscrewed aft from the airplane's spinning propeller tips, and its tail came up almost immediately in the stiff breeze. Williams deflected his rudder far to the right to counter the torque generated by his propeller and, near the bitter end of *Intrepid*'s bow, at what seemed the last moment, he raised his Avenger's nose. The airplane lifted begrudgingly off the flight deck but didn't climb; it sagged tail-first off the bow and disappeared below the level of *Intrepid*'s flight deck, completely out of sight of the men on deck.

The observers on Vultures' Row leaned over the catwalk railings, craning their necks for a better view. After a few agonizing seconds, Williams's Avenger staggered back into sight and inched above the horizon, climbing slowly like the overweight bird she was.

Will was greatly relieved by what he saw, and heartened. Williams's overweight takeoff hadn't looked that much different from the normal takeoff profile of a heavily loaded Avenger. The old Grumman Turkey and its R-2600-20 hadn't missed a lick.

Will had to concentrate on his own takeoff now. A yellow-shirted taximan appeared in front of Will's Avenger and pointed at its belly. The taximan drew a figure eight in the air with his hands, which was the signal to close the Avenger's bomb bay doors. Will complied immediately, raising the handle in the cockpit that actuated the doors. The red "door open" warning light in the cockpit blinked out, and Westmoreland, who could view the bomb bay through a portal at his flight station, confirmed over the intercom that the doors were closed. Next, the yellow-shirt patted his chest and walked backward into the wind, pumping his arms back and forth from his chest. This was the signal to taxi forward slowly. Will released his toe brakes and crept forward until the taximan held up closed fists, which was the signal to stop.

The yellow-shirt then extended his arms at his sides, and Will responded by repositioning the cockpit lever that extended his Avenger's wings. Driven by hydraulic pressure, the outer panels of number seven's wings rotated slowly at the joint and fell into place. A warning horn called a "howler" wailed in Will's cockpit and didn't stop until the wings were fully extended. Will looked at each wing. There were red-painted strips of metal, called "flags," linked to the folding mechanism near the leading edges of each span; if the flags were no longer visible, the Avenger's wings were fully extended and locked. By twisting around in his ball turret, Christman had a clear view of the wing roots. He, too, had a keen personal interest in locked wings—taking off with unlocked wings was a one-way ticket to Davy Jones's locker—and he reported "wings locked" over the intercom.

Will shifted his attention to his final takeoff checklist, fingering each switch and visually verifying the position of each control. Wings spread and locked; bomb bay doors closed; mixture control auto rich; blower control low-ratio; propeller pitch control set at high-r.p.m.; carburetor air direct; cowl flaps open; oil cooler flaps closed; fuel selector on main tank; rudder trim tab set one degree right to assist in maintaining directional control on takeoff; tail wheel castor unlocked until in position for takeoff; canopy locked open for emergency egress if necessary; auxiliary fuel pump on; wing flaps lowered; shoulder harness secure. Will keyed his intercom microphone and confirmed that Westmoreland and Christman were ready for launch; they were.

The yellow-shirt passed Will to Fly I, who motioned Will forward and halted him at the spot where Williams had begun his takeoff roll. Will locked his Avenger's tail wheel and held his control stick far aft to keep his tail wheel firmly planted on the flight deck; he pushed his stick from side to side, making a final check to ensure that he had full throw and proper rigging of his ailerons.

Fly I held up a red-and-white-checkered flag in his right hand, like a starter at a racetrack. Clenching his left fist, which was the signal to brake, Fly I twirled the flag above his head. Will pressed heavily on his brake pedals, and ran up his engine to maximum power by easing the throttle forward to its stop. Number seven's R-2600-20 stuttered briefly, and then erupted into a high-decibel roar.

Having a smoothly functioning engine is a life-or-death matter during a carrier takeoff. There is no long concrete runway ahead, no possibility of aborting and setting the airplane down on solid ground if the engine coughs or sputters. Once Will released his brakes he was committed. Today especially, with an Avenger as heavy as Will's, there was absolutely no margin for mechanical malfunction. Will would require every inch of manifold pressure and every rotation of his propeller to get airborne.

He sat bolt upright in his cockpit seat, his face a study in concentration. He now commanded seventeen hundred horsepower at the starting gate. Avenger number seven strained against her wheel brakes, wobbling and shaking as he held her in check. The thunder of her engine engulfed him, and wash from her spinning propeller flooded into Will's cockpit in a steady torrent, ripping at the fabric of his flight suit. He listened intently, straining to hear any misfire, sputter, whistle, or whine, and flicked his eyes over his engine instruments. The quivering needles on the dials told him his big Cyclone engine was producing maximum power, forty-four inches of manifold pressure, and twenty-six hundred r.p.m. His oil temperature and pressure gauges, canaries in the coal mine for engine failure, were within prescribed limits.

Fly I also listened to number seven's engine. He had the authority to scrub the launch if he didn't like the sound of the airplane's motor, unless the pilot insisted on taking off with a rough-running engine and overrode him.

Will held number seven's throttle forward with his left hand and gripped the control stick with his right. He looked at Fly I and nodded his head up and down in an exaggerated motion, his signal to Fly I that he was ready to go.

Fly I glanced forward to ensure that *Intrepid*'s bow was steady or swinging upward. Satisfied that Will would not take off on a downward plunge of the ship, Fly I whipped his checkered flag toward *Intrepid*'s bow.

Will dropped his feet from the wheel brakes and shoved his right rudder pedal to the stop. What mattered during the takeoff roll was not the airplane's speed relative to *Intrepid*, but her speed through the air. Almost instantaneously, Will's airspeed indicator registered forty-five knots, and he pushed forward on his control stick to lift his airplane's tail off the deck, steering himself down the centerline of the flight deck with his rudder pedals like a man steering a boat. The heavy Avenger accelerated more sluggishly than usual. At eighty knots and with not much flight deck remaining, Will hauled back on the stick and elevated number seven's nose to her maximum "lift-over-drag" angle of attack. He sensed his Avenger lighten on its main landing gear and begin to float. *Intrepid*'s bow flashed beneath him and he sailed out over the water. The sensation always reminded him of running full-tilt boogie off the end of a diving board.

Like Williams's Avenger, number seven began to sink toward the water. Will shifted his eyes between his airspeed indicator and his vertical speed indicator. With his engine running at maximum power, only two things mattered: maintaining maximum lift over drag and handling his controls smoothly. Fortunately for Avenger pilots, the performance of an airfoil improves slightly when compressed against the earth's surface, a phenomenon called "ground effect." Will counted on ground effect to arrest his plane's descent, and, after a few long seconds, number seven began to climb and her vertical speed indicator ticked upward. He angled his Avenger slightly to the right so the airplane taking off behind him would not be jostled by his wake turbulence.

Will's Avenger, like all carrier-borne aircraft of the period, was a "tail dragger," meaning it had two main landing gear and a tail wheel. The airplane's main landing gear were located on either side of the fuselage beneath the wing, and its tail wheel was located far aft beneath the radioman's compartment. Will yanked upward on his gear handle to raise his landing gear. Driven by hydraulic pumps, the main gear folded outward and upward into wheel wells beneath each wing. Relieved of the aerodynamic drag of its main mounts and wheels, number seven began to accelerate.

Will readied himself next to retract his wing flaps. Grabbing the ball-shaped flap actuation handle in the cockpit, he hesitated, remembering Williams's cautionary briefing. Flap retraction in an Avenger was a deadly trap under the best of circumstances. Avengers are configured with "split flaps" that flatten themselves against the undersides of the airplane's wings; whenever an Avenger's split flaps retract there is considerable loss in lift and a heavy shift in forward elevator pressure as the airplane's nose falls through. An Avenger will stall and sink if the pilot fails to counteract the loss of lift by forcefully raising the nose. The pilot's operating manual for the Avenger printed this cautionary ditty, which invariably flashed through Will's head whenever he touched the flap handle: "Here lies Dagwood Diddleworth Doakes, who might be called a goon. He made his last faux pas on earth when he raised his flaps too soon."

Will executed his flap transition without faux pas, and number seven settled into a steady climb at three hundred feet per minute. As his airplane accelerated through 120 knots, Will slowly retarded his throttle and decreased his r.p.m., thereby reducing engine power from full power to normal "climb power," which was about 60 percent of full power at sea level. He listened closely to the sound of his motor as he moved the controls. The most likely time for engine failure was during the first power reduction after takeoff, when things not screwed together properly tended to fly apart. Number seven's engine didn't miss a beat.

During his climb, Will squinted through his canopy windscreen to keep Williams, Vaughn, and Skelly in sight. Will had to lean from from side to side to see clearly over the upturned nose of his Avenger. The torpedo bombers flown by Williams, Vaughn, and Skelly looked like giant seabirds trailing one another into the morning sun. Passing eight hundred feet, Will remembered to buckle his parachute and survival pack to his harness.

Bud Williams's first job after takeoff was to combine his eight Avengers into a single formation for the journey to the Sibuyan Sea. Standard carrier doctrine required the flight leader to make a slight turn to the right after takeoff and then hold the carrier's Fox Corpen for a period of time equal to the number of planes in his division multiplied by the average launch interval (in seconds) for the type of aircraft in the division. After the prescribed time, the leader was expected to begin a gentle left turn back toward the carrier to collect his flock. The airplanes behind the leader were expected to cut across the arc of the leader's turn and join up with him one by one.

The rendezvous after takeoff was Will's favorite part of every formation flight. The maneuver always put him in mind of a childhood game of follow-the-leader or crack-the-whip. But the rendezvous after takeoff was a spatial puzzle played in three dimensions, and a much more serious and dangerous game. The game began as soon as the flight leader, flying at a constant airspeed and angle of bank, initiated his rendezvous turn, and the wingmen turned toward him to catch up. The trailing pilots had to monitor their closure rate and approach angle and constantly adjust their airspeed and angle of bank; they could not close so rapidly that they overshot the leader, nor close so slowly that they lagged behind him. Done correctly, the rendezvous after takeoff was a beautiful slow dance of airplanes in relative motion; flown recklessly or inattentively, it was fraught with the risk of a midair collision. As Van Antwerp preached repeatedly, how smoothly a pilot accomplished his rendezvous was a sign of his proficiency and professionalism; how quickly a division joined up was a mark of the squadron's competency and esprit de corps.

The basic building block of every formation was a two-plane "section" comprised of a lead aircraft and his wingman. Navy carrier doctrine in late 1944 left many of the details of formation flying to squadron commanders, but a navy wingman normally flew forty-five to sixty degrees aft of his leader and maintained twenty feet of separation from his leader, wingtip to wingtip. By late 1944, most combat squadrons required a wingman to fly a few feet below his lead in a "stepped-down" alignment that permitted the wingman to keep his lead's head and hands in sight at all times; line of sight was essential for the flight leader to be able to communicate by hand signal when his section was operating in radio silence. If the leader had a wingman on each side, his three-plane unit was still called a "section." Two- and three-plane sections were combined with other sections to create larger formations, such as divisions; the names and configurations of formations varied, depending on the total number of sections involved and the nature of the mission.

The torpeckers executed their much-dreaded overweight takeoffs without incident, and all eight Avengers rendezvoused exactly as Williams had briefed it. VT-18's join-up consumed no more than six minutes. Williams flew at the point of his assembled formation, with four Avengers trailing to starboard and three to port. This arrangement, called an unbalanced vee, resembled an arrowhead or a chevron of geese on the wing. Squatty Vaughn flew off Williams's port wing, while Ray Skelly, Will's former acey-deucey opponent, flew off Vaughn's port wing. Will was tail-end Charlie; he flew off Skelly's port wing and occupied the trailing position on the left leg of the unbalanced vee.

Will held his position by closely observing Skelly's torpedo bomber and making small adjustments of his flight controls to eliminate any relative motion between his airplane and Skelly's. By deflecting his ailerons and rudder pedals to the left, Will caused his airplane to move away from Skelly; by deflecting them right, he made his plane move closer. By adjusting his elevator and throttle, Will made his Avenger climb or descend, or slide ahead or behind the bearing line. Though focused primarily on Skelly, Will couldn't resist glancing up the line past Skelly's airplane toward Vaughn's airplane and Williams's. The picture thrilled him. The big blue torpedo bombers of Division 2 were suspended in space as if by an invisible hand, virtually motionless in relation to one another, and perfectly aligned on a forty-five-degree bearing line as if tethered together by the same string. The painted skin of the warplanes and their white star-and-bar insignia shone brightly in the sunlight. Their canopy glass sparkled in the clear Pacific air. The Avengers' potent Mark 13 torpedoes were concealed within the airplanes' bellies, but the black barrels of the Avengers' machine guns protruded threateningly from their ball turrets and ventral windows. The Avengers seemed to Will the embodiment of modern airpower, the very image of American military strength and lethality.

VB-18's Helldivers orbited high above the Avengers, and Ellis's Hellcats orbited higher still above the dive-bombers. Williams led Division 2 slowly upward to nine thousand feet, the Avengers' final cruising altitude en route to the target. _Intrepid_ had launched Strike 2 Able roughly forty nautical miles northeast of Samar. By nine fifteen a.m. _Cabot_'s contingent of warplanes had joined Strike 2 Able, and Commander Ellis had turned his combined strike group, now consisting of forty-five warplanes, to the west. Within minutes, the emerald shore of Samar drifted into view.

———

When Will first encountered the Philippines from the air in early September 1944, he was amazed by the sheer number of islands, and at just how small most really were. The Philippine archipelago consists of seventy-one hundred islands, scattered like the pieces of a shattered plate over eight hundred thousand square miles of ocean. But 90 percent of the islands have a landmass of less than one square mile; of the eleven major islands, only two, Luzon and Mindanao, have an area in excess of thirty-six thousand square miles, and the larger of these, Luzon, is only about the size of New York State. Will was also surprised by how mountainous most of the Philippine islands were, and how far above sea level many of the mountains soared, especially the massive volcanic cones on Luzon, which seemed always to be shrouded in clouds and rain. Will's navigational charts told him the elevations: The cordillera of Luzon and Mindanao rose more than eighty-five hundred feet above sea level; the cordillera of central Mindoro and Negros reach eighty-one hundred feet, and the cordillera of western Panay top sixty-one hundred feet. From the air, the islands appeared to be blanketed with an impenetrable hardwood jungle, except where the Filipinos had pushed back the forests to make way for their rice fields and farms, or had planted groves of coconut palms and banana trees, which seemed to flourish in dense abundance at the lower elevations. Surrounding the islands were turquoise waters of startling clarity and varying hue. Recognizable towns were few and far between, and most villages seemed to cling to the coasts. The fact that the Imperial Japanese Army occupied the Philippines did not prevent Will from appreciating the islands' wild and primitive beauty from afar, but he had no desire to set foot on them.

Traveling at a hundred and forty knots to conserve fuel, Commander Ellis led his strike group over the northern tip of Samar, then over the islands of Ticao and Masbate and a myriad of smaller islets that looked like stepping-stones in a pond. The shallows that surrounded them radiated every possible shade of blue. Here and there Will detected the geometric shapes of Filipino fish traps in the shallows. Passing Masbate, Ellis's warplanes crossed the eastern boundary of the Sibuyan Sea and headed toward Sibuyan and Romblon islands in the heart of the inland sea. The glistening waters spread out before them like a vast cerulean mirror, and the intensifying tropical sun deepened the palette of earth and sky. Will observed wistfully that October 24 was one of the loveliest days he had encountered in the western Pacific.

Commander Ellis had insisted on radio silence during the flight across the Sibuyan Sea, leaving Will and his fellow fliers alone with their private thoughts. Will tried not to dwell on the dangers ahead or the probability of returning to *Intrepid* unscathed. Forty-five airplanes against more than twenty Japanese warships, each bristling with antiaircraft guns, presented troubling odds, but nothing good would come from fretting about them. He diverted himself by flying rock-solid formation and by attending to the normal duties of an aircraft commander, just as if he were flying the entire mission by himself. Although Ellis was responsible for leading the combined strike group to the enemy, Will kept close track of the Avengers' progress westward. He periodically recorded his heading and airspeed, calculated his drift angle, and noted the exact time at which Division 2 passed over Samar and each of the islands on the path. He monitored number seven's fuel consumption and quantity, reassuring himself that his torpedo bomber was in fact pumping gasoline first from its ugly, drag-inducing drop tanks. He figured and refigured the division's elapsed flight time, estimated flight time to the target area, and remaining flight time. He plotted his return course to "point option," the fix from which he would navigate back to *Intrepid* at the end of the mission. Periodically, he called to his crew over the airplane's intercom, confirming his position with Westmoreland's radar track and prodding Christman unnecessarily to keep a sharp lookout for enemy planes. Not wanting to screw up his mission or run the risk of a torpedo attack for naught, he rehearsed in his mind his procedures for arming and dropping his torpedo. Adhering to old habits steadied his nerves.

As the strike group crossed into the Sibuyan Sea, Will observed two mountain ranges, one to the south and one to the west of his course, rising above the distant horizon. The blue-green peaks of the mountains crept slowly into view, as if they had been painted on scenery flats and pushed from the well of a stage. After an hour of flight, Will estimated the first mountain range was sixty miles south of his position and the second about the same distance off his nose. His navigational plot told him the southern mountains were those of western Panay, and the mountains ahead were those of Mindoro. He calculated that *Intrepid*'s strike group was rapidly approaching Tablas Island, a narrow spit of land roughly forty miles long and ten miles wide and oriented north–south along its length. Tablas Strait, the wide, deep-water channel that separates Tablas Island from Mindoro, lay directly ahead, only fifteen or twenty miles distant. *Intrepid*'s Sector Three search team had discovered the Japanese fleet entering Tablas Strait from the south; if Sector Three's contact report was correct, the enemy task force should lie somewhere in the strait off the northern end of Tablas Island. Will's heart began to pound in anticipation. Unless the enemy task force had turned back—part of Will wished this to be true—the enemy must be near. But where?

The northern half of Tablas Island was obscured by a thick blanket of low-lying cumulus clouds that appeared to extend all the way across Tablas Strait to the eastern shore of Mindoro. The cloud tops were dazzlingly white and peaked like whipped merengue. Under normal circumstances, the frothy cumulus would have offered a pleasant cloudscape, but on this morning they were simply a maddening obstruction. Will peered over his canopy rail, searching for breaks in the undercast, but there were none. By ten nineteen a.m., he figured the strike group had crossed over the western shore of Tablas Island and flown into the Strait.

At ten twenty, the clouds beneath Commander Ellis's attackers parted unexpectedly to reveal the wakes of the Japanese task force. The effect was as if someone had pulled away a blanket—a blanket frayed around the edges—to see what was beneath it. There were dozens of enemy warships steaming through the strait just east of Mindoro Island. The ships' wakes gleamed in the sunlight, as distinct against the royal blue waters of Tablas Strait as white chalk marks on blue fabric. The enemy task force appeared to be divided into two large groups; the ships of each group were sailing in parallel columns, apparently for mutual gunfire support.

Commander Ellis's attackers spotted the enemy task force at about the same instant. Will caught his breath at the sight. It suddenly occurred to him that there were far too many Japanese warships and far too few American airplanes.

The Japanese had monitored the approach of Commander Ellis's strike group on their air search radar. As soon as the American formation came within range of their guns, the Japanese opened fire.

Ellis's flyers were startled to see antiaircraft shells suddenly explode high above them, as high as sixteen thousand feet, detonating in bright, deadly kernels of red, yellow, and black. Some shells ruptured in pink feathers; others blossomed purple with white streamers. Commander Ellis promptly broke radio silence and radioed the position of the enemy armada back to *Intrepid*: latitude twelve degrees, forty minutes north, longitude 121 degrees, fifty minutes east, a position in the middle of Tablas Strait and abeam the northwestern tip of Tablas Island.

Nothing Bud Williams and his torpedo-plane pilots had experienced in three months of carrier warfare had prepared them for what they now saw beneath their wings in Tablas Strait. Below them lay the central core of the Imperial Japanese Fleet, more than a score of heavy enemy warships. Williams quickly tallied at least twenty-six or twenty-seven. He did not know their specific names, only their type and class. For months, using "plan and profile" diagrams of enemy warships, old Ernie Allen had drilled VT-18's pilots and aircrew relentlessly on how to identify Japanese surface ships, and Allen's persistent coaching now paid off. Williams recognized at least three older battleships of the *Kongo* or *Nagato* class, six heavy cruisers of the *Nachi* or *Mogami* class, three light cruisers, and thirteen destroyers. Two gigantic battleships of the *Yamato* class sailed in the lead group. With respect to these, Ernie Allen and the Sector Three search team had been right—and wrong. The massive wine-bottle-shaped forms of the *Yamato*-class ships were unmistakable, but the huge *Yamatos* were far heavier than forty-five thousand tons. They were wider in the beam than either an *Essex*-class aircraft carrier or an *Iowa*-class battleship. Williams estimated that the *Yamatos* displaced seventy thousand tons each if they displaced an ounce. By comparison, the smaller Japanese battleships and cruisers that sailed as the *Yamatos'* consorts looked like toy boats on a pond. Most of them were seasoned veterans, Williams guessed, participants in Japanese naval campaigns from the earliest days of the war.

Williams was right about the combat record of the warships beneath him. The Japanese formation included the battleship *Nagato*, which in the early days of the war had served as Admiral Isoroku Yamamoto's flagship (the Imperial Navy's plans for attacking Pearl Harbor had been finalized aboard *Nagato*) and more recently as an escort for Vice Admiral Jisaburo Ozawa's carriers in the Battle of the Philippine Sea; the battleships *Haruna* and *Kongo*, which had fought at Midway and in the Battle of Santa Cruz off Guadalcanal; the cruiser *Tone*, which had escorted Vice Admiral Chuichi Nagumo's carriers in the Pearl Harbor raid and seen combat at Midway, Guadalcanal, and in the Philippine Sea; the cruiser *Chokai*, which had repeatedly grappled with the American navy in the night battles off Savo Island; the cruisers *Kumano* and *Suzuya*, which had fought at Midway and the Battle of the Philippine Sea; and the crusier *Noshiro*, which as part of Vice Admiral Takeo Kurita's 2nd Fleet had attempted to prevent the American seizure of the Marianas. The enemy armada beneath Williams's wings was powerful and lethal, and had once ruled the Pacific.

As the American fliers peered down, the Japanese task force began to take evasive action. The warships altered course and accelerated, their screws carving sweeping white arcs on the blue table of the sea. The Japanese fleet commander clearly intended to keep his capital ships within a protective ring of antiaircraft fire and never offer an American attacker a predictable bearing on which to align. The enemy's fire intensified as Commander Ellis's fliers drew nearer. Japanese shells burst in dense Technicolor clusters, like the mad finale of a gigantic Fourth of July celebration. Some shells ejected silvery pellets or spewed white phosphorus, a dreadful chemical that stuck to any surface it touched and burned with inextinguishable ferocity. White phosphorus burned rapidly though metal and flesh alike, and pilots feared it like a snake in the cockpit. The angry explosions roiled the air, creating bone-jarring bumps in the sky.

Speaking calmly and succinctly, Commander Ellis broadcast target assignments over his strike group's tactical radio frequency. He ordered VB-18's twelve dive-bomber pilots to attack the two big *Yamato*-class superbattleships with their thousand-pound bombs, six planes to each ship. He directed Bud Williams's torpedo division to attack the easternmost *Yamato* and the *Nachi*-class cruiser that shielded her, and dispatched *Cabot*'s Avengers to the second *Yamato*. Last, he instructed the fighters of VF-18 and VF-29 to strafe the heavy enemy warships with their .50-caliber machine guns—each Hellcat mounted six wing guns—to divert enemy fire from the approaching torpedo planes.

Williams tautly acknowledged Ellis's order. He instructed two of his Avenger pilots to detach from the right side of his vee formation and attack the *Nachi*-class in a two-plane section. He signaled the remaining VT-18 torpedo plane pilots, including Squatty Vaughn, Ray Skelly, and Will Fletcher, to close up and remain with him for a hammer-and-anvil attack on the *Yamato*-class battleship farthest to the east—a superbattleship that American intelligence officers would soon identify as *Musashi*. Williams intended to split his flight of six planes into two three-plane sections during the descent, and attack *Musashi* on her port and starboard flanks.

The two-plane section broke away and headed for the *Nachi*-class cruiser, leaving Williams at the point of the Avenger formation, but with his vee now reduced to two torpedo bombers off his right wing and three off his left. Responding to Williams's close-up signal, the Avengers that remained with Williams, including Vaughn's, Skelly's, and Fletcher's, glided toward him along the bearing line. They eased in so close that Williams could see distinctly the features of several of the pilots and turret gunners. The men looked at him, awaiting his commands, their faces at once expectant, grim, determined, frightened, resigned, angry. Williams must have wondered in that moment which of these young men would emerge from the maelstrom ahead. Who would survive the morning, and who would not? Would any of them live through this ordeal? Williams raised his hand and signaled to the pilots arrayed off each wing: "Descend with me."

Then Bud Williams lowered the nose of his Avenger and led his boys down into the fire.

CHAPTER TWO

IN CALIFORNIA

★ ★ ★ ★ ★

Bud Williams had met most of his boys, including Ray Skelly and Squatty Vaughn, for the first time in early August 1943 at the Alameda Naval Air Station (NAS) in California. Commissioned at NAS Alameda on July 20, 1943, Torpedo 18 was comprised initially of sixteen junior officers and only a few airplanes. Before Van Antwerp arrived to take permanent command, Albert J. Long III, then a twenty-two-year-old lieutenant junior grade from Winnfield, Louisiana, had been appointed temporary commander and placed in charge of fifteen high-spirited young pilots of equal or slightly junior rank. Long's temporary command was a thankless job, akin to being team captain of an athletic squad on a road trip with no coach on the bus.

The first meeting between Williams and the boys probably occurred in one of the new airplane hangars the navy had constructed at Alameda. These were high-ceilinged, barnlike structures with repair shops, classrooms, and offices built into opposite walls; aircraft were stored in the space between, with two squadrons usually sharing the same hangar. Located on the western end of Alameda Island in the heart of San Francisco Bay, NAS Alameda was less than three years old when VT-18 was formed. The Navy Department had purchased the western end of Alameda Island, formerly an Indian burial ground and the terminus of a transcontinental railroad, for one dollar in 1935 and begun construction in 1938. When the airfield was officially commissioned in November 1940, it sprawled over one thousand acres, built partly on the original island and partly on landfill. Seen from the air, the airfield was a rectangular plain sitting a few feet above the chilly waters of San Francisco Bay. There were two sets of concrete runways and adjacent aprons, seaplane ramps, repair facilities for ships, office buildings, barracks, recreational facilities, warehouses, long quays for docking aircraft carriers and tenders, ship repair facilities, and, of course, aircraft hangars. The new naval air station and carrier base had served its purpose admirably early in the war. On April 2, 1942, the aircraft carrier *Hornet* departed Alameda loaded with sixteen U.S. Army Air Corps B-25 bombers on a secret mission. Eighteen days later, *Hornet* deck-launched these B-25s on Colonel James Doolittle's morale-boosting bombing raid over Tokyo.

World War II, a "two-ocean war," in Admiral Samuel Eliot Morison's succinct phrase, had caused an unprecedented expansion of the United States Navy, whose prewar fleet consisted of only eight big-deck aircraft carriers. By mid-1943, the number of American carriers, both big-deck and small, had mushroomed to more than thirty, with eighty more ships on the ways or the drawing boards. The new American carrier force required thousands of pilots skilled in naval aviation's principal combat specialties—fighter attack and defense, dive-bombing, glide-bombing, and torpedo attack—as well as in the art of taking off from and landing back aboard a moving ship at sea. Carrier operations also demanded that each squadron, regardless of its specialty, be trained to fight as part of a multisquadron carrier air group. Virtually all carrier combat operations were a joint effort by squadrons within a single air group, or by a combination of air groups from multiple carriers. By mid-1943, Alameda had become a busy rookery for carrier-based squadrons and air groups destined for the Pacific. VT-18, as the number implied, was the eighteenth torpedo-bomber squadron formed by the Navy Department. Before war's end, the navy would commission more than forty.

Lieutenant Commander Lloyd Wilbert Van Antwerp took charge on August 2, 1943, and the squadron undoubtedly held a change-of-command ceremony to commemorate the event. The pilots, clad in their dress white uniforms with gloves and swords (or dress blues if the weather was cool), would have stood at attention in the hangar bay with the squadron's Avengers parked behind them. (VT-18 had only four Avengers in the beginning, and these were older

TBF-1 models.) Long would have saluted Van Antwerp and handed over the squadron. Van Antwerp would likely have made a short speech to the assembled officers and men about the importance of their work and the challenges ahead. Williams, standing in the front rank, would have received Van Antwerp's first order, which was probably something routine, such as, "Carry out the plan of the day." Williams then would have saluted, wheeled about smartly, repeated the order, and dismissed his troops to their duties.

VT-18's plan of the day for the first day, and for nearly every day into the future for an indeterminate period of time, would be devoted to a singular objective: becoming proficient in carrier operations and combat. Achieving this objective would take time and training. Although every pilot in the squadron had learned the basics of flying an Avenger before arriving at Alameda, and a few of the pilots had logged many hours in the airplane, they had never flown together as a unit. Van Antwerp's fundamental task was to teach his pilots how to use their torpedo bombers as weapons of war and sharpen their collective combat skills.

Though untested as a squadron commander, Van Antwerp had all the tools to succeed. An intelligent and disciplined man, he had overcome the early obstacles life had thrown at him. His parents had both died when he was young, and he had been raised by his aunts and uncles. When he lost his football scholarship at Michigan State due to injury, he had supported himself by driving a taxi and earned his degree. He had chosen the military as a career, first the army and then the navy, and become an experienced naval aviator. Physically imposing, he was tall and broad shouldered, and naturally commanded a measure of respect from other men because of his physicality. But his chief leadership attributes seem to have been his youthful exuberance for the job of flying a torpedo plane—and flying it well—and his congenial nature. As his men soon learned, Van Antwerp was not a martinet. He was approachable and unusually talkative for a commanding officer; he punctuated his sentences with reflexive chuckles and chortles, a speech pattern that gave him an upbeat, happy-go-lucky air. He was surprisingly casual in his own uniform dress for a regular officer, preferring a soft khaki fore-and-aft cap to the more formal officer's bridge cap with visor, and eschewing a tie whenever possible. He possessed an oval face, slightly oversize ears, and an irrepressible grin, a combination that made him appear much younger than his twenty-nine years, and slightly mischievous.

Van Antwerp was a firm believer in the time-honored navy maxim that pilots who drink together, heavily and often, become brothers in arms and fight well together. On the day he assumed command of the squadron, he hosted VT-18's first official party for his pilots and their wives—several of the pilots, including Van Antwerp and Williams, were married—at the Alameda officers' club. He also formed the "CIS committee" for the purpose of improving squadron performance and boosting morale simultaneously. The exact meaning of the committee's initials is lost to time ("Committee on Infractions: Serious," is one possibility), but the purpose of the committee, consisting of Van Antwerp, Williams, and senior division leaders, was to levy fines on pilots for boneheaded mistakes. Because Van Antwerp intended to use CIS monies to fund future squadron parties, the pilots received his announcement of the new policy with warm and raucous approval.

With so few airplanes at the squadron's disposal, VT-18's initial tactical training was not arduous. The pilots spent the balance of August 1943 flying between Alameda and Clear Lake, an ancient freshwater lake that lies eighty miles northeast of San Francisco. The pilots made one or two simulated torpedo runs over the sparkling waters of the lake and flew home again.

The CIS committee assessed fines liberally in August, collecting enough money to throw a second party at the Alameda officers' club before the first training month was complete. It was a well-liquored and boisterous affair, and presented Van Antwerp with his first disciplinary challenge involving an officer. Lieutenant Junior Grade John L. "Robbie" Robinson of Baltimore, Maryland, had been stationed in California long enough to develop a steamy romance with a young woman in Oakland. As the squadron party broke up, Robbie decided to visit his girlfriend, but he had no car. The officer of the day (OD), the senior duty officer at Alameda responsible for maintaining security and good order, had parked his station wagon outside the officers' club with the keys still in it. Robbie decided to "borrow" the OD's car for a few hours. The OD later telephoned the main gate looking for his missing station wagon, identifying himself as the OD. The sentry snorted, "The hell it is. The OD just drove outta here." Robbie didn't get very far. He wrecked the station wagon a few blocks from the gate, and city police escorted him back to the base. They delivered him into the custody of the shore patrol and a very irate OD, and Van Antwerp placed Robinson "in hack" for ten days, meaning that Robbie was confined to his room at the bachelor officers' quarters (BOQ) except for meals and daily duties.

Torpedo attack was a form of aerial warfare nearly as old as the airplane itself, and Van Antwerp's fliers were among the latest practitioners of the art. That they honed their skills at Alameda was fitting. The birth of U.S. naval aviation is officially credited to Eugene Ely's demonstration in 1911 of the feasibility of landing an airplane aboard ship, when Ely dropped his flimsy biplane on the fantail of the cruiser *Pennsylvania* as she lay at anchor in San Francisco Bay. As a result of Ely's demonstration, the navy formed a small experimental aviation unit that same year, and the pioneering civilian aviator and aircraft designer Glenn Curtis taught the first naval aviator, Lieutenant Theodore G. Ellyson, how to fly.

The navy's fledgling air unit experienced battle for the first time in 1914 when it flew reconnaissance missions over Veracruz in support of President Wilson's punitive expedition against the Mexican revolutionary Victoriano Huerta. The navy fliers received counterfire in the form of rifle shots, and the Veracruz expedition thus became the first combat mission in the history of American military aviation.

Despite Veracruz and the obvious utility of aircraft as the eyes and ears of the fleet, the naval establishment did not embrace airplanes as offensive weapons. Big-gunned surface warships, such as the heavy cruisers with which Admiral George Dewey's Pacific squadron had so gloriously dispatched the Spanish fleet at Manila, were the darlings of the navy before World War I. The navy established a training base for seaplane pilots and aircrew at Pensacola, Florida, but relegated its nascent naval air arm largely to a support role. Navy airplanes and lighter-than-air aircraft patrolled the seacoasts or provided over-the-horizon scouting and gunfire control for surface warships, but they did not fight.

Certain officers, such as Admiral Bradley A. Fiske, perceived the potential of aviation as an offensive striking force, one that fit perfectly with the navy's primary mission of controlling the seas. In 1912, Fiske recommended the navy establish four air bases on Luzon, each equipped with a hundred planes. (With remarkable prescience, Fiske had been concerned about the navy's ability to defend the Philippine Islands against attack by a large Japanese fleet. Fiske believed a large force of suitably armed airplanes could do the job by sinking or turning back the enemy's warships.) Fiske believed airplanes should be configured to carry weapons heavier than the sidearms of their pilots, and torpedoes were among the first weapons he considered. Surface warships and submarines had launched self-propelled torpedoes for more than a decade, and the idea of an airplane dropping a self-propelled torpedo required no great leap of imagination. Fiske acted on his vision; he filed a patent application in 1912 for a device that allowed an airplane to carry and release an aerial torpedo, thus becoming the unofficial father of the torpedo plane.

But neither American naval temperament nor aircraft design were up to Fiske's vision. British designers were the first to successfully launch a heavy torpedo from an airplane in 1914, and British seaplane pilots patrolling the Aegean Sea in 1915 were the first to sink an enemy ship, albeit a slow, vulnerable Turkish merchantman, with torpedoes.

By the end of World War I, few doubted the military potential of the airplane, but there was widespread disagreement over its proper role. Aviation zealots overstated the case for aviation. General William "Billy" Mitchell argued publicly that airpower had "completely superceded sea power or land power as [the nation's] first line of defense." Within the navy, debate centered on the proper role of surface ships and air forces in naval operations. Infighting raged between traditional battleship-first admirals and more forward-looking officers who saw a glorious future for naval aviation, such as Rear Admiral William A. Moffett. Ironically, General Mitchell's spectacular sinking in 1921 of the captured German dreadnought *Ostfriesland* with fragile, biwing army bombers seemed to prove the case for naval aviation even as it doomed Mitchell's career. Mitchell's stunt greatly advanced the cause of naval aviation, although, as his critics pointed out, he had attacked *Ostfreisland* in decidedly unwarlike conditions, without the ship putting up any defensive fire and without any damage control parties working to save the ship. Moffett campaigned publicly for the development of combat aircraft and ships—aircraft carriers—that could accompany battleships and cruisers and yet attack enemy warships and mechantmen far beyond the range of the surface fleet's guns. In 1921, Moffett became the first chief of the navy's new Bureau of Aeronautics, the agency responsible for the development of naval aircraft.

That same year, the bureau took delivery of the first navy warplane capable of carrying a torpedo, the DT-1. This was also the first military airplane produced by the Douglas Aircraft Company, which later became famous for its reliable World War II dive-bomber, the SBD Dauntless, and its ubiquitous troop transport and cargo plane, the DC-3 Skytrain. The DT-1 was a boxy single-seat biplane powered by a four-hundred-horsepower liquid-cooled engine. The airplane was designed with folding wings and interchangeable wheel and pontoon-float chassis, features that made the DT-1 capable of operating from a runway or a seaplane ramp. The DT-1 carried a 1,835-pound torpedo externally under its fuselage, but the airplane was not exclusively a torpedo plane. The Bureau of Aeronautics reasoned that any airplane capable of dropping a heavy aerial torpedo should also be capable of dropping conventional bombs. Thus, the bureau required manufacturers to design dual-purpose torpedo bombers, easily adaptable to either form of aerial attack. Although the development of the DT-1 coincided with the commissioning in 1922 of *Langley*, the U.S. Navy's first aircraft carrier (the *Langley* was a converted collier named after a pioneer of powered flight, Professor Samuel P. Langley), the DT-1 saw carrier duty aboard *Langley* only as an experimental aircraft, not as a warplane.

Douglas Aircraft Company's competitor, the Glenn L. Martin Company, produced the next-generation torpedo bomber for the navy in 1924, the SC-1. The SC-1 bore a close resemblance to its predecessor—also a bulky biplane with an inline, water-cooled engine and interchangeable landing gear and floats—but carried a crew of three and boasted a 575-horsepower engine. Like the DT-1, the SC-1 saw little carrier duty and operated primarily from land bases. Finally, in 1925, Martin delivered the first torpedo bomber capable of operating routinely from an aircraft carrier, the T3M. The navy equipped two squadrons with an improved model, the T3M-2, two years later. Torpedo Squadron 1 (VT-1) flew T3M-2s from the deck of the navy's second aircraft carrier, *Lexington*, commissioned in 1927, and Torpedo Squadron 2 (VT-2) flew them from *Langley*. Although the T3M was still a biwing design, it was much more powerful than its predecessors. The final version of the Martin T3M torpedo bomber, the TG-2, had a steel-tube fuselage, a 620-horsepower air-cooled radial engine, and a maximum speed of 102 knots. The Martin family of torpedo bombers remained the fleet standard until 1935.

The Bureau of Aeronautics applied the same dual-purpose policy to fighter planes, reasoning that fighters should be capable of dropping bombs as well as shooting down enemy fighters and observation balloons. Manufacturers responded with a series of two-man fighter-bombers, or bomber-fighters, such as the F8C Falcon biplane introduced by Curtiss Aircraft Company in 1927.

The navy and Marine pilots who flew the early fighter-bombers in the late 1920s, such as the F8C, experimented with near-vertical dive-bombing techniques. The idea was to improve accuracy by diving straight at the target from a high angle, releasing the bomb, and pulling out at the last possible moment. A few catastrophic in-flight failures persuaded the bureau that a tougher, more heavily reinforced airplane was necessary to withstand the high accelerations and structural stresses associated with dive-bombing. Martin responded to the call in 1930 with the first special-purpose dive-bomber, the Martin BM-2. Reluctant to abandon the dual-purpose concept, however, the bureau first assigned the new BM-2 dive-bombers to a torpedo squadron.

The early navy warplanes were biplanes. A simple biwing design permitted an airplane to become airborne at relatively low airspeeds, and a biplane required minimal engine power to keep it aloft. Aircraft designers and manufacturers understood, however, that monowing designs had certain aerodynamic advantages and disadvantages. A single wing generates less structural drag and permits an airplane to achieve higher airspeeds and greater maneuverability, but a monowing must also move through the air faster to generate comparable lift. In the early 1920s, the advantages of a monowing design were largely theoretical. The chief obstacle to a practical monowing warplane lay in finding an aircraft engine with sufficient horsepower to pull the airplane through the air fast enough. Structural strength is also limited by the available engine power. An airframe fashioned of metal ribs and skin is stronger than a frame made of wood and fabric, but a metal airplane is also much heavier, demanding more engine power in the calculus.

During the late 1920s and early 1930s, metallurgical science and aircraft engine design improved. Air racers, with their stub-winged all-engine monoplanes, contributed greatly to the advance. The Bureau of Aeronautics pressed manufacturers to develop monoplane designs that would operate from the navy's new *Ranger* class of carrier. One of the first of the new monowing designs was a torpedo bomber built by Douglas, known as the TBD-1 Devastator. The Devastator was typical of the early monoplane era. It flew on low, wide, oval-shaped wings and had semiretractable landing gear. The airplane's maximum speed was 165 knots and it carried a thousand-pound torpedo externally beneath its fuselage. For self-defense, the Devastator mounted one forward-firing gun in its left wing, operated by the pilot, and one .30-caliber machine gun aft of the cockpit along its fuselage dorsal fin operated by a navigator-gunner. (Navy aircrewmen also served dual purposes from the earliest days.) The Devastator entered active naval service in 1937.

At about the same time, the Northrup Corporation developed a new monoplane dive-bomber for the navy called the BT-1. By 1939, Northrup had become a subsidiary of Douglas Aircraft Company and the BT-1 had evolved into the SBD Dauntless. The Dauntless carried its bomb load externally and had a top-end speed of 195 knots. It was distinguished by perforated panels or "dive brakes" along the trailing edges of its wings; these permitted the Dauntless to dive at angles of seventy to eighty-five degrees without accelerating beyond its maximum safe structural airspeed. The airplane was also fitted with a bomb sling or bridle beneath its fuselage; the sling rotated forward and released the bomb below the propeller arc so the airplane would not self-destruct in a steep dive.

The Curtiss Aircraft Company, the Grumman Aircraft Engineering Corporation, and the Brewster Aeronautical Corporation had long vied for the navy's fighter-bomber business. Brewster landed the first navy contract for a monoplane fighter in 1936 and delivered the Brewster F2A Buffalo, aptly named for its thick-bodied, big-shouldered look. Grumman won a contract in 1939 with its design for the F4F Wildcat, a tough, stubby midwing fighter capable of more than 250 knots. Early versions of the Wildcat carried two hundred-pound bombs (one beneath each wing), while later, more powerful versions introduced in early 1942 achieved airspeeds in excess of 290 knots and carried a bomb load of up to five hundred pounds.

When the United States declared war on Japan in December 1941, most large carrier air groups in the U.S. Navy were equipped with one squadron of Wildcat or Brewster fighters, two squadrons of Dauntless scout-dive-bombers, and one squadron of Devastator torpedo bombers. None of these air groups—their machines, their crews, or their tactics—had been tested in combat; most naval aviators had flown only in fleet exercises. But the American navy had learned from the experiences of the British navy, which by late 1941 had been at war for over two years.

Great Britain had been a longtime innovator in naval aviation, especially in the design and development of aircraft carriers. Determined that Britannia should continue to rule the waves, Great Britain had launched an experimental aircraft carrier, the *Argus*, in 1918, three years before the United States' *Langley*. At the outbreak of hostilities in Europe in September 1939, the British navy mustered seven aircraft carriers to America's four (which included the by-then obsolete *Langley*). His Majesty's carriers operated fewer airplanes than American carriers—HMS *Illustrious* carried only thirty-three aircraft, while USS *Ranger* carried seventy-six—but British carriers were more heavily armored and displaced greater tonnage.

In November 1940, the British navy demonstrated to the world the power of a well-executed aerial torpedo attack launched by carrier-borne aircraft. Mussolini had invaded Egypt from Libya the previous month, and British troops were fighting the Italians in North Africa in defense of Egypt. The British supplied their troops by sending convoys through the Straits of Gibraltar, and the job of the Italian navy was to intercept and destroy British convoys as they entered the Mediterranean. The Italian battle fleet was based at Taranto, a magnificent harbor on the instep of the Italian boot. Operating from Taranto, Italian warships could effectively block Britain's path to Egypt, protecting Mussolini's lifeline to North Africa and disrupting Britain's.

On November 11, the British Mediterranean fleet launched a surprise attack against Taranto, not by big-gunned surface warships but by torpedo planes launched from the carrier *Illustrious*. Twenty-four Swordfish torpedo bombers—biplanes similar in appearance and performance to the U.S. Navy's T3M-2—attacked the Italian ships as they lay at anchor or at their berths. Launched 180 miles from Taranto, the Swordfish attacked in two waves an hour apart and achieved total surprise. Three Italian battleships, including the new forty-five-thousand-ton *Littorio*, and a cruiser were sunk or damaged by aerial torpedoes, all at a cost of two Swordfish downed by shore-based antiaircraft fire.

Winston Churchill later wrote, "By this single stroke the balance of power in the Mediterranean was decisively altered. . . . Half the Italian battle fleet was disabled for at least six months, and the [British] Fleet Air Arm could rejoice at having seized one of the rare opportunities presented to them." Swordfish, called "Stringbags" by their crews, continued to serve the British fleet well: On May 26, 1941, Swordfish operating from the carrier *Ark Royal* torpedoed the German pocket battleship *Bismarck*, damaging *Bismarck*'s steering mechanism and leading to her destruction later in the day by naval gunfire.

The lesson of Taranto was not lost on the Imperial Japanese Navy. The British torpedo attack on Mussolini's warships greatly influenced Japanese planning for the raid on Pearl Harbor in late 1941, both inspiring the emperor's aerial torpedomen and forcing them to improvise. Since the early 1930s, the Japanese navy had built torpedo-capable carrier planes and experimented with aerial torpedo tactics, but Japanese torpedoes required a water depth of seventy-five to a hundred feet to launch successfully, like the aerial torpedoes of most navies. The water depth within Pearl Harbor averaged only about forty feet. To accommodate their equipment and tactics to the target, the Japanese reconfigured their torpedoes to run at shallow depths and repeatedly rehearsed their torpedo runs in Kagoshima Bay, Kyushu (the closest analog to Pearl Harbor in the Japanese home islands), until they achieved drop depths of only thirty-six feet. Like the British at Taranto, the Japanese achieved total surprise at Pearl Harbor on December 7, and aerial torpedo strikes accounted for much of the carnage. Battleships *West Virginia*, *Oklahoma*, *California*, *Nevada* and *Arizona*, and cruisers *Raleigh* and *Helena*, all sustained torpedo hits that caused catastrophic damage.

The U.S. Navy's aerial torpedo attacks in the early stages of World War II were far less successful than the Japanese raid on Pearl Harbor. Devastator squadrons sank or damaged a few Japanese ships during the Marshall and Gilbert islands campaigns, but neither the navy's torpedo planes nor its tactics were up to the standards of modern aerial warfare. Torpedo Squadron 8, equipped predominantly with Devastators, met with disaster at the Battle of Midway in June 1942. Launched from *Hornet*, fifteen VT-8 Devastators became separated from their strike group and attempted torpedo runs on Japanese carriers without the support of American fighters. Only one Devastator pilot got within range of his target, and most never released their weapons. Japanese carrier-borne fighters shot at least fourteen of the slow-footed, undergunned torpedo bombers out of the sky, while shipboard antiaircraft fire accounted for the final kill. Of the thirty aircrewmen who manned VT-8's ill-fated Devastators, twenty-nine were lost; only one man, pilot Ensign George H. Gay, survived the encounter. Most of the Devastator crews from VT-3 and VT-6 (launched, respectively, from *Yorktown* and *Enterprise*) also fell victim to enemy fighters at Midway; VT-3 and VT-6 committed a combined force of twenty-six torpedo bombers to battle but only four returned to their carriers.

Midway brought an abrupt end to the Devastator; the navy withdrew the airplane from operational use almost immediately following the battle and thereafter outfitted torpedo squadrons exclusively with new Avengers. The tactical lesson from the Devastators' annihilation at Midway was painfully clear, if dearly purchased: Making an uncoordinated and unsupported torpedo attack in the presence of enemy fighters was foolhardy and likely to fail. At Taranto, in the *Bismarck* engagement, and at Pearl Harbor, torpedo bombers did not have to contend with swarms of opposing fighters or intense antiaircraft fire; the attackers were able to bear down on their targets relatively unmolested and inflict substantial damage. At Midway, the unprotected Devastators had become slow, plump targets for the faster, nimbler Japanese fighters. After Midway, many naval aviators viewed torpedo attacks as suicidal and regarded torpedo bombers as little better than flying coffins.

But the American public had lionized the torpedo bomber crews at Midway for their courage and sacrifice, and VT-18's pilots considered themselves the proud legatees and successors of the Midway heroes. No one in Van Antwerp's squadron expected the same disasterous outcome when their day of battle arrived. Much had changed since June 1942. VT-18's Avengers were far superior to Devastators; they were state-of-the-art torpedo bombers, much faster and more powerful, better armed for self-defense, and more maneuverable. Tactics had also changed. The navy conceded (privately, not publicly) that torpedo bombers had inflicted little if any damage on the enemy at Midway. The sacrifice of VT-3, VT-6 and VT-8, while heroic beyond measure, was partly a consequence of poor strike group discipline and poor coordination within the air group. Post-Midway, the navy reemphasized among all squadron skippers and air group commanders the importance of coordination and mutual support in any carrier strike.

The carrier air group of which VT-18 was part, Carrier Air Group 18, was organized the same day as the torpedo squadron, July 20, 1943, and at the same place, the Alameda Naval Air Station. Commander William Edward Ellis, a fighter pilot by trade, was the air group's first commander. Born in Burlington, North Carolina, Ellis had graduated from the U.S. Naval Academy in 1930 and passed through Pensacola in 1932. He was a tall, patrician-looking man with a Roman nose, a pronounced Adam's apple, and the long-muscled physique of a fencer or a long-distance runner. He had been, in fact, a javelin thrower on the Naval Academy track team. Although his fellow midshipmen described him as something of a Don Juan, with a "winning personality, a captivating smile, a love of amusement . . . a general good nature" and a fondness for "dance[s] at Carvel Hall," he had matured into a no-nonsense sort of fellow, rather reserved and demanding of subordinates. He spoke forcibly, with traces of a Tidewater accent. Ellis's responsibility at thirty-five years of age was to forge the three squadrons that comprised Air Group 18—Torpedo 18, Fighting 18, and Bombing 18—into a cohesive striking force and lead them personally in battle when the time came.

Air Group 18 was far from combat-ready when Ellis assumed command, but a rumor surfaced nevertheless in late August 1943 that the entire outfit would be assigned to an aircraft carrier within a couple of months. No one at the squadron level could verify the rumor, or refute it. The Navy Department's war plans, including unit assignments and ship movements, were secret; the department tended to communicate its intentions only to persons with an operational need to know, and only in sufficient time to execute its directives. But the navy's war effort was so vast, with so many different sub-bureaus and agencies involved, that disconnected bits of information inevitably trickled down the chain and fueled speculation among ordinary sailors and airmen who lacked any insight into the bigger picture. In almost every conversation about the navy's intentions and the squadron's future, scuttlebutt filled the vacuum of knowledge. As they always have and always will, sailors accepted scuttlebutt as irrefutable fact and spread the rumors, finding ready acceptance among other young men who shared a destiny over which they had no control and hungered for certainty. Everyone was at the mercy of someone higher up the chain; even squadron commanders couldn't squelch or confirm persistent rumors. Men tended to believe what they wanted to believe.

In the expectation of shipping out in September 1943, several of the married pilots in VT-18 sent their wives home to live with parents or siblings. The men soon learned they had been misled by the rumors, and were now poorer for the train or bus fare. One recorded his disgruntlement in the squadron logbook the morning he was told the air group would remain in California indefinitely: "Sept. 15 0800. [I]f the guys who run this damed [sic] outfit would make up their feeble minds as to when the hell we leave this SNAFU base, maybe guys wouldn't send their wives home early and the Squadron could make plans."

And so VT-18's pilots trained, day after day, practicing the maneuvers and tactics that would serve them when they went to sea. They shifted their torpedo runs from Clear Lake to Monterey Bay, where the Pacific Ocean elbows aside the California coast and arcs south from Santa Cruz to Pacific Grove. On a typically glorious Golden State day, under dry azure skies and balmy temperatures, these torpedo exercises were thrilling and great fun. The Avenger pilots would swoop down over the rolling brown hills of Santa Cruz and fly low and fast over the slate blue waters of the bay. Maneuvering toward a target ship at an altitude of only five hundred feet above the water, they would accelerate to a speed of 250 knots and simulate launching their torpedo within fifteen hundred yards of their target. Then they would break off their torpedo run, banking sharply away from the target at low altitude, and climb to rejoin their buddies in formation. For the pilots, the whole experience was a payoff, proof of why they had chosen to fly in the first place and why they had worked so hard to become naval aviators. Perceptions of speed and power were heightened down low. The shimmering blue water rushing beneath your airplane, the cool sea air streaming into your cockpit, the engine noise and the hiss of the slipstream, the powerful airplane thrumming around you—these were addictively exhilarating sensations.

But it was in beautiful Monterey Bay that VT-18 experienced its first casualties. On September 5, Ensign Lyman A. Matthews of Oakland, California, Aviation Radioman 3rd Class Fred McCann of Mahanoy Plane, Pennsylvania, and the turret gunner, Aviation Ordnanceman 3rd Class James Sirrine of Phoenix, Arizona, vanished over Monterey Bay after a practice torpedo run. No one saw them go down, not even the crew of the target ship. Van Antwerp organized an aerial search but none of his searchers could find any trace of Matthews's Avenger or its crew. Had Matthews misjudged his altitude and flown his Avenger into the water at high speed, or had he become disoriented and flown away from the coast until he ran out of fuel? No one knew.

Over-water navigation hops were part of the training syllabus at Alameda, and Matthews's loss may have motivated a bit more concentration on the subject among VT-18's pilots. By late 1943, radio wave technology had evolved to the point that homing and directional beacons were commonplace navigational aids for aviators worldwide, but there would be few functioning radio beacons over vast areas of the Pacific Ocean. The Japanese had disabled homing beacons within their areas of occupation, and, when at sea in a combat zone, American aircraft carriers would operate largely in radio silence, using their YE homing equipment only intermittently. The same radio transmissions that helped American pilots find their way back to the aircraft carrier could, if intercepted, steer Japanese fliers to the ship and betray the position of an entire task force. Thus, naval aviators devoted much of their training time to learning how to navigate by dead reckoning and without the benefit of radio beacons.

Dead reckoning was the art of flying from point to point by tracking the airplane's magnetic heading, airspeed, and time, and by constantly adjusting for magnetic variation, compass deviation, windspeed, and direction. Success depended on accurately calculating drift angles—this is why plotting boards were standard equipment aboard every carrier-borne airplane—and on closely monitoring the weather outside the cockpit. Meteorological data, except of the grossest kind, were nonexistent at sea, and naval aviators were taught to be their own weathermen. They gauged the velocity of the wind by studying the sea state beneath them, estimating the distance between the crests of the waves, and consulting a handheld chart that translated these observations into rough approximations of wind direction and speed. They marked frontal boundaries and predicted changing weather conditions by detecting wind shifts and by reading the shape and drift of the clouds.

VT-18's pilots flew over-water navigation training hops alone or in two-plane sections. The idea was to build the pilots' skill and confidence by requiring them to navigate outbound to a predetermined fix over the water and return to a point somewhere down the coast of California. These were not easy flights. After the shoreline recedes behind you, the ocean looks the same in every direction—a broad, undifferentiated disk of blue or gray extending from horizon to horizon. If the sun is high, east and west are indistinguishable, and on hazy days the sky blends with the sea, making height above water impossible to judge without a functioning altimeter. Poor weather frequently obscures the coast, making the return path as trackless as the outbound path. Avenger pilots had the advantage of flying with a radar operator who could assist in locating the coastline, but radar equipment could fail, and pilots had to maintain a careful dead-reckoning track to ensure a safe return.

Navigation hops over the California countryside were far less stressful. The Golden State offered distinctive mountain ranges and ample roads, rivers, railroad tracks, and water towers for ready reference. Except when poor weather forced pilots to fly solely on instruments, overland navigation flights were a piece of cake compared with over-water flights. Pilots looked forward to overland flights, especially if the flight would "RON," or remain overnight, in a destination city that offered some nightlife. Lieutenant Commander Van Antwerp endeared himself to his pilots by scheduling frequent navigation hops to Reno, Nevada, and he never lacked for volunteers to fly the airplanes. These took off with one official functioning pilot and five or six extra "turret gunners" or "radiomen" in the dress blue uniforms of officers crammed into the airplane's fuselage.

Van Antwerp's training syllabus included many hours of formation flying, a skill that he viewed as the touchstone of professionalism. He demanded that every pilot fly precisely in formation, whether as a member of a two- or three-plane section, or of a larger division of four, six, eight, or more airplanes. He drilled his pilots in joining up expeditiously and holding their positions exactly. Van Antwerp prescribed close, tight formations for short periods of parade flying, and allowed more open formations for extended periods of cruising so as to conserve fuel and make station keeping less tiresome for his wingmen. But the forty-five-degree bearing line (or sixty-degree bearing line in cruise) was all-important. Van Antwerp tolerated neither creeping ahead of the bearing line—this was called flying "acute" in the jargon of naval aviation—nor falling behind, which was called flying "sucked." He probably lectured his pilots to this effect, which is the time-honored injunction of navy instructor pilots: "If you fly as my wingman in parade, you will stay on the bearing line, not one foot sucked nor one foot acute. If I lead the formation into a fucking mountainside, I want them to find your wreckage exactly forty-five degrees aft of mine and twenty feet to the left." Van Antwerp publicly displayed his squadron's prowess by leading it in parade formation over San Francisco Bay and by making simulated bombing runs on Alcatraz Island to promote the sale of war bonds.

VT-18 conducted real bombing runs on a range near Point Reyes, a rugged, forested spit of land that sits atop the San Andreas fault and juts into the Pacific Ocean north of San Francisco. Avengers were designed for horizontal bombing (the customary method of releasing bombs over a target from level flight) and for glide-bombing, a special bombing technique in which the pilot nosed over from eight or nine thousand feet and dived toward the target at an angle of between fifteen and sixty degrees. Depending on the weight and number of his bombs, the pilot pulled out of his glide-bombing run between a thousand and two thousand feet, released his ordnance over the target, and streaked away at low altitude and high airspeed to evade enemy antiaircraft fire. The heavier the bomb, the higher the release altitude. In combat, glide-bombing had proved to be somewhat more accurate than horizontal bombing, but less accurate than dive-bombing, which was the sole province of the Helldiver pilots, who dived at angles of seventy to eighty-five degrees. Avengers accelerated rapidly in a glide, and they were not designed for the stresses of dive angles in excess of sixty degrees.

VT-18 experienced its second set of casualties on the bombing range. Coming off a glide-bombing run over Point Reyes, Lieutenant Junior Grade Marvin Perry Horton Jr. flew into a flock of seagulls at high speed and crashed near Olema, California, killing himself and his radioman, Aviation Radioman 3rd Class Edward J. Kwiatkowski of Cleveland, Ohio. (Horton had no turret gunner aboard at the time.) The squadron was shocked at the incident, and disbelieving. Avengers were supposed to be rugged enough to withstand high accelerations and Japanese antiaircraft fire. Multiple bird strikes seemed a highly improbable cause for a fatal crash, but a postcrash investigation revealed that the leading edges of Horton's Avenger had been heavily pockmarked and dented by multiple seagull strikes before the airplane hit the ground. The bird strikes had caused catastrophic structural failure, and Horton and his radioman had no chance. VT-18's young pilots came to the sobering realization that hitting enough heavyweight birds at a sufficiently high airspeed was the equivalent of gunfire and could bring down any airplane, even their sturdy torpedo bombers.

Avengers were designed to be flown in combat by a three-man team, and VT-18's turret gunners and radar operators—all young enlisted petty officers, fresh from naval aviation technical schools—were as much a part of the squadron's training program at Alameda as the officer-pilots. Turret gunners and radar men rode along on most training flights, except for carrier landing practice, and gained real-world experience operating the Avenger's weapons systems and radar and communications equipment. In the process, they became familiar with the idiosyncrasies of the pilots.

Aviation Ordnanceman 3rd Class Wallace H. "Red" Russell, a turret gunner, was one of VT-18's original crewmen. Raised in Durham, North Carolina, Red had enlisted in the navy in early 1943 at age twenty-four and attended the navy's aerial gunnery school at Whidbey Island, Washington. On graduation, he had been assigned to a Carrier Air Service Unit (CASU) at NAS Alameda, which was a replacement unit for carrier-based pilots and aircrew. Red had performed exceptionally well at gunnery school and was an excellent ordnanceman. He had been offered a teaching position at Alameda but turned it down, volunteering instead for duty with VT-18 as a gunner. Red was the prototypical Avenger turret gunner: He possessed superb eyesight and the compact build of a gymnast. He also had excellent spatial awareness and was immune to motion sickness. These were fortunate traits for someone who flew backward much of the time and whose job it was to operate a ball turret that slewed about two axes while the airplane dipped or climbed in a third.

On weekend liberty, the pilots of VT-18 frequented the bars and dance halls in Oakland. Bud Williams and a clique of junior officers—Ray Skelly, Squatty Vaughn, Frank "Doc" Doyle, Kenny Barden, Joe Rubin, and Bill Bates, all then lowly ensigns—were leaders of the pack. Bud and his "boys" (as they called themselves) officially adopted the Lake Merritt Hotel bar as their liberty "headquarters," although this designation later caused some confusion. Skelly and Doyle had gone to a late movie one night. They had just settled comfortably into their seats, uniform ties loosened, shoes off, when the houselights came up and the manager announced that he had received an urgent call demanding that ensigns Skelly and Doyle report immediately to headquarters. The two young men leaped from their seats. Sailors in the audience saluted, and civilians wished them good luck as the two fliers bolted up the aisle and jumped a bus back to Alameda, where they promptly awakened the duty officer and demanded to know where VT-18 was being sent. The duty officer was not amused; nor were Skelly and Doyle when they learned the call from "headquarters" had come from the Lake Merritt Hotel bar.

In late October 1943, the squadron shifted from Alameda to the Monterey Peninsula for more training. The Monterey Peninsula is a lovely place, with a dry Mediterranean climate and a topography of pine-covered mountains and rolling brown hills. The American continent drops precipitously to the sea at Monterey, offering spectacular ocean vistas from high cliffs along the coast. The town of Monterey, one of the oldest in California, lies in the southern crook of Monterey Bay, sheltered to the east and south by the foothills of the Santa Lucia Mountains.

At the Naval Air Auxiliary Air Station (NAAS) Monterey, the squadron began an important new phase of training. Although each of VT-18's pilots had landed aboard an aircraft carrier before receiving his wings and earning his "naval aviator" designation, he would have to requalify for carrier duty in an Avenger by successfully completing five or six more actual carrier landings and takeoffs. Those who failed to requalify would not deploy with the squadron when it sailed with the fleet, and the squadron as a whole had to demonstrate carrier proficiency. At Monterey, Van Antwerp and his pilots engaged in field carrier landing practice (FCLP), an exercise designed to simulate landing aboard a carrier by "bouncing" on a small section of runway. After a few weeks of intensive FCLP, the squadron would requalify aboard a real carrier.

FCLP procedures were routine and invariable. Six or eight aircraft would take off one behind another. The lead pilot would climb to an altitude of two hundred to three hundred feet and fly upwind for three or four miles until all aircraft behind him were airborne. The lead would then initiate a shallow left-hand turn and fly back toward the airfield. The pilots behind him would turn in sequence, adjusting their airspeed to establish intervals of approximately fifteen hundred feet between airplanes. Entering the downwind leg of the landing pattern, the lead would decelerate and extend his airplane's landing gear and flaps, and the pilots behind the lead would do the same. The lead would slow his Avenger to a few knots above its stalling speed and, when he reached the approach end of the runway on the downwind leg, he would commence a descending left turn and look for the landing signal officer, or LSO.

The LSO stood at the approach end of the runway holding yellow-painted paddles. Using his paddles, the LSO would signal instructions to the pilot during his final approach, such as "add power," "decrease power," "turn right," "turn left," "raise your nose," "lower your nose." The LSO expected the pilot to adhere strictly to his instructions. If the pilot responded correctly and positioned his airplane over the runway threshold with proper airspeed, altitude, and alignment, the LSO would signal "cut." This was the signal for the pilot to immediately reduce power by retarding or chopping his airplane's throttle to idle. With engine power reduced, the Avenger would drop heavily into the landing area, a painted rectangle on the runway about three hundred feet in length. Once safely on the runway, the pilot would quickly reset his airplane's flaps and trim, advance his airplane's throttle, and roar off again for another circuit around the landing pattern. But if the pilot's approach was sloppy or dangerous, the LSO would wave him off with the paddles. A wave-off signal was mandatory, and the LSO expected the pilot to add full power immediately and go around for another try. The pilots flying behind the lead would execute their landings in precisely the same manner as the lead, and everyone would bounce around the landing pattern six or eight times in a big daisy chain behind the lead. When they completed their last approach and landing, they would taxi their Avengers to a ramp beside the runway and, without shutting down their engines, turn their airplanes over to the next group of six or eight pilots.

Although enlisted men usually did not accompany pilots during FCLP, they were vitally interested observers of the exercises. Turret gunners and radiomen knew they would be little more than passengers during a carrier takeoff and landing, and that their health and longevity would depend entirely on the skill of their assigned pilots. Red Wallace and his fellow turret gunners often watched FCLP from the bed of a pickup truck parked adjacent to the runway. They were attentive and critical, grading each pilot on his approach and landing like fence-sitters at a rodeo judging cowboys on their cutting and roping skills. Red preferred the pilots who were deliberate and cautious, not hot dogs like Lieutenant Junior Grade George Benson Riley. Ben Riley was a twenty-three-year-old pilot from California, Pennsylvania (a home of record that caused much confusion among navy personnel clerks). Riley had movie-star good looks and a penchant for pushing his Avenger to the far edges of its operating envelope. On touch-and-go landings during FCLP, Riley had a habit of retracting his landing gear shortly after advancing his throttle to full power. His Avenger appeared to accelerate more quickly when he did this—Red conceded the trick was pretty impressive to onlookers—but it required only an unexpected gust of wind or a hiccup of the engine to drop the airplane onto the runway in a grinding crash. Van Antwerp and Williams had not yet assigned aircrew to specific pilots, and Red made a mental note not to sign up as Riley's regular gunner if he could avoid it.

VT-18 pilots also flew instrument refresher hops at Monterey to keep their foul-weather flying skills sharp, piloting SNJ Texans, a low-wing, tandem-cockpit trainer that the navy used as an advanced trainer. Every VT-18 pilot had flown the SNJ during the intermediate stage of his flight training. On an instrument training flight, one pilot would sit in the front cockpit and keep lookout, while the second pilot sat in the rear cockpit beneath a canvas tent (called a bag) and flew the airplane solely by reference to instruments.

Accidents were inevitable in training. The causes were various, but they usually could be traced to pilot fatigue, distraction in the cockpit, unfamiliarity with the correct procedure, failure to use a checklist, ignoring warning lights and horns, or poor airmanship. One aspiring VT-18 pilot named Johnson exhibited all of these faults when, after a night on the town, he went ripping down the runway for takeoff at Monterey with his Avenger's wings folded. Johnson explained that he had done it just to see whether his turret gunner and radioman were observant, but Van Antwerp didn't buy his explanation. Johnson left the squadron shortly after the incident, but not before the CIS committee fined him heavily.

To replace their social headquarters at the Lake Merritt Hotel bar, Williams and the boys sought out hospitable bars and pubs in Monterey, which was then very much a workingman's town, populated largely by seafaring fishermen, immigrant cannery workers, ranchers and caballeros, as well as sailors. The small NAAS Monterey officers' club didn't offer much diversion, so Van Antwerp distributed money from the CIS fund for squadron parties at taverns like the Pine Inn, a popular establishment in Carmel-by-the-Sea, a charming oceanside town frequented by friendly young women. Van Antwerp fraternized enthusiastically with Williams and the boys, convinced that a skipper must demonstrate leadership in the barroom as well as in the air to be effective. He manned the rail with his pilots often, drinking and carousing with them into the wee hours. This leadership approach had its risks. A California Highway Patrolman pulled the skipper over in his jeep late one night as he weaved home from a squadron gathering. Van Antwerp was zipped up in his flight suit, complete with helmet over his head and flying goggles over his eyes. Somehow he persuaded the officer he was on important government business and the officer let him go.

In mid-November, the squadron flew en masse down the California coast to San Diego for carrier requalifications aboard the *Cohapee*, a small escort carrier built on the narrow-beamed hull of a freighter. The *Cohapee* was about 500 feet long, and her flight deck was only about ninety feet wide. She had the usual equipment of a larger fleet carrier, such as hydraulic catapults, elevators that descended into her hangar bay, and crash barriers, only less of it. Landing an Avenger with a fifty-four-foot wingspan on a flight deck only ninety feet wide required precision and finesse. Although FCLP at Monterey had prepared most of the pilots for the task, the novelty of landing aboard a ship for real was an inescapable distraction. Each of the pilots executed five landings and takeoffs, some more skillfully than others. Van Antwerp collected CIS heavily for blown tires and a few barrier crashes. Ensign Kurt W. Schonthaler, a tall Rhode Islander, broke an arresting cable on landing (not his fault) and careened over the side of the ship into the sea. Fortunately, his Avenger landed right-side up. Schonthaler stepped out of his airplane as it sank and was picked up unhurt.

When their carrier checkout was complete, the boys repaired to the Hotel del Coronado, a rambling, white-framed resort hotel of the Gilded Age located on the beach at Coronado Island. They celebrated their status as newly requalified carrier pilots in the hotel bar. Because each pilot had successfully engaged an arresting gear cable with his Avenger's tail hook, the men toasted one another with Flaming Hookers, a concoction of volatile liquors that the bartender poured into a shot glass and ignited. Each pilot raised his blazing glass to his squadron mates, extinguished the fire with a mighty huff, and quaffed the liquor in one swallow.

VT-18's next duty station was Hollister, California, then a tiny farming and ranching community in the Salinas River valley, forty miles northwest of Monterey. At NAAS Hollister, Van Antwerp's pilots began an extensive night flying syllabus (in addition to working through a training schedule devoted to more daylight navigation, bombing, and gunnery practice, torpedo tactics and FCLP). The squadron's night flying syllabus included night formation flying, which was an exciting new experience for most of Van Antwerp's pilots and a dangerous one. Even under ideal night flying conditions—a clear night with a full moon— a pilot has far fewer visual references than during daylight hours; the night sky significantly impairs a pilot's perceptions of his airplane's altitude, attitude in space, and relative motion. The boys learned quickly that mixing night flying with formation flying compounds exponentially the inherent risks of each.

To rendezvous at night, a wingman maneuvers chiefly by reference to his section leader's running lights. To hold his position, a wingman concentrates on a blue "section light" embedded in the top of his leader's fuselage and on blue "formation lights" in his leader's wings. The wingman must keep the apparent distance between his leader's formation lights constant. The whole experience is like trying to catch a constellation and fly alongside it. In the rural Salinas River valley, there were very few visual references at night and relatively little light. VT-18's blue-painted torpedo bombers became indistinct shadows in the night sky, except for the leader's formation lights and the ghostly blue flame that flared from the Avengers' engine exhausts. Any pilot who fixated on a single light did so at his peril, as Ensign Leon S. Vannais discovered one gloomy, moonless night in early December 1943. Taking off from Hollister, Vannais mistook a farmhouse light for his wingman's wingtip and pancaked his Avenger on the ground at 150 knots. Miraculously, no one was killed, although Vannais's radioman suffered serious injuries.

Night flying dampened the boys' nightlife, but taverns were fewer in rural Hollister in any event. Ensign John T. McKee of Livingston, Texas, whom Van Antwerp had appointed the squadron's athletic officer, arranged softball and pool tournaments to amuse the boys in their off-duty hours. Pool was the more popular pastime, except among squadron athletes like Barden who preferred softball. The pool tournaments were played in the BOQ recreation room, a smoky hall furnished with overstuffed chairs, a Ping-Pong table, magazine racks, and a pool table. Van Antwerp and Lieutenant Junior Grade Vernon A. "Duke" Delaney, a beefy pilot from Evansville, Indiana, dominated play, staying consistently atop the standings in eight-ball.

If Van Antwerp granted weekend passes for liberty, the boys usually traveled by bus or car to San Francisco. Kenny Barden found romance in the City by the Bay, just as Robbie Robinson had found love in Oakland. Barden, the Arkansan, met a dark-haired beauty from Mississippi, Margaret McWhorter, whose father, Herbert, was a successful salesman for the U.S. Rubber Company. Herbert's employer had transferred Herbert from Hattiesburg, Mississippi, to New Orleans, and from New Orleans to San Francisco; Herbert had purchased a handsome two-story house for his family off Market Street, not far from the Embarcadero and the Market Street trolley line. Barden's pal, Joe Rubin, a rich, ebullient, and very un-Orthodox Jewish pilot from Manhattan, had been introduced to Margaret's younger sister, Dickie, at a dance in San Francisco and asked her the sailor's timeless line, "Are there any more at home like you?" In this case the answer was yes, so Joe and Dickie arranged a blind date between Kenny and Margaret. The latter two fell instantly for each other, and the two pilots thereafter double-dated with the two sisters whenever the opportunity arose. The sisters' mother, Honey McWhorter, took pity on the two young naval aviators who were so very far from home and invited them to dine at the McWhorter house often.

The wives of the married pilots—those who had remained in California or returned to their husbands when the rumors of a September deployment proved false—followed their husbands from base to base. The Gypsy life of a navy wife is never easy; the husband is absent much of the time, confined to base or off at sea. VT-18's wives encouraged and supported one another. They socialized like sorority sisters, bolstering one another's spirits and comparing notes on how to make ends meet on a junior officer's salary. There was a liberating egalitarianism among the women in knowing exactly what everyone else's husband earned. The young married couples lived in small apartments or duplexes off base, and two or three couples sometimes shared the same automobile for transportation. The bond among the wives provided stability and security, a bond that was as important for the psychological well-being of the husbands as it was for the wives. Most of the wives enjoyed Hollister in all its dusty, Western charm. A few of the pilots struck up acquaintances with local farmers who allowed them to hunt on their land, and several wealthy ranchers hosted cookouts on the manicured lawns of their haciendas. The pilots and their wives feasted on venison and lamb under the oak trees and eucalyptus, and dreamed of the day when the war would end and they might buy a little place of their own.

A rash of accidents afflicted VT-18 in late December. In addition to Vannais's mishap, Ensign Frank D. Doyle, called Doc by his buddies, landed wheels-up in the squadron's SNJ instrument trainer. Van Antwerp restricted Doc to the base at Hollister for ten days, including the Christmas holidays, a punishment that seemed more severe than it actually was. Doyle's family lived in Fort Worth, Texas, and Doc wasn't going home for Christmas anyway.

The holiday season spawned an epidemic of homesickness among the young pilots, especially the unmarried ones. The single boys descended on San Francisco for Christmas liberty, although most had no place in particular to go. Kenny Barden and Joe Rubin were among the lucky ones; they had arranged double dates with Margie and Dickie on Christmas Eve. Awakening early on Christmas morning, Honey McWhorter descended the stairs of her San Francisco home to find a dozen VT-18 pilots sound asleep on the floor, curled into chairs and sprawled on the carpets. Honey quietly retreated upstairs and poked through her husband's wardrobe, looking for packages of new handkerchiefs or socks that she could wrap and place under the Christmas tree so each of the boys would have a gift. With Herbert's blessing, she invited all her night visitors to stay for Christmas dinner, and none declined. Breaking into his wartime liquor reserve, Herbert McWhorter ensured each young pilot had a shot of whiskey to celebrate the day.

After he returned to Hollister from the Christmas holidays, Kenny Barden pushed the squadron's string of December accidents to three after he inadvertently landed wheels-up in his Avenger, plowing up the runway with his propeller and surveying (destroying) the airplane's engine. Van Antwerp restricted Barden to base for ten days, a punishment made all the more severe by Margie's proximity and his inability to visit her on the weekends.

Barden's restriction gave him plenty of quiet time to think, and he thought mostly about Margie and marriage. The war had accelerated everything, and the idea that someone special would write him while he was gone and pray for his safe return was a powerful aphrodisiac. Planning confidently for the future was also an excellent way of coping with the uncertainty of the present. When his restriction ended, Barden proposed marriage to Margie and she accepted.

Joe Rubin had been considering marriage, too, and he decided Dickie was the one for him. But Dickie was unsure. One year younger than her sister, Dickie had enjoyed the attentions of several handsome, eligible young officers in addition to Joe. She found Joe funny and cosmopolitan, but different. Joe's father, Louis, who owned a fancy apartment on Central Park West, traveled from New York to San Franscisco to help plead his son's case. Louis treated the entire McWhorter family to a lavish night on the town and extolled the virtues of living in New York City, specifically on Central Park West. Louis Rubin's visit had the unintended consequence of cooling the relationship between Joe and Dickie. Raised in Hattiesburg, Mississippi, Dickie had always figured she'd return to Mississippi. New York seemed to her a distant and foreign country where she'd never fit in.

Training continued at Hollister, in fair weather and foul. VT-18 hadn't yet experienced any weather-related accidents, but the squadron's luck ran out in January 1944. Departing NAS Alameda on a short flight to Hollister in low ceilings and rain, Lieutenant Junior Grade Stephen Dragan, a young pilot from New York City, simply disappeared in his Avenger. When the weather lifted, Van Antwerp ordered a search of the Bay Area for the missing airplane. Dragan's squadron mates searched for him for two weeks but found nothing. Two months later, after VT-18 had left the States, a farmer walking his fields near San Jose discovered the wreckage of an Avenger with Dragan's remains still in the cockpit.

Scuttlebutt had predicted Air Group 18 would ship out after the first of the year. Most of the pilots had discounted the rumor at first, since they had been deceived by "Get ready, boys; we're shipping out next week" gossip before. But the rumors persisted, and in early January there was tangible proof the story might be true: The Bureau of Aeronautics outfitted VT-18 with eighteen brand-new TBM-1C Avengers, the latest-model torpedo-bomber fresh off the assembly lines of Eastern Aircraft Corporation. The pilots and aircrew crawled all over their new flying machines, excited as teenagers with a hot new car, which was fitting, because Eastern Aircraft was a division of General Motors Company. A new pilot, Ensign Nicholas J. Roccaforte from Houston, Texas, also joined the squadron as a replacement for Dragan, bringing the squadron back up to strength. Roccaforte had a high opinion of himself. One of the older pilots noted sarcastically in the squadron log, "Roccaforte joined the squadron. For almost three days he left us in ignorance as to who the hottest pilot in the fleet was; after that he told us."

Kenny and Margie were married on February 7 at a Presbyterian church in downtown San Francisco. Herbert and Honey McWhorter hosted a quiet ceremony that evening in the parlor of their home. Bud Williams, Squatty Vaughn, and Joe Rubin attended the celebration; Ensign William C. "Bill" Bates of Castle Point, New York, who was another of Barden's squadron mates and liberty buddies, served as Kenny's best man. A few days later, as if Barden's wedding celebration had roused the Navy Department from slumbering indecision, Air Group 18 received orders to transfer all equipment and personnel from Hollister to NAS Alameda and board the aircraft carrier *Lexington* for transport to Hawaii.

On the morning of February 24, 1944, at about nine a.m., the men of Air Group 18 assembled on the carrier pier at NAS Alameda in the shadow of *Lexington*. Most of VT-18's pilots had spent several extremely damp nights—damp from alcohol, not the weather—in San Francisco and Oakland in the days leading up to their departure. For some, the drinking and revelry were an extended celebration marking the end of training in California and the beginning of a great adventure. But for the married men, especially the newly married men like Barden, the pall of separation hung heavily over the celebrations, and the parting was bittersweet. At the appointed day and hour of embarkation, officers and enlisted men filed up their separate gangways to *Lexington*'s hangar deck. A few, like Squatty Vaughn, nearly missed the ship's departure because of too much bourbon in San Francisco the night before; he ran down the wharf and dashed breathlessly up the gangway at the last minute. Family, sweethearts, and friends were not invited to the naval station to say their good-byes. The movements of ships and squadrons were not shared with civilians, and the pilots and aircrew were enjoined not to tell a soul, not even their mothers and wives, the name of the vessel on which they were booked to sail.

After everyone had boarded, Air Group 18 mustered on the carrier's flight deck, officers in the front ranks and enlisted in the rear. Lieutenant Commander Van Antwerp stood at the head of VT-18's formation looking tired and a bit unsteady to Red Wallace's critical eye, and, later that day, *Lexington* got under way. She was packed with a full complement of her own ship's company sailors, the airplanes, pilots, aircrew, and staff of two air groups, 18 and 19, and a navy construction battalion (nearly two thousand Seabees) as passengers. At about two forty p.m., the big *Essex*-class carrier passed under the Golden Gate Bridge into the Pacific Ocean, and the men of VT-18 were bound for war at last. Or so they thought.

CHAPTER THREE

IN HAWAII

★ ★ ★ ★ ★

Lexington's flight deck was crowded with the air groups' airplanes and other tarpaulin-covered equipment destined for the war zone, and flight operations of any kind were impossible. Pilots and aircrew had little to do but attend lectures, play poker, and learn shipboard routines, customs, and rules—including the official prohibition against drinking any amount of alcohol not prescribed by the ship's doctors or the air groups' flight surgeons.

Most of VT-18's officers and airmen had never been to sea before. No one regarded VT-18's carrier qualifications aboard *Cohapee* as real sea duty. The torpedo-plane pilots had flown their Avengers to *Cohapee* from a land base, executed the required number of carrier landings and takeoffs, returned to the airfield, and adjourned directly to the Hotel del Coronado bar. Now, wandering around the big new *Essex*-class carrier, with its multitude of full decks, half decks, and narrow passageways cluttered with pipes and conduit, the aviators adjusted to the unfamiliar sensations of being under way, such as the constant motion of the ship and the omnipresent sound of machinery and ventilation blowers. No place aboard ship was silent, they learned; every space had its rattle or hum. There was also an ever-present cornucopia of smells to which the newcomers became accustomed. Fresh paint and machine oil were the predominant odors, but the mix of smells changed as men weaved their way through the maze of passageways. Paint and oil gave way to coffee, and coffee gave way to disinfectant and floor wax. Near the galleys and wardrooms, the odor of steam-heated food hung in the air like the aroma of a school cafeteria; in the hangar bay, the smell of aviation gas pervaded. The airmen had to learn how to negotiate steep shipboard ladders—an old salts' manner of descending was to grab the handrail with both hands, swing both feet forward to the third or fourth rung, and then slide downward like a gymnast on parallel bars, pedaling lightly down the steps—and pass through watertight hatches without banging their shins or smacking their foreheads. *Lexington*'s leisurely four-day passage to Pearl Harbor offered the airmen a pleasant, if somewhat unrealistic, introduction to life aboard an aircraft carrier. Barden was impressed with *Lexington*, exclaiming enthusiastically in his diary, "Whatta ship!"

Lexington arrived at Pearl Harbor midday on February 28. As tugs eased the ship through the channel toward the carrier berth at Ford Island, the men of air groups 18 and 19 congregated on the flight deck to gawk at the harbor sights. Barden was astonished at the number of ships in the port. There were heavy cruisers at anchor, and nests of submarines, tenders, destroyers, minesweepers, and transports. Gray-painted warships seemed to stretch in every direction as far as the eye could see. Near Ford Island, three battleships sunk by the Japanese during the Pearl Harbor raid still lay at their moorings, unmoved from where they had settled on the morning of December 7, 1941. The upturned hull of the battleship *Oklahoma*, looking like a massive turtle shell, brown and scarred, was a somber reminder to the men standing on *Lexington*'s flight deck of why America fought. As the carrier glided slowly past each wreck, *Lexington*'s officer of the deck ordered, "Attention to starboard," over the ship's 1MC. The men on deck snapped to attention and stood in silent tribute to their dead comrades, many of whom were still entombed inside the battleships' hulls. After *Lexington* had passed by each wreck, the officer of the deck intoned, "Carry on," leaving the men on deck to reflect upon what they had seen. The understated ceremony was a powerful motivator. Most of the men standing on *Lexington*'s flight deck had enlisted because of the Japanese attack on Pearl Harbor. Viewing the destruction with their own eyes steeled their resolve to avenge it.

Lexington docked at the Ford Island carrier pier. Much to the disappointment of VT-18's entire complement, Commander Ellis announced there would be no liberty in Honolulu. Air Group 18 was scheduled to transfer the next day to a new training base at Hilo on the Big Island of Hawaii. Ellis permitted air group personnel to go ashore that afternoon but confined them to Ford Island. There was little for the pilots to do. Barden, his best man Bates, Vaughn, and Rubin entertained themselves at the bar of the Ford Island Tennis Club while *Lexington*'s deck crews and shipyard workers carefully off-loaded VT-18's airplanes with cranes. The following afternoon, VT-18's pilots fired up their eighteen Avengers and departed the Ford Island airfield in a driving rainstorm. They flew two hundred nautical miles south to their new home at Naval Air Station Hilo on the Big Island of Hawaii.

The Big Island is a place of stark physical contrasts. The island was formed by at least five massive volcanoes that erupted from the sea floor and overlapped to create a landmass of more than four thousand square miles, the largest in the Hawaiian archipelago. Two of Hawaii's volcanic cones, Mauna Kea and Mauna Loa, soar thirteen thousand feet above sea level, high enough for their peaks to be snowcapped in winter. Three of the island's volcanoes are still active, and one of these, Kilauea, regularly spews rivers of molten rock into the sea, gradually expanding the island's southeastern shore. Hawaii's uplands are brown and arid and covered with volcanic scree, while the lowland valleys are green and lush and filled with tropical rain forests. In the 1940s, the island's arable flatlands were devoted primarily to growing sugarcane. Air Group 18's new home, NAS Hilo, lay on the eastern shore of the Big Island near the town of Hilo and in the lee of the high volcanoes; as a consequence, Hilo was among the wettest places in the Hawaiian chain. NAS Hilo occupied an old Army Air Corps airfield a couple of miles east of town, refurbished to accommodate at least two carrier air groups for training.

Commander Ellis completed the transfer of his entire air group from Ford Island to NAS Hilo within a few days of arriving at Pearl Harbor. After his men had settled into their new quarters, he convened a meeting of staff officers and pilots and announced that Air Group 18 would remain at Hilo indefinitely for more training. Whatever hopes the airmen had of an early deployment to a new fleet carrier like *Lexington* were dashed. Ellis's news especially grieved the newly married pilots, like Kenny Barden, who were eager to do their part in the war and return to their wives as soon as possible. But there were good reasons for more training and a delay in deployment. The Bureau of Aeronautics had replaced VB-18's aging SBD Dauntless dive-bombers with brand-new SB2C-3 Helldivers. Manufactured between 1939 and 1944, the Dauntless had been the navy's frontline dive-bomber at the outbreak of the war, and Dauntless-equipped dive-bomber squadrons had inflicted all of the damage on the Japanese carrier fleet at the Battle of Midway in June 1942. But the SBD Dauntless possessed serious combat limitations. The SBD—the airplane's initials stood for "scout bomber Douglas," although loyal Dauntless pilots insisted the initials meant "Slow but Deadly"—carried its bomb load on an external fuselage mount which greatly reduced the airplane's speed and maneuverability. The Dauntless also had ordnance constraints; it could not drop any single bomb weighing more than a thousand pounds from its fuselage mount. The Helldiver was a much bigger, faster, and more powerful dive-bomber. Curtiss had designed the Helldiver to carry bomb loads of up to two thousand pounds internally and to dive on targets at very steep angles of up to eighty to ninety degrees. Because Bombing 18's pilots and aircrew had trained exclusively in Dauntlesses, they would require additional training time in Hawaii—Barden grumped that it would take a hell of a long time—to grow accustomed to their new airplanes. The introduction of Helldivers would also require Ellis's entire air group to adjust its tactics to the greater speed and capabilities of the new dive-bombers.

The Helldiver had a troubled developmental history. Test flights (and crashes) of early prototypes revealed structural weaknesses, directional instability, and a lack of range and power. These defects would be unnerving in any airplane but were especially problematic for a warplane expected to carry heavy ordnance, absorb enemy counterfire, and perform high-stress maneuvers. Curtiss redesigned the airplane and delivered the first Helldivers, SB2C-1 models (also called "A" models colloquially), to VB-4 operating from *Yorktown* in May 1943. The commander, Naval Air Force, Atlantic fleet reported "continued malfunctioning, structural failures, and other operational difficulties which affect [the Helldiver's] use of armament and safety in flight. . . ." The same admiral declared the Helldiver "unsuitable for assignment to combatant carriers at this time." Curtiss again went back to the drawing board, and the navy restricted the airplane's speed and dive angle until Curtiss's engineers could make further modifications. To most naval aviators of the time, the Helldiver's problem-plagued introduction into the fleet confirmed the wisdom of the old aviation adage, "Never fly the A model of anything." By early 1944, Curtiss had substantially corrected the design deficiencies of the Helldiver and improved the company's manufacturing processes, and the navy began equipping its dive-bombing squadrons with more powerful and reliable SB2C-3 models.

VB-18 wasn't the only squadron slated to receive new equipment. Commander Ellis announced that VT-18's Avengers would be fitted with "rocket guns," which were in fact wing-mounted "rails" capable of launching five-inch high-velocity aircraft rockets (HVAR). More time would be necessary to teach VT-18's torpedo-plane pilots how to shoot their newfangled rockets and develop techniques for effective air-to-ground rocket attack.

Air Group 18's training at Hilo was slow getting under way. Day after day of drenching rain over eastern Hawaii scrubbed many training missions, and the pilots found themselves with plenty of time on their hands. Classroom sessions, playing poker and eight-ball, writing letters home, and attending movies at the base theater occupied the rainy days. The boys rode a bus into Hilo, where they wandered the streets, idly window-shopping in the downpour or chatting with the shop owners. The citizens of Hilo were welcoming and generous to the navy boys. City leaders offered the pilots free use of the swimming pool at the Hilo Yacht Club when the weather cleared, and extended invitations to attend cocktail parties at the club. The boys of VT-18 eagerly accepted the latter. In the assessment of the squadron's unofficial historian, the women at the Hilo Yacht Club proved to be "really lovely" and "the liquor was excellent."

When the weather finally cleared, air-to-air gunnery practice consumed much of VT-18's initial training time. Avenger pilots and turret gunners practiced air-to-air gunnery by shooting at a cloth streamer called a banner. A single Avenger pulled the target banner across the gunnery range, much like a civilian airplane drags an advertising banner above a crowded beach, while six or eight other Avengers in the division shot at it. The attacking Avengers would dive at the banner one at a time from "high perch," which was the starting position in the gunnery pattern roughly one thousand feet above the banner and a few thousand yards to one side. The pilot would drop one wing and angle down toward the banner, firing his .50-caliber wing guns at the streamer as he came within range; he would break off his gunnery run slightly above and behind the banner and pull up into a steep climb for a second run at the target from the other side. As the Avenger swept past the banner and entered the climb, the turret gunner would hammer away at the banner with his .50-caliber turret gun.

The aerial gunnery pattern combined the thrill of a roller-coaster ride with the pleasure of a carnival shooting gallery. The hardest part for the shooters—aside from hitting the target—was switchology, remembering in the excitement to charge and arm the guns. The Avenger's machine guns were hydraulically actuated, and if the pilots and gunners didn't charge their weapons with hydraulic pressure, the guns wouldn't fire. Everyone in the gun pattern enjoyed the experience, except the tow-plane pilot, who was expected to fly straight and level and hold a slow, steady airspeed. He was fated to worry constantly whether his engine would overheat from the strain of pulling the banner, whether he might accidently jettison the banner into the sea, whether a bullet would sever his tow cable, or, worst of all, whether a stray shell might smack into his tow plane.

To practice air-to-ground gunnery, Avenger pilots and gunners fired at one of the stationary targets the navy had established on uninhabited rocks near the Big Island, or at a moving target sled that was towed by a fleet tug or destroyer. In air-to-ground gunnery practice, Avenger pilots pushed over into dive angles of between fifteen and sixty degrees and bore down on the target at high speed, firing their wing-mounted .50 caliber machine guns in short bursts. They practiced aiming slightly below and behind the target and "walking" their bullets over the target as they approached it. The pilots were sternly and repeatedly warned by their commanding officers and flight leaders not to fixate on their target. If a pilot became mesmerized with the flight of his bullets toward the target, he could easily lose track of his minimum safe altitude for recovery and have insufficient altitude to pull out of his gunnery run. To minimize the risk of colliding with the earth on a strafing run, Avenger radiomen reported the changing altitude to their pilot over the intercom as the airplane descended.

The squadron's new high-velocity rockets presented special challenges. Pilots fired them at stationary targets or moving target sleds, just as they did with their machine guns, but they had to adjust for a different trajectory. Unlike a machine gun bullet, which exits the gun muzzle at terminal velocity, a rocket leaves its launcher at a fraction of its terminal velocity and accelerates. To the pilot, the rocket appears to rise above the flight path of the airplane before falling back toward its target. Mastering the aiming point of an HVAR required considerable practice for the pilot and considerable recalibration for the aviation ordnancemen, whose job it was to adjust the torpedo bomber's gun sight for rocket firing. Hitting the target required considerable luck in any event, since the new weapons were notorious for sailing off in unanticipated directions.

In early March, Kenny Barden, Squatty Vaughn, Joe Rubin, Bill Bates, and a fourth VT-18 ensign, Thomas P. Spaulding, received promotions to lieutenant junior grade. Naturally, the officers celebrated their new status. Each had purchased one share of the squadron's official whiskey ration—one share entitled the purchaser to one quart of whiskey every two weeks—and all four pilots donated one quart to the promotion celebration. The result was a good-natured party brawl. Barden had his shirt ripped off his back by one of the celebrants, and the promotees' biweekly whiskey ration was drunk up completely in one night. The following week, Kenny Barden, presumably remorseful and determined to exercise some restraint, sold his next whiskey ration to Lieutenant Commander Van Antwerp, who was delighted to have two quarts available for the long two-week period ahead. Barden used the proceeds from the sale to stake himself in poker and blackjack games for the next month.

VT-18's pilots and aircrew practiced their specialty—torpedo attack against enemy shipping—by making torpedo runs against target ships in a patch of ocean off Hawaii known as "Area Two Sugar North." The target ship, usually a destroyer, steamed on a north–south course between two torpedo recovery groups, each of which consisted of an oceangoing tug and two sampans. The first recovery group stationed itself two miles east of the target ship, and the second group two miles west. The attacking Avenger pilots would circle low over the target ship for recognition purposes, and then set up for their simulated torpedo runs. In practice, Avenger pilots launched a standard Mark 13 aerial torpedo that had been disarmed and set to a running depth that would allow it to pass beneath the target ship. The practice torpedo would either "strike" the target or streak past it. After the torpedo had run its course and bobbed to the surface, one of the recovery groups would fish the spent torpedo from the water and salvage it for reuse.

The commander, Naval Air Force, Pacific fleet, the officer to whom Commander Ellis and Lieutenant Commander Van Antwerp reported while their units trained in Hawaiian waters, had sternly enjoined all torpedo plane pilots to "be on hand" when torpedoes were loaded into their Avengers and to "take an active interest in the procedure." He urged his torpedo-plane pilots to know how to release their torpedoes before they flew into Area Two Sugar North— switchology was a challenge in launching torpedoes as well as in firing machine guns—and he cautioned them to identify the target ship positively before beginning a practice torpedo run. There was always the chance that friendly vessels other than the target ship might be operating in or near Area Two Sugar North;

a nontarget warship was likely to react defensively to a surprise torpedo run. The opportunities for mishap on or around the torpedo range were many.

VT-18's pilots discovered early in their training the difficulty of hitting a moving ship with an aerial torpedo. They began their practice torpedo runs with an accelerating glide toward the target ship. During their approach, they jinked violently from side to side, practicing the twists and turns that would be necessary to evade enemy antiaircraft fire. At a distance of about fifteen hundred yards from the target, they leveled their wings and launched their torpedoes. A successful torpedo run required precise airmanship, concentration, a good eye during the approach for closure rates, and a steady hand on the control stick at the moment the torpedo was released. The commander, Naval Air Forces, Pacific fleet tallied the number of "hits" by torpedo squadrons practicing in Area Two Sugar North. The results were excellent for a baseball player but disappointing for proponents of torpedo attack. On average, only about 40 percent of the torpedoes launched by Avenger pilots in simulated attacks found their target. Forty percent was the success rate under ideal training conditions, with the target ship limiting its evasive maneuvering to a turning circle of seven hundred yards, and with torpedo squadrons conducting most of their training exercises in the early morning hours to avoid rough water. In actual combat, the torpedo plane pilots would have to contend with a host of complicating factors, such as enemy fighters, concentrated gunfire from the target, unpredictable maneuvering by the target ship, a wingman's mistake (such as fouling the approach to the target), high winds, rough seas, and reduced visibility from smoke, clouds, and rain squalls.

Rumors of imminent deployment percolated at Hilo just as they had in California. Ernie Allen, VT-18's intelligence officer, boldly predicted the squadron would be in combat by the first of April and return stateside by October. Barden hoped Allen was correct—Kenny wanted to get home to Margie as soon as possible—but Barden secretly doubted the squadron would return from combat so soon. In mid-March, Allen's prognosticating gained a bit of credence when new scuttlebutt predicted that Air Group 18 would board *Bunker Hill* by mid-April. This report proved false, but two weeks later another rumor blossomed that VT-18 would go aboard *Yorktown* at the end of April. This too proved false.

The truth of the matter was that Air Group 18 was not yet ready for combat as an air group. Although the pilots and aircrew of all three squadrons, VF-18, VB-18 and VT-18, had trained extensively in their respective specialties, they had not yet received sufficient training in joint operations. To be effective as a carrier air group, each squadron had to learn to operate safely and efficiently with the other two and work under the direction of Commander Ellis or his designees. In a typical carrier air strike, the ship would launch fifteen to twenty fighters, twelve to sixteen dive-bombers, and six to eight torpedo bombers. Each squadron would rendezvous by type, and all three squadrons would then proceed to the target together. The attacking warplanes, all thirty or forty of them, would cruise at about the same ground speed but fly at different altitudes, separated by a few thousand feet. Normally, fighters would fly at the highest altitudes, torpedo bombers at the lowest, and dive-bombers in between. They would arrive over the target en masse—air group strikes were called "massed attacks"—and hit the target rapidly in a prescribed sequence. Dive-bombers would usually roll in first over the target, fighters second, and torpedo bombers last. A well-coordinated strike lasted no longer than four or five minutes. With dozens of airplanes concentrated in the same airspace, coordination and timing were critical. Absent flight discipline and adherence to plan, pilots courted midair collisions when rolling in or pulling off the target, and risked flying through the path of friendly machine-gun fire or into the concussive cloud of a friendly bomb.

Massed attacks were difficult to execute properly, even without enemy opposition. Pilots were delayed taking off and joining up, and airplanes sometimes malfunctioned and returned to base, creating offensive and defensive gaps in the formation that compelled flight leaders to make adjustments in their dispositions literally on the fly. Communications, essential for coordination, were a constant challenge. Unnecessary radio chatter often blocked the tactical frequency. Some strike group leaders, like Commander Ellis, insisted on radio silence and practiced it, relying on visual signals to communicate with his strike group rather than on radio transmissions, except in an emergency. But visual signals weren't foolproof. Although U.S. Navy pilots were expected to have memorized a whole lexicon of visual signals—bewildering combinations of head nods, finger pointing, fist twisting, hand waving, waggling of the wings, dipping of the nose, and gunning of the engine—they sometimes misinterpreted the signals, like a batter missing a bunt sign. The weather did not always cooperate, of course. Clouds, rain, fog, and mist complicated both navigation and coordination by concealing elements of the strike group from one another and by obscuring the target. Massed attacks became especially complex when strike groups from two or three different air groups attacked the same target only minutes apart. When multiple air groups participated in the same bombing exercise, there would be more than one hundred blue-painted warplanes in the vicinity of the target, some headed inbound, some headed home, and some orbiting nearby, awaiting their turn.

Pilots and aircrews referred to massed-attack training missions as "group gropes," largely because of the perception among the participants that no one was really in charge of the exercise. Even when all elements of the strike group got airborne and were headed toward the target, no one was sure what would happen if or when they located it. Wags complained, only half in jest, that group gropes were more hazardous to the participants than to any enemy on the ground. It was no coincidence that Commander Ellis acquired the nickname "El Gropo" at Hilo, a nickname that blossomed naturally from the combination of "Ellis" and "group commander," but also seems to have been a good-natured jab at his navigational skills. Ellis took to flying with another Hellcat on his wing at all times, not only for mutual protection against enemy fighters but also to assist him with navigation.

In the early days at Hilo, El Gropo was unhappy with his air group's performance. Fighters, dive-bombers, and torpedo bombers were too slow in rendezvousing, too dispersed en route to the target, inaccurate in their bombing and strafing of the target, too slow to regroup afterward, and too dispersed when returning to the airfield, resulting in excessive landing intervals. Barden didn't disagree; in his estimation the first few group gropes by Air Group 18 were TARFU: Things Are Really Fucked Up. Not only was VT-18's bombing inaccurate, but too many of the pilots failed to release their ordnance at all—the air group usually practiced with lightweight hundred-pound bombs or fifty-pound bombs containing smoke markers instead of explosives—making the whole exercise a waste of time and gasoline. In some cases, the pilot's failure to release his ordnance was due to mechanical or electrical defects in the airplane or in the ordnance itself, but more often, the failure to drop was the result of pilot distraction and switchology error. Barden, who had failed to release his bombs once or twice on the practice range, recorded that Ellis was pulling his hair at the air group's poor performance.

VT-18 trained harder, not only to execute group gropes with greater efficiency, but to sharpen its performance in all manner of Avenger operations. Van Antwerp cycled his divisions though the mine-laying and smoke-laying school located at Naval Air Station Barbers Point, Oahu. This school was not popular among VT-18's pilots; mine laying and smoke laying were far too dull and defensive for most of the boys. But Van Antwerp also rotated his divisions through live-ordnance bombing exercises at a range off Barbers Point called the Rock, where his crews dropped heavyweight bombs instead of lightweight practice bombs. Dropping a thousand-pound bomb on the range was exhilarating. Nothing demonstrated the Avenger's offensive power more spectacularly than the boom and rumble of the bomb's explosion and the geyser of smoke and debris that shot into the air. Blimps hovered high above the Rock while the blimp's crew, called gas baggers or bag pilots, carefully recorded the Avengers' hits and misses. Over time, VT-18's scores improved.

Although the live-bombing exercises at Barbers Point were exciting, Van Antwerp's torpeckers didn't think much of the living accommodations there. The temporary quarters for those officers training at Barbers Point, called transient officers' quarters, were a collection of overheated Quonset huts infested with mosquitoes; VT-18's pilots were only too happy to relinquish their beds to the next group of trainees. The return flight to Hilo also offered the torpeckers an opportunity to replenish NAS Hilo's whiskey supply and their liquor ration. Barden, Kurt Schonthaler and his buddy Duke Delaney, Robbie Robinson, and two other VT-18 Avenger pilots flew home to Hilo from Barbers Point in late March with fifty-one cases of bourbon for the Hilo officers' club. Barden bragged that he had given a navy chaplain a ride to NAS Barbers Point and "replaced him with 9 cases of Seagram's."

On April Fools' Day, Bud Williams caused considerable mirth within the squadron by scheduling Lieutenant Commander Van Antwerp to fly the tow plane, normally a chore reserved for the most junior pilot in the squadron. The skipper laughed along and flew the hop. A few days later Van Antwerp announced that VT-18 would "be doing nite [sic] low level radar bombing off our carrier." This news, which several pilots probably dismissed as the skipper's own version of a good April Fools' joke, came as a big surprise.

Launching airplanes from an aircraft carrier at night and recovering them is a whole different kettle of fish from launching and recovering airplanes in the daylight, and flight operations at night dramatically increase the risks for aircrews and flight deck crews. World War II carrier operations were almost exclusively a daylight affair, with task group commanders and air officers normally scheduling operations so that the first strike launched at dawn and the last strike recovered before sunset. By mid-1944, however, the navy had formed small units of night fighters that served with regular fighter squadrons as detachments. Night-fighter detachments usually consisted of four or five specially equipped Hellcats flown by pilots who had been schooled intensively in instrument flying and night carrier operations. Their primary mission was to shoot down Japanese "snooper" planes, or "Washing Machine Charlies," that came out at night to reconnoiter and disturb the sleep of the American task force. Although VT-18's pilots had been trained for routine night flying at Hollister, they had not been trained to take off or land aboard a carrier at night.

Van Antwerp's expanded night-flying syllabus began with radar-directed night bombing and torpedo attacks. Pilots roused themselves from bed between one and three a.m. and took off in the dark between three and five a.m. They navigated to the target—usually a target ship—using their Avengers' airborne radar and dropped flares over the target. They simulated their torpedo or bombing attacks beneath the pale white light of the flares, and returned to Hilo in the darkness. The pilots often flew a second training mission later in the same day, completing a daylight navigation flight or ordnance run before dusk. The night syllabus made it difficult for the boys to find a little time to relax. Some of the pilots sandwiched visits to the officers' club between training hops, although the official rule was eight hours bottle-to-throttle. In early May, Barden had scheduled a night radar bombing mission with a three a.m. wake-up call. Bud Williams, Squatty Vaughn, Ray Skelly, and Doc Doyle, all slightly drunk, barged into the bachelor officers' quarters at one a.m., awakened Barden, and insisted everyone fly the scheduled radar hop immediately. Barden went along and, surprisingly, everyone completed the flight and landed safely back at Hilo by four thirty a.m.

The opportunity for night qualifications aboard a real aircraft carrier never materialized for VT-18, but most of the pilots regarded night takeoffs and landings at NAS Hilo as a good-enough approximation. The ocean area east of the airfield became black as the ace of spades at night, and the glooming hills to the west of the airfield offered scant visual references, only the chance to collide unexpectedly with the earth in the dark. The pilots flew their night approaches at Hilo hugging the runway as carefully as if they were landing aboard ship.

The Pacific land war had evolved into an amphibious island-hopping campaign, with U.S. Marines in the vanguard of the attack. In amphibious operations, navy warships stood offshore and bombarded the beachhead. Marine riflemen lowered themselves over the sides of transports into smaller landing craft. At the appointed hour, the warships ceased their heavy bombardment and waves of boats and amphibious vehicles laden with marines motored toward the shore. As the landing craft discharged their human cargo on the beach, carrier-based warplanes would execute strikes on demand against enemy troop concentrations and gun emplacements. That was the theory, anyway.

As part of its daylight training syllabus, VT-18 practiced "close air support" for marines as they rehearsed large-scale amphibious landings on the beaches of Maui. Avengers laid smoke low over the water to shield the transports and landing craft, and made simulated bomb gunnery, and rocket runs over the beach. Effective close air support required constant communication between the boys on the ground and the boys in the air. The Maui exercises were designed to teach Marine infantry how to go ashore and school navy and Marine pilots on how to bomb and strafe the beachhead without killing their countrymen below. These amphibious support exercises—there were several in March and April alone—generated six to ten hours of flight time per day for each pilot as VT-18 constantly shuttled Avengers among NAS Hilo, NAS Maui, and the landing beaches. Barden grew weary of the training, complaining that the "Marines should recognize every pebble on that beach by now."

The boys sought diversion and escape in Hilo's nightlife, such as it was. NAS Hilo supplied a school bus to transport officers and enlisted men into town for liberty and to return them to the air base before midnight. Red Wallace was often assigned to drive the bus. His job was to drop off passengers at restaurants and bars in town, such as Volcano House, Seaview Inn, Naniolas, Hilo Hatties, and the Hilo Yacht Club, and carry the airmen safely home again. The boys supplied Red with free drinks as he made his rounds of the bars. On many nights, Red couldn't drive the bus home; with Red incapacitated, one of the boys usually maneuvered the vehicle back to the base while Red slept in the backseat. Fights sometimes broke out in the bars or on the bus. The boys quarreled over anything debatable: women, sports, politics, bad flying, inequitable scheduling, aircrew assignments, perceived affronts, and stupid remarks. One night in April, Squatty Vaughn punched Lieutenant Junior Grade Robert McKee over some indignity, and McKee, in turn, cut Squatty's lip. Someone blackened Lieutenant Junior Grade Robert "Ole" Olsen's eye in the same fracas. A couple of weeks later, Ensign "Bris" Brisbin decked a loudmouthed enlisted Marine who was also riding on the bus back from Hilo, and Ensign Roccaforte, the Texan, pasted Lieutenant Junior Grade Schonthaler, the Rhode Islander, in the nose for some offense.

The fighting cost Bud Williams his job as squadron executive officer, at least temporarily. Bud was responsible for discipline and order among the troops, and he hadn't delivered. In fact, he was often in the middle of things. Van Antwerp appointed Ernie Allen to the job, and demoted Bud to operations officer. Kenny Barden resented the change, remarking sourly in his diary, "From now on anything can happen."

By May 1944, the boys had been training together for nine months, and the repetition and monotony had strained the pilots' fraternal bond. Most of the men believed they were ready for war. They were frustrated at not knowing when their training would end. They were impatient, eager to get on with the war, and irritable at being held back. But VT-18's bombing accuracy and efficiency were still unsatisfactory in Van Antwerp's and Ellis's view. Van Antwerp presided over a squadron gripe session in mid-May, during which he raised hell with his pilots about their performance and invited any pilot to speak his piece. Many accepted, complaining about a lack of military discipline, too much fraternization with enlisted men, shuffling of aircrewmen without the pilots' consent, and other grievances. Van Antwerp's gripe session cleared the air, but what most of the pilots really wanted was an end to the ceaseless training and an opportunity to apply their skills in combat against the enemy, something that was beyond Van Antwerp's ability to deliver.

Then, on May 23, 1944, Air Group 18 received word that it would transfer from Hilo to Oahu within two weeks and go aboard *Intrepid* in June. The mood in the squadron changed overnight; disgruntlement gave way to renewed enthusiasm. Reenergized by the new timetable for deployment, VT-18's pilots spent the few remaining days in May shuttling their Avengers between Hilo and Barbers Point, where they battled the ever-present mosquitoes and executed more practice bombing runs with live ordnance.

On June 2 the long-anticipated transfer order arrived. Commander Ellis directed Lieutenant Commander Van Antwerp to shift VT-18 to Naval Air Station Kaneohe located on the eastern shore of Oahu. Everyone knew NAS Kaneohe was the final way station for all air groups destined for assignment aboard an aircraft carrier operating in the Pacific. Word also had it that VT-18 would board the fleet carrier *Franklin* on June 9 for carrier requalifications. If the squadron performed satisfactorily around the boat—and no one doubted it would—VT-18 would go aboard *Intrepid* as soon as she returned to Pearl Harbor from the West Coast. Air Group 18 would be off to war at last. Delighted that their days at Hilo were at an end, Bud Williams, Doc Doyle, Ray Skelly, Frank Scrano, and Kenny Barden made a final, celebratory round of the Hilo taverns on June 4 to bid farewell to the town barkeeps, and the next day VT-18 moved all aircraft, personnel, and equipment to NAS Kaneohe. Kenny Barden was so hopeful and confident the word was true that he didn't unpack his bags when he arrived at Kaneohe. He figured he'd be aboard *Franklin* in a day or two.

On June 8, Van Antwerp abruptly announced that carrier qualifications aboard *Franklin* had been canceled. He explained that *Franklin* had become unavailable—Air Group 19, destined for duty aboard *Lexington*, had taken the carrier requalification slot on *Franklin*—and VT-18 must now delay its carrier requalifications until *Intrepid* herself arrived in mid-June.

Kenny Barden unpacked glumly, and he and the boys settled into much the same training routine they had followed at Hilo. They flew group gropes led by El Gropo, bombing and torpedo runs, rocket and gunnery practice, over-water navigation hops by day and by night, and FCLP by day and by night. Commander Ellis addressed the "growing resentment among a certain few members of Air Group EIGHTEEN that the war is not being waged exactly as they wish" with an open letter to all hands. He cataloged the complaints—orders issued and retracted; plans to move out and stay put; exercises scheduled and canceled at the last minute; flying secondhand airplanes; getting new airplanes and having them snatched away and replaced by even older airplanes—and acknowledged that "these things are exasperating." But, he reminded his men, "military matters do not and never will run smoothly on schedule," and they must "adapt themselves to uncertainties and discomforts." Ellis counseled them, "Air Group EIGHTEEN will move up into combat soon enough. In the meantime let every man condition himself physically and mentally, prepare himself mentally in every way possible for the job ahead."

Van Antwerp's boys took some consolation from the fact that the seaside air base at Kaneohe was far larger than Hilo and boasted superior recreational facilities. The officers' club was "a thing of beauty" in Barden's assessment, with four bars, two dance floors, slot machines, a swimming pool, and excellent food. The air base offered sandy beaches, tennis and basketball courts, baseball diamonds, and the opportunity to watch some of the world's best baseball players. None other than Joe DiMaggio played for an Army Air Corps team on Oahu, while Johnny Mize played for the Kaneohe Klippers. A starstruck Barden watched DiMaggio's team defeat Mize's in eleven innings and recorded afterward, "What a game!" Although Barden and the boys conceded that Kaneohe was a pleasant spot to pass the time, living a relatively pampered life at Kaneohe wasn't getting them any closer to war or home.

Carrier Air Service Unit One (CASU-1), based at Barbers Point, Hawaii, was a squadron of replacement pilots and aircrew, most of whom were recent graduates of navy flight training. CASU-1 supplied Pacific-bound squadrons with trained airmen, either to bring established squadrons up to full strength before deployment or to replace crews lost to illness or training accidents. In mid-June, four ensigns from CASU-1 joined VT-18, raising Van Antwerp's total complement of torpedo-plane pilots to twenty-seven. Among these new pilots was Ensign Willard M. Fletcher, a twenty-year-old from Illinois.

Will Fletcher's path to the Pacific was typical of the three young naval aviators who joined VT-18 with him. A 1941 high school graduate with an aptitude for flying, Will enlisted in the Navy Reserve in August 1942 at the age of nineteen and enrolled three months later in the Naval Aviation Cadet Training Program, Murray State Teachers College, Murray, Kentucky. These cadet training programs, which the navy had established at small colleges throughout the country, were intended to prepare young men with little or no college education for the academic demands of pilot training, and to supply qualified candidates for the navy's formal preflight training schools. The cadet training program consisted of a six-week crash course in mathematics, physics, civil air regulations, navigation, meteorology, and aircraft identification. Cadets at Murray State received military indoctrination training, physical conditioning, and thirty-five hours of primary flight instruction from a local civilian flight instructor in a high-wing civilian monoplane, such as a Taylorcraft or Cub. Cadets were lodged separately from the regular college students on campus and lived a quasi-military life of fixed schedules, concentrated training, and obligatory attendance. They wore fore and aft caps and military coats and trousers of navy blue or khaki. Each day they awoke at five thirty a.m. and breakfasted by six. Sunday was a free day, unless a cadet was scheduled to fly, something that happened frequently when bad weather forced the cancellation of flights the preceding week. The cadets received no salary, only a small stipend for expenses.

Those who successfully completed the cadet preparatory program, such as Will Fletcher, were assigned to one of the five official preflight schools the navy had established at large state universities around the country. Will received orders in January 1943 to the U.S. Navy Pre-Flight School on the campus of the University of Georgia at Athens. As the school's name implied, the navy provided no in-the-air training at its preflight schools. The curriculum was devoted entirely to mathematics, physics, military discipline and courtesies, infantry drill, basic military tactics, seamanship, navigation, ordnance, first aid, signaling, and more physical conditioning. There was ample physical conditioning. A public relations brochure for the Athens preflight school trumpeted that "the physical training program is the most strenuous and complete that has ever been undertaken by any college or organization in this country." The cadets performed calisthenics, ran track and hurdles, boxed, wrestled, played basketball and football, swam, and bounced on trampolines. They ran cross-country obstacle courses that challenged them to climb ten-foot walls, clamber over log pyramids, vault ditches, shinny up poles, and traverse ravines by clinging to rope bridges. Instructors hounded cadets to improve their performance with each running. Every cadet, although he was not yet a commissioned officer, was outfitted with a set of the standard white, khaki, and dress blue uniforms of a naval officer with all the accoutrements, except for an officer's sword. Each was housed in a college dormitory that had been converted to a military barracks, fed five thousand calories per day, and paid sixty-nine dollars a month. They were subject to naval discipline. The navy forbade cadets to drink alcohol and strictly enforced the prohibition. Nineteen-year-old Will Fletcher wrote home from Athens to his mother, Naomi:

The awful-est thing happened last night. They don't allow cadets to drink or even go into a saloon or they get washed out of the service. But last

night being Saturday night and pay-day and everything, a group of cadets,
about eight, went into a saloon and was drinking pretty heavy (so I hear)
and about 9:00 some military police caught them. You should see their
faces today. They are ready to bawl because they know they will be kicked
out in a couple of days.

Perhaps thinking of his own father, who was a profound alcoholic, Will went on, "I don't see why they don't pour all the damn stuff in the river and many more lives would be happier today." Will showed little sympathy for the cadets who had erred. "But on the other hand, if a fellow hasn't got enough common sense and willpower to leave it alone, I guess he has to learn. You'd be surprised at the number of fellows that has tried to get [my friend] Bill and I to take a drink and we just politely say, 'no, thank you, I'll take an orange soda.' And boy, what I mean, that's the way it's going to be for me all the time!"

Every cadet at Athens was a child of the Great Depression, but Will Fletcher's material disadvantages as a child were greater than most. His father, Norman, a draftsman and machinist by trade, was caught up in the sweeping tides of the unemployed, and drifted from town to town in southern Illinois in search of a job, uprooting his family whenever there was promise of work. When he found employment, he could not hold it because of his weakness for drink. Within the space of ten years, Norman moved his family—Naomi, Will, and his two younger sisters, Betty and Gerry—from Edwardsville, Illinois, to Glen Carbon, from Glen Carbon to Roxanna, from Roxanna to Granite City, from Granite City to Peoria, from Peoria to Edwardsville, from Edwardsville to Springfield, and then back to Edwardsville. Notwithstanding three attempts at taking the cure, Norman could not overcome his alcoholism, and Naomi divorced him when Will was ten.

Naomi and her children moved in with relatives who were themselves living at the margins economically. But Naomi was strong and resourceful. She cleaned the houses of the well-to-do in Edwardsville and worked two or three other jobs part-time to make ends meet. Will also worked part-time from the age of twelve as an elevator operator, potato digger, and stock boy, contributing whatever he earned to the family finances. Ultimately, Naomi found steady work as a school librarian and moved the family into a tiny, four-room walk-up flat above a dry-goods store in Edwardsville. Will was six months out of high school when the

Japanese struck Pearl Harbor, living at home and working as an apprentice draftsman at Emerson Electric, a factory in St. Louis.

The war offered Will the opportunity to escape his circumstances, and he pressed Naomi to allow him to enlist. Charles Lindbergh and Wiley Post were Will's heroes as a child, and he had always wanted to learn to fly. While in high school, he had bartered flying lessons from a local barnstormer and had flown solo a few times in a biwinged Waco. Naomi consented to Will's enlistment, even though he was exempt from military service as the sole male provider for his family. Will departed for cadet preparatory school at Murray full of excitement—and guilt at abandoning his family. When he entered navy preflight school and began to receive a regular salary, he sent the bulk of his paycheck home each month to his mother and sisters.

Tragedy struck in April 1943 while Will was still at the Athens preflight school. Naomi had taken a full-time job working on the assembly line at Emerson Electric. She collapsed on the factory floor and died of a heart attack at the age of thirty-seven. Will could not afford to go home for his mother's funeral. His older sister, Betty, mailed him a lock of Naomi's hair wrapped in a pink bow. Will tucked the lock of hair in his wallet and carried it with him always as a talisman and remembrance.

For those who successfully completed preflight school, such as Will Fletcher, the next step was primary flight training at one of several naval auxiliary air stations the government had constructed in rural areas around the United States where there was ample flatland and plenty of open airspace to accommodate large numbers of airplanes. Will Fletcher received orders in mid-May 1943 to Naval Air Station Norman, Oklahoma, where he learned to fly the navy's primary trainer, the Stearman N2S-3. The Stearman was a two-seat biplane with fixed landing gear and a radial engine, the cylinders of which were exposed to the air. The Stearmans at Norman were painted bright yellow to attract attention and minimize the risk of midair collisions around the airfield. New cadets grappled with the challenge of learning to fly the N2S-3, an underpowered airplane that demanded its pilot comprehend basic aerodynamic principles and control the airplane from the moment its propeller began to spin. The cadets nicknamed their trainer the "Yellow Peril."

Will Fletcher loved the Yellow Peril from the instant he lifted off the ground on his first instructional flight. This was flying in its purest form, powered flight as close to the flight of birds as was possible for man. The Stearman's cockpit opened to the sky; the instructor sat in the rear cockpit and the student up front. Nothing separated Will and his instructor from the elements but a Plexiglas windscreen and a skin of painted fabric stretched over an airframe made of wood and aluminum. In a Stearman, the drone of the engine and the rush of the slipstream enveloped the pilots; there was no electronic means of communicating between cockpits. Will and his instructor communicated by shouting through a voice tube, or by resorting to hand signals and wagging the control stick. They glided above the Oklahoma countryside, above pastures and fields greening in the spring, above tree-filled gullies and mud-brown cow ponds. They occasionally overtook a hawk or a buzzard that rolled left or right and dived away from the airplane, as if inviting them to follow. Sometimes Will and his instructor accepted, chasing the hawk or buzzard and winging low to the ground. Will inhaled the sweet odor of fresh-mowed hay.

Aerobatics were a large part of the curriculum at Norman, and Will excelled at them. Like all good aerobatic pilots, Will had the capacity to visualize things in three dimensions and the ability to make the airplane an extension of himself. He could inscribe in the sky whatever maneuver he envisioned. Will loved overhead maneuvers the best. These were the 360-degree loops, the Immelmanns, and the Cuban Eights and Half Cuban Eights. He thrilled at the whine of the propeller and the flutter of the wind in the guy wires as he dived to gather speed for his maneuver. The Stearman's engine thrummed and ticked like an old sewing machine. He relished the acceleration that forced him into his seat as he began his pull upward. And then, as the airplane floated over the top of the loop upside down, as his flight controls became light and unloaded, he bent his head back as far as he could manage to pick up the rising horizon and checked that his wings were level. He always grinned at the sights and the sensations. Everything inverted, upside down, high above the earth, with nothing holding him in his seat but his lap and shoulder belts, the force of gravity diminished to less than one. And then, as the airplane dived toward the earth gathering speed, as aerodynamic acceleration pressed him back into his seat and the ground rushed up at him, he pulled the nose back up and through and felt as if he could repeat the maneuver again and again and again and stay in the loop forever.

Will flew his last flight at Norman on August 10, 1943, three days before his twentieth birthday. He had flown seventy-eight hops in the Yellow Peril, logging

107 total hours in the air since leaving Athens. Within the week, he had transferred to the naval air training center at Corpus Christi, Texas. By August 23, Will was training in the SNV-1 Vultee "Valiant," a slow, underpowered monoplane that the navy used primarily as an instrument trainer. The Vultee's landing gear did not retract, and she had an oversize greenhouse canopy that rattled noisily. Aviation cadets referred to the non-retractable-gear Valiant as "stiff-legged" and dubbed her the "Vultee Vibrator."

The navy training program required students to endure only about forty hours of flight instruction in the Vultee. They moved next to the SNJ-4 Texan, built by the North American and Boeing aircraft companies. The Texan was a real airplane. She was fully aerobatic, with retractable landing gear and a powerful radial engine enclosed within an aerodynamic cowling. The SNJ-4 approximated the complexity and agility of combat aircraft, yet was forgiving of mistakes, if they were committed with enough airspeed or altitude to recover. Will logged more than 135 hours in the SNJ-4 between October 1943 and January 1944, learning the fundamentals of gunnery, formation flying, more acrobatics, night flying, navigation, glide-bombing, and torpedo attack.

The naval air training center at Corpus Christi, Texas, had been commissioned in March 1941. By the time of Will's arrival in mid-1943, Corpus Christi was the largest naval aviation training center in the world. It consisted of the main naval air station and six outlying, or auxiliary, airfields. Will thought it odd the navy had chosen to name most of these auxiliary training fields, such as Chase Field located near Beeville, Texas, for naval aviators who had died in airplane crashes. He joked to his pals that it was an honor to which he did not aspire.

The main base at Corpus Christi had the look of a hastily built college campus, underlandscaped and not quite finished. With the exception of the base chapel, which was a Currier & Ives–style church with a soaring white steeple, the main buildings at Corpus Christi were boxy and unadorned structures, constructed mostly of whitewashed clapboard or cinder blocks. There were administrative offices, a hospital, mess halls, dozens of long double-storied barracks buildings, classroom buildings, a library, an auditorium, a gymnasium, and recreational buildings. The air station had been constructed on the flattest, sandiest, and most desolate acreage Will had ever seen. The navy had planted a few spindly trees, but none had grown to more than shoulder height; the decorative shrubs around the buildings were dwarves, entirely out of proportion to the structure. Although the navy had sown the grounds with thick-bladed Bermuda grass, the lawns were thin and weedy. Anyone who ventured off the sidewalks or roadways would collect sand spurs in his cuffs and socks.

Will had never before experienced heat or humidity like the heat and humidity that suffocate south Texas from August through late September. He couldn't walk more than fifty yards without breaking into a sweat. The training airplanes, hundreds of SNVs and SNJ-4s, were tied down on vast concrete aprons adjacent to the hangars and runways. By ten in the morning, heat radiated off the apron in shimmering waves, and the metal skin of the airplanes became a griddle to the touch. When it rained—and it rained heavily almost every afternoon between three and five thirty—the concrete apron steamed like a Turkish bath.

While Will trained at Corpus Christi, the war ground on, with the Allies taking the offensive in Europe and in the Pacific. Axis resistance collapsed in Sicily, and Allied forces landed at Reggio di Calabria on the toe of the Italian boot and at Salerno below Naples, beginning the Allied campaign to oust the Axis from Italy. The United States Army Air Corps continued its campaign of daylight bombing raids against targets deep in the heart of Germany. American losses on such raids were staggering. On August 17, 1943, the American 8th Air Force attacked German ball-bearing factories at Schweinfurt and Regensburg, losing in a single day 147 of 376 bombers dispatched over the target. In the Pacific, American and Australian infantrymen and airmen continued to battle the Japanese for control of New Guinea, and in November 1943, United States Marines landed at Tarawa in the Gilbert Islands. The Tarawa invasion marked the beginning of the United States' island-hopping offensive across the central Pacific. The Japanese commander of Tarawa had boasted that his defenses in the Gilberts could not be breached by a million men in a million years. The U.S. Marines secured the islands in three days, but at a cost of 1,009 Americans killed and 2,101 wounded.

On January 19, 1944, Aviation Cadet W. M. Fletcher officially completed navy flight training and was commissioned Ensign Willard M. Fletcher, United States Naval Reserve. A senior officer pinned above Will's left breast pocket the yellow-gold wings insignia that distinguished Will as a naval aviator. After the ceremony, Will stood at attention on the steps of the administration building at Corpus Christi in his dress blues for his graduation photograph. He stood with twenty-six other former cadets who had been newly commissioned and newly winged that same week, all looking fit and confident.

The decision as to who would fly what type of airplane for the fleet was less a matter of pilot choice than the needs of the navy. Although most aviation cadets probably hoped for an assignment after graduation to a fighter squadron, bombing and torpedo squadrons furnished most of the offensive clout for a carrier air group, and in terms of sheer numbers, the navy required more pilots for dive-bombing, torpedo attack, transport, patrol, and reconnaissance than for tangling with Japanese Zeros. One of the primary missions of the Naval Air Training Command was to ensure adequate numbers of skilled pilots for further training in all specialties and to replace pilots of all aircraft types who were lost in advanced training and combat. Will had been assigned to torpedo planes, and within two weeks of commissioning he had been transferred from Corpus Christi to Naval Air Station Miami, Florida, to begin his tactical training as a torpedo-plane pilot in the TBM Avenger. He flew his first two flights in a TBM on February 3, 1944. Will piloted the airplane on these first training missions by himself, without any instructor pilot riding along, and he did so on every training flight thereafter. Avenger instructor pilots led formations and taught tactics; aside from delivering basic familiarization lectures and offering ground-school coaching, they didn't teach people how to fly the airplane itself. Read the manual; fly the airplane. This was the navy's approach to introducing a designated naval aviator to a new airplane.

Will logged more than 130 hours in the TBM at Miami, familiarizing himself with the airplane's systems and performance and learning to use the plane as a weapon of war. He flew practice bombing, torpedo, and gunnery missions, and he learned to navigate over open water by dead reckoning from NAS Miami to NAS Bermuda and back to NAS Key West. In contrast to the heat and torpor of Corpus Christi in August and September, Miami was a tropical paradise, with day after day of high blue skies, balmy temperatures, and soft, clear nights. Miami was a sophisticated town, a city built for sun-seeking tourists. There were cabarets and dance clubs. And women. Near the end of his training in Miami, Will met a pretty, wide-eyed girl named Margie of whom he was sufficiently proud to send home a photograph. In the picture, Will in his dress white uniform and Margie in a flower-print dress sit together at a dinner table holding hands. Visible in the foreground are half-filled drinking glasses with straws in them. "This is Margie!!" Will scribbled on the back of the photograph. "One of the last evenings in Miami, Florida." Still a twenty-year-old teetotaler, Will assured his sisters, "Ginger ale in the glasses!"

Will's training at Miami lasted only three months. By May 1944, the Navy Department had transferred Will thousands of miles west to CASU-1.

Will Fletcher and fellow CASU-1 ensigns Vernon J. Sistrunk of Los Angeles, Daniel Laner of Marcola, Oregon, and Owen F. Williams of San Pedro, California, arrived at Kaneohe in mid-June like freshmen on campus, excited and a bit overwhelmed. Barden was the squadron duty officer when they reported aboard. He cheerfully welcomed them to "this broken-down outfit" and assigned them to their quarters. After two days of squadron indoctrination, the new ensigns began flying with VT-18's old guard.

Will was in awe of Kenny Barden and the boys at first. They were all three or four years older than Will and had trained with VT-18 since its inception. They were far more seasoned pilots, having logged on average about 920 hours of flight time, more than double Will's total military flight time of 410 hours. Several had gone to college. Some had wives back home. They drank a lot of whiskey and beer and seemed to play poker like professionals. They had well-established relationships and inner circles. They cracked private jokes and shared personal histories that were foreign to Will. But Will was determined to break in and compete. He conceded the older guys nothing but a little age and experience.

One week after the new ensigns arrived, the pilots of VT-18 requalified for carrier duty by landing aboard the *Ommaney Bay*, CVE-79, a small escort carrier. Each pilot made at least two passes and two landings. The new guys did well, but two of the older hands, Lieutenant Junior Grade Donald Pieper and Ensign Nicholas Roccaforte, slammed into the barrier. Barden was irked because Pieper had been flying Barden's favorite Avenger, number fourteen, when he hit the barrier, and number fourteen was a total loss. The accidents didn't dampen the pilots' enthusiasm that night at the Kaneohe officers' club. The pilots lustily celebrated VT-18's requalification, and the new guys began to bond with the old boys.

Commander Ellis was still not satisfied with Air Group 18's bombing performance. He scheduled more group gropes and training missions, sternly warning his pilots to get better quick or expect six more months of training. *Intrepid*, Ellis threatened, could go to someone else if everybody didn't shape up.

In July, Van Antwerp reshuffled his personnel like a coach reshuffling his lineup. He created four divisions of six (instead of three divisions of eight) and appointed new division leaders for at least two of the four divisions. Lieutenant Junior Grade George Riley, the hotshot who seemed indifferent to the laws of aerodynamics and the limitations of his airplane, became the leader of Division 4. Kenny Barden retained his slot in Division 2 as Lieutenant Leo M. "Chris" Christensen's wingman, much to Kenny's relief. Barden and Chris had learned to work together well; they communicated efficiently and supported each other, anticipating each other's moves like good doubles partners in tennis. Van Antwerp also integrated the new ensigns into the lineup, giving them a chance to prove themselves by flying on the wing of more experienced pilots. Will Fletcher seized the opportunity, flying nearly every day during the month of July and sometimes twice a day. He eagerly flew the whole mix of torpedo-bomber missions, including rocket runs, bombing runs, radar and navigation hops, gunnery runs, torpedo runs, combined navigation and bombing hops, day FCLP, and night FCLP.

Night FCLP at Kaneohe was as challenging as at Hilo. A few days after Van Antwerp's reshuffling of personnel, Barden's lead pilot, Chris Christensen, disappeared on a night FCLP flight after just one touch and go. Apparently, Christensen had become disoriented while turning out to sea for a second pass at the runway and had crashed in the black water east of the airfield. VT-18 dropped flares over the water until one a.m. in an effort to locate him, and boats from Kaneohe searched the area with floodlights. They found no trace of Christensen or his airplane. Barden flew his scheduled predawn hop at three thirty a.m., and took off again with Bud Williams at dawn to search for Christensen's wreckage or—they hoped—a life raft. They landed two hours later without finding any sign of their buddy. Christensen had simply vanished, his Avenger swallowed up by deep water. Barden and Williams retired to the BOQ, saddened and mystified.

Christensen's death was a blow to Barden personally. The man with whom Barden had flown daily for months, the division leader whom Barden trusted with his life, was gone. The senior staff intelligence officer for Air Group 18, Lieutenant George Race, offered his condolences to the squadron and sent a bottle of Old Taylor whiskey to Barden's BOQ room. That night, Barden, Joe Rubin, Frank Scrano, George Riley, and Bud Williams held an Irish wake of sorts in the BOQ, consuming the entire bottle of whiskey in toasts and remembrances to Chris.

VT-18 was not the only squadron in the air group to lose men at Kaneohe. During an air interception exercise, one of VF-18's Hellcats collided head-on with one of VB-18's Helldivers. The poor dive-bomber pilot had been part of a three-plane Helldiver section that was flying along straight and level and playing the role of an unsuspecting Japanese bomber formation. A VF-18 fighter division had "intercepted" the Helldivers, and the fighter pilots had taken turns making simulated gunnery passes on the dive-bombers. During the ill-fated pass, one of the fighter pilots made a slashing, nearly head-on approach, focusing his attentions on the Helldiver flying on the far right-hand side of the dive-bomber vee. The fighter pilot flew aggressively but gravely misjudged his closure rate of more than 450 knots. He rolled left sharply at the last instant to avoid a collision, but his airplane's momentum carried him forward. In the blink of an eye, the Hellcat sliced through the Helldiver, severing the dive-bomber's right wing. The fighter pilot sheared off his own right wing in the process, and the two warplanes spun together into the sea like falling leaves. Both pilots and the Helldiver gunner were lost.

While the men of Air Group 18 trained at Kaneohe, *Intrepid*'s crew prepared to receive the carrier's new air group. The aircraft carrier *Intrepid* was the fourth U.S. Navy warship to bear the name. (The first was a French-built ketch captured from pirates off Tripoli in 1803 by Commodore Edward Preble; the dashing Preble renamed his prize *Intrepid*.) The modern carrier's keel was laid down in Newport News, Virginia, on December 1, 1941 and she was commissioned CV-11 in Norfolk, Virginia, twenty months later. The letter "C" stood for carrier, "V" stood for heavier-than-air aircraft, and the numeral "11" indicated that *Intrepid* was the eleventh carrier authorized by Congress. She was the third carrier constructed in her class, known as the *Essex*-class "short-hull group."

Intrepid with Air Group 6 embarked had first seen action on January 29, 1944, as part of Task Group 58.2. The carrier and her air group furnished air support for Marine assaults on Roi-Namur and Kwajalein Atoll in the Marshall Islands. On February 16, 1944, off Truk Atoll in the central Caroline Islands, a Japanese aerial torpedo struck *Intrepid* just below the waterline. The blast killed eleven men and warped *Intrepid*'s rudder into a "huge potato chip," as her damage control officer described the injury. *Intrepid* retired from the combat area with her rudder jammed hard to port and sailed slowly and erratically back to Pearl Harbor for repairs. Her skipper, Captain Thomas L. Sprague, tried to hold the crippled *Intrepid* on a northeasterly course to Pearl Harbor by idling her starboard screws, but she swung like a pendulum when the breeze freshened.

"She had a tendency to weathercock right into the wind . . . [and] turn her bow toward Tokyo," Captain Sprague reported, "but right then I wasn't interested in going there." Sprague was compelled to rig an improvised sail on her forecastle to steady her. Describing *Intrepid*'s erratic track back to Pearl Harbor, Sprague said, "No enemy sub could have figured out her zig-zag plan." *Intrepid* sailed on to Hunters Point Naval Shipyard in San Francisco to replace her rudder, and there she remained until June 1944.

Repairs to *Intrepid*'s rudder took longer than anticipated. Rather than return the aircraft carrier immediately to combat duty, the Navy Department assigned her temporary transport duty. Packed with airplanes and heavy equipment, *Intrepid* departed NAS Alameda on June 9, 1944, bound for Pearl Harbor. When she arrived at Pearl Harbor, *Intrepid* exchanged her cargo of war material for Air Group 19, which had been training at Kaneohe concurrently with Air Group 18. Air Group 19 had been assigned to the aircraft carrier *Lexington* (CV-16), which was then operating in the Marshall Islands. *Intrepid* transported the men and machines of Air Group 19 to Eniwetok Atoll, twenty-five hundred miles west of Hawaii. On Independence Day, 1944, *Intrepid* embarked hundreds of soldiers, sailors, and marines as passengers, some of whom had been wounded in the assault on Eniwetok, and weighed anchor for passage back to Hawaii.

One week later, *Intrepid* returned to the Pearl Harbor Naval Shipyard and tied up at the pier, made fast to the bollards by eight hawser wires and six heavy manila lines, each thicker than a man's wrist. She received fresh water, electricity, telephone service, and steam and air from the dock. Yard workers and crewmen from *Intrepid* immediately went to work replenishing the ship, loading the tons of supplies necessary to feed, clothe, shoe, cleanse, arm, exercise, heal, discipline, train, amuse, berth, and comfort her complement of nearly thirty-two hundred officers and men for weeks at a time at sea. They also loaded the staggering variety of materials necessary to sustain and operate *Intrepid* herself. The ship required lubricants, paints, varnishes, bottled gases, solvents, waxes, electrical wire, tubing, conduit, tools of all kinds, jigs, dyes, instruments, gauges, carbon paper and ink, staples, paper clips and tape, replacement flight deck timbers, steel and aluminum sheeting, electronic components, testing equipment, and much more. The carrier consumed enormous amounts of fuel, and dockworkers topped *Intrepid*'s capacious fuel bunkers with nearly sixty-five hundred tons of navy special, a fuel oil similar to the diesel fuel that powers locomotives and over-the-road trucks. To power Air Group 18's warplanes, dockworkers and sailors pumped aboard nearly 130,000 gallons of highly volatile one-hundred-octane aviation gasoline.

On July 24, Commander Ellis announced that Air Group 18 would board *Intrepid* in about four or five days. Barden and the boys were cautiously optimistic. Ellis ordered all ground personnel—the term "ground personnel" encompassed all air group officers and enlisted men whose principal duties did not involve flying as a pilot or aircrewman—to prepare to transfer from Kaneohe to Ford Island. The normal practice was for ground personnel to board the ship while she was tied up at the pier; most of the pilots and aircrew would fly aboard the carrier after she put to sea. The transfer of airplanes and pilots from Kaneohe to the ship would be accomplished as part of a shakedown cruise, a joint training exercise between the air group and the carrier, the chief purpose of which was to test the air group's readiness for carrier operations and begin the process of melding the carrier and her new air group into an efficient fighting unit before they sailed off to war together.

On July 25, Will Fletcher loaded Leon Vannais, recently promoted to lieutenant junior grade, and four VT-18 ground personnel into his Avenger at Kaneohe and flew them over Pali Pass to Ford Island. Will's passengers had been tasked with supervising the embarkation of VT-18's ground personnel and equipment, and Will used the opportunity to inspect the ship that would become his home.

Intrepid had shifted her berth to dry dock number four when he first saw her. He stood on the pier and gazed up at her, dumbfounded at her size. He had traveled to Pearl Harbor on an escort carrier and had never before seen an *Essex*-class "fleet" carrier up close. The ship's flanks towered above him, stretching in both directions like an infinite wall of steel. *Intrepid*'s hull had been painted in bold trapezoidal shapes of black, gray, and blue. This cubist paint scheme, Will learned, was a "dazzle" camouflage pattern intended to confuse enemy submarines. Seven hawsers to port, and seven more to starboard, held *Intrepid* securely in her place. She pumped seawater constantly from her bilges; streams of bilge-water shot from her drainpipes like water from a fire hydrant. Her ventilation fans and blowers droned noisily. Sailors trudged up the aft gangway carrying heavy boxes on their backs like beasts of burden, while others, freed of their lading, bounded back down the forward gangway to gather up more. A yard worker sat high up in the cab of a dockside crane, lifting pallets of bombs from the quay and gently depositing his deadly lading on *Intrepid*'s flight deck. Sailors pushing wheeled carts hauled the bombs away to stowage as soon as they settled on deck. Will was astonished by the bustle of activity and excited by the prospect of going to sea aboard *Intrepid*. This would be a great undertaking, a great adventure, a great movement of men and material and machines. The ultimate fruits of America's wartime science and industry had been invested in this warship, and in many others like her.

On July 26, 1944, President Roosevelt arrived in Hawaii aboard the heavy cruiser *Baltimore* for a conference with his Pacific commanders. The following day the president, accompanied by Admiral Chester Nimitz and General Douglas MacArthur, visited Honolulu and toured the Pearl Harbor naval base. The crew of *Intrepid*, resplendent in their dress white uniforms, manned the rail and stood shoulder-to-shoulder around the periphery of *Intrepid*'s flight deck in honor of the dignitaries. The celebration also included a massive flyover of warplanes, seemingly comprised of every serviceable navy and Army Air Corps airplane in the Hawaiian Islands. Will did not participate, but Kenny Barden spent two hours in the air practicing the flyover and three hours more in the air on the day of the big event. Barden protested, "Now I know I'm voting for Dewey," and VT-18's squadron historian reported, "Listening to the general talk after the [flyover] hop landed, it was assumed Dewey would win the Election by Service-men's votes alone."

What most servicemen in Hawaii did not know (but many suspected) was that the president had come to Honolulu for a high-level conference with General MacArthur and Admiral Nimitz to plot the future course of the Pacific war. The decisions made at the Honolulu Conference would likely determine where and when *Intrepid* and Air Group 18 would fight. The conference lasted only three days. Not much was said publicly at the time. The war leaders disclosed their plans to the press in only the most general terms. President Roosevelt announced simply that America was "going to get the Philippines back" and that General MacArthur would take part in the effort.

When not rendering honors to the brass, *Intrepid*'s sailors, aided by Pearl Harbor dockworkers, scurried to make the carrier ready for war at sea. Between July 25 and 27, crews loaded and stowed massive amounts of ordnance: 36 torpedoes and associated components, such as gyros, warheads, igniters, boosters, and detonators; 520 general-purpose bombs of various weights ranging from 250 pounds to 1,000 pounds; 625 rocket bodies; 1,600 five-inch .38-caliber projectiles; 600,000 rounds of .50-caliber machine gun ammunition (divided into equal quantities of incendiary, tracer, and armor-piercing bullets); 30,000 rounds of 40-millimeter ammunition; and 60,000 rounds of 20-millimeter ammunition.

On July 27, Air Group 18's ground personnel packed the air group's equipment and baggage aboard a caravan of trucks and transported the lading across Pali Pass from the Kaneohe airfield to Pearl Harbor. VT-18's baggage included more than thirty sea chests; these were heavy wooden footlockers, each of which contained the personal belongings of one of the squadron's officers. Most of Air Group 18's pilots and aircrew—Will Fletcher among them—remained at Kaneohe, eagerly awaiting the order to fly their airplanes out to sea and land aboard *Intrepid* for the first time.

Intrepid departed Pearl Harbor for the shakedown cruise on the afternoon of July 28. As the big carrier slowly backed out of dry dock four, Air Group 18's ground personnel loitered on deck like the passengers they were and observed the proceedings with interest. Air Group 18's sailors had been trained for aviation specialties; they had no notion of how a ship put to sea, and they had no responsibilities for making the carrier ready or casting her off. The boatswain's call over *Intrepid*'s 1MC, "Set the special sea and anchor detail," meant nothing to them. They leaned over the rails and enjoyed the warm sunshine and the harbor views.

Intrepid's ship's company had its own way of doing things, and there was always a period of adjustment when a new air group reported aboard a carrier. Ship's company regarded air group sailors as quasi-sailors, as men who wore the same uniform but who knew nothing about seafaring; ship's company tended to treat new air group personnel with a measure of indifference or disdain until the airmen proved themselves worthy of the ship. Many of *Intrepid*'s ship's company were "plank owners," meaning they had been members of the carrier's original commissioning crew. Plank owners were proprietary; they regarded *Intrepid* as their private vessel and were resistant to any suggestion that they do things differently. The distinction between ship's company and air group personnel was reinforced by subtleties of dress and tribal nicknames. Officers in *Intrepid*'s ship's company were called "black shoes," because ship's company officers were usually attired in standard navy-issue black work boots, or wore black dress shoes with their summer khaki uniforms. Officers of the air group were known as "brown shoes," because pilots usually wore brown flying boots, or brown dress shoes with their summer khaki uniforms. Ship's company sailors, regardless of rank or station, referred to air group personnel as "Airedales," a mildly derisive label that conjured images of exuberant but dim-witted puppies. For their part, air group personnel referred to ship's company as "squids" and to ship's engineering personnel as "snipes."

The shakedown sortie of July 28 was short-lived. *Intrepid* maneuvered gracefully though the submarine nets protecting the approaches to Pearl Harbor and began a full-power run-up to thirty knots. But as the big ship accelerated, she suddenly began to shake and shudder to her core. *Intrepid*'s skipper, Captain Joe Bolger, reduced speed and ordered his engineers to investigate the problem. The snipes' report was grim. The lubrication system associated with one of *Intrepid*'s propeller shafts had failed and damaged a bearing. A rumor circulated among the crew, probably apocryphal, that a careless sailor or yard worker had dropped a rag into the machinery and clogged the system. Whatever the cause, the big ship was forced to turn around and creep ignominiously back to Pearl Harbor for major repairs.

Air Group 18's ground personnel disembarked at Ford Island, berth F2, within sight of the still-weeping hull of *Arizona* and the other sunken American battleships. VT-18's ground personnel carried the officers' heavy sea chests ashore and trucked the stuff back across Pali Pass to NAS Kaneohe. The returning Airedales amused their comrades at Kaneohe with tales of the aborted sortie.

They swore the harbormaster had been forced to assign extra tugboats to prevent *Intrepid* from turning automatically into dry dock of her own accord. The Airedales began to refer to their future home waggishly as the "Decrepit," "Queen of the Dry Docks," or simply the "Dry I."

For the next two weeks, while *Intrepid* underwent repairs to her shaft bearing at the Pearl Harbor Naval Shipyard, VT-18's pilots entertained themselves by playing baseball, horseshoes, cards, and cork ball, or by loitering around the swimming pool and bar of the Kaneohe officers' club. Van Antwerp hosted a luau on the Kaneohe beach for the entire squadron, at which he personally carved the pig and dished out meat, cold beer, and poi to his sailors. To maintain his pilots' flying edge, Van Antwerp scheduled more practice bombing, torpedo, gunnery, and rocket runs, and Commander Ellis led the air group on more group gropes.

Ellis's group grope of August 2 ended tragically. Commander Ellis led a strike group in a simulated attack against the battleship *Massachusetts* and several destroyers. During the second torpedo run against *Massachusetts* by a three-plane section of VT-18's Avengers, Lieutenant John L. "Robbie" Robinson—the lovesick pilot who had borrowed the OD's car at Alameda—collided with Lieutenant Junior Grade Bill Bates, Kenny Barden's best man. Robinson's Avenger disintegrated and plummeted into the sea, killing him and his two crewmen, Aviation Radioman Second Class George E. Siegrist and Aviation Ordnance Man Second Class George H. Stewart, both from the Bronx. Bates nursed his crippled Avenger back to Kaneohe with a large piece of its wing missing. He crash-landed on the runway, lost control of his airplane, and demolished a B-24 Liberator bomber parked on the concrete apron. Miraculously, Bates and his crew escaped serious injury.

The deaths of Robinson and his crew, coming on the heels on Christensen's loss, left the squadron understrength. To maintain four Avengers divisions comprised of six pilots each, plus adequate reserves, Van Antwerp required at least one new pilot, and one new turret gunner and radioman. The replacement pilot would not step into Robinson's role as a section leader; Van Antwerp would pick one of the lieutenants junior grade to step up and become a section leader. The new pilot would become a floater, filling in as a wingman where needed. Van Antwerp and his administrative officer, Frank Scrano, requested a replacement Avenger crew from CASU-1, and CASU-1 complied, dispatching Ensign

Bernard J. "Ben" St. John and two crewmen over the Pali to join VT-18 at Kaneohe.

Ben St. John was a wiry redhead from Adams, Massachusetts. Before the war, he had driven a bakery truck, delivering bread, cakes, and cinnamon rolls door-to-door. Ben had nearly washed out of flight training once or twice because of problems with high overhead maneuvers such as loops, but he had impressed his instructors with his desire and perseverance. In joining VT-18, Ben would be going to war with a group of men he didn't know. He would be expected to pull his weight, notwithstanding that he had fewer flight hours and less training than the other pilots in the squadron, including his fellow ensigns. Ben's relative inexperience bothered him not at all. He was thrilled at the opportunity of joining a torpedo squadron heading to war aboard a big-deck carrier like *Intrepid*. Though he would not be the youngest pilot in the squadron—Will Fletcher held that distinction—Ben would be the most junior ensign by date of rank, the "boot."

On August 7, with her damaged bearing repaired, *Intrepid* commenced in-dock engine trials in preparation for getting under way. Commander Ellis again ordered his ground personnel to transfer the air group's baggage to Pearl Harbor—the officers' sea chests were now much resented by the enlisted men who had to manhandle them on and off the trucks and up the ship's gangway—and for the third time VT-18's ground personnel transported the lot across the Pali to Ford Island in a caravan of trucks. All air group personnel reembarked on *Intrepid* later that afternoon, and the carrier departed Pearl Harbor early the next morning. This time, *Intrepid* accelerated smoothly to high speed when she hit open water, and her air department made ready to receive the new air group.

The pilots of Air Group 18, led by Commander Ellis, ferried their warplanes directly from Kaneohe to *Intrepid* on the morning of August 10. Van Antwerp led his squadron of eighteen Avengers to the carrier en masse in three divisions of six. Van Antwerp was eager to make a good first impression on *Intrepid*'s crew and to deliver all eighteen of his torpedo bombers aboard the carrier without incident. He had selected the squadron's most proficient pilots for the ferry flight, including Barden, Skelly, Vaughn, and Bates. Van Antwerp had also picked Will Fletcher, who believed he deserved to be chosen because he had performed exceptionally well in FCLP and in carrier requalifications aboard *Ommaney Bay*. Nine pilots, including Ben St. John, who was too new and untested to be tapped for the ferry flight, hitched rides as passengers. On the trip to the ship, Ben was impressed with VT-18's formation flying. The torpedo-plane pilots rendezvoused quickly and held their parade positions precisely; wingmen remained exactly twenty feet wingtip-to-wingtip from their leaders, no more, no less, and held fast to the forty-five-degree bearing line.

The pilots had no difficulty locating *Intrepid* on the broad table of the sea. The wakes of the aircraft carrier and her screen of destroyers and cruisers, collectively designated Task Group 19.11 for the shakedown cruise, were visible for twenty miles from the air. VT-18's Avengers would be the last to land; they would recover behind VF-18's fighters and VB-19's dive-bombers.

Will piloted one of the Avengers in the second section of the third division. He had eagerly anticipated his first arrested landing aboard a big fleet carrier, and resolved to execute his approach and landing aboard *Intrepid* exactly as he had been taught. He wanted to perform flawlessly, to give his division leader, the LSO, his skipper, and Commander Ellis no cause for reproach or criticism. When Task Group 19.11 came into view, Will flipped the switch that activated his Avenger's APX-2 IFF equipment. This equipment signaled to the ships of the screen in a series of electronic interrogations and replies that his Avenger was a friendly aircraft. Will's division leader had repeatedly lectured that the IFF radio—IFF meant "identification, friend or foe"—was among the most important radios in the airplane. More than one pilot had tried to return to his carrier after a patrol or combat mission, only to be shot at by anxious antiaircraft gunners who failed to make a correct visual identification. The torpedo bomber's IFF equipment did not guarantee safety, but it offered some protection against accidental fratricide. Although this precaution was unnecessary on a ferry flight in a large group of airplanes only fifty miles off Oahu, Will practiced setting the proper code in his APX-2.

Van Antwerp steered his formation directly over *Intrepid* and banked into a wide circle two thousand feet above the carrier, a pattern known as the "group breakup circle." On Van Antwerp's signal, the entire flight of Avengers would begin a slow, spiraling descent to the squadron breakup circle, an elliptical pattern one thousand feet above the ship. Once established in the squadron breakup circle, Van Antwerp's three divisions would separate from one another and descend division by division to the approach circle, a racetrack pattern three hundred feet above the carrier. The approach circle was the final carrier landing pattern. In the approach circle, each division would further subdivide into two sections of three airplanes, and each section would then pass abeam *Intrepid* on her starboard side. When each three-plane section reached a point one thousand yards ahead of *Intrepid*'s bow, the lead pilot would break left, turn across *Intrepid*'s path, and enter the downwind leg of the landing pattern. His wingmen would follow him at thirty-second intervals.

Will gathered himself for the challenge ahead. He must land his Avenger on a moving ship at sea within a confined space no more than one hundred feet wide and three hundred feet long. He rehearsed his carrier landing procedures in his head and visualized himself making a precise carrier approach and arrested landing. The recovery would be performed in complete radio silence, based solely on standard approach signals and procedures, except for an emergency. Will tried not to think about the possibility of a wave-off or go-around. A wave-off for reasons other than a fouled flight deck was a public rebuke for poor airmanship. A wave-off for sloppy air work undermined the pilot's confidence and increased the pressure on the pilot to get the airplane aboard on the next pass. Will knew his first approach and landing aboard *Intrepid* would be closely scrutinized. Lieutenant R. N. "Dick" Moot, the air group's LSO, would be standing at the edge of the landing area with his paddles. He would assist Will in getting aboard, but he would also critique Will's approach and grade his landing. Van Antwerp would be very much interested in Moot's grades, because the precision and efficiency of VT-18's pilots in the carrier landing pattern was a direct reflection on Van Antwerp himself, and an indication of how well he had prepared his squadron for shipboard duty. A pilot scoring unsatisfactory marks might be disqualified for deployment and sent home. Last but not least, scores of ship's company sailors would be standing on *Intrepid*'s catwalks during flight operations. They would form their own unofficial opinions of Will's airmanship and technique and, by inference, of the squadron's professionalism. Will's objective was to score nothing less than an "okay" pass and landing, which was the best grade a pilot could get.

Will's division leader led Will and four other pilots down to the approach circle, maneuvering the division in a wide arc toward the initial approach point off the carrier's starboard side, roughly two miles behind the ship. During the descent, the division leader signaled division breakup by shaking his Avenger's wings and elevators with a quick rotary motion of his control stick. Will's section leader angled right, taking Will and one other pilot with him in right-echelon formation. This maneuver opened the distance in the descent between Will's section and the division leader's section. When both sections leveled off at three hundred feet behind the carrier, all six airplanes were angling back toward the ship to parallel her course. Will's section trailed the first section by one thousand yards.

Intrepid lay ahead, looking impossibly small. A ribbon of white foam trailed from her stern, and a brown wisp of stack gas streamed from her uptake vents. If a pilot screwed up his landing and couldn't get aboard the ship out here, he could divert to Oahu. Diverting for landing at Barbers Point or Ford Island would be humiliating but survivable. But when the air group went to war, an aircraft carrier would be the air group's only refuge in a dangerous and indifferent sea. Will's heart rate rose perceptibly; he was confident and determined to get aboard.

As Will's section passed abeam *Intrepid* on her starboard side, he stole a glance at the ship, but he dared not gawk. The carrier was a blur of gray shapes and shadows. He perceived airplanes in the landing pattern and airplanes parked forward on the flight deck, and glimpsed the antlike forms of hundreds of men milling about on the ship's catwalks and balconies. He detected Fox flags and pennants snapping gaily at the masthead.

Will's section glided past *Intrepid* and reached the break point ahead of the carrier's bow. There, the section leader shook his Avenger's wings and elevators rapidly, placed the fingers of his left hand to his lips, and blew Will a kiss. The kiss signified the leader was leaving the formation. The leader banked left across *Intrepid*'s bow and made a crosswind turn to enter the downwind leg of the landing pattern. Will, flying the number two position in the section, waited until the leader's airplane had turned abeam Will's left wing. Then Will blew his wingman a kiss and rolled left to follow his section leader.

Will flew his crosswind turn partly on instruments at a standard rate of three degrees per second. He had set his radar altimeter to beep if he descended below 250 feet, because height above water was exceedingly difficult to judge. After one minute, he rolled out of his crosswind turn and steadied his Avenger on the downwind leg of the landing pattern. His Avenger was now a thousand yards off *Intrepid*'s port bow, three hundred feet above the water, and headed in the opposite direction of the ship. Will concentrated on maintaining the proper separation on the downwind leg of the landing pattern between his airplane and the airplane ahead. This was essential for deck handlers to recover airplanes safely and efficiently. If Will's Avenger followed too closely behind the leader, the landing interval between the airplanes would be too short. A shortened interval would likely result in a wave-off or fouled deck, and Ellis and Van Antwerp would be displeased. If Will lagged too far behind his leader, the aircraft recovery process would be delayed, and Ellis and Van Antwerp would be equally displeased. Will gauged his Avenger's distance from the section leader's airplane to be fifteen hundred feet, a correct interval.

Will lowered his landing gear and pulled back on his control stick to counter the downward pitch of his Avenger's nose. As his torpedo bomber slowed through 130 knots, he lowered his wing flaps and countered the upward pitch of the nose by rolling in handfuls of nose-down trim. Will's Avenger quickly decelerated to her approach circle airspeed of ninety knots. He slid back the side panes of his cockpit canopy, and a torrent of warm air poured into the cockpit, carrying with it the roar of his engine.

Will glanced around his cockpit to ensure that he had properly configured his Avenger to land. He muttered the landing checklist to himself. Bomb bay doors closed. Landing gear down. Wing flaps down. Tail wheel caster unlocked. Canopy locked open. Fuel state, main tank selected, and sufficient fuel for two more hours of flight. Mixture automatic rich. Carburetor air direct. Propeller control twenty-four hundred r.p.m. Throttle set at eighteen to twenty inches of manifold pressure. Blower (the turbocharger used for high-altitude flight) set low-ratio. Oil cooler flap open. Cowl flaps open. Tail hook up. Will flipped his arresting hook switch to the down position and waited expectantly for the indicator gauge in the cockpit to register. On this flight, a malfunctioning tail hook would mean a diversion to Oahu. In the war zone, it would mean a wave-off and a water landing, or a collision with the barrier. To Will's relief, the arresting hook indicator clicked down, and Will asked Westmoreland, the radioman, to verify visually through the rear tunnel window that the hook had extended fully.

Will insisted on silence among his aircrew in the carrier landing pattern, except in response to a direct inquiry from him or an emergency. Will wanted no chatter, no distractions, only reports essential to safety. His crewmen honored this rule not only because the pilot had ordered it, but because their lives depended on the precision of his approach and landing.

Will's Avenger and *Intrepid* closed on each other at about a hundred knots.

This was the combined speed of Will's airplane as it decelerated to its landing speed of eighty-five knots and *Intrepid*'s speed as she churned through the water on the opposite course at fourteen knots. Will again stole a glance at the great ship that would be his home. She was clearly bigger than *Ommaney Bay* and the Great Lakes training carrier on which Will had landed before, but from the air *Intrepid* still appeared miniature and compact, incapable of housing thirty-two hundred men and carrying nearly a hundred airplanes. The forward half of *Intrepid*'s flight deck area was now jammed with air group warplanes that had landed ahead of Will. The carrier's deck-edge catwalks were crowded with Lilliputian crewmen.

Will suppressed the urge to sightsee. His goal on the downwind leg of the landing pattern was to arrive at the start position at the correct airspeed and altitude.

The start position was a point in space a thousand feet off the carrier's port side and directly abeam her stern, three hundred feet above the water. The constant refrain of Will's flight instructors echoed in his head: "A good carrier landing begins with a good start." When Will reached the start position, he would simultaneously descend to 150 feet above the water and turn ninety degrees back toward the ship for landing. Because *Intrepid* would be moving away from him as he was angling toward her, Will would have to make slight adjustments during the last ninety degrees of turn to intercept *Intrepid*'s extended centerline at the proper distance, roughly a thousand feet behind the carrier. If Will executed the second turn correctly, he would roll out with his Avenger established on *Intrepid*'s centerline, a thousand feet aft of her landing area, and a hundred feet above the water. Will would be squarely "in the groove," ready for a straight-in descent for landing. But he would not descend further until he had Moot and his signal paddles clearly in sight.

Will made final preparations for his approach. He twisted his propeller control knob clockwise and advanced his propeller r.p.m. to twenty-six hundred. The whine of the propeller increased in pitch. Will switched on his engine's auxiliary fuel pump and retarded the throttle slightly. The Avenger slowed. He eased his airplane into a semistalled attitude, trimming his Avenger's nose upward until eighty-five knots showed on his cockpit airspeed indicator. This was ten knots above the Avenger's stalling speed in her "dirty" configuration, with landing gear, flaps, and tail hook extended.

When Will reached the start position, he simultaneously dropped his

Avenger's nose and reduced power. The roar of his Avenger's engine subsided, as if he had unplugged a huge floor fan. Will banked sharply left toward *Intrepid*'s stern and looked over his left shoulder, searching for the location of the Avenger ahead of him and for the solitary figure of Lieutenant Moot standing somewhere on the left side of the flight deck. Will shifted his eyes constantly among his airspeed indicator, altimeter, the carrier, Moot, and the water below. *Intrepid*'s centerline was well defined by the carrier's wake, and Will used the wake as a reference for his approach and lineup.

Will's Avenger arced gracefully toward the ship like a big-winged gull. After turning ninety degrees, Will checked his position relative to the ship. Van Antwerp had urged his pilots to strive for a carrier landing interval of no more than thirty or forty seconds between airplanes. Will confirmed that the airplane ahead of him was where it should be, crossing *Intrepid*'s ramp and about to touch down.

Will turned gradually to *Intrepid*'s heading and intercepted the extended centerline of the ship, taking great pains not to overshoot the centerline in his turn. *Intrepid*'s stack gases produced an area of warm, choppy air behind the ship's island. Stack gas turbulence was treacherous; it tended to suck an airplane too far right of the centerline and bounce it off the proper glide path. If a pilot overshot to the right, he might also lose sight of his LSO, which was a guaranteed wave-off. As Will intercepted *Intrepid*'s centerline and rolled wings level, he glimpsed the lead Avenger touching down and jerking to a stop. Three or four sailors dashed from deck-edge catwalks to quickly disengage the leader's tail hook.

Will fixed his eyes on Moot. There was no point in watching the lead aircraft any longer. If the lead aircraft did not clear the landing area, Moot would wave Will off for a fouled deck.

Will inched his throttle backward and descended directly toward the ship. He hung his Avenger on its propeller and held her barely above stalling speed. The airplane's flight controls were heavy and trucklike. Will had trimmed his controls to reduce the forces necessary to deflect his stick and rudders, and he made constant corrections and adjustments, countering each movement of his controls with a small opposite movement to avoid overcorrecting in one direction. His eyes flicked between Moot and his Avenger's most critical cockpit instruments in this phase of flight, its airspeed and rate-of-descent indicators.

Moot held a solid yellow paddle that was about the size of a squash racquet in each hand. He extended his arms high above his head and formed a "Y" with his body. This signal indicated to Will that his Avenger was too high on final approach and too far above the proper glide path. Will corrected immediately by dropping his nose and retarding his throttle very slightly. Moot lowered his paddles and held them straight out at his sides, signaling to Will that his airplane had settled on the correct glide path. From the corner of his eye, Will detected the pointer of his airspeed indicator sliding from eighty-five to eighty knots. He dipped his nose again and advanced his throttle, thereby increasing engine power and arresting his descent, but he sensed immediately that he might not have applied enough power. Moot wagged his paddles back and forth like a man rowing a boat. This was the "come on" signal, the order to add more power. Will inched his throttle forward and simultaneously pressured his stick forward. These corrections further checked Will's deceleration and rate of descent. He held his airplane as steady as possible, making minute corrections and counter-corrections with his control stick and visualizing a stable-state glide path to the middle of *Intrepid*'s landing area. Moot now held his paddles reassuringly out to his sides, the signal to Will that his Avenger was now on the right glide path at the right speed.

Will flew precisely at eighty knots, descending at three hundred feet per minute. *Intrepid*'s wake boiled and frothed beneath him, sparkling white like a snow-covered highway. Will sensed his airplane approach the ramp, the after-most edge of *Intrepid*'s flight deck, but he forced himself not to fixate on the flight deck. The cautionary refrain of Will's flight instructors rang in his head: "Watch your landing signal officer all the way to the cut signal. Do not—repeat, do not—spot the deck. Ignore this advice, and you will strike the ramp and bury your airplane in the spud locker." Will's grip on his throttle and stick tightened as he waited for Moot's signal. Cut and land or wave-off were the only options at this point. Will tensed to react to either signal. Spring-loaded was how Will thought of himself at this moment.

When Will's Avenger was about twenty feet aft of *Intrepid* and twenty feet above her flight deck, Moot slashed one of his paddles across his chest, the signal to Will to cut his engine and land. Will instantly yanked his throttle to the rear stop and held up his Avenger's nose as she decelerated. The Avenger's big radial engine sputtered and sighed, and Will waited for the jolt of his airplane's wheels hitting the flight deck.

It didn't take long. With her engine at idle, Will's Avenger dropped heavily into the landing area on her main landing gear. The toe of the Avenger's tail hook—the device looked like a horse's hoof—snatched a steel arresting wire and yanked the cable though its pulleys. After a run of forty or fifty feet, Will's airplane careened to a stop. Cockpit debris from some earlier mission, a piece of broken pencil and a cigarette butt, shot past Will's head and hit the instrument panel in front of him. Will's body lurched forward involuntarily, pressing him against his shoulder harness and lap belt. The sensation was like crashing an automobile at high speed into a giant balloon. Her forward momentum spent, Will's Avenger settled back on her tail wheel. Arresting gear crews wearing green jerseys quickly disengaged Will's tail hook and freed him from the arresting gear. The deckhands moved with practiced urgency. The last plane in the section was rolling into the groove on its final approach to the carrier.

A flight deck director wearing a bright yellow shirt appeared off the port side of Will's airplane. He stood near the Avenger but well clear of the deadly arc of its idling propeller. The yellow-shirt showed Will the backs of his hands and pumped his arms vigorously toward his chest. This was Will's signal to taxi straight ahead and clear the landing area. Will checked that his airplane's tail wheel was unlocked and advanced the throttle. His Avenger's engine roared again, and Will taxied forward, toeing his Avenger's wheel brakes to control his speed and steer his airplane.

Will glanced up at *Intrepid*'s island as he taxied forward, surprised at the height of the superstructure and impressed with the size of *Intrepid*'s five-inch gun turrets located fore and aft of her island. He saw knots of sailors clustered on the island's catwalks. They rested their elbows on the rails and gazed down at him, regarding him with a mixture of curiosity and respect. Will allowed himself a smile of relief and exhilaration. He couldn't resist a friendly wave to the men on the island. He had performed what relatively few men had accomplished in the history of aviation: He had landed his airplane on the moving deck of a ship at sea. For Will, his first landing aboard *Intrepid* had come three days before his twenty-first birthday. Later in the day, an aviation yeoman recorded in Will's flight logbook and in the logbook of every pilot in Air Group 18 who had flown aboard that day, "All landings from this date carrier landings."

On August 11, Commander Ellis led Air Group 18 in a simulated air attack against the ships of Task Group 19.11. This was a massive group grope, in effect, but the first one to begin with a carrier takeoff and end with a carrier landing. Van Antwerp scheduled Will Fletcher to fly this first mission, and Will was exceedingly pleased to have been chosen, just as he had been pleased to fly the ferry flight to the ship. Ellis's simulated attack against the task group was the air group's first opportunity to prove to *Intrepid*'s captain and crew that Air Group 18 was ready for war. All of Ellis's pilots launched satisfactorily and pressed home their attacks admirably, but one fighter pilot clipped a gun mount on landing, and one dive-bomber pilot missed a wire and hit the barrier. The torpeckers were flawless. For the next two days, *Intrepid*'s air department and her new air group conducted flight operations of all kinds—more simulated bombing runs, rocket runs, torpedo runs, antisubmarine patrols, combat air patrols—and at the end of the period *Intrepid*'s skipper, Captain Bolger, pronounced himself satisfied with the air group's performance. Bolger reported to the commander, Naval Air Forces, Pacific fleet that Air Group 18 was ready for war.

Intrepid's ship's company gained a measure of confidence in Air Group 18 and began to accord the Airedales guarded respect, but there was still a divide between the veteran surface sailors and the rookie airmen, a schism between black shoes and Airedales, a sense of "us and them." Despite Captain Bolger's official acceptance of the air group, many ship's company sailors remained inexplicably frosty and aloof. According to Air Group 18's chief intelligence officer, Lieutenant George Race, the black-shoe sailors in *Intrepid*'s air department "did not seem particularly pleased" to have the air group aboard. They often acted "as if they thoroughly disliked the whir and clatter made by airplanes." Whenever an Airedale offered a suggestion, he was sharply reminded by personnel in the air department that Air Group 6, Air Group 18's predecessor aboard *Intrepid*, had done it differently. Race wondered in his diary "if the carrier would prefer to operate without airplanes."

With her shakedown cruise completed, albeit belatedly, *Intrepid* reentered Pearl Harbor on the afternoon of August 13 to reprovision and load additional ammunition. For the next two days, *Intrepid*'s ship's company and Airedales labored together to load and stow additional high explosives of all kinds, both naval and aerial. Almost all of Air Group 18's pilots, elated at their performance on the shakedown cruise and eager to celebrate the end of their training, descended on the Ford Island Tennis Club bar to drink, overwhelming the small woodframed clubhouse with boisterous enthusiasm and consuming large amounts of alcohol. They knew there was a long, and mostly dry, spell ahead of them.

Finally, on August 16, 1944, *Intrepid*, fully manned, armed, and provisioned, sortied from Pearl Harbor with her new air group on her second war cruise. Once clear of the harbor's antisubmarine netting, she joined Task Unit 12.3.2, a temporary unit comprised of *Intrepid*, the fleet carrier *Enterprise*, the escort carrier *Independence*, and four destroyers. Known as the "Big E," *Enterprise* was the most venerable and decorated carrier in the American fleet, a participant in nearly all the major naval engagements of the war, and already a mythic ship in the annals of naval aviation. *Enterprise* had fought most famously at the Battle of Midway in June 1942; in the naval battles off Guadalcanal between August and November 1942; in strikes on the Gilbert and Marshall islands in 1943; in attacks on Eniwetok in early 1944, and at the Battle of the Philippine Sea in June 1944. With *Enterprise* serving as guide, Task Group 12.3.2 set a westerly course for Eniwetok Atoll in the Marshall Islands. As the task group formed up, Will Fletcher leaned on *Intrepid*'s rail and gazed across the blue water at *Enterprise*. She carried Air Group 20, which had a reputation for being a hot outfit; Will hoped Air Group 18 would earn the same reputation.

Will got a chance to contribute to Air Group 18's war record later that same afternoon, when Kenny Barden assigned him and three other VT-18 ensigns to antisubmarine patrol duty (ASP) for the task group. ASP was a chore normally reserved for junior pilots in the squadron. The flight was usually boring as hell, except for the over-water navigation part and the carrier landing. But, as Barden noted, the antisubmarine patrol was VT-18's first official operational mission of the war, and Will was eager to fly it. The Avenger pilots launched uneventfully and droned over open water for four hours. They landed without incident, having sighted nothing but the ships of their own task group. But no matter. After fourteen months of preparation, the airmen of VT-18 were finally headed to war and glad of it.

Many thousands of miles to the west, the enemy prepared to meet them.

CHAPTER FOUR

IN LINGGA ROADS

★ ★ ★ ★ ★

Vice Admiral Takeo Kurita, commander of Japan's powerful 2nd Fleet, sat at his desk in the sea cabin of his flagship, the heavy cruiser *Atago,* and studied the latest naval war plan prepared by the staff of his immediate superior, Admiral Soemu Toyoda, commander of the Japanese Combined Fleet. Distributed by Combined Fleet headquarters in early August 1944, Toyoda's war plan outlined the Imperial Japanese Navy's revised strategy for defeating the United States Pacific Fleet in a decisive naval battle, one that would bring the Pacific war to a satisfactory conclusion. Toyoda's plan was not new in its fundamental assumptions, namely that the United States would sue for peace if it suffered a sufficiently large-scale military defeat, one bloody enough to shock the American conscience, and that superior Japanese fighting spirit would inevitably produce a victory for Dai Nippon—or at least a stalemate that preserved Japan's imperial gains. Japan's decisive-victory dogma was based partly on hubris and partly on historical experience. In 1905, the Japanese navy had achieved a resounding victory over the Russian navy at the Battle of Tsushima Strait, a battle that proved decisive geopolitically in securing a Japanese foothold on the Asian continent.

Winning a decisive battle had been the Imperial Navy's goal from the earliest days of the war. Japanese naval strategists had planned the surprise attack on Pearl Harbor as a decisive blow, and they had attempted to provoke decisive confrontations at Midway island in June 1942, and again in the Marianas two years later. In his latest plan, Admiral Toyoda proposed to fight a decisive naval battle in the waters surrounding the Philippines, where Japanese strategists expected the Allies to invade next on their westward march. He had dispatched Vice Admiral Kurita's 2nd Fleet, which included Japan's superbattleships *Musashi* and *Yamato* and a score of other heavy warships, to Lingga Roads to train intensively and make final preparations for the upcoming battle.

Lingga Roads was a sheltered anchorage that lay off the eastern shore of Sumatra, roughly 130 miles below Singapore and six thousand miles west of Oahu as the crow flies. Bisected by the equator, Lingga Roads sweltered in unrelenting heat and humidity, its sea breezes blocked by jungle-covered islands to seaward. The Imperial Japanese Navy favored the anchorage because of its proximity to the Palembang oil fields of Dutch Sumatra, which had been among the most coveted spoils of Japan's seizure of the Dutch East Indies in 1942.

As he absorbed Admiral Toyoda's newest war plan, Kurita must have reflected on how drastically Japan's military fortunes had declined.

The war had gone very well for the Japanese in the beginning. Between 1937 and late 1941, the Japanese had driven the Nationalist Chinese from Nanking and forced the Chinese Communists into the hills, thereby placing the riches of northern China firmly under Emperor Hirohito's control. To enforce Dai Nippon's new world order, the Imperial Japanese Army had quartered more than two million troops on Chinese soil. By early December 1941, the Imperial Japanese Navy had eliminated the principal military obstacle to further Japanese adventurism in Asia, the United States Pacific Fleet, with a brilliantly executed surprise attack on Pearl Harbor; as a result, six American battleships lay on the harbor bottom, and two more had been reduced to smoking ruin. Within three months of the Pearl Harbor raid, the Japanese blitzkrieg had swept over vast areas of the western Pacific. The emperor's ground and naval forces had seized the Philippines, overrun British colonies in Hong Kong and Singapore, occupied the principal cities of the Dutch East Indies, a far-flung colonial empire encompassing nearly three thousand islands, and transformed the South China and Java seas into Japanese lakes. Japan's armed forces had seized the wealth of nations, including the verdant rice and hemp fields of the Philippines, the prized oil fields of Sumatra and Borneo, and the rich rubber plantations of the Celebes, at little cost.

American, British, Dutch, and Australian forces in the western Pacific had attempted to resist the onslaught. They had hastily organized themselves into a joint command called ABDACOM and attempted to mount a multinational defense of European and American colonial interests in Thailand, Burma, the Malay Peninsula, and the Dutch East Indies. But ABDACOM had failed to stem the relentless Japanese tide. The Allied effort was largely doomed from the outset by the joint British-American policy of "Europe first," which limited the supplies of men and material available for a vigorous defense of the western Pacific (much less for a major counteroffensive), and by the Allies' inability to coordinate joint military operations. The emperor's air forces achieved and maintained air superiority everywhere within the combat radius of their warplanes, and the emperor's warships dominated the South China and Java seas, handily dispatching the brave but overmatched and outnumbered ABDA warships that dared challenge them. Without sufficient naval transport and air cover, most ABDA soldiers remained in their Australian camps, far removed from the fight. ABDACOM disbanded when the Japanese invaded Java in late February 1942, and the ABDACOM commander, General Archibald Wavell, decamped to India.

The American Joint Chiefs of Staff (JCS) quickly assumed responsibility for devising an Allied military strategy that would halt Japan's southern advance toward Australia. The JCS, a committee comprised of General George Marshall (army chief of staff), Fleet Admiral Ernest J. King (commander in chief of the U.S. fleet), General Henry Arnold (commanding general of the United States Army Air Corps), and Admiral William D. Leahy (as chairman), divided the Pacific into two main operational areas, the Southwest Pacific Area and the Pacific Ocean Area. The JCS appointed General MacArthur, safely headquartered in Australia following his escape from Corregidor, as the commander of Allied forces in the Southwest Pacific Area. This was a new theater of military operations encompassing Australia, New Guinea, the Solomons, the Philippines, Borneo, and the Dutch East Indies. MacArthur's chief task was to prevent a Japanese invasion of Australia, and, when the Allies had built up their forces sufficiently, to dislodge the Japanese from the territories they had captured. The JCS also designated Admiral Chester Nimitz as the commander of the Pacific Ocean Area. Nimitz's task, simply put, was to destroy the Japanese navy and eliminate any threat from Japanese air and naval forces in the immense region of the Pacific east of the 159th parallel. Nimitz, in turn, appointed Admiral Robert L. Ghormley (and later Admiral William F. Halsey) as the commander of the South Pacific Area. Ghormley's (and Halsey's) primary task in the early days of the war was to keep open the vital sea-lanes by which the United States supplied Australia with arms and matériel.

The initial JCS strategy was simple in concept. When reinforced and ready for battle, Allied troops under MacArthur's command would sail north from Australia and secure a foothold in southeastern New Guinea. MacArthur's forces would then move west, dislodging the Japanese from their island bastions, such as those on Rabaul and Biak. The United States Navy, weakened by the Pearl Harbor disaster but able to muster seven aircraft carriers (not counting the aged *Langley*) and a flotilla of surface combatants and transports, would shield MacArthur's New Guinea operations and keep the Australian lifeline open.

But the insatiable Japanese were on the move. In March 1942, Japanese troops landed at Lae and Salamaua on the northeastern shore of Papua New Guinea with the ultimate objective of seizing Papua's capital, Port Moresby, and taking control of the straits of Dampier and Vitiaz. These moves threatened to block the sea-lanes north of New Guinea and isolate the Australian continent. If the Japanese established airfields in southeastern New Guinea, the emperor's warplanes could bomb Australian cities with impunity.

In May, a large Japanese invasion force, accompanied by a striking force of three aircraft carriers, six cruisers, and seven destroyers, sailed from Imperial anchorages at Truk and Rabaul to seize Port Moresby directly. Alerted to enemy intentions by British and American cryptanalysis of Japanese naval codes, Admiral Nimitz dispatched American task forces centered on the carriers *Lexington* (the predecessor of the *Lexington* that transported Air Group 18 to Hawaii) and *Yorktown* to intercept and destroy the Japanese invaders. The opposing surface ships never came within sight of each other but, on May 7, pilots from *Lexington* and *Yorktown* found and sank *Soho*, a light carrier that had escorted the Japanese transports bound for Port Moresby. The Japanese invasion force turned back, but the emperor's fleet carriers *Shokaku* and *Zuikaku* did not withdraw. The next day, Japanese naval aviators torpedoed and disabled *Lexington*—she was sunk by American destroyers at the end of the battle to prevent the Japanese from salvaging her—and severely damaged *Yorktown*. In exchange, American dive-bombers so disabled *Shokaku*'s flight deck that she could neither launch nor recover her airplanes. The Japanese canceled the invasion, and Port Moresby was spared. The American navy had delivered the first check to Japanese expansionism in defense of Port Moresby, but the loss of *Lexington* in this engagement, called the Battle of the Coral Sea, severely depleted American carrier strength.

Less than one month later, the Americans managed to deliver a much more crippling blow to Japanese ambitions. To draw the American fleet into a decisive battle and extend Japan's defensive perimeter farther east, the Imperial Japanese Navy dispatched a massive invasion force comprised of 145 warships and transports to seize Midway, a lonely American outpost eleven hundred miles northwest of Oahu, and the Aleutian islands of Adak, Attu, and Kiska. The Japanese flotilla destined for Midway included a striking force comprised of four aircraft carriers, *Akagi*, *Kaga*, *Hiryu*, and *Soryu*, all under the command of Vice Admiral Chuichi Nagumo, an experienced carrier commander who had led these same ships in the Pearl Harbor raid. Acting on the brilliant intelligence work of Commander Joseph Rochefort and his cryptanalysis unit at Pearl Harbor, Admiral Nimitz had deployed two carrier task forces northeast of Midway to ambush the Japanese invasion force as it approached. The Americans were heavily outnumbered. Task Force 17 under the command of Rear Admiral Frank Jack Fletcher consisted of only nine surface ships and a single carrier, *Yorktown*, which had been hastily repaired at Pearl Harbor following the Battle of the Coral Sea. Task Force 16, led by Rear Admiral Raymond Spruance, consisted of only fifteen surface ships and two carriers, *Enterprise* and *Hornet*.

On the morning of June 4, Nagumo launched half his total complement of warplanes on a first strike against the American airfield at East Island, a tiny spit of sand that lies within the encircling coral reefs of Midway Atoll. As Nagumo prepared to launch a second strike against Midway, a Japanese search plane reported the presence of American carriers in the area. Surprised by the discovery, Nagumo ordered his squadron commanders to cease preparations for a second attack on Midway and to prepare instead for an attack on American warships. This order required deck crews aboard Nagumo's carriers to switch their airplanes' ordnance from general-purpose bombs (which were more appropriate for attacking land targets) to torpedoes and armor-piercing bombs suitable for attacking ships. While Nagumo's crews shifted ordnance for the second strike, warplanes from Nagumo's first strike returned to their carriers for refueling. In the midst of all this rearming and refueling, with gasoline hoses and bombs strewn across the decks of Nagumo's carriers, American SBDs from *Enterprise* caught *Kaga* and *Akagi* without fighter cover, and SBDs from *Yorktown* descended on *Soryu*. Spruance's and Fletcher's dive-bomber pilots executed textbook-perfect bombing runs on the Japanese flattops, and within minutes, all three enemy carriers had become raging infernos. *Hiryu*'s fliers retaliated against *Yorktown*, causing her fatal damage with torpedoes, but an attack group from *Enterprise* struck back at *Hiryu* and damaged her so badly that she had to be scuttled the following day. All four of Nagumo's carriers sank, depriving Japan of the jewels of her carrier fleet. These were not the carriers themselves, but the hundreds of skilled and irreplaceable naval aviators and aircrew who had perished in fearsome shipboard explosions and conflagrations or had gone down with their carriers. The Battle of Midway had been decisive, but not in the way the Japanese had imagined it.

Despite the crushing defeat of the Imperial Navy at Midway, the emperor's land, sea, and air forces remained in firm control of nearly forty million square miles of Pacific territory and the lives of untold millions. They would not yield these lightly.

In July 1942, General MacArthur's Southwest Pacific forces took the offensive. American and Australian soldiers sortied from toeholds at Port Moresby and Milne Bay in southeast Papua New Guinea, and launched a series of air and ground attacks designed to drive the Japanese from the country. The fighting in Papua, a mountainous island covered with primordial jungle, was brutal, and Allied soldiers in the field were additionally burdened with enervating heat and humidity and plagued by tropical diseases, such as malaria, dengue fever, scrub typhus, bacillary and amoebic dysentery, jungle rot, dhobie itch, athlete's foot, and ringworm. The South Pacific would prove to be a miserable place to wage war.

In August 1942, Admiral Robert L. Ghormley's South Pacific naval forces landed ten thousand United States Marines at Guadalcanal, one of the principal islands of the Solomon archipelago. Ghormley's mission was to deny the Japanese the use of a new airfield they had begun to construct on Guadalcanal, a development that the Americans perceived as a threat to MacArthur's New Guinea campaign and the Australian sea-lanes. The Japanese resisted fiercely, sending squadrons of warships from Rabaul to bombard the Marines ashore and cut off their lines of reinforcement and supply. The Japanese also landed their

own first-line troops on the island, ultimately committing thirty thousand soldiers in an effort to oust the Marines. Between August and November 1942,
Ghormley's and William F. Halsey's South Pacific naval forces fought five major
naval battles off the coast of Guadalcanal. These were ferocious sea fights with
exotic names, such as the Battle of Savo Island, the Battle of Cape Esperance,
and the Battle of Tassafaronga Strait, engagements in which United States naval
forces suffered grievous losses, but also inflicted heavy damage on Japanese surface forces. The American Navy lost the carrier *Wasp* to an enemy submarine but
retained sufficient control of the seas to sustain the Marines, if only by the nar-
rowest margin. U.S. Army soldiers relieved the Marines on Guadalcanal in December, and, after two more months of desperate jungle fighting, the Americans
ejected the Japanese from the island.

The Guadalcanal campaign was a turning point, militarily and psychologi-
cally. The seemingly invincible Japanese military juggernaut had been stopped, a
reversal of fortune that Japanese strategists themselves recognized. The emperor's
defeat in the jungles of Guadalcanal and the surrounding waters had assured
MacArthur's troops in New Guinea of reinforcement and resupply. MacArthur's
Southwest Pacific force and Halsey's South Pacific force could now advance together, moving westward on mutually supporting parallel tracks through the
Solomon and Bismarck seas.

In November 1943, Vice Admiral Spruance's central Pacific forces, strengthened by America's prodigious output of new ships, aircraft, and weaponry, and
the soldiers, sailors, and Marines to operate them, added pressure to Japan's
defensive perimeter by commencing a major naval offensive across the central
Pacific. The idea was to capture the emperor's island outposts and turn them
against him in an island-hopping campaign toward Tokyo. Spruance attacked
Japanese garrisons in the Gilbert and Marshall islands, seizing Tarawa, Makin,
Kwajalein, and Eniwetok. By February 1944, MacArthur had reclaimed Lae
and Salamaua on New Guinea, and Halsey had advanced up the Solomon chain
as far as Bougainville. By April 1944, MacArthur's forces in New Guinea had
outflanked concentrations of Japanese troops on Papua and had seized smaller
islands to the northeast of New Guinea, such as Los Negros and Manus in the
Admiralties. MacArthur had "leapfrogged" centers of Japanese resistance, bypassing enemy strongpoints to capture weaker ones, and his air and naval forces
had prevented the Japanese from reinforcing and resupplying their soldiers in

the field. But Allied casualties in MacArthur's New Guinea campaigns were high. One Allied serviceman in eleven died during MacArthur's Papua campaign, as compared to one man in thirty-seven during Halsey's sea and land campaign to invade and subdue Guadalcanal.

Despite the disasters at Midway and Guadalcanal, leaders of the Imperial Japanese Navy held fast to the strategic dogma of decisive battle, and schemed to engage the American Pacific fleet on the most advantageous terms. As the Americans moved steadily westward, Japanese strategists pointed to the practical benefits of fighting from interior lines. The Japanese navy would have shorter lines of communication and logistics than the Americans, and the Japanese navy would have the ability to concentrate its forces rapidly against the point of American attack. The leadership also believed fervently that the samurai spirit would produce ultimate victory, a belief shaken but not broken by the experiences of Midway and Guadalcanal.

On May 4, 1944, on the occasion of assuming command of the Japanese Combined Fleet, Admiral Soemu Toyoda, commander in chief, issued a message to his subordinate commanding officers. Admiral Toyoda wrote:

Our combined fleet in several occasions has crushed the main enemy forces with lightning speed. In the two and one-half years since, together with our armies, we occupied the areas essential to greater east Asia, officers and men of the fleet have voluntarily sacrificed their lives and inflicted great damage on the enemy. The fate of the enemy was nearly sealed, but in the midst of this period, the enemy recovered his fighting strength and, taking advantage of our supply difficulties, moved over to a full-scale counterattack. The war is drawing close to the lines vital to our national defense. The issue of our national existence is unprecedentedly serious, and unprecedented opportunity exists for deciding who shall be victorious and who defeated. This autumn we will make this great task our responsibility.

By giving all possible thought to basic plans, by utilizing opportunities for advance or retreat and by placing faith in the great fighting ability of our officers and men, we will carry out the decisive operations which mean certain enemy defeat.

Orders and instructions will be issued separately regarding operation policy and measures for carrying it out. We must achieve our objectives by crushing with one stroke the nucleus of the great enemy concentration forces, thereby reversing the war situation, and, together with our armies, shifting directly to the offensive. Officers and men of the decisive battle force must trust in God, train thoroughly in the art of warfare, and in one battle determine the fate of the Empire.

Realizing the gravity of responsibility for the fate of our Empire, with its history of more than two thousand years, full of reverence for the glory of the imperial throne and trusting in the help of God, I will endeavor to comply with the Emperor's wishes. The desire of officers and men of the entire fleet must be to respond wholeheartedly to this great honor and duty.

Admiral Toyoda had decided to provoke the next decisive battle with the American navy in the Philippine Sea, southwest of the Marianas. Saipan, one of the principal islands of the Marianas, was an administrative center essential for Japan's governance and control of its central Pacific empire. Admiral Toyoda and his staff had anticipated that the Americans would attempt to invade Saipan and perhaps her sister islands of Guam and Tinian. Admiral Toyoda's battle plan for the defense of the Marianas, named A-Go, called for Japanese carriers to lure the American fleet away from the Marianas and attack it with masses of warplanes launched from land bases on Yap, Palau, and Luzon, as well as from the Japanese carriers themselves. Dozens of Japanese submarines and a score of heavy surface warships would also lie in wait for the Americans when they took the bait.

Toyoda's A-Go Plan relied heavily on "shuttle-bombing," a tactic which fed into the fight as many warplanes as possible in the shortest space of time. Flying from aircraft carriers stationed west of the Marianas, Japanese carrier pilots would open the battle with long-range air strikes against the American invasion force off Saipan; but instead of returning to their ships, the carrier pilots would divert to Japanese land bases on Saipan, Guam and Tinian, there to rearm and refuel. Joined by squadrons of land-based naval aircraft that had been prepositioned on these islands, the carrier planes would shuttle back and forth between the emperor's land bases and the American invasion force, bombing and torpedoing the American ships in repeated air attacks. Toyoda's A-Go plan also presupposed that aggressive American fleet commanders would try to counterattack the Japanese carriers. To locate the enemy carriers, the Americans would be compelled to move their own aircraft carriers west of the Marianas; if the Americans did not move west, their carrier planes would have insufficient fuel to reach the enemy and return safely to their ships. As the American carrier force pursued the Japanese carrier force, it would be ambushed by waiting Japanese submarines and surface ships, and by more aircraft from Yap, Palau, and Luzon. A-Go assumed a third of the American fleet would be destroyed by shuttle-bombing tactics and submarine attacks, and that the remainder would be annihilated by follow-up carrier-plane attacks, submarine attacks, and heavy naval gunfire.

The American Joint Chiefs had, in fact, marked the Marianas for capture, not only for the political and psychological importance of the islands to the Japanese—most Japanese regarded the Marianas as Japanese "home islands"—but because Saipan, Guam, and Tinian afforded air bases from which the new American long-range bomber then in the final stages of deployment, the Boeing B-29 Stratofortress, could reach the Japanese mainland.

When Admiral Spruance's Task Force 58 obligingly appeared off Saipan on June 15, 1944, to protect American amphibious landings on Saipan, Toyoda set A-Go in motion. The Japanese Mobile Fleet, consisting of nine carriers, five battleships, thirteen cruisers, and twenty-eight destroyers, approached the Marianas from the southwest, and twenty-five Japanese submarines submerged to lie in wait. But American preparations for the Saipan invasion doomed the A-Go plan from the beginning. In the month before the invasion, American destroyer escorts sank at least seventeen Japanese submarines and American bombing raids destroyed many of the enemy airfields in the Marianas, thereby depriving Japanese carrier pilots of operational land bases for shuttle-bombing. Spruance also possessed a decided advantage in numbers over his enemy, unlike his circumstances at Midway two years before. Task Force 58 boasted fifteen carriers, seven battleships, twenty-one cruisers, and sixty-nine destroyers; Spruance's carriers were capable of putting up more than 950 warplanes, double the number of aircraft available to the commander of the Mobile Fleet, Vice Admiral Jisaburo Ozawa. When Ozawa's carrier planes collided with Spruance's on the morning of June 19, the more experienced and better-trained American pilots shot them out of the air in droves. In a single day of dizzying air battles, Ozawa lost 350 planes to Spruance's 30. American submariners also bested the Japanese by far, sinking the carriers *Taiho* and *Shokaku*. Ozawa's Mobile Fleet withdrew to the west, and a final counterstroke by Spruance's carrier pilots late the following day sank the carrier *Hiyo* and damaged *Zuikaku*.

By July 1944, the Americans had captured Guadalcanal, New Georgia, Vella Lavella, Tarawa, Bougainville, Kwajalein, Truk, Eniwetok, Saipan, Guam, Tinian, and scores of other enemy island outposts. They had cut off and neutralized Japanese garrisons on the mainland of New Guinea. Warplanes operating from American aircraft carriers and American land bases in New Georgia and Bougainville had subjected the giant Japanese naval base at Rabaul to constant aerial attack. Rabaul had become isolated and untenable as a naval anchorage, and the Imperial Army and navy simply abandoned in place more than a hundred thousand Japanese troops and laborers there. The strategic question for the Allies in midsummer of 1944 was, "Where next in the Pacific?"

At the Honolulu Conference in July 1944, while *Intrepid* refitted at Pearl Harbor and Air Group 18 readied itself at Kaneohe for carrier duty, President Roosevelt discussed this strategic question with admirals Leahy and Nimitz and with General MacArthur. Admiral Leahy and the Joint Chiefs had proposed a strategy of seizing Formosa and bombing Japan into submission from Allied airfields in China. The Joint Chiefs viewed any attack on the Philippines merely as a "prerequisite to taking Formosa," a step they regarded as necessary to cut off the flow of war material to Japan from Southeast Asia. But recent events in China—the Japanese army had overrun American air bases in eastern China and eliminated China as a platform for launching land-based air strikes against Japan—had undermined the Joint Chiefs' proposal. Fleet Admiral King, who had briefed Admiral Nimitz on his personal views but did not attend the Honolulu Conference, urged an alternative strategy of bypassing the Philippines altogether and invading Formosa. Some American strategists had advocated an even more aggressive strategy of using the United States' massive battle fleet to bomb the Japanese home islands directly, ignoring both the Philippines and Formosa. Arbitrating the differences among his commanders over America's next steps in the Pacific War, Roosevelt is reported to have tapped a large map of the Pacific Ocean with a bamboo pointer and asked General MacArthur, "Well, Douglas, where do we go from here?" MacArthur is said to have replied immediately, "Mindanao, Mr. President, then Leyte and then Luzon."

MacArthur presented his case for a Philippine invasion before all else, passionately and forcefully. Seizing control of the Philippine archipelago would sever Japan's economic lifeline to Southeast Asia as effectively as seizing Formosa, he claimed, and would provide a secure base for further advances toward the Japanese home islands. The civilian population of the Philippines, he observed, was far less hostile to the Allies than the civilian population of Formosa, which had much stronger economic and cultural ties to Japan. The Philippines were also "American territory," MacArthur asserted. Bypassing the Philippines would be a geopolitical mistake, proving the claims of Japanese propagandists who preached that Americans were indifferent to the plight of Asians. President Roosevelt faced election for a fourth term in November 1944, and MacArthur warned him privately that the American public would be "aroused and resentful" if the president ignored the Philippines and abandoned the many thousands of American soldiers and civilians who were confined in squalid prisoner-of-war and internment camps throughout the islands. The general was determined to fulfill his "I shall return" promise to the Filipino people, and navy proposals to bypass the Philippines infuriated him.

Swayed by MacArthur's moral and political arguments, President Roosevelt agreed not to bypass the Philippines. He approved a go-forward strategy in the Pacific that accommodated the views of both General MacArthur and Admiral King. General MacArthur, in cooperation with the United States 7th Fleet, would execute an amphibious invasion of the Philippine Islands from New Guinea in October or November of 1944. Admirals King and Nimitz would concurrently pursue the navy's central Pacific strategy of seizing island air bases from which American aircraft could bomb the Japanese homeland. The United States 3rd and 5th fleets (which were the same fast carrier attack forces and logistics groups at their core, but were designated 3rd Fleet under Halsey's command and 5th Fleet under Spruance's) would seek out and destroy Japanese fleet elements in wide-ranging raids and support American amphibious landings on enemy-held islands. The ultimate decision on whether to invade Japan itself would await the fruits of this strategy.

The war plans that Vice Admiral Kurita studied at Lingga Roads were styled, "Outline for Task Force Operations [and] . . . Combined Fleet Operations in the SHO Operations." The plans had been distributed by Admiral Toyoda's staff on August 10, 1944, the same day that Air Group 18 flew aboard *Intrepid* for the first time. SHO plans one through four were the Japanese navy's ultrasecret operational orders for the defense of the Philippines, Formosa, and the Japanese home islands. In them, Admiral Toyoda's staff concluded the Pacific war had entered a "crucial stage . . . upon which the fate of the empire depends." Toyoda's staff acknowledged that the battle situation had become more serious since the Battle of the Philippine Sea, but observed optimistically that American "lines of communication are becoming extended as [the enemy] approaches our inner defenses." The staff characterized the heavy surface ships of the Japanese Combined Fleet as "the last line of home defense," and predicted the revised SHO-1 plan for the defense of the Philippines "will crush the enemy advance, smash his plans, change the trend of battle and establish bases for future operations and advances."

SHO-1 required Japanese fleet units to sortie from the Japanese home islands to Brunei, Borneo, or, alternatively, to the north-central Philippines "as soon as the enemy landings are ascertained." SHO-1 divided the Combined Fleet into a "diversion attack force" and a "main force." These naval forces were to cooperate with Japanese air forces based in the Philippines "in an all-out attack." SHO-1 described the mission of the diversion attack force as follows:

> Depending on the supply situation, it will aim to reach the landing point at the time the enemy invasion force is making its landings. Avoiding the attack of the enemy task force, it will push forward and engage in a decisive battle with the surface force which tries to stop it. After annihilating this force, it will then attack and wipe out the enemy convoy and troops at the landing point.

SHO-1 directed the main force to attack one flank of the enemy task force and "come down on the enemy supply force and annihilate it."

On the day Toyoda's staff issued the outline of SHO operations, Japan's "last line of home defense" included the superbattleships *Musashi* and *Yamato*, then riding at anchor in Lingga Roads as elements of Kurita's 2nd Fleet. *Musashi* and *Yamato*, nearly identical sister ships of the *Yamato* class, had been built during the late 1930s, *Musashi* at the Mitsubishi Nagasaki Shipyard in Nagasaki Harbor and *Yamato* at the Kure Naval Yard on the Inland Sea near Hiroshima. They were the two most powerful warships on earth, built for world conquest and designed specifically to outclass the largest British and American battleships in terms of size, firepower, and armor.

Before the development of the *Yamato* class, the largest battleship in the Japanese fleet was *Nagato*, with a displacement of forty-three thousand tons and a beam of ninety-four feet. The Japanese Bureau of Naval Construction designed *Musashi* and *Yamato* with a displacement of seventy-three thousand tons and a beam of 127 feet to surpass anything afloat. Japanese naval architects had calculated that the girth and displacement of any American battleship would be constrained by the width of the Panama Canal, and in this they were correct. The American *Iowa*-class battleships, first laid down in 1940, had a canal-friendly beam of 108 feet and displaced only fifty-seven thousand tons fully loaded.

In terms of armament, *Musashi* and *Yamato* each mounted nine eighteen-inch (forty-six-centimeter) naval guns, as well as secondary batteries of twelve conventional six-inch (15.5-centimeter) naval guns, twelve four-inch (12.7-centimeter) dual-purpose guns capable of destroying small ships and aircraft (later in the war *Yamato* mounted twenty-four such guns), and more than one hundred thirty twenty-five-millimeter antiaircraft guns. The eighteen-inch naval guns of *Musashi* and *Yamato* were monster weapons, each capable of firing a 3,220-pound projectile across a distance of twenty-six miles and to an altitude of thirty-five thousand feet. By contrast, the newest and finest American battleships of the *Iowa* class mounted nine sixteen-inch guns, each capable of firing a 2,700-pound projectile across a distance of twenty-three miles. The greater shell weight and range of the Japanese eighteen-inch naval guns were a murderous advantage in any conventional ship-against-ship duel, where capital warships lobbed armor-piercing, high-explosive shells at opponents steaming beyond the horizon.

Musashi and *Yamato* were the most heavily armored warships in history. All capital ships of the 1920s and 1930s were constructed with an "armor box" that shielded vital areas of the ship from the destructive force of enemy shells and torpedoes. Plates of hardened steel were riveted inside the hull to protect vulnerable machinery and steering spaces, boiler rooms and engine rooms, and ammunition magazines and handling rooms. Armor plates were also riveted beneath the main deck to prevent bombs and plunging shells from reaching the ship's mechanical heart. In combat, a battleship's captain and senior officers would seal themselves within a central command-and-control center, called a conning tower. The conning towers of most capital ships were also encased in heavy steel armor; officers would observe the action through apertures in the bulkhead, like medieval archers peering through slits in a castle wall.

The hull armor of *Musashi* and *Yamato* was sixteen inches thick below the waterline, and tapered vertically up her flanks to a thickness of seven or eight inches, whereas the hull armor of an *Iowa*-class battleship was 13.5 inches thick at the base and tapered vertically to 1.6 inches. The deck armor of a *Yamato*, which ran the length of her hull from her forward main gun turret (number one turret) to her aft main turret (number three turret), was eight inches thick, and the armor surrounding the conning tower of a *Yamato* was an astonishing twenty inches thick along the sides. By contrast, the deck armor of the *Iowa* class was no more than six inches thick, and the armor of an *Iowa*-class conning tower was a modest 17.5 inches thick at the sides. The *Iowa* class, capable of more than thirty-three knots, bettered the *Yamato*'s maximum speed of twenty-seven knots, but the *Iowa*'s greater speed would be an advantage only in maneuvering or disengaging, not when sailing in line of battle and exchanging broadsides. The greater range of the *Yamato*'s guns would almost always assure the Japanese of the first volley.

Musashi and *Yamato* were conceived while Japan was still subject to the tonnage restrictions and inferior capital ship ratios of the Washington Naval Treaty. As a consequence, the two new warships were built in great secrecy. In 1933, the Japanese Bureau of Naval Construction informed senior officials at the Nagasaki Shipyard (located on the southern island of Kyushu) of an ultrasecret plan to build two large warships of identical design and of immense size and weight. The battleship to be built at Nagasaki would be referred to during construction simply as Battleship No. 2.

The engineers at the Nagasaki Shipyard were stupefied at the general dimensions they were given for Battleship No. 2. The ship was so large they would be compelled to modify Nagasaki's dry docks and construction facilities to accommodate it. The projected length, girth, and tonnage of Battleship No. 2 required them to dredge the harbor; lengthen the shipyard's slipway; build a launch platform thirteen feet wide to support the new warship's keel—this was a platform twice the width required to support the launch of contemporary ships such as *Lexington* and the *Queen Mary*—and cut away portions of the mountainside opposite the slipway to have sufficient room to launch the great ship in Nagasaki's narrow harbor.

The Bureau of Naval Construction delivered blueprints to the Nagasaki yard in July 1937, and construction began eight months later with a ceremonial toast of cold sake among the engineers and workers. Tight security pervaded every aspect of construction. Workers, more than twenty-five hundred of them, were photographed, sworn to an oath of secrecy, and made to wear armbands that specified the areas of the yard in which they were authorized to work. Engineers distributed drawings from a windowless concrete bunker each morning and locked the drawings in a vault each night. Blueprints were carefully inventoried and accounted for like top-secret messages, and woe to anyone who misplaced a plan. The Japanese secret police, the Kempeitai, brutally interrogated workers for suspected breaches of security or lapses of construction protocol. The Kempeitai also forcibly evacuated an entire village of Chinese civilians from the heights overlooking the shipyard and established observation posts in the hills around Nagasaki Harbor to detect any suspicious activities. Huge construction gantries—each gantry was a movable framework of steel girders that supported cranes and winches for heavy-duty lifting—enclosed the slipway where *Musashi* was being built. To shield the dockyard and the emerging ship within from the eyes of curious onlookers and spies, engineers draped heavy curtains of hemp rope over the sides of the gantries like window blinds. The project consumed so much hemp that local fisherman complained about having insufficient sisal rope for their nets.

Like most vessels, Battleship No. 2's hull was constructed first. The interior of her hull was such a complicated maze of voids, bunkers, passageways, shafts, and spaces that workers marked their paths in and out of the ship with chalk and mustered after each shift to ensure that no one had been left behind. Battleship No. 2 was launched with minimal ceremony on the morning of November 1, 1940, after nearly three years of construction. On the day of launch, the Kempeitai conducted "inspections" of houses around the harbor to divert the residents' attention from the shipyard. To prevent the massive hull from shooting across the harbor during launch and running aground on the shore opposite the slipway, engineers rigged heavy chains to slow her descent down the ways. Once Battleship No. 2's hull was in the water, engineers anchored another ship outboard to conceal the warship's size, and yard workers began erecting Battleship No. 2's superstructure and outfitting her for sea.

Battleship No. 2's superstructure housed her conning tower, bridges, and gunfire control towers. The gunfire control towers mounted optical range finders (used to determine the range and bearing to a target) and gun directors (used to calculate azimuth and elevation orders for the battleship's naval guns). Generally speaking, the taller the gunfire control tower, the greater the distance at which an enemy surface force could be detected and engaged, and Japanese naval architects characteristically designed fire towers of great height. Battleship No. 2 was no exception. Her superstructure soared more than a hundred feet above her main deck, with compartment stacked above compartment like toy blocks. Above the conning tower sat the compass bridge; above the compass bridge sat the range finders used for close-in targets; above the close-in range finders sat the combat bridge; above the combat bridge sat the air defense command post; above the air defense command post sat the main gunfire control directors; and above the gun directors sat the optical range finders for long-distance targets. An additional long-distance range finder was also mounted on each of Battleship No. 2's three main eighteen-inch gun turrets. Although *Yamato*-class battleships were equipped with radar sets for air and surface search, neither *Yamato* carried radar systems that directed or controlled naval gunfire or anti-aircraft fire. When completed, Battleship No. 2's superstructure boasted thirteen decks from her main deck to the top of her superstructure, and featured an interior high-speed elevator that connected them all. From the bottom of her keel to the top of her superstructure, Battleship No. 2 was as tall as a sixteen-story building; if set on dry land beside the Washington Monument, *Musashi* would have blocked a third of the obelisk.

Most Japanese warships of the period were cramped below the main deck, with few amenities for ordinary seamen. Sailors slept in hammocks, ate in their berthing spaces, and bathed in saltwater showers on the weather decks. But Battleship No. 2 featured sleeping bunks, mess rooms, interior showers, 282 electric fans for cooling, and even some air-conditioned spaces. The ship contained 1,147 watertight compartments. To maintain internal communications among the men inside them, workers installed 491 telephones and 461 speaking tubes. To furnish electric power for the ship, workers installed electrical generators capable of producing forty-eight hundred kilowatts, enough electricity for a city of thirty thousand people.

Battleship No. 2's nine eighteen-inch naval guns were housed in three main gun turrets. Each gun house was more than forty-two feet wide, and each turret, fully outfitted, weighed 2,510 metric tons, or about 5,532,040 pounds, which was 10 percent more than the weight of a fully loaded American destroyer of the *Fletcher* class. A single eighteen-inch gun weighed 165 metric tons, or about 364,000 pounds; with three guns per turret, total gun weight per turret reached 495 tons, or nearly one million pounds. Three guns were mounted about twelve feet apart centerline-to-centerline on a huge turntable that weighed 350 metric tons, or about 772,000 pounds. The balance of the turret's weight was attributable to 875 tons of elevating and training gear and 790 tons of gun house armor. Gun armor was more than twenty-five inches thick at the front of the turret, and ten inches thick at the roof and sides.

The Japanese built only twenty-seven eighteen-inch guns, nine for Battleship No.1 (which became *Yamato*), nine for Battleship No. 2, and nine for a third *Yamato*-class battleship that the Bureau of Naval Construction later converted to the ill-fated aircraft carrier *Shinano*. The Imperial Japanese Navy had experimented after World War I with 18.9-inch guns, but suspended the project when Japan signed the Washington Naval Treaty. In designing the *Yamato* class, the Bureau of Naval Construction had specified eighteen-inch naval guns to assure undisputed superiority over any foe. The crew of Battleship No. 2 anxiously test-fired her giant eighteen-inch guns for the first time during sea trials in June 1942. Sailors placed guinea pigs in wire cages on the main deck to measure the concussive effects of the gun blast; when the smoke cleared, the sailors discovered the poor guinea pigs had been ripped to shreds.

Battleship No. 2 received her name, *Musashi*, during the period of her final outfitting and sea trials in mid-1942. She was named after the Musashino Plain, a fertile agricultural region northwest of Edo (the ancient name for Tokyo), which now lies within Saitama Prefecture. *Yamato* was similarly named for a feudal province of Honshu, and Yamato was an ancient name for Japan herself. *Yamato* was commissioned in December 1941 and *Musashi* in August 1942. The two superbattleships were, in name and aspiration, the embodiment of the nation.

Despite their immense power, *Yamato* and *Musashi* had seen little combat since entering fleet service. Both ships had been employed primarily in headquarters duty in the central Pacific. *Yamato* had served as the flagship of the Combined Fleet under Admiral Isoroku Yamamoto during the Battle of Midway in June 1942 but did not enter the fray.

By late 1942, Japan had lost the bloody battle for Guadalcanal and the Solomons, and Japanese strategists were determined to stem the Allies' westward advance by reinforcing the Japanese air and naval base at Rabaul, which was located on the island of New Britain, northwest of the Solomons in the Bismarck archipelago. Rabaul was the principal Japanese bastion in the Southeast Pacific, regarded by the Japanese as essential to their continued control of the region. In early 1943, the Imperial Navy dispatched numerous ships of the Combined Fleet, including *Yamato* and *Musashi*, to Truk Atoll, a naval anchorage in the central Carolines roughly eight hundred nautical miles north of New Britain, to further support and defend Rabaul.

After completing training exercises with the carrier *Zuikaku* in the Inland Sea, *Musashi* made her first sortie of the war on January 18, 1943, sailing from Kure Naval Base to Truk with an escort of three destroyers. Arriving at Truk four days later, *Musashi* joined *Yamato* and other elements of the Combined Fleet already at anchor there. In February, Admiral Yamamoto transferred his flag from *Yamato* to *Musashi*, much to the pride of *Musashi*'s crew, but the two great warships remained largely in harbor.

Two months later, as Admiral Yamamoto flew from Rabaul to Ballale Island to inspect Japanese air bases there, American P-38 fighters from Guadalcanal (alerted by decrypted Japanese message traffic) shot down Admiral Yamamoto's airplane over Bougainville. The admiral was killed in the crash, though his body was recovered. Yamamoto's death was a great blow to the Imperial Navy; the chief architect of the Japan's maritime strategy and the revered father of her modern navy was gone. His death was kept a state secret. In mid-May 1943, in reaction to the American invasion of Attu Island in the Aleutians, *Musashi* and a group of carriers and cruisers sortied from Truk to the Yokosuka Naval Base near Tokyo. In the process, *Musashi* had the honor of transporting Admiral Yamamoto's ashes home for burial. At Yokosuka, *Musashi* was placed at the core of a large task force of carriers, battleships, and cruisers bound for Alaska and the defense of Attu, but before she and her consorts could put to sea to contest the Attu invasion, the island fell to the Americans.

For the next four months, *Musashi* remained in home waters. In June, her senior officers entertained Emperor Hirohito and a cadre of high-ranking military officials. *Musashi*'s officers and men regarded an imperial visit to the ship as a great honor, a sign of *Musashi*'s singular importance to the nation. Like all warships of the Imperial Japanese Navy, *Musashi* mounted Emperor Hirohito's chrysanthemum crest on her bow and displayed the emperor's portrait in her wardroom. The emperor is reported to have toured his newest battleship for two hours, visiting crew quarters and dining in the senior officers' mess.

In September 1943, *Musashi* returned to Truk and rejoined *Yamato* and the Combined Fleet. In mid-October, *Musashi* and the Combined Fleet sortied in strength to attack an American task group believed to be intent on raiding Wake Island, but the Japanese armada returned to Truk two weeks later without ever making contact with the enemy.

Musashi was pressed into transport duty in February 1944, tasked with delivering troops, fuel, and ammunition to the Palau Islands. This reinforcement and resupply mission did not go well. En route to Malakal Harbor, the principal naval anchorage within the Palaus, *Musashi* encountered a powerful typhoon that pounded the ship relentlessly. Fearing that the fuel drums and ordnance lashed to the battleship's weather decks would explode, *Musashi*'s captain ordered the lading jettisoned into the sea. Then in March, while still at Malakal, *Musashi* made an emergency sortie from the harbor to escape an American air strike (which never materialized), and this precaution placed her squarely in the path of other dangers. The American submarine *Tunny*, SS-282, sighted *Musashi* off Babelthuap and torpedoed her. *Tunny*'s torpedoes damaged *Musashi*'s bow and forced her to return to the Kure Naval Yard for repairs.

Yamato, too, had been sighted and attacked by American submarines. *Flying Fish*, SS-229, had torpedoed *Yamato* in August 1942 as the giant battleship steamed off Truk, but *Flying Fish*'s missiles did no damage. In late December 1943, again in the waters off Truk, *Skate*, SS-305, fired a spread of torpedoes at *Yamato*, one of which punctured her starboard side near her stern, forcing her to withdraw to Kure. Despite these submarine encounters, or perhaps because of them, American intelligence had grossly underestimated the size of *Yamato* and *Musashi*. Intelligence officers calculated the displacement of the *Yamato* class at forty-five hundred tons, when, in fact, each battleship displaced seventy-three thousand tons. The difference between the ships' actual and estimated displacement, twenty-eight thousand tons, would fill ten or eleven Olympic-size swimming pools.

While dry-docked at Kure for hull repairs, *Musashi* was fitted with additional antiaircraft guns, an acknowledgment by Combined Fleet headquarters of the increasing potency of American airpower. Yard workers removed two triple-mount six-inch auxiliary gun turrets and installed more than seventy additional twenty-five-millimeter antiaircraft machine guns on her superstructure and main deck, thereby raising the total number of twenty-five-millimeter antiaircraft guns on *Musashi* to 115. (*Yamato* received a similar upgrade of sixty-two additional antiaircraft guns at Kure, raising her total to ninety-eight.)

On May 10, 1944, the same day Admiral Toyoda issued his A-Go plan for a decisive battle in the Philippine Sea, *Musashi* weighed anchor at Kure for Tawi-Tawi, a Japanese naval anchorage in the Sulu Sea northeast of Borneo, there to join Admiral Jisaburo Ozawa and his Mobile Fleet. As she eased out of the Inland Sea, *Musashi*'s topsides bristled with the upturned barrels of her new antiaircraft guns like the spikes of an angry porcupine. One month later, the Americans invaded Saipan, and Admiral Toyoda ordered Ozawa's Mobile Fleet to sortie north and attack. *Musashi* and *Yamato*, then en route with 2nd Fleet to oppose American landings at Biak Island off the coast of Borneo, broke off their mission to join Ozawa in the fight.

Neither *Musashi* nor *Yamato* was a factor in the First Battle of the Philippine Sea, the great aircraft carrier clash that erupted in the waters northeast of Luzon and west of Saipan on June 19, 1944. Ozawa held the Japanese 2nd Fleet in reserve, hoping first to sink or disable most of the American ships with submarine attacks, massed carrier air strikes, and shuttle-bombing, and then to bring the big naval guns of 2nd Fleet to bear against the remnants of Task Force 58. As a consequence of Ozawa's tactics, *Musashi*, *Yamato*, and the bulk of the 2nd Fleet had been miles from the center of the fighting on June 19, and *Yamato* had done more harm than good by firing mistakenly on a flight of Japanese fighters and downing several. At dusk, Ozawa withdrew his Mobile Fleet—diminished by two aircraft carriers and hundreds of warplanes—to Okinawa. The 2nd Fleet, with Japan's two superbattleships at its core, trailed him there in vicarious defeat.

The First Battle of the Philippine Sea forced Admiral Toyoda to devise a new plan for engaging the American Pacific fleet in decisive battle. In the interim, Combined Fleet headquarters recalled the Mobile Fleet to home waters and directed Ozawa to accelerate the training of replacements for the hundreds of carrier pilots and aircrew lost in the Marianas. Recognizing the likelihood that *Musashi* and *Yamato* would have to fight without the benefit of friendly air cover, headquarters also ordered the two *Yamatos* home to Kure Naval Yard to be fitted with additional defensive weapons. In late June and early July, *Musashi* received fifteen more twenty-five-millimeter antiaircraft guns, raising her total twenty-five-millimeter armament to 130 guns; *Yamato* received an additional fifteen twenty-five-millimeter antiaircraft guns, raising her total to 113.

With the *Yamatos'* antiaircraft defenses strengthened, Combined Fleet headquarters dispatched Kurita's 2nd Fleet, comprised of *Musashi*, *Yamato*, and an armada of veteran battleships, cruisers, and destroyers, to Lingga Roads. By stationing Kurita's heavy surface ships at Lingga, Admiral Toyoda and his staff had placed a powerful striking force within three days' sail of the Philippines, which was where they expected the next American blow to fall. The move was also necessary. To conduct training exercises and execute any attack on the American fleet in defense of the Philippines, Kurita's 2nd Fleet would require enormous supplies of fuel oil. The *Yamatos* were especially voracious: to fill the bunkers of a single *Yamato*-class battleship to capacity required sixty-three hundred tons. At top speed, a *Yamato*-class consumed nearly sixty-three metric tons of fuel per hour and, when sailing with consorts, she also would be expected to transfer a portion of her fuel to smaller ships, such as destroyers. American submarines had substantially choked off the flow of fuel oil from southeast Asia to Japan; by stationing *Musashi*, *Yamato*, and their consorts at Lingga, Admiral Toyoda had placed his main battle fleet near a plentiful fuel source (close to the Palembang oil fields) and mitigated the risk that his superbattleships would be fuel-starved and inert when the opportunity for the decisive battle arrived.

As *Musashi* lay at anchor in Lingga Roads, her crew looked forward to writing the next chapter in their superbattleship's history. *Musashi*'s war record had been disappointing so far, but the officers and men of *Musashi* were confident in their ship and eager to unleash its immense destructive power against the American fleet. *Musashi*'s sailors had memorized a battle song composed especially for their ship, and they sang it often. "*Musashi* is unsinkable," the first verse went. "If *Musashi* sinks, Japan will sink with her."

CHAPTER FIVE

IN THE MIDDLE LATITUDES

★ ★ ★ ★ ★

Navy air groups developed reputations, and joint training exercises between them became undeclared competitions where the efficiency and effectiveness of one air group as compared with another were judged by how quickly the pilots got airborne, how quickly they formed up, and how precisely they executed their massed attacks. En route to Eniwetok, Air Group 18 and *Intrepid* conducted joint tactical exercises with Air Group 20 from *Enterprise*. The men of Air Group 18 still viewed Air Group 20 as friendly rivals in the game of "proficiency around the boat," and Commander Ellis and his boys were eager to acquit themselves. On August 18, Ellis led fifty-four of his pilots, flying thirty Hellcats, eleven Helldivers, and thirteen Avengers, in the first of several simulated air attacks on Task Unit 12.3.2's three carriers and their escorts. Air Group 18 recovered all aircraft within forty-two minutes, a pace that Barden described as "No record, but good for a green Air Group." Afterward, Captain Bolger announced over *Intrepid*'s 1MC that "Flight operations were exceedingly well handled," and Admiral Frederick C. Sherman, the task unit commander, blinkered from *Enterprise*: "From OTC [officer in tactical command], Well Done." The plaudits of Bogan and Sherman boosted the confidence of Air Group 18 and elevated its standing with *Intrepid*'s ship's company.

VT-18's pilots also flew more mundane missions during *Intrepid*'s passage to Eniwetok, such as practice search-and-rescue missions and "message drops." The latter were similar to old-fashioned airmail flights; pilots would deliver messages to other carriers in the task group by flying low and slow over the ship and dropping weighted canvas bags on the recipient's flight deck. Lieutenant Commander Van Antwerp designated Squatty Vaughn as the message pilot for one of *Intrepid*'s first message flights, a dry run intended to get everyone accustomed to the procedure. Vaughn, piloting his Avenger expertly down the length of *Intrepid*'s flight deck just a few knots above stalling speed and within a few feet of the carrier's superstructure, dropped his message bag in the middle of the flight deck. A signalman seized the message bag, rushed up the ladders to *Intrepid*'s navigation bridge, and handed the bag to Captain Bolger. Bolger opened it and scanned the special message that Vaughn had composed for purposes of the drill with Van Antwerp's blessing:.

"If you have two, turn one in. If you have one, draw one."

Captain Bolger reportedly guffawed at the absurdity of the message—the skipper's reaction no doubt bewildered the signalman at first—and word of the incident spread quickly throughout the ship. No one was surprised at Vaughn's cheeky text. Before leaving Hawaii, Van Antwerp had nicknamed his squadron "The Carrier Clowns," and Vaughn had developed a reputation within the air group as VT-18's Chief Prankster.

Nicknaming a new squadron was a long-standing tradition in the U.S. Navy. Each aviation unit in the navy was, in many respects, a self-defined tribe of warriors. All torpedo plane crews were known as "torpeckers," for example, but the airmen of VT-18 were a unique tribe within the larger nation of torpeckers; they had been forged together by many months of training and merited their own identity. The skipper of the squadron usually chose the nickname. Some skippers held a contest, and most tried to pick a clever nom de guerre that reflected the unit's tactical mission and the temperment of its members. Humorous nicknames were prized, especially if they conveyed double entendre or menace. After the skipper made his choice, he deputized someone (usually an amateur artist in the squadron) to design a unit patch or emblem that incorporated the nickname. The emblem would be painted on the ready room door and on the "photo board," which was a collage of individual head shots of all pilots in the unit. Aboard ship, photo boards were hung in the passageways outside the air group's office spaces so everyone in the air group would know who was who.

It was also customary for parachute riggers to embroider the unit emblem on a cloth patch, which crewmen would then stitch to their flight suits and jackets. As of late 1944, U.S. Navy aircrew were permitted to wear unit patches in home waters only. Once the squadron deployed to a combat zone, members were required to remove all patches to prevent the Japanese from identifying American units in the area simply by looking at the flight suits of downed airmen.

The origins of "Carrier Clowns" are obscure; in this case, the squadron emblem may have preceeded the nickname. According to Red Russell, the emblem was designed by a VT-18 enlisted man who was fond of Walt Disney cartoons. This fledgling artist (who aspired to work in Disney's animation studios after the war) incorporated into his drawing a degree of symbolism that would have confounded anyone unfamiliar with a torpedo squadron's mission. His design depicted a barking seal—the seal apparently represented the quasi-amphibious ability of an Avenger to operate from land bases or a carrier at sea—balancing a large antiship mine on its nose. A zebra—VT-18's radio call sign was "Zebra"— tiptoed atop the mine, which the artist bisected with an aerial torpedo and ringed with six stylized bombs. The result was this: A barking seal in the middle of the picture, juggling a mine, a zebra, and the whole panoply of Avenger-borne ordnance on its nose, as if everything were part of a circus act. No one could deny the artist had captured the tactical versatility of an Avenger squadron, but the Carrier Clowns' emblem and nickname weren't especially warlike. Van Antwerp apparently liked them; privately, Will Fletcher thought they were a little sappy.

The airmen of Bombing 18 called themselves "the Sunday Punchers." This is boxing slang for a knockout blow, and VB-18's nickname may have been an oblique reference to seeking revenge for the Sunday sneak attack on Pearl Harbor. The squadron emblem consisted of a winged bomb encased in a boxing glove. The men of Fighting 18 called themselves, rather unimaginatively, "Fighting Eighteen." VF-18's squadron emblem depicted a horned red devil with a mischievous expression on his face and a halo encircling his head. Whether VF-18's emblem was a nod to the philosophical conundrum of doing extreme violence for a righteous cause or simply artistic license, no one today can say.

On the voyage to Eniwetok, Will was surprised to learn how hazardous a place an aircraft carrier could be—even for those who didn't fly airplanes. Everything aboard the ship was made of steel and slippery when wet, an ideal environment for falling down and breaking bones. There were unpadded edges, low-hanging pipes, steep ladders, watertight hatchways with shin-banging thresholds that grabbed at the feet, and heavy hatches with knuckle-cracking dog handles. Machinery of all kinds—pumps, fans, blowers, generators—operated twenty-four hours a day. Airplanes, forklifts, tool chests, scaffolds, and ordnance carts moved constantly about the ship on decks that pitched and rolled ceaselessly. Men slipped, knocking heads and fracturing limbs; arresting gear cables snapped and lacerated arms and legs; fingers became entangled in bomb hoists; bombs fell off carts and crushed feet; hand cranks kicked back and broke jaws. *Intrepid* had been at sea for only one day when a mechanic sitting in the cockpit of a Hellcat accidentally discharged the fighter's wing guns in the hangar bay, spraying .50-caliber rounds across the deck and wounding six men with shrapnel. Will learned quickly to keep his head on a swivel.

Task Unit 12.3.2 crossed the International Date Line on August 21 and entered Eniwetok Atoll on the afternoon of August 24. Eniwetok—the name means "the land between east and west"—was a mid-Pacific naval anchorage nearly forty miles in diameter. Lying 2,300 nautical miles southeast of Japan and 2,370 nautical miles southwest of Hawaii, Eniwetok had served as strategic naval base for the emperor's warships until February 1944, when American marines seized the atoll at a cost of 339 American lives and nearly 2,800 Japanese. By August 1944, the sheltering islands had become a refuge for the United States Pacific Fleet and a principal staging area for further American attacks against Japan's bastions in the western Pacific.

As *Intrepid* passed through the so-called deep entrance to the harbor, most of Air Group 18's pilots loitered at the ship's rail, fascinated by their first glimpse of a major Japanese military outpost purchased with American blood. The perimeter islands were little more than low mounds of white sand that bore ineradicable scars of combat. Most of the palm trees had been splintered by naval gunfire, and the brush beneath them had been burned away. The ground was studded with blackened tree stumps. Only a sun-bleached airstrip and a few hastily constructed Quonset huts of corrugated metal were visible on the shore. The consensus among the boys was that Eniwetok would be a piss-poor place for liberty if they ever got ashore. But inside the harbor lay a stunning sight. As far as the pilots could see, an enormous collection of ships rode calmly at anchor. There were aircraft carriers both big-deck and small, battleships, cruisers both

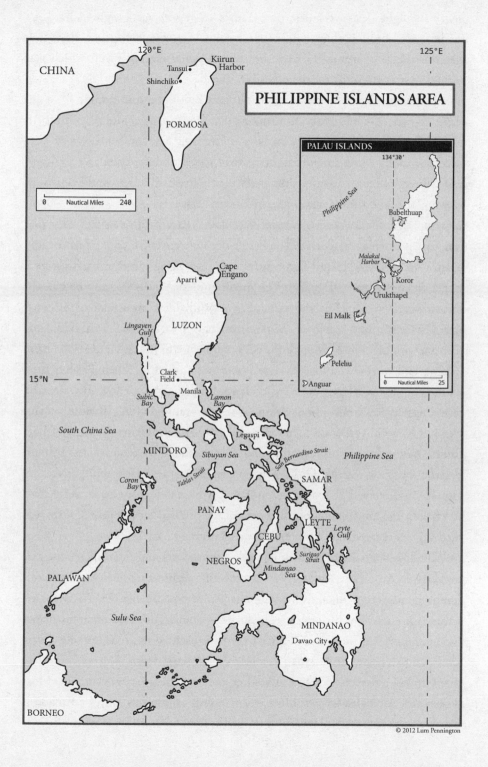

PHILIPPINE ISLANDS AREA

CHINA

120°E

Tansui •
Kiirun
Harbor
Shinchiko •

FORMOSA

125°E

0 Nautical Miles 240

Cape
Engano
Aparri •

LUZON

Lingayen
Gulf

15°N

Clark
Field •
Manila •

Subic
Bay

Lamon
Bay

South China Sea

Legaspi •

MINDORO

Sibuyan Sea

SAMAR

Philippine Sea

Coron
Bay

Tablas Strait

San Bernardino Strait

PANAY

LEYTE
Leyte
Gulf

CEBU

Surigao
Strait

NEGROS

Mindanao
Sea

PALAWAN

Sulu Sea

MINDANAO

Davao City •

BORNEO

PALAU ISLANDS

134°30'

Philippine Sea

Babelthuap

Malakal
Harbor

Koror

Urukthapel

Eil Malk

Peleliu

▷Anguar

0 Nautical Miles 25

© 2012 Lum Pennington

heavy and light, destroyers, destroyer escorts, minesweepers, freighters, tankers, tenders, ammunition ships, and support ships of every description. Eniwetok was the assembly ground for Admiral Halsey's massive 3rd Fleet, which was gathering strength daily for the offensives ahead.

Task Unit 12.3.2 dissolved on arriving at Eniwetok, and no one from *Intrepid* went ashore on liberty. On August 25, 1944, *Intrepid* and Air Group 18 sortied from the harbor to begin two days of training exercises with *Bunker Hill*, CV-17, and Air Group 8; the light carriers *Cabot* and *Independence* and several cruisers and destroyers accompanied them. These exercises would consist of group gropes and simulated attacks on the carriers.

Impatient for battle, Air Group 18's pilots referred derisively to task group war games as "playing carrier," but even the mock attacks could turn deadly when they involved firing live ammunition. In making a rocket run against a target sled on August 26, Ensign Vernon Sistrunk of VT-18 (Vernon had joined the squadron at Kaneohe the same day as Will) blew away half of his own Avenger's horizontal stabilizer. Sistrunk managed to land safely back aboard *Intrepid* with his crew of two uninjured, but Lieutenant Junior Grade Bob "Bris" Brisbin and his crew, also of VT-18, were not so lucky. When Brisbin fired his rockets, his Avenger pitched up violently and sheared a wing. The airplane rolled upside down and plunged into the water, taking with it Brisbin's turret gunner, Aviation Ordnance Mate Third Class William Henry Besoain of Fort Jones, California, and his radioman, Aviation Radioman Second Class William Patrick Young of Warren, Ohio. Brisbin leaped clear of his tumbling, gyrating airplane and opened his parachute just before he hit the water. He badly fractured a leg and ankle, and poor Bris, one of the original members of VT-18, was medically evacuated to a hospital at Pearl Harbor.

The loss of an Avenger crew to exploding rockets and Sistrunk's close call shocked the air group. An angry Ellis ordered an immediate investigation, but the probe proved inconclusive. Like many kinds of ordnance, HVAR were assembled from several major components before being mounted on an airplane; the best guess was that an ordnance man had installed the rocket vanes incorrectly. In Bris's case, he had inadvertently shot himself down.

Intrepid returned to Eniwetok after her exercises to await orders. Most sailors and Airedales were confined to the ship. Those few who had made it ashore reported back unfavorably, "It [is] hotter than hell . . . Warm beer is dished right out from the case, and the whiskey is Schenleys," wrote one of Air Group 18's intelligence officers, Lieutenant George Race, who also groused about the lack of intelligence. No one seemed to know precisely where *Intrepid* and the Air Group 18 would strike first, including the air group's intelligence officer. Messengers raced about the ship with locked metal boxes containing dispatches, but the dispatches were accessible only to those with a key, and Race didn't have a key. Irritated at the lack of information, and perhaps at the oppressive heat, Race complained, "You would think we were on Times Square surrounded by Jap spies, rather on an American warship in Eniwetok Harbor on the way to fight the Japs."

On the morning of August 29, *Intrepid* weighed anchor and sortied again from Eniwetok Harbor, this time departing her anchorage as a unit of Task Group 38.2 (TG 38.2), one of three fast carrier task groups formed by Admiral Nimitz for the purpose of raiding Japanese island bases throughout the Pacific. In addition to *Intrepid*, TG 38.2 consisted of her sister *Essex*-class carriers *Hancock* and *Bunker Hill*; light carriers *Independence* and *Cabot*; the heavy cruisers of Cruiser Division 14: *Vincennes*, *Houston*, *Miami*, *San Diego*, and *Oakland*; and fifteen destroyers of Destroyer Squadron 53, including *The Sullivans*, a destroyer named for five brothers who died together on the same ship, the cruiser *Juneau*, in the night sea battles off Guadalcanal. Rear Admiral Gerald F. Bogan, who had shifted his flag to *Intrepid* at Eniwetok, commanded Task Group 38.2.

On the same day, Task Group 38.3 (TG 38.3), under the command of Rear Admiral Frederick C. Sherman, also sortied from the massive anchorage at Eniwetok. Sherman's task group consisted of *Essex* herself, first of her class of large fleet carriers, and her sister carrier *Lexington*, light carriers *Princeton* and *Langley*, four battleships, four heavy cruisers, and more than a dozen destroyers. Two other fast carrier task groups of slightly smaller size had also formed in or near Eniwetok. These were Task Group 38.1 (TG 38.1) under Vice Admiral John Sidney McCain, with fleet carriers *Wasp* and *Hornet* and light carriers *Cowpens* and *Monterey*, and Task Group 38.4 (TG 38.4) under Rear Admiral Ralph E. Davison, with fleet carriers *Franklin* and *Enterprise* and the light carriers *San Jacinto* and *Belleau Wood*. All four task groups comprised Task Force 38 (TF 38) under the command of Vice Admiral Marc A. Mitscher, one of the heroes of the carrier battles in the Philippine Sea.

Mitscher flew his flag from *Lexington* and reported to Admiral William F.

Halsey, commander of 3rd Fleet. (After the Battle of the Philippine Sea, the Navy Department had redesignated Spruance's 5th Fleet as Halsey's 3rd Fleet.) Halsey flew his flag from the battleship *New Jersey*, which steamed in company with one of the task groups. All combined, Task Force 38 mustered at least eight big deck carriers and six small deck carriers.

Not until Task Force 38 had put to sea, when there was no possibility of unwanted disclosure, did the men of Air Group 18 and *Intrepid* learn their destination. Third Fleet staffers distributed operational orders to task group and air group commanders, and air group intelligence officers summoned pilots and aircrewmen to their respective squadron ready rooms for briefings from folders conspicuously stamped "Top Secret." Van Antwerp and Allen advised the pilots and aircrew of VT-18 that their first combat mission would be flown against the Palau Islands. Most of them had never heard of the place.

Known to the Japanese as Parao-shoto, the Palau Islands lie 520 nautical miles east of the Philippine island of Mindanao and roughly five hundred nautical miles north of the equator. They are the westernmost of the Caroline Islands, a group of six hundred islands and atolls scattered across the central Pacific from longitude 134 degrees east to 162 degrees east. Babelthuap, only sixteen miles long and ten miles wide, is the northernmost island of the Palau archipelago. Koror Island sits immediately below Babelthuap in the chain, followed in succession by the lesser islands of Urukthapel, Eil Malk, Peleliu, and Angaur. West of the Palau Islands lies an immense barrier reef, where schools of brightly colored fish with faces like harlequins dart among the shallows. Palau's western reef runs for more than seventy nautical miles, greater than the entire length of the Palau archipelago itself.

The Palau Islands' nearest neighbors are very far away. North by northeast of the Palaus, 550 nautical miles distant, lie Guam, Tinian, and Saipan, principal islands of the Marianas. Seventeen hundred eighty miles due east of the Palaus lie the tiny volcanic islands of Ponape and Kusaie, the easternmost links of the Caroline chain. Eniwetok lies 360 miles above Ponape and Kusaie. To the south of the Palaus, 690 miles distant, sits New Guinea, the largest landmass between the Palau Islands and Australia. Between and among them all rolls the primeval sea, incomprehensibly vast, restless, and deep.

Germany purchased the Palau Islands from Spain in 1899 to establish a naval coaling station and support its colonial presence in the equatorial Pacific.

Japan seized the islands in 1917 while Germany was preoccupied with World War I in Europe, and the nascent League of Nations rewarded Japan for her initiative by granting the government of Emperor Yoshihito, Hirohito's father, a political mandate over the islands in 1920. During the 1930s, the Japanese military secretly transformed the Palau Islands from tropical coaling station to military fortress. They built airfields and hangars, dry docks and repair stations, fuel and ammunition storage dumps, seaplane ramps, boat basins, communications stations, lumberyards, barracks and hospitals, and they constructed elaborate ground defenses to protect the islands from invasion. From Palau's three air bases, the emperor's warplanes had patrolled the central Pacific in all directions for five or six hundred miles, and the emperor's warships had sheltered and re-provisioned in Palau's waters. The emperor's aircraft carriers had sortied from Palau's Malakal Harbor in December 1941 to attack U.S. forces in the Philippine Islands following the raid on Pearl Harbor, and the emperor's proud Kawaguchi Brigade had embarked at Malakal for Guadalcanal in September 1942, destined for destruction in the jungles of the Solomons.

Lieutenant Commander Allen briefed his torpedo-bomber crews on what to expect. Task Force 38 would sail west-southwest from Eniwetok, giving wide berth to the Japanese naval base at Truk where *Intrepid* had come to grief in February 1944. The task force would pass beneath Truk and proceed nearly due west toward the Palau archipelago. Once there, Mitscher's carrier air groups would begin a three-day bombing campaign.

The emperor's occupying forces on Palau outnumbered the native population five to one. The six main islands of the chain held an estimated twenty-one thousand soldiers of the Imperial Japanese Army, four thousand sailors of the Imperial Japanese Navy and ten thousand laborers. The number of enemy warplanes based on Palau's three airfields was not well-known. Allen believed the Japs had withdrawn most of their aircraft to the Philippines or Formosa after the Philippine Sea battle, but the Japanese could easily return to the Palaus if their airfields and harbors remained intact. Admiral Nimitz regarded the Palaus as an impediment to the American advance across the central Pacific and as a threat to any attempt by MacArthur to liberate the Philippine Islands. Nimitz did not want a Japanese-occupied Palau in the navy's rear when the time came to attack the Philippines, and he viewed the Palaus as a necessary staging point for a Philippine invasion. Major General William Rupertus, the commander of the 1st Marine Division charged with invading and securing the Palaus, had predicted a quick American victory. After three days of bombing the Palaus, Allen announced, Task Force 38 would head west to bomb Mindanao, where heavy air opposition was expected.

Kenny Barden listened intently to Allen's briefing, especially the part about heavy air opposition. The reality of what VT-18 faced sank in. Looking beyond today's game to the next, Barden memorialized his anxieties in his diary that night: "Mindanao. Oh God!!"

On the weeklong voyage from Eniwetok to the Palaus, Barden and his fellow torpedo-plane pilots made final preparations for their first strike. They attended more intelligence briefings and lectures and studied recognition diagrams of ships and aircraft so they could quickly identify enemy airplane types by their silhouettes against the sky, and enemy ship classes by their plan and profile views. They had studied these drawings from the earliest days of their training, but the task took on new urgency when making the correct identification might mean the difference between life and death. Ernie Allen tested his pilots over and over with identification flash cards, like a schoolmarm teaching her pupils vocabulary or math. The pilots also studied maps of the Palaus and the target areas assigned to Air Group 18. Third Fleet's staff had divided the Palaus into different target areas so that different air groups did not interfere with one another. Air Group 18 flew more group gropes to hone its combat edge. VT-18 performed well in these exercises, but VB-18 suffered two barrier crashes, one of which smashed a Helldiver to pieces. The Helldiver's crew was uninjured, but a ship's company sailor leaped over *Intrepid*'s side to avoid being struck by the careening dive-bomber. Admiral Bogan dispatched two destroyers from the Task Group to search for the sailor, but he was never seen again.

In off-hours, the pilots played poker and acey-deucey, reread letters from home, wrote return letters that wouldn't be mailed for days or weeks, watched movies that were projected nightly on a temporary screen erected in the hangar bay—the hangar bay was blacked out at night and stiflingly hot—and fired their .38-caliber pistols off the carrier's fantail. *Intrepid*'s master-at-arms cracked that the safest place to stand when the pilots took pistol practice was directly in front of the target. *Intrepid*'s Catholic chaplain, whom the sailors called Padre, distributed a pocket-size prayer book to all hands entitled *Prayers for the Dead and Dying*. Padre's gesture was prescient, but it didn't do much to inspire confidence.

Will Fletcher didn't accept a copy of Padre's prayer book, not because he was irreligious—he had been an altar boy at his mother's Episcopal church, much to Naomi's pride and delight—but simply because Will didn't think much about death, his or anyone else's. His mother's passing had been too painful and he had no further interest. Death was an abstraction to him, a sad and mysterious passage reserved for someone else, for the unlucky or incapable. Those whom Will knew had experienced it—his mother, his buddies killed in training—had simply gone away. Will understood that he might be killed in combat—he'd done the responsible thing and purchased a government life insurance policy for the benefit of his sisters, which he paid for by pay allotment—but he figured the odds were in his favor, and that his first combat mission would come off exactly like the dozens of bombing exercises and group gropes he had flown in training. Will was absolutely confident he wouldn't die because of his own mistake; he believed himself too good a pilot for that. What concerned him most on the eve of battle was that he might make a mistake that embarrassed the squadron, like botching his engine start or joining up late. Will didn't fear losing his nerve in the face of enemy fire, but he dreaded the possibility of exhibiting stupidity or poor judgment in front of his pals. "Better dead than look bad," his buddies had quipped whenever one of the VT-18's pilots erred publicly, but only half jokingly.

Will did worry about the possibility of capture. Van Antwerp and Allen had briefed VT-18's pilots on what to do if their airplane was hit and disabled over the Palaus. The two senior officers had offered the standard advice: Get as far out over the water as possible before bailing out or crash-landing, and avoid capture by all means. Jap soldiers tortured downed American pilots for information and then executed them, usually by beheading. Jap soldiers also cannibalized their dead enemies, not out of famine but as part of a depraved samurai-warrior ritual. The pilots talked among themselves about the horrific possibilities. Will wondered whether he'd hold up under interrogation if captured, and he confided his fears to Lieutenant Junior Grade John Savage, who was among Will's closest friends in the squadron. Did Savage really think the Japs on Palau ate the flesh of dead men?

Savage could think of no reason why the enemy soldiers on Palau would be any different from their comrades elsewhere.

Will had pressed him. "What would you do if you got shot you down over the Palaus and you survived the parachute ride or water landing but fell into Jap hands?"

Savage had patted the holster of his .38 revolver and answered ambiguously. "Won't happen, Fletch."

The big day finally arrived. Task Force 38 and *Intrepid* steamed into the Palau Islands area on September 6, 1944, and Air Group 18 launched its first two strikes of the war that same day, beginning with an eight fifteen a.m. fighter sweep over the Palau Islands in combination with Hellcats from other air groups. Air Group 18 concluded the day with a solo strike against the Japanese airfield on Babelthuap, the largest and northernmost island of the Palau chain, by a co-ordinated force of fighters, dive-bombers, and torpedo bombers.

Will did not participate in the strikes of September 6, and he sensed that those who had flown that day had come away mildly disappointed. The attacking forces encountered minimal antiaircraft fire and no fighter opposition. Pilots reported seeing "little of interest." VF-18's fighter pilots, acting with too little discipline and too much aggression, attacked and sank three native sampans on their return trip to *Intrepid*, an incident that Lieutenant Race described as "regretful."

Task Force 38 began the aerial bombardment of the Palau Islands in earnest on September 7. Air Group 18 had been charged with "neutraliz[ing] Babelthuap pending the landing of our Marines on Peleliu to the south." Every airman in the outfit understood the word "neutralize" was a military euphemism for obliterate, and they relished the opportunity to avenge Pearl Harbor personally at last.

Air Group 18's first mission of September 7, Strike 2A as in "Able," began at six a.m. with the takeoff of sixteen fighters, fifteen dive-bombers, and eight torpedo planes launched in that order. The strike group rendezvoused after takeoff at fifteen hundred feet and, minus one Helldiver whose starboard wing flap would not retract, arrived over the Japanese airfield at Babelthuap ninety minutes later. Hellcats attacked first, strafing the airfield and the surrounding buildings from forty-five-degree dive angles. Helldivers attacked second, nosing over from ten thousand feet into eighty-degree dives and pulling out at two thousand to one thousand feet. Avengers attacked third, pushing over from thirty-eight hundred feet into thirty-five-degree glide-bombing runs and pulling out at twenty-five hundred feet. Prestrike intelligence had predicted that the Japanese airfield would be fully operational, but the attackers saw no enemy airplanes on the ground and none in the air. In the words of the strike leader, Strike 2 Able had encountered "negligible" resistance.

While Strike 2 Able was in progress, *Intrepid* launched Strike 2B as in "Baker," beginning with the takeoff of fifteen Hellcats at eight fifteen, one of which was piloted by Commander Ellis himself. These were followed in rapid sequence by fifteen Helldivers and eight VT-18 Avengers. By eight thirty-five a.m., all thirty-eight aircraft of Strike 2 Baker had successfully rendezvoused above the ship. Their objective was to destroy the main Japanese runway at Babelthuap and any antiaircraft positions that surrounded it.

Strike 2 Baker arrived over the Babelthuap airfield at about nine-oh-five a.m., and VT-18's Avengers, led by Bud Williams, attacked first this time. Bud's four-plane division concentrated on knocking out enemy gun positions north of the runway. His torpedo bombers nosed over in synchrony from eighty-five hundred feet and established a thirty-five-degree glide-bombing run at 320 knots. They released their combined payload of sixteen five-hundred-pound bombs simultaneously at twenty-five hundred feet and pulled out of their bombing run at eighteen hundred feet. The second four-plane division of Avengers focused on cratering the runway itself. Attacking next from 11,500 feet, VB-18's Helldivers concentrated their bombs on antiaircraft emplacements and a barracks building. VF-18's Hellcats swept down in the aftermath, machine-gunning the smoldering gun positions around the perimeter of the airfield, shooting up an adjacent warehouse, and strafing a Japanese harbor tug or two. Strike 2 Able was effective but not flawless; the Avenger flown by VT-18's Ensign Owen F. Williams had developed a hydraulic leak after takeoff, and Williams had been unable to open his bomb bay doors.

By eight fifty a.m. on September 7, all of the aircraft that had participated in Strike 2 Able had landed safely back aboard *Intrepid*, and sailors from the air department immediately began to refuel and rearm many of these same warplanes for a third attack on Babelthuap, Strike 2C as in "Charlie." By nine forty a.m., Strike 2 Baker had finished its business over Babelthuap and departed the target area. Heading home to *Intrepid*, Commander Ellis scribbled approvingly on his plotting board that the bombing of VT-18 and VB-18 had been "accurate," and noted, perhaps with a mild degree of disdain, that the intensity of Japanese antiaircraft fire over Babelthuap had been "negligible."

If asked, Lieutenant Junior Grade M. A. "Andy" Anderson of VB-18 probably would have disagreed with Ellis's characterization of the enemy's anti-aircraft fire. During Anderson's dive-bombing run on Strike 2 Baker, a thirty-seven-millimeter shell struck the port side of his Helldiver's engine cowling and exploded in the engine accessory section. A piece of the shell ripped through the cockpit, singeing the hair off Anderson's left leg and knocking out his airplane's electrical system. On his return to *Intrepid*, Anderson attempted to land aboard the ship, but *Intrepid*'s landing signal officer waved him off because of a fouled deck. With his propeller stuck in fixed pitch at 1,250 r.p.m. and his Helldiver incapable of maintaining flying speed, Anderson landed in the water near the destroyer *Colahan*. The Helldiver remained afloat for one minute, ten seconds, sufficient time for Anderson and his radioman to escape the airplane. Sailors of the *Colahan* fished the men from the water uninjured.

Although Ellis concluded in his after-action report for Strike 2 Baker that "no further bombing of this airfield was . . . necessary," no one canceled *Intrepid*'s third strike. Strike 2 Charlie's targets were various structures adjacent to the Babelthuap airfield that hadn't been blasted on the earlier missions, such as barracks buildings and warehouses. Lieutenant Commander Van Antwerp contributed eight VT-18 Avengers to the effort and designated Lieutenant George Benson "Ben" Riley, the hot-dog pilot from Pennsylvania with whom Red Russell was reluctant to fly, to lead the Avenger flight. Each of Riley's Avengers was armed with twelve hundred-pound general-purpose bombs fused to explode instantaneously on hitting the earth. VF-18 contributed sixteen fighters and VB-18 fourteen dive-bombers.

Will Fletcher made his bombing debut on Strike 2 Charlie. Piloting the fourth Avenger in Riley's division, Will pulled back the control stick of his torpedo bomber and lifted off *Intrepid*'s flight deck at about ten fifty a.m. He had been slotted to fly the mission as Lieutenant Junior Grade John Savage's wingman in the first division, which was led by Riley himself, but all that changed almost as soon as the Avengers launched. Minutes after takeoff, Will was startled to see the number two Avenger up ahead of Savage belch black smoke from its exhausts and level its wings. Reflexively, Will ran his eyes over his engine instruments to assure himself his own engine was maintaining power. Trailing puffs of smoke like a string of black pearls, the stricken Avenger sank below Will's line of sight.

Counting noses in his rendezvous turn, Riley realized his flight of eight torpedo bombers was now reduced to seven. He had briefed his pilots for the possibility that one or more airplanes would develop mechanical problems and be forced to return to the carrier—this was all too common an occurrence—and he shrugged off the loss. Riley would execute the strike with whatever airplanes he had available. The two four-plane divisions that comprised the flight had been assigned different targets near the airfield anyway, and Riley's first division would simply attack shorthanded as a three-plane section. As soon as he collected his six wingmen, Riley jabbed upward with his gloved index finger, signaling a climb to the Avengers' cruising altitude of nine thousand feet. Seven torpedo bombers rose as one, climbing slowly at 150 knots and three hundred feet per minute. In the climb, Riley signaled Savage to shift from his right side to his left and placed Will, as the most junior pilot in the division, off his right wing.

Strike 2 Charlie had launched at six degrees, nine minutes above the equator, and 134 degrees and eleven minutes east, a position roughly seventy nautical miles south of Babelthuap. This is a region of the world where sea, earth, and sky bask in perpetual summer; the nights never cool and the days turn sultry within minutes of sunrise. The midmorning air temperature on September 7 had already soared to eighty-five degrees Fahrenheit at the surface. Will welcomed the marked decrease in air temperature as his Avenger climbed. He unlocked his shoulder harness and leaned forward in his seat, allowing the slipstream to swirl behind his shoulders and cool his back. He shifted his flying goggles to the top of his head and mopped the sweat from his brow with the back of his glove.

Will had acquired a permanent skier's tan, the result of months of exposure to the Pacific sun. His forehead, ears, eye sockets, and upper cheekbones—shielded by his goggles—were Caucasian pink, but his naked nose, lips, jaw, and jowls were now bronzed and ochered like a desert dweller. Squinting through his windscreen, Will eyed VB-18's two divisions of Helldivers lumbering upward to their cruising altitude of 10,500 feet, arrayed in a "vee of vees" formation and headed northeast to the same initial approach fix northeast of Babelthuap. Much higher still, sections of VF-18 fighters weaved gracefully back and forth above the dive-bombers in a Thach Weave, an air-defense maneuver named for the fighter pilot who had devised it. The combined strike group resembled a mass migration of large birds.

Intrepid and her consorts had quickly receded from view, and Will sensed that he and his companions were flying through a vast empty space, an infinite room without boundaries or dimensions. The floor of the room was the surface of the sea itself, which lay flat and featureless beneath them, stretching from horizon to horizon in every direction. The room had no roof, except for a gossamer layer of white cirrus clouds that streaked the sky high above them. Every direction across the trackless sea looked the same to Will in the midmorning sun. Without a navigational fix, no man could have divined where he was; without an altimeter, no man could have known how high above the water he flew; without a compass, no man could have ascertained his course.

Will's turret gunner on Strike 2 Charlie was Aviation Machinist Mate Second Class George E. Christman Jr., from Rye, New York. Christman had first flown with Will at Kaneohe in July 1944. Since Kaneohe, the young New Yorker had become Will's regularly assigned turret gunner, and the two men had flown more than a dozen training missions together. En route to Babelthuap, Christman's job was to search the sky for enemy fighters. By slewing his ball turret from side to side, and by elevating and depressing the barrel of his .50-caliber machine gun, he could cover the areas directly above and behind his Avenger and on each flank. Will heard the electric buzz and whir of the turret motors in his earphones. The sound was reassuring—Christman was doing a good job of maintaining a constant lookout. Will envisioned him squinting into the sunlight for signs of the enemy, probably with his trigger finger itching.

Will's radioman and radar operator was Aviation Radioman Third Class Robert G. Westmoreland, from Atlanta, Georgia. Will had flown only four prior training missions with Westmoreland, and the two men were still growing accustomed to each other. The radioman's principal duties were to operate the airplane's VHF and UHF transmitters and receivers, provide radar search and navigational assistance, configure the Avenger's electrical armament system to properly release bombs and torpedoes, and, on a torpedo run, track the target. Seated at his primary flight station inside the tunnel, Westmoreland operated the Avenger's Westinghouse air-to-surface type-B radar set and peered at his radar screen. He searched for the phosphorescent blotches that would indicate the islands of Angaur and Peleliu, the southernmost of the Palaus; he constantly tuned and adjusted the rakelike radar antennae assemblies that protruded beneath the Avenger's wings. He could also see inside the Avenger's bomb bay through an access portal in the tunnel floor, and he periodically checked the bomb bay to ensure that none of the bombs had vibrated loose from their shackles. Every few minutes, he reported to Will his estimates of the strike group's remaining distance and flight time to the target.

Strike 2 Charlie's group leader—the skipper of VB-18, Lieutenant Commander Mark Eslick, Jr., served as the group leader on this strike, as well as the leader of VB-18's two Helldiver divisions—had the responsibility for leading all thirty-seven warplanes to a predetermined initial approach point for the attack. Eslick led his attackers toward the initial approach point—a fix fifteen miles northeast of Babelthuap out over the Pacific Ocean—as a group, but with fighters, dive-bombers, and torpedo bombers flying at different assigned altitudes. Riley's Avengers leveled off at nine thousand feet, VB-18's dive-bombers at 10,500 feet, and VF-18's fighters at sixteen thousand feet, an altitude suitable for flying "top cover" for the entire group. After leveling off, the strike group accelerated en masse and buzzed toward the initial approach point like a three-layer swarm of hornets.

Will glimpsed Angaur and Peleliu up ahead, small disks of mottled brown and olive green, surrounded by sparkling ribbons of white sand. Seemingly adrift on an immense sea of turquoise and blue, the islands looked insignificant and innocuous. Peleliu supported a large, multirunway airfield, but "neutralizing" that airfield was the responsibility of some other air group. Will's objective, Babelthuap, lay in the distance at the northern end of the archipelago. Babelthuap was gourd shaped and hilly, easily distinguishable from the other islands in the chain by Mount Ngerchelchuus, an eight-hundred-foot-high hump that dominated the northern half of the island.

Will reviewed in his head what was about to happen. Like Air Group 18's earlier strikes on Babelthuap, Strike 2 Charlie had been planned as a "massed attack," in which Hellcats, Helldivers, and Avengers would pummel the airfield in rapid succession. In theory, massed attacks concentrated the attackers' bullets and bombs, suppressed counterfire from defending antiaircraft batteries, and impaired the enemy's ability to recover his casualties. The strike group leader would issue the order to attack, but VF-18's Hellcats would attack first. Three divisions of fighters, twelve F6Fs in all, would descend rapidly from the initial approach fix and execute high-speed, low-level strafing runs over the target. These were intended to suppress enemy antiaircraft fire in advance of the dive-bombers and torpedo bombers. One Hellcat division would remain at altitude to shoot down any Japanese fighters that might rise up to challenge the attackers. VB-18's Helldivers would initiate their dive-bombing runs before the fighters pulled off the target. The dive-bomber leader would roll into a near-vertical bank, add full power, and pitch down from 10,500 feet into an eighty-degree dive. His wingmen would pitch over and follow him down in sequence, descending single file and maintaining about four hundred feet of separation airplane-to-airplane. With their dive brakes extended, the Helldiver pilots would accelerate to 320 knots, unload their bombs at twenty-eight hundred feet, and pull out at fifteen hundred feet. If each dive-bomber pilot pickled his bombs as the target centered in his bomb sight, the effect would be a continuous rain of bombs on the target at two- to four-second intervals. A well-executed dive-bombing attack by fourteen Helldivers, from the moment the leader nosed over until the last dive-bomber pulled out, required no more than four or five minutes.

Lieutenant Riley's seven Avengers would swoop down on the airfield immediately on the heels of VB-18's dive-bombers. VT-18's torpedo bombers would execute thirty-five-degree glide-bombing runs in two or three-plane sections. Glide-bombing permitted the Avengers to attack at higher airspeeds, a tactic that greatly minimized the aircrews' exposure to antiaircraft fire. Although Avengers were designed to glide-bomb at angles as high as sixty-six degrees, bombing angles were restricted by the class and weight of the bombs. Light- and middle-weight bombs, if dropped at too steep an angle, were likely to strike the airplane's fuselage or propeller; the lighter the class and weight of the bomb, the shallower the allowable glide angle. When carrying twelve hundred-pound class bombs, the Avenger's maximum glide-bombing angle was thirty-five degrees. When bombing in section, the Avengers flew side by side during the entire bombing run and released their ordnance simultaneously. In a section attack, the leader of the formation controlled the run; he selected the target and maneuvered the section for the attack. The wingmen were along for the ride.

The strike group arrived at the initial approach point about fifty minutes after leaving *Intrepid*, and Riley led his seven torpedo bombers into a racetrack holding pattern at nine thousand feet to await the attack signal from the strike group leader. Will flew off Riley's right wing and Savage flew off Riley's left. As Riley banked left into the holding pattern, Will and Savage banked with him. Will flew slightly above Riley in the turn and Savage flew slightly below him, but both wingmen oriented themselves in space solely by reference to Riley's Avenger. To Will, Riley's Avenger and Savage's appeared to be skimming only inches above a sheet of royal blue water; to Savage, Riley's airplane and Will's appeared to be suspended in the air against an azure sky.

Riley's three-plane section would be the first group of Avengers to attack; the second division of four torpedo-bombers would follow Riley down. Riley readied his section for its bombing run with a flurry of hand signals. He extended his arm forward and made a fist, twisting it at the wrist. This was the signal to Will and Savage to increase their Avengers' propeller r.p.m. to twenty-six hundred. In response, Will twisted his propeller control knob and the thrum of his engine rose perceptibly. Next, Riley held up his fist and popped it open. This was the preparatory signal to open the Avengers' bomb bay doors. Will grasped his bomb bay door control handle, which was located just above his left knee on the lower instrument panel, and held it in anticipation. A few seconds after giving the preparatory signal, Riley waggled his wings, the signal to execute, and Will yanked down on the control handle. He sensed his Avenger decelerate slightly as the torpedo bomber's hydraulically actuated bomb bay doors folded open into the airstream. A red light on his instrument panel illuminated and glowed like a ruby. The light was installed in the cockpit to warn the pilot when his bomb bay doors were open, but Will didn't need the light to tell him. The Avenger's bomb bay doors were twenty feet long. When opened, they created a hole in the bottom of the Avenger's fuselage nearly half the airplane's length. The open doors created additional drag, and the slipstream moaned loudly past the gaping bomb bay like someone blowing across the mouth of a beer bottle, a noise the pilot couldn't miss. Last, Riley pointed at Will and Savage and patted the sides of his fuselage, signaling his men to tighten up the formation for the section bombing run. Will and Savage complied, each inching closer to Riley along their respective bearing lines.

As he maneuvered closer, Will ensured the twelve bombs nestled in his bomb bay—they had been loaded in two tiers of six bombs each, one tier atop another—were ready to fall. He had worked a long time for this opportunity, and he wasn't about to screw it up now by inattention to detail. Switchology was key. He called Westmoreland over the intercom to verify that his radioman had configured the Avenger's electrical release circuitry to drop the bomb load "in train" (meaning the bombs would fall nose-to-tail, one immediately behind another like the cars of a railroad train). Westmoreland eyed the Avenger's main armament panel, which was located on the port side of the tunnel next to the radar operator's flight station, and confirmed that he had set the "select-train" switch on the intervalometer switch (this device spaced the fall of the bombs from the Avenger's bomb bay) to "train" and moved the station distributor (this device controlled the sequence in which the bombs would fall) to "station 9." Westmoreland reported over the intercom that the armament panel was set and the bomb bay doors were open and clear.

Will acknowledged Westmoreland's reply with a curt, "Roger," and instructed him to move the main armament switch from "safe" to "armed." Westmoreland shifted the "arm-safe" lever on the main armament panel to "armed—nose and tail" with no fuse delay, and confirmed that the armament panel was now hot. Will again acknowledged Westmoreland's report and flipped his own cockpit armament selector switch, labeled "bomb-torpedo-R.P.," to the "bomb" position.

Intrepid's radio call sign was Lucky or Lucky Base. Strike 2 Charlie hadn't completed its first circuit of the holding pattern before the flight leader broadcast over the tactical frequency the customary command, "Lucky Strike Two Charlie, Lucky Strike Two Charlie. Check all switches and begin a high-speed run." The fight was on.

Will glimpsed VF-18's Hellcats nosing over high above him in two-plane sections, streaking toward Babelthuap. The fighters chased one another downward, weaving from side to side like children playing crack-the-whip. As the last of the Hellcats descended below 10,500 feet, VB-18's flight leader rolled up on one wing and shoved his nose into a near-vertical dive; thirteen Helldivers plummeted after him. With their barrel-shaped fuselages, thick wings, and oversize vertical tails, the Helldivers appeared to be falling out of the sky like cormorants plunging after prey. Riley's Avengers were next.

Will flipped the red master switch on his cockpit armament console to the closed position. This was the final step in the ordnance arming process. Will's bombs would fall as soon as he squeezed the bomb button on his control stick. He glanced at the emergency bomb release handle on the lower instrument panel. He could find the release handle blindfolded, but he imprinted its location again in his mind to avoid fumbling for it in the final seconds of the bombing run. The Avenger's electrical release was quirky and didn't always work. Will's practice was to pull the manual bomb release handle in the cockpit as a backup to the electrical bomb release.

As the last of the Helldivers dropped from sight, Riley waggled his wings and shoved the nose of his Avenger into a thirty-five-degree dive. Will and Savage mimicked the movements of Riley's airplane exactly and pushed over with him.

The pushover was a negative-gravity maneuver. Will and his crewmen floated upward for an instant, forced against their lap belts; their foreheads grew warm and tingly as negative gravity flooded their brains with blood. The Avenger's airframe creaked and popped, and the Klaxon horn that warned of unlocked wings honked loudly until the airplane stabilized in the descent and positive gravity took over once more. The pushover was exhilarating, like cresting the high point of a roller coaster and starting down.

The two Avengers accelerated quickly to three hundred knots, descending side by side toward Babelthuap at twenty-five hundred feet per minute. Will took his eyes off Riley's Avenger for an instant and glanced forward through his windscreen at the target. The enemy airfield was a sand-colored rectangle bulldozed from the jungle. It occupied much of the southern half of Babelthuap; the verdant foothills of Ngerchelchuus bordered the airfield on the north side. The main runway, paved with finely crushed rock or concrete, ran east–west across the clearing; aircraft revetments and a few boxy buildings, some still smoldering from earlier air strikes, ringed the perimeter of the field. Wisps of whitish smoke, the residue of earlier strikes, drifted upward like the plumes of dying campfires.

Will had expected Lieutenant Riley to zig and zag during the bombing run in an effort to disrupt the aim of enemy antiaircraft gunners, and Lieutenant Riley didn't disappoint him. Riley snapped his torpedo bomber violently back and forth at irregular intervals, and Will struggled to keep his bucking airplane in place. Will focused intently on the right side of Riley's Avenger, constantly working his flight controls to hold the proper step-down and stay on the bearing line. Small details about Riley's airplane registered in Will's peripheral vision: The wheel tucked into Riley's starboard landing-gear well leaked red hydraulic fluid from its brake assembly; the slipstream blew a drizzle of engine oil aft from Riley's engine cowling, soiling the white undersides of his fuselage; ordnancemen had chalked messages to Hirohito, probably obscene, on the lower tier of slate-colored bombs clustered in Riley's bomb bay. (Will couldn't read the messages; his eyes were good but not that good.) The air had grown warmer and more turbulent as the three Avengers descended. Will had shut his canopy side panels for the attack, and the combination of warm air and sunshine streaming through the Plexiglas overwhelmed his Avenger's ventilation system. Will broke into a sweat, and beads of perspiration dripped into the cups of his flying goggles.

Riley's three Avengers closed rapidly on their target. Will glimpsed fresh geysers of gray and black smoke erupting over the airfield, the handiwork of VB-18's Helldivers. Seen from a distance, the Helldivers' bombs exploded as soundless puffs, as if the whole scene of destruction were a film without a sound track. Dust and smoke from the bombs drifted north toward Ngerchelchuus, giving its foothills the look of a smoldering pile of leaves.

Will had kept one eye on his rapidly unwinding altimeter during the descent. As the three airplanes plunged below thirty-five hundred feet, Riley slowly raised his Avenger's nose and arrested his section's glide. After a beat, Riley waggled his wings and Will saw the first of twelve finned canisters drop from the belly of his leader's Avenger. Will instantly pickled his own bomb-release button and simultaneously yanked upward on his emergency release handle. Savage released his bombs at the same time, and thirty-six hundred pounds of ordnance from the three Avengers filled the air. The bombs seemed to hesitate for an instant, wobbling in the slipstream as if gathering their bearings, and then nosed downward toward the earth.

The pullout was a positive-gravity maneuver. An Avenger traveling at three hundred knots is limited structurally to positive acceleration of no more than 4.8 times the force of gravity; if a pilot executes too abrupt a pullout at too high an airspeed he may overstress the airplane and cause structural failure. Riley's pullout was smooth and steady, well below the structural limit but still two or three times the force of gravity. As Will eased back on his control stick, the positive acceleration forced him into his seat and his arms and legs grew heavy; as he had been trained to do, he grunted and tightened his stomach muscles to keep blood from draining from his head. The three Avengers continued their descent side by side even as their noses started up, their momentum carrying them below the bomb release altitude. At about two thousand feet, they bottomed out their glide.

The kettledrum roll of thirty-six hundred-pound bombs detonating as they hit the ground overtook the retreating Avengers, and the shock wave of the explosions passed beneath Riley's section like a sharp bump in the road. Christman, who had ridden backward on the bombing run—this was akin to sledding backward down a bobsled run—was rewarded with an unobstructed view of the resulting fire and smoke. The gunner keyed his intercom button and yelled something like, "Take that, you sons of bitches!"

Lieutenant Riley, still jinking left and right to avoid enemy antiaircraft fire, led his three-plane section due west at high speed. He intended to rendezvous out over the ocean with his second Avenger division, which at that moment was somewhere behind him on its glide-bombing run, and join up with the balance of the strike group for the return flight to *Intrepid*. But suddenly and unavoidably, Riley's three torpedo bombers penetrated a dense cloud of smoke produced by the earlier attacks of the dive-bombers. A mix of odors flooded into Will's cockpit: the burned-firecracker smell of Explosive D (the navy's primary bomb-making material), whiffs of pulverized concrete and charred wood, and the chlorophyll smell of shattered vegetation, like the smell of mowed grass. Riley's blue-and-white-painted Avenger, which had been Will's singular lodestar during the bombing run, flickered out of sight.

Flying formation on Riley now became impossible and dangerous. To avoid a collision with his lead, Will yanked right on his Avenger's control stick and turned to a compass heading forty-five degrees off Riley's heading. Will hadn't anticipated flying instruments on his first bombing run. His Avenger bounced and yawed in the murk; his artificial horizon jiggled in the turbulence, and the altimeter and rate-of-climb indicator shot up and down erratically. Will worked the controls, trying to keep his Avenger upright. Then, as unexpectedly as his Avenger had entered the smoke, he bolted into sunlight and smoother air.

Beneath Will's airplane lay the western half of Babelthuap, an area thickly forested with ironwood and banyan trees. The emerald folds of Mount Ngerchelchuus sloped down to a meandering beach of glistening white sand. Farther west, the blue-green waters of Palau's barrier reef extended as far north and south as Will could see, the pale fingers of the reefs entwined with the darker blue waters of the deeper ocean. The sea shimmered in the sunlight. The tropical panorama was breathtakingly beautiful, picturesque as a postcard, but Will could not admire it. He had to rejoin Riley. He spied two Avengers orbiting west of the island; these were Riley and Savage, waiting for him. Farther out to sea, he saw the rest of the strike group waiting for the Avengers to catch up.

Drenched in sweat, Will slid back his canopy side panels and shoved his goggles to his forehead. He still had dangerous work ahead in landing his Avenger back aboard *Intrepid*, but he allowed himself a moment of self-congratulation.

He had completed his first real bombing mission and not screwed up. He had stayed glued to Riley's side, and he and his crew had dropped their bombs on cue. They had not embarrassed themselves and they had punished the Japs. A grin spread irrepressibly across his face. This was what he had trained for; he had accomplished what he had set out to do. He pointed his airplane in Riley's direction and headed for the poststrike rendezvous.

Air Group 18 launched a total of five strikes—five deck loads, in carrier jargon—against Babelthuap on September 7. At the end of the day, El Gropo judged that the available targets on the island did not warrant the expenditure of further bombs and ammunition. Nevertheless, Mitscher and Bogan ordered up one more strike, Strike 2 Able, for the morning of September 8. Ben Riley again led a division of eight VT-18 Avengers over Babelthuap, and Will Fletcher and John Savage again flew as members of Riley's division. VT-18's assigned target was an oil and ammunition dump on the western shore of Babelthuap, not far from the airfield the squadron had bombed the day before. Riley's Avengers were each loaded with a single two-thousand-pound bomb.

The strike began inauspiciously. For the second consecutive day, only seven of VT-18's eight Avengers were able to rendezvous off the carrier. Ensign Don Morris's engine began detonating after takeoff; he could not gain altitude and was forced to land back aboard *Intrepid* with his two-thousand-pound bomb still shackled in the bomb bay. Maintenance crews could find nothing wrong with Morris's engine and blamed the engine detonation on poor pilot technique in managing the airplane's throttle, mixture, and supercharger. Morris's mistake was exactly the sort of error Will dreaded.

After Ben Riley made the first bombing pass over the ammunition dump, Strike 2 Able turned fatal. Riley had dropped his bomb and circled back to observe John Savage make the second bombing run. Riley saw Savage approach the target in a shallow twenty-five-degree dive, and he feared Savage's approach was much too low. Riley couldn't warn his pilot in time and watched in disbelief as Savage released his two-thousand-pound bomb at about eight hundred feet, roughly a thousand feet below the recommended altitude for a bomb of that weight. The explosion instantly disintegrated the empennage of Savage's Avenger, and the tailless, uncontrollable airplane spun in like a boomerang roughly a hundred yards offshore, killing Savage and his two crewmen, Aviation

Ordnanceman Second Class Ora H. Sharninghouse of Findlay, Ohio, and Aviation Radioman Second Class Albert P. Rybarczyk of St. Joseph, Michigan. Riley and two wingmen circled the spot where Savage's Avenger had crashed, but they found only a patch of water discolored by hydraulic fluid and a small amount of debris, including a deflated life raft floating on the surface.

The return flight to *Intrepid* was nearly fatal for Riley and his crew. When still fifty miles from the carrier, Riley's wingman yelled at him over the radio that his Avenger was on fire. Riley barked back to shut up and observe radio silence, but his instrument gauges told him his engine oil pressure was falling rapidly. He descended and made a forced water landing while he still had engine power. The force of impact jammed shut his canopy side panes and Riley had difficulty prying them open. The Avenger wallowed on the surface for nearly two minutes while Riley struggled with his canopy; he finally pried open one side and escaped with his crew to the airplane's three-man life raft before the aircraft sank in more than twenty-four fathoms of water. His wingmen had relayed the raft's position back to *Intrepid*, and the destroyer *Law* pulled Riley and his crew from the sea.

In the destroyer's wardroom that night, the tin-can skipper treated Riley to several rounds of medicinal rye whiskey, enough medicine that Riley had trouble picking out the skipper from the other officers around the dinner table. When Riley returned to *Intrepid* the next day, he recommended his fellow Avenger pilots jettison their cockpit side panes entirely before ditching to minimize the risk of being trapped in the cockpit of a sinking airplane.

John Savage's death reinforced three fundamental rules that Van Antwerp and Bud Williams had preached from the earliest days of VT-18's tactical training, rules that Savage undoubtedly knew but had inexplicably disregarded: A heavier, more powerful bomb requires a higher release altitude; pay close attention to your minimum release altitude; and do not fixate on your target. None of VT-18's pilots judged Savage too harshly. The lost pilot had been a superior naval aviator, and his buddies all realized they could have made the same fatal mistakes under the right circumstances. VT-18's pilots, Will Fletcher especially, were nevertheless shaken by the loss of Savage. Grief pervaded the ready room that night, tinged with some bitterness. El Gropo had declared Babelthuap a waste of bombs only the day before, and the deaths of Savage and his crew over an undefended oil and ammunition dump seemed disproportionate and unnecessary. Savage's friends, Will among them, sadly gathered up the lost pilot's personal effects and packed them in a wooden footlocker for shipment home. Though he didn't drink alcohol himself, Ben St. John purchased Savage's share of the squadron liquor mess and placed the money in the footlocker for Savage's next of kin.

VT-18 had lost two pilots, one dead, and four aircrewmen, all dead, in less than two weeks of operations. Five had been killed out of a squadron of about one hundred men, and none was dead as a result of enemy fire. Task Force 38's next theater of operations would be the eastern Philippines, where Ernie Allen had predicted heavy Japanese air opposition and intense antiaircraft fire over the targets. Some pilots wondered aloud: "If things are this bad on group gropes and relatively unopposed bombing runs, what will things be like when the Japs vigorously contest VT-18's attacks?"

They were about to find out.

CHAPTER SIX

IN THE VISAYAS

★ ★ ★ ★ ★

On September 7, 1944, the same day Will Fletcher flew his first combat mission against Babelthuap, Emperor Hirohito issued the eighty-fifth official decree of his reign, known as the 85th Imperial Rescript. The emperor's rescript acknowledged that the American offensive against Japan had intensified and the war situation had grown more critical. Like the official statement Admiral Toyoda had issued on assuming command of the Japanese Combined Fleet, the imperial rescript again reflected the unshakable belief of Japan's military government in decisive battle as the pathway to victory, notwithstanding the bitter experience of Midway and the Battle of the Philippine Sea. The emperor decreed:

> Today our imperial state is indeed challenged to reach powerfully for a
> decisive victory. You who are leaders of our people must now renew
> your tenacity and, uniting your resolve, smash our enemies' evil pur-
> poses, thereby furthering forever our imperial destiny.

Admiral Toyoda intended to smash the Americans' evil purposes in the Philippines. The American amphibious landings in the Philippines, regardless of where and when they occurred, would be supported by enormous numbers of heavily laden transports and support vessels. The concentrated presence of so many ships and men presented a prime opportunity for the Imperial Navy to inflict great carnage on the enemy and achieve a decisive victory. The stakes were high. If the Americans succeeded in retaking the Philippines, Japan's shipping lanes to the south, already constricted by American submarines, would be severed completely, and Japan's war machine would be starved of oil, rubber, rice, and other necessities. As Admiral Toyoda himself later explained his willingness to sacrifice the Japanese navy to preserve the Philippines, "There would be no sense in saving the [Japanese] fleet at the expense of the loss of the Philippines."

Although the Japanese navy possessed sufficient numbers of surface warships for a credible defense of the Philippines, it lacked adequate air forces. Warplanes were necessary not only to provide air cover for surface combatants such as *Musashi* and *Yamato*, but to carry out aerial bombing and torpedo attacks and grapple with Admiral Halsey's astonishing number of aircraft carriers and fighter planes. Because of interservice rivalries and divisions, Combined Fleet could not rely on the air forces of the Imperial Japanese Army to support naval operations, and Japanese naval air forces, which consisted of both carrier-based and land-based aviation units, had been decimated. Vice Admiral Jisaburo Ozawa's Mobile Fleet had lost more than two-thirds of its carrier-based planes in the Battle of the Philippine Sea, and Vice Admiral Kimpei Teraoka's 1st Air Fleet had lost nearly half of its land-based naval aircraft and airmen during the same battle.

After the failure of the A-Go operation, Admiral Toyoda had reorganized 1st Air Fleet and attempted to build up naval air strength in the Philippines. He had transferred surviving aviation units to Luzon and the Central Visayas and directed Admiral Teraoka to convert Philippine-area training bases into combat bases. Between August and early September 1944, Admiral Teraoka assembled a naval air force of over five hundred warplanes in the Philippines, consisting of day and night fighters, bombers, and reconnaissance and transport aircraft. Many of these were the newest models, fresh from the factories of Mitsubishi and Nakajima. By early September, roughly 280 of Teraoka's warplanes were operational and ready to fight, although most of his naval aviators were woefully undertrained and inexperienced when compared with their predecessors who had perished off the Marianas. Admiral Teraoka stationed his refurbished air groups primarily at Clark Field, which was General MacArthur's former air base near Manila, at air bases near Legaspi in southern Luzon, at Davao City on Mindanao, and on the islands of Cebu and Leyte.

Task Force 38 abandoned the waters around the Palaus midday on September 8 and zigzagged west toward Mindanao, one of the principal islands of the eastern Philippines. Aboard *Intrepid*, Lieutenant Commander Van Antwerp and Lieutenant Commander Allen assembled VT-18's pilots in the ready room and briefed them on Air Group 18's near-term assignments and objectives. Air Group 18, they reported, would conduct a series of bombing raids against Japanese air bases and port facilities on the eastern coast of Mindanao beginning on September 9. Later in the week, Task Force 38 would steam north and Air Group 18 would bomb airfields on Leyte and Cebu. The primary objective of 3rd Fleet's carrier raids was to destroy Japanese airpower in advance of any attempt by General MacArthur to retake the Philippines. But Admiral Halsey also had a parallel objective, one that mirrored the Japanese desire for decisive battle. Ever the aggressive naval commander—on taking command of the South Pacific Area, he had famously exhorted his sailors and Marines, "Kill Japs. Kill Japs. Kill more Japs"—Halsey hoped the sudden appearance of Task Force 38 off the eastern Philippines would entice the main Japanese fleet to do battle. Lieutenant Commander Allen expected strong air opposition over the Philippines, and he warned his attentive listeners that there would be precious few days of rest ahead.

Allen distributed to each of VT-18's pilots and aircrewmen a silk map of the Central Visayas, the region of the Philippines that lies between Luzon and Mindanao. The map, printed by the Royal Australian Air Force in waterproof ink, depicted lower Luzon and the Central Visayas in topographical detail. The map marked the principal towns and villages and noted the rotational frequency of lighthouses and the distances at which these navigational beacons could be seen from the sea. The map was not intended for navigational purposes but for survival, to help downed pilots avoid capture. Allen handed his aviators a hundred Philippine pesos and instructed them to avoid towns and villages and seek the sanctuary of Philippine guerrilla forces in the countryside if they were forced down. Catholic priests and nuns, he advised, were likely to be sympathetic to the Allied cause.

Third Fleet's Task Force 38 was designated a "fast carrier task force," and

Vice Admiral Mitscher's huge formation of aircraft carriers and escorts justified the name by steaming through the night at twenty to twenty-five knots. *Intrepid* rattled and hummed as she kept station. Inside her hangar bay, her air department worked around the clock to prepare eighty warplanes for a dawn launch. By sunrise on September 9, *Intrepid* had closed to within eighty miles of Mindanao, and at six-oh-two a.m. she launched the first of four deck loads against Japanese air bases on Mindanao.

Air Group 18's first target of the day was the Japanese airfield at Matina, which lay about five miles inland from Davao City, a seaport town situated in the northwest corner of Davao Gulf off Mindanao. Commander Ellis himself led the strike group, which was comprised of fifteen VF-18 fighters, eight VB-18 dive-bombers, and eight VT-18 torpedo bombers. Bud Williams led the Avenger division on the strike. Four of his torpedo bombers had been armed with twelve hundred-pound fragmentation bombs designed to destroy enemy airplanes and personnel on the ground, and four had been armed with a single two-thousand-pound general-purpose bomb designed to crater the enemy's runways and render them useless. Squatty Vaughn led one of the heavy Avenger sections, and Will Fletcher flew off Squatty's wing.

Admiral Teraoka's engineers had constructed the Matina airfield in the middle of a prewar coconut plantation and surrounded it with antiaircraft gun positions. The runways were easy enough to spot from the air. They had been constructed of concrete and stone, and they shone brightly in the sunlight, their wide straightaways accentuated by the bordering palm trees. The taxiways were less obvious, meandering through rows of coconut palms like country lanes or cow paths. The enemy antiaircraft positions and the airplanes on the ground were virtually impossible to detect from the air without prior photographic reconnaissance. The Japanese had concealed their gun positions in the trees and sheltered their warplanes in widely dispersed revetments camouflaged with netting and brush. To minimize his strike group's exposure to enemy antiaircraft fire, El Gropo approached Matina over the sparsely populated ground northwest of Davao City. Notwithstanding Ellis's precautions, Japanese antiaircraft fire intensified as the strike group drew near, and black kernels of smoke peppered the sky above the Matina airfield. Allen's warning echoed in the attackers' heads; the Philippine raids would be far different from the Palau raids.

VB-18's Helldivers attacked first, nosing over from eleven thousand feet with thousand-pound general-purpose and fragmentation bombs. Bud Williams's Avengers attacked second, beginning shallow glides from twelve thousand feet and releasing their bombs at about ten thousand feet in straight and level flight. Ellis, who orbited high above the airfield as the Avengers went in, noted with satisfaction that Williams and Vaughn placed their two-thousand-pound bombs dead center on the runway, and that another two-thousand-pound bomb obliterated a gun position. Half of VT-18's fragmentation bombs fell squarely within the Japanese aircraft revetment areas, but two VT-18 pilots were unable to release their payload over the target due to improper bomb loading and suffered the ignominy of jettisoning their ordnance harmlessly into the water. To the disappointment of VF-18's Hellcat pilots, whom Ellis had enjoined to remain at altitude to protect the dive-bombers and torpedo bombers, no Japanese fighters rose up to challenge the strike group. All thirty-one of Ellis's aircraft returned safely to *Intrepid*, but two Avenger pilots and one Helldiver pilot made the unsettling discovery after landing that their airplanes had been perforated with shrapnel. Will was one of the Avenger pilots. He and his crew poked curiously at the three-inch holes in the tail of their airplane and mused about what might have happened if the shells had hit twenty feet farther forward. The holed Helldiver was piloted by Lieutenant Junior Grade Andy Anderson, who, after also taking a thirty-seven-millimeter hit on one of the first bombing missions over Babelthuap, could be forgiven for thinking he was a magnet for antiaircraft fire.

Air Group 18 not only returned to Matina for a second strike later in the day, but also conducted two bombing raids against the Japanese air base at Daliao, which was another coconut-plantation airfield close by Davao City. The raids on Daliao were similar to the strikes on Matina but without the excitement of enemy antiaircraft fire. VT-18's Avengers attacked with a mixture of runway-busting two-thousand-pound bombs and lighter fragmentation bombs. As over Matina, no Japanese fighters contested the air.

Nearly every torpedo-bomber crew in VT-18 participated in the daylong action over Matina and Daliao, and some pilots, like Kenny Barden and Will Fletcher, flew twice. In VT-18's ready room that night, there was a sense of relief that none of the masses of Japanese fighters that American intelligence had predicted would defend the islands had shown up, but there was also puzzlement among the torpeckers. Was their intelligence about Jap capabilities really that poor, or were the Japs up to something?

Relations between Air Group 18 and *Intrepid*'s air department chafed a bit after the first raid on Matina. The source of the friction was photographs. Lieutenant Junior Grade R. C. "Beatle" Beatley, an F6F pilot, returned to the carrier at nine a.m. with excellent reconnaissance photos of Matina, which clearly showed the location of fifteen Japanese fighters in revetments. The pictures were developed and available by ten thirty, but they didn't reach air group intelligence until after the third strike had launched at one fifteen p.m. Lieutenant George Race had pleaded with the ship's photographic officer for copies, but had been rebuffed with the comment that Captain Bolger and the air officer ran the ship, and air group intelligence would get prints after Captain Bolger and the air officer, if and when the photo lab had time. Ellis complained to Bolger and the two commanders soon worked out a system for obtaining pictures in a timely manner.

On September 10, Davao City itself became Air Group 18's target. The objective was to destroy the city's business and commercial center and knock out port facilities. Commander Ellis's ordnance of choice for attacking Davao's city center was hundred-pound incendiary bombs, a weapon that Air Group 18 had never used previously. As Lieutenant Race trumpeted to Air Group 18's pilots and aircrew, "Burn Davao" was the order of the day. Commander Ellis assigned six Avengers, each loaded with twelve incendiary bombs, to attack Davao's business district, and he detailed eleven Helldivers, each loaded with thousand-pound general-purpose bombs, to execute dive-bombing runs on the piers, warehouses, and storage tanks that were located at the city's Santa Ana shipyards. In his preflight briefing, Ellis explicitly ordered his pilots not to drop their bombs on Davao City's residential districts or on the city's hospital.

Bud Williams led the Avenger incendiary attack and Will Fletcher was among the pilots who accompanied him. Will knew the Imperial Army and Navy employed or impressed Filipino civilians of all walks of life to support Japan's military occupation of the Philippines. He understood that his midmorning incendiary attack would catch many civilians at work in Davao City's shops and offices. But Will accepted without question El Gropo's distinction between killing Filipino civilians in their homes and sickbeds and killing them while they worked for their Japanese overlords. He viewed their deaths as regrettable, but necessary. Enemy troops had expropriated Davao City and its port facilities to sustain Japan's war effort against America and its allies. The Japanese occupiers must be destroyed. Any Filipino civilians who worked with Japanese soldiers and sailors, whether by choice or by compulsion, must share the fate of their Japanese masters. It would be death by association, but the war could not be fought with too many fine distinctions, and air warfare by its very nature made no fine distinctions.

El Gropo, flying a Hellcat, led the first strike on Davao City. Bud Williams's Avengers pushed over first from fourteen thousand feet and dropped half of their firebombs on the Santa Ana dock area in a glide-bombing attack. Then, in two plane sections, Williams's Avengers swept back and forth across the three principal streets of Davao's business district at a thousand feet, dropping the balance of their incendiaries. In his low-level run, Will detected the first antiaircraft bullets he knew were intended for his airplane. Intermittent dashes of burning light rose up at him from guns the Japanese had concealed in wooded areas on the edge of town. Will guessed the Japanese were firing twenty-millimeter impact shells with tracers. He felt or heard nothing from the guns; the bright dots of deadly light drifted well below him or sprayed far ahead. Fortunately, the Japanese gunners did not seem particularly skilled. Ellis's dive-bombers rolled in next to pummel the dockyards, but were forced to glide-bomb because of the smoke.

As his torpedo and dive-bombers departed Davao City, Commander Ellis recorded three tremendous fires burning in Davao's business district, and heavy clouds of smoke billowing up as high as eight thousand feet. Davao's industrial section and dock areas, Ellis wrote, "appear to be virtually gutted." Before returning to the ship, Ellis also circled high over Matina and Daliao, targets of the day before. He confirmed that both airfields were "still well cratered" and "apparently inoperative." When he got back aboard *Intrepid*, El Gropo canceled the last two strikes of the day.

On September 11, Task Force 38 shifted north two hundred nautical miles to the waters east of the Central Visayas. That same evening, VT-18's pilots gathered in the ready room to receive another briefing from Ernie Allen on the expected course of operations. For the next three days, Allen reported, Task Force 38 would bomb Japanese airfields on Samar, Leyte, Cebu, and Luzon, and perhaps raid as far north as Manila. The task force would then return to the Palau Islands to provide air cover for the U.S. Army's invasion of Angaur. Air Group

18 would fly up to four combat missions per day. As at Mindanao, the objective of Task Force 38's raids in the Visayas was to destroy Japanese airpower and draw out the Jap fleet for a "showdown battle." Barden penciled ambiguously in his diary, "Manila—here we come." His words didn't reveal whether he dreaded the possibility or welcomed it.

El Gropo scheduled three air strikes against Tacloban and San Pablo airfields on Leyte for September 12, and Ernie Allen once again predicted strong air opposition. Barden flew the first strike, Strike 2 Able, his Avenger armed with twelve hundred-pound incendiary bombs and four five-inch rockets. He arrived over his target, the San Pablo Airfield on Leyte, at about eight fifteen a.m., together with the crews of seven other Avengers, four VF-18 fighters, and eleven VB-18 dive-bombers. But to Barden's disappointment, there was very little on which to expend his Avenger's ordnance. The San Pablo Airfield appeared to be nothing but a farmer's field, a "large green pasture with shallow revetments scattered about." Strike 2 Able encountered no air opposition and no antiaircraft fire. Barden dropped his bombs on some rickety buildings near the airstrip, and headed home for *Intrepid*.

On the strike group's return to the carrier, Lieutenant Commander Van Antwerp, the Avenger division leader, spied a hundred-ton Japanese freighter off the southern coast of Samar. He detailed Barden and three other Avengers to attack the ship with rockets. As he descended on the freighter, Barden excitedly switched his armament selector switch to "R.P.," the rocket selector position. To Barden's relief, his rockets did not fire prematurely or whirl away from his Avenger like cheap Chinese fireworks, and he was able to place at least one rocket directly on the freighter. Barden's rocket penetrated the stern of the ship and caused an explosion and fire that, Van Antwerp later reported, "doubtless damaged the ship seriously."

Intrepid's strikes 2 Baker through 2 Dog were planned as bombing raids against Tacloban Airfield on Leyte and Le Hug Airfield near Cebu City, and against Japanese ships anchored inside Cebu Harbor. These were the first of Air Group 18's air strikes to target enemy shipping specifically.

Japanese cargo ships plied constantly between and among the Philippine islands and the Japanese home islands, carrying the men and material necessary to sustain the Japanese war effort and export the spoils of occupation, such as rice, hemp, and coconut oil. U.S. Naval Intelligence had code-named Japanese merchantmen and classified them by type and displacement. "Fox Able" was a Japanese freighter displacing more than six thousand tons, while "Fox Baker" was a freighter of lesser displacement. Tankers were code-named "Sugar" and classified by displacement in the same manner. Thus, a "Sugar Able" was a tanker displacing more than six thousand tons, and a "Sugar Dog" was a small tanker of a thousand tons or less.

On Strike 2 Charlie, Bud Williams's seven-plane Avenger division, which included torpedo bombers flown by Squatty Vaughn and Will Fletcher, joined with VB-18 in sinking two small freighters and damaging five others in Cebu Harbor with bombs. (The small, thin-hulled enemy freighters did not justify the expenditure of torpedoes.) By the end of the day, Air Group 18's pilots had upped their tally, claiming to have sunk in conjunction with carrier planes from other air groups two Sugar Ables, three Sugar Charlies, and four Sugar Dogs. They also claimed to have seriously damaged two more Fox Dogs, a Fox Charlie, and a Sugar Dog, to have "left sinking" one Sugar Able, and to have "probably sunk" another Fox Dog. Air group intelligence officers kept careful track of tonnage sunk; the air group's cumulative "tare" number was posted on *Intrepid*'s scoreboard, which was a large billboard in the hangar bay that tallied the air group's strike results in terms of enemy aircraft destroyed and ships sunk.

Despite his air group's successes against enemy merchantmen, El Gropo concluded that the day's results were "disappointing." Japanese fighters had not engaged, and if the enemy did not engage he could not be destroyed. Several pilots had also broken formation to strafe small native boats, and Commander Ellis "read them the riot act." He had given his pilots strict instructions not to strafe small boats unless they were clearly motor-driven. "Filipinos in sailboats are our friends," El Gropo likely bellowed, "and you may be goddamned glad to see a goddamned Filipino sailboat someday." El Gropo closed his aircraft action report for September 12 with the observation "The Japs seem strangely uninterested in combat."

Commander Ellis's mood brightened the next day when Air Group 18 encountered its first Japanese fighter opposition over Negros, an island in the Visayan Sea twenty miles west of Cebu. "Success at last!" Barden crowed in his diary on the evening of September 13. "Hit Negros today and found Jap planes galore—both on the ground and in the air."

The fighter encounter had come as something of a surprise to both the Japanese and the Americans. El Gropo had dispatched twelve Helldivers and six Avengers, escorted by eight Hellcats, to bomb and strafe Japanese airfields in northern Negros. The pilots assigned to the Negros strike—Will was not among the torpedo-plane pilots scheduled to fly that day, but Barden and his buddy Joe Rubin were—had received no prior photo reconnaissance of the airfields. They knew only that the Japanese had established multiple air bases in the vicinity of the city of Fabrica on the northern tip of the island. Lieutenant Commander Van Antwerp led Air Group 18's strike group, including VT-18's six-plane Avenger division. When the attackers arrived over the target area, they found the ground partially obscured by clouds. Through a break in the clouds, the leader of the Helldiver division, Lieutenant Commander Mark Eslick, located what he believed to be Silay Airfield. He pushed over into his dive-bombing run from fourteen thousand feet, and his fellow dive-bomber pilots dutifully rolled in after him, plummeting one by one through the cloud deck.

Van Antwerp's torpedo bombers, incapable of diving as steeply as the Helldivers, could not attack through the same hole in the clouds. Van Antwerp tarried at ten thousand feet, waiting for an opening in the clouds that would permit a more sedate forty-degree glide-bombing run on a nearby airfield he believed to be Bacolod. As his Avengers orbited above the target area, a lone Mitsubishi A6M fighter, known as a Zeke or Zero, popped out of the clouds from below and set up for a gunnery run on Van Antwerp's formation from behind. The leader of VF-18's Hellcat division, Lieutenant Cecil Harris, who was weaving protectively above the Avengers at fourteen thousand feet, spied the approaching Zeke. Harris left two Hellcats overhead to deal with any other threats and descended rapidly with three Hellcats on his wing to intercept the Zeke. (Harris's covering division was down to six F6Fs because Harris had earlier detached two Hellcats on a photographic mission.)

Seeing four Hellcats diving on him, the Zeke pilot prudently broke off his attack and rolled back into the cloud deck to escape. Harris and his three F6Fs pursued. All four Hellcats plunged through the base of the clouds at high speed and overshot their prey, but they discovered to their surprise ten to fifteen enemy Zekes "milling about" at twenty-five hundred feet. The Hellcat pilots found themselves directly above the Fabrica airstrip in fighter heaven. A "general melee" ensued, with Hellcats rolling in and among the gaggle of enemy aircraft. The Japanese fighter pilots appeared to be interested only in escaping the Hellcats. Some of the enemy pilots clearly did know what to do. Others engaged in purely defensive maneuvers, such as loops, split "S"s, and slow, tight turns. Chasing the Zekes flying at 180 to 200 knots, the faster Hellcats repeatedly overran their targets and had difficulty maneuvering into firing position on the tighter-turning Japanese fighters. But Harris and his wingmen adjusted quickly. Within minutes of dropping through the clouds in pursuit of the lone Zeke, VF-18's four Hellcats had downed eight enemy fighters. Harris alone had shot down four.

The attacks on Negros were not without cost. After VT-18's pilots completed their glide-bombing runs on Bacolod, they strafed a third air base about ten miles west of Fabrica, where Van Antwerp had observed the presence of aircraft dispersal pens. Van Antwerp believed the airfield to be Alicante Airfield. One of the Hellcat pilots whom Lieutenant Harris had left behind to provide fighter protection cover for Van Antwerp's torpedo bombers, Lieutenant James B. "Jim" Neighbours, joined in with the Avenger pilots who were strafing enemy aircraft parked on the ground. Neighbours had just leveled off from his strafing run at fifteen hundred feet when enemy antiaircraft bullets severed the tail of his Hellcat. Neighbours had no time to bail out; his Hellcat tumbled to the ground and exploded.

One of VT-18's Avenger crews suffered the same fate over Alicante as Lieutenant Neighbours. Ensign Daniel Laner of Marcola, Oregon, having dropped his bombs on Bacolod, was strafing Alicante when his Avenger was hit. Perhaps Laner was caught up in the excitement of the moment; perhaps he was simply too eager. Whatever the reason, he violated squadron doctrine and strafed the airfield at only three hundred feet, which was twelve hundred feet below the minimum strafing altitude prescribed for a defended target. Flak struck the right wing of Laner's Avenger and his torpedo bomber burst into flames. The aircraft wobbled through the sky for a instant and then slammed onto the runway and burned, killing Laner and his crewmen, Aviation Radioman Third Class Alfred B. Lankford of Seaford, Delaware, and Aviation Ordnanceman Third Class Francis R. Krantz, of Cross Plains, Wisconsin. Van Antwerp was both saddened and angered at the loss. He had taught Laner better, yet Laner had exposed himself unnecessarily. On the return flight to *Intrepid*, Van Antwerp nearly lost a second plane and crew. Joe Rubin's hydraulic system failed, which meant that Rubin's gun chargers were inoperative and he could not lower his landing gear or flaps hydraulically. Barden flew off Rubin's wing and nursed his buddy home with the welcome help of two of Harris's fighters.

Intrepid continued her air suppression raids, launching a fighter sweep and a bombing mission against small airfields in northern Fabrica on September 14. Bud Williams led a division of six Avengers on the bombing strike, each armed with either twelve hundred-pound fragmentation bombs or twelve general-purpose bombs and a full load of machine gun ammunition. Williams found no suitable targets over Fabrica for his bombs—the crude airfields looked like cow pastures hurriedly reconfigured to accommodate airplanes—and instead ordered his pilots to execute strafing runs on what appeared to be aircraft revetments around the periphery of the airfields. The gunnery runs were of indeterminate value. On their return to *Intrepid*, Air Group 18's pilots reported that the Japanese had camouflaged their parked aircraft with nets that stretched from the trailing edge of the airplane's wing to the tip of the airplane's tail. The netting made it difficult for attacking pilots to detect enemy aircraft during a strafing run and gave a parked airplane a false appearance of previous damage.

Notwithstanding Lieutenant Harris's singular success over the Fabrica airstrip earlier in the week, VF-18's fighter pilots began to grumble that "routine four-a-day fighter-bomber-torpedo strikes against nonspecific targets" were "a waste of power and bombs." They groused that they were tied up in escort duty and should be freed up instead for strafing or fighting. Most of the Hellcat drivers had yet to tally a kill, and they lusted for one. But the fighter boys would have to wait. The 1st Marine Division was scheduled to invade Peleliu on September 15, and heavy aircraft carriers were needed to provide air support for the amphibious landings. In the early evening hours of September 14, *Intrepid* pointed her prow to the east and set a base course for Peleliu in company with Task Force 38.

Admiral Halsey's first series of fast carrier raids against the Philippines was over.

As Task Force 38 steamed east toward the Palaus, which was roughly a twenty-four-hour journey, the recurring theme of conversation in Air Group 18's ready rooms—aside from the usual staples of conversation: women, poker winnings and losses, baseball, news from the hometown, favorite foods and drink, and the declining quality of shipboard food—was how surprisingly unaggressive the Japanese had been. *Intrepid*'s pilots had destroyed scores of Japanese warplanes on the ground but only a handful in the sky. The few Japanese fighter pilots whom Air Group 18 had encountered in the air seemed unwilling to press home their attack. Most of the enemy pilots had behaved in the air as if they were bewildered or incompetent. Japanese antiaircraft fire, while deadly against low-flying aircraft, had been largely ineffective, and Japanese warships had been absent completely. Although *Intrepid* and her sister carriers had often sailed within sight of the central Philippines, the Japanese had not sortied out to challenge Task Force 38. Even Admiral Halsey characterized Japanese passivity in the Visayas as "unbelievable and fantastic."

En route to the Palaus, *Intrepid* refueled, taking on nearly eight thousand barrels of fuel oil and 102,000 gallons of aviation gasoline from the tanker *Kaskaskia*. Captain Bolger used the lull in operations to attend to discipline. He conducted captain's masts, which were nonjudicial disciplinary hearings on relatively minor infractions of shipboard rules and naval tradition. Many of Bolger's crew were very young men or barely postadolescent boys, and some could be intractable and unruly. Bolger handed out punishment, usually in the form of extra duty or loss of pay, for offenses such as insubordination, threatening gestures, striking a fellow sailor, sleeping during flight quarters, breaking into the chow line, using profane language to a master-at-arms, and smoking when the smoking lamp was out.

In *Intrepid*'s ready rooms, aircrew listened to radio reports of the progress of the Peleliu invasion, which had begun on September 15, and basked in Admiral Halsey's accolades for Task Force 38. Halsey had messaged a "well-done" to the task force and promised that the Mindanao and Visayan raids were "only a preview of the real show—which will be staged for the benefit of the highest ranking individuals of the Asiatic Theater—Tokyo—here we come!"

Intrepid took station west of the Palau Islands on September 17. Air Group 18's missions were to provide air-to-ground support for the Marines on Peleliu and air cover for the U.S. Army's amphibious landing on Angaur, a small island to the south of Peleliu. The 1st Marine Division had encountered far stiffer resistance than expected on Peleliu. At the end of the first day, General William Rupertus's marines were badly bloodied and in grave danger of being hurled back into the sea by enfilading artillery fire on the landing beaches and by aggressive Japanese counterattacks, including combined tank and infantry assaults on the American beachhead. The Marines' progress inland was slow and costly. The Japanese had heavily fortified the island by burrowing interconnected tunnels, machine gun nests, and artillery positions within the island's coral and limestone ridges, and by blanketing the approaches to the high ground with heavy weapons fire. Water was in short supply ashore and the heat was suffocating. The Marines had suffered greatly.

Air Group 18 launched five strikes on September 17. The first was a strafing and bombing strike on Peleliu at five twenty a.m. Will Fletcher participated in the second strike at seven-oh-four a.m., a "Pre-George Hour" bombing and rocket attack on the red and blue beaches of the Angaur landing area. The overall air coordinator for the strike, VF-18's skipper, Lieutenant Commander E. J. Murphy, orbited high above the beach and observed the attack. He radioed back to *Intrepid*, "Very good attack. All bombs in target area." As Will pulled off his rocket run over the beach and banked his Avenger sharply back toward the sea, he stared down the length of his wing at the spectacle of the American troops going ashore. Hundreds of landing craft were headed determinedly toward the beach in uneven rows, their wakes trailing behind them like white ribbons. Some of the boats had reached Angaur's beach and were disgorging their human cargo. Will thought of his cousin Bruce Barth, a Marine sniper serving somewhere in the Pacific, and was gratified to see that the soldiers of the 81st Infantry Division who had landed on Angaur's beach appeared to be walking inland standing up, rather than crouching or falling.

Air Group 18 dropped napalm bombs for the first time at Peleliu. Instructions to use these new weapons, which consisted of drop tanks filled with a jellied gasoline mixture, had reached *Intrepid* less than two hours before the scheduled attack. The results of the air group's first napalm strikes were exceedingly poor. Six of eight bombs dropped by VF-18's Hellcats on Strike Dog failed to explode, and seven of eleven bombs dropped by VF-18's fighters on Strike Echo failed to explode. An unhappy El Gropo discovered the dud bombs had been miswired, 180 degrees out of phase. No one took any consolation in the fact that most of the bombs had been consistently miswired.

Task Force 38 remained off Peleliu for only one day. By late evening on September 18, Vice Admiral Mitscher's fast carrier task force was headed back toward the Philippines, there to resume Admiral Halsey's campaign to eliminate Japanese airpower in the western Pacific and, if possible, draw the Japanese fleet into battle.

CHAPTER SEVEN

OVER LUZON

★ ★ ★ ★ ★

Task Force 38 had not rested after leaving Eniwetok in late August. It had maneuvered constantly, not only to launch and recover airplanes and take on supplies from the at-sea logistics group, but to minimize the risk of discovery and attack by enemy submarines and aircraft. Steaming from one operational area to another, the four fast carrier groups of Task Force 38 sprawled across several hundred square miles of ocean.

As *Intrepid* plowed west toward the Philippines, Commander Ellis granted his airmen some much-needed rest—air group personnel were permitted to sleep through the morning call to general quarters—and airmen took time to read (and reread) personal mail that had been delivered while *Intrepid* was operating off the Palaus. Kenny Barden had received eleven letters from Margie, an event he described as "a bigger thrill than my first strike against the Japs." Commander Ellis also prepared his airmen for their reprise attacks in the Philippines by lecturing them on their objectives. He announced that *Intrepid* and Air Group 18 would again concentrate on suppressing Japanese airpower, this time on Luzon, the largest island in the Philippine archipelago. The air raids would have historic significance, Ellis noted. The strikes by *Intrepid* and Air Group 18 would be the first carrier air strikes against Luzon since the fall of the island to the Japanese in early 1942.

By September 20, 1944, Task Force 38 had returned to Philippine waters and taken up station roughly a hundred nautical miles east of central Luzon. With his carriers in position, Admiral Halsey wasted no time, ordering up wide-ranging air strikes across Luzon for the morning of September 21.

The first carrier air strike against Luzon since the island's fall, *Intrepid*'s Strike 2 Able, was delayed by heavy rain squalls and low visibility. Scheduled to launch at dawn, Strike 2 Able finally took off at eight ten a.m. (still in driving rain) with the objective of bombing Clark Field, the former American air base sixty-five miles north of Manila at which General MacArthur's detachment of Army Air Corps B-17s and P-40s had been destroyed on the tarmac by Japanese bombers on December 8, 1941. Leading Strike 2 Able personally, Commander Ellis guided his thirty-three-plane strike group directly inland from Dingalan Bay on Luzon's eastern shore. The strike group passed north of Mount Arayat, a towering volcanic cone that rises more than three thousand feet above sea level and lies about fifteen miles east of Clark Field, and then turned south. Twelve Hellcats flew escort, while twelve Helldivers and nine Avengers hauled the strike group's combined bomb load of thirty-two thousand pounds.

El Gropo's attackers arrived over Clark Field at nine thirty-five a.m. and achieved complete surprise—no Japanese fighters rose up to challenge them— but dense cloud cover hampered their target selection. Ellis's dive-bombers and torpedo bombers orbited Clark Field until they located breaks in the clouds through which they could release their bomb loads. El Gropo saw multiple explosions and secondary fires on the ground; he was confident that many of his strike group's bombs had found their mark, although he conceded in his after-action report that dense cloud cover had prevented him from making any comprehensive assessment of damage.

Ellis had no sooner departed on Strike 2 Able than *Intrepid*'s air department readied thirty-nine more warplanes for action over the Philippines. The primary objective of the second strike of the day, Strike 2 Baker, was not to bomb enemy airfields on Luzon but to sink a convoy of Japanese merchantmen that had been discovered heading for Subic Bay, a deep-water harbor on the western side of the Bataan Peninsula. Lying about sixty miles west of Manila, Subic Bay is shaped like an inverted "U" with its mouth open to the South China Sea; the city of Olongapo sprawls along the eastern shore of the bay.

Olongapo was an important port of entry and supply point, a lifeline for the Japanese occupation of Luzon and Manila.

Strike 2 Baker consisted of fifteen Helldivers, sixteen Hellcats, and eight Avengers. Because enemy shipping was the primary target, each of VB-18's Helldivers had been loaded with one thousand-pound armor-piercing bomb suitable for penetrating a ship's deck before detonating, and each of VT-18's Avengers had been loaded with one twenty-two-hundred-pound Mark 13 aerial torpedo.

Strike 2 Baker on September 21 had special significance for the Carrier Clowns. To this point in the war, VT-18 had not dropped any torpedoes. Even during their raids on Japanese shipping in Cebu Harbor earlier in the month, the torpeckers had carried mixed ordnance, but no torpedoes. Strike 2 Baker would be VT-18's first torpedo strike of the war, the first opportunity for Van Antwerp's torpeckers to apply in combat the unique skills they had trained so hard to perfect in California and Hawaii. Van Antwerp selected Bud Williams to lead the Avenger division. Doc Doyle, Squatty Vaughn, Will Fletcher, and Lieutenant Junior Grade Lloyd Karch, a quiet, unassuming Ohioan with a fondness for astronomy, were slated to be among the division members.

When Will got word he had been scheduled to fly Strike 2 Baker, he made a point of visiting the hangar bay to observe the torpedo loading process, just as he had been schooled to do at Kaneohe. He had been assigned bureau number 45924, the same airplane he had flown on his first bombing run at Babelthuap, which he regarded as a lucky draw. He watched as ordnancemen from *Intrepid*'s air department wheeled a fully assembled Mark 13 2A torpedo from its storage rack in the hangar bay and parked it beside Will's Avenger.

The torpedo, blunt and brutish-looking, lay on a four-wheeled dolly. The ordnancemen checked the torpedo's air pressure and alcohol quantity gauges to ensure that the torpedo's gas-turbine engine, which burned a combination of alcohol and compressed air, was adequately fueled. (Sailors were known to surreptitiously siphon a bit of torpedo alcohol and mix it with Coca-Cola or lemonade on the mistaken theory that anything called alcohol was potable alcohol. Not only did this sort of thievery impair the war effort, the resulting Torp Cocktail was sometimes fatal to the imbibers.) The ordnancemen also inspected the torpedo's contra-rotating propellers and the tail shroud that encircled the propellers and set the torpedo's running depth for the draft of the expected target. They pushed the torpedo cart between the Avenger's open bomb bay doors and, using electrical winches, hoisted the heavy weapon into the airplane's bomb bay. They positioned the topsides of the torpedo against two sway braces within the bomb bay, wrapped wire slings underneath the torpedo, and attached the slings to shackles, thereby securing the torpedo inside the airplane. They stretched a lanyard between the aft end of the torpedo and the back end of the bomb bay compartment. When the pilot released the shackles (electrically or manually), the slings would fall away and the torpedo would drop; the falling torpedo would yank the lanyard and ignite the torpedo's motor. When the torpedo hit the water and began its run, an impeller beneath the nose would arm the weapon.

Strike 2 Baker launched from *Intrepid* at nine ten a.m. With VB-18's fifteen Helldivers in the lead and sixteen VF-18 Hellcats flying fighter cover high above him, Bud Williams led his Avenger division west-southwest over the green hills of central Luzon at eleven thousand feet. One hour and thirty minutes later, the strike group reached Subic Bay, 190 nautical miles west of *Intrepid*'s position in the Philippine Sea.

To Williams's relief, Strike 2 Baker encountered none of the obscuring cloud cover that had plagued Commander Ellis's Strike 2 Able over Manila only an hour earlier. The waters of the bay shone in the midmorning sun. White cumulus clouds drifted languidly above the sea at three thousand feet like scattered popcorn puffs. Williams spotted a line of four merchant ships lying beneath the clouds just outside Subic Bay. Screened by four small escort ships, the merchant vessels were sailing slowly north into the mouth of Subic Bay, apparently headed for Olongapo like cows to the barn. Another ship lay just inside the entrance to the bay; she was anchored close to shore but with steam up, apparently ready to get under way. Williams could not discern from his altitude what types of merchantmen these were, but the vessels appeared to be big ones of Able or Baker size.

Williams passed the lead of the Avenger division to Squatty Vaughn and directed him to proceed with six Avengers, including those flown by Vaughn, Fletcher, and Karch, to attack the merchantmen outside the bay. Williams and Doc Doyle would concentrate on the ship near the shore.

With Doc Doyle on his wing, Williams glided down over the bay for a torpedo run on the merchant ship anchored inside the bay. Flying two abreast with about five hundred feet separating their wingtips, Williams and Doyle approached the anchored freighter from her port side. She was a large ship, a Fox Able. Williams didn't anticipate much antiaircraft fire from the merchantman, so he didn't bother to jink; he flew low and slow at only two hundred feet above the water and only two hundred knots. Williams and Doyle aimed their torpedoes amidships, released them within fifteen hundred yards of their target, and banked sharply back out to sea. Both missiles ran straight and true and struck the motionless freighter nearly simultaneously. The ship erupted bow and stern in two distinct, violent explosions and began to burn furiously. As Williams retired from his attack, his radioman reported weak antiaircraft fire coming from the ship, but no enemy bullets reached them. As Williams and Doyle climbed higher, Williams's radioman observed their erstwhile target through binoculars. The burning Fox Able was settling rapidly in shallow water and her crew was abandoning ship in life rafts.

Meanwhile, Vaughn led six Avengers, his and five others, in a coordinated torpedo attack on the column of four enemy merchantmen lying outside Subic Bay. Broadcasting over the tactical radio frequency, Vaughn divided up the four targets among his attackers, distributing his Avengers east and west of the enemy column and directing them to attack it from different directions. Vaughn selected the lead ship as his target and maneuvered to attack her from the northwest. He assigned a section of two Avengers to torpedo the second ship in the column, a smaller Sugar Able, directly from the east. He ordered Will, who had been flying on his left wing, to torpedo the third ship in line, a medium-size freighter or Fox Baker, from the east. He directed the last section of two Avengers to concentrate on the Fox Baker at the rear of the convoy and attack from the west.

Will initiated his torpedo attack four miles from the target, nosing over into a thirty-degree dive from seven thousand feet. The freighter appeared exactly like many of the small "Maru" Will had studied in recognition photographs. She had a high forecastle and a tall bridge structure amidships, with cargo booms fore and aft. Smoke wisped aft from her single stack, and she rode low in the water, which indicated she was heavily loaded with cargo. She looked like a toy in the distance. Will planned to release his torpedo at four hundred feet above the water and at an airspeed of no more than two hundred knots. He set his radar altimeter to beep at four hundred feet and aligned his airplane on the freighter's bow. Beginning his torpedo run at an altitude well above his torpedo release altitude was a technique that allowed him to keep his target in sight and accelerate in his glide to the proper airspeed for torpedo release. To ensure his torpedo entered the water at the proper angle of between eighteen and thirty-two degrees, Will would match his airspeed with altitude; generally, a faster approach required a higher release altitude and a slower approach required a lower release altitude. The trick was to arrive at the optimal torpedo release point one thousand to fifteen hundred yards from the target at the right combination of airspeed and altitude, with the nose of the airplane properly aligned. If the target ship was moving, the pilot had to lead his shot like a hunter shooting a bird on the wing.

Will's Fox Baker was plodding slowly and obediently behind the big Sugar Able ahead of her, barely making steerageway. Off the freighter's forward starboard quarter, a small patrol boat popped off small-caliber tracers at Will's approaching Avenger, but Will ignored the bullets. He was determined to hit the freighter.

The Avenger's Mark 13 optical gun sight served triple duty as wing gun sight, bomb sight, and torpedo sight. Based on target length, speed and flight path angle (the pilot entered these data by adjusting dials on the sight), the gun sight would place the bull's-eye, or "pipper," over the target at the proper release point. Most VT-18 pilots dispensed with the data entries, having grown accustomed to setting their gun sights in the "fixed" position on torpedo runs and aiming their Avengers ahead of the target like a rifleman taking his lead. Will's freighter was moving very slowly—she was nearly stationary relative to Will's speed—and he was approaching her broadside; his gun sight wasn't likely to be of much assistance in calculating the release point in any event. As he glided toward the target, Will adjusted his gun sight to its brightest setting—an illuminated ring appeared on the face of the glass—and "caged it" in the fixed position, at which point an illuminated pipper centered in the ring. He opened his bomb bay doors and snapped his "bomb-torpedo-R.P." switch to the "torpedo" position. Westmoreland confirmed to Will over the intercom that the Avenger's bomb bay doors were open and that the torpedo shackles were unlocked.

Will's target loomed larger as he drew nearer, and his Avenger's radar altimeter began to beep. Will leveled his wings and closed his master armament switch; he adjusted his heading to place the illuminated circle of his gun sight one-half ship-length ahead of the slow-moving freighter. Will tried to fly as smoothly as possible now. His heart pounded in his chest, beating so hard he feared the thumping would shake his control stick. He breathed deeply and deliberately, focusing on the gray silhouette of the freighter and the ripple of white water dribbling aft from her bow.

As he closed to within eleven hundred yards of the Fox Baker, Will held his Avenger rock-steady and pressed the bomb release button on the torpedo bomber's control stick. The torpedo slipped from the Avenger's bomb bay and nosed toward the water. Relieved of its twenty-two-hundred-pound payload, Will's airplane suddenly wanted to pitch nose-up. Will pressured the stick forward to remain low over the water, advanced his throttle to full military power, and banked sharply away. He had done all he could do. His goal now was to escape the target area as rapidly as possible.

After executing their torpedo runs on the large freighter anchored in the harbor, Williams and Doyle had loitered overhead to observe the runs of Vaughn's Avengers against the column of merchantmen. Williams saw Will's torpedo, marked by a ribbon of bubbles, bear down directly on the freighter and explode against the ship's forward beam. Will did not see his own torpedo strike, but Westmoreland and Christman did; they whooped with delight as a column of fire and black smoke erupted from the ship's starboard side. In all, four of the six torpedoes launched by Vaughn's Avengers found their marks; two torpedoes ran erratically, the result of mechanical defects in the torpedo or improper launch technique.

The ordeal of the Japanese merchantmen did not end with the Avengers' retirement from the scene. Helldivers from VB-18 attacked the same convoy with bombs immediately on the heels of VT-18's torpedo planes. Back aboard *Intrepid* an hour and a half later, VT-18 and VB-18 pilots claimed to have sunk a tanker and two freighters, "probably sunk" two freighters, and "seriously damaged" one tanker. Air Group 8, embarked aboard *Intrepid*'s sister carrier *Bunker Hill*, attacked the Subic Bay convoy immediately after Air Group 18 and reported similar results. El Gropo conceded in his after-action report that there may have been some duplication in the claims of air groups 18 and 8, but he was pleased with the professionalism of his aircrews and the results.

There was no doubt about the accomplishments of VF-18's Hellcats on the twenty-first. On the return trip to *Intrepid*, several of the F6F pilots who had flown fighter cover for Strike 2 Baker encountered enemy fighters near Clark Field. They downed seven enemy aircraft, knocking out of the air two Kawasaki fighters, code-named "Tonys," four medium Mitsubishi medium bombers, code-named "Bettys," and one Nakajima heavy bomber, code-named "Helen." Lieutenant Junior Grade C. M. Mallory accounted for three of these kills by himself, downing one Betty and two Tonys. The Hellcat drivers also reported inflicting damage on two additional enemy fighters. Things were looking up for the fighter boys, and they complained a little less about escort duty.

Kenny Barden had flown the first strike against Clark Field on the twenty-first, and he also flew Air Group 18's fourth strike of the day, a bombing mission to finish off a Japanese convoy discovered farther up the western coast of Luzon near Lingayen Gulf. Barden landed back aboard ship shortly before dark with only ten gallons of gas remaining; he confided to his diary at the end of the day that he had "never before been so completely exhausted."

Air Group 18 had launched four strikes against Luzon on the twenty-first, and all of its pilots and aircrew had returned safely to the carrier. There were some mishaps but no deaths. Rocky Roccaforte's Avenger absorbed a twenty-millimeter shell, and Lieutenant Junior Grade C. P. Amerman's F6F took flak on a strafing run, which froze the airplane's right aileron in the up position. Amerman had insufficient lateral control to land aboard the carrier, and he water-landed instead near a destroyer, the *Halsey Powell*. The *Powell*'s crew threw a cargo net over the side of the ship and hauled Amerman to safety. An SB2C-3 broke completely in half when landing back aboard *Intrepid* and careened into the barrier. Miraculously, neither aircrewman was injured.

Something of a fraternity-party atmosphere prevailed in Air Group 18's ready rooms on the evening of September 21. There was even a little whiskey. Doc Fish, the air group's flight surgeon, distributed small bottles of medicinal liquor to all pilots. The airmen joked and bragged and traded good-natured insults. In VT-18's ready room, the boys relaxed with a songfest. They coaxed the shy Lloyd Karch to the front of the room to sing "The Wabash Cannonball." Lloyd's audience whistled and applauded and convinced him he had delivered a brilliant performance when, in fact, poor Lloyd couldn't carry a tune in a bag. Will accepted the congratulations of his colleagues on his successful torpedo run, and he had never felt as fulfilled as he was that night. He was now as much a brother to these men as if they had been family from birth.

Air Group 18 had more work to do the next day, and El Gropo broke up the party early. The following morning, September 22, at six twenty a.m., nine

Avengers took off from *Intrepid* as part of Strike 2 Able, a bombing and strafing mission against Clark Field, in company with sixteen Hellcats and twelve Helldivers. Will Fletcher flew one of the Avengers, loaded with four five-hundred-pound general-purpose bombs. Although the weather over Luzon was clear below sixteen thousand feet, a high gray overcast foretold a change. At about ninety minutes after takeoff, VT-18's Avengers and VB-18's Helldivers cratered the runways at Clark Field and followed up with strafing runs through moderate twenty-millimeter antiaircraft fire. VF-18's Hellcats then swooped down and machine-gunned the enemy airplanes parked on the ground, which were an odd-lot collection of Zekes, Bettys, two Mitsubishi heavy bombers known as "Sallys," and a Mitsubishi reconnaissance airplane known as a "Dinah." Ensign W. L Passi, a recent VF-18 replacement pilot, was credited with destroying two Zekes on the ground, but on Passi's second or third strafing run at low altitude his Hellcat was struck by antiaircraft fire. Passi's airplane spun in and exploded.

Air Group 18's day was not over. Strike 2 Baker launched from *Intrepid* at seven fifty a.m. and set course for the Lingayen Gulf on the western coast of northern Luzon. Its mission was to destroy enemy merchant shipping near San Fernando Point. Arriving over the gulf at about nine thirty-five a.m., Strike 2 Baker discovered no fewer than nine small cargo ships nestled close to shore, and Air Group 18's warplanes attacked them through low stratus clouds. Returning pilots claimed to have sunk three freighters, "probably sunk" four others, and set afire a ship that "appeared to have military personnel aboard." There was no antiaircraft fire, and Lieutenant George Race recorded afterward that "everybody had a picnic."

The recovery of strikes 2 Able and 2 Baker aboard *Intrepid* was not a picnic, however. Will returned to *Intrepid* from Strike 2 Able at about nine twenty a.m. to find low clouds and heavy rain over the carrier. Visibility was poor, and *Intrepid* wallowed through heavy seas. Wind gusts buffeted Will's Avenger on his landing approach to the carrier, and the landing signal officer staggered on his platform as the great ship heaved and rolled beneath him. Will landed safely, but he was completely spent by the effort.

By the time Strike 2 Baker returned at eleven ten a.m., *Intrepid* was nearly closed in by clouds and driving rain. She was pitching and rolling violently, and pilots could not see the landing signal officer until they were very close in on final approach. Despite the foul weather, every returning warplane on Strike 2

Baker landed safely, if not smoothly. El Gropo was pleased. He said the recovery was "the best work in the worst weather he had ever seen." The skipper of *Intrepid*, Captain Bolger, and the commander of Task Group 38.2, Admiral Bogen, both issued Air Group 18 a "well-done," which was about the highest accolade naval aviators should expect from their commanders.

The nasty weather was a precursor to a typhoon that was building in the eastern Philippine Sea and bearing down on northern Luzon. Admiral Halsey's staff canceled all remaining strikes for September 22, and Task Force 38 headed south to escape the storm.

That night in their ready rooms, Air Group 18's pilots and aircrew listened to Tokyo Rose, the English-speaking woman whom Japanese propagandists featured on "Zero Hour," a radio broadcast from Tokyo. (There were actually several English-speaking Japanese women who played the role of Tokyo Rose.) Between interludes of American swing music, Tokyo Rose disseminated misinformation about the progress of the war and toyed with the emotions of American soldiers and sailors, reminding them pointedly of home and the sweethearts they had left behind. For American sailors at sea, the strangely seductive voice of Tokyo Rose was about the only female voice they heard routinely. Tokyo Rose announced to the men of 3rd Fleet on September 22 that the Philippine Islands had declared war on the United States for its "unprovoked assault."

As Task Force 38 moved south, 3rd Fleet intelligence officers puzzled again over the lack of vigorous Japanese resistance from the air. Air group intelligence officers, such as Lieutenant George Race and Lieutenant Commander Ernie Allen, estimated that the enemy had hundreds of combat aircraft on the islands, but none of these had ventured out to attack the American carriers. American radar had detected an occasional bogie or snooper plane at night but, as Admiral Halsey wired home to Admiral Nimitz at Pearl Harbor, there was "nothing on the screen but Hedy Lamarr."

Admiral Halsey would have been overjoyed had he known his fast carrier raids were largely to blame for the lack of air opposition. Task Force 38's bombing attacks on Davao, Cebu, Legaspi, Tacloban, and Clark Field had destroyed on the ground nearly two-thirds of the aircraft Admiral Teraoka had so carefully husbanded for the decisive battle. By the time Task Force 38 withdrew in late September, 1st Air Fleet in the Philippines had been reduced to a hundred operable warplanes, down from 280 at the beginning of the month. The loss of so many aircraft forced imperial headquarters to reconsider its approach to waging the decisive battle and seek new leadership. Imperial headquarters relieved Admiral Teraoka of command of 1st Air Fleet in late September and appointed Vice Admiral Takijiro Onishi in his place.

Onishi had proposed to imperial headquarters a nontraditional approach to aerial warfare, grounded in the belief that Japan's ever-escalating inferiority in numbers demanded extreme measures. Onishi suggested that 1st Air Fleet employ "special tactics" against the American 3rd Fleet. The tactics were simple: Squadrons of Japanese pilots would be trained not to duel with American fighters in the sky or drop bombs from on high, but to crash, or "body-slam," bomb-laden airplanes directly into American ships. The advantages of Onishi's approach were obvious. Special tactics did not require pilots with extensive flight time or combat experience; the navy's pilot training and replacement programs could be accelerated, and more pilots could be funneled into the theater of operations more quickly. One-way suicide missions focused on the destruction of enemy ships carried a higher probability of success than dropping bombs or launching torpedoes; a single determined pilot could sink or disable an American aircraft carrier and thereby eliminate more than ninety enemy warplanes in one sacrificial blow. In the cold calculus of war, Onishi's special tactics were a more efficient use of men and machines. Special tactics would also convince the American public of Japan's indomitable warrior spirit and ultimately tip the asymmetric balance of airpower in Japan's favor. Imperial headquarters embraced Onishi's plan and, toward the end of September 1944, the Japanese navy began shifting more airplanes to the Philippine theater and recruiting pilots for its new special tactics units—the kamikaze.

In early August 1944, *Musashi* received a new commanding officer, Captain Toshihira Inoguchi. The new captain of Japan's superbattleship had strong familial ties within the Imperial Japanese Navy. Toshihira, his son, and his brother had all graduated from Etajima, Japan's prestigious naval academy. Toshihira's brother, Captain Rikihei Inoguchi, was then serving as the senior staff officer for Admiral Teraoka's 1st Air Fleet in the Philippines, and Toshihira's son, Lieutenant Junior Grade Satoshi Inoguchi, was then a young navy fighter pilot stationed in Japan. Toshihira Inoguchi had developed a reputation within the Imperial Navy as a superior gunnery officer, and Admiral Toyoda presumably ranked Toshihira among the officers most capable of deploying *Musashi*'s monster guns to greatest advantage in the coming decisive battle.

As *Musashi* lay at anchor in the furnace of Lingga Roads, Captain Toshihira Inoguchi studied Admiral Toyoda's Sho-1 plan and prepared his ship for battle (while his brother Rikihei struggled to build up Japanese naval airpower in the Philippines). Concluding that *Musashi* would likely be involved in night operations, Inoguchi instructed his sailors to paint his battleship a deeper gray, the better to conceal her huge bulk from enemy surface ships and submarines. By September's end, Inoguchi's sailors had procured the paint, reportedly from stores of the former British naval station at Singapore. Dangling over *Musashi*'s massive superstructure and hull by the hundreds, Inoguchi's sailors completed the herculean job of painting the ship in a matter of days; the dark paint job also gave *Musashi* a more sinister appearance to match her deadly purpose.

The proximity of the Palembang oil fields allowed Inoguchi the luxury of training at sea and bringing his sailors up to a higher state of combat readiness. He sortied from the anchorage and drilled his crews incessantly in gunnery with a view toward making his ship's already formidable antiaircraft defenses as impenetrable as possible. With the loss of so many Japanese warplanes over the Marianas in the A-Go operation, Inoguchi suspected *Musashi*'s crew would have to defend their ship without the benefit of friendly fighter cover. Inoguchi also trained his crew intensively in damage control procedures. The crew's training routine included at least two drills daily in setting watertight conditions and establishing a condition of complete closure. His damage control engineers rehearsed counterflooding to correct lists, and Inoguchi required his engineers to demonstrate their proficiency by deliberately inducing lists and removing them. *Musashi*'s crew was "exceptionally well-trained by Japanese standards."

Intrepid steamed off the eastern Philippines for two more days in September, remaining well south of the typhoon. On September 23, Air Group 18 launched one of the longest carrier-based strikes of the war. Admiral Bogan ordered twelve of VB-18's Helldivers, each equipped with wing tanks containing 116 extra gallons of fuel and armed with one thousand-pound bomb, to attack Japanese shipping inside Coron Bay, a rocky, remote anchorage that lay 350 miles to the southwest in the Calamian Group of the western Philippines. VB-18's skipper, Lieutenant Commander Mark Eslick, led the bomber group departing *Intrepid* at dawn.

Eslick's raiders surprised about fifteen enemy freighters in Coron Bay with masthead-level bombing attacks. Eslick claimed to have sunk seven of them. Three Helldivers did not return, the victims of enemy antiaircraft fire. One of the downed Helldivers safely water-landed and the two crewmen escaped to a rubber life raft. They were last seen paddling their life raft for shore. Eslick and eight other Helldiver pilots landed safely back aboard *Intrepid* after a round-trip combat mission of seven hundred nautical miles, an extreme distance for carrier aircraft of the day.

On September 24, VF-18's Hellcats conducted fighter sweeps over Leyte and Cebu. El Gropo specifically instructed the pilots of his photo-equipped VF-18 Hellcats to "lay off shooting down Zekes and get some photographs." When Will and the other Avenger pilots learned of El Gropo's order, they immediately surmised that General MacArthur wanted good reconnaissance photographs of his invasion beaches. On the same day, VT-18's Avengers attacked a lone freighter in Ormoc Bay on the western shore of Leyte with bombs and rockets, leaving the freighter gutted and burning. Van Antwerp led the attack on the freighter, even though he had contracted the measles and was blotchy as a pimpled adolescent. VF-18 grieved the loss of Ensign William H. Sartwelle Jr., who was shot down by antiaircraft fire while on a strafing run later in the day at Cebu Airfield.

Will Fletcher did not fly on either September 23 or 24. He tended instead to his collateral duties as assistant squadron maintenance officer. Despite his title, Will had no responsibility for actually repairing VT-18's Avengers; *Intrepid*'s air department performed all aircraft maintenance. Will's duties were entirely administrative; he mostly read directives issued by the commander, Naval Air Force, Pacific Fleet relating to aircraft readiness and acted as a liaison with the air department in sorting out what should be done when. The directives of the commander, Naval Air Force, Pacific Fleet covered a seemingly endless variety of technical subjects, such as stenciling an aircraft wing between its rocket launcher rails, installing outer brake spring plugs on propellers, mounting aircraft clocks, inspecting supercharger drain valves, adjusting manual bomb release mechanisms, placing electrical receptacles for rocket launchers, and installing oil dilution systems. The commander issued stern prohibitions against taking maintenance shortcuts, such as jump-starting one airplane from another, and warned pilots and aircrew of the dire mechanical consequences of failing to comply with aircraft engine limitations and failing to observe correct engine start procedures. The commander's directives were voluminous, and Will spent much of every nonflying day in VT-18's cramped maintenance office surrounded by gray metal filing cabinets, browsing through sheaves of message traffic, thumbing through ring binders, and moving papers from wire in-baskets to wire out-baskets. Flying a desk, Will called it.

Will had a mechanical bent. He enjoyed watching air department maintenance crews disassemble Avengers, repair them, and reassemble them. He enjoyed eavesdropping in the background when chief petty officers in the maintenance department, like surgeons lecturing interns on a difficult case, gathered around junior enlisted men to diagnose a difficult mechanical problem. Will often asked questions, but he never ventured suggestions without first vetting the ideas beforehand with the chief. As the saying goes, CPOs run the navy, and Will learned early in his career never to question a CPO too closely in front of his men.

As assistant maintenance officer, Will learned the mechanical idiosyncrasies of every torpedo bomber in the squadron. Some Avengers consumed excessive amounts of engine oil, no matter how often the mechanics replaced the rings; some airplanes bled hydraulic fluid profusely, no matter how often the mechanics tightened the gaskets; other Avengers exhibited high engine cylinder-head temperatures, like a child running a persistent fever. In several airplanes, communications radios malfunctioned consistently in the air but always "checked out good on deck." A few of the squadron's Avengers were notorious hangar queens, incurable hypochondriacs, that pilots returned to the hangar bay repeatedly for the treatment of multiple maladies real and imagined.

Will believed in the psychology of machines. Identical airplanes performed differently depending on who flew them. Some pilots never seemed to experience a mechanical malfunction no matter which airplane they flew, while others invariably returned to the ship with a maintenance gripe. Will suspected each Avenger had a rudimentary personality of sorts, not a soul exactly, but a nature or disposition like that of a horse or a dog, a presence that was energized whenever the airplane's switches were thrown and its engine cranked. The airplane's inert parts became a functioning thing, capable of moving, ingesting, and excreting like a life-form, and perhaps they were capable of favoring some pilots over others. Could an airplane really have sensitivities or preferences? Will had discussed the idea earnestly with John Savage once.

A bunch of crap, Savage had scoffed. Psychological projection. Anthropomorphism. Sheer nonsense. Poor maintenance and ham-fisted pilots break airplanes. Furthermore, airplanes don't reproduce.

Will was unpersuaded, and he treated each airplane he flew with gentleness and respect. He patted their sides when he preflighted them, and talked to them under his breath, calling them "friend" or "old girl."

Task Group 38.1 withdrew from the Philippines on September 24 and set course for Saipan to replenish and rearm. Air Group 18 stood down en route, except for flying routine patrols, such as antisubmarine patrol or ASP. ASP was not a popular assignment; it involved three or four hours of monotonous flying over open water, and required the search crews to fly far from the relative security of the task group. The emptiness, the immensity, the tracklessness, and the unrelenting sameness of the sea were unsettling. Each search unit, comprised of two Avengers and a Hellcat, would fly outbound from the ship on an assigned heading for one hundred fifty nautical miles or so, turn left or right, travel an arc of fifty miles or so, and return to the carrier. But the carrier would have moved on in the meantime, and the search unit would have to navigate back to where the carrier was supposed to be, not to the original point of departure. The search unit would have to contend with thunderstorms, rain showers, squall lines, falling barometers, and wind shifts. VT-18's Avengers were equipped with airborne radar, and search units climbed steadily during their outbound leg to maintain radio contact with the ship, but pilots relied heavily on their dead-reckoning skills to bring them safely home. Whenever Will flew ASP, he fretted about his navigation the whole time, checking and double-checking his heading, airspeed, and elapsed time and compensating for diversions around the weather. He took comfort from the knowledge that his wingmen were plotting the unit's position independently, but he never relaxed until Westmoreland announced over the intercom that he was painting the ships of the task group's screen on his radar scope and that *Intrepid* and her sister carriers, their only refuge in Neptune's watery domain, were in sight.

Intrepid anchored in Tanapag Harbor, Saipan, at dawn on September 28. Three months earlier, on June 15, more than seventy-seven thousand United States Marines had invaded Saipan, intending to subdue the island in three days. The thirty-two thousand Japanese defenders had resisted fiercely, inflicting four thousand Marine casualties in the first forty-eight hours of combat. The fighting dragged on for three weeks. On July 5 and 6, Japanese soldiers mounted a series of fanatical banzai charges, losing more than four thousand men, 10 percent of their defense force, in two ghastly nights of hand-to-hand fighting. On July 9, organized Japanese resistance on the island ended, but twenty-two thousand Japanese civilians and Saipanese, convinced they would become the victims of American atrocities, had jumped to their deaths from the high cliffs at Marpi Point on the island's northern shore or committed suicide by other means. When *Intrepid* anchored in the harbor, American soldiers were still engaged in burying the dead and ferreting unsurrendered defenders from their caves.

To Will and the crew of *Intrepid*, at sea for nearly two months, any land looked inviting, even the scorched and bludgeoned shores of Saipan. Captain Bolger did not grant *Intrepid*'s crew liberty, but Lieutenant Ben Riley and a few other Air Group 18 officers and men went ashore with the dubious excuse of scrounging necessary spare parts for their airplanes and "locating a bore sight." Will's collateral duty as a maintenance officer got him ashore. He tagged along behind Riley, who made a beeline straight for Saipan's makeshift officers' club, an open-sided tent with rough wooden tables. Will set aside his scruples about alcohol and joined Riley and the crowd in drinking a few tepid beers. The visitors from *Intrepid* wandered past the prisoner-of-war stockade and were startled at the sight of Japanese men and women bathing together in the open. These were the first native Japanese Will had seen in the flesh. They were small, brown, and undernourished, pitiable in their nakedness, but Will allowed himself no pity for any of them. Marines who had fought the battle of Saipan hawked souvenirs to the sailors, offering them captured Japanese money, swords, knives, guns, and helmets. The prices were high, and Will declined to buy.

Intrepid departed Saipan on September 29 bound for Ulithi, a giant naval anchorage in the western Carolines roughly equidistant from the Philippines, Formosa, and Okinawa, and a way station to the front lines. Seized from the Japanese without opposition earlier in the month, Ulithi consisted of more than forty islets surrounding a central lagoon of 270 square miles. The lagoon could accommodate nearly seven hundred warships and support ships, and the U.S. Navy had quickly converted Ulithi into a staging area for further operations in the central and western Pacific.

En route to Ulithi, Van Antwerp and Allen briefed the Carrier Clowns on the bigger picture. The war news was sobering and offered little prospect for an early end to hostilities. Although the tide in the Pacific seemed to have turned in America's favor, China was weakening. In April 1944, the Japanese army had mounted a massive ground offensive in China, called Ichi-Go, with the twin objectives of closing the gap between Japanese forces in central China and those in Indochina, and of depriving the Allies of their air bases in southern China, from which American fighters and bombers had attacked Japanese shipping in the China Sea and provided air support for Chiang Kai-shek's Chinese Nationalist Army. Ichi-Go had accomplished its goals. By September, the Japanese had overrun at least eleven Allied airfields, and Chiang's army was in full retreat. With the loss of the Chinese airfields, the best the Allies could hope for was that a million Japanese troops would be tied down on the Asian continent while American forces seized new island bases from which they could mount a bombing campaign against the Japanese mainland. Establishing new airfields on islands south of Japan, such as Formosa and Okinawa, was now necessary to support the anticipated invasion of Japan, and recapturing the Philippines was necessary to tighten America's stranglehold on Japanese shipments of war material.

No sooner had *Intrepid* dropped anchor at Ulithi on October 1 than wind and waves began whipping across the central lagoon, tossing smaller ships in the anchorage like tethered corks. The Naval Weather Service helpfully reported another typhoon bearing down on Ulithi and Task Group 38.2, but most sailors could read the signs in the glowering sky. Admiral Bogan and his staff, ferried across the ruffled waters of the lagoon in barges, transferred from *Bunker Hill* to *Intrepid*, making *Intrepid* the new flagship of Task Group 38.2 and adding the twenty officers and fifty men of Bogan's staff to *Intrepid*'s roster. The weather did not improve, and on October 3 Admiral Bogan ordered his task group to weigh anchor and put back out to sea. The big carriers and their escorts would be far safer riding out the tempest in open water than in the confines of the atoll.

Aboard *Intrepid*, sailors scurried to make the ship ready for the typhoon.

They sheltered as many warplanes as possible inside the hangar bay and lashed down the remainder on the flight deck. They rigged foul-weather lines that men could grip as they walked about the decks, and secured loose gear that, if dislodged during the storm, might shift or slide. Ship's cooks hurriedly prepared gallons of soups and trays of sandwiches, meals that could be sipped from coffee cups or eaten with the hands. In VT-18's maintenance office, Will gathered up loose papers and stuffed them into filing cabinets. As the storm intensified, personnel stood down from daily routines, and general quarters drills were canceled. When veteran sailors lay down to sleep, they strapped themselves to their sleeping racks with their uniform belts.

The typhoon spawned monstrous waves that swept beneath *Intrepid* like mountain ranges on the move. The wind blew steadily from the west at forty to fifty knots, decapitating the peaks of the waves and depositing gray webs of foam on the surface of the sea. *Intrepid* heaved and twisted in every axis. The carrier's hull had been constructed in three main sections; as the big ship slid into the trough of one swell and climbed the face of the next, her bow section rose, her center section fell perceptibly, and her stern section rose, as if she were snaking across the watery ridges. Waves broke over her flight deck fifty feet above her mean waterline, and heavy rain lashed the ocean around her.

On the cusp of nausea, Will spent a sleepless night in his bunkroom, listening to *Intrepid*'s bulkheads creak and pop and the wind moan through *Intrepid*'s ventilation ducts. He pitied the sailors on lighter ships with narrow beams, such as destroyers and cruisers that were top-heavy with deck guns and high superstructures. If a giant like *Intrepid* could be so punished by the waves, what must it be like for the smaller ships and their crews? Will remembered something John Savage had once said. Savage, who loved flying but was less enthusiastic about ships, was fond of quoting an eighteenth-century British writer whose words now seemed apt: "No man who has the wit to get himself into jail would go to sea. For being at sea is like being in jail with the chance of being drowned."

The storm abated on October 4, and Task Group 38.2 returned to the sanctuary of Ulithi. Miraculously, no ships were lost in the typhoon, and the damage to *Intrepid* was insignificant. As *Intrepid* rode at anchor in Ulithi's lagoon, most of her crew were shipbound, and Air Group 18's flight crews had little to do. Barden whiled away the hours playing cribbage and bridge, and played a little basketball in the hangar bay.

The situation briefings continued. There was grave concern over the circumstances in China. Ernie Allen reported that American troops under the command of General Douglas MacArthur would be transported from New Guinea to the Philippines by the United States 7th Fleet and would land in the central Visayas on or about October 20. The ships and planes of Task Force 38.2 would support General MacArthur's invasion, but to mask American intentions and further degrade Japanese airpower, Task Force 38.2 would first conduct diversionary raids on Okinawa and Formosa between October 9 and 18. On or about October 18, Allen predicted, Task Group 38.2 would return to the central Visayas to help protect MacArthur's amphibious landing force.

On October 6, Task Group 38.2, with *Intrepid* serving as Rear Admiral Bogan's flagship, departed Ulithi and steamed northwest to join Task Force 38. Task Group 38.2 consisted of heavy carriers *Intrepid* and *Hancock* and light carriers *Cabot* and *Independence*. The four aircraft carriers were escorted by battleships *New Jersey* and *Iowa*, by cruisers *Vincennes, Houston, Miami, San Diego,* and *Oakland*, and by eighteen destroyers of Destroyer Squadron 52.

When Task Group 38.2 rendezvoused with Task Force 38 on October 7, 1944, Task Force 38 became one of the largest battle fleets ever assembled. Comprised of four fast carrier task groups, each of which was about the size of Task Group 38.2, Task Force 38 boasted a total of nine heavy carriers, eight light carriers, six battleships, eight heavy cruisers, eight light cruisers, and no fewer than forty destroyers. In addition to these combatants, the supply ships of 3rd Fleet's at-sea logistics group (which replenished the warships at sea) added no fewer than thirty fleet oilers, twelve escort carriers with replacement pilots and aircraft, numerous fleet tugs and ammunition ships, and dozens of screening destroyers and destroyer escorts. Much of this massive naval force set course north by northwest on October 7, trailing the stormy remnants of the typhoon that had swept over Ulithi.

The Ryukyu Islands would be the next enemy stronghold to experience the combined striking power of Task Force 38.

The largest island in the Ryukyu archipelago, Okinawa, lies 250 nautical miles south of Japan and three hundred miles off the coast of China. The island is wasp-shaped, roughly sixty miles long and twenty miles wide at the widest. Although the Ryukyuan language and culture were distinct from Japan's, the

Ryukyuan people had maintained close political and economic ties with Japan for hundreds of years (notwithstanding that many native Japanese regarded Ryukyuans as primitive cousins and racially inferior). In the 1870s, Okinawa and her sister islands, known to the Japanese as Nansei Shoto, became a prefecture of Japan. To Emperor Hirohito and his government, Okinawa was indisputably Japanese soil.

Okinawa was also Japanese territory as far as Admiral Halsey was concerned, and he was eager to assail it. He and Admiral Mitscher had divided the island into different sectors for attack by different task groups, and assigned Task Group 38.2 the northern sector. By the morning of October 10, Task Force 38 lay one hundred miles southeast of Okinawa.

At about six-oh-five a.m., *Intrepid* launched Strike 2 Able against the Japanese airfield on Ie Shima, a small island off Okinawa's northwestern coast. Commander Ellis, who had promoted the upcoming raids on Okinawa to his pilots as "the first attack on [the] Japanese home islands," led the strike group. Although nine Avengers, twelve Helldivers, and eight Hellcats departed *Intrepid*'s flight deck on Strike 2 Able, two aircraft failed to rendezvous. One Hellcat pilot was forced to return to the carrier immediately, because his airplane's engine cut out whenever he advanced his throttle, and one SB2C-3 lost power and settled into the water on launch. The Helldiver pilot escaped his sinking airplane, but his rear-seat man was knocked unconscious on impact and drowned.

The Avengers assigned to Strike 2 Able had been armed with a mixture of ordnance. Two aircraft had each been loaded with a two-thousand-pound general-purpose bomb; the remaining seven Avengers had each been loaded with six hundred-pound general-purpose bombs and six hundred-pound incendiary bombs. Strike 2 Able arrived over Ie Shima at about seven forty a.m. under clear skies with the enemy airfield in plain view. The airfield was a large one, consisting of three runways, each five thousand feet in length; two of the main runways intersected each other like the legs of an "X." El Gropo directed Ben Riley, who led the two-plane Avenger section armed with two-thousand-pound bombs, to crater the runway at the intersection.

Riley began his attack three miles east of Ie Shima, nosing over from nine thousand feet into a forty-five-degree glide. The maximum permissible airspeed in a dive for an Avenger was 315 knots in smooth air, and diving at forty-five degrees while carrying a two-thousand-pound bomb was a recipe for exceeding the torpedo bomber's structural limits. But Riley had never exhibited much concern for structural limits; the morning air was calm, and Riley had confidence he could keep the wings attached to his airplane. He reached the drop point at two thousand feet and three hundred knots—he had fifteen knots to spare—and pressed his bomb release button. Much to El Gropo's delight, Riley's bomb hit dead center on the runway intersection, throwing up a boiling cloud of smoke and debris. Riley's wingman dropped his bomb on the runway apron near Riley's, and El Gropo ordered the remaining Avengers and Helldivers to loose their loads on the enemy barracks, storage buildings, and revetments that were adjacent to the airfield. Commander Ellis watched with satisfaction as his strike group's general-purpose bombs erupted in smoky plumes, and its incendiary bombs sparked and flamed like struck matches. The entire target area was ablaze when El Gropo led the warplanes of Strike 2 Able away from Ie Shima and took up a southeasterly course back to *Intrepid*. El Gropo considered his mission accomplished, but he was displeased with the maintenance problems that had reduced his strike group by one fighter and one dive-bomber from the outset.

VT-18 was not immune from maintenance issues that plagued the other squadrons. Three Avenger pilots on Strike 2 Able had been unable to drop their entire ordnance load over Ie Shima due to faulty electrical wiring. One Avenger pilot, unable to release all of his incendiaries, returned to *Intrepid* with his bomb bay doors open as a precaution. When his airplane hit the flight deck, loose incendiary bombs scattered over the deck like bowling pins. Things did not improve on Strike 2 Baker. Lieutenant Junior Grade Al Long's engine quit after takeoff, and he water-landed his Avenger near the carrier. Fortunately, Long and his two crewmen got out quickly and were rescued by the destroyer *Colahan*.

Air Group 18 launched a total of four deck loads against Okinawa on October 10. Although flight leaders complained that the close proximity of other carriers and the large number of airplanes circling near the island had impeded the rendezvous phase, Air Group 18 had found plenty of targets on the ground. Ellis's attackers bombed Yontan Airfield in northern Okinawa and set fire to several of the larger towns on the island; VT-18's Carrier Clowns, Will Fletcher among them, sank or damaged with bombs and rockets more than twenty-five small freighters, luggers, lighters, and sampans anchored near shore. The pilots and aircrew returning from Strike 2 Dog reported that the entire island appeared to be burning. VF-18's fighter boys were disappointed, however. They had encountered only one Japanese fighter over Okinawa, and that fighter appeared to be attempting to flee the island when Lieutenant Junior Grade Beatley casually shot it down from behind. Commander Ellis counted the day's raids a success, although he judged the accuracy of the bombing on Strike 2 Dog to have been "far below Air Group 18's standards." One man had been lost in the Helldiver takeoff mishap, but none to enemy fire.

Task Force 38 withdrew to the southwest at sunset, and the men of Air Group 18 retired for the night. They were exhausted, confident, and a bit disdainful of their enemy. Formosa was next on 3rd Fleet's list, and things would be very different there.

CHAPTER EIGHT

OVER FORMOSA

★ ★ ★ ★ ★

Formosa—the name means "beautiful island" in Portuguese—lies in the South China Sea about a hundred miles off the Chinese coast and 230 miles north of Luzon. Portuguese sailors, among the first Europeans to encounter the island, bestowed the island's name in the sixteenth century. Covering an oblong area of about thirteen thousand square miles, Formosa is split longitudinally by a ridge of mountains. The western half of the island is relatively flat and arable, while the eastern half is densely forested and broken by rugged hills and valleys. Several of Formosa's mountain peaks rise to more than ten thousand feet, and one, Mount Niitaka, reaches 14,500 feet. Malayan seafarers were the island's aboriginal peoples. Although Chinese fishermen and traders visited Formosa's shores for millennia, the Chinese had been discouraged from permanent settlement by the ferocity of the native tribes. The Dutch East India Company first colonized the island in the 1620s and named the place Taiwan; in the mid-1600s, the Spanish occupied portions of the island, including what is now the northern port city of Keelung. By the late 1600s, Chinese warlords had ousted the Europeans and imposed a primitive form of government over the eastern coastal regions, although much of the island remained an unruly frontier. In 1894, attracted by political weakness and disunity in China and coveting an Asian market for Japanese textiles, the government of Emperor Meiji (Emperor

Hirohito's grandfather) dispatched an invasion force to Korea, which was then a Chinese province. Not long after Japanese troops landed on the Korean Peninsula, the Qing Dynasty sued for peace. In the Treaty of Shimonoseki of 1895, China ceded Taiwan to Japan as one of the spoils of war and also paid Japan substantial monetary indemnities, which Emperor Meiji devoted to further strengthening Japan's army and navy.

Under Japanese rule, Nipponese farmers, merchants, and manufacturers dominated the island's agriculture and economy, even though Japanese immigrants comprised only about an eighth of Formosa's total population. Formosans traded almost exclusively with Japan, exporting for the benefit of the empire 90 percent of the island's production of rice, sugarcane, sweet potatoes, tropical fruits, camphor, tea, coal, oil, phosphorous, copper, gold, and other minerals. But the natives of Taiwan were not easily subdued; as late as 1938, tribes of head-hunting aborigines still stalked the forests and mountains along Formosa's eastern coast, forcing the Japanese government to erect electrified fences to prevent the savages from preying on civilized communities.

Formosa was one of the success stories of nineteenth-century Japanese imperialism, proof of the economic rewards of an aggressive national policy of military adventurism. The Japanese had constructed numerous airfields on the island and improved the island's harbors and defenses, and the island had played a prominent role in Japan's twentieth-century military expansion. In the 1930s, Japanese warplanes flying from Formosa had attacked Chinese coastal cities in support of the emperor's incursions in Manchuria, and, from December 1941 through May 1942, Japanese warplanes flying from Formosa had attacked MacArthur's troops in the Philippines. The Imperial Japanese Navy had headquartered its southern command on Formosa—Admiral Toyoda visited the island frequently—and the country served as an unsinkable aircraft carrier from which Japanese warplanes could patrol the East China Sea and hopscotch from air bases in southern Japan to air bases in Indochina and the South Pacific. Typically, the emperor's pilots flew from Kyushu to Okinawa, thence to Formosa, thence to the Philippines, and thence to islands farther south.

Following the Battle of the Philippine Sea, the Japanese navy had attempted to rebuild its air forces in Formosa as well as in the Philippines. By early October 1944, Vice Admiral Shigeru Fukudome, commander of Japan's 6th Base Air Force, had assembled more than 450 aircraft on Formosan airfields. Fukudome patiently awaited the American onslaught. The American 3rd Fleet had recently struck at Okinawa, and Fukudome understood that his island might be next.

Task Force 38 steamed south from Okinawa on the evening of October 11 and then looped west, taking up station seventy miles off the eastern coast of Formosa the following morning. As at Okinawa, Task Force 38's objective at Formosa was to destroy as much of Japan's airpower as possible and vitiate future Japanese air attacks against General MacArthur's ground forces in the Philippines. Vice Admiral Mitscher had warned the sailors and airmen of Task Force 38 that carrier air raids on Formosa would come as no surprise to the Japanese. The Japanese had hundreds of combat aircraft on the island, and the Americans should expect attacks and counterattacks. As at Okinawa, Mitscher had assigned primary responsibility for attacking different areas of the island to different task groups; he had assigned Formosa's northern coast to Task Group 38.2 and *Intrepid*.

On October 12, Air Group 18 had the honor of leading one of the first strikes of the war against northern Formosa by carrier-based warplanes. Admiral Bogan selected Commander Ellis to act as target coordinator for the first sorties launched by all five carriers of Task Group 38.2: *Intrepid, Hancock, Bunker Hill, Cabot*, and *Independence*. Bogan's staff had briefed Ellis and his flight leaders from detailed aerial photographs of the primary target areas and had assigned them alternative targets. There would be no confusion or uncertainty as to where the targets were, or which targets were which, as there had been during Task Group 38.2's raids on Negros back in September. Task Group 38.2 would strike first at the dockyards and warehouses in Kiirun Harbor (now Keelung Harbor) on Formosa's northern shore. Kiirun Harbor was fed by the Tansui River, which flowed through a narrow valley past the city of Taipei and emptied into the sea; the harbor was rimmed on three sides by mountains. The alternate target was a Japanese seaplane base farther west up the Tansui River. Ellis had picked Lieutenant Commander Van Antwerp to lead *Intrepid*'s Strike 2 Able, which would consist of nine Avengers, five Hellcats, and twelve Helldivers. Van Antwerp's first Avenger division would include Bill Bates, Kenny Barden, Joe Rubin, and Ben St. John, VT-18's boot ensign. VB-18's skipper, Lieutenant Commander Mark Eslick, would lead the dive-bombers in two divisions of six aircraft.

Red Russell, scheduled to fly as Barden's turret gunner, suspected he was in for a very rough morning over Formosa. All airmen were fed steak and eggs for breakfast, a sure sign that someone higher up thought the strike would be challenging. The hearty meal augured heavy air opposition, intense enemy anti-aircraft fire, or both. After delivering his intelligence briefing, Lieutenant Commander Allen gave his airmen wads of Japanese currency with which to bribe native Formosans if the American fliers were forced to bail out or crash-land on Formosa, but he candidly warned his torpeckers to expect little help and no mercy.

Don't bail out over land if you can help it, and do everything you can to reach the sea, was Allen's counsel. If you reach the water, there is a chance one of our submarines assigned to air-sea rescue can pick you up.

As target coordinator, Commander Ellis launched at six-oh-five a.m. and proceeded to Kiirun Harbor ahead of *Intrepid*'s strike group with his VF-18 fighter escort. Strike 2 Able took off immediately thereafter, climbing into skies "black as the inside of your hat" and threatening. One Avenger sprang an oil leak that mushroomed into an engine fire and forced the pilot to return to the carrier. Van Antwerp guided the remainder of *Intrepid*'s strike group 150 miles northwest to Kiirun Harbor through cloudy, rainy skies.

As Strike 2 Able approached Kiirun Harbor, angry black puffs of antiaircraft fire dotted the sky. The Japanese gunners did not seem to be firing blindly through the clouds either. The bursts of gunfire tracked the movements of Van Antwerp's airplanes no matter which direction they turned. El Gropo, orbiting nearby, deduced that the Japanese medium and heavy antiaircraft guns were radar-controlled; he ordered the crew of an Avenger equipped with a radar intercept receiver to determine the frequency of the Japanese radar pulse. After some experimentation, the radioman confirmed signals on two hundred and six hundred megacycles, both of which were known to have been used by the Japanese for radar fire control purposes. Ellis made a mental note: He would direct crews on subsequent missions to try to jam the enemy's radar signals by dropping "window."

"Window" consisted of strips of aluminum foil cut into lengths that corresponded to the wavelength of the enemy's radar signals. When scattered from an airplane, window provided a false return. For a two-hundred-megacycle signal, the aluminum strips were cut precisely to 28.2 inches; for six hundred megacycles, the strips were cut to 9.4 inches. The navy hadn't used window in combat before, and the techniques for deploying window were still experimental and primitive. Avenger and Helldiver radiomen simply shook bags of precut aluminum strips into the airstream, like emptying the garbage. The aircrews on Strike 2 Able had not been supplied with window, so they had no choice but to press home their attacks without it.

Van Antwerp's strike group arrived over Kiirun Harbor to find it blanketed by weather. A nearly unbroken mass of towering cumulus sat directly over the harbor, and the spaces between the clouds were streaked with scud. Estimating the ceiling to be only a thousand to fifteen hundred feet, Van Antwerp picked his way around the clouds, looking for an opening through which to attack; he found none. Van Antwerp consulted Ellis on the tactical frequency, and El Gropo directed Van Antwerp's strike group to divert west and bomb the Japanese seaplane base on the Tansui River. As Van Antwerp acknowledged Ellis's command and turned west, he suddenly realized his strike group was short one division of six Helldivers. While maneuvering around a billowing rain cloud in low visibility, VB-18's two Helldiver divisions had become separated. The second division, led by Lieutenant Edward H. Eisengrein, had lost visual contact with the first, led by Lieutenant Commander Eslick. This was a mistake. Regardless of the weather, Eisengrein's primary duty as division leader was to remain with Eslick's division unless Eslick ordered otherwise. But Lieutenant Commander Eslick had also lost contact with Van Antwerp's main group while circumnavigating the clouds. Eslick and his five wingmen were now on their own.

Eslick's odds of quickly relocating either Van Antwerp's main group or Eisengrein's division in lousy weather were low, and Japanese antiaircraft fire coming from the vicinity of Kiirun Harbor discouraged him from loitering over the target area to look for them. Eslick decided to proceed with his primary attack on the harbor rather than divert to the seaplane base; he either didn't hear Ellis's order to divert upriver or chose to disregard it.

Unable to execute a standard high-angle dive-bombing run because of low weather, Eslick led his five Helldivers in shallow glide-bombing runs over Kiirun Harbor. As they had at Negros, Eslick's dive-bomber pilots pushed over unhesitatingly through the clouds to find their targets, following their leader down in close-order single file. But Eslick and his dive-bomber crews were not as fortunate at Kiirun Harbor as they had been at Negros. Kiirun Harbor was ringed with antiaircraft positions, and the antiaircraft fire intensified as the Helldivers descended. When Eslick's Helldivers pulled off their bombing runs and rendezvoused for the return to *Intrepid*, there were only four aircraft in formation, and Lieutenant Commander Eslick's Helldiver was not among them; neither was the Helldiver flown by Lieutenant Junior Grade John W. Gruenewald, Eslick's section leader. Lieutenant Junior Grade John Forsyth, one of the dive-bomber pilots who had trailed Eslick in his run, believed that Eslick's bombs had fallen squarely on a dockside warehouse, but Eslick, Gruenewald, and their rear-seat men were never seen or heard from again. Their Helldivers had simply disappeared on their bombing runs, the victims of antiaircraft fire or a collision with cloud-shrouded hills.

The surviving Helldiver crews had little time to absorb the loss of their skipper. They no sooner had rendezvoused north of Kiirun Harbor than five Kawasaki twin-engine fighters, known as "Nicks," and a twin-engine Nakajima navy fighter known as an "Irving" jumped them at low altitude. The enemy fighters were painted mottled brown or khaki, with yellow stripes around their fuselages. The Helldiver pilots firewalled their throttles and headed for open water, while their rear-seat men sprayed the pursuing Nicks and Irving with twin .30-caliber machine guns, desperately trying to hold off the attacking Japanese airmen until VF-18's Hellcats could come to the rescue. The five Hellcats assigned to Strike 2 Able as fighter escorts quickly swooped in among the Nicks and the Irving and, within a space of two or three minutes, the Hellcats had shot down two Nicks and the Irving and driven off the remaining three Nicks.

Meanwhile, Van Antwerp had led his Avengers and Eisengrein's Helldiver division up the Tansui River toward the Japanese seaplane base. Visibility over the seaplane base was fair, and Van Antwerp gave the order to attack. The Avenger and Helldiver pilots selected their targets carefully and distributed their bomb loads among the seaplane ramp and secondary targets, such as adjacent warehouses, oil storage tanks, a freight yard with standing railcars, riverside docks, and dockside buildings. Unchallenged by enemy fighters and faced with only meager antiaircraft fire, Van Antwerp's attackers lingered over the target area to machine-gun small boats anchored in Tansui Harbor. Lieutenant Junior Grade Bill Bates strafed a gunboat at low altitude and received an unexpected jolt when the two-hundred-foot vessel, apparently loaded with ammunition or explosives of some kind, detonated before his eyes and sank beneath an anvil cloud of smoke.

Van Antwerp collected his Avengers and Helldivers, including the four survivors of the Kiirun Harbor attack and their fighter escorts, and led them southeast across Formosa's mountains toward *Intrepid*, while Ellis orbited north of the harbor in his Hellcat and continued to direct the strikes of other air groups. But the Japanese were not yet finished with Air Group 18.

Within minutes of forming up, Van Antwerp's flight came under attack by ten to fourteen "Tonys" and "Oscars." (These were different types of single-engine fighters manufactured, respectively, by Kawasaki and Nakajima.) VF-18's Hellcats leaped in among the enemy fighters and scattered a few of them, but the American fighter pilots were outnumbered in the skirmish. Unengaged Tonys and Oscars made aggressive low side runs against the flanks of the Avengers and Helldivers, like sharks slashing at their prey.

Van Antwerp's torpedo bombers were far less maneuverable than the Tonys and Oscars. Their best hope lay in combining the defensive fire of eight Avengers, each armed with a single .50-caliber turret gun, two forward-firing .50-caliber wing guns, and a single .30-caliber stinger gun. The Helldiver pilots were in a similar fix; they would have to rely on the massed fire of their twenty-millimeter wing cannons, two to each airplane, and the twin .30-caliber guns operated by each Helldiver's rear-seat man. Van Antwerp signaled his Avenger pilots to close up and maintain a tight division-vee formation with Van Antwerp's torpedo bomber flying the point. The Helldiver flight leaders did the same, arranging their divisions into two tight defensive vees and positioning themselves below and astern of Van Antwerp's Avengers.

Ben St. John had been flying near the rear of the Avenger division when the Japanese fighters first appeared. Obeying his skipper's hand signals, Ben had nudged his torpedo bomber forward and taken up the trailing position on the right leg of Van Antwerp's vee. He had nestled his Avenger beside and slightly below Joe Rubin's, flying so close to Rubin's airplane that Ben's left wingtip overlapped Rubin's right. Ben felt uncomfortably exposed on the right wing of the vee, as if he were flying the tow plane in a gunnery pattern and the shooters were determined to hit his airplane instead of the banner. Ben heard his turret gunner firing at the Japanese fighters, but he had no idea from which direction the Japanese were coming or where his gunner was aiming. Ben could not take his eyes off Rubin's airplane for very long and still hold his position. In his peripheral vision, he glimpsed Rubin's turret gun sparking furiously and deduced that an attacker must be close by. Suddenly, a shadow flashed over Ben's airplane, not more than a hundred feet above him, and rolled to one side like a man swan-diving off a high dive. A ball of orange flame erupted around the shadow and it plummeted out of sight. Ben took heart that at least one of the enemy fighters had been put out of action.

VF-18's fighters engaged the first wave of Tonys and Oscars in a snarling dogfight that lasted fifteen minutes and covered seventy miles. In the meantime, Van Antwerp's strike group cleared the eastern mountains of Formosa and descended to 1500 feet. Van Antwerp's group was without fighter cover, but the low-layered clouds that had been such a dangerous impediment at Kiirun Harbor now became Van Antwerp's ally. Van Antwerp fishtailed his flight through gaps in the clouds, hoping his blue-painted torpedo bombers and dive-bombers might escape the notice of any more Japanese fighters. But less than five minutes after the first fighter attack ended, a second wave of twelve to sixteen Oscars and "Tojos" (a third type of single-engine fighter manufactured by Nakajima) descended on the strike group and began making gunnery runs on Van Antwerp's unprotected Avengers and Helldivers from ahead and behind.

To discourage the enemy's head-on attacks, Van Antwerp turned his Avenger formation directly into the path of the oncoming enemy fighters. Van Antwerp's seven wingmen—Long, Bates, Barden, Rubin, and St. John included— all banked with him, flying as close to one another as possible. Maintaining a tightly packed division-vee formation was imperative now, not only for preservation of the group but for individual airplanes. As he rolled out of the turn, Van Antwerp opened fire with his wing guns, spraying .50-caliber shells in the face of the Japanese attackers. Van Antwerp's wingmen all did the same, although none of them took aim at anything in particular. The eight Avengers were frozen in formation; the pilots simply fired their weapons forward, dividing their attention between the oncoming fighters and holding their position in Van Antwerp's vee.

Ben St. John glanced down at his cockpit armament panel, confirming that he had depressed his gun-charging control valve and activated his wing guns and armament master switches. As the dark forms of enemy fighters passed in front of his windscreen—they darted through his field of vision like finches—

Will Fletcher, age seventeen, indulges his love of flying at a Midwest air show in 1940. Aviation pioneers Wiley Post and Amelia Earhart were among Will's childhood heroes; both set aviation records in the 1930s while flying modified Lockheed Vegas. The airplane in the background appears to be a "businessman's" late-model version of a Vega.

Courtesy of Mrs. W. M. Fletcher

Torpedo 18 with Air Group 18 personnel, probably taken at NAS Hilo, Hawaii, prior to the squadron's transfer to NAS Kanehoe. (*Front row, left to right*) Lt. j.g. Kurt W. Schonthaler; Lt. George B. Riley; Lcdr. Ernest Allen; Lt. John G. "Bud" Williams; Cdr. William E. Ellis; Lcdr. Lloyd W. Van Antwerp; (unidentified, but perhaps Lt. Leo M. Christensen, killed at Kaneohe); Lt. Albert J. Long. (*Second row, left to right*) Lt. j.g. Lloyd E. Karch; Lt. j.g. Thomas P. Spaulding; Lt. j.g. John T. McKee; Lt. j.g. Donald W. Morris; Lt. j.g. John Robinson (killed at Kaneohe); Lt. j.g. Raymond J. Skelly (killed in action 10/24/44); Lcdr. John W. "Jack" or "Doc" Fish (flight surgeon, killed in a kamikaze attack 11/25/44); Lt. j.g. Robert E. Olsen; Lt. j.g. Leon S. Vannais; Lt. j.g. Kenneth P. Barden. (*Third row, left to right*) Lt. j.g. Joseph L. Rubin; Lt. j.g. Frank D. Doyle; Lt. j.g. Elmer B. Vaughn; Lt. j.g. Robert Brisbin; Ens. Nicholas J. Roccaforte; Lt. j.g. John Savage (killed in action 9/8/44); Lt. j.g. William Bates; Lt. j.g. Donald B. Pieper; Lt. Vernon A. Delaney; Lt. j.g. Frank Scrano. Pilots not pictured but who joined VT-18 at Kaneohe and deployed with the squadron in August 1944 include Ens. Willard M. Fletcher; Ens. Daniel Laner (killed in action 9/13/44); Ens. Vernon J. Sistrunk; Ens. Bernard J. St. John; and Ens. Ralph R. Ursch.

Courtesy of Mrs. Mildred Schonthaler

Kenneth P. Barden, 1943.

Courtesy of Peggy Paulson

Ens. Willard M. Fletcher, 1944.

Courtesy of Mrs. W. M. Fletcher

Ens. Vernon J. Sistrunk, 1943,
shown in his cadet flight helmet
with "Gosport tubes" attached to
his earpieces.

Courtesy of Steve Sistrunk

Lt. j.g. Bernard J. St. John,
after returning from the Pacific
in December 1944, but before
receiving his awards.

Courtesy of Bernard St. John

Lt. j.g. Kurt W. Schonthaler with
an unidentified war correspondent
aboard *Intrepid*, late 1944.

Courtesy of Mrs. Mildred Schonthaler

A TBM-1C Avenger with the "white cross" tail insignia of Air Group 18, off Hawaii. The pilot is likely Kurt Schonthaler. *National Archives*

An F6F Hellcat fighter takes off from the USS *Lexington*, 1943. *National Archives*

Avengers of VT-18 form up for a simulated attack (a "group grope") against Task Group 12.3.2 as *Intrepid* steams between Pearl Harbor and Eniwetok, on August 19, 1944, preparatory to first strikes on the Palau Islands. *National Archives*

These photos capture SB2C Helldiver dive-bombers returning to their carriers. *National Archives*

Admiral William F. Halsey, commander of the U.S. Third Fleet. *National Archives*

Vice Admiral Marc A. Mitscher, commander of Task Force 38.

National Archives

Rear Admiral Gerald F. Bogan, commander of Task Group 38.2. *National Archives*

Captain Joseph F. Bolger, commander of USS *Intrepid*. *National Archives*

Commander William E. Ellis, commander of Carrier Air Group 18. *National Archives*

Intrepid (CV-11) on station in the Philippine Sea in November 1944. Visible forward of her island are two five-inch .38-caliber gun turrets; an F6F is parked with its fuselage hanging over the starboard side (the "white cross" of Air Group 18 is visible on the F6F's tail); more F6Fs, SB2C-3s, and TBM-1Cs are parked aft. Note the numeral "11" on the flight deck in dark paint. *Intrepid* would be struck and disabled by two kamikazes only days after this photograph was taken. *National Archives*

Vice Admiral Takeo Kurita, commander of Force A (Center Force). *National Archives*

BELOW A long-distance photograph of *Yamato* (*left*) and *Musashi* (*right*) at anchor. (Location unverified. Perhaps at Brunei, Borneo; perhaps in the Inland Sea near Kure.)

National Archives

IJN *Yamato*, sister ship of *Musashi*, during sea trials, 1942.

National Archives

Musashi's foredeck, probably photographed from her compass bridge. Approximately one hundred men stand in ranks forward of her No.1 turret.

National Archives

BELOW *Musashi*'s gunfire control tower, port side, looking aft. The two dark rectangles visible directly above the two sailors standing closest to the camera in the foreground are the "slits" in her armored conning tower. The compass bridge sits above the conning tower; the combat bridge and the air defense command post sit higher up still. The thick "arm and fist" protruding from her foretop is the port wing of her fifteen-meter range finder. The port side of her No. 2 eighteen-inch gun turret is visible in the left foreground; the boxlike structure in the foreground is the port wing of the turret's range finder.

National Archives

Musashi's starboard side, adjacent to the No. 1 turret, looking aft at her gunfire control tower. Visible in the right half of this photograph is the barrel of one of her monster eighteen-inch naval guns, three of which were housed in the No. 1 turret.

National Archives

Musashi's forecastle facing aft and staring into the muzzles of six of her eighteen-inch guns and three of her 15.5-centimeter .60-caliber guns.   *National Archives*

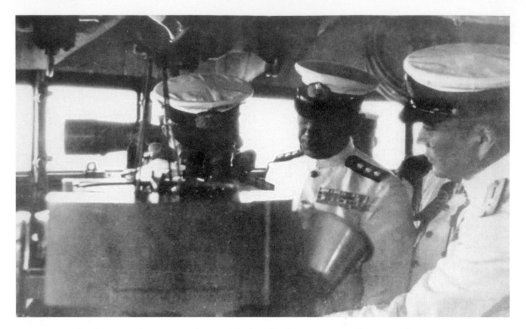

Japanese naval officers confer on one of *Musashi*'s three bridges on her gunfire control tower.

National Archives

RIGHT   *Musashi* at an unconfirmed location. This photograph—probably taken from about two thousand yards, a common distance between warships when riding at anchor or cruising—illustrates how *Musashi* would have appeared to an attacking Avenger pilot at the optimal torpedo release point (absent the intense counterfire, of course).   *National Archives*

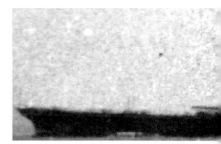

BELOW   An honor guard bears the ashes of Admiral Isoroku Yamamoto down *Musashi*'s foredeck.   *National Archives*

Part of the Japanese Center Force in the Sibuyan Sea is seen here in this aerial photograph taken on October 24, 1944, immediately before the attack by Air Group 18's Strike 2 Baker. Note ships taking evasive action.
National Archives

A battle-damaged Avenger, flown by Kenny Barden, returns to *Intrepid* after Air Group 18's strike against Vice Admiral Ozawa's carriers off Cape Engano on October 25, 1944. Note the huge hole in the airplane's fuselage. Miraculously, Barden's control cables were not severed and he landed safely.
Courtesy of Peggy Paulson and Kenneth P. Barden Jr.

Guerrilla officers on Luzon load a dinait—a native Filipino sailboat—November 1944. Will Fletcher was transported to Panay in the hold of a wooden sailboat of this type, crewed by guerrillas of the 6th Mountain Division's sailboat brigade. Note the outrigger and the sailcloth made of woven grass or reeds. *National Archives*

A Filipino guerrilla camp on Leyte, December 1944.
National Archives

A Filipino lieutenant interrogates a Japanese prisoner captured on Leyte in December 1944. The guerrillas took few prisoners.
National Archives

A Filipino guerrilla sergeant on Leyte explains the bolo knife to an American soldier, December 1944.

National Archives

Filipino guerrillas on Leyte demonstrate the use of bolo knives in hand-to-hand combat, 1944. *National Archives*

Bud Williams, VT-18's executive officer, stands on *Intrepid*'s flight deck while she is anchored at Ulithi, December 1944. A TBM-1C Avenger is in the background. *Courtesy of Bernard St. John*

Squatty Vaughn aboard *Intrepid*. F6F Hellcats with belly tanks are parked in the background.
Courtesy of Bernard St. John

Ben St. John stands beside the starboard main mount of an Avenger. *Courtesy of Bernard St. John*

A party in VT-18's ready room. The boys celebrate the news, delivered at Ulithi Atoll in early December 1944, that *Intrepid* would return home by Christmas. Kenny Barden is lower right, with his right arm on the shoulder of an unidentified officer. Bud Williams stands in the second row, third from left, wearing his bridge cap askew. Ben St. John, shirtless, stands in the last row, third from right. *Courtesy of Bernard St. John*

Air Group 18 pilots drink beer under the palms at Crowley's Tavern, Mogmog Island, Ulithi Atoll, in December 1944.　　*Courtesy of Bernard St. John*

Naval Aviation Cadet William Shackelford stands before a N2S-3 Navy Primary Trainer, the "Yellow Peril."　　*Courtesy of William Shackelford*

Kenny Barden (*center*) enjoys a picnic lunch with his wife, Margie, and an unidentified officer in San Francisco, 1945. Note the "Carrier Clowns" patch on Barden's flight jacket.　　*Courtesy of Peggy Paulson*

Captain Willard M. Fletcher with his Navy Cross, about 1968.

Courtesy of Mrs. W. M. Fletcher

Lloyd Karch, age eighty, poses next to an Avenger at a California air show in 2001.

Courtesy of Ed Auld

Ben St. John in his Long Island home in 2011, at age ninety. The photograph beside him shows him piloting an Avenger in 1945; the airplane belonged to a San Diego reserve squadron. *Author's Collection*

Ben squeezed the trigger switch on his control stick. He felt his wing guns hammer and glimpsed his tracer bullets racing forward into the middle distance, but he didn't dwell on the sight. Ben turned his attention back to Rubin's airplane and the critical business of flying in formation.

Van Antwerp's idea had been to throw a wall of lead at oncoming fighters, and his tactic seemed to work. The enemy fighters broke off their headlong attacks, but Oscars and Tojos continued to harass the Avengers from above and behind, both singly and in pairs, setting up for their runs as if they were taking air-to-air gunnery practice.

VF-18's five overworked Hellcats, having driven off the first wave of Japanese attackers, rejoined Van Antwerp's formation in the middle of the second wave of attacks and did what they could to protect the torpedo bombers. Lieutenant R. D. Van Dyke of VF-18, having shot down three Tonys moments earlier, made repeated runs on the enemy Oscars and Tojos and broke up their attacks, even though Van Dyke himself was completely out of ammunition. For Van Antwerp and his torpedo bombers, now separated from the dive-bombers and beset by a gaggle of Japanese fighters, the situation had become desperate. There appeared to be dozens of enemy fighters in the sky. The few friendly fighters available to help were low on ammunition, and Van Dyke's dry runs would keep the enemy at bay only so long.

Van Antwerp elected to take his Avenger formation into the clouds, notwithstanding the difficulty of keeping everyone together in reduced visibility and turbulence. Ben St. John sensed the formation tilt right, then back to the left again. Beads of moisture streamed across his windscreen, and Ben suddenly found himself jostling through cumulus clouds gray as slate. His lead aircraft—this was Joe Rubin's Avenger flying to Ben's left—became a ghost, appearing and disappearing through the veil of clouds like a winking apparition. Suddenly, Rubin's airplane veered sharply toward Ben's, as if Rubin's airplane had been punched in the side. Ben jerked away reflexively to avoid a collision and, to his dismay, lost sight of Rubin completely.

Ben did what he had been trained to do: He turned ninety degrees away from Van Antwerp's heading and, knowing the sea was below him, descended. When he bottomed out of the clouds, he found himself all alone. Formosa's dark shore lay off his right wing and his buddies were nowhere in sight.

———

As they did with every returning mission, sailors gathered on *Intrepid*'s island and deck-edge catwalks to observe the recovery of Strike 2 Able. They counted the airplanes in the landing pattern and knew immediately how many aircraft had been lost and of what type, if not who had been lost specifically. The sailors had learned long before Formosa never to count an airplane recovered until it was safely aboard ship, and this rule proved itself again on Strike 2 Able. The engine of one of the five Hellcats returning from Strike 2 Able began to sputter on approach. The Hellcat pilot, Ensign Harry R. Webster, water-landed near *Intrepid* but did not survive the landing; apparently knocked unconscious, he went down with his plane.

Van Antwerp's torpeckers—minus Ben St. John—escaped the pursuing Japanese fighters in the clouds and landed safely back aboard *Intrepid* after three harrowing hours in the air. Van Antwerp attributed his division's survival to tight formation flying and the skill and aggressiveness of VF-18's fighter pilots; he also credited Lieutenant Al Long with destroying an enemy Oscar with machine gun fire and credited "all [Avenger] aircrewmen" with destroying another. When Bill Bates inspected his Avenger in the parking area after landing, he was astonished to learn how close he had come to not making it home. A wire cable from the exploding patrol boat in Tansui Harbor had blown into the air and wrapped itself around his Avenger's propeller shaft.

Ben St. John, flying from cloud to cloud for concealment, navigated his way back to the task group by dead reckoning. Any airplane approaching the task group alone was in grave danger of being shot down by the destroyer screen, even if the pilot was broadcasting on the right IFF identification channel. The Japanese had captured an American IFF and learned to mimic its signal (there were only four IFF channels to choose from), so American pilots were briefed to execute a 360-degree recognition turn in addition to broadcasting on the IFF channel designated for the day. The direction of turn also changed daily, and if the pilot turned the wrong way he would be shot down. Ben did things right and landed thirty minutes after the rest of his squadron. The torpeckers in the ready room were relieved to see him.

Of the twenty-three airplanes that had sortied as part of Strike 2 Able, three were lost; five men—three pilots and two Helldiver aircrewmen—did not return. Three of the Hellcat pilots who had taken off ahead of Strike 2 Able on the fighter sweep also did not return, the victims of antiaircraft fire or enemy fighters. The total losses for Air Group 18 that morning were six aircraft and eight men.

The news of Lieutenant Commander Eslick's death spread quickly throughout the ship. Men reacted with a mixture of disbelief, mystification, and anger. Eslick had been a conscientious and aggressive dive-bomber commander, always confident and seemingly invincible, but his admirable warrior qualities had not saved him. One of Eslick's wingmen on Strike 2 Able, Lieutenant Junior Grade John Forsyth, was furious that Lieutenant Eisengrein had failed to stick with Eslick in the clouds; Eisengrein's mistake had left Eslick with too few dive-bombers for the attack and permitted the Japanese antiaircraft gunners to concentrate their fire. Eslick's former executive officer, Lieutenant Commander George D. Ghesquiere, assumed command of the squadron and smoothed the waters. He showed support for Eisengrein by scheduling him to lead the second division again the next morning.

Air Group 18 had no time to mourn. *Intrepid* launched three more deck loads against northern Formosa on October 12.

Strike 2 Baker took off at eight twenty a.m. and hit Matsuyama Airfield at about ten ten a.m. Visibility was poor and Japanese flak was intense and accurate. VB-18 lost one Helldiver over the airfield to antiaircraft fire. A second Helldiver was struck by antiaircraft fire while pulling out of its dive-bombing run and sent tumbling. Unable to communicate with his pilot and believing his gyrating airplane to be mortally wounded, the rear-seat man bailed out. The pilot, Lieutenant John A. Thvedt, somehow regained control of his damaged dive-bomber, notwithstanding that much of its empennage had been shot away, and limped back to the task group. Rather than attempt a landing, Thvedt parachuted from his Helldiver and was rescued by a destroyer. A third Helldiver crash-landed back aboard *Intrepid* with its pilot and rear-seat man both bleeding profusely from bullet and shrapnel wounds. Four of the eight VT-18 Avengers assigned to Strike 2 Baker, including torpedo bombers flown by Bud Williams and Will Fletcher, returned from the Matsuyama Airfield riddled with bullet holes and shrapnel.

Strike 2 Charlie, launched at eleven fifteen a.m., bombed Kiirun Harbor for the second time that day at twelve thirty p.m. VB-18 suffered heavily again, losing two more Helldiver crews to antiaircraft fire. VT-18 nearly lost two Avengers. Lieutenant Ben Riley, leader of VT-18's Avenger division, returned with his airplane holed and streaming gasoline, and Lieutenant Junior Grade Donald W. "Moe" Morris returned with three feet of his right wing shot away.

Demonstrating superb airmanship, Morris managed to land back aboard *Intrepid* notwithstanding the damage to his airplane.

Strike 2 Dog, led by Lieutenant Commander Van Antwerp, launched at one fifteen p.m. with the objective of bombing Matsuyama Airfield for the second time that day. The weather, marginal at takeoff, deteriorated badly en route, so badly, in fact, that one division of dive-bombers became separated from the main group and turned back. Van Antwerp's pilots, forced to fly instruments and maintain tight formation for nearly the entire trip, arrived over Matsuyama Airfield to discover the target area completely socked in. Van Antwerp's bombers were obliged to jettison their loads over the Tansui River seaplane base, the same alternate target that Van Antwerp's strike group had bombed on Strike 2 Able. A weary Van Antwerp, who had led two strikes and logged seven hours of flight time on October 12, complained after his return to the ship that "the advisability of risking planes and pilots, and spending bombs, in weather such as this strike encountered is questionable."

The day had been costly for Air Group 18. The air group had lost nine pilots, including the skipper of the dive-bombing squadron, and six aircrew. Fifteen men had been killed within the space of six hours. Kenny Barden, who had flown with Van Antwerp in the first and fourth strikes of the day, recorded in his diary, "The picnic is now over."

The defense of Formosa was costly for the Japanese. Vice Admiral Fukudome had ordered aloft more than 230 fighters to ambush the attacking Americans on October 12 and had lost nearly a third of them. Fukudome's optimism had turned to despair as he watched American bombers and fighters press home their attacks and realized that the "long arching trails of smoke" he saw in the sky were burning Japanese fighters, not the enemy's. Fukudome bitterly observed that his young and undertrained fighter pilots were like "so many eggs thrown against the stone wall of the indomitable enemy formation." He nevertheless went on the offensive that night, dispatching bombers and torpedo planes from Formosan airfields to punish Task Force 38 for its trespasses.

Aboard *Intrepid* at seven p.m. that evening, radar operators detected an estimated forty-six enemy aircraft bearing down on the ship. Captain Bolger sounded general quarters, and, within minutes, the antiaircraft guns of the task group, including those of *Intrepid* and *New Jersey*, began firing into the sky.

Tracers soared into the dusk, and the sea was illuminated by the huge yellow-orange explosions of Japanese aircraft crashing into the water. *Intrepid* and her escorts also maneuvered defensively, changing course and speed every five minutes to confound the aim of Japanese bombers and torpedo planes. Drawn by the booming guns, Lieutenant George Race and a few pilots sneaked from the ready room to the flight deck to watch the light show. They didn't stay long. Someone in Race's party yelled that there were bullets ripping across *Intrepid*'s flight deck, and the group quickly retreated to the relative safety of the ready room. One of *Intrepid*'s escorts, firing at low-flying attackers, accidentally hit two of *Intrepid*'s sailors, who were stationed in a gun tub near her bow.

Firing ceased about ten thirty that night, but everyone remained at general quarters. Cooks carried buckets of hot coffee and sandwiches to men at their gun stations. Will Fletcher and his fellow pilots, trying to sleep in their ready room chairs, were awakened by a dull thud. Scuttlebutt reported that a Japanese torpedo had hit the ship but failed to detonate. One hour before dawn, exhausted plane handlers who had fallen asleep on the deck—they were lying side by side in the cramped quarters of *Intrepid*'s island—were awakened by their petty officers for the morning air strikes. The passageways reeked of sweating men.

Task Group 38.2 bombed Formosa again on October 13, a Friday. Superstition plays no role in modern war, or shouldn't, and no one dared suggest that Friday the thirteenth was too unlucky a day to fly. Besides, the men of Air Group 18 had learned that any day over Formosa was likely to be unlucky for some of them. *Intrepid*'s Strike 2 Able included six VT-18 Avengers, eight VF-18 Hellcats, seven of which were armed with five-hundred-pound general-purpose bombs, and twelve VB-18 Helldivers. VB-18's former executive officer and newly appointed skipper, Lieutenant Commander Ghesquiere, led the first dive-bomber division, and Lieutenant Eisengrein led the second.

The weather over northern Formosa was worse than the day before. The strike group was forced to climb through a solid overcast and didn't break into the clear until it reached thirteen thousand feet. The attackers then discovered their primary targets, Kiirun Harbor and Matsuyama Airfield, were closed in by clouds. Determined to inflict some damage on the enemy, the target coordinator directed the strike group to bomb an airfield and railyard at Shinchiku, a city on Formosa's northwestern shore. Strike 2 Able's fliers were compelled by the poor weather to fly west—nearly to the China coast, recorded Kenny Barden—

before they found a hole in the overcast through which they could descend for their attacks. The wind blew in from the China Sea at forty knots or more, making the bombing runs difficult. Strike 2 Able encountered no Japanese fighters over Shinchiku Airfield, perhaps because of the bad weather, but the enemy's antiaircraft fire over Shinchiku was radar controlled, intense, and accurate.

Air Group 18 dropped window for the first time in combat over Shinchiku. Each Avenger and Helldiver on Strike 2 Able had been supplied with thirty-five canvas bags of precut aluminum strips. As soon as the Japanese began shooting, Avenger radiomen and Helldiver rear-seat men emptied their bags of window into the slipstream, dispensing one bag of six hundred strips every four seconds. The slipstream sucked the aluminum strips into the air and they wafted through the sky like clouds of silver-sided leaves. Some of the strips blew back inside the airplanes—crews complained afterward that they needed a more efficient device for dispensing tinsel than a canvas bag—but enough of the stuff reached the atmosphere to have an effect. With window in the air, Japanese antiaircraft shells burst behind the American warplanes. As the American fliers nosed over into their bombing runs, the enemy's shells continued to explode at altitudes the attackers had vacated, rather than tracking them down in their descent. To the Americans' delight, the Japanese continued firing at "window clouds" for several minutes after the Helldivers and Avengers had dropped their bombs and made their getaway. El Gropo reported at the end of the day, "The use of window has an excellent effect on morale."

But window was not a shield. One of VB-18's Helldivers was hit during its dive-bombing run. The pilot headed for open water, just as he had been instructed, but the damage to his airplane was too severe. The smoking Helldiver rolled inverted and nose-dived for the water. The dive-bomber's wingman observed two silk canopies blossoming just before the Helldiver struck the water, but the parachutes disappeared quickly in the high wind and waves. Lieutenant Commander Ghesquiere broadcast an air-sea rescue message immediately to alert nearby American submarines of the crash site about a mile off Shinchiku, and Lieutenant Junior Grade John Forsyth orbited the scene looking for survivors. Forsyth saw nothing on the windswept sea but an empty, deflated life raft. When he landed back aboard *Intrepid*, Forsyth learned that the downed Helldiver pilot was Lieutenant Eisengrein, the man whom Forsyth had criticized the day before for losing contact with Eslick's division over Kiirun Harbor.

Northern Formosa remained closed in by weather on October 13, so Air

Group 18 launched two more deck loads against the only unclouded target of value that day, Shinchiku Airfield. On Strike 2 Baker, Bud Williams led an Avenger division comprised of only four airplanes. Battle damage from earlier strikes over Formosa had reduced the number of torpedo bombers available. Will Fletcher piloted one of the Avengers on Strike 2 Baker; he nosed over from nine thousand feet into a forty-degree glide-bombing run, dropped his thousand-pound on a nearby railyard, and then circled back to release four rockets on a string of freight cars. Westmoreland fed window out the tunnel hatch during Will's bombing and rocket runs, and their Avenger came through unscathed.

Fukudome's fliers ventured out again on the evening of October 13 to punish Task Force 38. Thirty-odd Japanese bombers, whose crews had been specially trained in night attack, took off at dusk. Some followed a path of float lights that Japanese scout planes had strung between the northern tip of Formosa and the last-known position of Halsey's warships. The attackers skimmed low over the water to avoid detection and attempted to deliver their bombs and torpedoes close in. The fleet carrier *Franklin* of Rear Admiral Davison's Task Group 38.4, and the heavy cruiser *Canberra* of Vice Admiral McCain's Task Group 38.1, were both struck. A Japanese bomb exploded on *Franklin*'s deck-edge elevator, setting her port side ablaze, and a Japanese aerial torpedo penetrated *Canberra* astern. *Franklin*'s damage-control crews quickly extinguished the fire, but *Canberra* ingested tons of seawater and lay immobile only ninety miles from Formosa.

The third day off Formosa, October 14, was scheduled to be a day of rest and refueling for Task Force 38, but Admiral Halsey ordered additional bombing raids and fighter sweeps over the island. VT-18, low on serviceable torpedo bombers, did not participate. For his part, Admiral Fukudome sent more than a hundred Japanese warplanes against Task Force 38 in at least three separate strikes, but only a few successfully eluded Halsey's combat air patrols or penetrated the wall of antiaircraft fire raised by Task Force 38's screen. VF-18's Hellcats jumped about forty of Admiral Fukudome's fighters, and the Devils claimed to have destroyed twenty, with no losses of their own.

Some of Fukudome's fliers did get through. *Intrepid* came under attack around three fifteen p.m., and her gunners shot down a Tony off her starboard bow. The light cruiser *Reno* of Rear Admiral Sherman's Task Group 38.3 was hit, apparently by a suicide attacker—the burning remnants of the Japanese aircraft and its pilot lay scattered across her weather decks—and the heavy cruiser *Houston*, then steaming as part of Rear Admiral Bogan's Task Group 38.2 (she was the namesake of the *Houston* sunk in February 1942 in the Java Sea), was torpedoed and disabled. But the Japanese attackers sank none of Halsey's ships. By the end of the third day of aerial combat over Formosa, nearly four hundred of Admiral Fukudome's fighters and bombers had been destroyed. On the morning of October 15, Halsey formed Task Group 30.3, code-named "Cripdiv" or "Baitdiv 1," to tow the crippled *Houston* and *Canberra* to Ulithi.

Japanese pilots who returned to Formosa from the night raids of October 12 and 13 were heartened by the explosions of their near-misses and inspired by their fiery successes against *Franklin* and *Canberra*. They reported a great naval victory to Fukudome and to his superior, Admiral Toyoda at Combined Fleet headquarters. These reports coincided with Admiral Halsey's shift of Task Force 38 northeast of Formosa on October 15 to regroup. Toyoda interpreted Halsey's movement as a retreat and he ordered Fukudome to attack "the remnants of the Third Fleet" with every remaining fighter and bomber.

For a time, the Japanese believed they had achieved a stunning victory off Formosa. The Japanese government announced to the nation that the Imperial Navy had sunk eleven American carriers, two battleships, three cruisers, and a light cruiser or destroyer, and damaged many more American ships. The Japanese admitted the loss of 312 aircraft, but claimed to have shot down 112 American warplanes. Emperor Hirohito decreed a celebration. Tokyo Rose reported in her radio broadcast that six carriers had been sunk and fifteen other warships had been damaged, and she assured the surviving pilots of Task Force 38 in her broadcast that the "Third Fleet is demoralized, scattered, and fleeing as a result of the day's action."

The Americans knew better. Secretary of the Navy James Forrestal telegraphed his congratulations to the men of the 3rd Fleet on their successes at Formosa, and Admiral Nimitz granted them a "well-done." Nimitz wrote, "In its recent crucial offensive, the Third Fleet has been a source of pride to us all and has inflicted destruction and disaster on our enemy which he will not forget." Referring to the exaggerated claims of the Japanese and the 3rd Fleet's upcoming attacks in the Philippines, Admiral Halsey radioed Nimitz, "The Third Fleet's sunken and damaged ships have been salvaged and are retiring at high speed toward the enemy."

As *Intrepid* steamed east of Formosa on October 15, Rear Admiral Bogan, Captain Bolger and Commander Ellis granted the men of Air Group 18 and *Intrepid* a few hours of well-deserved rest and relaxation—except for those on-duty airmen who were scheduled to fly combat air patrols and antisubmarine patrols, and those on-duty sailors who were preoccupied with running the ship and attending to essential chores, such as refueling *Intrepid* from the fleet oiler *Schuykill*. Off-duty aircrew and sailors caught up on their sleep, wrote letters home, read magazines, sunned themselves in the catwalks, or played basketball in the forward elevator shaft. Will Fletcher joined in a Ping-Pong tournament in the junior officers' recreation room. He had achieved a measure of shipboard notoriety as a crafty Ping-Pong player who had advanced through the brackets by playing defensively and picking just the right moment for his counterattack. When an opponent slammed a ball over the net, Will retreated and caught the ball below the lip of the table, slicing at the ball just out of his opponent's view. The ball usually looped back over the net like a combination changeup and curveball and bounced nearly ninety degrees to its flight path after it hit the table. His opponents fell out of their shoes trying to catch up and usually netted the ball or whacked it over the side.

That afternoon, Lieutenant Commander Allen advised VT-18's pilots that their next objective would likely be northern Luzon and perhaps Manila. This news brought a sense of relief to the boys in the ready room. Barden thought "the Manila assignment should be duck soup compared to the Formosa strikes." Air Group 18's pilots held an impromptu jam session in VT-18's ready room after the briefing. Several pilots had brought musical instruments aboard *Intrepid*, including a violin, a clarinet, two guitars, an accordion, and a mouth harp, and the aviators' little band—the musicians called themselves the "Peckerville Fighting Funsters"—convened in VT-18's ready room to celebrate the end of the Formosa ordeal. Lieutenant Junior Grade Doc Doyle acted as master of ceremonies, and Lieutenant Junior Grade Moe Morris, who two days earlier had landed his Avenger back aboard with a damaged wing, danced a jitterbug with Lieutenant Junior Grade Leon Vannais. Even El Gropo joined in; he strummed an old ukulele and rasped the lyrics to "Lovely Hula Hands," apparently the only song he knew. Nonmusical pilots, such as Will Fletcher and Lloyd Karch, crowded around the players to heckle and clap appreciatively.

These musical diversions evoked mixed emotions in Will. On the one hand, singing familiar songs with his buddies amused him and bound him ever closer to his squadron mates; on the other hand the music made him feel homesick and pine for simpler times. The tunes were the same ones Will had listened to at home on his mother's Motorola, but Will was no longer the same callow boy who had once enjoyed them. The familiar melodies emphasized the gulf between the riskless civilian life he had once led and the dangerous job of grim reaper he now performed almost daily. The songfest after *Intrepid*'s withdrawal from Formosa was especially bittersweet; too many voices had gone missing forever from Air Group 18's chorus of singers.

The air battles over Formosa caused the boys to reflect. They admitted to one another that the war seemed much tougher now, much less the great adventure. War was an exhausting and dangerous undertaking, with no rules and little predictability. The enemy was plentiful and tenacious, determined to defend their homeland. The path to ultimate victory seemed far steeper than it had appeared on the Palau Islands or in the Visayas. After the very first day of combat over Formosa, El Gropo had approved an entry in Air Group 18's aircraft action report that read, "It is generally agreed that northern Formosa can be considered a serious obstacle on the road to Tokyo." The subsequent days had confirmed Ellis's assessment.

The boys were relieved to abandon Formosan waters and return to the Philippines, where Japanese resistance had been far less aggressive and costly, but their relief turned to disappointment on the night of October 15. Admiral Halsey had received intelligence reports indicating that Japanese fleet units were on the move north of Okinawa. Ever eager to engage Japanese fleet units wherever he could find them, Halsey ordered Mitscher's task group commanders to locate and destroy the enemy surface force. Advised that planes from Task Group 38.2 would search for the enemy fleet units at first light, Barden closed his diary on the fifteenth with the lament, "I knew the Leyte operation was too good to be true."

Enemy warships were, in fact, on the move. A squadron of three cruisers and seven destroyers commanded by Vice Admiral Kiyohide Shima had sortied from Japan's Inland Sea to search for the remnants of 3rd Fleet. Emboldened by the exaggerated reports of a great Japanese victory off Formosa, imperial headquarters had dispatched Shima's surface warships, which normally served as a screening force for Admiral Ozawa's Mobile Fleet of aircraft carriers, to administer the coup de grâce to Halsey's 3rd Fleet. Shima had cautiously probed the waters east of the Ryukyu Islands looking for damaged American aircraft carriers waiting to be sunk.

Bunker Hill launched long-range searches at dawn looking for Shima, and Task Group 38.2 prepared once again for combat. *Intrepid* and Air Group 18 set Condition 11, which for VT-18 meant there were eight Avengers spotted on *Intrepid*'s flight deck armed with torpedoes and ready for takeoff on ten minutes' notice. Commander Ellis had ordered the Avengers equipped with wing tanks to extend their range, but there was disagreement in VT-18's ready room—a "big uproar" was how Barden described it—about whether the torpedo bombers would get airborne with such a heavy load. Barden thought it "doubtful" that the Avengers would get off the deck.

VT-18's torpeckers spent a tense day in the ready room waiting. At about four twenty-five p.m. on October 16, Halsey's searchers spotted an enemy formation northeast of Formosa, reported to include twelve Japanese surface ships, four of them heavy, and a light aircraft carrier. Five minutes later, Van Antwerp advised his boys that Air Group 18 would launch a strike against the enemy warships within the hour. The skipper's announcement compounded the usual precombat anxieties among VT-18's pilots. A daylight strike was dangerous enough, but a late-afternoon launch would mean a late return to the ship, with the likelihood of men landing in the water at night with no gas, as had happened to many of Spruance's carrier pilots during the Battle of the Philippine Sea. After a three-hour wait, the squadron secured from flight quarters without launching anyone, to everyone's relief. The prospect of launching late in the day had been "chilling," in Barden's words. He wrote simply, "Thank God we weren't launched."

By sunset on October 16, Vice Admiral Shima had learned from the reports of Japanese scout planes that Task Force 38 was far from battered and impotent. Mitscher's many aircraft carriers, even those that had been hit by Japanese bombs, were fully operational, and Task Force 38's battleships, cruisers, and destroyers seemed numerous as the stars. Shima sensibly broke off his ill-founded search for cripples and retreated to Japanese home waters. Imperial headquarters had decided to assign Shima a supporting role in Admiral Toyoda's Sho-1 plan for a defense of the Philippines, and Shima stood by patiently for further instructions.

Expecting an order to attack Shima's force, VT-18's torpeckers sat in their ready room suited up in flight gear until noon on October 17, when Van Antwerp finally placed VT-18's third division on standby status and permitted the balance of his weary pilots to stand down from flight quarters. American search planes had lost contact with the enemy surface force off Okinawa. Van Antwerp assured his torpeckers that Task Group 38.2 would steam south during the night and bomb northern Luzon in the morning.

The boys were tired. Tired from the sleepless nights. Tired from the pace of flying. Tired from the stress of standing by to fly. Tired from the tension of enemy air attacks. Tired from the strain of trying to keep an edge. Kenny Barden and the boys yearned for a respite, for a return to port. Any port would do, even desolate Ulithi.

But rest was not in the cards for VT-18.

CHAPTER NINE

IN THE SIBUYAN SEA

★ ★ ★ ★ ★

On October 16, 1944, the same day Barden and the boys sweated through the prospect of launching a late-afternoon long-range strike against Shima's cruisers and destroyers, General Douglas MacArthur's huge Philippine invasion force departed Allied bases on New Guinea's northern coast. Japanese passivity in defending the Philippines during Task Force 38's carrier raids of September 1944, and the loss of Allied air bases in China, had persuaded the Joint Chiefs to accelerate their timetable for the Philippine invasion. They had selected the eastern beaches of Leyte Island as the initial invasion point, with the ultimate goal of seizing Mindoro, landing on Luzon at Lingayen Gulf, and eliminating Japanese ground forces concentrated near Manila. MacArthur himself sailed aboard *Nashville*, a light cruiser that would serve as the flagship of his invasion armada. The U.S. 7th Fleet, under the command of Vice Admiral Thomas C. Kinkaid, provided transport and seaborne defense for Lieutenant General Walter Krueger's landing force of 174,000 men.

Kinkaid's invasion convoy, consisting of 420 transports and nearly 160 warships, steamed northward from New Guinea on a three-day journey. As MacArthur himself described the scene from the deck of the *Nashville*, there were "ships to the front, to the rear, to the left and to the right, as far as the eye could see. Their sturdy hulls ploughed the water, now presenting a broadside view, now their stems, as they methodically carried out the zigzag tactics of evasion."

An American naval force under the command of Rear Admiral Jesse Oldendorf had preceded Kinkaid's armada to the waters east of Leyte Gulf. This preinvasion force included minesweepers, destroyer-transports loaded with an Army Ranger battalion, and a small naval bombardment group comprised of the battleship *Pennsylvania*, three cruisers, and a number of supporting destroyers. The principal objectives of Oldendorf's preinvasion force were to seize several small islands at the entrance to Leyte Gulf, thereby eliminating Japanese radar installations on the outlying islands, and to clear the minefields that floated north of Dinagat Island at the entrance to Leyte Gulf.

Fifteen hundred miles to the southwest of Leyte Gulf at Lingga Roads, Vice Admiral Takeo Kurita prepared to execute Admiral Toyoda's plan for defeating the American 3rd Fleet in Philippine waters. Privately, Kurita had come to the conclusion that Japan had already lost the war, but he had been schooled in the doctrine of decisive battle and understood that his First Striking Force offered Japan her last real hope of checking the seemingly inexorable American advance. Although Imperial Headquarters did not yet know precisely where the Americans would land in the Philippines (opinion was divided among Japanese strategists as to whether the Americans would attempt an amphibious landing on Luzon or elsewhere in the Philippines), Kurita had readied his First Striking Force to sortie north at a moment's notice. He had trained his squadron in gunnery and maneuver for more than two months and had provisioned, fueled, and armed his warships for the great confrontation.

In selecting Takeo Kurita to lead the First Striking Force, Admiral Toyoda had chosen a veteran naval commander. A descendant of scholars and academics, Kurita had enrolled at Etajima in 1905, the year of the great Japanese naval victory over the Russians at Tsushima. Takeo means to "be a great warrior" and Takeo Kurita had lived up to the name, having led a cruiser division in the battles of the Java Sea and Midway and commanded the battleship *Kongo* at the battles of Santa Cruz and Guadalcanal. Kurita had spent much of his adult life at sea but had never attended any of Japan's postgraduate war colleges. His contemporaries did not regard him as an intellectual officer, but he had performed admirably in war games and competently in combat. He had become a specialist in surface torpedo attack, an aggressive style of naval warfare highly favored by the Imperial Navy in which cruisers and destroyers maneuvered at high speed and launched deadly Long Lance torpedoes at the enemy. When he assumed command of the First Striking Force, Kurita chose the cruiser *Atago*, rather than one of the palatial *Yamatos*, as his flagship, because Japanese fleet commanders traditionally served aboard cruisers, and Kurita himself preferred a more nimble, torpedo-launching cruiser beneath his feet. Kurita had a reputation as a congenial commander, unlike other senior Japanese naval officers, who, as a class, were notorious for their aloofness and severity.

Oldendorf began reconnaissance and minesweeping operations near Dinagat Island on the morning of October 17. These preinvasion activities alerted Japanese Imperial Headquarters that the long-anticipated American invasion of the Philippines was imminent and that the Americans intended to land somewhere within Leyte Gulf. By midafternoon on October 17, Admiral Toyoda had ordered Kurita's First Striking Force and Vice Admiral Ozawa's Mobile Fleet, which now consisted of four aircraft carriers, two hybrid battleship-carriers (called "hermaphrodites" by the Americans), and a handful of light cruisers and destroyers, to stand by for further orders to execute the Sho-1 plan. Ozawa, who had been working feverishly in Japan's Inland Sea to train new carrier air groups to replace those destroyed in the Marianas, abruptly ceased training and marshaled his Mobile Fleet for the dash south to the Philippines. Ozawa could muster no more than 116 combat aircraft for his six carriers, and most of these warplanes were piloted by inexperienced aviators.

Vice Admiral Kurita directed his subordinate commanders to strip their warships for action. Aboard *Musashi*, sailors removed bedding, curtains, wooden furniture, and other flammables from the crew's quarters and swept the officers' wardroom bare of accoutrements, except for the sacred portrait of Emperor Hirohito. Sailors who only a month before had brushed a coat of dark paint on the battleship's exterior now chipped paint from the ship's interior passageways to prevent the spread of fire. To complement the ship's dark exterior, Captain Inoguchi ordered his crew to blacken *Musashi*'s weather decks with soot from her boiler tubes to better conceal her in the darkness.

At about one a.m. on October 18, Kurita's First Striking Force sortied from Lingga Roads and set course for the Japanese naval base at Brunei Bay, Borneo, eight hundred miles southwest of the Leyte landing beaches, there to refuel and await final instructions for the run northward to the Philippines. By dawn, the giant *Yamatos* and their consorts, which had dotted Lingga Roads like a score of man-made islands, had vanished from the anchorage.

In an emotional meeting at Imperial General Headquarters in Tokyo on October 18, Admiral Toyoda disclosed to officers of the Imperial Japanese Army his plan to destroy the American landing force on the beaches of Leyte and engage the United States Navy in a decisive battle. Toyoda pledged his Combined Fleet to the destruction of American naval forces in Leyte Gulf "with every available ship." When senior army officers protested that the loss of the Imperial Navy would leave the Japanese home islands open to invasion, Toyoda's chief of operations pleaded with Imperial General Headquarters to allow the Combined Fleet to "bloom as flowers of death." That same afternoon, Emperor Hirohito personally assented to the execution of Toyoda's Sho-1 plan.

Sho-1 required coordinated movements among Kurita's First Striking Force, Vice Admiral Ozawa's Mobile Fleet, and Japanese naval air forces based in the Philippines. (The last were denominated "5, 6, and 7 Base Air Forces.") Under Toyoda's initial plan, the Mobile Fleet would steam south from Japan's Inland Sea and attempt to draw Admiral Halsey's carrier forces away from the invasion area to the north. Meanwhile, the First Striking Force would steam north from Brunei Bay: "Avoiding the attack of the enemy task force, [First Striking Force] will push forward and engage in a decisive battle with the surface force which tries to stop it. After annihilating this force, it will then attack and wipe out the enemy convoy and troops at the landing point." The base air forces were to "concentrate all the airpower at their disposal, proceed at a favorable opportunity, and await the approach of the enemy invasion force." After the Americans landed, the air forces were to "shift to an all-out attack upon the enemy task force and invasion force." Japanese troops based in the Philippines were to "make every effort to annihilate the enemy on the beaches, but if [the enemy] succeeds in landing, [the defense force] will fight to the death to prevent [the enemy's] occupation and use of the airfields."

Task Force 38 announced its return to the Philippines by bombing Luzon on October 18. *Intrepid* and Air Group 18 launched two deck loads, a total of fifty-one sorties, against the Japanese airfield and harbor at Aparri on Luzon's northern coast. Commander Ellis, leading a combined strike group from *Intrepid* and *Bunker Hill*, found little of interest at Aparri, but discovered four transports in a secluded bay near Camiguin Island. Ellis's attackers blazed two of the transports, sank the other two, and left "three or four hundred Japs . . . swimming around in the water." Ellis characterized the Camiguin strike as "a fruitful morning's work," but complained that the second strike of the day had been "a poor one" due to the lack of suitable targets. Ellis pleaded with Rear Admiral Bogan, "[W]hen advance intelligence is lacking and targets are an unknown quantity, the first strikes [should] be fighter and reconnaissance sweeps." Targets should be carefully preselected based on photographic reconnaissance, and aircraft and ordnance should be matched to the targets. Ellis grumbled, "Routine four-a-day fighter-bomber-torpedo plane strikes against nonspecific targets result in a prodigious waste of power and bombs, in addition to tying up fighters who might otherwise be strafing or fighting, unhampered by escort duties."

Though intended to suppress Japanese airpower in the Philippines, Task Force 38's air strikes on northern Luzon probably had less to do with inflicting meaningful damage on the enemy than with keeping the Japanese off balance as to American designs. But on October 19, the Americans showed their hand unmistakably. Oldendorf's bombardment and fire-support group, comprised of twenty-six surface warships, opened fire on Violet and Yellow beaches near Dulag and on White and Red beaches near Tacloban, the capitol city of Leyte. At dawn on October 20, "A-day," assault day, the day of the invasion, Oldendorf's battleships and cruisers again cannonaded the landing beaches at Leyte, and Avengers, Hellcats, and Wildcats from the eighteen escort carriers of Task Group 77.4, commanded by Rear Admiral Thomas L. Sprague, *Intrepid*'s old skipper, strafed and bombed the invasion area. The heavy bombardment of Oldendorf's surface ships, supplemented by rocket fire from innumerable naval gunboats, transformed the Leyte beachheads from a verdant jungle of palm trees and brush into "a solid sheet of blinding and exploding flame." When the bombardment lifted at about nine forty-five a.m., waves of landing craft laden with American troops and material motored across the placid waters of Leyte Gulf toward the shoreline.

Unbeknownst to the Americans, the two main elements of the Combined Fleet were converging on the Philippines in force. By midday on October 20, A-day,

Vice Admiral Kurita's First Striking Force of nearly forty warships had rumbled to anchor in Brunei Bay, Borneo, completing the first stage of its journey to Leyte Gulf. Twelve hundred miles north of the Philippines, Vice Admiral Ozawa's Mobile Fleet of aircraft carriers and escorts had weighed anchor for Luzon, departing Japan's Inland Sea only hours after General MacArthur waded ashore at Red Beach to broadcast his message of liberation to the Filipino people.

The next day, October 21, General Krueger's landing force moved inland from the American beachhead on Leyte and seized the town of Dulag and Tacloban Airfield. To suppress Japanese airpower in the area, Task Force 38 launched multiple air strikes across its old familiar bombing grounds, the central Visayas. For their part, *Intrepid* and Air Group 18 struck Japanese airfields in eastern Panay and Negros. On Strike 2 Able, Van Antwerp's division of Avengers executed a combined rocket and bombing attack on a Japanese freighter off Panay, but inflicted minimal damage. Several rockets failed to fire, and the torpeckers' bombing proved uncharacteristically inaccurate. Commander Ellis judged the enemy airfields on Panay and Negros to be worthless targets, with no enemy airplanes on the ground (or in the air, to the disappointment of VF-18's fighter boys), and with the enemy's supporting facilities built of "flimsy, shack-like construction easily and cheaply replaced."

The day got worse. Admiral Bogan had launched Strike 2 Able more than two hundred nautical miles from its objective. VT-18's Avengers had taken off without auxiliary wing tanks, and the long-range mission had nearly sucked the torpedo bombers dry. Three Avengers, including Barden's, Van Antwerp's, and Bates's, each landed back aboard *Intrepid* with less than fifteen gallons of fuel remaining, sufficient for only ten to twelve minutes of flying time at low power. Avengers flown by Joe Rubin and Duke Delaney were forced to divert to *Lexington*, which was then operating closer to Samar as part of Task Group 38.3; they landed with less than five gallons each. A sixth fuel-starved Avenger, piloted by Lieutenant Albert Long (VT-18's original temporary commander), water-landed alongside *Intrepid*. This was Long's second water landing within a week. Although Long and his turret gunner escaped the sinking Avenger, the radioman did not. Long, afloat in his Mae West, watched helplessly from the water as his radioman, Aviation Radioman Third Class Billy Hunter of Seattle, Washington, struggled frantically to open the torpedo bomber's tunnel hatch. High waves made it impossible for Long to assist Hunter, and the torpedo bomber sank, taking Hunter with it. Billy Hunter had been a popular man in the squadron, and his buddies whispered angrily among themselves that Long had mismanaged his Avenger's fuel consumption and was responsible for Hunter's death.

Strike 2 Able had been poorly executed, minimally productive, and fatal. Barden judged the mission the worst of his career and summed up the day with the comment, "Everything went wrong."

On October 21, Admiral Toyoda ordered Vice Admiral Kurita to break into Leyte Gulf on the morning of October 25. Kurita convened his division commanders aboard *Atago*, still riding calmly at anchor in Brunei Bay, to discuss the Sho-1 plan. There was consternation among Kurita's division commanders, including *Musashi*'s skipper, Rear Admiral Inoguchi (who had been promoted while at Lingga Roads), that the plan now required a daylight attack on the American warships and transports in Leyte Gulf. Most Japanese naval officers had been trained to fight their ships at night, and they prided themselves on their night-fighting skills; the planned daylight attack deprived them of this tactical advantage and of the element of surprise. Inoguchi also strongly disapproved of turning the monster guns of *Musashi* and *Yamato* against the American landing force. He preferred a confrontation with American battleships and other warships of the line, not transports. Japan's two mightiest battleships, the pride of the Imperial Navy and the puissant symbols of Japan's fleet in being, deserved a worthy foe.

Privately, Kurita may have agreed with the fiery Inoguchi, but he silenced disagreement among his officers by reminding them of the "glorious opportunity" that Imperial Headquarters had presented them. Kurita acknowledged that First Striking Force had been assigned a difficult mission, one that might result in the destruction of half of the Combined Fleet, but he asked his officers rhetorically to sacrifice themselves, saying, "Would it not be a shame to have the fleet remain intact while the nation perishes?" Kurita transformed the likelihood of defeat into hope by reminding his officers that "there are such things as miracles." He challenged his captains pointedly, asking, "What man can say that there is no chance for our fleet to turn the tide of war in a Decisive Battle," to which his officers responded with lusty cries of, "Banzai!"

Kurita informed his subordinate commanders of recent refinements to Admiral Toyoda's original plan for destroying the American invasion force. Although Vice Admiral Ozawa would proceed with his feint against northern Luzon to draw the American carriers away from the landing area as initially planned, Kurita's First Striking Force would be split into two groups of unequal size to permit an attack on the American landing beaches from different directions. The smaller group, known as Force C (which the Americans would later dub "Southern Force"), would be commanded by Vice Admiral Shoji Nishimura. Consisting of two battleships, a cruiser, and four destroyers, Nishimura's Force C would steam northeast from Brunei Bay and enter Surigao Strait, the narrow seaway between southern Leyte and northern Mindanao, during the night of October 24. Kurita himself would retain command of the larger part of the First Striking Force, known as Force A (which the Americans would later call "Center Force"), consisting of battleships *Musashi*, *Yamato*, *Nagato*, *Kongo*, and *Haruna*, eleven cruisers, and sixteen destroyers. Force A would approach Letye through the Sibuyan Sea, remaining west of Leyte for as long as possible to avoid American search aircraft, and pass through San Bernardino Strait, the east–west passage between southern Luzon and northern Samar, on the night of October 24. Early the next morning, Force A and Force C would converge on the Americans at Leyte, pressing home their attacks from opposite directions and crushing the Americans in a naval vise. A third surface force, commanded by Vice Admiral Shima, would lend weight to Force C and trail Nishimura's warships through Surigao Strait during their night passage.

On October 22, Admiral Halsey withdrew Task Force 38 to a position roughly two hundred miles east of the central Philippines and considered his next moves. The tactical situation in the Visayas seemed to have stabilized. General MacArthur's ground forces were safely ashore at Leyte and progressing inland. Admiral Sprague's escort carriers, aided by Admiral Oldendorf's battleships and cruisers, were protecting the American transports at anchor in Leyte Gulf and providing close-air support for troops on the ground. Third Fleet's air suppression raids over Okinawa, Formosa, Luzon, and the Visayas appeared to have virtually wiped out Japanese naval airpower; very few enemy aircraft had contested the American amphibious landings. Although Halsey was concerned over the exact whereabouts of the Japanese carrier fleet, American intelligence had received no indication of any significant movements by Japanese fleet units. Personally, Halsey did not believe the Japanese navy would commit to a decisive battle until it had rebuilt its carrier-borne air forces.

Worried about the continuing strain on his pilots, Halsey decided to use the combat hiatus to rotate his carrier air groups through Ulithi and Manus to rest, rearm, and refuel. Halsey reassigned the heavy carrier *Hancock* from Task Group 38.2 to Task Group 38.1, and ordered Task Group 38.1 under Vice Admiral John McCain to retire east to Ulithi. Aboard *Intrepid*, pilots welcomed the respite from combat flight operations, even though they were not among the lucky ones chosen for a Ulithi vacation. Air Group 18 flew nothing but routine antisubmarine searches and combat air patrols over the task force on October 22. Barden, who hadn't scheduled himself for any searches, settled into a daylong bridge tournament with his buddies. "Bridge, bridge and bridge—nothing else," was his diary entry for the twenty-second. But nothing was about to change to something. As Kenny Barden dealt the cards in the ready room that morning, Kurita's First Striking Force departed Brunei Bay for the western Philippines.

American submarines operating from Allied bases in southeast Australia routinely patrolled the South China Sea and the western approaches to the Philippines. About three a.m. on October 23, submarines *Darter* and *Dace*, whose commanders were unaware that major elements of the Combined Fleet had shifted from Lingga Roads to Brunei, detected Kurita's Force A steaming off the western coast of Palawan Island near an area of reefs and shoals known as "the Dangerous Ground." Kurita had arrayed Force A in five parallel columns, stationing his flagship *Atago* at the head of the far port column of capital ships. Over the next two hours, *Darter* and *Dace* tracked Kurita's formation and maneuvered into firing position. At about five thirty a.m., *Darter*'s skipper elected to attack the head of Kurita's column. Firing from the submarine's bow and stern tubes, *Darter*'s crew methodically loosed multiple torpedoes at the first and second ships in the enemy van. At least four of *Darter*'s torpedoes struck *Atago* broadside as she maneuvered in the midst of an evasion turn, and two others slammed into the cruiser *Takao*, which was next in line behind *Atago*. Holed and burning, *Atago* began listing heavily.

Admiral Kurita quickly abandoned his dying flagship. Kurita and the surviving members of his staff slid over *Atago*'s side, and crewmen of the destroyer *Kishinami* fished them from the oily water and transferred them to *Yamato*. *Atago* sank rapidly, taking with her nearly 360 of her crewmen. Meanwhile, the submarine *Dace* had assaulted the starboard column of capital ships headed by the cruiser *Myoko*. *Dace*'s torpedoes exploded against the third ship in line, the heavy cruiser *Maya*, causing her to break up and sink within minutes. *Takao* was heavily damaged, but did not sink. She retired to Borneo and became one less warship with which the Americans at Leyte would have to contend.

Although the attacks of *Darter* and *Dace* resulted in the loss of three enemy warships—a spectacular feat of arms—the submarines' encounters with Kurita's Force A were perhaps of greater tactical value for the information they provided 3rd Fleet. The Americans at Leyte had been uncertain of the precise location of Japanese fleet units. Reports by *Darter* and *Dace* of at least eleven enemy warships, three of them battleships, approaching the western Philippines from the south alerted the Americans that a significant Japanese naval force was on the move. The submarines' intelligence reports, first radioed to 7th Fleet headquarters in Australia, reached *New Jersey* shortly after breakfast on October 23. Admiral Halsey's staff officers were divided and undecided over Japanese intentions. Was this Japanese naval force simply running troop reinforcements to the Philippines, or did it pose a serious threat to the Leyte invasion area? Halsey discounted the latter, observing that the enemy formation lacked aircraft carriers. The Japanese would not provoke a decisive battle without their carriers, Halsey insisted. He believed he had sufficient carrier forces to deal with any surface threat, and he initially rejected the idea of recalling *Bunker Hill* or McCain's Task Group 38.1 from Ulithi, thereby leaving Rear Admiral Bogan's Task Group 38.2 with only three aircraft carriers, *Intrepid* and two light carriers, *Cabot* and *Independence*.

But Halsey decided to hedge his tactical bet by shifting Task Force 38, minus McCain's Task Group 38.1, closer to the Philippines during the night of October 23. Under Halsey's precautionary plan, three of Vice Admiral Mitscher's fast-carrier task groups would be deployed off the eastern shore of the Philippines on a north–south line, roughly a hundred nautical miles apart, by dawn the next day. Task Group 38.3 under Rear Admiral Forrest Sherman would be stationed farthest to the north, about ninety miles off central Luzon; Rear Admiral Bogan's Task Force 38.2, containing *Intrepid*, *Cabot*, and *Independence*, would be positioned about seventy miles off the entrance to the San Bernardino Strait; and Task Group 38.4 under Rear Admiral Ralph Davison would be stationed about sixty miles off southern Samar, not far from the northern approaches to Leyte Gulf. Halsey also directed task groups 38.2 and 38.4 to conduct air searches of the central and southern Philippines at first light on October 24.

Aboard *Intrepid* on October 23, VT-18's torpeckers waited for word of where Air Group 18 would strike next. Barden played more bridge in the ready room and seized on late-afternoon scuttlebutt that predicted Task Group 38.2 would head north to look for Japanese ships and provide protection for the injured *Houston* and *Canberra*. That night, Admiral Bogan and El Gropo marshaled fighters and dive-bombers for a dawn search of the Sibuyan Sea, and discussed equipping their Avengers with wing tanks. Barden scheduled Van Antwerp's 1st Division for a possible first strike, and the boys retired for the night, knowing they would be on standby to launch in the morning. Shortly after midnight on October 24, Bogan detached *Independence* for night operations close to Samar, leaving Task Group 38.2 with only two carriers off Samar, *Intrepid* and *Cabot*.

At four a.m. on the twenty-fourth, reveille sounded in the darkness of Will Fletcher's bunkroom.

CHAPTER TEN

ON STRIKE 2 ABLE

★　★　★　★　★

Vice Admiral Kurita had anticipated air attacks from Halsey's aircraft carriers as Force A approached the western Philippine island of Mindoro and entered Tablas Strait, the broad seaway between the islands of Mindoro and Panay. In the early morning hours of October 24 Kurita rearranged his armada under cloak of darkness to concentrate its antiaircraft fire, deploying his warships in two defensive circles of thirteen ships each. He placed seven capital ships—the the big-gunned battleships and heavy cruisers—at the center of each defensive circle and stationed six destroyers around the perimeter. He compressed the distance between the ships in each circle to between fifteen hundred and two thousand yards. Kurita's new flagship, *Yamato*, and her sister ship, *Musashi*, sailed at the center of the lead circle, with *Musashi* steaming off *Yamato*'s starboard rear quarter. The battleships *Kongo* and *Haruna* sailed at the center of Kurita's second defensive circle and trailed the first circle of warships by five or six miles.

Kurita had requested Japanese headquarters in Manila to provide fighter cover for Force A while it traversed the Sibuyan Sea, but as dawn broke on October 24, no friendly aircraft appeared overhead with the sun. Commanders of Japanese naval air forces in the Philippines had decided to commit their warplanes to concentrated air strikes on American aircraft carriers operating in the Philippine Sea off Leyte Gulf, not to Kurita's defense. At about eight a.m., Kurita's radar operators detected enemy airplanes circling near his formation. These were Commander Ellis's sector three search planes from *Intrepid*.

At about eight ten a.m., Rear Admiral Inoguchi ordered *Musashi*'s twenty-four hundred sailors to battle stations. Above *Musashi*'s main deck, antiaircraft gun crews quickly unlimbered their weapons and readied their ordnance. Many of the gunners tied white hachimaki or "victory" headbands around their heads. A hachimaki was, in essence, a white scarf marked with a bloodred rising sun; when the hachimaki was tied properly, the rising sun blazed from the wearer's forehead. Belowdecks, *Musashi*'s sailors rushed to their assigned battle stations. Once there, they dogged watertight doors and hatches behind them to minimize flooding from compartment to compartment, and shut ventilation ducts to prevent the spread of fire and smoke. The sailors belowdecks effectively sealed themselves inside their compartments and cut themselves off from comrades in adjacent compartments. Their only means of communicating during the coming battle would be via electric telephone or voice tube. Aboard *Musashi* and the other ships of Kurita's Force A, thousands of Japanese sailors waited anxiously but confidently for the inevitable American air assault. Few of them believed American pilots possessed the skills or the fortitude to press home their attacks and do the emperor's ships much harm. The American search planes, unmolested by Japanese antiaircraft fire or fighters, had shadowed Kurita's formation from nine thousand feet at a distance of three to five miles until about nine ten a.m. and then disappeared.

Petty Officer Second Class Shiro Hosoya's battle station was in a signal booth connected to *Musashi*'s compass bridge, the second of three bridges built into the battleship's mountainous gunfire control tower. Hosoya had a clear view of *Musashi*'s main deck forward of her conning tower, including the ring of antiaircraft guns at the base of *Musashi*'s conning tower and her forward gun turrets. As a supervisor of signalmen, Hosoya had few duties in combat. On the morning of October 24, he enjoyed the panoramic views from his battle station and the beautiful weather. The blue-green mountains of Mindoro Island, their volcanic peaks brightly illuminated by the morning sun, lay far to his left. The low emerald hills of Tablas Island glided by *Musashi* off Hosoya's right. The sky was clear, except for a cluster of cumulus clouds that hovered over Tablas Island.

At about ten a.m., *Musashi*'s radar operators detected a large formation of unidentified airplanes, presumably American, heading toward the Center Force from the east. *Musashi*'s officers sounded the alert, and Hosoya observed *Musashi*'s gunners training their weapons expectantly toward the sun. At about ten twenty, *Musashi*'s long-range antiaircraft guns opened fire at targets Hosoya could not see. Only minutes later, Hosoya spied through the smoke a cluster of dark specks northeast of his ship, very high in the sky. The specks arranged themselves into smaller groups of twos and threes, like dash marks in the heavens. One by one, or in groups of two and three, the specks separated from their companions. Some dived at steep angles toward the sea, veering either toward *Musashi* or the nearby battleship *Nagato*. The diving specks plummeted vertically toward the water, like stones tossed off a cliff, and they grew larger and more distinct as they descended. Hosoya knew each falling stone was a dive-bomber pressing home an attack.

Hosoya swelled with pride and confidence as *Musashi*'s gunners fired at the dive-bombers, filling the morning sky with exploding shells and clouds of white phosphorous. Iridescent streams of varicolored machine gun fire swept across the heavens, intersecting and converging on the descending warplanes. The noise of *Musashi*'s guns was deafening, and smoke billowed aft in dark, angry clouds. Hosoya was awestruck by the spectacle. He thought it inconceivable that a seabird or a butterfly, much less an enemy airplane, could evade such a murderous barrage. Unexpectedly, two bombs exploded close by *Musashi*, sending up huge columns of smoke and spume. *Musashi* sailed on serenely, seemingly unfazed, and Hosoya concluded that the American bombs had not done his ship any serious injury. A third bomb clanged off *Musashi*'s number one gun turret near her forecastle and bounced into the sea; the bomb stripped the heavy armor plate from the turret but did not explode. Hosoya recited the words of a song he had sung many times as a member of *Musashi*'s crew. They were lyrics in which he fervently believed: "The *Musashi* is unsinkable. . . ."

As he descended with Bud Williams for the attack, Will Fletcher anxiously eyed his target. The big *Yamato*-class battleship was maneuvering in the middle of Tablas Strait, weaving back and forth across a northeasterly base course. She was surrounded by a ring of older battleships, heavy cruisers, and fast destroyers. Even at a distance of fifteen miles, his target seemed to be a floating castle, a dark fortress of malevolence. Her immense size distorted the scale of things. The ships of her screen, all powerful and dangerous warships in their own right, were mere toy boats on a pond by comparison. Several thousand yards northwest of Will's target sailed a second *Yamato*-class battleship, a mirror image of the first. Although Will did not know it at the time, his target was *Musashi*, and the distant battleship was *Yamato* herself, with Vice Admiral Kurita aboard.

Williams led his division southwest toward Tablas Island, intending to duck into the cloud deck that stretched across the northern end of the island. Williams's plan was to conceal his division's approach to *Musashi* in the same blanket of clouds that had initially obscured the Japanese armada, and thereby escape the murderous gunfire coming from the battleship and her screen. The plan was a good one, so long as the Japanese guns were not radar controlled. Unfortunately, the bases of the clouds were high; Williams estimated the ceiling to be four or five thousand feet. His torpeckers would have to press home their torpedo runs clear of the clouds, and with good visibility for attackers and defenders alike.

Williams signaled his pilots to jettison their Avengers' external fuel tanks. Will had earlier shifted to his center main tank for fuel, and he toggled the electrical switches that released his external tanks into the air. He glimpsed the drop tanks of the other Avengers in Williams's division tumbling toward the water like so many empty barrels; he asked Westmoreland over the intercom whether his own drop tanks had fallen away cleanly, and Westmoreland reported that they had.

Colored bursts from the enemy's medium-range antiaircraft guns tracked Williams's six-plane division as it descended from nine thousand feet. The Japanese navy fired dual-purpose artillery shells that contained dyes of blue, red, yellow, green, and orange; the exploding Technicolor puffs enabled the gunners to gauge the range and fall of their shot and make adjustments. Shells detonated close by Williams's torpedo bombers, generating shock waves that rattled the Avengers like gusts from a thunderstorm. To throw off the enemy's aim, Williams rolled his Avenger from side to side and altered his rate of descent. Williams's wingmen worked strenuously to stay with him; Will Fletcher, flying on the far left leg of Williams's vee, felt like Tail-end Charlie in a game of crack-the-whip.

Williams's six Avengers penetrated the rumpled tops of the cloud bank at seven thousand feet, jostling together in vee formation through skies white as milk. Will Fletcher kept his eyes fixed on Skelly's Avenger to his right. The blue-and-white-painted airplane flickered in the clouds, brightening and darkening in hue in proportion to the density of the water vapor. Moisture condensed on Will's windscreen, and the air whistling through his open cockpit ventilation vents turned warm and sticky.

Will prepared himself mentally for the next phase of the approach. When Williams's Avenger division bottomed out of the clouds, it would split up into two three-plane sections. Williams would take two Avengers to the west of *Musashi* and set up for torpedo runs on her port side; Vaughn would take Skelly and Fletcher to the east of *Musashi* and set up for torpedo runs on the battle-ship's starboard side. The two sections would execute a standard hammer-and-anvil torpedo attack. Williams's section of three airplanes would be the hammer; Vaughn's would be the anvil. No matter which way *Musashi* turned, she was likely to collide with one or more of VT-18's torpedoes. By attacking simultane-ously from opposite sides, the six Avengers also would divide enemy counterfire coming from the ship's centerline guns. Timing was everything. The torpeckers also relied on Commander Ellis's dive-bombers and fighters to divert the atten-tion of *Musashi*'s antiaircraft gunners upward and away from the low-flying tor-pedo planes.

Will's radioman, Westmoreland, reported the relative position of the target to Will every ten or fifteen seconds based on his radar returns. "Target bearing three fifty degrees relative, range twenty thousand yards. Target maneuvering. Base course approximately oh-one-oh degrees true, estimated speed twenty-two knots."

Will visualized the relative positions of the division and the target. When Williams's six Avengers bottomed out of the clouds, they would be pointed at *Musashi*'s bow like the tines of a fork.

At five thousand feet, Williams's Avengers plunged into clear air. The scene beneath the clouds was beautiful and chaotic. *Musashi* lay in the middle of Ta-blas Strait, directly ahead of Williams's division, roughly fifteen thousand yards distant. The mammoth battleship was framed by the blue-green mountains of Mindoro and surrounded by the ships of her screen. The Helldiver attack was in full swing, and *Musashi* and her escorts were turning at high speed to evade VB-18's dive-bombing runs. The enemy warships churned the placid waters of the strait, tracing graceful arcs and S-turns across the blue water and emitting angry puffs of black and colored smoke as their antiaircraft gunners fended off the Helldivers' attacks. Will saw huge plumes of water erupt suddenly on either side of *Musashi*'s bow, marking the near-misses of two of the Helldivers' bombs. He worried that the Helldiver division had attacked too soon. Williams's Avengers would not be in a position to make their final torpedo runs for two minutes. VF-18's Hellcats would strafe next, but if *Musashi*'s gunners were allowed too much time to recover, they could concentrate their guns on the torpedo bombers.

Williams signaled "division breakup and attack" by rocking his Avenger's wings rapidly from side to side. Vaughn shoved his nose low and banked hard left, leading Skelly and Fletcher downward on a southeasterly heading; Williams broke hard right, taking two Avengers with him southwesterly across *Musashi*'s bow.

Vaughn angled his three-plane section toward *Musashi*, aiming for a turn-in point roughly a thousand yards ahead of the gigantic battleship and ten thousand yards off her starboard bow. His immediate objective was to lower his section's silhouette against the eastern horizon and to make his three Avengers as inconspicuous as possible for as long as possible. Once he reached the turn-in point, Vaughn would break up his section; Vaughn, Skelly, and Fletcher would maneuver their Avengers independently for a shot at *Musashi*'s starboard flank. They would attack the big battleship at about the same time, but on separate headings. Vaughn signaled Skelly and Will to cross beneath him and take up echelon positions off his right wing—this was so Vaughn could keep the target and his wingman continuously in sight during the descent—and directed them to open their bomb bay doors and arm the torpedoes.

Skelly and Will glided below and behind Vaughn's Avenger and settled into position off his right wing. Will simultaneously jammed his bomb bay door handle down to "open" and switched his cockpit armament selector to "torpedo." He instructed Westmoreland over the intercom to unlock the torpedo's shackles by shifting the "arm-safe" lever on the airplane's main armament panel to "arm." Will then flipped the armament master switch located in his cockpit to "torpedo" and set his Mark 13 gun sight in the fixed position, dispensing with setting target speed or target angle. *Musashi* was a big target and moving fast; he would aim his torpedo like a man shooting clay pigeons on a skeet range. Anticipating a torpedo release altitude of three hundred feet, he set his radar altimeter to beep at 250 feet. He glanced anxiously at the western horizon beyond *Musashi*, hoping to see Williams's three Avengers descending on the battleship from her port side. He saw nothing but enemy ships and open sky and peppercorn puffs of antiaircraft fire. A knot formed in his stomach at the realization that Vaughn's three-plane anvil might be compelled to attack *Musashi* without the diversion of Williams's three-plane hammer.

Vaughn's path took his section directly over a Japanese destroyer in *Musashi*'s outer screen. Squatty had no choice. He could not avoid the destroyer and yet close the distance to *Musashi*. The destroyer shifted its guns and began firing at Vaughn's Avengers. Dashes of yellow light sparked toward Will's airplane and drifted behind him like shooting stars. The Japanese gunners had underestimated the speed of Vaughn's torpedo bombers. Vaughn ignored the destroyer and continued his descent.

Passing a thousand feet, Will heard Westmoreland sing out over the intercom, "Target bearing oh-eight-oh degrees relative, range ten thousand yards and closing." Vaughn's section was roughly abeam *Musashi* and headed in the opposite direction. At the same instant, Vaughn waggled his wings, which was the signal to Skelly and Will for "section breakup and attack."

Will, flying closest to the target, banked hard right, pushed his throttle to the stop, and pointed his nose directly at *Musashi*'s starboard bow. Skelly continued straight ahead for a beat and then broke right at a shallower angle, pointing himself at *Musashi*'s starboard midsection. Vaughn pressed ahead for two beats, broke right, and pointed himself at *Musashi*'s starboard quarter. Vaughn's three Avengers, now separated from one another for their final torpedo runs, began to jink and weave toward the giant battleship.

Will had never lost sight of *Musashi* after leaving the clouds. The battleship's massive gunfire-control tower loomed constantly above the horizon, and a gray-black cloud of smoke marked her position like a beacon. With about nine thousand yards separating him from *Musashi*, the battleship's gunners spied Will.

First came the 12.7-centimeter, .40-caliber shells. Each of these shells was comparable to an American five-inch, .38-caliber naval shell and carried nearly nine pounds of high explosive. The shells detonated directly ahead of Will's flight path, erupting in brilliant orange-yellow kernels of fire and puffs of colored smoke. Will could hear them detonate, the explosions producing an arrhythmic *crump, crump*, like the beat of a distant drum. The sound of the exploding shells reached his ears a millisecond after their light reached his eyes. Will made a quick calculation. He was flying at 310 knots, a little more than five nautical miles per minute. His run-in from nine thousand yards to a torpedo release point roughly fifteen hundred yards from *Musashi* would require about forty seconds; his breakaway and retirement would keep him within *Musashi*'s range for one minute, fifteen seconds more. *The next three minutes*, Will concluded, *will be the longest of my life. Or the shortest.*

He jinked as violently as he could manage. The Avenger flew like a truck under normal flight conditions, but at high speeds her flight controls grew especially stiff and heavy. Will shoved his control stick to the left and then pulled it back to the right, putting his Avenger into a steep turn to the left, and then forcing her to reverse into a steep turn to the right. He stomped alternately on his left and right rudder pedals to maintain a coordinated turn, and yanked his control stick back into his belly to keep his Avenger's nose from falling through. The acceleration forced Will into his seat and tugged at his arms and legs. His Avenger creaked and groaned, and Will grunted with her through every turn. For Westmoreland and Christman, the final approach to the target was a nauseating roller-coaster ride, but they accepted the wild zigs and zags as necessary. Anything to confound the enemy's antiaircraft gunners.

Westmoreland excitedly reported the range to the target over the intercom: "Eight thousand yards and closing." This was a critical number. Inside eight thousand yards, Will's Avenger was within range of *Musashi*'s twenty-five-millimeter antiaircraft guns.

Within seconds of Westmoreland's report, *Musashi*'s machine gunners opened fire on Will's Avenger. Thousands of machine gun rounds, twenty-five-millimeter, .60-caliber, streaked toward Will's torpedo bomber in pulsating streams of light. Every fourth or fifth bullet was a tracer round that glowed bright red or yellow, seeming to crisscross and collide with one another in their eagerness to reach him. Will thought incongruously of fire hoses, of shining drops of water sprayed from a hundred fire hoses. He shoved his Avenger down to three hundred feet above the water, descending as low as possible to reduce his silhouette against the sky.

In pressing home his attack, Will had to keep an eye out for Skelly and Vaughn and avoid fouling their torpedo runs. Jinking to his left, Will spied Skelly's torpedo bomber gliding low over the water, roughly a thousand yards to the south. Skelly, too, was banking his Avenger steeply from side to side to throw off the aim of *Musashi*'s gunners. The wings of Skelly's torpedo bomber flashed alternately blue and white in the sunlight; to the uninitiated, his airplane appeared to be on the verge of flying out of control. Three Avengers would divide *Musashi*'s antiaircraft fire better than two. Will hoped Squatty was also in the midst of his final torpedo run, but he dared not level his wings to search for him.

Musashi loomed larger and larger in Will's windscreen as he bore down on her through the smoke. She presented her starboard side to him in full profile, as if she were passing on parade through a light morning fog. Her hull was long and graceful, with a blunt stern and a sharply angled prow. She rode low in the water and threw up a glittering bow wave of white foam. The barrels of her main naval guns, astonishingly long and thick, protruded ominously from three gigantic turrets, two forward and one aft, and her superstructure—her conning tower, gunfire control towers, and funnel—soared above her main deck like a castle keep. *Musashi*'s big naval guns were mute, but dots of light from her 12.7-centimeter and twenty-five-millimeter antiaircraft guns flashed in the shadows of her superstructure, and wisps of smoke streamed aft from their muzzles, creating the impression that the battleship was skimming across the water at high speed. She was the biggest floating object Will had ever seen, bigger than any American aircraft carrier, and more massive than any American warship by far. He marveled at her even as he tried to destroy her.

Will detected dark blue specks swooping low over *Musashi* like hawks descending for a kill. These were VF-18's Hellcats, armed only with bullets, strafing the battleship along her length. Will realized he could never have approached this close to *Musashi* without the benefit of the Hellcats' suppressing fire.

Westmoreland called out over the intercom, "Target bearing three hundred fifty-five degrees relative, four thousand yards." Less than twenty-five hundred yards to the torpedo release point, only fifteen seconds to go, Will calculated.

Will glanced left to get a good fix on Skelly's whereabouts. His eyes had no sooner focused on Skelly's Avenger than he detected colored bursts of 12.7-centimeter gunfire cluster around it like party balloons. A blink of the eye later, Skelly's torpedo bomber exploded in a ball of pink-orange vapor. The airplane's wings sheared aft, spinning crazily away from the fuselage like leaves blown from a tree, and the wingless fuselage nosed over and slammed into the sea, throwing up a wave of white foam.

Will was stunned. Reflexively, he yanked his airplane away from the fireball. His turret gunner, Christman, had also seen the explosion. Christman keyed his intercom microphone to report the downing of Skelly's airplane but then said nothing; he was either at a loss for words or thought better of breaking his pilot's concentration.

The gunners on *Musashi* who had shot down Skelly's torpedo bomber now shifted their attention to Will. A barrage of 12.7-centimeter shells detonated ahead of Will's Avenger, splattering the sky with smoky color and temporarily obscuring his view of *Musashi*. Will heard the unmistakable ping and clatter of spent shrapnel hitting his propeller and windscreen. As his Avenger buffeted through the turbulence, he encountered new streams of twenty-five-millimeter machine gun fire converging on him. It seemed impossible not to be struck by the Japanese bullets.

Everything suddenly seemed to have inexplicable vibrancy to Will. The colored puffs. The sounds. The sunlight. The glittering blue sea beneath him. The blue metal skin of his airplane. The white pointers of his cockpit instruments shuddering in front of him. The idea of breaking off his torpedo run flashed through Will's mind. He had lost his wingman and was entirely on his own. He was flying through the Valley of Death. His torpedo attack had become Kipling-esque, and pressing home his attack in the face of *Musashi*'s concentrated counterfire now seemed suicidal. He thought of his crewmen. Saving them was reason enough for abandoning the run, excuse for any rational man. But it was too late to break off the run, of course. They had come too far, and breaking off the run was now as deadly as continuing on.

Westmoreland sang out, "Two thousand yards."

The gargantuan mass of the battleship lay a mile ahead. Instinctively, Will leveled his wings and pointed his torpedo bomber's nose two ship lengths ahead of *Musashi*, making a last-second rudder-swerving adjustment to his alignment. Will glanced at his instrument panel: 295 knots and three hundred feet above the water, a perfect box. He did not see how he could miss. He held his torpedo bomber's wings level, perfectly still with zero slip or skid, and squeezed the torpedo release button on his control stick.

The torpedo dropped from the belly of Will's Avenger like a log and splashed into the sea. In the interstices of his concentration, in the final milliseconds before he dropped his torpedo, Will Fletcher remembered his mother and prayed to be reunited with her if death came.

Aboard *Musashi*, Petty Officer Hosoya watched the dark blue American fighters diving on his ship. They rolled in one after the other, pointing their blunt noses directly at *Musashi*. As the Hellcats swooped toward him, Hosoya detected tiny flickers of light coming from the fighters' wings. He understood the winking bits of light were tracer rounds, and that for every lighted tracer round he could see there were two or three nontracer rounds he could not detect. Hosoya knew the enemy's machine gun bullets were at that very moment ricocheting along *Musashi*'s main deck, fragmenting into pieces of deadly shrapnel, but he could see nothing of the damage they caused because of the smoke swirling beneath him.

Glancing to starboard, Hosoya was startled to see a thick-bodied American torpedo plane flying low over the water and closing rapidly on the ship through the smoke. He saw *Musashi*'s antiaircraft gunners shift their short-range weapons toward the attacker and concentrate their fire on the plane, but the attacker kept coming on. Hosoya watched in disbelief as a torpedo slipped like a log from the belly of the American airplane and splashed into the sea. He searched frantically for the torpedo's wake but he could not see it. Less than forty-five seconds later, the ocean exploded in front of him. A geyser of seawater shot two hundred feet into the air along *Musashi*'s starboard waterline, inundating the sailors on *Musashi*'s main deck. *Musashi* shuddered at the blow and Hosoya staggered. Like all Japanese, Petty Officer Hosoya had experienced earthquakes in his homeland; *Musashi*'s steel deck swayed beneath his feet, filling him with the same sickening sense of fear and dread.

Will Fletcher had no interest in watching the results of his torpedo run. Survival depended on exiting the killing zone as quickly as possible, and the quickest escape route lay to the north. Will yanked upward on his bomb bay door control handle, rolled his Avenger into a steep right turn, and held his plane's throttle lever against the stop, squeezing every inch of manifold pressure from his engine. Without its heavy weapon, Will's Avenger seemed suddenly agile as a kite, and the acceleration of the turn pressed the young pilot lower in his seat. Will held his control stick tightly aft to keep his airplane's nose from dropping and riveted his eyes on the horizon. The airplane's radar altimeter beeped loudly, protesting that Will had allowed his Avenger to descend to only two hundred feet above the water.

Westmoreland's voice crackled over the intercom. "Clean drop, bomb bay closed—" he began, but he never finished his sentence.

A brilliant white light, a flash of blinding phosphorescence, of star-white incandescence, pierced the middle of Will's left wing, and a loud crack like the hammer of Thor himself rent the air. Will's Avenger shuddered violently and snapped farther right—it was as if the airplane were being flipped on her back— and a blast of searing air shot past Will's left cheek. His heart seized. He saw nothing through his windscreen but blue water coming up at him. Instinctively, he kicked hard on his left rudder pedal and slammed his control stick left, hoping to level his wings and raise his nose. The Avenger responded grudgingly to Will's control inputs and slowly righted herself.

Will saw a jagged hole in the trailing edge of his left wing about six feet from the fuselage. The hole was at least three feet in diameter, and a magnesium-white fire burned fiercely at the center, yellow-orange sheets of flame streaming aft with the slipstream. A 12.7-centimeter shell had pierced Will's left wing a few inches aft of the main wing spar as he was in his breakaway turn. Had the shell struck a few inches forward, Will's Avenger would have suffered a catastrophic in-flight breakup like Skelly's.

The shell had blown away the left side of Will's cockpit canopy, shredding the fuselage abaft of his flight station and sucking out of the cockpit everything that was not secured. Gone were Will's charts and pencils. He noted a triangular piece of metal about the size of a fifty-cent piece protruding from his left thigh just above the knee. The wound oozed blood, but Will felt no pain. Through the roaring slipstream, he heard pieces of aluminum creaking and banging behind him, as if the airplane were about to disintegrate.

Will grabbed his handheld microphone, jammed his intercom button, and shouted for Westmoreland and Christman. Nothing came back in reply, not even the hiss of a side tone.

The burning hole diminished the lift generated by the Avenger's left wing and increased the airplane's aerodynamic drag. The Avenger pulled left like a badly aligned car, and Will had to hold his control stick far right of center to keep the wings level. The torpedo bomber's airspeed began to deteriorate rapidly. The pointer of Will's airspeed indicator sagged inexorably through 250 knots, 240, 230, 220, 210. Had Will's Avenger been hit at altitude, he would have dived to extinguish the fire, like blowing out a candle. But this option was not available to him; he had little room to descend. Will nosed over to fifty feet above the water, seeking the aerodynamic advantages of ground effect.

In his struggle to regain control of his stricken airplane, Will wandered into the middle of the Japanese formation and flew directly between two Japanese heavy cruisers. The cruisers were probably *Myoko* and *Noshiro*, but Will cared nothing for their names. To his astonishment, neither ship fired at him, perhaps out of surprise, perhaps from fear of hitting a sister ship. But a point destroyer that was steaming a few hundred yards ahead of the cruisers had no such inhibitions. The destroyer, probably *Shimakaze*, opened up on Will's Avenger with a vengeance as he passed her.

There was nothing Will could do to evade the Japanese gunfire. His Avenger was dying. The fire had spread along her left wing like a torch. She wobbled above the wave tops, barely above stalling speed, yawing right and left like an oscillating weather vane. Her propeller tips were kicking up spray. Will felt as if he were holding his burning airplane aloft through sheer physical effort. He dared not attempt a turn; his controls were heavy and sluggish, and he doubted he had sufficient throw in his control stick to execute a turn without stalling and spinning into the sea. Will's legs quivered from the strain of pushing on his rudder pedals to counteract the yaw.

The degraded performance of Will's Avenger had an unexpected benefit. The gunners on *Shimakaze* misjudged Will's airspeed and fired too far ahead, their shells consistently smacking the water twenty or thirty yards in front of the airplane, throwing up a thicket of white saltwater plumes. The plumes subsided just as the nose of Will's Avenger reached them, but salt spray showered into the cockpit, splattering his goggles and drenching his clothes.

Will perceived a sharp pain in his left foot; he thought at first he'd been hit in the sole by *Shimakaze*'s gunfire. He looked down, expecting to see a mangled foot and blood. Instead, yellow-orange flames licked through the cockpit floorboards. Will absorbed details that were absurdly trivial under the circumstances. His left shoelace was untied. The fire had melted the wax from both of his uniform shoes, and the sole of his left shoe had begun to smolder. He stared, mesmerized, as fingers of flame slithered up the cockpit bulkhead and reached for his Avenger's throttle control quadrant. A blast of scalding air boiled up from beneath the cockpit floorboards, striking him in the face like the breath of a furnace, and fire leaped toward the Avenger's communications console at Will's right elbow. Only the saltwater shower from *Shimakaze's* near-misses had pre-vented Will's khaki flight suit from igniting.

Will jammed the intercom button to warn his aircrew. "Ditching now," he yelled. "Fire in the cockpit . . . can't keep feet on the rudder pedals anymore. . . . Brace."

Will had neither the time nor the stomach to describe to Westmoreland and Christman what was likely to happen next. The airplane was wallowing at ninety knots only a few feet above the water. When he yanked his feet off the rudder pedals, the Avenger's left wing would drop immediately and strike the waves. The water, incompressible as concrete, would snatch the left wing out of the air and the Avenger would cartwheel nose over tail and disintegrate in a fireball. He and his crew would be torn apart.

Will resigned himself to death. He embraced the calm that comes to men in extremis when they realize there is nothing more they can do, when no amount of physical strength or agility, no degree of intelligence or quick thinking, no skill or trickery can alter the situation. He had reached the moment when men consign themselves to God or chance. At least the sea would quench the flames.

Will lifted his feet from the rudder pedals and hauled back on the Avenger's control stick to slow the airplane as much as possible.

The American attackers disappeared as quickly as they had arrived, and *Musashi's* gunners ceased firing. Captain Kenkichi Kato, *Musashi's* executive officer, im-mediately called for assessments of damage to his ship.

Damage-control officers aboard *Musashi* recorded the location of battle damage by reference to "frame number." A "frame" was a steel rib within the battleship's hull, and each frame was numbered consecutively from bow to stern. *Musashi's* hull contained approximately 230 frames, with frame 136 located roughly amidships beneath her huge funnel. Damage-control officers confirmed to Captain Kato that an aerial torpedo had struck *Musashi's* starboard side amid-ships, roughly 350 feet aft of her prow at frame 130. The explosion had fractured *Musashi's* inner hull and damaged the bulkheads of her seventh and eleventh holds. Seawater had flooded into the number eleven fire room, forcing engineers to evacuate the compartment and shut down one of the ship's twelve steam boil-ers. *Musashi* had taken on a five-degree list to starboard and shipped three thou-sand tons of seawater through the hole in her hull, but her damage-control parties had counterflooded by pumping seawater into empty bunkers on *Musashi*'s port side. Counterflooding gradually lessened her port list to one degree. A second torpedo was reported to have struck *Musashi*'s starboard side farther aft at frame 140 near a starboard hydraulic machinery compartment, and a third may have hit at frame 150 near the ship's starboard outboard engine room, but neither detonated. Only the torpedo that hit at frame 130 had inflicted any real structural damage to the heavily armored battleship. The near-misses of the American dive-bombers had caused little damage to the ship itself, but bomb blasts and shrapnel had dismembered and killed many of the antiaircraft gunners who had been exposed on *Musashi*'s main deck and superstructure. During the American fighters' strafing runs, the chief of *Musashi*'s number one machine gun squad had been pierced through by enemy machine gun fire.

The concussion from the torpedo hit at frame 130 had also partially disabled the gunfire control system for *Musashi*'s turret number two, making it impossible for the turret's gun crew to fire two of their three big eighteen-inch naval guns simultaneously. The inability to fire two guns concurrently impaired *Musashi*'s capacity for knocking out an American warship with a tight salvo of three heavyweight eighteen-inch shells all striking the target within seconds of one another.

Although angered and depressed by the damage to his battleship's gunfire control system, Admiral Inoguchi knew more American fighters, dive-bombers, and torpedo planes would arrive over *Musashi* very soon, probably within the hour, and he prepared his crew for a second attack. He relaxed watertight conditions throughout the ship long enough for sailors to carry wounded shipmates to *Musashi*'s infirmaries and for cooks to distribute lunches to sailors at their battle stations. He directed his engineers to begin repairs on damaged equipment immediately, and ordered his gunners to replenish their stocks of ammunition. Like their captain, *Musashi*'s sailors expected the blue-painted carrier planes to return soon, and they diligently went about their preparations. Many were too busy or too anxious to eat the lunch the cooks had brought them.

Despite Air Group 18's opening attacks, *Musashi* remained a fearsome and formidable weapon, and she steamed onward with Kurita's Force A undeterred.

When Will lifted his feet from the rudder pedals of his burning Avenger, the plane's left wing sagged toward the water just as he feared it would. Will glimpsed the wingtip clipping the tops of the waves, and, in the next instant, the airplane jerked violently to the left. He heard a shriek of tearing metal and pitched forward against his shoulder harness and lap belt as if he had been shot from a cannon, his arms and legs flailing uncontrollably about the cockpit like a rag doll's. An avalanche of seawater cascaded over the windscreen, slamming him back into his seat and ripping his goggles and helmet from his head. The Avenger bounced for fifty yards across the waves on its left side and slid to a stop with its nose buried in a swell.

Will was dazed, but conscious. He was still strapped into his cockpit seat but lying on his left side. His Avenger's right wing was pointing straight up in the air, projecting high above the starboard side of the fuselage like a jib sail. The wing wobbled back and forth in the air, as if debating whether to roll right or roll left. Will dully perceived that if his airplane rolled to the left he would be trapped upside down in his cockpit seat, fully submerged with his airplane sinking on top of him. He fumbled clumsily for his lap belt but, before he could find the release lever, the upturned wing rolled right and smacked the water like the fluke of a whale. Will slammed against the starboard bulkhead of his cockpit, and seawater gushed over the canopy rail, drenching him anew.

Will's torpedo bomber was sinking rapidly by the nose; her hot metal surfaces hissed and steamed as she settled. Will recalled his cockpit escape procedures from his training in the Dilbert Dunker in the Corpus Christi swimming pool: Grab the canopy bow, pull yourself out of your seat, exit the starboard side, and remove the life raft. Will unbuckled his lap belt and shoulder harness and seized the longitudinal canopy bar above his head. He hauled himself out of his seat and crawled over the canopy rail onto the upper surface of the right wing, which was already awash. He intended to extract the Avenger's three-man inflatable life raft, known as the Mark IV, from its stowage compartment immediately aft of his flight station. The footing along the wing root was slippery, and he inched his way aft. He had not moved very far when he stopped short, horrified at what he saw. What had once been the Avenger's ball turret was a basket of twisted metal and shattered Plexiglas. Christman, the turret gunner, had been decapitated. His torso was still strapped into his seat; his right arm was frozen grotesquely upward in midgesture, as if he had tried to fend off the blow that had killed him. Christman's flesh had splattered against his machine gun, and his flight suit was black with blood.

A wave of nausea and revulsion swept over Will, like the seawater swirling around his knees. Fighting the urge to retch, he pounded on the side of the fuselage, yelling at Westmoreland to get out of the tunnel. But then Will's eyes fell on the holes in the Avenger's fuselage. There were uncountable holes clustered at the spot where his radioman would have been sitting, some clean and round, about the diameter of a fifty-cent piece, others gaping and irregularly shaped, as if someone had punched through the skin of the Avenger from the inside with an ax. The cables that connected the Avenger's control stick with her elevator and rudder ran along the interior bulkhead of the tunnel on the port side. Will wondered by what miracle they had not been severed. He banged again on the fuselage with his fist and listened for a reply. He heard nothing but the gurgle of seawater flooding into the perforated fuselage. Will could not reach the exterior handle to open the tunnel hatch; it was too far aft and already submerged. The Avenger suddenly lurched nose down, and Will slipped off the trailing edge of the wing and fell into the sea.

Burdened with his parachute harness, his .38-caliber revolver, his bandolier containing twenty rounds of ammunition, his survival knife, his shoes and baggy clothing, his parachute bag, and his survival kit, Will sank into the Sibuyan Sea like a brick. He desperately kicked his way back to the surface and, gasping for air, dog-paddled furiously away from the fuselage, fearful of becoming entangled with his sinking airplane. He managed a glance backward at the wreckage, hoping by the grace of God his radioman had emerged from the tunnel, but there was no sign of Westmoreland. Will saw nothing but the blue empennage of Avenger number seven, bureau number 73202, well holed by bullets, slip forever into the deep.

She had sunk in less than thirty seconds, taking the remains of Westmoreland and Christman to the bottom with her.

The standard procedure for escaping the cockpit after a water landing called for the pilot to strip off his parachute harness first, then detach his survival kit from the harness (the kit contained the pilot's inflatable one-man life raft and other survival gear), leave the parachute pack behind in the cockpit seat, and take the survival kit with him. There was good reason for shedding the parachute. A parachute pack absorbed water like a sponge, gallons of it. In his eagerness to abandon his sinking airplane, Will had not removed his parachute, and it now pulled at him like an anchor. Scissor-kicking to keep his head above water, he groped for the buckles to his parachute harness and suddenly realized he had also failed to remove his flying gloves. His soft, calf-leather flying gloves, so tactile when dry, had turned slick as snot in water. To his horror, he discovered he couldn't feel or grip the harness buckles or locate his survival kit. Frantically, he bit into the cuff of his right glove and peeled it from his hand with his teeth.

The leaden parachute won out and dragged Will under. No matter how furiously he kicked, he could not overcome its weight. An indigo abyss yawned beneath him, and he sensed himself free-falling rapidly, as if he were racing his airplane to the bottom. The water grew cooler as he sank deeper, forcing its way into his ears and nostrils with steadily increasing pressure. He dared not exhale—the oxygen in his lungs was all he had—and his chest ached. He brushed the chest buckle of his parachute harness with his bare right hand and unsnapped it, but he could not locate the buckles for the leg straps that encircled his thighs. The more he struggled to find them, the more terrified he became. He knew he had only seconds of consciousness remaining. He seized one of the leg straps and traced its course with his naked fingertips. The buckle had somehow rotated behind his buttocks. He pried open the buckle and kicked himself free of the leg straps. The parachute harness fell away, taking with it not only his sodden parachute pack but his survival kit.

Though relieved of the weight of the pack, Will did not ascend. He hung weightless and inert in the inky water, drained by the effort of shedding his parachute and confused, uncertain of up or down. His ears ached; his extremities tingled. He dimly understood that he must pull a lanyard to inflate his Mae West. He pressed his hands to his chest and felt for the bladders of his life preserver, but couldn't find the lanyard. He probed the edges of the bladder until a small plastic marble floated into his fingers. It was the bitter end of one of the inflation lanyards, and Will tugged on it.

A carbon dioxide capsule popped and one-half of the Mae West inflated. Will sensed himself ascending. The water grew warmer, its color brightening gradually from deep purple to sapphirine, from sapphirine to turquoise. The surface shimmered above him, refracting light in a million facets, but it seemed impossibly far away. He knew he should swim toward the light, but his arms and legs were too heavy, too distant, too immobile. His ascent was maddeningly slow, interminable. He told himself he must inflate the second bladder of his Mae West to ascend more quickly, but he couldn't command his fingers to search for the second lanyard. He was too tired. He wanted to sleep. He shut his eyes.

Will's head broke the surface and bobbed on the water like a cork. The collar of his half-inflated Mae West held his head afloat, while the remainder of his body dangled limply from the life preserver as if he were a corpse hanging from a noose. The sun shining on Will's face roused him from his torpor and he gagged, ejecting cupfuls of salt water and vomit into the ocean. When he had recovered his senses, he looked around him.

He was adrift now in the middle of the Sibuyan Sea. Alone, and without a raft.

When Commander Ellis's attackers joined up for the return flight to *Intrepid*, it was that clear that Strike 2 Able had lost two torpedo bombers. Williams knew who they were, and he carried a pit of sadness in his stomach all the way home to the ship. Although Williams's three-plane section had carried out the anvil portion of the attack with a fair degree of alacrity and coordination, it had scored only one or two "possible" hits on *Musashi*'s port side. The heavy antiaircraft coming from *Musashi* and her screen had made it difficult to observe the results. Vaughn had managed to release his torpedo but missed *Musashi* entirely; he thought he had seen Skelly release his torpedo seconds before he was shot down, and he credited Skelly and Fletcher with the two confirmed hits on *Musashi*'s starboard side. Of the two Avenger pilots who had attacked the *Nachi*-class cruiser, one scored a hit and one failed to release his torpedo. In all, VT-18's torpedo planes had tallied three torpedo hits out of seven drops and eight attempts. Commander Ellis, who had orbited high above the watery battlefield during the Avengers' torpedo attack, verified the results.

Lieutenant Junior Grade John Forsyth was one of the Helldiver pilots returning with Commander Ellis to *Intrepid*. Forsyth had flown one of VB-18's dive-bombers on Strike 2 Able and had attacked *Musashi*. He had completed his dive-bombing run only moments before Williams's six Avengers began their torpedo runs and had observed the torpeckers' approach. A man well qualified to judge the courage of others, Forsyth later wrote, "As I pulled through, I saw the torpedo planes, their attack perfectly timed—but what a job, low, close to the water, just zooming the guns of the enemy. The guts and courage to press home a torpedo attack go unexcelled in the annals of flying."

Will's shoulders stung. He discovered the skin covering his collarbones had been rubbed raw, chafed away by the straps of his shoulder harness during his violent crash-landing. His left thigh ached and throbbed; he probed cautiously for the piece of shrapnel and winced when his fingers touched the cut. Although the shrapnel had dislodged itself during his frenetic kicking, the open wound still bled. Will worried about sharks. The navy had experimented with shark repellent in early 1944, but hadn't issued any to Air Group 18.

A ragged flap of blue-painted fabric about the size of a hand towel bumped against Will's shoulder. He recognized the debris as part of the skin of his Avenger, ripped from the airplane's ailerons, elevators, flaps, or rudder. He fished the fabric from the water and pressed it tightly against his trouser leg, hoping to prevent more blood from oozing into the water until the wound coagulated.

Then Will heard a noise, a faint thrum that rose above the slap of the waves. It was an engine of some kind. He forced himself higher up in the water and squinted in the direction of the sound. What he spied coming at him over the horizon was as unwelcome as a shark. The mast and funnel of a ship.

The ship was bearing down on him at high speed. The vessel was undoubtedly part of the enemy formation he had just attacked. Will feared the Japanese would spot him if the ship sailed close by; his Caucasian skin and bright yellow Mae West would be a beacon in the azure water. The thrumming grew louder, and he made out the ship's superstructure clearly. She was a destroyer with the bloodred battle flag of the rising sun snapping from her masthead. She may have been one of the ships of *Musashi*'s screen that had fired on him. Could she have been dispatched to find him? He pulled the blue fabric from his leg and draped it over his head, camouflaging himself to look like a piece of flotsam. Will hadn't yet thought to inflate both bladders of his Mae West, and his oversight became a blessing. The single bladder allowed him to ride low in the water.

The enemy destroyer passed by Will at high speed, steaming within thirty yards of him. Will peeked at the warship from beneath his blue fabric. He was close enough to discern the facial features of men on deck. Japanese sailors stood at their antiaircraft gun stations; most had their faces turned upward toward the sky, obviously on the lookout for more American planes. Japanese officers in blue tunics stood on the navigation bridge; several had binoculars in their hands and they too scanned the heavens. Will heard the hiss of seawater rushing past the destroyer's hull and felt the cavitation of her screws in his chest. He expected a sharp-eyed officer to see him and point him out. Cowering low in the water, he tried to make himself as small as possible. He bobbed up and down in the wake of the passing destroyer like a crab pot, holding his breath and waiting for splashes of small arms fire to erupt all around him.

No shots were fired. The destroyer sailed on by. The Japanese clearly had more pressing business than to search for a downed American pilot.

Will was utterly alone now, adrift on a bottomless sea with only his Mae West to keep him afloat. No one knew where he was, and no one would be coming to his rescue. His buddies had retired from the fight and soon would be two hundred miles to the east. Even if his squadron mates had mounted a search for him—and the exigencies of war clearly did not permit this—they were not likely to find him; he was nothing but a tiny pebble on a vast watery plain. Whether Will survived was entirely up to him.

Will knew he was in for a very long swim. He stuffed his blue fabric into the breast pocket of his flight suit and inflated both sides of his Mae West. He had a rough idea of where he had crashed and of where the closest land might lie. Mindoro lay to the west. Even from Will's sea-level perspective, the green mountaintops of the island were visible above the western horizon, but very far away. Tablas Island lay to the east and was probably much closer. A bank of cumulus clouds, the same clouds through which Will had flown, still marked the position of the island. Will decided Tablas Island offered the best chance for making landfall. He looked at his wristwatch, a government-issue Bulova. To his surprise, the Bulova had survived the water landing and was still ticking. The time was ten fifty a.m. No more than ten minutes had elapsed since he had begun his final torpedo run on *Musashi*.

Will stretched out into the water and began pulling and kicking himself toward the clouds over Tablas Island.

Chapter Eleven

ON STRIKE 2 BAKER

★ ★ ★ ★ ★

Admiral Onishi's naval air forces were among the first to draw American blood in the decisive battle for the Philippines. At about eight a.m. on October 24, fifty minutes before *Intrepid* launched Strike 2 Able, Japanese warplanes based on Luzon attacked Admiral Forrest Sherman's Task Group 38.3, then stationed about a hundred miles east of central Luzon and three hundred miles north of Leyte Gulf. Hellcats from fleet carriers *Essex* and *Lexington*, and light carriers *Princeton* and *Langley*, shot down or turned back many of the attackers, but at about nine forty a.m. at least one Japanese bomber penetrated the fighter screen and dropped a single bomb on *Princeton*'s flight deck . . . The bomb pierced three decks before exploding, and ignited aviation gasoline that had been stored in *Princeton*'s hangar deck.

The conflagration quickly spread to armed aircraft in the hangar bay that were awaiting refueling. Torpedoes and bombs detonated, blowing *Princeton*'s forward aircraft elevator into the air. Nearly continuous explosions racked the carrier, and *Princeton*'s skipper immediately ordered all hands, except for a damage-control party of about five hundred men, to abandon ship. Admiral Sherman dispatched three destroyers to assist in rescuing *Princeton*'s crew, and the cruisers *Reno* and *Birmingham* eased alongside *Princeton* to help suppress the fires raging aboard her. The rescuers' plan was to extinguish the fires and take the carrier under tow. It was not to be. *Princeton*'s torpedo storage room exploded and catapulted huge sections of her flight deck into the sky. The storm of fire and steel killed 229 of the sailors crowded on *Birmingham*'s exposed main deck—firefighters, antiaircraft gunners, and line handlers—who stood by to assist, as well as many still aboard *Princeton*.

Sherman's preoccupation with Onishi's air attacks prevented the carriers and air groups of Task Group 38.3 from supporting *Intrepid* and *Cabot* in the first air strikes against Kurita's Center Force. Mitscher's third task group on line, Rear Admiral Davison's Task Group 38.4, was out of range, simply too far south to assist, and Vice Admiral McCain's Task Group 38.1 was still en route to Ulithi for replenishment. At ten forty-five a.m., about the same time Will Fletcher began his swim toward Tablas Island, *Intrepid* launched its second deck load of the morning against *Musashi* and the Center Force, Strike 2 Baker, comprised of ten fighters, twelve dive-bombers, and nine VT-18 torpedo bombers.

Van Antwerp led VT-18's first division on Strike 2 Baker, including Bill Bates, Kenny Barden, Ben Riley, Joe Rubin, Moe Morris, and Vernon Sistrunk, the last being one of the young ensigns who had joined the squadron at Kaneohe at the same time as Will Fletcher. Because the position of the enemy formation was known precisely, Van Antwerp's Avengers launched without the added weight and worry of wing tanks. Heading outbound on Strike 2 Baker, Van Antwerp's formation passed Commander Ellis's fliers as they returned to *Intrepid* from Strike 2 Able. El Gropo urged Strike 2 Baker's target coordinator over the tactical frequency to concentrate his attacks on *Musashi*; better to focus on one target of significance than to scatter precious bombs and torpedoes among many.

Strike 2 Baker reached the target area after an hour of flying and discovered the Japanese had split their force into two large formations about five miles apart. The enemy warships threw up the same intense barrage of multicolored, long-range gunfire that had threatened Strike 2 Able. Following the Helldivers' dive-bombing and the Hellcats' strafing runs, Van Antwerp split his nine Avengers into two groups and led them in a standard hammer-and-anvil torpedo attack against *Musashi*. Scores of *Musashi*'s gunners had been killed by Air Group 18's earlier dive-bombing attacks and strafing runs, but the volume of antiaircraft fire coming from *Musashi* was intense nonetheless. Van Antwerp's tactics had divided the enemy fire, but several of his Avengers were hit during their run-in.

A large shell passed through Kenny Barden's right wing and fuel cell; fortunately the shell did not explode or cause any serious structural damage.

None of the torpeckers hung around after making their torpedo runs to gawk at *Musashi* or assess the fruits of their labors. They all jinked away from the killing zone like scalded dogs. Based on the observations of VB-18 dive-bomber crews and photographs taken of the Avengers' torpedo wakes, Van Antwerp's division recorded three torpedo hits on *Musashi*'s port side and one on her starboard side; Vernon Sistrunk was the second ensign of the day to be credited with a confirmed hit.

Musashi and her screen continued to fire at the American strike group as it fled the scene. Ben Riley's Avenger was struck by forty-millimeter gunfire on retirement, and he was forced to ditch his wounded torpedo bomber about fifteen miles east of the enemy formation with zero oil pressure showing on his engine gauge. Van Antwerp's division orbited over Riley's three-man raft long enough observe a large sailboat lower a smaller native boat and snatch up Riley and his crew. Van Antwerp's fliers all hoped the men in the sailboat were friendly Filipinos, not Japanese, but no one could be sure.

Will Fletcher swam on through the morning. The Sibuyan Sea was calm, except for the gentle cradling of the swells. The tropical sun beat down on his bare head. His scalp, forehead, and cheeks tingled, alerting him to incipient sunburn. He couldn't avoid gulping seawater as he swam. He spit out the brine like poison but it left his mouth dry and parched. Sunlight, as if reflected by a million tiny mirrors, glinted off the water's surface. His eyes burned from the glare and his cheeks ached from squinting. He swam as smoothly as he could, in the belief that too much commotion would attract sharks. He breaststroked with his head up, alert to any shape moving in the water other than his own. His knife was at hand, and he was ready to slash at any sea beast that approached him.

To navigate, he had picked out a distinctive cloud shape on the eastern horizon and swam doggedly for it. The clouds had drawn perceptibly nearer to him, but he worried the cloud cover itself had simply drifted farther west and that he had not closed the distance to shore at all. The clouds appeared to be thinning in the heat, and he dreaded losing his directional beacon; he feared circling endlessly across the water until he exhausted himself, like a hiker lost in deep woods.

He puzzled over why his Avenger had not disintegrated in the crash landing. As best he could figure, the white-hot wing fire that had spread toward his fuselage and cockpit had weakened his left wing at the wing-fold joint. When the wing hit the water, it had sheared away at the joint instead of digging into the water and flipping the airplane into a cartwheel. As the Avenger skidded across surface on its left side, the stub of the wing had sliced through the water like a boat keel, stabilizing the fuselage and holding the right wing upright. Will wondered whether his extraordinary luck in surviving the crash landing would hold long enough for him to reach dry land.

Aboard *Musashi*, Captain Kato received reports of the new damage inflicted on his battleship by Air Group 18's second strike of the morning. At least two bombs had struck *Musashi,* but they had caused little damage to the ship. As in the prior attack, near misses had taken a bloody toll among machine gun crews, who were obliged to fire their weapons from open gun tubs with minimal protection from concussion and shrapnel. The main deck was strewn with bodies and parts of bodies. One bomb had penetrated two decks on *Musashi*'s port side amidships before detonating; it had ruptured a steam line, filling the number two engine room with superheated steam and forcing the crew to abandon their stations. As a consequence, the battleship lost the use of her port inboard propulsion shaft. To keep her place in Kurita's formation, she had to increase r.p.m. on her three remaining propeller shafts. Three torpedoes were reported to have struck her port side almost simultaneously, throwing men to the deck and causing serious flooding in machinery spaces that were necessary to pump water from side to side and maintain her trim. She took on a five-degree list to port, which her engineers lessened to one degree by counterflooding, but she had ingested huge volumes of water, which weighed down her bow. One torpedo strike was confirmed on her starboard side, but this hit had caused only minimal flooding.

Captain Kato ordered his engineers to do what was necessary to repair the damage and enable *Musashi* to keep pace with the remainder of Force A, which plowed eastward through the Sibuyan Sea toward San Bernardino Strait at twenty-two knots.

The southern passage into Leyte Gulf lies through the Mindanao Sea and Surigao Strait. At about same the time that *Intrepid* launched Strike 2 Able on

October 24, Vice Admiral Nishimura's Force C, the southern component of Admiral Kurita's two-pronged Leyte Gulf attack force, entered the western boundary of the Mindanao Sea. The supporting warships of Rear Admiral Shima's Second Striking Force trailed Nishimura by several hours. Adhering to the Sho-1 plan, Nishimura intended to pass through Surigao Strait at night and surprise the Americans within Leyte Gulf at dawn on October 25.

The Americans knew the Japanese were coming at them through Surigao Strait. Vice Admiral Thomas Kinkaid, commander of all 7th Fleet units within Leyte Gulf, had dispatched patrol aircraft over the southwest Philippines on the morning of October 24. These searchers, joined by aircraft from *Enterprise* and *Franklin* of Davison's Task Group 38.4, had spotted Nishimura's Force C in the Sulu Sea at about ten a.m. Kinkaid had directed the commander of his shore bombardment force, Admiral Jesse Oldendorf, to prepare for the defense of the American landing beaches and transports.

Admiral Oldendorf's bombardment group consisted of six battleships—four of the battleships in Oldendorf's group, *Pennsylvania*, *California*, *West Virginia*, and *Tennessee*, had been salvaged from Pearl Harbor and refitted to fight again— eight cruisers, twenty-six destroyers, and nearly forty small torpedo boats. Because Oldendorf's battleships had been outfitted predominantly with high-capacity shells suitable for shore bombardment, they carried enough armor-piercing shells for only five salvos against the oncoming Japanese battleships. But Oldendorf was confident of success; he had the advantage of position, the naval equivalent of defending from the high ground.

Oldendorf had stationed his battleships, heavy cruisers, and destroyers across the northern end of Surigao Strait on an east–west line between Dinagat Island and Leyte Island, precisely at the point where Nishimura's Force C would enter Leyte Gulf. To navigate the strait, the Japanese would have to approach Oldendorf's battle line in column. Oldendorf could bring many naval guns to bear on the enemy, while the Japanese could reply with only relatively few. Tactically, Oldendorf had blocked the entrance to Leyte Gulf with his bombardment group like the cap on a "T," and Nishimura and Shima would have to breach a wall of heavy naval gunfire to reach the beaches. Oldendorf had also stationed torpedo boats at the southern end of Surigao Strait to interdict and harass the Japanese as they entered the strait from the Mindanao Sea.

Under the Sho-1 plan, the task of Admiral Ozawa's Northern Force was to draw Mitscher's carriers away from the Philippine Sea east of Samar and Luzon and clear the way for Kurita's Center Force to pass through San Bernardino Strait and descend on Leyte Gulf. By one a.m. on October 24, Ozawa's Northern Force lay two hundred miles north of Luzon, in position to execute its duty as a sacrificial decoy for the pincer movement of Kurita and Nishimura.

At about eleven forty-five on October 24, Ozawa launched fifty-eight aircraft, half his striking force, south toward central Luzon. Ozawa's attackers soon tangled with Hellcats from Admiral Sherman's Task Group 38.3, who had successfully repulsed the early morning raids by Onishi's land-based warplanes, except for the lone *Princeton* bomber. Sherman's Hellcats shot down most of Ozawa's attackers or drove them back to their carriers or air bases on Luzon, but Sherman's task group now faced multiple demands. Not only were Task Group 38.3's aircraft required for strikes against Kurita's Center Force in the Sibuyan Sea, but they had to defend the crippled *Princeton* and search for possible Japanese carriers. The sudden appearance of Ozawa's carrier planes prompted Sherman to dispatch aircraft from *Lexington, Essex,* and *Langley* (a new light carrier named after the original) at about one p.m. to seek out the enemy carriers far to the north.

Although Ozawa's midday strike inflicted little damage on the American 3rd Fleet, he had accomplished his primary mission under the Sho-1 plan, which was to capture the attentions of the American carrier commanders off Luzon and Samar. Ozawa had alerted admirals Sherman, Mitscher, and Halsey unmistakably to the presence of enemy carriers somewhere on their northern flank.

CHAPTER TWELVE

ON STRIKE 2 CHARLIE

★ ★ ★ ★ ★

In the aftermath of the second air attack against Force A, Vice Admiral Kurita pleaded for friendly air support to fend off the American carrier planes. He radioed Imperial Headquarters in Manila and Admiral Ozawa off Luzon: "We are being subjected to repeated enemy carrier-based air attacks. Advise immediately of contacts and attacks made by you on the enemy."

At the very moment Kurita broadcast his plea for information and assistance, Ozawa's 58 carrier planes were winging their way south and about to encounter the Hellcats launched from Sherman's Task Group 38.3. Although Ozawa had ordered his fliers to attack any American warships they stumbled upon, the Japanese carrier planes were too far away to lend Kurita any direct aid, and they were, in any event, scattered by Sherman's fighters. Manila never responded to Kurita's request.

At about one thirty p.m., twenty-four aircraft from *Essex* and *Lexington*, which Admiral Sherman had dispatched to the Sibuyan Sea two hours before he became aware of the Japanese carriers on his northern flank, arrived over Kurita's Force A. *Essex's* Air Group 15 and *Lexington's* Air Group 19 split their attacks between *Musashi* and *Yamato*, executing the customary series of strafing runs, dive-bombing runs, and hammer-and-anvil torpedo attacks.

Musashi received little attention and suffered minimal damage in the third attack of the day. She absorbed no bomb hits, although near-misses again took their toll on her antiaircraft machine gun crews; one torpedo pierced her starboard side, causing flooding in forward compartments that lowered her bow another seven feet. *Musashi*'s chief gunnery officer had requested permission from Admiral Inoguchi to fire Sanshikidan shells at the American planes from *Musashi*'s eighteen-inch guns, but Inoguchi had denied the request. Each of the monster guns had a service life of 200 to 250 rounds; gunnery training had already shortened the life span of the big guns, and the admiral insisted on preserving them for the expected encounter with American surface ships in Leyte Gulf.

Forty minutes after the third strike, sixty-five warplanes from *Enterprise* and *Franklin*, part of Admiral Davison's Task Group 38.4, hit *Musashi* and the Center Force, just as the last aircraft from *Essex* and *Lexington* were retiring from the scene. Davison's strike groups, totaling twenty-six Hellcats, twenty-one Helldivers, and eighteen Avengers, focused their attacks on the wounded *Musashi*, assaulting her with multiple waves of strafing, dive-bombing, and torpedo attacks.

Musashi and her crew suffered greatly from the fourth attack. Damage-control parties reported to Captain Kato at least one direct bomb hit on *Musashi*'s weather deck amidships, which caused more frightful carnage among the ship's machine gun crews. Three more bombs struck in the vicinity of her number one gun turret forward; they penetrated *Musashi*'s main deck and detonated belowdecks, killing surgeons and patients alike in the infirmary. But a far more serious blow to *Musashi*'s ability to fight were the four or five torpedoes that penetrated the battleship's forward storerooms and machinery spaces. These hits caused substantial structural damage internally and flooded much of *Musashi*'s hull forward of her armor box. Although her armor box itself remained fairly intact despite the torpedo hits, *Musashi* listed two degrees to starboard, and her bow trim was down by nearly twenty feet. Heavily burdened by flooding forward, with very little freeboard remaining at her bow, *Musashi*'s speed fell to sixteen knots, and she began to lag behind Kurita's formation.

In the face of the fourth American air strike of the day, *Musashi*'s chief gunnery officer had again pleaded with Admiral Inoguchi for permission to fire the ship's eighteen-inch Sanshikidan shells at the attacking carrier planes. This time Inoguchi assented, despite his grave concerns about the effect of the big guns' concussion on the ship's starboard list and nose-down trim. *Musashi*'s eighteen-inch naval guns fired for the first time in anger at about two twenty p.m., although only six of them were operational at the time. The three guns housed within the number one turret had been silenced completely by the earlier attacks. The great warship roared and shook and belched clouds of fire and smoke like a dragon, and the Sanshikidan detonated in spectacular fashion. But the results were disappointing. The American fliers kept coming on, and few American aircraft were observed to fall.

A fifth wave of attackers from Task Group 38.3 targeted *Musashi* on the heels of the fourth. Although the planes of the fifth wave scored no hits, they forced *Musashi* to evade their attacks, and the giant warship's performance deteriorated steadily, like a boxer who has absorbed too many body blows. At the conclusion of the fifth attack, one of her four engine rooms and three of her twelve boiler rooms were inaccessible and inoperable due to ruptured steam lines or blocked access. Most of her antiaircraft battery was destroyed. As a precaution against the heavy flooding forward, which could break the battleship's back if it became too severe, Captain Kato further reduced *Musashi*'s speed to twelve knots. Inexplicably, *Musashi*'s engineers made no attempt to remove seawater from the spaces they had flooded to correct her list, and *Musashi* gradually began to lose buoyancy and stability.

Aboard *Intrepid* at one p.m. on October 24, Air Group 18 prepared for its third strike of the day against *Musashi* and the Center Force. Strike 2 Able had returned to the ship at about twelve forty-five p.m. with two Helldivers badly shot up and two Avengers missing. Strike 2 Baker was still airborne and not expected to return to *Intrepid* until two fifteen p.m., but radio reports relayed from the Sibuyan Sea indicated that Strike 2 Baker had lost no fewer than two divebombers and one torpedo bomber. In VT-18's ready room, Ernie Allen, Frank Scrano, and the torpedo-plane pilots who were scheduled to fly Strike 2 Charlie, including Al Long, Duke Delaney, Lloyd Karch, and Ben St. John, gathered to listen to the after-action reports from the first strike.

Bud Williams confirmed the loss of Fletcher, Skelly, and their crews, and each of the returning pilots recounted the morning's action from his own point of view. The unbelievable intensity of the warships' Technicolor antiaircraft fire and the massive size of the two *Yamatos* were common themes among the reports. One of the returning torpedo-plane pilots confessed that he had failed to arm and release his weapon during the excitement of his torpedo run; to his chagrin, he had landed back aboard *Intrepid* with his fish still in his Avenger's belly, having endured the danger of the run but contributing nothing except the diversion of antiaircraft fire. Williams warned his torpeckers to stay as high as possible, five hundred feet or higher, during their final approach to the target, and not to fly at low altitude when breaking off their torpedo runs. There was mild heresy in his advice; a low-level approach and retirement was the navy's textbook technique for executing a torpedo run, precisely the technique Skelly and Fletcher had used. Williams explained that the Japanese gunners had sprayed their naval guns ahead of his Avengers' flight paths, raising solid columns of water that would bring down an airplane as surely as if it tried to fly through a forest of trees.

There was a sense among VT-18's pilots and aircrew that they were up against the entire Jap fleet and all alone in the fight. By one p.m., the vacationing carriers *Hancock* and *Bunker Hill* had not yet rejoined *Intrepid* and *Cabot*, and VT-18 was down to only four serviceable Avengers. Although Task Groups 38.3 and 38.4 had launched, or were in the process of launching, strike groups from *Lexington*, *Essex*, *Enterprise*, and *Franklin* to attack the Center Force, none of their aircraft had yet reached the scene of battle. Air Groups 18 and 29 had executed the first two attacks on the giant *Yamatos* and their escorts by themselves and had attacked while the enemy's antiaircraft batteries were at full strength. VT-18 had lost two Avenger crews on Strike Able and one on Strike 2 Baker. The squadron's losses so far that day were a testament to the lethality of the enemy's antiaircraft fire and a stark reminder to the men in VT-18's ready room of the challenge they faced.

Despite all this, there was a powerful but unspoken conviction among the pilots and aircrew that the enemy had to be stopped. This was the fight they had trained for. Commander Ellis, especially, was determined to punish the enemy while he had warplanes and daylight available. Although Ellis had already logged a twelve-hour day and been shot at by an unprecedented number of Japanese warships, he personally led Strike 2 Charlie off *Intrepid*'s flight deck at one fifty p.m. Immediately behind him launched fourteen more VF-18 Hellcats, twelve VB-18 Helldivers, and four VT-18 Avengers, the last led by Lieutenant Al

Long. One of the Avengers in Long's division, flown by Duke Delaney, developed an engine oil leak immediately after takeoff and returned to the ship, leaving Long with Karch and St. John as his only wingmen. El Gropo gathered up his attackers and headed back to the Sibuyan Sea for the second time in five hours.

Following the third wave of attacks on *Musashi*, Admiral Kurita had renewed his urgent plea for air support, advising Imperial Headquarters, "First Striking Force is engaged in severe fight in Sibuyan Sea. Enemy air attacks are expected to increase. Request land-based air force and mobile force to make prompt attack on enemy carrier force estimated to be at Lamon Bay [off eastern Luzon]." Manila again ignored Kurita's request; Imperial Headquarters in the Philippines had assigned fewer than a dozen fighter planes to cover Kurita's passage through the Sibuyan Sea, and American pilots had encountered very few Japanese fighters in the vicinity of the Center Force throughout the day. *Intrepid*'s Hellcats had downed two enemy planes on Strike 2 Able, a single-engine Jill and a twin-engine Frances, but VF-18's pilots were unsure whether they were part of a covering force or merely unlucky strays. Neither had bothered to engage, and VF-18's pilots had shot them down from behind at low altitude.

Strike 2 Charlie found *Musashi* and the Center Force near Sibuyan Island at about three thirty p.m. *Intrepid*'s strike group had been joined by aircraft from *Cabot*, *Essex*, *Franklin*, and *Lexington*, and the boys from Air Group 18 were greatly heartened to see them. *Musashi* had fallen behind Kurita's main body and was slowly steaming in evasive circles north of Sibuyan Island, protected by at least three destroyers, two cruisers, and one *Nagato*-class battleship. Ellis concentrated Air Group 18's third attack of the day on *Musashi*, which obviously had been crippled by earlier strikes. Better to finish off one of the world's largest warships than to expend ordnance on her less damaged sister ship and her escorts. "Scratch one superbattleship" seemed to be El Gropo's single-minded objective.

Following on the heels of VB-18's Helldiver bombing runs and VF-18's Hellcat strafing attacks, Lieutenant Long led his three-plane Avenger section in a sweeping turn behind *Musashi* to set up for roughly parallel torpedo runs on her starboard side. Long signaled for division breakup several miles south of the battleship, and each pilot began jinking wildly as he closed the distance to the target.

Ben St. John, VT-18's boot ensign, who had never before dropped a torpedo in combat and had dropped only two in training, took to heart Williams's advice about making a high approach. He wove past a destroyer, soared directly over a cruiser, and launched his weapon at nine hundred feet and 290 knots, roughly two thousand yards from *Musashi*. His torpedo passed ahead of *Musashi* but exploded in the starboard side of a *Mogami*-class cruiser on the battleship's northern flank. Lloyd Karch also released his torpedo high, from about 650 feet, just as *Musashi* was beginning an evasive turn to the north. Karch's torpedo appeared to strike the battleship squarely in the stern, sending up a high column of yellowish smoke. To Karch and Commander Ellis orbiting overhead, Karch's torpedo appeared to have damaged *Musashi*'s steering; rather than continue her evasive maneuvering, the battleship settled into a lazy left-hand turn. El Gropo characterized *Musashi*'s movement after Karch's hit as that of an "aimless cripple."

Al Long did not drop his torpedo. He signaled to Karch and St. John after they had joined up with him for the return flight to *Intrepid* that he had been unable to release his weapon electrically or manually. St. John, who had flown through a maelstrom of antiaircraft fire from at least three warships to press home his attack and had dodged more gunfire on retiring, did not believe him. St. John, convinced Long had broken off early, was furious and unforgiving.

Karch had different concerns. His turret gunner, Aviation Ordnanceman Second Class Irving Dugas, had been hit by shrapnel in the left leg, resulting in a bloody compound fracture of his femur, and Karch's radioman, Aviation Radioman Third Class C. W. Fort, had received a flesh wound in the thigh. Fort had extracted Dugas from the turret and applied a tourniquet to the wounded man's mangled leg, but he couldn't ease Dugas's pain. When Fort opened the Avenger's first-aid kit, he discovered to his disgust that someone had removed the morphine syringes. During the ninety-minute flight home to *Intrepid*, Karch kept up a running conversation with his two wounded crewmen over the intercom. Dugas, bleeding profusely and terrified of sharks, asked Karch anxiously whether they would have to ditch. Karch nervously eyed the two eight-inch-wide, forty-millimeter holes in his right wing, but assured Dugas he would get him back to the ship.

Karch landed safely with a shot-out tire and his gunner in agony; Karch's Avenger was so badly holed that it required a wing replacement. As *Intrepid*'s medics prepared Dugas for surgery, the injured man begged Air Group 18's flight surgeon, Doc Fish, not to let the medics amputate his leg. Fish assured him he would see what he could do.

Air Groups 18 and 29 had the distinction of delivering the first blows to *Musashi* and of being among those to deliver the last. The sixth and final attack of the day by Mitscher's carrier planes—*Intrepid*'s Strike 2 Charlie participated in the sixth attack—had made a shambles of *Musashi*'s superstructure. No fewer than ten bombs had hit her amidships, with at least six of these detonating directly on her conning tower and bridges. Admiral Inoguchi, on duty in the conning tower, had been gravely wounded by shrapnel slicing through his left shoulder, and the ship's chief navigator, antiaircraft commander, and five other senior officers had been killed in the collapse of the combat bridge high above Inoguchi's battle station. Sailors had carried Admiral Inoguchi to his sea cabin, and Inoguchi had transferred command of *Musashi* to Captain Kato.

Musashi's new skipper had to deal not only with the loss of senior ship's officers in the sixth attack, but with the cumulative effects of no fewer than ten additional torpedo hits, seven of which had struck *Musashi*'s port side. These had flooded major ammunition magazines and machinery spaces and shut down two more of *Musashi*'s boiler rooms, leaving only seven of her twelve boilers online. The torpedo hits had also flooded an engine room on her port side, leaving only two of her four engine rooms operational, both on her starboard side. *Musashi* now listed twelve degrees to port. Her main deck was submerged at the bow, and seawater surged over the chrysanthemum crest of the emperor that was affixed to her prow. Engineers counterflooded again to correct her list, but her speed was down to six knots, insufficient to steer the giant ship.

The sixth attack against Force A had also persuaded Kurita of the folly of pressing onward in the face of continued American air attacks. At about four p.m., Kurita ordered Force A to reverse course to the west, away from San Bernardino Strait and the planned rendezvous with Nishimura's Force C. Kurita characterized his course reversal to Admiral Toyoda as a "temporary" retirement "beyond range of hostile planes until friendly planes could strike a decisive blow against the enemy force." He obliquely criticized his superior's battle plan and blunted any criticism of himself by explaining, "[W]ere we to have forced our way through as scheduled under these circumstances [meaning without adequate air cover to disrupt the enemy's persistent air attacks] we would merely make of ourselves meat for the enemy, with very little chance of success to us."

At about the same time that Kurita reversed course, the skipper of *Princeton*, having concluded that his crippled light carrier could not be saved, reluctantly directed his damage-control parties to abandon ship. When all of *Princeton*'s surviving crew members had been removed, Admiral Sherman ordered his destroyers to sink the carrier—now a drifting, burning derelict—to prevent her from falling into the hands of the Japanese or from interfering with further movements of Task Group 38.3's warships. Of *Princeton*'s total complement of about 1,370 men, 108 had been killed and scores more had been grievously wounded.

The loss of *Princeton* was the low point of the day for Admiral Halsey. For most of the morning of October 24 and deep into the afternoon, Halsey and his staff had held court in *New Jersey*'s smoke-filled combat information center, where they had received constant reports from Mitscher's fliers on the progress of the air-sea battle raging in the Sibuyan Sea. The fliers' reports had been uniformly positive throughout the day, from the first strikes by *Intrepid* and *Cabot* to the last. Mitscher's fliers claimed to have heavily damaged many capital warships, including two huge *Yamatos* and a *Nagato*, and to have sunk a *Mogami*-class cruiser. In the aftermath of the sixth strike of the day, Mitscher's fliers reported that the enemy's battle formation had disintegrated and his ships were circling in disarray. And then at about four forty p.m. came confirmation of possible victory in the Sibuyan Sea: A carrier pilot reported that the enemy armada had reorganized but had reversed course and was steaming west, away from Leyte Gulf. Halsey and his staff were jubilant, but their joy was short-lived.

Only minutes after learning of Admiral Kurita's course reversal, Halsey received confirmation of enemy carriers on his northern flank. A search plane pilot from Sherman's Task Group 38.3 had sighted an enemy striking force comprised of at least three aircraft carriers, six cruisers, and six destroyers roughly two hundred miles northeast of Luzon. This striking force was, of course, Admiral Ozawa's Mobile Fleet, although Halsey did not know its true identity at the time. What Halsey and his staff did know was that Task Force 38 was now faced with three enemy fleets: a powerful but degraded surface force in the Sibuyan Sea, apparently retreating to the west; a smaller surface force approaching Surigao Strait from the south; and a mixed force of carriers and surface ships threatening his northern flank. Although Admiral Halsey regarded destruction of the Japanese fleet as his paramount objective, he believed aircraft carriers had been the principal instruments by which Japan had crippled the United States Navy and achieved domination in the Pacific. Halsey considered Japanese aircraft carriers to be Task Force 38's most deserving and productive targets, and he was obsessed with sinking them. Nevertheless, Halsey paused to assess this new threat from the north—and evaluate this new opportunity. He and his staff relit their cigarettes, recharged their coffee cups, and considered their options.

Deep in the Sibuyan Sea, Will Fletcher had swum for nearly six hours since being shot down. He had alternated between breaststroke and backstroke to even the strain on his muscles, but his neck, shoulders, and legs ached nonetheless. His scalp and face were beginning to blister from the sun, and the skin of his hands was wrinkled from constant immersion in salt water. His lips were cracked, and he was afraid they had begun to split and bleed. He was desperately thirsty and hungry; he chastened himself for not having eaten his breakfast eggs that morning, and mourned the loss of the drinking water in his survival kit. He had reinflated his Mae West by blowing through the mouth tubes of his life preserver every ten minutes, but the bladders were steadily leaking air. The sun had settled lower in the western sky. Although the declining sun helped orient him, the sun would soon set with tropical suddenness. The prospect of being adrift at night filled him with dread.

As he despaired of reaching land before nightfall, a swell lifted him up and he spied on the distant horizon a green nub. As the swell passed, he sank in the trough and lost sight of it. As the next swell bore him up, he confirmed the nub was the top of a sugarloaf hill, or perhaps the tops of trees. He could not tell which, but no matter. The green hump meant land. He was instantly exhilarated, reenergized, filled with hope. He forced himself not to weep with joy, because he could ill afford to lose the tears, and he pulled and kicked toward the green nub with renewed determination and purpose. His salvation was within reach.

Admiral Kurita had sailed westward aboard *Yamato* for an hour. No American carrier planes had attacked Kurita's armada since the end of the sixth strike, and he knew there would be no more air attacks today. The sun was declining and the American carriers were too far away; the American pilots could not reach Kurita's warships and yet make a safe return to their carriers in daylight.

Although his rendezvous with Nishimura in Leyte Gulf had been delayed by several hours, and his ships and crews had been punished by daylong American bombing and torpedo attacks, Kurita resolved to keep the appointment. At about five fifteen p.m., he ordered Force A to reverse course again and head east toward San Bernardino Strait.

At dusk, Kurita passed the stricken *Musashi* and his heart was filled with sorrow. Petty Officer Hosoya, who had survived the bombing of *Musashi*'s bridges and conning tower, signaled *Yamato* at Captain Kato's insistence: "*Musashi* taking on water."

Kurita's replied, "*Musashi,* go forward or backward at top speed and ground on nearest island and become a land battery."

But Captain Kato could not comply with Kurita's orders. *Musashi* was unsteerable, and she wallowed in a wide arc, sinking ever lower by the bow. Kato's engineers also could no longer halt *Musashi*'s flooding forward. Seawater had surged unchecked through huge torpedo holes in her shoulders and spread progressively aft. As a consequence of the repeated American air attacks, Kato's battleship had become a charnel house; intact corpses and dismembered bodies, human viscera and entrails were scattered about her decks. Pools of blood were mixed with the soot that Inoguchi's sailors applied to *Musashi*'s weather decks before she departed Brunei. The wounded cried out for help but had little hope of aid or succor; *Musashi*'s medical personnel had been decimated, and those who remained alive were overwhelmed. The injuries to the living were horrific: burns, broken and severed limbs, deep shrapnel cuts and punctures. Scores of uninjured sailors were trapped belowdecks; they were sealed within their compartments by collapsed overheads and bulkheads, by passageways filled with debris, or by flooded spaces above and beneath them. There were no damage-control parties to rescue them; even if *Musashi* did not sink, many of these trapped sailors were fated to suffocate at their battle stations. If there was any good fortune for *Musashi*'s crew, it was that secondary fires and smoke were minimal, the consequence of Inoguchi's order to remove unnecessary flammables before sailing for battle. The sailors who were able to emerge from belowdecks for fresh air were stunned at the scenes of carnage and destruction topside; they had misinterpreted the thunder and shaking of the American bombs and torpedoes as the concussive effects of *Musashi*'s own guns, not as the accompaniment to disaster.

At six p.m., *Musashi* lost all power. She was listing twelve degrees to port and her hull was fully submerged as far aft as her number one gun turret.

Will Fletcher swam toward the green hump on the horizon for nearly an hour. Gradually, the hump revealed itself as a canopy of trees. Palm trees. Beneath the trees ran a thin ribbon of white sand. All that separated Will from the safety of the beach was a narrow reef that lay fifty yards offshore and was marked by a line of white breakers.

Will paddled furiously across the reef. In the foamy water beneath him he detected a bed of brain coral, looking like cauliflower buds in a cook pot. His left foot struck a head of coral and his uniform shoe gave way, sliced open by the rock. Fearful of cutting open his shins and hands, he tucked himself into a ball and allowed the following swells to propel him across the reef. He tumbled though the breakers and drifted into a pool of warmer water. The bottom of the pool was a rippled bed of sand. His feet could not touch the bottom at first, so he dog-paddled toward the beach until the water grew shallow and his knees struck the sand. He gathered himself slowly, his body trembling from exhaustion, and crawled out of the water on all fours.

Aboard *Musashi*, Admiral Inoguchi had resolved to go down with his ship. The wounded Inoguchi handed Captain Kato his last will and testament and his written apology to the emperor for his errors in judgment, which included a too-passionate belief in the power of capital ships and naval guns and, by extension, a failure to appreciate the power of airplanes. Inoguchi forbade Kato to remain with him; he instructed Kato to remove the emperor's portrait and lower the ship's battle flag. Admiral Inoguchi handed his sword to a young officer and then locked himself in his sea cabin.

Kato mustered his surviving crew members on *Musashi*'s fantail. He instructed them to shift debris from port to starboard to counteract the battleship's steepening list. The wounded, those who were easily accessible and had a chance to survive, had been carried topside to the main deck. Kato had summoned the destroyers *Kiyoshima* and *Shimakaze* to assist in taking off the wounded, but the destroyers stood off passively in the distance; their skippers were apparently reluctant to risk damage to their ships by moving in too close to the dying *Musashi*. Signal officers, having tried unsuccessfully to burn *Musashi*'s secret codebooks, resorted to throwing the books over the side in canvas bags weighted with machine guns. Petty Officer Hosoya supervised the lowering of the flag at *Musashi*'s stern. A trumpeter played the Japanese national anthem as the ensign was lowered, and Hosoya entrusted the flag to a capable swimmer. Three officers jumped over *Musashi*'s side, taking with them the ship's ensign and the emperor's portrait.

At seven twenty p.m., *Musashi* lurched farther to port. Debris that sailors had earlier shifted to the starboard side slid back across the deck, crushing scores of men who were awaiting the order to abandon ship. The sea around the battleship was black with oil that had leaked from her ruptured bunkers. Ten minutes later, *Musashi* tilted to thirty degrees and her rate of list increased. Captain Kato bellowed at his sailors to abandon ship, yelling almost as an afterthought, "Every man for himself."

Musashi's stern rose as her bow descended, revealing her massive screws and rudder, and she began a slow death roll to port. Sailors by the hundreds leaped into the oil-coated sea. Some were unable or too terrified to swim; others were simply determined to die with their ship and clung fiercely to the battleship's stern rails. Currents of seawater rushed in and out of her hull in boiling confusion. Some men were captured by the rushing streams, unable to overcome the force of the current and swim away; others were spit out by the capricious currents and offered the chance to live. Petty Officer Hosoya found himself sprinting across the battleship's barnacled hull, dodging the gaping torpedo holes in her sides that became visible as she capsized. He reached the water and swam desperately away from the undertow of the sinking ship. The ship created a massive swell as she rolled on her side, inundating men who were struggling in the water to remain afloat. *Musashi* turned bottom up and began to slide under bow-first, her enormous bulk generating a swirling vortex as she descended to her resting place.

At seven thirty p.m., the ocean swallowed *Musashi* completely. Her stern disappeared in a hissing cloud of steam and she began her final journey to the seafloor, four thousand feet beneath her, at latitude thirteen degrees, seven minutes north and longitude 122 degrees, thirty-two minutes east. The hiss and rumble of her sinking quickly subsided. The water covering her grave had become a hellish stew of oil and debris, of bodies living and dead. More than twelve hundred enlisted men and forty officers were adrift in the water; more than a thousand officers and men were lost, either killed during battle or drowned with their ship.

Petty Officer Hosoya and Captain Kato were among the survivors. They shared a wooden box for flotation. Japanese destroyers crept through the watery graveyard, shining searchlights in the darkness to locate survivors, whose heads looked like melons floating in a pond. To bolster their spirits in the darkness, the survivors sang songs, but a few refused rescue and swam off into the darkness to die.

Shortly after Vice Admiral Kurita reversed course for the second time and headed back toward San Bernardino Strait, his superior, Admiral Toyoda, had radioed him instructions from Tokyo. "Trusting in divine help," the message had read, "resume the attack." Kurita's subordinates had disparaged Toyoda's order, noting that, "Not even a god can direct naval battles from shore," but Kurita dutifully led his Force A steadily eastward with the goal of making a night passage of San Bernardino Strait and breaking into the Philippine Sea at dawn. At about seven thirty p.m., Admiral Nishimura confirmed to Kurita by radio that his Force C would also "storm the center of the eastern shore of Leyte Gulf at 0400 on the 25th." The planned envelopment of American forces in Leyte Gulf had been delayed but not derailed.

The mood in VT-18's ready room that night was grim. Barden, the scheduling officer, noted that the squadron's torpedo bombers had been shot to hell and that VT-18 had only seven Avengers still in commission. Far more painful were the losses of Skelly, Fletcher, Riley, and their crews. Nine men from a single squadron lost in a single day. Although there was hope Riley and his crew had been rescued by friendly forces, there was no hope for the others. In his stateroom that night, Lieutenant Commander Van Antwerp wrote letters to the next of kin of Skelly, Fletcher, and their crewmen. The letters included the same grim sentence, "I am of the opinion that the airplane was destroyed by the intense enemy fire." Lieutenant Scrano drew the same conclusion in his administrative report with respect to the loss of Fletcher and his crew: "The attack commenced at [10:30 a.m.]. The aircraft was hit by the intense antiaircraft fire from the Japanese fleet, and was forced to land or crash in the sea at or near the scene of action. Search was impossible due to the proximity of the enemy fleet. It is the opinion of the CO that the subject men are missing as a result of intense enemy AA by reason of which their aircraft was forced to land or crash in the sea."

Mass was held on board for Christman, a Catholic. Friends of the missing men collected the personal effects of the lost sailors and packed the belongings in sea chests for shipment home. Items that could not be easily shipped, such as a musical instrument or a bulky souvenir, were auctioned off and the proceeds were placed in the sea chest for the next of kin. Barden recorded in his diary, "Formosa was a set-up compared to the AA I saw today. To say today was terrible doesn't begin to explain." Lieutenant Race echoed the sentiment. Despite Air Group 18's losses over Formosa, "Pilots agreed this was the roughest day they have had thus far."

At about the same time that *Musashi* slipped beneath the waves, Admiral Halsey and his staff made their tactical decision. Admiral Oldendorf's battleships and Admiral Sprague's escort carriers could deal with the enemy surface force approaching from the south, they decided. The enemy surface force in the Sibuyan Sea had been turned back, and the enemy carrier force to the north presented the greatest threat. Halsey feared the Japanese carrier planes might shuttle-bomb the Task Force, as they had tried to do off Saipan. Vice Admiral Willis A. Lee, who commanded all Battleships Pacific Fleet and flew his flag in *Washington*, warned Halsey of a potential course reversal by Kurita and urged Halsey's staff to leave behind a group of surface ships to guard San Bernardino Strait. Halsey disregarded this advice and ordered task groups 38.1, 38.2, and 38.3 to rendezvous off northern Luzon and prepare for an attack on the Japanese carriers the following morning.

By nine p.m., Admiral Bogan's Task Group 38.2, still comprised only of two carriers, *Intrepid* and *Cabot*, was racing northward with the battleships *New Jersey* and *Iowa*, three cruisers, and fourteen destroyers. In VT-18's ready room, Barden scheduled Bud Williams's division for the first mission in the morning, a torpedo strike. Barden entered names on the flight status board other than Skelly, Fletcher, and Riley, a duty that underscored the day's losses.

Several VT-27 Avenger crews assigned to the unlucky *Princeton* had taken refuge aboard *Intrepid*. VT-27 and VT-18 had trained contemporaneously at Hollister, and Barden had drinking and card-playing buddies among VT-27's pilots. He was very glad to see them. Relieved that task groups 38.3 and 38.4 were now scheduled to join Task Group 38.2 by morning, Barden also took comfort that VT-18 would no longer be alone in the fight. He wrote, "This business of A.G.18 battling the entire Jap Navy is damned rough."

CHAPTER THIRTEEN

OFF BANTON AND CAPE ENGANO

★ ★ ★ ★ ★

Will Fletcher sat on the crest of the beach, exhausted from his struggle to get ashore. Checking his Bulova, he saw that he had been in the ocean for nearly seven hours. Despite the sand beneath him, his inner ear told him he was still rolling through the waves. His first thought was to conceal himself and find water. He rose unsteadily to his feet and shuffled inland to a cluster of coconut palms that leaned over the beach at crazy angles, like fence poles about to topple over from neglect. He picked up a palm frond, something he had never lifted before; it was surprisingly heavy. Dragging the palm frond to the water's edge, he retraced his steps back to the palm trees, erasing in the sand any sign of where he had come ashore. When he reached the shelter of the palms, he leaned wearily against a tree trunk and surveyed his surroundings.

Will had landed on the western shore of a flat, sandy island. Narrow at the spot where he had swum ashore, the island was no more than fifty yards wide, and the highest elevation appeared to be no more than four or five feet above sea level. Less than one hundred yards south of where Will stood, the sandy beach vanished beneath turquoise-colored water. How far north his refuge extended he could not tell; a dense grove of storm-swept narra trees and tall coconut palms that grew along the central spine of the island blocked his view. A thicket of brush and bamboo grass flourished in the shadows beneath the trees. The dense undergrowth raised Will's hopes of finding freshwater.

He was surprised to discover three other islands in the distance, none of which he had seen as he swam ashore. About five miles to the east was a pyramid-shaped island with uplands high enough to have ensnared some rosy evening clouds. The island to the south was a low hummock, like a sugarloaf hill or an Indian mound, perhaps six miles distant. To the west lay a hazy bump on the horizon, too far away for him to judge its size or true distance. The high mountains of Mindoro to the west were silhouetted by the setting sun; Will was certain the highest peaks were Mount Baca and Mount Halcon. Before he had launched from *Intrepid* that morning, he had drawn circles around these two mountains on his navigational chart, marking them as the unmistakable western boundary of the Sibuyan Sea and noting that they rose eight thousand feet above sea level, obstacles to be avoided.

Will pulled out his silk survival map of the Philippines and pinpointed where he had crashed and begun his daylong swim. He had flown over Tablas Island and attacked *Musashi* at the northern end of Tablas Island, pretty much in the middle of Tablas Strait. He had been headed in a northerly direction before he crashed. If Mindoro's mountains lay southwest, he reasoned, the islands to the east should be Banton and Simara.

Will concluded that the pyramidal island was Banton. His silk map reported Banton's highest elevation to be 2,016 feet above sea level, which corresponded with his seaman's eye. The hummocky island to the south of his islet must be Simara, with an elevation of only 772 feet. The hazy bump to the west he took to be the uplands of Maestre de Campo. Will's map revealed no other large islands in the triangle of the Sibuyan Sea bounded by Banton, Simara, and Maestre de Campo. He had beached on an uncharted islet, one of the many in the Visayas that are unmapped and unnamed. He realized that his plan of swimming directly toward Tablas Island by following the clouds had been naive. He had been swept far north of Tablas Island. The winds and currents of the Sibuyan Sea had commanded his path, not him; they had borne him where they willed and deposited him where they pleased.

Will took stock of his possessions, carefully laying out each item on the map in front of him: his Bulova watch; his survival knife; his deflated Mae West; his .38-caliber revolver; his holster belt with twenty rounds of ammunition; a few

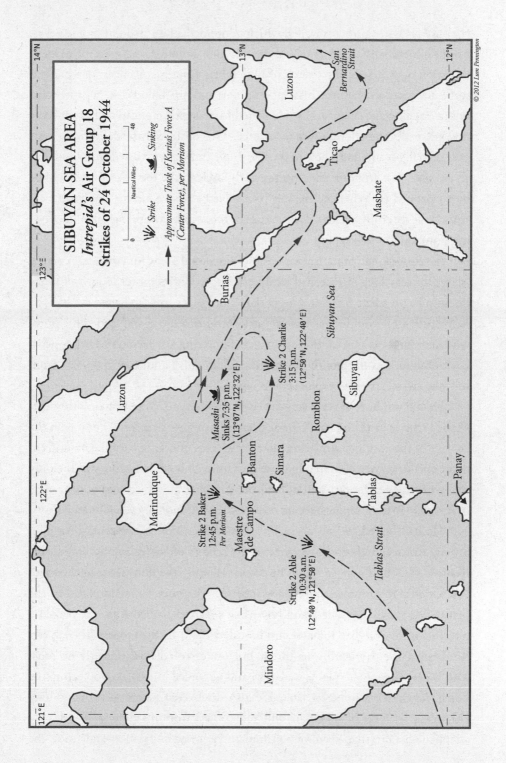

SIBUYAN SEA AREA
Intrepid's Air Group 18
Strikes of 24 October 1944

Nautical Miles
0   40

🖐 Strike

⚓ Sinking

→ → → Approximate Track of Kurita's Force A
        (Center Force), per Morison

14°N
13°N
12°N

121°E   122°E   123°E

Luzon

San Bernardino Strait

Ticao

Masbate

Burias

Luzon

Musashi
Sinks 7:35 p.m.
(13°07'N, 122°32'E)

Strike 2 Charlie
3:15 p.m.
(12°50'N, 122°40'E)

Sibuyan

Sibuyan Sea

Romblon

Strike 2 Baker
12:45 p.m.
Per Morison

Banton

Simara

Tablas

Marinduque

Maestre
de Campo

Strike 2 Able
10:30 a.m.
(12°40'N, 121°50'E)

Tablas Strait

Panay

Mindoro

© 2012 Lam Pennington

sticks of chewing gum; his wallet, which contained a hundred Philippine pesos, his military identification card, and the lock of his mother's hair; his metal identification or dog tags; the swatch of blue fabric from his Avenger; one pack of wet Lucky Strike cigarettes; his Zippo lighter; and his "blood chit," a paper written in Tagalog and Spanish that identified him as an American and promised a reward to anyone offering him assistance. He considered the condition of his gear. His flight suit had a hole in the left thigh and was encrusted with sand, but serviceable. His uniform shoes were nearly useless; the toe box of his left shoe had separated entirely from the sole. He craved a smoke but his cigarettes were ruined; he carefully preserved the shreds of tobacco by wrapping them in chewing gum foil for safekeeping.

Nothing he had brought ashore with him would allow him to remain on the island for very long. He needed food and especially freshwater soon, and knew he must begin a search for these essentials and a place to sleep before the sun set. Will stuffed his worldly possessions back into his pockets and loaded his pistol with six rounds as a precaution against encountering any Japanese. He popped a stick of gum into his mouth to stimulate some saliva and, sore and weak from his long swim, set off to explore his refuge.

He did not have to walk very far. Will's refuge proved to be a tiny crescent-shaped strip of sand and coral. It was disappointingly small, a mere bump on the surface of the vast sea, displacing only a few acres of ocean. Reeflike mounds of coral and sand were clustered in close proximity, but his little islet was the only one with any vegetation. Will walked the complete circumference of his refuge in less than fifteen minutes, seeing no signs of habitation or even human visitors.

He had hoped to find a source of freshwater, perhaps a spring or a pool among the trees and brush that grew in the center of his islet, but his hopes were dashed. He found none; as far as he could tell, only the rains watered the islet's vegetation. He stumbled upon a few scraggly wild cherry tomato plants in the brush. Why they grew here and how they survived baffled him. He picked a handful of marble-size tomatoes and stuffed them in his mouth. Their bitter fluid eased the dryness in his throat but underscored how urgently he must find water. The tomato plants were few, and he forced himself to stop eating the berries to preserve some for later. He also discovered palmetto plants among the trees, the roots of which are edible, he knew from his time in Florida. He snapped off a fan-shaped palmetto frond and gnawed at its celery-stalk root; the

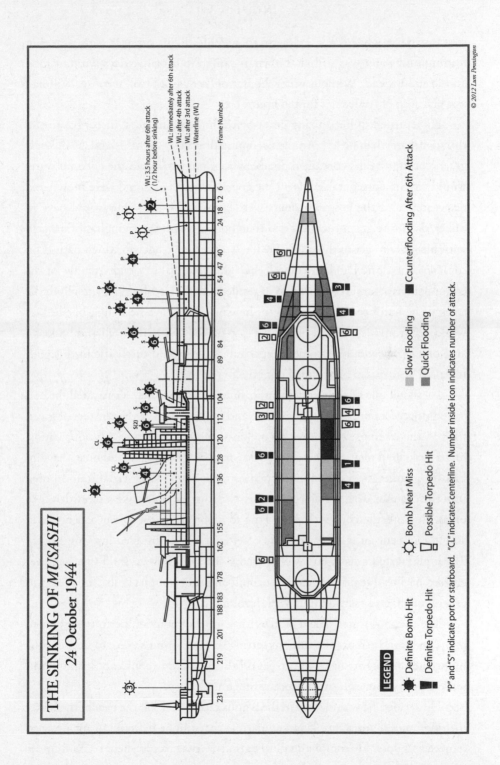

THE SINKING OF *MUSASHI*
24 October 1944

WL: 3.5 hours after 6th attack
(1/2 hour before sinking)

WL: immediately after 6th attack
WL: after 4th attack
WL: after 3rd attack
Waterline (WL)

Frame Number

© 2012 Liam Pennington

LEGEND

Definite Bomb Hit
Definite Torpedo Hit

Bomb Near Miss
Possible Torpedo Hit

Slow Flooding
Quick Flooding

Ccunterflooding After 6th Attack

"P" and "S" indicate port or starboard.   "CL" indicates centerline.   Number inside icon indicates number of attack.

root tasted like a brazil nut. Palmetto root would fill his stomach for a time, but finding freshwater was still vital. A man can go four or five days without food and keep his head. Without water, he has only a day or two at most. Will had not had a sip of freshwater for ten hours.

He returned to his starting point beneath the palm trees, disconsolate and thirstier than when he left. Ample coconut palms grew on his island. Will knew green coconut palms contained potable water, but getting to the coconut water would require considerable effort. The coconuts on the ground were brown and desiccated, and the green coconuts were high in the trees. He would have to knock down the green coconuts and then bore through their tough, fibrous skin with his knife to get to the water. He had seen a movie once in which natives on some Pacific island had half crawled, half slithered up the slender trunks of coconut palms to harvest the fruit. Will mulled whether he should try to climb the trees. If he had been at full strength, he would not have hesitated, but he was weakened from his swim. If he lost his grip on the trunk, if he fell and broke an arm or a leg, he would become incapacitated and would surely die in this godforsaken little place. He decided not take to the risk.

He shook one of the slender trunks but no coconuts fell. Frustrated, he collected dried coconuts from the ground and hurled them at the clusters of green fruit in the treetops. He threw the melon-size nuts overhead with both hands, like a basketball player making a pass downcourt. He missed, and missed again. Finally, a large green coconut plopped into the sand. Will seized it and bored into the coconut with his survival knife, twisting the point like a screwdriver to break through the coconut's skin. True to its promise, the green coconut held about a half cup of tepid water at its core, which Will dribbled into his mouth. The liquid tasted grassy, but Will judged it the most blessed fluid that had ever crossed his lips. He pried open the coconut and sliced out its flesh. The meat was green, tough, and tasteless, but Will devoured it.

The coconut water slaked Will's thirst for the moment, permitting him to focus on his next steps. The sun was setting. He must find a place to sleep for the night and then figure out a way to get off this island. He could not sustain himself on cherry tomatoes and coconuts indefinitely.

He decided he would sleep in the woods rather than on the beach, the better to hide himself from any Japanese patrols that might be looking for downed American pilots. He found a mature narra tree that would shelter him, but decided he shouldn't sleep on the ground. The surrounding brush and bamboo looked to be a fine habitat for snakes. He pulled himself up into the tree and nestled into a crook where three branches came together. To keep from falling in his sleep, he strapped himself to a branch with his pistol belt.

As he lay in the tree, he grappled with the problem of how to escape his refuge to a larger island, perhaps to Banton, where he could obtain freshwater and the assistance of friendly guerrillas. Building a fire to signal for help would be foolish. There were no American forces within hundreds of miles, and his smoke signal might attract the Japanese rather than curious Filipinos. He dreaded the idea of getting back in the ocean for a swim to an adjacent island. Without ample food and freshwater, he doubted he would have the endurance for another six or seven mile swim. He had also escaped the attentions of sharks on today's desperate journey, but would he be so lucky tomorrow?

The solution was growing all around him. A dense break of bamboo grass stood within a few yards of Will's narra tree, and he suddenly hit upon the idea of building a raft made of bamboo. He had no doubt there were large stalks of bamboo grass growing in the break. If he could harvest some bamboo poles and lash them together with bamboo strips, he could build a raft large enough to support his weight and enable him to paddle himself over to Banton, or wherever he chose to go. He imagined a bamboo mattress, woven together like a piece of rattan furniture. His plan excited and comforted him. He would not be marooned here; there was a way to get himself off this island after all.

He was tired, and decided to start building his raft at first light. He closed his eyes and listened to the sea breeze rustling the narra leaves and the palms. Will had first enjoyed the evening song of palm trees while walking along the Miami Beach boardwalk at night, an attractive young woman on his arm. The music of the palms, the gentle hiss and slapping of the fronds, had been as soothing as a violin adagio. He had been enchanted. But tonight, the clattering of palms became the whispering of ghosts, and he played and replayed in his mind the images of the day. He saw Skelly and his crew die again in the disintegration of their airplane. He relived the terrifying explosions of *Musashi*'s guns all around him. He thought of the cockpit fire and of the wrenching violence of his crash landing. He remembered the horror of Christman's headless corpse and his futile effort to save Westmoreland. He envisioned the bodies of Westmoreland and Christman decomposing in the depths of the Sibuyan Sea and shuddered at the narrowness of his own escape from the airplane, at the terror of his near drowning, and the ordeal of his daylong swim. He wondered at his bad luck and his good fortune. The difference of an inch here, or a split second in time there, and he would have been among the dead, not the living.

Will could not sleep despite his weariness. He climbed down from his narra tree and ventured onto the beach. The night sky over Tablas Strait was clear and the stars were brilliant. They glittered like diamond dust from horizon to horizon.

On the evening of October 24, while Will Fletcher tried to sleep on his un-inhabited islet and Task Force 38 raced north to intercept Ozawa, Admiral Nishimura's Force C entered the Mindanao Sea, intent on passing through Su-rigao Strait during the night and rendezvousing with Kurita's Force A off southern Samar at dawn. Nishimura had been aware of the American air attacks on Kurita's warships in the Sibuyan Sea, and he had slowed his progress toward Leyte Gulf in the expectation that Kurita would be delayed.

At about ten forty p.m. that night, a section of Admiral Oldendorf's wooden-hulled motor torpedo boats (called "PT boats") discovered Nishimura's Force C off Bohol Island in the Mindanao Sea. The American PT boat section—three PT boats comprised one section—radioed its sighting to Oldendorf, and then im-mediately attacked the Japanese formation with torpedoes. Nishimura's heavier-gunned destroyers drove the PT boats away, but their skippers had alerted Oldendorf to Nishimura's presence. For the next three hours, Force C churned through the eastern waters of the Mindanao Sea, evading a series of resolute but largely ineffectual torpedo attacks by multiple PT boat sections. By two thirty a.m., Force C had exited the Mindanao Sea and turned north into Surigao Strait, the narrow stretch of water between Leyte and Dinagat islands. The channel is no more than twenty miles wide at the widest; the southern entrance to Leyte Gulf lies only forty miles to the north. The seven warships of Force C steamed northward through the middle of Surigao Strait at eighteen knots. The three heavy warships, battleships *Yamashiro* and *Fuso* and the cruiser *Mogami*, were aligned in column; two destroyers of Force C screened ahead of *Yamashiro*, and two remaining destroyers shielded *Yamashiro*'s flanks.

At about three a.m., after Force C had traveled roughly halfway up the strait, five American destroyers from Oldendorf's Destroyer Squadron 54 materialized out of the darkness on Nishimura's flanks. Launching torpedoes in high-speed hit-and-run attacks, the American destroyers sank three of Nishimura's destroyers and disabled the battleship *Fuso*, setting her ablaze. Nishimura, aboard his flagship, *Yamashiro*, ignored the loss of *Fuso* and three of his four destroyers and pressed onward toward Leyte Gulf with his three remaining warships. Nishimura had received little reconnaissance on the size or disposition of the American forces he faced, and he was determined to execute his mission. The remnants of Force C, the battleship *Yamashiro*, the cruiser *Mogami*, and the destroyer *Shigure*, continued north in column, zigzagging defensively back and forth across their base course. At about four a.m., the remnants of Force C sailed within range of the six American battleships and five cruisers that Admiral Oldendorf had positioned to block the exit from Surigao Strait into Leyte Gulf.

Oldendorf's battleships opened fire on Nishimura's Force C from about twenty-three thousand yards. With *West Virginia* in the lead, the six American battleships, mounting fourteen or sixteen-inch naval guns, steamed west to east, trailing behind one another bow-to-stern like ducklings in a row. They fired salvo after salvo, creating man-made thunder and lightning in the night. When the big ships had run their course in one direction, they reversed course and steamed east to west, this time with *California* in the lead, and opened fire again. Oldendorf's five cruisers, stationed farther south in the channel, also paraded west to east across the neck of the strait. With *Louisville* in the lead, the cruisers opened fire on Force C from eighteen thousand yards at about the same time as the American battleships. To one American observer, the "arched line of tracers [from the American guns] in the darkness looked like a continual stream of railroad cars going over a hill." Oldendorf's warships had "crossed the T" on Nishimura's approaching column; American "ships of the line" had fired broadside on an approaching enemy column and brought all of their weapons to bear concurrently. Crossing the T was a consummate naval tactic as old as the days of wooden warships. By four thirty a.m., *Yamashiro* had been reduced to an inferno and sunk, taking Admiral Nishimura and most of *Yamashiro*'s crew with her. *Mogami* had been mortally wounded, while *Shigure* had escaped to the south. *Fuso* had blown up and sunk in two burning halves.

Admiral Shima's Second Striking Force of three cruisers and four destroyers, which had trailed Nishimura's Force C through the Mindanao Sea by several hours, entered Surigao Strait at about the same time as *Yamashiro* met her fiery end. Shima learned of the disaster that had befallen Nishimura, and he prudently reversed course to the south, quickly retiring from the fight and almost certain annihilation by Oldendorf's battle line.

The southern jaw of the Japanese vise had been broken. But Admiral Halsey had led Task Force 38 north in hot pursuit of Ozawa's aircraft carriers. In doing so, Halsey had left San Bernardino Strait unguarded, and the narrow east–west seaway between Luzon and Samar, the gateway to the Philippine Sea and Leyte to the south, lay wide-open to the enemy.

Vice Admiral Kurita's Force A skillfully navigated San Bernardino Strait during the night of October 24 and entered the Philippine Sea at about twelve thirty a.m. on the morning of October 25. Since leaving Brunei on October 20, Kurita's Force A had been reduced by the loss of three cruisers in the submarine attacks off Palawan on October 23, and further weakened by the loss of *Musashi* and the heavy cruiser *Myoko* in the daylong air attacks in the Sibuyan Sea. The battleships *Yamato*, *Nagato*, and *Haruna* had been damaged by the Sibuyan Sea air strikes, but not to the extent that Halsey's carrier pilots had reported or his staff believed. Kurita's Force A remained strong and lethal, fully capable of executing its mission. Kurita had at his command four battleships, including *Yamato*, six heavy cruisers, and no fewer than eleven destroyers.

All that stood between Kurita and the landing beaches in Leyte Gulf, roughly two hundred miles to the south, were three amphibious support groups comprised of American escort carriers and undersize surface combatants. The northernmost of these American support groups, designated "Taffy 3," consisted of six escort carriers, three destroyers, and four smaller warships classed as "destroyer escorts." As the sun rose on October 25, Taffy 3 lay about forty miles east of Anitaquipan Point off central Samar. The second group of escort carriers and destroyers, "Taffy 2," lay about sixty miles south of Taffy 3 and patrolled the eastern entrance to Leyte Gulf. The third group of escort carriers, "Taffy 1," lay another seventy miles south off the eastern coast of Mindanao. These three groups of escort carriers and small surface ships were part of Vice Admiral Thomas C. Kinkaid's 7th Fleet. Their principal mission was to provide air support for the amphibious landings at Leyte and for the movement of MacArthur's troops inland, not to engage the main body of a powerful enemy surface force.

As the sun rose on October 25, Rear Admiral Oldendorf's bombardment

group, although victorious over Nishimura's Force C in the night action in Surigao Strait, was in no position to challenge Kurita's capital ships as they moved
south toward Leyte. Oldendorf's cruisers had moved deeper into Surigao Strait
during the night to pursue Admiral Shima's Second Striking Force and the
damaged *Mogami*; Oldendorf's battleships had retired to Leyte Gulf to replenish their ammunition.

The Taffy groups were all alone.

At five thirty a.m. on October 25, Task Group 38.2 was steaming off Luzon 150
miles north of San Bernardino Strait. At flight quarters aboard *Intrepid* that
morning, Lieutenant Commander Allen informed the torpedo-plane pilots assembled in VT-18's ready room that a battle line of eleven Japanese surface warships had been discovered fifty miles northeast of *Intrepid*'s position and that
the ultimate prize, four Jap carriers, was arrayed thirty miles astern of the enemy's battle line. Air Group 18 would launch Strike 2 Able against the enemy
carriers within the hour.

Intrepid's air department had repaired VT-18's battle-damaged Avengers
overnight, increasing the number of warplanes available from the pitifully few
that were serviceable after the previous day's strikes in the Sibuyan Sea. Kenny
Barden, who had gone to sleep thinking he wouldn't fly early the next morning, learned at flight quarters that Commander Ellis had specifically requested
Van Antwerp lead an eight-plane Avenger division on Strike 2 Able. Barden,
Bud Williams, Doc Doyle, and Joe Rubin would all join their skipper. VT-18's
Avengers, armed with Mark 13 torpedoes, would be accompanied by ten VB-18
Helldivers, each armed with a thousand-pound armor-piercing bomb and two
hundred-pound general-purpose bombs. Because the primary objective was to
sink or disable the enemy carriers, six out of the seven VF-18 Hellcats assigned
to Strike 2 Able would each carry one five-hundred-pound general-purpose
bomb.

Ellis led Strike 2 Able off the flight deck at six oh three a.m. into clear skies.
The strike group orbited *Intrepid* for forty-five minutes, climbing slowly to fifteen thousand feet. Ellis's attackers arrived over the enemy battle line at eight
thirty a.m., where they were joined by strike groups from four other American
carriers. Vice Admiral Mitscher had designated Commander T. H. Winters,
commander of Air Group 19 based aboard *Lexington* and code-named *Mohawk*,

as strike coordinator. Mitscher had also strictly enjoined his pilots to maintain radio discipline and keep the airwaves clear. Winters calmly talked over the situation with his fellow group leaders and assigned targets over the tactical frequency. Surprisingly, the Japanese carriers made no attempt to launch any fighters, and there were no airborne Zekes to hurry Winters along. When all was ready, he broadcast, "Check all switches and make a high-speed run," and the attack began.

VB-18's Helldivers pushed over from eleven thousand feet into dive-bombing runs of fifty to ninety degrees, targeting two *Zuiho*-class light carriers. The dive-bombers released at twenty-five hundred feet and pulled out at fifteen hundred feet. The Japanese carriers and their screen threw up intense antiaircraft fire, but the Sunday Punchers scored at least five confirmed and two probable hits. VB-18's skipper credited John Forsyth with one of the confirmed hits.

Van Antwerp split up his eight-plane Avenger flight five-three, with Van Antwerp leading a five-plane Avenger division against *Zuikaku*, a fleet carrier and veteran of the Pearl Harbor raid, and with Bud Williams leading a three-plane section against a light carrier, believed to be *Zuiho* or *Chitose*. The torpeckers endured a gauntlet of intense antiaircraft fire from the carriers' surface escorts, but the counterfire coming from the carriers themselves was weaker than the volume raised by yesterday's superbattleships. Williams's three Avengers scored two probable and one possible hit on the *Zuiho*-class; Van Antwerp's four Avengers put three fish in the water, all of which appeared to hit home on *Zuikaku* (which Ellis and Van Antwerp later misidentified in their aircraft action reports as *Shokaku*). One VT-18 pilot was unable to release manually or electrically.

Kenny Barden scored one of VT-18's torpedo hits on *Zuikaku* but nearly paid the ultimate price. An antiaircraft shell pierced the underside of his fuselage just aft of his radioman's flight station, passed upward through the tunnel, and exploded above his airplane but not in it. Miraculously, Barden's radioman didn't receive a scratch, and his Avenger's control lines weren't severed. Barden's Avenger nevertheless lost its ventral fin and a huge piece of its fuselage; in silhouette Barden's torpedo bomber looked like a fish with a big chunk of meat chewed out of its spine. Barden was able to land his wounded Avenger back aboard *Intrepid* without incident. Other VT-18 aircrew returned to *Intrepid* with battle damage—Van Antwerp landed back aboard ship with his engine afire, and Doc

Doyle landed with his radioman, Aviation Radioman Second Class F. Bellamy, bleeding from a shrapnel wound to his leg—but all returned.

By nine thirty a.m., *Intrepid* had safely recovered all of her aircraft from Strike 2 Able. As of that moment far to the south off Samar, Admiral Kinkaid's Taffy groups had been engaged for nearly three hours in a desperate fight for survival.

At about six fifty a.m. on October 25, search planes from the northernmost Taffy group, Taffy 3, discovered Kurita's armada less than twenty-five miles away, menacingly arrayed along a thirteen-mile front, and sounded the alarm. The commander of Taffy 3, Rear Admiral Clifton A. F. Sprague—not to be confused with Rear Admiral Thomas L. Sprague, Commander of Taffy 1 and the entire escort carrier task group—reacted decisively to the unhappy surprise. Knowing his thin-skinned, slow-footed escort carriers could not withstand shelling by Kurita's warships and would be quickly overrun by Kurita's faster surface ships—the Japanese vessels were capable of nearly twice the speed of the American escort carriers—Sprague turned Taffy 3 due east at 17.5 knots, the maximum speed his carriers could sustain, and tried to open the distance between himself and the enemy. He summoned help from Taffys 1 and 2, and ordered all Taffy 3 aircraft aloft to attack Kurita's formation. He gathered his escort carriers like pioneers circling their wagons, and sought the cover of rain squalls.

As he descended on Taffy 3, Kurita reshaped his formation for battle, grouping his battleships and cruisers into four separate divisions and dividing his destroyers into two divisions. Instead of coordinating the movements of these six battle groups, Kurita ordered a "general attack," an open-ended directive that gave each of his subordinate group commanders the freedom and discretion to attack as he saw fit.

The Japanese opened fire on the Americans at about seven a.m., and heavy-caliber Japanese shells began to fall around the ships of Taffy 3 with escalating accuracy and intensity. Sprague doubted his escort carriers would survive five minutes absent extreme measures. At seven-oh-six a.m., he ordered his destroyers and destroyer escorts to make torpedo runs against the onrushing Japanese. Under cover of a rain shower, Sprague turned his carriers back to the southwest to close the distance to Leyte Gulf, where, he hoped, he would receive air support from Taffy 1 and 2 and from American aircraft on Leyte.

Taffy 3's destroyer screen responded with alacrity and heroism. Destroyers *Hoel*, *Heermann*, and *Johnston* were the first to dash to the attack against the much more powerful Japanese warships. Laying clouds of smoke to cover their approach as they maneuvered within range of the enemy, the American destroyers launched torpedoes, fired their five-inch guns, and endured withering counterfire from much heavier Japanese naval guns. Some of the Japanese armor-piercing shells passed through the thin hulls of the American destroyers without exploding; others wreaked havoc belowdecks and above. At about seven forty-five, with Taffy 3's circumstances still desperate, Sprague ordered a second torpedo attack by the destroyers of his screen. Once again, the American destroyers responded aggressively and selflessly. *Hoel* was struck by more than forty enemy shells; at about nine a.m., she rolled over and sank with great loss of life. But the attacks of *Hoel* and her sister destroyers had disabled at least two of Kurita's cruisers, and the destroyers' sacrifice had confused the Japanese and disrupted the southward advance of the Center Force.

Taffy 3's fighters and torpedo bombers joined in the counterattacks, and some of Sprague's warplanes made diversionary runs on the Japanese ships without any ammunition. Kurita's formation fell into disarray. Because the heavy Japanese warships had to maneuver to evade the American counterattacks, both real and feigned, they failed to close the distance on Sprague's vulnerable escort carriers.

Not all of Clifton Sprague's carriers escaped the onslaught. Although harassed by *Johnston* and the destroyer escort *Samuel B. Roberts* (destroyer escorts were about half the tonnage of a destroyer), four of Kurita's heavy cruisers closed within range of the escort carrier *Gambier Bay* and sank her with gunfire at about eight thirty a.m.; twenty minutes later they also sank the brave *Johnston* and *Samuel B. Roberts*. As if in retaliation for these losses, aircraft from Taffy 3 and Taffy 2 pummeled the Center Force in well-coordinated torpedo and bomb attacks and sent cruisers *Chokai* and *Chikuma* to the bottom at nine a.m. Admiral Kurita and his staff interpreted the American air attacks as coming from a strong American force, perhaps from Task Force 38 itself. At nine eleven a.m., he ordered his cruisers and battleships to break off their attacks and regroup. Kurita's withdrawal order unintentionally spared escort carriers *White Plains* and *Fanshaw Bay* from imminent destruction by Kurita's remaining cruisers, *Tone* and *Haguro*, and allowed Taffy 3 to escape Kurita's reach.

But at about ten a.m., Sprague's escort carriers, and those of Taffy 1 stationed near the entrance to Leyte Gulf, faced a new and unexpected threat. Flying from bases on Luzon, Japanese warplanes appeared overhead in groups of three or four. The enemy pilots dived at the American ships as expected, but instead of releasing their bombs and flying away, they attempted to steer through the antiaircraft fire and crash their airplanes deliberately into the American ships. These attacks were Admiral Onishi's first official aerial kamikaze raids of the war (although his suicide pilots had been trying for several days, unsuccessfully, to locate suitable American targets for their body-slamming tactics). American sailors watched in horror and disbelief as Japanese suicide pilots targeted the escort carriers *Santee* and *Suwannee* of Taffy I, and escort carriers *Kitkun Bay*, *Fanshaw Bay*, *White Plains*, and *St. Lo* of Taffy 3. One of the suicide bombers struck *St. Lo* with full force, and she suffered much the same fate as *Princeton* the day before. The kamikaze's bomb exploded ordnance and fuel on *St. Lo*'s hangar deck and touched off uncontrollable fires. The carrier sank twenty-five miles east of southern Samar at about eleven a.m.

At about twelve thirty p.m., more than seventy American warplanes from Taffy 2 and 3 attacked the Center Force, damaging the battleship *Nagato* and the cruiser *Tone*. These attacks likely convinced Kurita to disengage completely. Kurita had learned earlier in the day of Nishimura's fate in Surigao Strait, and he knew any sortie by Force A into Leyte Gulf would be unsupported. He feared further heavy air attacks from Task Force 38, or from land-based American warplanes on Leyte. He decided he must preserve Force A and *Yamato*, the very embodiment of the Japanese nation, as a fleet in being to fight another day.

At twelve thirty-six p.m., Kurita radioed Admiral Toyoda and Combined Fleet Headquarters that Force A was retiring toward San Bernardino Strait.

Admiral Halsey first learned of the Taffys' desperate struggle with Kurita's warships through Rear Admiral Sprague's pleas for assistance, which had been relayed by Vice Admiral Kinkaid and reached *New Jersey* at about eight twenty a.m. This was only a few minutes before Commander Winters unleashed five air groups, including Air Group 18, on the four Japanese aircraft carriers off Cape Engano. At about eleven a.m., Halsey ordered Task Group 38.2 to about-face and head south. Aboard *Intrepid*, Strike 2 Baker was abruptly canceled, notwithstanding that Air Group 18's warplanes were ready on deck, fueled, armed, manned, for a second attack on Ozawa's carriers. Halsey directed task groups 38.3 and 38.4 to continue bombarding Ozawa's carrier force while *Intrepid* and a flotilla of battleships, cruisers, and destroyers came to Sprague's assistance and tried to intercept Kurita.

By one forty p.m., *Intrepid* had disengaged from the fight with Ozawa and was running south at speeds of between sixteen and twenty-three knots, accompanied by *New Jersey* with Halsey aboard, by the battleships *Iowa*, *Massachusetts*, *Alabama*, *South Dakota*, and *Washington*, and by three cruisers and ten or more destroyers. In VT-18's ready room that afternoon, there was frustration, disappointment, and anger among the pilots. After only one strike against the Japanese carrier force, Task Group 38.2 was being withdrawn and thrown against the same powerful surface force it had confronted the day before in the Sibuyan Sea, while other task groups stayed behind to polish off the Japanese carriers off Cape Engaño. Barden wrote, "Everyone (including the Admiral [Bogan]) is really p.o.'d at this move. We started it, then someone else gets the soft job of finishing off the cripples." That night, Dr. Jack Fish delivered medicinal bottles of whiskey to the ready room. Barden noted with understatement that the whiskey was "most welcome."

Will Fletcher had no whiskey. He had subsisted on coconut water drained laboriously from green coconuts. He had passed the night fitfully in the arms of the narra tree and awakened on the morning of October 25 at first light. On climbing down from the tree, stiff and sore, he had resolved, "Snakes be damned, I will sleep on the ground tonight." He had nibbled some cherry tomatoes and sipped some more coconut water for breakfast.

Will had decided to abandon his refuge and strike out for Banton Island, whose lush hills beckoned him across a channel of deep blue water that was about five or six miles wide. He had chosen Banton over Simara Island, the only alternative destination within reasonable reach, because Banton appeared to be a mile or two closer. Banton also appeared to be no more than six or eight miles in diameter, too insignificant to house a Japanese garrison—he hoped. His silk survival map showed a town, improbably named Jones, situated on Banton's northern shore. Jones, he hoped, would have ample food and water, and perhaps friendly guerrillas among its residents.

He had begun the day working in the bamboo brake, cutting stalks of bamboo with his survival knife to build an escape raft. Cutting the bamboo was strenuous labor; the living stalks were tough-skinned and his knife was short-bladed. The thicket was humid and airless and flies and gnats appeared from no-where to torment him. He perspired heavily, losing fluid he could not replace. He disturbed a large green snake that slithered past his feet. Will leaped backward reflexively when he saw the creature; he was too startled to think about killing the snake for food. By the time he recovered his nerve, the snake had disappeared deeper into the brake. He changed his mind about sleeping on the ground.

Will had drawn the shape of his escape raft in his mind and he built it on the fly, improvising and modifying the design as he went. First, he stacked three large bamboo poles—these were four-inch-diameter poles about six feet long that he had hewn out of the thicket—and wrapped them tightly with bamboo strips. These formed a tritubular pontoon, of sorts. He experimented with his pontoon, dropping it into the lagoon to test its buoyancy. The pontoon floated passably, but he decided he would need at least two additional pontoons to bear his weight. Will bound together three more large poles to create a pontoon for the opposite side of his raft, and three more to form a center support pontoon. He laid his three pontoons side by side and connected them all with four sturdy cross members of bamboo, forming a rectangle of about six feet by four feet. Next, he gathered palm and palmetto fronds and thatched a rude covering for the raft on which he could sit. The idea struck him that he should weave a hat from the palm fronds, so he interrupted his work on the raft to fashion himself a conical-shaped coolie hat to ward off the sun. He lashed his thatched covering to the raft frame with more bamboo strips until the whole contraption resem-bled a large mattress of green leaves. To stabilize his raft, he fashioned an outrig-ger by tying a long, sturdy bamboo pole perpendicular to the axis of his raft, and by tying a cluster of shorter bamboo sections to the outboard end of the outrig-ger pole. The shorter sections would supply buoyancy, and the outrigger pole would provide leverage against capsizing in the swells.

Will worked single-mindedly on his raft; it was a matter of life or death. Whenever he flagged from the heat, or felt himself slipping into self-pity or de-spair, he thought of Westmoreland and Christman and rebuked himself. They were dead; either man would change places with him in an instant. Will ignored the insects, the humidity, the scorching sun, his persistent hunger and thirst. He shed his flight suit to remain cool, although every exposed area of his body—his face, arms, hands, neck, legs, feet—grew scarlet with sunburn. To stretch his supply of coconut water, he sucked on a pebble-size seashell and tricked a little saliva to flow around his tongue.

At the end of the day, Will stripped off his skivvies at the water's edge and waded naked into the surf. He stood in water up to his chest, allowing the rippling waves of the lagoon to cleanse and refresh him. The irony of bathing in the sea did not escape him. Only twenty-four hours earlier he had fought to escape the sea; now he took pleasure from the ocean, like a tourist at Miami Beach. A line of evening thunderstorms began to build far out over Tablas Strait, obscuring the distant peaks of Mindoro. Will watched the cumulus clouds grow higher and higher in the western sky; the clouds piled on top of one another like a mountain of snowy boulders. The sun tinted the highest of the clouds red, and sheets of slate-colored rain fell into the sea from beneath them. The storm clouds over Tablas Strait looked no different to him than the towering summer thunderstorms that swept across the American Bottom from Missouri into southern Illinois, dropping curtains of rain on farmers' corn and potato fields. The memory of home loosed in Will a flood of emotions, as unstoppable as the waves that rippled into the lagoon from the sea. He surrendered to homesickness and despair and self-pity. He thought of his dead mother whom he had abandoned; he had left her to pursue his dream of becoming a flier when he didn't really have to go, only to end up here in this desolate place. He thought of his sisters who had depended on him, and of his aunts and uncles and cousins who had loved him. Would he ever see them again; would they ever know what became of him? No person in the living world knew where he was, no one but himself. No one would be looking for him; his skipper and his VT-18 squadron mates would reasonably assume him dead, lying at the bottom of the Sibuyan Sea with Westmoreland and Christman. He did not exist in the familiar world he knew yesterday, and his isolation weighed on him. He was utterly alone; he would have to make his way back into the world alone.

Lightning flashed from the bottom of the storm clouds, piercing Will's despondency. The clouds had drifted slowly toward him, raising his hopes that the clouds would dump rainwater on his islet and deliver him freshwater to drink, his first in two days. He had prepared for this possibility. When harvesting his raft poles, he had observed that each green bamboo stalk contained a fibrous membrane below the joint; if he sawed below the joint, he could preserve the membrane and fashion a cup of sorts. He had made several of these rudimentary bamboo cups and, when the lightning flashed closer, he eagerly retrieved his cups from beneath his narra tree and set them out in the sand, mouths open to the sky.

Will thought of Naomi as he waited for the rains to come. She had loved stargazing in a clear night sky and was fond of the old saying, "If the stars revealed themselves only once a year, no man would doubt the existence of God." Will knelt in the sand and tried to pray. He thanked God for his salvation, but he couldn't bring himself to pray for anything more. The faces of his two dead crewmen crowded out his thoughts. To pray for himself—to pray for freshwater, for food, for rescue and safe passage home—seemed ungrateful when he still had life and they did not.

The rain clouds didn't move any closer to Will's island; his bamboo cups remained empty of rainwater and sat forlornly in the sand. He bedded down again in his narra tree as lightning flashed again far to the west, silhouetting the mountain peaks of Mindoro. Will cursed at the injustice of freshwater falling uselessly as rain into the strait and tried to sleep.

Halsey and his cavalry arrived too late to be of assistance to Sprague's Taffys or to catch Kurita. Task Group 38.2 and the additional battleships, cruisers, and destroyers that accompanied it did not reach San Bernardino Strait until about one a.m. on October 26, several hours after Kurita's Force A had withdrawn through the strait into the Sibuyan Sea. But Halsey was determined to engage and destroy the Japanese task force as it retreated. At first light on October 26, *Intrepid* launched a strike group to find and attack Kurita.

Commander Ellis led the strike group—comprised of twelve Hellcats, sixteen Helldivers, and seven Avengers—southwest toward Panay, where the Center Force had been sighted by search aircraft and Filipino coast watchers. The fighters carried five-hundred-pound bombs; the dive-bombers were armed with their usual mix of thousand-pounders, and the Avengers were armed with torpedoes. After an outbound flight of more than two hours, El Gropo's attackers located Kurita's warships at the southern entrance to Tablas Strait, roughly 210 nautical miles from *Intrepid*. Kurita had essentially retraced the path he had taken through the Sibuyan Sea two days earlier, but he had far fewer warships in his formation than when he had begun his journey. Since leaving Borneo, Force

A had lost *Atago*, *Takao*, and *Maya* on the twenty-third, *Musashi* and *Myoko* on the twenty-fourth, and the cruisers *Chikuma*, *Chokai*, *Suzuya*, and *Noshiro* on the twenty-fifth. Many of Kurita's surviving warships were damaged and low on ammunition.

VB-18's dive-bombers rolled in first from thirteen thousand feet and concentrated their attacks on a *Nagato*-class battleship. Van Antwerp tried to be deliberate in his target selection; VT-18 had been given the final opportunity to sink or disable the heavy warships of the Center Force before they retreated beyond the range of American carrier planes, and Van Antwerp wanted to make his torpedoes count. He split his seven-plane division into three sections, dispatching three Avengers against a *Nagato*-class battleship, three against a *Kongo*-class battleship, and one against a cruiser. Cloud cover over the area hampered target coordination. Dive-bombers and torpedo planes became separated in the cloud layers, and the results were disappointing. At the end of the day, Van Antwerp could claim only two definite hits on one battleship, one probable hit on a second, and one possible hit on a cruiser. Afterward, the torpeckers all described the volume of antiaircraft fire coming from the enemy ships as less intense than on October 24, with less "heavy stuff," and reported that the Japanese gunners had delayed putting up a heavy barrage until the planes turned in on the attack, perhaps to conserve ammunition.

Commander Ellis had pressed home Air Group 18's final attacks on the Center Force to the limits of his warplanes' endurance. Despite resorting to extreme fuel conservation measures on the return flight to *Intrepid*—the dive-bombers flew home at only a thousand feet and 130 knots—four Helldivers were forced to water-land before reaching the carrier. The pilot of one Helldiver became trapped beneath the wing of his airplane after ditching. The rear-seat man, Aviation Radioman Third Class Louis D. Vaughn, rescued his pilot but ingested much seawater himself in the process. The pilot managed to inflate his own Mae West and was holding his radioman's head above water when one of the battleships of *Intrepid*'s screen passed close aboard; the ship's wake ripped Vaughn from his pilot's grasp and he was swept away, never to be recovered. Six of Van Antwerp's Avengers landed safely, notwithstanding having been airborne for five and a half hours on average, but several landed short of *Intrepid* on other carriers.

Van Antwerp led another strike into the Sibuyan Sea at about three p.m., looking for a Japanese battleship and two cruisers that were reported still afoot. He insisted either Bill Bates or Kenny Barden fly on his wing, and Barden lost the coin toss. They returned at sunset without finding their targets and landed with their torpedoes securely in their Avengers' bellies. Barden was not disappointed. He had flown three combat missions against the Japanese fleet on three consecutive days, and he was relieved not to have to fly through any more heavy antiaircraft fire. He wrote that he could "hardly see how any man can be lucky enough to fly through that AA three consecutive times." Duke Delaney's Avenger lost power on returning to the ship, and he was forced to water-land; he and his crew were picked up quickly by the destroyer *Cushing* and returned to *Intrepid*.

That night in *Intrepid*'s ready rooms, the men of Air Group 18 reflected on the events of October 24, 25, and 26, balancing their accomplishments against their disappointments. On the positive side of the ledger, Air Group 18 had been the first American carrier air group to attack the mighty *Yamatos* in the Sibuyan Sea on the twenty-fourth, and among the last carrier air groups to attack the Center Force before it withdrew temporarily to the west. Air Group 18 had been among the first to attack the once-invincible Mobile Fleet off Cape Engano on the twenty-fifth, and the last to attack the wounded Center Force as it withdrew from the Sibuyan Sea on the twenty-sixth. Air Group 18 had contributed to the sinking of *Musashi*, *Myoko*, and other cruisers, and two of Ozawa's carriers. On the negative side, Air Group 18 had been denied the opportunity of finishing off the Japanese carriers, and the airmen complained bitterly about it. The air groups that had remained with Mitscher off Cape Engano (instead of racing south with their carriers to aid the Taffys) had sunk all four of Ozawa's carriers, *Zuikaku*, *Chitose*, *Chiyoda*, and *Zuiho*, two cruisers, and two destroyers. Air Group 18 had been deprived of that prize. And the airmen griped that "[o]ur big beautiful battleships—as yet they haven't fired a damned shot." Aircrew were exhausted, and Barden doubted the squadron could take many more missions without some extended rest.

The pilots listened to Tokyo Rose on the evening of October 26. They were surprised to hear her admit the loss of one Japanese carrier, three battleships, and one cruiser, and amused when she reported that the Japanese had sunk eight American carriers and several battleships and cruisers off Samar. But many of

Intrepid's sailors and airmen also perceived that the Battle off Samar had been a very close-run thing for Admiral Kinkaid and his Taffys. The Japanese had in fact sunk three carriers, Sherman's light carrier *Princeton* and Kinkaid's escort carriers *St. Lo* and *Gambier Bay*; two Taffy 3 destroyers, *Hoel* and *Johnston*; and one destroyer escort, *Samuel B. Roberts*. If Kurita's Center Force had been only slightly more aggressive and persistent, if *Musashi* not been sunk, if the Taffy destroyers and carrier pilots had been less self-sacrificial, Tokyo Rose's exaggerated claims of American losses might have been grimly understated.

Halsey sent his sailors and airmen a dispatch that cheered them: "For brilliance, courage, and tireless fighting heart, the all-hands performance of the THIRD FLEET since early October will never be surpassed. It has been an honor to be your commander. Well-done."

At home in America, the news of the battles around Leyte Gulf electrified the nation. The *New York Times* late city edition on Thursday, October 26, proclaimed in one-inch headlines, "U.S. Defeats Japanese Navy; All Foes Ships Sunk in One Fleet Hit; Many Sunk; Battle Continues." The secondary headline elaborated, "Battleship Is Sunk. Seventh Fleet Smashes Two Japanese Forces Converging on Leyte. Remnants in Flight. They Are Hotly Pursued—Third Enemy Force Is Hit off Formosa." The lead article by Lewis Wood reported: "President Roosevelt exultantly announced late today the receipt of a report from Admiral William F. Halsey saying that the Japanese Navy in the Philippine area has been 'defeated, seriously damaged, and routed' by our forces. Two hours earlier Admiral Ernest J. King, Commander in Chief of the United States Fleet and Chief of Naval Operations, had disclosed that virtually all of the long elusive Japanese Fleet had been engaged at last in the furious sea battle of the Philippines. These two startling revelations, exciting Washington as nothing has done since the European invasions, were taken here to mean that the vaunted Japanese naval power had been seriously crippled and the road to Tokyo made much easier. At last, it was presumed, the principal part of the Japanese naval strength had been nettled out of hiding and then decisively beaten."

A parallel article on the front page observed:

"Pending official word from Pearl Harbor, it appeared the greatest surface and air action in the history of naval warfare was being fought and won by the Pacific Fleet, the greatest naval force that ever went down to the sea."

———

Will rose with the sun on the morning of October 26 hungrier and thirstier than the day before. He resolved to set off for Banton Island at sunset; he would travel at night to minimize the risk of being detected by Japanese air and sea patrols. He hoped to complete the passage across the channel in six or eight hours.

He devoted the day to final preparations, testing the buoyancy of his raft in the lagoon—it floated passably and supported his weight—and stockpiling green coconuts, palmetto root, and cherry tomatoes for his passage. He stuffed his provisions into a loosely woven basket he had fashioned from palmetto fronds. He also cut two bamboo poles to serve as paddles and a third pole to serve as a mast. He lashed a crosspiece to his mast pole, which made his mast look like a crucifix; he intended to slip his flight suit over the yardarm and catch the westerly sea breeze. He scouted the eastern side of the island for a suitable place to launch his raft. In his quest for freshwater he had discovered that the reef he had swum across two days before encircled his island almost entirely; remembering his shredded left shoe, he feared the coral rocks might rip his raft apart. He climbed a narra tree and searched for a clear path through the reef into the channel. He sighted a stretch of blue unruffled water that lay between shoulders of turquoise and foam about fifty yards offshore and decided that this stretch of water would be his gateway into the channel.

Just before sunset on October 26, Will dragged his raft to the eastern shore of his islet. He stripped to his T-shirt and boxer shorts and donned his coolie hat; he secured the hat beneath his chin with laces salvaged from his shoes. He strapped his pistol belt tightly around his waist for safekeeping and for ready access to his pistol and his survival knife. He placed his food basket, his flight suit, and his Mae West in the center of his raft and eased her into the waters of the eastern lagoon.

The mountains of Banton Island had turned purple in the fading light. The sea was calm, and Will thanked providence for good weather. He pushed his raft through the shallows until he could no longer touch bottom. Then he flopped stomach-first on the rear half of his raft and began kicking toward the opening in the reef, like a surfer headed out to sea on his surfboard. The raft proved about as steerable as a barn door, and kicking was exhausting work. After a time, he gave up kicking and crawled atop the raft. Grabbing one of his bamboo paddles, he knelt on his Mae West and began paddling for the break in the reef, like an Indian paddling a canoe. The raft creaked like a wicker chair, and seawater swirled around his knees, but his little bamboo mattress bobbed steadily toward the opening in the reef.

Clearing the reef took more time than Will had anticipated; the sun had been sunk an hour by the time he reached open water. A light breeze blew from the southwest, and Will decided to try to take advantage of the wind. He unzipped the front of his flight suit and inserted the mast's yardarm through the sleeves. He tied the left pant leg of his flight suit to the left side of his raft and held the other leg in his right hand; he wedged the base of the mast into the frame of the raft and hoisted the mast upright between his knees. To Will's delight, his flight suit billowed in the breeze like a sheet hung out to dry on a clothesline, and the raft began to mush through the water at a perceptibly faster clip. Will was elated. He wrestled his little sail to keep it filled with air, but fill it did.

The fickle zephyr soon died and Will found himself becalmed in the middle of the channel. He stowed his sail and resorted once again to paddling from his knees. The dark pyramidal mass of Banton Island loomed on the horizon. He paddled toward the island with as much strength and persistence as he could muster, but he couldn't gauge in the darkness whether he was closing the distance to the island or merely holding his ground. Soon he lost his bearings entirely; a thick haze had built up in the channel like vapor rising from a jungle floor, reducing the visibility around Will's raft to only a few hundred yards and obscuring Banton Island from Will's view. The air turned silver and the water black as oil in the night. Will had no idea which way to steer. He set his paddle aside and decided to sleep. He donned his Mae West and inflated the bladders of the life vest through its mouth tubes; he lay on his back, with the collar of his Mae West serving as a pillow and his bare feet hanging off the end of the raft. He nibbled a few cherry tomatoes and closed his eyes, listening to the constant slap of water around his hips and shoulders. He drifted off to sleep wondering where he was headed in the night, borne like a leaf on a stream, and what the dawn would reveal.

CHAPTER FOURTEEN

OFF BANTON AND LUZON

★ ★ ★ ★ ★

Intrepid remained in a high state of readiness on October 27 as she zigzagged off the eastern coast of Samar. She took on fuel oil and aviation gasoline from the fleet oiler *Patuxent*, and VT-18 received seven replacement Avengers from VT-11, which had been operating from *Hornet*. That lucky carrier was headed to Ulithi with Task Group 38.1 for rest and replenishment. VT-11 no longer needed its torpedo bombers, while VT-18 badly needed replacements. The boys of VT-18 welcomed the slightly worn airplanes but looked forward eagerly to *Hornet*'s return to the line. When *Hornet* came back from Ulithi, *Intrepid* would be withdrawn from the line, or so the boys believed. Barden managed to log a few hours of rest and diversion. He slept until nine a.m. for the first time in weeks and received a batch of mail from Margie, delivered via the Fleet Post Office San Francisco and by destroyer to *Intrepid*.

With the remnants of the Japanese fleet on the run, Task Group 38.2 and *Intrepid* resumed the mission of supporting of General MacArthur's Leyte operations by striking at Japanese airfields and shipping in the northern Philippines. On October 28, Lieutenant Commander Van Antwerp advised his torpeckers of Air Group 18's next anticipated assignment. The Japanese had heavily reinforced Clark Field with fighters, Van Antwerp reported, and Air Group 18 would execute a series of bombing raids and fighter sweeps over northern Luzon. Barden dully absorbed the briefing and returned to his stateroom to write a long letter home to Margie. As he wrote the letter he despaired of her receiving it anytime soon. "God only knows when it will be mailed, 'cause it seems we're never going back to Ulithi—Hit Clark Field tomorrow—3 deck loads."

As the sun rose over the Sibuyan Sea on October 27, Will Fletcher sat on his raft, becalmed under cloudless skies. The uninhabited, waterless islet from which he had set out the evening before had vanished beyond the western horizon; Banton Island, his destination, lay several miles to the southeast. Banton's hills, silhouetted by the rising sun, displayed a different aspect than they had the day before. Will sensed that he had drifted north in the night, far north of where he had begun his voyage. A combination of currents and tides had carried him parallel to Banton's western shore, but not closer.

Will sat cross-legged, hunched over at the shoulders, with his legs and buttocks awash in an ever-present puddle of seawater. Although he had donned his flight suit during the night to stay warm, he shivered in the morning air. The temperature of the Sibuyan Sea was slightly above eighty degrees, much lower than his body temperature, and the inestimable volume of water had slowly sapped his body heat. He welcomed the intensifying sun, never mind that he had cursed the heat the day before as he labored to complete his raft. He discovered in the pale morning light that the workings of his bamboo mast had loosened the rattan strips that bound together the frame of his raft, and that his bamboo mattress rode lower in the water than it had the day before. This was an alarming development; he feared his raft might disintegrate under the strain if he hoisted his makeshift sail. He decided not to attempt the sail again even if a sea breeze arose. His only option now was to paddle.

To nourish himself for a day of hard paddling ahead, Will ate a breakfast of cherry tomatoes and palmetto root. Boring a hole in a green coconut, he dribbled the water into his mouth to chase down his food. He was about to slip from his raft into the sea to relieve himself when his eye detected movement beneath his raft. He peered cautiously over the side into the water and glimpsed a dark shape, obviously a large fish of some kind, gliding beneath him. The fish suddenly disappeared and, as Will searched anxiously around his raft to see where the fish had gone, a second fish larger than the first flashed beneath him. The second fish appeared to have a large dorsal fin on its back, and Will's blood froze. A shark. He sat motionless on his raft, not daring to breathe.

The two creatures broke the surface of the sea about thirty yards beyond Will's raft and circled back toward him. Both fish had dorsal fins, the tips of which betrayed their track through the water. Two sharks. Will reached for his revolver and took aim; if they came too close, he intended to shoot them, the echoing report of a gun be damned. The two fish glided toward him side by side and, when they had closed to within a dozen yards of Will's raft, they arched their backs gracefully like a pair of synchronized swimmers and dived out of sight. Will lowered his pistol. They were porpoises, not sharks. They were harmless, gray, gregarious, torpedo-shaped, bottlenosed little whales of some Pacific breed; they were not sharks and they were not fish.

Will watched the mammals circle back toward his raft and pass close by him. One of them dared to nudge the starboard side of his raft with his flank as he passed, like a trained porpoise in an aquarium show. The raft swayed and rocked, but the outrigger pole prevented the craft from swamping or capsizing. Will's visitors swam away as quickly as they had appeared. They were the first living creatures of consequence he had encountered in three days, other than the snake in the bamboo brake. They were a momentary diversion from his predicament. He felt a little less alone in the world. He picked up his paddle and began paddling his raft toward Banton Island.

To conserve his strength Will disciplined his paddling. He stroked ten minutes at a time per his Bulova and then rested for two, repeating this pattern throughout the morning. By noon, he had drawn closer to his destination. Banton's green hills filled more of the eastern horizon, and the island's topographical features had become more distinct. Will thrilled at his first sight of Banton's beach, a thin white streak running along the island's shore. He had paddled himself within a mile of the beach, but currents or tides unseen prevented him from closing the final gap. He had to paddle almost constantly to hold his position in the channel. A flight of six or eight airplanes passed high overhead at noon. Will was certain they were Japanese, and he endured an anxious afternoon worrying whether the airplanes would return for a closer look, or whether the flight leader would dispatch a boat to investigate him more closely.

Will thought of little as he paddled except reaching shore and finding food and water. He daydreamed about food and water. He had consumed no meat since the fried bologna he had eaten for breakfast aboard *Intrepid* on October 24, nearly four days earlier. He remembered his grandmother's Christmas pot roast, Yorkshire pudding and gravy, and Naomi's Sunday meat loaf. He vowed he would never complain again about food, even the tough, gamy Australian lamb the mess stewards had served him aboard *Intrepid*.

By sundown on October 27, after nearly twenty hours aboard his raft, Will had exhausted himself and his rations. His palms were blistered from nearly constant paddling, and his knees were raw. Despite sipping coconut water, Will's lips and tongue had begun to swell from dehydration, and he had learned from painful and nauseating experience that too much palmetto root acted as a powerful laxative. Despite his coolie hat, his face had turned scarlet from sunlight reflecting off the water.

Will had miscalculated the difficulty of crossing the channel. His bamboo raft had proven unwieldy; he could not propel it at speeds sufficient to break the grip of the currents and tides. The physical effort was draining, and he had not carried sufficient food to sustain himself. In abandoning his little island refuge, he had jumped from the frying pan to the fire, and his situation had become desperate. He decided he must abandon his raft in the morning. At first light, he would inflate his Mae West to its fullest, slip from his raft, and swim for shore, gambling everything on the chance that he had the strength to swim the distance. As he lay back on his raft to sleep, he prayed the morning sky would be overcast and that he would be spared the merciless sun.

He awoke on October 28 aching and chilled to the bone. He was weaker than the day before, with nothing left on his raft to eat or drink. He had floated farther from the island during the night. Daylight revealed that he now faced a swim of several miles. The sky was overcast and gray; God had answered his prayer in this respect, at least. A blanket of rain clouds, the misty bottoms of which touched the surface of the sea in places, cloaked Banton's hills. In hopes of catching some rainwater, Will fished a bamboo cup from his basket of provisions, now empty, and waited for the squall to drift his way. But the rain clouds did not move. Gray sheets of rain drenched the shoreline, obscuring it entirely, but nary a drop splashed out in the channel; a mischievous God had caused the rain to fall beyond Will's grasp.

Will's hearing had been dulled by ambient noises of the sea, by the constant sound of water slapping around his raft and the murmur of the sea breeze. But at about seven a.m., according to Will's Bulova, he heard the unmistakable clatter of a two-cycle motor. The sound appeared to be coming from Banton. He strained his eyes in the direction of the noise and saw a small boat emerging from behind a curtain of rain. It was a native longboat, narrow and weathered, with a high prow and outrigger pontoons that extended over each side. Will had seen these native boats from the air; they were called bangkas. Filipinos commonly used them for fishing and commuting among the islands. This one had a mast pole leaning across one gunwale and nets piled up on its prow.

There were two men sitting in the bangka, and they saw Will at the same instant he saw them. The men in the boat appeared to be as startled as Will at this chance encounter in the channel. The bangka's motor sputtered and died and the boat coasted to a stop. The men eyed Will across the distance, and Will eyed them back.

The boatmen wore broad-brimmed straw hats and sleeveless ponchos; their naked arms were brown and well muscled. Will debated what he should do. *Should I begin a small naval war right here and shoot them*, he wondered, *or hail them as friends?*

The men in the bangka made no move, no sound. Will reasoned that they would have steered directly for him if they had been Japanese, or Filipino collaborators intent on capturing him. The man sitting in the bow of the bangka reached down and pulled a bolo knife—a long-bladed weapon similar to a machete—from the bottom of the boat and laid the knife conspicuously across his knees. He displayed his weapon not as a threat but as a cautionary sign; he clearly wanted Will to know he and his companion were armed and that they were not men to be trifled with.

Will waved at the men and beckoned them toward him. He had no choice but to accept the risk that they were unfriendly. He desperately needed food and water and a boat ride to shore. He had his revolver; if they tried to harm him he could shoot them and seize their boat or force them to take him ashore.

The bangka's motor sputtered back to life and the two men warily approached Will's raft. Will was no expert on Asian races, but the men appeared to be native Filipinos; their faces had the rough-hewn look of farmers or fishermen, not of soldiers or city dwellers. He decided to reveal himself. He removed his coolie hat and bellowed at them with as much voice as he could muster. "American," he shouted. "American."

The bangka sped up, and within minutes the boat drifted to a stop alongside Will's raft. The two men in the bangka stared curiously at Will with bemused looks on their faces, as if Will were a crazy man and his raft the oddest seagoing contraption they had ever encountered. They couldn't be blamed for this. Will was hollow-eyed, sun-blistered, unshaven and shoeless, half-clothed in a khaki coverall; his raft was a primitive bundle of sticks not very tightly lashed together. Filipinos were experts at constructing bamboo rafts; they used them for poling their way across shallow rivers or through marshes but never for sailing on open water.

"I am an American pilot," Will rasped, in the hope that one of the Filipinos understood English. "Can you help me, please?"

The two men nodded approvingly and grinned. "Yes, yes," said the man in the bow, "we help you please."

The Filipino in the bow tossed Will a manila rope and motioned for him to wrap the line around his chest and tie it under his arms. Will did as he was told, and the two Filipinos pulled him through the water, dragging him across the short distance that separated his raft from the bangka and hauling him into the boat like a tuna. Will was weak; he collapsed in the bottom of the bangka and nearly passed out. The Filipinos, who introduced themselves in broken English as fishermen from Banton, gave Will fresh water from a tin cup, which he gulped down ravenously.

The Filipino in the stern revved up his two-cycle motor and swung the prow of his bangka in the direction of Banton. Trailing blue smoke, the little boat puttered noisily toward the island, carrying Will and the two fisherman through the same curtain of rain from which the Filipinos had first emerged. The ride to shore took nearly half an hour, according to Will's Bulova, and Will realized he would never have been able to swim the distance in his weakened condition. They motored toward a tiny fishing village on the beach. Will counted about fifteen native huts clustered along a narrow strip of sand. The huts were elevated on wooden stilts and shaded by thickets of palm and narra trees. The walls of the huts were made of bamboo mats, their roofs constructed of thatched palm fronds and banana leaves. Behind the village lay a grassy marsh; beyond the marsh, a ridge of emerald and olive-colored hills rose steeply into the clouds and mist.

The return of the bangka brought villagers down to the water's edge. By the time the fishermen grounded their bangka on the beach, a crowd of men, women, and small children, twenty or thirty in all, had gathered to see what strange cargo the fishermen had brought back from the channel so prematurely. To Will's astonishment, the villagers grew angry when they saw him sitting in the bangka; they clenched their fists at him and shouted at him. Men brandished steel bolo knives. Will did not understand their words, but he clearly sensed their fury. He was confused and afraid; his pistol would be useless against all these angry people. He feared he had fallen in with collaborators or cannibals.

The men in the boat grinned at Will. "They think you Jap," said the man in the bow. "We fix."

The man in the bow shouted back at the villagers in Tagalog. The only word Will comprehended was "American," but the mood of the villagers changed instantly. A cheer went up, and applause. The women jabbered excitedly among themselves, and men waded into the water to help bring Will ashore. The two men in the bangka eased Will over the side of the boat into the arms of three villagers. Will was too light-headed to walk unaided, and the villagers carried him ashore. When he reached dry land at last, he lost consciousness and collapsed on the sand.

Intrepid's brief respite from combat ended on October 29. At seven a.m., Commander Ellis led Strike 2 Able back to Clark Field with the objective of obliterating the airfield and destroying as many Japanese aircraft as possible. Strike 2 Able was a relatively heavy strike, composed of twelve Hellcats armed with five-hundred-pound bombs, twelve Helldivers armed with thousand-pound general-purpose bombs, and eight Avengers armed with fragmentation bombs and incendiaries. Ellis's warplanes arrived over the target at about eight forty-five and unloaded their ordnance on the airfield. A group of Oscars unexpectedly jumped VB-18's Helldivers after they pulled off their dive-bombing runs, and the Helldiver rear-seat man shot down four of the enemy fighters, an extraordinary tally.

Commander Ellis ascribed the Helldivers' success in fending off the enemy fighters to luck. Given the large numbers of Japanese fighters in the area, VB-18's Helldivers easily could have been overwhelmed. Ellis went on record in his aircraft-action report to state, "VB-type aircraft are not suitable for attacks against areas where the destruction of airpower is the prime consideration.

Planes in revetments are almost impossible to hit by bombs; they can be destroyed by strafing. For this reason," Ellis continued, "it would seem that a large enough flight of fighters should be assigned to such missions that one group could give protection against airborne opposition while another destroyed grounded planes by strafing."

VF-18's fighter boys were too busy tangling with Japanese fighters over Clark Field to bomb effectively. Of the eight Hellcat pilots who attempted to bomb the airfield, only one succeeded in making an aimed drop. To the Americans' surprise, the Japanese pilots over Clark Field were more aggressive and better tacticians than any VF-18 had encountered previously. Although VF-18's Hellcat pilots claimed eight enemy fighters shot down on Strike 2 Able, they had spent much of the morning protecting one another's tails. The Devils' skipper, Lieutenant Commander E. J. Murphy, also vented his frustrations in his aircraft action report: "This squadron strongly disapproves of the practice of sending in [bomb-laden] VF as an escort when heavy air opposition is anticipated. While it is true that bombs may be jettisoned, the dangers of being caught out of position, as in this instance, are too great to justify the risk."

El Gropo had grown frustrated, too, over the predictability of American tactics. He urged Bogan's staff and Mitscher's "to vary the pattern of our attack. At present we are launching a dawn VF sweep followed by three or four strikes, all of which have the same composition and takeoff times. The enemy knows what to expect and when." Ellis also complained that the rendezvous points had become a trap: "It is urgently recommended that when repeated strikes are launched against the same area, a different rendezvous point be selected for each strike. When the logical rendezvous point (i.e., the most prominent landmark) is used time and again, the enemy soon disposes his airborne fighters in the best attack positions."

Ellis's and Murphy's recommendations were too late to be of assistance to Strike 2 Baker, which launched from *Intrepid* at eleven thirty a.m. to hit Clark Field for a second time that day. Van Antwerp led VT-18's first division, which included Avengers flown by Bill Bates, Kenny Barden, Joe Rubin, and Nick Roccaforte, and ran smack into the same hornets' nest of Zekes, Judys, and Oscars as Strike 2 Able. The Japanese fighters had orbited at high altitude above the previously used rendezvous point and waited for the Americans to make their attacks. Then they swarmed down on Strike 2 Baker's dive-bombers and torpedo planes while the Americans were in the midst of their runs. In the ensuing melee, VF-18's covering fighters shot down eleven enemy fighters and later claimed five more probable kills and significant damage to five others. But enough of the enemy fighters got through to badly maul the strike group. Three Helldivers, nine Hellcats, and three Avengers were riddled by bullets. Joe Rubin was wounded in the left shoulder by shrapnel from an enemy fighter and forced to water-land near *Intrepid* on the return flight. More seriously, Nick Roccaforte, the tall-talking Texan, was forced to ground over Luzon by a Japanese fighter. Van Antwerp listed Roccaforte and his crewmen, Aviation Ordnanceman Second Class Rodger W. Jones of Syracuse, Kansas, and Aviation Radioman Second Class Carl M. McLerran of Boulder, Colorado, as missing in action and presumed dead (and in fact they were).

October 29 was a rough day for *Intrepid* herself. Minutes after the last Avenger took off on Strike 2 Baker, *Intrepid* absorbed her first kamikaze hit of the war. A Japanese bomber crash-dived the ship and struck a glancing blow on *Intrepid*'s port side aft of the number two elevator near gun tub number ten, which contained a twenty-millimeter antiaircraft gun manned by a team of stewards (who, in the U.S. Navy of 1944, were all African-Americans). The gunners kept up unflinching fire, but the suicide plane kept coming; six of the men were killed outright when the airplane hit the gun tub, and several others were seriously burned. Three of these later died of wounds. Fortunately for the aircrews airborne at the time, the crash caused little damage to the carrier's flight deck, and *Intrepid* maintained her station in formation.

Air Group 18 was not finished with Clark Field for the day. *Intrepid* launched a third bombing mission, Strike 2 Charlie, at two-oh-eight p.m., comprised of fifteen Hellcats, six Helldivers, and six Avengers. Bogan's staff dispensed with any bombs for VF-18's Hellcats, the better to grapple with Japanese fighters, but Ellis's intelligence assistant, Lieutenant George Race, objected to the inclusion of any torpedo planes or dive-bombers on the strike at all. Race noted caustically that "the flag [Bogan] had sufficient evidence that fighter opposition was fierce and that Clark Field was an unhealthy place for slow-moving torpedo and bomber groups."

Bud Williams led the Avenger division on Strike 2 Charlie. Although the distance to Clark Field was not excessive, weather forecasters predicted low clouds and poor visibility over the target. With his usual attention to detail, Bud reminded his pilots during their prestrike briefing of VT-18's doctrine of "close unity" in the event a water landing became necessary, meaning that all aircraft should land together.

Strike 2 Charlie arrived over Clark Field at four p.m. to find the airfield obscured by clouds at two thousand feet. The cloud cover complicated the bombing runs; the torpeckers and dive-bomber pilots were forced to execute low-level attacks through breaks in the undercast. The attacking pilots reported seeing about two hundred enemy planes, including many twin-engine bombers, parked on the airfield, but none of the pilots was sure whether his bombs found their mark. VF-18's fighter boys were certain of their score; they reported downing eleven enemy fighters in air-to-air duels, and Lieutenant Cecil Harris claimed four of them.

The day's excitement was not over for Strike 2 Charlie. About fifteen minutes before the strike group was due to recover, *Intrepid* steamed into a squall line. Although the carrier was shrouded in heavy rain, most of the returning aircraft were low on fuel, and the pilots had no choice but to attempt an instrument landing. The Hellcats flew in first on the gauges, and all but one made it back aboard ship. Lieutenant William R. Thompson, whose instruments had failed him, wasn't as lucky as his squadron mates. He elected to water-land rather than fly blindly toward the carrier; he did not survive the landing. The Helldiver pilots were next to attempt a recovery. Two were forced by heavy rain and low visibility to break off their approach and water-land; the remaining dive-bombers careened back aboard the carrier with minimum fuel, their crews lucky to be home.

Bud Williams, orbiting with his six-plane Avenger division in clear air outside the squall, had monitored the chaos of recovery aboard *Intrepid* and requested via radio that *Intrepid* alter course to recover his division in the clear. The time was about seven p.m.; night was about to fall with tropical abruptness, and Williams's Avengers were low on fuel. Inexplicably, *Intrepid* tersely declined Williams's request, and he was faced with difficult choices. Should he attempt a low-fuel instrument approach to the ship; should he continue orbiting, on the chance Captain Bolger would sail *Intrepid* clear of the squall; should he water-land? Williams knew his wingmen were likely to have less fuel remaining than he, and that a water-landing with engine power in the fading light would be far more survivable than a low-fuel instrument approach to the ship or a dead-stick approach in the dark. He had presciently briefed the "close unity" doctrine, but he didn't really think they would have to use it.

Williams signaled his pilots to close up and gave them a thumbs-down, his signal for a water-landing. They would land in sequence and as close together as possible.

Williams's torpedo bomber splashed down first. Ensign Ben St. John, who was flying the Tail-end Charlie position in Williams's formation, ditched last. St. John had alerted his crew to prepare for ditching and begun a slow gentle descent toward the water. He had lowered his Avenger's flaps to maintain minimum flying speed and held a normal rate of descent for landing. Hanging on its propeller, St. John's Avenger settled into the water and nosed forward in a tsunami of spray. Ben catapulted into his harness when his airplane hit the water but stayed in his cockpit seat; his airplane held together. After Al Long lost his radioman to botched evacuation procedures, Ben had devised his own ditching and evacuation procedures. He had gone over them with his crew before every flight, and he used them now. He scrambled out of his cockpit, pushed the airplane's three-man raft through the fuselage to his turret gunner on the port wing, and tossed his radioman his own one-man raft as the radioman emerged from the tunnel. The turret gunner inflated the larger raft and Ben and his radioman clambered aboard; the airplane sank in less than one minute. Afterward, Ben's crew told him his water landing was no worse than his carrier landings; Ben wasn't sure whether his crew intended to compliment his water landing or criticize his carrier landings.

All of Williams's Avenger crews, eighteen men in all, had escaped their sinking airplanes and climbed safely into their three-man rafts. Williams had reported his ditching coordinates to *Intrepid*, and his little "Goodyear navy" settled down for a night at sea, bobbing and rolling on the Pacific swells, with several of the rafts lashed together. The men got seasick and vomited repeatedly over the side of their rafts. They heard airplane engines above them and debated whether to signal; Williams ordered them not to, because the noise sounded like a multiengine airplane, and Williams doubted it was friendly. The night sky cleared and the men waited for rescue, miserable from the ceaseless motion of the sea.

About midnight, Williams's ocean rafters heard the distinctive rumble of a Hellcat motor overhead. With Williams's permission, Ben St. John fired off some tracer rounds from his pistol to attract the pilot's attention. As the airplane circled, the men in the rafts shone their flashlights in the night sky to give the pilot a good fix on their position. Two hours later, the destroyer *Halsey Powell* crept toward Williams's rafters in the darkness, and the excited torpeckers waved their flashlights in a frenzy to guide her closer. The *Halsey Powell*'s crew dropped cargo nets over the destroyer's side, and the seasick, tired, wet, grateful aviators hauled themselves aboard. The next day, *Halsey Powell* delivered the rescued airmen to *Intrepid* via high line and boatswain's chair. In return, *Intrepid* highlined back the customary ransom of ice cream.

Losing the services of six Avengers and eighteen men on a single mission—none to enemy action—provoked some discussion. Bud Williams had water-landed his entire division rather than expose any of them to the extreme hazard of finding the ship in foul weather while running low on fuel. Ellis defended Williams's decision, noting in his aircraft action report that "eighteen flight personnel were returned to the carrier early on the 30th, all ready to fly again." Williams had clearly made the right decision under the circumstances; airplanes could be replaced easily, trained crews not so easily. What Williams and his men did not know until they returned to the ship was that Captain Bolger's refusal to steer *Intrepid* clear of the squall line was a "flag" decision, presumably Admiral Bogan's. A large flight of enemy aircraft had been detected on radar, and Bogan had elected to shelter his entire task group in the rainstorm, despite the probability of losing some of his returning warplanes.

George Race invited Barden, Bates, and Squatty Vaughn to his stateroom the night after the Clark Field bombing raids to close out a day of sad loss and extraordinary danger. They drank from Race's cache of whiskey and ate a big steak dinner in the wardroom. Later, Doc Fish distributed his tonic among the torpeckers assembled in VT-18's ready room. The whiskey healed some wounds and opened others. Lloyd Karch, who had asked to be removed from Al Long's division, requested to fly again; Al Long decided to turn in his wings.

Will awoke and dully absorbed his surroundings. He lay in one of the native huts he had seen from the bangka on his approach to the village. The roof was constructed of thatched palm fronds; the walls were made of bamboo. His bed was Western-style, a plain, cast-iron, steel-spring type one might find in a hospital or a cheap hotel. A carved crucifix bearing the figure of the dying Christ hung on the wall adjacent to Will's bed. The carving depicted the moment when

Jesus cried out to God for forsaking him; the artist had inserted white mother-of-pearl into Christ's upturned eyes.

Will sensed he was lying naked beneath a cotton blanket. An elderly Filipino woman sat in a wooden chair at the foot of his bed, mixing something in an earthen bowl with her fingers. She had once been heavyset and not too long ago; folds of excess skin draped from her chin and her upper arms. She wore a cotton-print coverall; her dress hung on her body as loosely as her skin. The woman's hair, salt-and-pepper-colored, was tied tightly behind her head. Her face was leathery-brown, heavily lined and creased by the sun. Beside the old woman stood a native girl of nine or ten clad in a frilly white dress, a dress like those worn by Catholic girls at first communions. When the girl saw that Will had awakened, she dashed from the hut calling out to someone in a tongue he did not understand.

Will's eyes met the old woman's and she smiled. He noticed many of her teeth were missing, and those that showed themselves were tea-brown. The woman shuffled to the head of his bed. She dabbed paste from her bowl, applying it gently to Will's brow and smoothing it along the ridge of his nose. The paste smelled of fish oil and coconut, but it extinguished the fire of Will's sunburn. Will asked for water.

The old woman handed Will a tin cup of cool water and he drank it down. The water tasted faintly of lime. She handed him another cup, this one of warm broth with a few lumps of fish. Will gulped the broth hungrily, straining the lumps with his teeth and chewing them. They were tough and rubbery, but he savored them like the finest steak. Will's flight suit and skivvies were draped over the foot rail of his bed to dry; his pistol belt and Mae West lay on the mattress at his feet. The old woman must have undressed him. The thought embarrassed him.

The little girl ran back into the hut, followed by another young girl dressed in white and a smiling Filipino man of about thirty. The man spoke English. He announced that he was the mayor of the village and the father of the two young girls standing beside him in the hut. "The Americans are our liberators," said the mayor. "You are most welcome here." As if to prove the point, the mayor nudged his daughters forward; the two girls began to sing to Will in perfect English, though shyly, "Let Me Call You Sweetheart," while their mayor-father beamed with pride.

Will was overcome. He shook the mayor's hand and blubbered his thanks. The mayor offered him a cigarette, an Alhambra brand. To Will's amusement, the mayor lit it with a matchbook stamped, "I shall return. Douglas MacArthur."

The mayor pulled up a chair and the two men talked. Will revealed to the mayor that he had been shot down over the Sibuyan Sea in a great air-sea battle and that he had swum a long distance to an uninhabited island. The mayor acknowledged that he had seen the flights of blue airplanes overhead and heard the crash of guns coming from Tablas Strait. The villagers had interpreted the fighting in the strait as a hopeful sign, he said. Also, word had reached Banton Island of General MacArthur's landings in Leyte Gulf; the Americans had returned, keeping their promise to rid the Philippines of the hated Japanese, and the mayor and his villagers were overjoyed at the prospect of their liberation.

Will asked how he could rejoin American forces, or locate friendly guerrillas. The mayor confided to Will that only a small band of guerrillas operated on Banton, and that most of them were not based permanently on the island. The mayor promised to deliver Will into the guerrillas' hands quickly, but he cautioned that Will must leave the village for the hills as soon as he had the strength. "This is necessary," the mayor said, "to avoid capture by the Japanese, whose motorboats patrol the strait and visit the village routinely."

The next morning, the mayor introduced Will to a wiry Filipino boy of about fifteen. The mayor assured Will that the young Filipino would lead him to a secret cave in the mountains above the village, a kind of safe house where Will could hide until the local guerrillas could decide what to do with him. The mayor was confident the guerrillas would meet him at the cave within the next day or two, and he gave Will a broad-brimmed straw hat and sandals to replace his ruined shoes. He urged Will to wear his hat and roll down the sleeves of his flight suit at all times when he was in the jungle, despite the heat. The mayor shook Will's hand, and the old woman who had tended to Will after his rescue handed the Filipino boy a rucksack of food and a goatskin of water for the journey into the hills.

Will followed the boy out of the village, which was surrounded by dense growths of coconut palm, banana, mango, breadfruit, and papaya trees—the trees were largely stripped of their fruit, Will noticed—and climbed up a steep, rocky trail through the jungle. He quickly discovered why the mayor had urged him to cover up as much as possible. A leech dropped from a bush along the trail and attached itself to Will's naked ankle. Will was horrified, but his Filipino guide calmly showed him how to remove the leech with a burning cigarette.

They climbed to fifteen hundred feet above sea level and paused before a stand of enormous trees wedged in a vale of rocks. Will gawked at the size of the trees. Supported by cathedral-like buttresses that were covered with moss, they towered at least ninety feet above the earth. Beneath them grew a dense thicket of foliage; there were liana, climbing bamboo, jasmine, and tree ferns in wild profusion. The boy drew his bolo knife from its sheath and hacked at the undergrowth, motioning for Will to follow him deeper into the jungled vale. The trail turned sharply upward, and Will found it difficult to keep his footing among the mossy roots. Hanging vines slapped him in the face; branches snatched at his arms and legs; and mosquitoes, clouds of them, assaulted him in the climb. Will detected brilliantly colored orchids entwined about the trees, but he couldn't appreciate their beauty; he had to concentrate on remaining upright. The humidity, which never drops below 70 percent in the forests of the Philippines, even in the dry season, weighed him down like a sack of bricks. By the time Will reached the cave in the late afternoon, he was exhausted.

The cave, which was hidden among a jumble of volcanic rocks atop Banton's highest peak, was mostly man-made. Its interior had been enlarged with hand tools to accommodate about a dozen men. Will stooped to enter it. The detritus of a military camp lay about: several three-legged stools, empty food tins, a bucket, an iron kettle, tin cups and plates, bits of charcoal from old campfires, boxes splintered for firewood. Other men had visited the cave not long before him; the clay floor bore the imprints of both naked and sandaled feet. Will and the Filipino boy each settled on a stool to rest. The boy, who spoke a little English, opened his rucksack and handed Will his supper, which consisted of a green plantain and a rice ball. The rice ball was a pasty compaction of brown rice and gray slivers of something Will could not identify. The slivers were sweet and tender, and Will devoured the rice ball quickly. He asked the Filipino what the slivers were. The boy pointed at the roof of the cave; "Bats," he said. As Will soon learned, Filipino peasants were protein-starved during the war, and smoking bats out of caves was a common method of securing meat.

Will spent an uncomfortable night in the cave, worried about centipedes and scorpions. The air was heavy and motionless and damp. The jungle below the cave was alive at night with rustling noises and strange clicks and snaps.

Midmorning the next day, two Filipinos materialized out of the woods. They were diminutive men of uncertain age, each armed with a bolo knife and an old U.S. Army Springfield '03 rifle. They carried ammunition bandoliers around their necks and were dressed in faded trousers cut off at the knees. One of them wore a khaki U.S. Army–style uniform shirt with sergeant's stripes, the only evidence he wasn't a cutthroat, and he spoke good English. He offered Will a cigarette and explained that he and his companion were guerrillas attached to the 6th Military District, which was headquartered on Panay, a much larger island to the south. They had received orders that any American sailors or airmen who came within their area of operations were to be transferred to Panay for safekeeping and, ultimately, for repatriation. The sergeant assured Will the guerrilla forces on Panay were strong and that he would be far safer there than on Banton. He informed the young pilot that he had arranged for a sailboat. Will would depart the next day from the same fishing village where he had come ashore. He would travel by daylight. Filipino fishermen do not fish by night, the sergeant said, so a sailboat traveling by day was less likely to arouse the suspicions of the Japanese.

The two guerrillas spent the night at the cave, sharing with Will and the Filipino boy a meal of boiled rice and canned meat. The next day, they escorted Will and the boy back to the fishing village. As the little party descended from the mountaintop cave, they glimpsed through the trees columns of white smoke rising from the direction of the village. The guerrilla sergeant called a halt and ordered the Filipino boy to run forward to the village and investigate.

After a time, the boy returned with frightful news. Japanese soldiers had set fire to much of the village, he reported. Enemy soldiers had arrived at dawn on a coastal patrol boat and searched the village. The soldiers had torched many huts and killed some villagers. The Japanese had departed in their patrol boat only hours earlier. The village was now clear of Japanese, and the survivors were still trying to quench the fires.

The guerrillas, with Will and the boy following close behind, dashed into the village. They arrived to a scene of confusion and despair. Men ran to and fro through the smoke carrying buckets of seawater to extinguish the smoldering huts. Women of the village clutched their children to their breasts and wept. The hut in which Will had spent his first night on Banton was in ruins, and Will feared for the fate of his benefactors.

The mayor, grim faced and angry, emerged from the smoke with his young daughters in tow. Will was greatly relieved to see them alive. The girls were still dressed in their nightshirts; they had been crying. The mayor and his family had escaped into the hills when the Japanese patrol boat first appeared offshore. They had been spared, but others had not.

The mayor recounted to Will and the guerrilla sergeant what had happened, adding detail to the Filipino boy's story. A platoon of Japanese soldiers had entered the village to search for evidence of guerrilla activity, as they had done many times before. On this visit, the Japanese platoon leader announced that his soldiers were searching for any downed American airmen who may have survived the big fleet battle in Tablas Strait. He demanded that all survivors be turned over to him. Fearing reprisals, villagers had remained silent at first. None revealed that an American had come ashore on their beach. But the platoon leader had grown suspicious. He began interrogating villagers privately, one by one. A villager had either broken under questioning or turned collaborator. Someone had revealed that two fisherman had brought an American pilot ashore and that an old woman had assisted them.

The mayor led Will and the guerrilla sergeant to a copse of narra trees at the edge of the village. There, from the branches of the trees, hung three dead bodies. They were the two Filipino fishermen who had plucked Will from Tablas Strait and the old Filipino woman who had nursed him. The soldiers had impaled all three villagers on bamboo stakes and slung them in the trees to die. The corpses' arms and legs were akimbo, as if they were in the act of falling; their blood had stained the earth beneath the trees black. The Japanese squad leader had enjoined the villagers not to remove the bodies; he threatened to impose even more severe punishment on the village if anyone disobeyed. The corpses would decay in the trees as gruesome reminders of the consequences of aiding the Allies.

Will sickened at the sight, guilt-ridden that he had been the cause of the villagers' deaths. These innocents had paid for their generosity and humanity with their lives.

Only the mayor's early morning escape had spared him and his young daughters a similar fate. The mayor vowed that he and the guerrillas would identify and deal with the traitors in his village. He promised his retribution would be as summary and brutal as the punishment the Japanese had inflicted on the old woman and the fishermen.

The raid on the village disrupted the guerrilla sergeant's plans to transfer

Will to Panay. The sergeant had commandeered a large sailboat for the trip, but he was uncertain whether the Japanese patrol boat was still lurking in the vicinity of Banton. The risk of sailing immediately was too great. The mayor and the sergeant agreed it would be best for Will to depart in the morning.

Will helped extinguish the fires and spent a sleepless night in the village. He was profoundly shaken by the deaths of the Filipinos and burdened by guilt. Had he not come ashore here, this horror might never have happened. Before the killings in the village, Will did not hate the Japanese people as a race, even though their government was his nation's bitter enemy. But the atrocities on Banton changed his view. After the killings, he began to hate the Japanese people with a righteous and biblical hatred.

The next morning, Will bade farewell to the mayor and his daughters, the guerrilla sergeant and his trooper, and the Filipino boy who had been his guide. Will had been utterly ignorant of the Filipino people before he landed among them. Their warmth, their generosity, their childlike eagerness to help had taken him completely by surprise. Without the villagers' kindnesses, Will would have been dead by now. He had no words to convey the depth of his gratitude. He offered the mayor and the guerrilla sergeant his pistol and survival knife in thanks, but they declined. His journey was far from over, they said. "Use your weapons against the Japs."

Will waded into the surf and climbed aboard the sailboat. Like the bangka that had carried Will ashore, the sailboat, called a dinait, was a wooden outrigger with a narrow hull. The boat had a single mast and a lateen rig; its sailcloth was made of woven straw like a floor mat. The boat's hold, where Will would be hidden, was covered by a bamboo hatch. The boat was crewed by two Filipino men who spoke virtually no English. They were young, athletic-looking men with round faces and amiable smiles. The Filipino in charge of the boat motioned for Will to lie down in the hold. He covered him with fish netting and lowered the hatch. With the sun breaking over Banton's hills, the dinait put to sea. All of Will's hopes for a safe repatriation depended on the fidelity and nautical skill of two small brown native men whom he did not know and with whom he could barely communicate.

On October 31, *Intrepid* was still standing by off Luzon, held on station by 3rd Fleet while other carriers replenished at Ulithi. Tempers among Air Group 18's pilots and aircrew were short, and patience was thin. *Intrepid* and her air group had been continuously at sea since August. The stress of combat operations, exacerbated by the Japanese suicide attack of October 29 and the ever-present threat of more, coupled with the perception that *Intrepid* had been forgotten in the rotation through Ulithi for rest, provoked much bickering and complaining.

VT-18 continued to fly routine antisubmarine patrols, but there were pilot shortages and personnel issues. Barden, the flight officer responsible for scheduling, noted glumly, "Things are so bad I had to fly an ASP today." Joe Rubin had rejoined the squadron but was still too weak to fly as a result of his shrapnel wound over Clark Field. Duke Delaney was not flying. Al Long had removed himself from flight status and been transferred to *Intrepid*'s air plot. Long had managed to keep his wings "by pulling strings," according to Barden. On November 2, Air Group 18 learned that Commander Ellis was being relieved as air group commander and appointed *Intrepid*'s air officer, the officer in charge of the carrier's air department. Van Antwerp was appointed the temporary air group commander until the new air group boss, Commander Wilson McConnell Coleman, USN, originally from Eutaw, Alabama, arrived to take charge.

Ellis's appointment as air officer was a promotion. In the chain of command aboard a carrier, the air officer was senior to the air group commander and served not only as head of the air department but as chief adviser to the ship's captain on all aviation matters. Ellis's pilots viewed his move to *Intrepid*'s air department as a positive development, not because they were happy to lose Ellis—El Gropo had been an effective combat leader and was highly respected by his pilots and air crew—but because *Intrepid*'s air department needed a kick in the butt. Although Air Group 18 and *Intrepid*'s air department had operated together for nearly three months, turf battles and disagreements between the air department and the air group had persisted. Barden, with his usual understatement, predicted that the air department "should see some changes soon." George Race, highly partisan and less circumspect, predicted that Ellis would eliminate the "inertia, red tape, and incompetence known as the Air Department." A few days later, Race later reported with glee, "Lopping off heads left and right, quietly laying down the law all along the line, within three days [Ellis] had the department streamlined under a few able officers who were willing to work. Within a week, the new air department was running slick as a whistle."

On November 3, Air Group 18 learned dispiriting news. Not only was Task

Group 38.2 not returning to Ulithi to rest and refit, but the task group would resume bombing raids over Luzon on November 5 and 6, together with task groups 38.1 and 38.3. An irritated Barden complained to his diary, "No food, no bombs, no pilots, no morale, no love. No nothing—but we still are not returning to Ulithi to reload." He mocked the indifference of 3rd Fleet planners to Air Group 18's contributions. "We (38.2) stayed out here and fought all alone while other groups went back—now we must continue here—to help them! Oh well—'That's the way it goes'!!" The only silver lining for Barden was that VT-18's first bombing mission over Luzon would not be flown against heavily defended Clark Field, but against Legaspi Field in southern Luzon, where fighter opposition was expected to be less fierce.

The Legaspi mission proved unproductive. Despite intelligence reports of numerous enemy airplanes on the ground at Legaspi, Air Group 18's pilots found few targetable aircraft and expended their ordnance on buildings instead. Later that afternoon, the air group reprised their earlier raids on Clark Field, also for the purpose of destroying airplanes on the ground. The strike group encountered little fighter opposition—VF-18's fighter boys saw only ten Japanese fighters and shot down the two that dared to engage them—and found few airplanes on the ground. The attackers ended up bombing and strafing coconut groves near the runways in the expectation that the enemy had concealed their warplanes in dispersal areas in the trees. The next day, with VT-18 down to only nine flyable airplanes, Air Group 18 bombed the Japanese airfield at Lipa Field near Manila, where the story was much the same: little or no fighter opposition, weak antiaircraft fire, few visible targets, and little smoke or fire or other evidence by which to judge the effectiveness of the raid.

Air Group 18 finally received word that Task Group 38.2 would be withdrawn from the line on November 8 and sent to Ulithi for replenishment and rest, "unless," as Barden acidly recorded, "some shoe clerk changes the present plan." No one changed the plan. En route to Ulithi, *Intrepid* passed through a modest typhoon, an experience that reinforced everyone's eagerness to quit the sea for a while, and arrived safely at Ulithi on November 9.

Replenishment came before rest in the navy. As soon as *Intrepid* anchored in the harbor, torpedoes were the first things to be loaded, followed by bombs. There was no mail, no fresh food, and no liberty. "Grr! Another day and you can expect a mutiny," Barden scribbled. Loading of essential stores continued throughout the night and well into the second day, and four new pilots reported to VT-18 to replace the squadron's losses. The ship suddenly seemed crowded. To Barden's delight, mail was delivered on the second morning in harbor; to his irritation, officers were strictly prohibited from drinking their whiskey cache while aboard ship. Barden and the boys didn't receive permission to go ashore until two full days after *Intrepid* arrived at Ulithi. As they motored toward shore in a liberty launch—they were headed for the beach bar dubbed Crowley's Tavern—Barden mused that he had not set foot on land since leaving Pearl Harbor in August.

Will's journey to Panay was slow and uncomfortable. The Filipino fishermen sailed the dinait languidly from island to island, tacking against the prevailing southwesterly breeze. They allowed Will out of the hold when they sailed in the offing, but they motioned him back down into the hold whenever they came close to shore and covered him head to toe with heavy fishing nets made of hemp. The dinait's hold was cramped, hot, and airless. Bilgewater sloshed constantly around Will's hips and shoulders, and his flight suit soon stank of sweat, brackish water, and stale fish. At night, the fishermen poled the boat close to shore. Will slept on the beach while one of the Filipinos stood watch; they fed him boiled fish and rice, and bananas when they could find them.

On Will's third day in the dinait, the fisherman made a detour to a small island. Will was delighted to see an American standing on the shore. He was a navy pilot, probably Lieutenant Junior Grade James Ritchie, a downed Hellcat pilot from VF-37 based aboard the escort carrier *Sangamon*, CVE-26. Ritchie, who had ditched off Samar on October 26 during a combat air patrol, was in the company of two brown natives who seemed to know Will's boatmen well. The four natives exchanged a few words in Tagalog and Ritchie boarded the dinait. The boat captain stowed Ritchie and Will side by side in the narrow bottom of the dinait and covered them with netting. The two fliers laughed that war had made them bedfellows on nothing more than a quick hello and a handshake.

After two more days of circuitous sailing—two days of claustrophobia, nauseating heat, the relentless motion of the sea, and the anxiety of being captured—Will and Ritchie reached Panay. The Filipino fishermen poled their dinait ashore on a remote stretch of beach on Panay's northern coast, twenty or thirty miles west of the town of Kalibo. Will and Ritchie thanked the Filipino crew profusely for safe passage but quit the sailboat gladly for the shore.

The two fliers were met on the beach by a small party of guerrillas commanded by a young Filipino officer dressed in the khaki uniform of the Philippine Scouts. The officer spoke excellent English. He introduced himself as Third Lieutenant Ricardo Duremdes, commander of M Company, 2nd Battalion, 61st Infantry Combat Team. Duremdes welcomed Will and Ritchie to Panay with an earnest handshake. He explained that the 61st Infantry Combat Team (ICT) was a regimental-size fighting force, one of six on Panay, comprised of approximately 130 officers and twenty-two hundred men and commanded by Lieutenant Colonel Cirillo Garcia. Although Lieutenant Colonel Garcia had recently established new headquarters at Kalibo, a provincial capital abandoned by the Japanese only a few weeks before, Garcia had instructed Duremdes to escort the two Americans to the main guerrilla camp in the mountains of northwestern Panay. The hike would be arduous, Duremdes warned, but the Americans would be far safer in the mountain camp than in Kalibo.

Ritchie, the more senior officer, asked how quickly he and Will would be repatriated. Duremdes replied that he did not know; the 61st ICT was in constant radio contact with General MacArthur's headquarters in Australia, and the guerrillas would advise Australia that Will and Ritchie had been rescued. Duremdes disclosed that the crew of the dinait were guerrillas. The 61st ICT was attached to the 6th Mountain Division, a division of United States Armed Forces Far East, or USAFFE. The "fishermen" were members of the 6th Mountain Division's Sailboat Brigade, a clandestine unit that the guerrillas used for intercoastal and interisland transportation and communication. A message boat had preceded Will and Ritchie to Panay and alerted the 61st ICT of where and when the two downed fliers would arrive. Will now understood why his passage to Panay had been so painfully slow.

A guerrilla sergeant offered the two Americans a meal of cold rice and bananas. Duremdes urged them to eat quickly; the journey to the camp would take several days, and Duremdes was eager to set off. Duremdes cautioned Will and Ritchie not to speak along the way with natives—other than the six or eight guerrillas in Duremdes's squad—and not to tell anyone they were Americans. Although Duremdes's party would avoid towns and villages where Japanese troops were garrisoned, Japanese spies and collaborators were everywhere on Panay, Duremdes warned.

With this welcome, Will and Ritchie fell in with the guerrillas, and Duremdes led his squad, plus two, off the beach into the foothills of northern Panay.

At Ulithi, VT-18 received another replacement pilot, raising the total number of untested torpedo-plane pilots to five. Task Group 38.2 was scheduled to return to combat duty within a few days, and Barden worried that the squadron wouldn't be "halfway ready." Scuttlebutt abounded regarding the air group's next objectives. There was serious talk of raiding the Japanese naval base at Yokohama or bombing Tokyo itself. These rumors subsided within a day or two, and the best guess was that more "strategic support" in the Philippines or Formosa was in the works. The latter target was about as appealing to Barden as Tokyo itself.

Air Group 18's officers and men went ashore at Ulithi for beer parties. The new air group commander, Commander Coleman, formerly skipper of *Franklin*'s VF-13, met most of his pilots for the first time in the officers' club bar. A few of the boys managed to spill a drink on their new commander, but Coleman was good-natured about it. VT-18's Duke Delaney was returning to *Intrepid* on the liberty barge when a loudmouthed pilot from *Lexington*'s Air Group 19 bragged that his air group had sunk the entire Jap fleet off Luzon single-handedly. This braggart compounded his error by disparaging *Intrepid* as "Queen of the Dry Docks" and referring to Air Group 18 as "that green air group." Delaney quietly walked up to the man and decked him with one blow. Delaney stood over the body and asked, "Anyone else from Nineteen?" Apparently there wasn't.

Truth was, the men of Air Group 18 considered themselves second to none after the ordeals of Formosa and Clark Field and the terrible days in late October. Barden pointed with pride to statistics, apparently compiled by George Race, that showed Air Group 18 had flown more hours and sorties in September and October than Spruance's Task Force 58, the heroes of the First Battle of the Philippine Sea, had flown in its entirety during any two months of the task force's deployment. "Small wonder we were tired when we got back to Ulithi," he scribbled.

On November 14, Barden recorded in his diary "the best news of the week." VT-18 had received a dispatch reporting that "Fletch has been picked up and is with our forces on Panay."

CHAPTER FIFTEEN

ON PANAY

★ ★ ★ ★ ★

"Our forces on Panay" consisted of six battalion-size infantry combat teams, each of which was responsible for guerrilla operations within a defined geographic district. The guerrilla combat teams on Panay were members of a confederation of indigenous military and paramilitary groups that General MacArthur had gathered beneath USAFFE's military umbrella to provide intelligence to the Allies and resist the Japanese occupiers.

Guerrilla groups had sprung up quickly on the islands of Luzon, Samar, Negros, Mindanao, and Panay after the surrender of the Philippine-American Army on Bataan. Many of these guerrilla bands were led by former Filipino officers who refused to surrender and were determined to continue armed resistance. They were the successors to earlier Filipino guerrilla leaders who had opposed Spanish imperialism in the late nineteenth century and confronted American colonialism in the early twentieth century. Some guerrilla groups were led by Filipino revolutionaries or insurgents whose political philosophies coincided with neither Japanese imperialism nor Western democratic ideals. The Hukbalahap on Luzon, initially branded by General MacArthur's headquarters as a "radical communist-tainted outfit," was one of these. A few guerrilla groups were led by gangsters and political opportunists who, while acting the role of anti-Japanese nationalists, indulged in "coercion, extortion, criminality and score-settling."

Operating from his headquarters in Australia, MacArthur had established a "Philippine Subsection" of USAFFE dedicated to gathering intelligence on Japanese activities throughout the Philippines. In the early days of the war, MacArthur's staff relied on contacts within the old Philippine Constabulary and on a clandestine Filipino intelligence network that had been developed in January 1942 by Brigadier General Simeon de Jesus. Captured by the Japanese shortly after the fall of Bataan, General de Jesus was tortured by the Japanese secret police, the Kempeitai, at Santiago Prison in Manila, and died there.

By mid-1942, General MacArthur's staff had strengthened Allied ties with the Philippine guerrilla movement by establishing the "Philippine Regional Section" under the direction of General Courtney Whitney. Using submarines of the U.S. 7th Fleet for the delivery of supplies, General Whitney furnished Filipino guerrilla units with arms, ammunition, radio transceivers, code ciphers, money, and medicines. Ultimately, Whitney's staff was able to communicate with most major guerrilla organizations by radio and furnish command direction. General Whitney established a Filipino "coast-watcher" system for reporting the movements of Japanese aircraft and shipping, and later formed the Allied Intelligence Bureau (AIB). The AIB communicated regularly with Philippine resistance groups, gathered intelligence, identified escape routes for Allied soldiers, sailors, and airmen, engaged in covert activities, and disseminated Allied propaganda.

The Japanese occupation of the Philippines produced widespread hunger among the Filipino people. Agriculturally, the islands had not been self-sustaining before the war. To feed the islands' population of nearly eighteen million people, the government of the Philippine Commonwealth had imported rice from India and Japan. The Japanese occupiers reversed the flow of rice, confiscating Philippine rice harvests to feed the Imperial Army and Japan's populace. Japan's seizure of Philippine rice not only created severe shortages throughout the islands, but inflated the prices of other food staples. The Japanese occupation of the Philippines fundamentally damaged the nation's economy and belied imperial propaganda about establishing a Greater East Asia Co-Prosperity Sphere in cooperation with the occupied countries. Before the war, exports to the United States and Great Britain of Philippine sugar, sugarcane, hemp, and coconut products accounted for 80 percent of the islands' exports. The Japanese occupation shut down these markets entirely.

In central Luzon, MacArthur's "communist-tainted" Hukbalahap, or People's Anti-Japanese Army, emerged as the dominant guerrilla group, while "President Quezon's Own Guerrillas" dominated southern Luzon. The President's Own was closely tied to Manuel Quezon, the Philippine president in exile. Son of a Spanish army officer, Quezon was the president of the nascent Philippine Commonwealth at the time of the invasion. A friend and admirer of General MacArthur, Quezon personified the new, fully emancipated, and democratic Philippines that many Filipinos hoped to build. But Quezon did not lead the President's Own personally. In February 1942, Quezon had escaped from Corregidor in a U.S. Navy submarine; he led the "Free Philippine government," a government in exile, from the safety of Washington, D.C.

On Panay, Macario Peralta, a lawyer by training and a former officer of the Philippine-American infantry, had disobeyed the general order to surrender after the fall of Bataan and fled to the rugged mountains of western Panay. There he had organized a political and paramilitary force of unusual effectiveness. He had divided Panay into multiple administrative and military districts and worked to undermine the Japanese occupation. An underground shadow government of civilian officials led by Peralta's chief political rival, Tomas Confessor, had also arisen on Panay. Confessor's administrators were ostensibly loyal to the Free Philippine government and the Allied cause, but were often the same native civil officials on whom Japanese army officers were forced to rely to manage their occupation.

Peralta had organized his infantry combat teams (ICTs) on the U.S. Army model. Each combat team consisted of a headquarters battalion, three infantry battalions composed of three companies, and special-purpose units, such as signal and encryption units, medical units, and a "sailboat pool," of which Will and Ritchie were beneficiaries. The ICTs operated from multiple camps within their assigned districts; they established separate command posts, training centers, primitive hospitals and infirmaries, and even prisoner pens. (The prisoner pens were used primarily to detain Filipino collaborators; the guerrillas took few Japanese prisoners.) Peralta expanded his organization to include much smaller guerrilla units operating on Tablas, Romblon, Sibuyan, and Banton islands north of Panay.

In February 1943, General MacArthur officially recognized Peralta's guerrilla forces and incorporated them into USAFFE. He designated the Panay–Negros Island area as the "6th Military District," and placed Colonel Peralta in overall command. By December 1943, MacArthur's headquarters, which broadcast from station KAZ in Darwin, Australia, was in regular radio contact with Peralta's command post located near Kalibo on the northern coast of Panay, and American submarines were delivering supplies to the island routinely.

Resistance to the Japanese occupation was not universal among the Filipino people. Some Filipinos saw personal economic or political opportunity in collaborating; some genuinely believed the Filipino people had been exploited by Western powers and embraced Japan's promise of equal partnership in a Greater East Asia Co-Prosperity Sphere. Some actively betrayed their countrymen, such as Franco Vera Reyes, a denizen of the Manila underworld who became an agent for the Japanese and did much to expose USAFFE's intelligence network in the Philippines. Other Filipinos—perhaps the majority, who were simple farmers, fishermen, or shopkeepers preoccupied with day-to-day living in a subsistence economy—simply withdrew, indifferent whether East or West prevailed in the struggle, and fearful of reprisals from the victor if they chose sides. The peasants carried on as they had for centuries.

Panay, which anchors the Central Visayas, lies forty miles east of southern Mindoro. The island is shaped like an equilateral triangle. Tabung Point marks the northwestern angle of Panay; from there, Panay's shoreline arcs southeasterly for thirty miles to form Pandan Bay, and then runs due south for roughly ninety miles past Bugasong and the capital city of San Jose, Antique. Below Antique, the coastline bends sharply east again and runs northeasterly for one hundred miles past the port city of Iloilo and the smaller island of Guimaras, which lies off Iloilo like a nursing child, to Balacaue Point. From Balacaue Point, Panay's shoreline turns abruptly west again and runs one hundred miles past the towns of Pilar, Capiz, and Kalibo to Tabung Point. The island is mountainous, with high cordilleras paralleling Panay's western shore for much of its length. Within this western range, Mount Madiac soars forty-three hundred feet above sea level; Mount Nangtud rises sixty-seven hundred feet, and Mount Baloy fifty-six hundred feet. These mountains decline gradually to the east, forming a hilly, central lowland that stretches for twenty or thirty miles. The land rises up again in the northeastern corner of Panay to three thousand feet, and then crumbles once more into the Visayan Sea.

Panay's aboriginal people were the Ati, who were subsistence farmers and

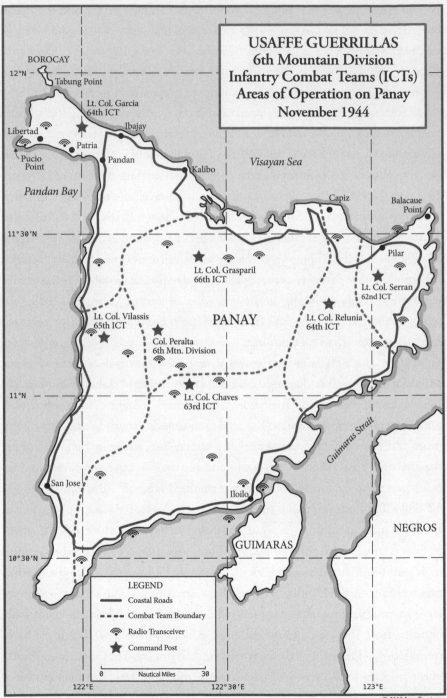

fishermen. The Ati people and their descendants were predominantly Negrito, shorter in stature than Filipinos of Malay or Chinese descent, with broad faces and very dark skin. Legend says an Ati chieftain sold Panay's lowlands in the twelfth or thirteenth century to ten tribal leaders from Borneo for a hat and a gold necklace. When the Spaniards colonized the island in the sixteenth century, the Ati accepted Christianity but otherwise clung stubbornly to their tribal culture. During four centuries of Spanish rule, the Ati lived in small villages scattered throughout the hinterlands, coexisting uneasily with Spanish overlords and Augustinian monks. Many Ati resisted Spanish efforts to resettle natives permanently in town centers, and Panay became the site of repeated uprisings against Spanish officialdom. Americans also experienced the intractability of the Ati and their descendants firsthand. During the so-called Philippine Insurrection—that bloody guerrilla war against American colonialism that followed closely on the heels of the Spanish-American War—U.S. troops landed on Panay in early 1900 and battled guerrillas there for more than a year until the conflict ended.

Japanese troops landed at Iloilo in April 1942 and soon after occupied the island capital of San Jose, Antique and numerous other towns on Panay. By October 1944, the Japanese army had concentrated its forces in the larger coastal cities, such as Iloilo, Capiz, and San Jose. At the zenith of their occupation, the Japanese had constructed eleven air bases on Panay, a submarine base at Iloilo, and a motor patrol boat base on Guimaras. To exploit the island and assert imperial authority, the Japanese dispatched patrols by land and sea to confiscate food and livestock, intimidate the populace, and seize suspected guerrillas. The Japanese patrols were a favorite target of Peralta's soldiers.

Duremdes led his party westward. With his two American fliers in tow, the Filipino lieutenant skirted the main coastal road, the better to bypass Japanese checkpoints and avoid enemy patrols. The squad hiked through coconut groves and farmers' fields. Will saw few houses of substance. Filipino farmers on Panay, like the fishermen on Banton, tended to live in primitive bamboo huts, usually clustered close together and concealed within a thicket of banana trees, narra trees, and palms. Many of the huts were surrounded by rickety fences that once may have held sheep or goats but were now empty. The fields were empty too. Although the farmers had once delimited their plots with hummocks of earth, the borders had become overgrown with grass and were now indistinct. Will saw no crops in the fields to speak of, and no livestock, not even a stray dog. Duremdes told him meat was scarce on Panay and nearly every dog on the island had been eaten long ago.

On the second day of their journey, Duremdes and his squad stumbled upon an unexpected sight. Four Japanese fighters sat wheels-up in an open field, the victims of a very recent crash-landing en masse. One of the airplanes was burning furiously. Will recognized the olive green warplanes as Kawasaki Tonys, sleek, bullet-nosed fighters operated by the Japanese army. A clutch of Filipino peasants stood over four Japanese pilots, holding them captive with shotguns and the sharp blades of their bolo knives. The captives sat quietly in the grass with their heads bowed. Duremdes learned from one of the pilots that his flight of four Tonys had left Negros on a training and reconnaissance mission and become lost. Low on fuel, the pilots had made emergency landings in the open field.

Will studied the enemy. These were the first Japanese he had seen since Saipan. The thought never occurred to him that he might have much in common with these young men, none of whom was much older than he. These men knew how to fly. Did they share Will's fascination with machines, his appreciation of the breathtaking power and beauty of a distant thunderstorm, the inexplicable serenity and oneness with God that comes with flying on a calm summer evening? Will made none of these associations. They were the enemy, and he could not separate in his mind these men from the Japanese soldiers who had committed the atrocities on Banton.

Duremdes ordered the captured pilots to strip off their flying boots. The guerrillas gathered up the pilots' shoes and distributed them among the guerrillas who wanted them. Will observed that most of the Filipino enlisted men were shod in sandals (if they were shod at all), and many of the guerrillas seemed to prefer bare feet to sandals or shoes. Will needed a new pair of shoes as much as anyone, but all of the Japanese boots were too small to fit him. The guerrillas rifled through the pockets of the pilots' coveralls. They found several Japanese flags, each of which had been inked with vertical rows of flowery Japanese script. Duremdes explained that the calligraphy was the prayers and well-wishes of the pilot's family and friends. Duremdes handed one of the flags to Will as a souvenir and a welcome gift to Panay.

The guerrillas stripped the enemy aircraft of easily removable items, such as magnetic compasses, radios, and charts, and hid the booty in the trees. Duremdes explained that he would summon a work party from Kalibo to remove the heavy machine guns and transfer the entire load to a guerrilla supply camp. The guerrillas conferred over what to do with their prisoners. The nearest prisoner pen was in the opposite direction from the guerrillas' destination in the western hills of Panay. Duremdes assigned two well-armed guerrillas to march the prisoners back to Kalibo. Based on the sullen demeanor of the guards, Will doubted the Japanese would reach the prisoner pen alive, and he admitted to himself that he was indifferent whether the prisoners did. He rather hoped they didn't.

Duremdes resumed the march to camp. Along the way, he told the story of how his company's executive officer, Second Lieutenant Conrado Aguila, had been killed in a recent skirmish with the Japanese. He offered the story as a cautionary tale about the Japanese way of fighting. Two months earlier, the 61st ICT had mounted a campaign to drive the Japanese back into their garrisons at Capiz, Kalibo, and Ibajay, which were towns along Panay's northern shore. The guerrillas had targeted Japanese patrols in a concerted effort to isolate enemy units from one another and destroy them. One of these confrontations had gone very badly for the guerrillas. The Japanese had outflanked the 1st Platoon of M Company, 61st ICT, and attacked it from the rear. As M Company's executive officer, Second Lieutenant Aguila, was rushing to the aid of 1st Platoon, he was hit in the hips by enemy machine gun fire and dropped to the ground. As Aguila attempted to crawl back to safety, Japanese soldiers set upon him. Aguila's men later found his naked body, minus its nose and right ear. Aguila's left arm had been skinned.

Duremdes's squad reached the main camp of the 61st ICT after a four-day journey, having traveled roughly forty miles on foot from the spot where Will and Ritchie had come ashore. The guerrilla camp was hidden in the forested mountains above Pandan Bay, six miles north of the village of Patria. To reach the camp, Duremdes had led his men up a jungle trail past well-concealed sentries who challenged their passage at several points along the trail. The jungle was dense and disorienting; Will once again endured the assaults of leeches and omnipresent mosquitoes in the climb through the woods.

The camp was set in a jungle clearing twenty-five hundred feet above sea level. The living quarters were primitive wooden huts and lodges covered with thatched grass or tarpaulin roofs; drinking water was drawn from a nearby stream. Only one of Lieutenant Colonel Garcia's infantry companies was in the Patria camp when Will arrived; Garcia had stationed his other companies, six or eight of them, in temporary camps scattered throughout the battalion's area of operations, which was officially designated as the First Administrative District.

The guerrillas in camp did not resemble any military unit Will had ever seen before. The troops ranged in age from young boys of sixteen or seventeen to older men of fifty or sixty. Most were only partially outfitted with uniforms; they wore khaki military shirts with civilian trousers, or civilian shirts with military trousers, but not both. Many wore knee-length shorts. Few had regulation footwear or headgear of any kind; some had no footwear at all. Most wore straw hats. Bolo knives and daggers were ubiquitous, but only about a third of the troops seemed to carry rifles; a few of the guerrillas appeared to be armed with only spears.

Duremdes escorted Will and Ritchie to the headquarters hut to meet Lieutenant Colonel Garcia. The office was sparsely furnished; it boasted a single typewriter and few supplies. Writing paper was especially scarce. Orderlies had typed their reports on lined school paper, sheet music, tax records, the back sides of ledger sheets, and newsprint. There were no communications radios in the Patria camp; Garcia had three transceivers hidden on mountaintop sites to the west, the closest being Mount Pinatubo eight miles away, but only a trusted few knew the precise locations of the radio sets. The guerrillas communicated among themselves primarily through messengers and runners. The code name for the 6th Mountain Division was "Tunis"; the code name for the 61st ICT was "Hubag."

Garcia, a gruff, tough-looking officer of Malayan descent, greeted the Americans in English and welcomed them to his camp. He spied Will's .38-caliber revolver and instructed Duremdes on the spot to make Will an officer in M Company. Will protested that he had no infantry training and could speak neither Spanish nor Tagalog. Garcia waved him off. "You have a pistol," he said. "You will be an officer."

Garcia did not suffer contradiction. He was also strict, tactless, and generally disliked by his subordinates, most of whom were Visayan Filipinos from Panay. Garcia by birth was Tagalog, a term that not only defines the official language of the Philippine Islands but generally describes persons of Malayan ancestry. Before the war, Garcia had held the rank of captain in the army of the Philippine Commonwealth, serving as a liaison officer with the 41st Infantry Division in the town of Tayabas in southern Luzon. He had arrived on Panay from Bataan in February 1942 and organized a powerful guerrilla force in northwest Panay well before Macario Peralta became the principal guerrilla commander on the island. Garcia was ambitious and jealous of his authority; he had initially refused to cooperate with American soldiers who had escaped capture on Panay in 1942. Garcia tolerated Peralta's leadership but maintained considerable autonomy. Garcia's First Administrative District encompassed the critical submarine rendezvous and supply areas in Pandan Bay, and Garcia derived much of his power and influence from his control over the distribution of American largesse. MacArthur's headquarters suspected him of graft, and MacArthur's chief of staff, Lieutenant General R. K. Sutherland, complained of Garcia's alleged misappropriation of supplies and the loss of thirty tons of matériel "due to poor organization and planning for the shipment."

Will was privy to none of this, and probably wouldn't have cared if he'd known. He viewed Garcia's guerrillas as his saviors, as his protectors in a strange and dangerous land. Will felt obliged to repay the guerrillas' kindnesses, and duty-bound to serve with them as allies. He accepted Garcia's commission and earnestly set about learning something of army life and tactics from Duremdes.

He began by reading the guerrillas' general orders, which prescribed in English the rules for camp life. Securing a source of pure drinking water and protecting it was first on the list. Drawing water from unpolluted springs was always the preferred choice, according to the rules. If drinking water must be drawn from a surface well or river, the water must be boiled or treated with halazone before drinking. To protect the water source, streams and rivers were never to be polluted by throwing garbage waste in them or by defecating in them. If a stream must be used for multiple purposes, the following order of use must be observed from upstream to downstream: (1) water for drinking and cooking; (2) water for bathing (bathing was recommended at least twice a week); (3) water for drinking by animals, such as mules and donkeys; and (4) water for washing clothes. These stream usage areas must be appropriately flagged, according to the rules.

Palatability of food was to be sacrificed for cleanliness, according to the rules. Fruits and vegetables were to be boiled for one minute before eating, and partially decayed meats and fish were to be thrown out. Proper disposal of garbage and human excreta was essential for fly prevention and to avoid the spread of disease. Troops on the march were instructed by the rules to dig small holes for the purpose and, when in camp, to dig latrine trenches that were scaled in size and complexity to the length of stay and the number of troops in camp. Guerrillas were expressly prohibited from urinating out of windows; they were required to construct urine soakage pits and place urinal cans in bivouac areas at night. Mosquito nets were required for sleeping at night, and insect repellent was to be used, if available. (There wasn't any repellent in Garcia's camp, anyway.)

The rules decreed principles of personal hygiene: Wash hands before every meal; brush teeth after every meal; cut hair short every two weeks; cut nails short; and treat cuts and bruises without delay using tincture of iodine or tincture of Merthiolate. If shoes and socks were worn, guerrillas must ensure they were well fitting. Last, hospitals and aid stations were required to maintain prophylactic stations for the prevention of venereal disease. The rules directed that "[a]ll Officers and E.M. [enlisted men] who subject themselves to exposure with women of doubtful virtues or with disreputable women must go to one of these aid stations for prophylactic treatment immediately after exposure and not later than twenty-four hours thereafter."

To learn infantry tactics, Will studied old U.S. Army field manuals and accompanied Duremdes on patrols through the countryside. The primary purpose of these patrols was not to harass the Japanese, but to hunt and forage for food. Like all guerrilla organizations in all wars, the 61st ICT depended heavily on the civilian population for support and sustenance. But sufficient food, especially cereals, was a serious problem. In some districts and towns on Panay, nearly 85 percent of the people ate only once a day, subsisting primarily on roots such as cassava, gabi, and camote. In Panay's south-central regions, conditions were only slightly better; people there consumed a diet of corn, rice, or balinghoy once or twice daily.

Requisitioning food from hungry civilians was not easy. There were several different currencies in circulation on the island, including official occupation "pesos" issued by the Japanese government and "Emergency Circulating Notes" (also denominated in pesos) printed by "currency committees" of the Free Philippine government, which secreted their presses in various regions of the island. The general populace viewed all island currencies with skepticism, suspecting the scrip, whether Japanese or Filipino, of being worthless or nearly worthless. Although guerrilla officers strictly prohibited their troops from seizing food from civilians without paying compensation, civilians sometimes refused to give up precious foodstuffs in exchange for the devalued currency, and hungry soldiers occasionally resorted to force. Confiscating food could be very expensive for the soldier who indulged in the practice. A guerrilla private earned twenty pesos a month (when he actually got paid); shooting a village woman's chicken without her approval would cost the soldier two hundred pesos in reparations.

In the Patria camp, cooks served up meals of boiled rice mixed sparingly with whatever meat was available: boiled fish, stewed chicken, wizened goat or carabao. Bananas, plantains, or coconut meat were staples, and brown candy made from sugarcane was a rare treat. Without refrigeration—the guerrillas had none—uncooked meat lasted one day in the heat and cooked meat no more than two days. Meat supplies fluctuated wildly, and the guerrillas ate (or didn't eat) like primitive hunter-gatherers. Not long after Will arrived, the Patria camp exhausted its usual sources of meat, and the cooks offered the soldiers a choice between two entrees: rice with monkey meat, or rice with bat meat. Will chose the bat meat, and for several days thereafter monkey meat or bat meat were the only culinary alternatives. But cigars and cigarettes were plentiful in camp and everyone smoked. The cigars and cigarettes were exotic brands Will had never heard of, such as La Indiana cigarettes and General MacArthur cigars. Smoking lessened the appetite, calmed the nerves, and kept the mosquitoes at bay— somewhat. Occasionally in the evening after dinner, young guerrilla officers would share whiskey with their American guests and tell them something of themselves and their struggles.

The guerrillas on Panay were a diverse group, comprised of Panay natives and refugees from many parts of the archipelago. The officers were predominantly unsurrendered soldiers of the Philippine-American Army, but most had not been commissioned officers before the fall of Bataan. Of the 1,560 officers on the roster of the 6th Mountain Division, only about 370 were regular or reserve officers; the balance were merely "acting" or "probationary" officers in temporary positions of authority. About five hundred of the division's officers had college degrees; six hundred more had attended college before the war; and another four hundred had graduated or attended high school. Of the 21,500 enlisted men on the 6th Mountain Division's roster, 13,200 were classified as "volunteers." Keeping volunteers in ranks was difficult; pay was poor and irregular. A guerrilla private was supposed to be paid twenty pesos monthly in Emergency Circulating Notes, a sergeant between thirty and fifty pesos, and a captain one hundred pesos, but the soldiers' wages were months overdue.

The chronic pay shortage was a source of tension between the military authorities and the Free Philippine shadow government of Tomas Confessor. In letters to General MacArthur, Colonel Peralta and Governor Confessor each charged the other with treasonous neglect in their respective spheres. At bottom were bitter jealousies and disagreements over the control and allocation of scarce government monies and food supplies. Peralta argued that paying and feeding troops in the field should be the Free Philippine government's highest priority. Confessor countered that paying troops in the field would merely drive up prices and create black markets, and that civilian administrators must control the treasury and the food supply for the broader benefit of the people. Peralta accused Confessor of not living up to his promises to deliver food to the military, by refusing to release cereals in favor of the army except on a cash-and-carry basis. The military had done its part to expand the food supply, Peralta insisted. As district military commander, Peralta had personally encouraged his troops to "utilize every spare second of [their] time to planting something edible, camotes, bananas, camoteng, cahoy, corn and even palay," and had formed military units that managed, or attempted to manage, fishponds; Peralta had even appointed an "administrator of fishponds." Peralta charged that Confessor's refusal to provide funds was "nothing more than an attempt to beat the Army Forces to its knees and compel them to take order[s] from Gov. Confessor." Peralta suspected Confessor of scheming to replace Quezon as president of the Philippines after the war, and wrote angrily to MacArthur, "I fully understand the role of a military commander in a democracy, but under these times and conditions, I do not think that I must swallow [Confessor's insinuations to MacArthur of dishonesty among Peralta's officers, including Lieutenant Colonel Garcia] without inviting serious disaster. Only thing holding me back from putting him in jail is that such action may be misinterpreted and followed by other military comdrs [sic] in adjacent islands who may have similar problems. Another is that the Nips may capitalize on it."

Peralta's civil affairs officers reported monthly, and district by district, on the state of relations between Panay's guerrilla units and the people. Generally, the natives of Panay supported Peralta's guerrillas and complied with their policies, but there were civilian complaints. As cataloged by guerrilla officers, civilian complaints centered on "the lack of courtesy, discipline and tactfulness" among some of the soldiers, and many civilians "harbor[ed] in their hearts ill feelings against abusive soldiers who break rules and orders." Among the most persistent grievances were soldiers who forced natives to pound and haul palay without pay and to repair roads and bridges. Notwithstanding the diminishing supply of pigs and chickens on the island, farmers had been "discouraged" from raising more animals "because of the abuses of our soldiers shooting left and right without giving consideration whether it is a mother hen, a mother pig or for breeding purposes."

By the time Will reached Panay in early November 1944, the morale of the people on the island was "excellent," in the estimation of Lieutenant Colonel Garcia's adjutant, notwithstanding the deprivations caused by war. Most civilians had learned of the Allied landings at Leyte Gulf, and many Filipinos had personally observed "frequent passing of Allied planes overhead." The civilian populace of Panay "expected the Americans to land at our shores within this month or early next month," and they hoped the Allies would quickly defeat and expel the despised Japanese.

Will mustered with Duremdes's platoon each morning in the camp assembly area. The men in the ranks were a mix of Negritos, Filipinos, and Malays. Regardless of rank, age, or race, they were thin and wiry, their skin stretched tautly over their cheeks and collarbones. Most of Duremdes's soldiers were friendly and open; they were ingenuous, eager to please, and reasonably disciplined. But some of Duremdes's guerrillas had a look of innate savagery in their faces; the whites of their eyes and the flare of their nostrils betrayed a primitivism and unpredictability that Will had never encountered before. Will imagined himself standing before a primeval war party. Only fire, drums, and war dances were missing.

After two weeks in camp, Will himself cut a comical figure. His flight suit was soiled and patched. He wore a bandanna and a straw hat over his head to ward off leeches and mosquitoes. He had no shoes; he still wore the sandals the Banton mayor had given him. He had contracted a mild case of dysentery in camp and lost much weight; his pistol belt and holster hung loosely around his hips. His beard had grown out. To Will's surprise, his beard had a strawberry tinge, which greatly amused the Filipinos. As he trailed behind Duremdes during morning inspections, Will looked more harlequin or beggar than military officer.

Intrepid returned to the Philippine coast on November 19, and Commander Coleman led his first strike as the new commander of Air Group 18. Coleman's air group bombed Nichols and Clark fields near Manila, but the effectiveness of the strikes was difficult to assess, because the enemy had widely dispersed his aircraft. On Strike 2 Able, VT-18's Avenger division, led by Duke Delaney, was unable to keep up with VB-18's Helldivers en route to the target and fell behind by about four miles. Three Japanese fighters trailed the torpedo bombers for several miles but never pressed home an attack. Delaney reported the enemy fighters simply "indulged in aerobatics." On landing, one of Delaney's Avengers lost its tail hook, causing a barrier crash and major damage to the airplane but none to its crew. At the end of the day, Commander Coleman praised the bombing of his VT and VB crews for its accuracy.

A dispatch arrived on November 19 announcing some welcome news to Barden and the boys: Air Group 18's relief, Air Group 9, would arrive in Manus on December 21. But the same message also contained disappointing details: Air Group 9 was not yet ready for combat and would not relieve Air Group 18 until February 1, 1945, at the earliest. Even if the schedule held, Air Group 18 would be on the battle line for a minimum of ten more weeks.

Doc Fish came to the pilots' rescue that night, distributing bottles of beer to the weary airmen in their ready rooms.

In the third week of November, Will Fletcher and Jim Ritchie also learned welcome news. Lieutenant Colonel Garcia informed them that they would be moved soon to Libertad, a remote fishing village on the shore of Pandan Bay twenty miles west of the Patria camp. There they would be joined by other American servicemen who were currently hiding in guerrilla camps scattered around Panay. The entire group would be evacuated to Australia by an American submarine within the month.

Will Fletcher and Jim Ritchie were not, of course, the only American pilots sheltered by the guerrillas on Panay. There were many others, such as Ensign William G. "Bill" Shackelford.

Bill Shackelford, called "Shack" by his buddies, was an F6F pilot assigned to *Monterey*'s VF-28. While strafing a Japanese airfield during one of Halsey's airpower-suppression raids over the Visayas in early September 1944, Shack's Hellcat was hit by antiaircraft fire. He crash-landed in a rice field near Iloilo City and was rescued by a Filipino in civilian clothes who spoke flawless English. The Filipino was Carlos Copaghe, a former UCLA law student, who served as the staff judge advocate of the 63rd Infantry Combat Team. Copaghe led Shack safely past enemy garrisons situated in and around Iloilo City and delivered him to the headquarters camp of Lieutenant Colonel Jules P. Chaves, who served as commander of the 63rd ICT and as executive officer of Colonel Peralta's 6th Mountain Division.

Chaves's camp was located in the foothills of south-central Panay adjacent to a river. His "headquarters building" was a crude one-room bamboo hut with a raised wooden floor and a thatched roof. The hut also functioned as living quarters for Chaves and his wife, Magaliena, whom Chaves called Madge. Lieutenant Colonel Chaves and Madge invited Shackelford to share their office-house, and native mountain people (whom Bill curiously observed preferred to squat in the trees like monkeys rather than rest on the ground) constructed a bamboo addition to Chaves's house to accommodate him. To Shack's amazement, the mountain people built the bamboo addition overnight.

Shackelford's hosts treated him well. They furnished him with a bamboo plate, a tin cup, a sleeping blanket, mosquito netting, and an oil lamp for his room, shared their food, whisky and cigars, and gave him money with which to purchase toiletries, such as toothpaste and soap, from local merchants. (Enterprising Filipino vendors hawked such things to guerrillas from mobile kiosks that they could hide from Japanese troops.) Madge, who owned a pedal-powered sewing machine, stitched a Filipino-style shirt for Bill from the cloth of his parachute, and tried to teach him the Tagalog language. Chaves also assigned Bill a Filipino manservant, whom Chaves introduced simply as "Boy," to sleep outside Bill's room and to prepare him hot water each morning and night. Boy was unusually stout for a Filipino and much taller than Bill; armed with a heavy Browning automatic rifle, Boy carried Bill and the BAR on his back whenever they forded a stream.

Bill accompanied Chaves on a few guerrilla raids, but mostly as an observer. On one occasion, Chaves's guerrillas planned to ambush a group of Japanese staff officers as they traveled outside Iloilo to inspect nearby waterworks and a power plant. The guerrillas had filled a bamboo pipe with explosives and buried it in the road leading to the plant. On the day of the attack, Chaves and Bill rode horses to the top of a hill that overlooked the ambush site and concealed themselves in the trees. As the motorcade of Japanese officers passed over the pipe, the guerrillas detonated their makeshift land mine. Pieces of cars and body parts flew in all directions. Guerrillas with rifles and bolo knives emerged from the woods to finish off the survivors. Bill observed firsthand that the guerrillas preferred not to bury dead Japanese on Philippine soil, but rather to burn the corpses and dump the ashes into the sea.

In late October, Shackelford learned from Lieutenant Colonel Chaves that he would be sent on a "special mission" to the far western regions of Panay controlled by the 61st ICT. Although Bill's orders did not say so explicitly, Bill understood that his "mission" would involve possible evacuation from the island by an American submarine. Bill was excited and eager, but first he would have to travel more than a hundred miles through enemy-infested territory to reach the 61st ICT area of operations. Chaves helpfully assigned a Filipino officer and two enlisted men to guide Bill and protect him along the way. Chaves also loaned Shackelford five hundred pesos in Emergency Circulating Notes, printed by the Filipino shadow government in nearby Iloilo, to pay for food and the services of boatmen on the trip.

Shack's party departed Chaves's camp in early November. Along the way, the travelers picked up four U.S. Army Air Corps fliers, one of whom, Second Lieutenant John M. Wilder, was a B-24 bombardier and the nephew of Billy Wilder, the Hollywood movie director. Wilder and his crew had bailed out over Panay, and, luckily, they had fallen into the hands of the guerrillas instead of the Japanese. The party's journey from Chaves's camp to Libertad, partly overland and partly by sailboat, took two weeks. The Americans picked up new guides at intervals and traveled by boat whenever possible, but it was sometimes difficult to get Filipino fishermen to assist them for fear of Japanese reprisals. John Wilder was sickly, and his poor physical condition impeded the party's progress. On one overland stretch, Wilder had to be transported on a bamboo travois pulled by a mule. Wilder smoked cigarettes heavily and hoarded them. One evening, while wading from the boat to shore to bivouac for the night, he stepped into a hole; cigarettes by the hundreds floated out of his pockets and washed away with the waves. Shack found John a tiresome traveling companion; Wilder subsisted mostly on bananas, complained incessantly about the poor food, and boasted how one day he would get his famous uncle to make a movie about his escape from Panay.

Libertad lay at the mouth of a narrow river that emptied into Pandan Bay. The village consisted of a large wooden schoolhouse and a few native huts of bamboo. The inhabitants of the village were predominantly fishermen, many of whom had been involved from the earliest days of the war in smuggling supplies ashore to aid the guerrilla movement on Panay. The smuggling process was simple and efficient. MacArthur's headquarters in Australia would advise Peralta's guerrillas by radio of the place, date, and time of delivery. Assuming no Japanese patrols were sighted in the area, American submarines would surface inside Pandan Bay, or farther out in Tablas Strait, at a designated navigational fix. Using native fishing boats from Libertad, the guerrillas would rendezvous with the American submarine, transfer supplies into the fishing boats, and ferry the stores to the beach and hide them. A large cache of nonperishable war material had accumulated over time at Libertad; hundreds of fifty-gallon drums of gasoline lay buried near the village in anticipation of an Allied invasion.

Bill Shackelford's party arrived in Libertad on November 20 to find a large group of Americans already there. The group included Will Fletcher and Jim Ritchie, and Lieutenant John Wesley Williams of VT-29 and his two crewmen. Williams had piloted one the four Avengers from *Cabot* that had accompanied Commander Ellis on *Intrepid*'s Strike 2 Able on October 24. After making a torpedo run on *Yamato*, Williams and his crew had crash-landed ten miles south of Marinduque Island and were quickly rescued by Filipino fishermen. The group included other survivors of the Battle in the Sibuyan Sea, such as Ensign Robert K. McAdams, an Avenger pilot from *Lexington*'s VT-19. McAdams had attacked the Center Force at dusk on October 24 and become separated from his group. Lost and low on fuel, he had water-landed in a cove at Romblon Island. McAdams and his crew were close enough to shore to call out to some Filipinos for help. "We're Americans," they shouted. "MacArthur sent us." The Filipinos launched a boat to pick up McAdams and his crew and happily escorted the Americans across the mountains to a house that overlooked a bay. The house on Romblon was occupied by a family of White Russians, and McAdams and his crew hid there, except for spending an occasional night in the mountains to avoid Japanese patrols, until they were taken by sailboat to Libertad.

The Americans at Libertad knew they would be evacuated from Panay by submarine, but they didn't know precisely when. They had taken refuge in the Libertad schoolhouse while they awaited their deliverance, protected by the guerrillas of M Company, including Third Lieutenant Duremdes, and attended to by the Filipino women of the village, who cooked for them.

The Libertad schoolhouse was an old wood-frame building about forty feet wide and eighty feet long and had the look of a campground assembly hall. Although the schoolhouse was the largest building in the village, it had only one room. The arrival of Shackelford and his party raised the total number of American servicemen in Libertad to twenty-nine. The American airmen, officers and enlisted alike, were quartered together; each man was given a straw mat on which to sleep, and a wooden plate and a tin cup with which to eat and drink. Possessions were few. The idea was to be able to move quickly if a Japanese patrol suddenly appeared, and to evacuate the schoolhouse without leaving any evidence of habitation by outsiders. Lieutenant Williams was the senior American officer in the group, and he had assumed command of the Americans. He set up a watch schedule, and drilled his troops in rolling up their mats and escaping into the woods. The men slept in the schoolhouse fully clothed, not only to make a quick getaway if necessary but to avoid the stings of scorpions and the bites of spiders.

The Americans dined in an area of the village removed from the schoolhouse, subsisting on the same spare diet of rice and meat scraps that they had consumed in their respective guerrilla camps. The Americans who had been on Panay the longest were easy to distinguish from those who had been rescued recently. Recent arrivals were sunburned and relatively fat; the old hands were thin from an inadequate diet and pale from jungle living. Shackelford was among the skinniest and palest; he had come down with dysentery from drinking bad water and he had contracted malaria, despite sleeping beneath the mosquito netting that Lieutenant Colonel Chaves had given him.

The Americans' common goal at Libertad was to get fed long enough to get out of there. They tried to supplement their food supply by hunting in the hills above Libertad. Fletcher and Shackelford hunted together, escorted by a squad of guerrillas armed with rifles (more for the Americans' protection than to bring down any game). Will and Shack intended to shoot any edible animal, small or large, that wasn't obviously domestic. They usually returned from the hunt with nothing but leeches, which they were not yet desperate enough to eat. Although they urged Duremdes to let them try their hand at fishing in the river or the shallows offshore, Duremdes discouraged it. The jungle would conceal a hunter, but a fisherman would be exposed. The entire village would be in danger if the Japanese discovered an American fishing from Libertad's beaches or riverbanks.

The Americans spent most of their time lounging in the schoolhouse, sleeping, playing cards or dice, and talking about what they would eat when they got home. There were few vices available for the Americans at Libertad, except for cigars and cigarettes tobacco was abundant—and a faux coffee that the Americans made by roasting rice grains on a metal sheet, grinding them up, and then boiling the brown powder in a pot. The guerrillas did not interfere with the Americans' daily routine, but an armed guerrilla guard accompanied the Americans wherever they ventured outside the schoolhouse, whether walking to meals, to the river to bathe, or to the latrine. Occasionally, when the guerrillas had confirmed that the coast was clear, a few Americans would walk down to the beach at dusk under armed guard to swim. Will Fletcher did not join the swimmers; he had swum for miles after crashing in the Sibuyan Sea, and he had no interest in voluntarily entering water over his head ever again.

On the afternoon of November 24, Duremdes disrupted the Americans' coffeehouse complacency. He burst into the schoolhouse and shouted excitedly, "Get your weapons and follow me to the beach!" The startled Americans gathered up whatever weapons they had—most of them, like Fletcher and Shackelford, carried nothing more than their .38- or .45-caliber pistols—and rushed outside. As they jogged toward the water, the Americans learned why Duremdes had rousted them: A Japanese patrol boat was headed to Libertad and would arrive within the hour.

When, back in 1943, Lieutenant Colonel Garcia and General MacArthur's staff first arranged to supply Panay though Libertad, Garcia had created a network of guerrilla coast watchers and stationed them in the hills above Pandan Bay to observe and report on the movements of the enemy. The hills offered a commanding view of the bay and of the seaward approaches to Patria and Libertad. It was one of Garcia's coast watchers who had alerted Duremdes to the approaching patrol boat.

Duremdes had to decide quickly whether to stand and fight, or to evacuate

346 • INTREPID AVIATORS

the Americans to the hills. Duremdes was reluctant to withdraw his platoon from the village. Thirty guerrillas and twenty-nine American servicemen would be difficult to move on such short notice, despite Lieutenant Williams's evacuation drills. In their hurry to leave, the Americans or the guerrillas inevitably would leave behind some evidence of their presence. The Japanese were not stupid; the purpose of their visit was to search for evidence of guerrilla activity and to exact retribution from the populace if they found a trace. The Japanese patrol would seize on whatever evidence was left behind—a piece of uniform clothing, a dropped letter, or cigarette butts in abundance—and the entire village would suffer the enemy's wrath.

Japanese patrol boats had visited Libertad before, Duremdes knew. The Japanese habitually anchored their patrol boats in the shallows and allowed their troops to wade ashore. Duremdes hurriedly assembled his troops and announced that they would ambush the Japanese patrol boat just after it dropped anchor.

The numbers favored Duremdes. A Japanese coastal patrol boat—like the one that had raided Banton—normally carried between twenty and twenty-five soldiers and a crew of three or four. With his platoon of about thirty guerrillas, reinforced by twenty-nine armed American servicemen who knew how to shoot, Duremdes's ambushers should enjoy a two-to-one advantage. The coastal terrain at Libertad also favored Duremdes. The jungle below the village ran down to the shore, nearly to the water's edge. Even at low tide, only a few yards of hard sand separated the waters of Pandan Bay from a tangled bramble of palms, banana trees, and brush. The undergrowth along the shore was dense as a hedgerow and provided excellent cover. Anyone standing at the water's edge would have a difficult time seeing Duremdes's men concealed behind the foliage, even though they were only a few feet away.

Duremdes's guerrillas distributed additional rifles and ammunition among the Americans to bolster their firepower. The guerrillas handed Shackelford a zip gun that fired .38-caliber shells, and offered Will an old Springfield '03 rifle. The guerrillas had no machine guns or mortars in their arsenal, not even a Browning automatic rifle. The plan, Duremdes explained, was to lie in wait in the thicket and fire at the boat on his signal. The boat must be destroyed, Duremdes warned. If the boat escaped, the Japanese would return in greater force and the village would become untenable. We must catch them by surprise, he warned. "Do not fire until I give the signal."

The Americans understood without question that the stakes were high, not only for the native Filipinos who had become their friends and protectors but for themselves. If the Japanese got ashore in force, the Americans would have to retreat into the jungle with the guerrillas, and their longed-for repatriation would be delayed indefinitely, perhaps until war's end. The Americans resolutely took their positions in the thicket along the beach, standing side by side with Duremdes's Filipinos in the prickly heat, and waited.

The defenders of Libertad heard the Japanese patrol boat approaching from the east long before they saw it. The boat puttered slowly toward the village and coasted to a stop roughly thirty yards from shore, directly in front of the ambushers. The boat was seventy or eighty feet long, diesel powered and made of wood. The boat's pilothouse was festooned with radio antennae, and a heavy machine gun was mounted on the boat's foredeck like a harpoon gun. A Japanese rising-sun flag fluttered from the boat's bow. The figures of enemy soldiers were visible in the stern area; a sailor stood on the bow deck waiting to release the forward anchor. Diesel fumes wafted toward the hedgerow, carried landward by the sea breeze.

Duremdes's ambushers, crouching behind the hedgerow and sweating profusely in the heat, waited impatiently for their leader's signal to open fire. The tension became palpable, but still Duremdes did not signal. The Japanese sailor standing on the foredeck of the patrol boat, oblivious to the danger, released the bow anchor, and the boat's pilot shifted his engines in reverse to take up slack in the chain and secure the anchor to the bottom.

The strain of being in close proximity to the enemy became unbearable for one of Duremdes's ambushers. A single shot suddenly rang out from the hedgerow. Whether fired by an American or a guerrilla, no one knew for sure, but it was clearly not fired by Duremdes.

The ambush sprung, Duremdes immediately bellowed the order to fire, and the sixty Allied men in the thicket loosed a ragged first volley at the enemy gunboat. The noise was deafening. A wall of lead spewed from the hedgerow, shredding leaves and branches and betraying the guerrillas' position. Will worried the Japanese would rake the hedgerow with their machine gun, so he fired his Springfield at the sailor standing in the bow. The sailor crumpled to the deck, whether from Will's shot or someone else's, Will could not tell. From the corner of his eye, he detected the patrol boat's wooden sides splintering from the impact of the guerrillas' bullets, and saw Japanese soldiers in the stern of the boat taking cover behind the gunwale.

Duremdes's ambushers launched a second roaring volley on the heels of the first, and then the gunfire quickly subsided. The Japanese had not gotten off a shot in return. The stern of the patrol boat was on fire, and most of the Japanese who had exposed themselves appeared to be dead or dying; a few Japanese who had leaped into the water to escape the flames in the rear of the boat were now treading water. Aviation Electrician First Class Bronislaw Raczynski, Lieutenant Williams's turret gunner, bolted from the thicket to the astonishment of everyone else still hidden in the brush, hopped through the shallows, flopped onto his belly, and began swimming toward the patrol boat, apparently intent on seizing the Japanese flag before the boat sank.

Several fishing bangkas had been beached on the sand not far from the ambush site. Duremdes ordered a squad of guerrillas to launch the boats and bring ashore all survivors for interrogation. Will watched from the beach as the guerrillas carried out Duremdes's order. Some of the Japanese in the water refused to be rescued. These survivors the guerrillas shot point-blank or bludgeoned with their bolo knives, staining the surf with blood. Will lost count of the number killed in this manner; when the guerrillas beached their bangkas at last, they had collected only six survivors. Three were badly burned, and these unfortunates the guerrillas laid out on the sand to die. Three survivors were uninjured; the guerrillas forced the three uninjured soldiers to their knees and bound their arms tightly behind their backs.

The gunfire, and the abrupt cessation of gunfire, had attracted curious villagers to the beach. The villagers crowded around the Japanese prisoners, cursing them and spitting on them. An angry woman grabbed a bucket from a bangka and doused the burned Japanese soldiers with salt water. Other women took turns at this, and the agonized cries of the soldiers only seemed to fuel the women's fury. The Filipino women tormented the three burned soldiers until the men lost consciousness and died.

The guerrillas also ransacked the burning patrol boat, hurriedly stripping it of everything pilferable before fire overtook the vessel. They were overjoyed to find weapons and ammunition, tinned meats and fruits, and, best of all, bottles of sake. When the guerrillas had looted everything they could remove easily, they stoked the smoldering fire in the boat and shot more holes in the hull to sink it quickly. The guerrillas intended to erase the patrol boat from the face of the earth. The Japanese occupiers must never learn how, or where, one of their coastal patrol boats had been lost. The boat must simply vanish without a trace.

Duremdes ordered the angry villagers to back away while he interrogated the three uninjured Japanese. A guerrilla sergeant hauled each man to his feet, and the victorious ambushers, Filipino and American alike, crowded around Duremdes and his prisoners in a semicircle to observe the interrogation. The most senior of Duremdes's prisoners was a sergeant, a wiry man of indeterminate age with a shaved head. Duremdes questioned the three Japanese prisoners using English and Japanese phrases, but all three men remained stubbornly silent. The Japanese sergeant seemed especially sullen and defiant.

Will Fletcher happened to be standing at Duremdes's shoulder as the Filipino lieutenant interrogated the prisoners. Will made eye contact with the Japanese sergeant, who seemed deaf to Duremdes's questioning. The two men glared at each other. Neither was willing to be the first to look away. The Japanese sergeant's face twisted into a sneer. Then he tilted his head back and spat in Will's face.

Will could not restrain himself. A rage unlike anything he had ever experienced exploded inside him. He struck the Japanese sergeant with his fists, hitting him first in the face and then in the stomach. The sergeant buckled at the blows, and Will kicked the man in the groin with as much force as he could muster. He sank to his knees in the sand, groaning, and Will struck him again in the head with his fists, toppling him over on his side. A cheer went up from the guerrillas, but Will didn't hear it. He was insensible to anything except his rage. He kicked again at the man on the ground, punishing him for the deaths of Savage and Laner and Skelly and Christman and Westmoreland and the Banton villagers who had been impaled in the narra trees, and for the whole senseless war his people had started.

Duremdes pulled Will away from the Japanese sergeant, who lay gasping on the ground and bleeding from his mouth and ears. Two guerrillas lifted the sergeant to his knees and propped him unsteadily in the sand. Then one of the guerrillas raised his bolo knife high in the air and—on whose order no one really knew—decapitated the man on the spot. The effort required two blows; the prisoner's neck spurted a geyser of blood, and his severed head rolled toward Duremdes's feet. The guerrillas and villagers roared their approval.

Bill Shackelford had turned away when he saw the blade strike the sergeant's neck. He knew what was coming and didn't care to watch. But the guerrillas did not behead the other prisoners. Duremdes stopped the bloodshed and ordered a squad of guerrillas to escort the two remaining survivors to a prison pen near Patria. The prisoner detail didn't get very far; gunshots soon rang out from the woods east of Libertad, and the squad leader and his guards returned to the village without their prisoners.

"The Japanese tried to escape," the squad leader explained. "I was forced to shoot them."

No one believed him, but neither did anyone chastise him. There were now no survivors of the Japanese patrol boat, and no one left to tell the tale to the enemy.

The guerrilla who had beheaded the Japanese sergeant presented his bolo knife, still stained with blood, to Will as a souvenir, and Will accepted it. That night in the schoolhouse, the Filipinos shared their captured rations and sake with the Americans. The two groups of Allies celebrated their victory with toasts to liberation and freedom, to brave friends and good fortune. Lieutenant Colonel Garcia proudly reported to Colonel Peralta and the adjutant of the 6th Mountain Division that the men of M Company, 61st ICT, had sunk a motorboat off Libertad, Pandan, on November 24. Garcia issued to each American serviceman a typed letter certifying that the American airman had participated in the ambush of a Japanese motorboat "resulting in the sinking of said boat and a casualty [sic] of an estimated twenty (20) Jap soldiers and crew."

On the morning of November 25, as the Americans at Libertad slumbered in the village schoolhouse, Task Group 38.2 resumed its bombing raids over the Central Visayas. Commander Coleman had begun the day by leading Strike 2 Able back across the Sibuyan Sea to attack enemy shipping south of Luzon. The men of Air Group 18 were in good spirits, and they were well rested and well fed. After blasting Lipa and Nichols airfields on November 19, Air Group 18 had flown only routine patrols, and on November 23, Intrepid's ship's company and Coleman's Airedales had enjoyed a Thanksgiving Day dinner with turkey and all the trimmings. Barden had worried at the time, "This is too easy—Am afraid it won't last long." He was right.

Strike 2 Able had returned to the ship at about eleven a.m., and Commander

Coleman was finishing his aircraft action report in the ready room when general quarters sounded at twelve fifteen p.m. for the fourth time that day. *Intrepid*'s radar operators had detected several enemy aircraft closing fast on the task group, which consisted of *Intrepid* and her old battle companions *Hancock* (now serving as Vice Admiral Mitscher's flagship), *Cabot*, *Independence*, *New Jersey*, *Miami*, and *Vincennes*, the battleship *Iowa*, and seventeen destroyers.

Strike 2 Baker was circling overhead *Intrepid* awaiting recovery when general quarters sounded, and Strike 2 Charlie was on deck preparing to launch. At twelve twenty-seven p.m., as *Intrepid*'s antiaircraft gun crews trained their weapons in the direction of the oncoming enemy, *Intrepid*'s flight deck crews began launching Strike 2 Charlie. Ben St. John's Avenger lifted off the deck at twelve forty-four p.m., the last of the strike group's airplanes to get airborne. Vernon Sistrunk had launched ahead of St. John, but Sistrunk's Avenger had developed engine trouble and he was forced to circle back to the ship and land. At twelve forty-seven p.m., Vernon's sick Avenger glided into the arresting gear. Quickly shutting down the airplane, he and his crewmen abandoned their torpedo bomber to the care of plane handlers, who shoved the airplane to the forward elevator and hustled it belowdecks. Sistrunk and his crew scampered across the flight deck and ducked through a hatch in *Intrepid*'s island.

At twelve fifty-three p.m., *Intrepid*'s gunners let loose a cacophonous barrage of twenty- and forty-millimeter antiaircraft fire at an approaching Japanese fighter, a Mitsubishi Zeke. Though hit and burning, the Zeke bore down on *Intrepid* and, less than one minute after the American gunners commenced firing, the airplane struck her flight deck aft of the island. The deck erupted in orange and yellow flame, as shards of metal and burning gasoline spewed in all directions. The Zeke's bomb pierced the unarmored flight deck and detonated in ready room five on the gallery deck; the blast blew a hole in the flight deck and shot a geyser of flame and smoke high into the air. Inside the island, Sistrunk and his crew staggered at the concussion, temporarily deafened by the noise; they had narrowly escaped incineration.

Shortly after he had taken command in early November, Commander Coleman had issued standing orders to all Air Group 18 personnel that ready rooms were to be abandoned during an enemy air attack. Coleman had learned from painful experience aboard *Franklin* that ready rooms located directly beneath the flight deck were much too vulnerable to enemy bombs. Thus, there were only a few men in *Intrepid*'s ready rooms when the kamikaze struck, but twenty-one enlisted men working in a nearby Link trainer office and radar repair shop were killed instantly. The Zeke itself skipped toward the bow, breaking up and ejecting its pilot. The pilot's corpse, a mangled, bloody heap, dropped to the flight deck near *Intrepid*'s forward catapults.

Five minutes later, as *Intrepid*'s crew battled the fires from the first kamikaze's hit, another Zeke approached the carrier from low astern on her port side. Flying through the dense smoke that boiled aft of the ship, the second Zeke successfully evaded *Intrepid*'s counterfire. The Zeke's low stern approach and the billowing smoke from the first hit made it difficult for *Intrepid*'s gunners to bring their weapons to bear until the last moment. The pilot of the second Zeke pulled up over the fantail, dropped one wing as if executing a wingover, and plummeted into the middle of the flight deck aft of the island. The enemy airplane punched a huge hole in the flight deck and penetrated to the hangar deck before both the airplane and its bomb exploded in a fountain of flame. The explosions instantly triggered secondary fires the length of the hangar bay that destroyed seventeen warplanes parked there. Fortunately, none had been loaded with bombs or torpedoes, but the raging fires cooked off ammunition, which exploded like firecrackers and flung machine gun bullets randomly throughout the hangar bay. The second Zeke pilot bounced clear of his airplane on impact and sailed past the island; his parachute came loose and snagged itself on *Intrepid*'s signal bridge.

Lieutenant George Race, who had been slow to comply with Commander Coleman's standing directive to evacuate the ready room during air attacks, had bolted from the air group commander's ready room area after the first kamikaze hit. He was making his way through choking black smoke from the gallery deck to the flight deck when the second kamikaze hit the carrier, "jarring the ship from stem to stern." On reaching the flight deck, Race was greeted by a "terrifying sight. Flames and great billows of smoke were coming from a gaping hole in the after part of the deck. Fire hoses were strung everywhere. Men were running back and forth, clearing debris from the deck, swinging axes into the deck to release more of the smoke that was building up below. Officers and men were lying on the deck all around the island structure, some of them gasping for air, some of them vomiting, some of them peacefully relaxed, obviously dead."

Thanks to Coleman's directive, most of the pilots and aircrew still aboard the carrier were one level below the hangar deck in the officers' wardroom when the kamikazes hit. But no place is safe aboard a ship when it catches fire. Asphyxiation is the primary mechanism of death in a shipboard fire, a killer as sure as shrapnel wounds, burns, or concussions. After the second kamikaze struck, ventilation blowers sucked up the oily smoke from the hangar bay and pumped it into the wardroom. Everyone there dropped to the deck, pressing napkins and handkerchiefs soaked in iced tea to their noses to filter the air as best they could. The men gathered in the wardroom managed to escape death by asphyxiation, but others were not so fortunate. Scores of sailors who had been trapped in smoke-filled compartments were laid out on the deck on their stomachs, right cheeks on the backs of their right hands, all bleeding from their mouths.

Lieutenant Race learned that Dr. Jack Fish was among the wounded and went looking for him. Doc's post had been in the battle dressing station located on the gallery deck just aft of where the second kamikaze had hit. When Race found him, Doc was laid out on the flight deck near the island and receiving artificial resuscitation. In Race's words, "a spatula held [Doc's] mouth open and his protruding tongue looked black and thick. A corpsman held a bottle of plasma, although it was soon apparent that Jack was absorbing none of it." Unwounded officers and enlisted men worked with the medical corpsmen "trying to urge a spark of life" back into Doc and the many others who were laid out beside him. At one point, Admiral Bogan himself knelt beside Doc's body and quietly asked the corpsman whether the doc would make it. At about four p.m., the ship's surgeon told Race and the others gathered around Doc to stop working. Doc was gone.

Admiral Halsey, watching the conflagration from *New Jersey*, initially wrote the carrier off as a total loss. Flames belched from *Intrepid*'s fractured flight deck, and plumes of thick smoke billowed thousands of feet into the air, like the breath of an erupting volcano. But by three thirty p.m., *Intrepid*'s firefighting crews brought the fires under control, despite the early death of the ship's fire marshal, Lieutenant D. D. Dimarzo, in the second hit. In the space of ten minutes, sixty men had been killed and one hundred more injured.

The next morning, crews began the grisly business of cleaning up. In Race's words, "The stench was terrific. Commander Coleman put some men to work searching behind all the pipes [in the ready rooms] for bits of human flesh. It is likely that odor came from flesh that had been blown from the hangar deck against the gallery deck, and was inaccessible. In the Link trainer room workmen found a dismembered head. In another compartment a leg." At four p.m., burial services were held on the hangar deck. Bud Williams, Ernie Allen, and George Race were among the air group officers who served as honorary pallbearers for Doc Fish. Race recorded, "Sailors carried 60 neat white canvas bags to the rail and lined them up. Chaplins Herlihy and Stafford had their say. In the distance *Iowa* and *New Jersey* fired a salute. Hardly able to stand the horrible odor of burned and mortifying flesh, sailors managed to hoist the canvas bags over the side. They went into the sea with a dull plop. The bugler sounded taps. The marines fired a salute, and everyone jumped as the guns went off. That was all. Joe [Purdy, VB-18's Air Combat Intelligence Officer] and I walked up to the room and drank a bottle of whiskey."

Seeing their ship in flames, the pilots of *Intrepid*'s Strike 2 Baker had diverted to other carriers or to the old Japanese airstrip at Tacloban on Leyte, now securely in the hands of MacArthur's troops. The pilots of Strike 2 Charlie, oblivious to *Intrepid*'s agony, had continued with their mission, which was to sink Japanese destroyers and minelayers anchored in Balanacan Bay off the island of Marinduque. Kenny Barden bombed a destroyer, and Ben St. John concentrated on a minelayer anchored a few hundred yards off shore. St. John flirted with the fate of Lieutenant Junior Grade John Savage at Palau by sweeping in low to drop his four five-hundred-pound bombs, but Ben somehow got away with it. St. John's bombs broke the back of the minelayer, which blew up in a secondary explosion and cracked in two. One piece of the hull sank stern-first, the other bow-first.

On the return trip to *Intrepid*, Strike 2 Charlie learned that *Intrepid* could not recover her aircraft. The pilots were ordered by radio to proceed to Tacloban and land. The strike group had no trouble locating the airfield, but, after executing nothing but carrier landings for the past four months, the pilots had to readjust to landing on an earthen runway. The runway wasn't moving, and it was surfaced with prefabricated, interlocking steel mats that could be slick as ice in the rain. None of the customary markers by which the torpeckers gauged their approach was applicable, and there was no LSO to assist them. Ben St. John touched down long and had to remember at the last minute to use his wheel brakes.

While *Intrepid*'s crew battled the shipboard holocaust, *Intrepid* never wavered from her appointed station in Task Group 38.2's formation. But the two kamikaze strikes had rendered the great carrier useless operationally. She had huge holes in her flight deck, and most of her arresting gear was gone. Two of the three elevators necessary to shuttle planes between the flight deck and the hangar deck, elevators two and three, were inoperable. Third Fleet ordered *Intrepid* to retire to Ulithi for possible repairs, there to be reunited with her scattered air group.

Air Group 18's refugees remained at Tacloban for two days, subsisting on food and coffee provided by the Salvation Army and the United States Army, and then flew six hundred miles to Peleliu, where they remained overnight. The next morning, they flew another three hundred miles to Ulithi. The refugee pilots arrived on November 28 to find *Intrepid* burned and blackened, and to learn that Doc Fish had been killed. Barden described Fish's death as "Air Group 18's biggest loss," and mourned him simply as "a helleva swell fellow."

Third Fleet ordered *Intrepid* back to Pearl Harbor for repairs, and scuttlebutt in *Intrepid*'s wardroom and mess decks focused on Air Group 18's future. The big question was whether Air Group 18 would return to Pearl Harbor with the ship, or whether its airmen would be reassigned to other carriers still on the line. The Japanese navy had been soundly defeated in the battles off Leyte Gulf, and the danger to American forces from Japanese warships was minimal. But 3rd Fleet had decided that more fighter pilots were necessary to deal with the new threat from the kamikazes, the idea being to have more Hellcats in the air to shoot the bastards down. Rumors abounded that all Helldiver squadrons would be replaced by fighter squadrons, and that VT-18's Avenger pilots would be required to check out in Hellcats at Ulithi for immediate reassignment to fighter squadrons already on station. The latter rumor did not sit well with the torpeckers, especially since there was truth to it. Admiral Bogan, Captain Bolger, and Commander Ellis all had to argue forcefully against such stopgap measures to bolster Task Force 38's fighter strength. VF-18's fighter boys did not fare so well in the debate; on November 30, VF-18 was transferred to *Hancock*. Barden thought VF-18's fighter pilots, whom he regarded as "our best buddies [and] also the best fighter squadron in the Navy," had received a "rotten deal." As VT-18's Avenger pilots waited for news of whether they would be converted to Hellcat pilots, Barden sulked: "This is now one big unhappy family."

Although morale was low aboard *Intrepid*, morale among the American airmen at Libertad was sky-high. The Americans had learned from Lieutenant Colonel Garcia that they would be taken off the island by submarine on December 5. The navy's instructions, radioed from 7th Fleet Headquarters in Australia to Garcia at Patria, required the guerrillas to display an "all-clear" signal if there were no Japanese troops or patrol boats in the vicinity of Libertad. The pre-scribed signal was two white circles, each eight feet in diameter, displayed on the beach below Libertad by midday on December 5. The implication of 7th Fleet's instructions was plain: No white circles, no rescue.

The Americans were at first perplexed and annoyed at 7th Fleet's demand for two eight-foot white circles as the all-clear signal. A few of the fliers took the instructions as proof of the idiocy of military staffers. The guerrillas and their American guests had few tools, little lumber, and no white paint. Why not ask for a neon sign?

Lieutenant Williams consulted with Duremdes, and the Filipinos devised an ingenious solution. White bedsheets were virtually nonexistent in the village, but some of the village women wore slips and brassieres. The guerrillas would borrow the local women's lingerie, stitch their underthings together, and stretch the white fabric across bamboo frames, which could then be propped up in the sand. The plan worked. After only a few hours of construction, the Americans had fabricated two white circles eight feet in diameter, each of which resembled a small trampoline, and carefully concealed the signals in the schoolhouse against the day of their rescue.

While the Americans at Libertad awaited their repatriation, the crew of *Hake*, SS-256, a diesel-powered American submarine of the *Gato* class, eagerly antici-pated the end of their boat's seventh war patrol. Although *Hake*'s crew had tor-pedoed a Japanese cruiser off Luzon in mid-November, their patrol had been marred by loss.

On October 20, 1944, the day of the Leyte invasion, *Hake* had departed Fremantle, Australia, under the command of Commander F. E. Haylor. On reaching her assigned patrol area in the South China Sea, *Hake* had joined a search-and-attack group with two other *Gato*-class submarines, *Growler*, SS-215, and *Hardhead*, SS-365. The skipper of *Growler*, Commander T. B. Oakley Jr., commanded the three-boat group.

In the predawn hours of November 8, *Growler* made radar contact with a group of Japanese warships cruising west of the Philippines. Commander Oakley ordered *Hardhead* and *Hake* by radio to converge on the enemy warships with *Growler* in the lead. As *Hardhead* and *Hake* maneuvered closer to the enemy, the crews of both submarines detected several large underwater explosions. No one ever saw or heard from *Growler* again; the submarine and her entire complement of about of eighty sailors had vanished in an instant, and no one knew what had happened. Was *Growler*'s destruction the result of internal mishap or enemy action?

Later, not far from where *Growler* disappeared, *Hardhead* encountered and sank a Japanese tanker. While prowling in the vicinity of *Hardhead*'s target, *Hake* endured ferocious and persistent depth-charge attacks, probably initiated by Japanese destroyers that had been charged with protecting the tanker. For more than twelve hours on November 8, Japanese warships chased *Hake* to and fro, dropping depth charges and punishing *Hake* for *Hardhead*'s kill. A direct hit by a depth charge or an aerial bomb is not necessary to sink a submerged submarine; a near-miss can create sufficient overpressure to rupture the hull and cause catastrophic flooding. The enemy's depth charges rattled *Hake* to the core. Bracing himself within *Hake*'s inner hull as the submarine's battle lanterns flickered and her hull creaked ominously, Commander Haylor dutifully logged nearly 150 explosions. Ten days later, *Hake* stumbled upon her chance for revenge, and Commander Haylor seized it. *Hake* torpedoed and damaged the Japanese light cruiser *Isuzu* off northern Luzon about sixty miles west of Corregidor.

Not long after torpedoing *Isuzu*, Commander Haylor received via radio orders from 7th Fleet to proceed to western Panay, to a position approximately eleven degrees, thirty-eight minutes north and 121 degrees, fifty-three minutes east, there to rendezvous with Filipino guerrillas and evacuate American airmen shot down by the enemy.

On the morning of December 5, Will and his fellow Americans awoke early and mustered for breakfast. Instead of the usual fare of boiled rice and lumps of bat meat or fish, the Filipino cooks served up a special farewell dish of boiled rice and stewed chicken, a treat much appreciated by the Americans, never mind that the meat had come from roosters killed in a cockfight. After breakfast, the

Americans gathered up their few possessions and readied themselves for departure. Will had very little. He still wore the flight suit, now ragged and thin, in
which he had been shot down, and the sandals given him by the Banton mayor;
his only possessions were his dog tags, his wallet, his watch, his swatch of blue
airplane fabric, his pistol and survival knife, his Zippo lighter, the flag taken
from the downed Japanese pilot, and the bolo knife with which the guerrillas
had beheaded the Japanese sergeant.

Duremdes confirmed that the Pandan coast was clear and that the rescue
would go forward as planned. Lieutenant Colonel Garcia's coast watchers had
reported no Japanese movement or activity in the Pandan Bay area. The Americans applauded the report, but weren't much concerned about any Japanese
presence. "Frankly," Fletcher later said, "we didn't care if there were Japs in the
next hut; we were going to set out those two goddamn white circles."

At about noon on December 5, Duremdes's guerrillas escorted the Americans from the schoolhouse to the beach at Libertad, to the same strip of sand
from which Duremdes had ambushed the Japanese patrol boat. Two large
round-bottomed sailboats, crewed by members of the guerrillas' 6th Mountain
Division Sailboat Brigade, wallowed in the surf. Colonel Garcia and a few officers of his staff stood on the beach, waiting for the American fliers to arrive.
Duremdes had assigned a squad of Filipinos to erect the all-clear signal in the
sand. The guerrillas propped up the bamboo circles against two palm trees at
the water's edge and lashed them securely to the trunks to keep the signals from
blowing away in the sea breeze.

The Americans bade farewell to their hosts and protectors. Will warmly
shook Duremdes's hand and gave him his revolver as a parting gift. The two
men promised to correspond after the war. Will bestowed his survival knife on
a young guerrilla who had acted as something of a tour guide and orderly for the
Americans at Libertad. The boy had lost a leg in the fighting on Bataan but had
escaped to Panay; he had hopped about Libertad on his crutches, carrying messages between the Americans and Duremdes and loitering in the schoolhouse,
where he entertained the Americans with stories of Filipino life.

Lieutenant Colonel Garcia and his staff officers boarded one sailboat, and
the Americans boarded the other. The American fliers waded through the surf
and hoisted themselves over the gunwales of the larger vessel. Filipino crewmen
draped sailcloth over the well of the boat to shield the Americans from the sun

and from the eyes of any Japanese patrol planes that might appear overhead. The Filipinos then shoved their heavily laden craft into deeper water and set sail into the offing with much creaking of ropes and snapping of canvas.

Just before dawn on the morning of December 5, *Hake* slipped beneath the surface of the waters of Tablas Strait and descended to a depth of 120 feet. She ran submerged on a course of 115 degrees, proceeding cautiously at four knots toward the navigational fix off western Panay where she was to rendezvous with USAFFE guerrilla forces. At about ten a.m., *Hake* reached the rendezvous point. She altered course and circled to hold her position, creeping slowly beneath the water at only two to three knots. At two thirty p.m., *Hake*'s officer of the deck, Lieutenant Junior Grade G. W. Evans, whose primary duty was to serve as *Hake*'s assistant communications officer, brought the submarine to periscope depth. Evans sighted a sailboat bearing 059 degrees true. At four-oh-four p.m, Evans's relief, Lieutenant Junior Grade A. R. Metzger, *Hake*'s assistant electrical and commissary officer, sighted through his periscope "two white discs" on the beach bearing due north from the submarine. Metzger had read the all-clear signal.

At five twelve p.m., Metzger spotted two sailboats bearing northeasterly from the submarine; thirty-five minutes later, he brought *Hake* to the surface. Metzger opened a pressure hatch and climbed the ladder through *Hake*'s conning tower to her bridge. Crewmen opened the aft main pressure hatch, and a dozen submariners clambered onto the submarine's weather deck. The sailors wore blue dungaree trousers, white undershirts, and life vests; a few of them were armed with rifles. Commanding the boat from *Hake*'s conning tower, Metzger steered his submarine cautiously at "various courses and various speeds" for a rendezvous with the nearest sailboat. Metzger noted weather conditions in *Hake*'s log: "overcast, visibility good, calm sea."

At about six fifteen p.m., under the command of Lieutenant J. F. Maier, *Hake*'s first lieutenant, the submarine coasted to a stop. Speaking through a bullhorn, Lieutenant Maier commanded his boatswain's mates to help bring one of the Filipino sailboats alongside. The Filipino fishermen handling Lieutenant Colonel Garcia's vessel maneuvered as close as they dared and tossed a bowline to the American sailors, who eased the sailboat close abeam and hauled Colonel Garcia aboard. A petty officer saluted Garcia and led him belowdecks to confer with Commander Haylor, while *Hake*'s sailors and Garcia's staff exchanged pleasantries.

The American refugees sat cheek by jowl in their cramped sailboat, waiting impatiently for Garcia to conclude his conference and for their sailboat's turn to nestle beside the submarine. The Americans knew that the sudden appearance of a Japanese patrol plane could disrupt the whole rescue operation. If a plane appeared, the sailboats would immediately cast off, and *Hake* would submerge to save herself. But for now *Hake* lay on the surface like a slumbering leviathan, a monster from the deep. All she revealed above the water's surface were her weather deck, the rounded shoulders of her pressure hull, and her conning tower. Her mass lay below the surface, dark and mysterious. The airmen joked among themselves about being sealed up in an underwater boat. "I signed up for aviation so I wouldn't have to get in one of those sons of bitches," joked one cheerfully, but he was as eager as the rest of the Americans in the sailboat to get aboard and under way. Will thought *Hake* the most beautiful warship he had ever seen. Best of all, she represented America. She was made in America. She was part of America. When he stepped on her deck, he would be as good as home.

At six twenty-five p.m., Garcia's sailboat pulled away from *Hake* and the Americans' moment of repatriation arrived. At six fifty, the Filipino fishermen skillfully placed the second sailboat alongside *Hake*, and the twenty-nine Americans, led by Lieutenant Williams, clambered aboard the submarine under the watchful eye of her chief boatswain's mate.

The chief inspected the rescued airmen before they descended through the pressure hatch into the bowels of the submarine. He groused to all within earshot that his new passengers had spent too much time in the jungle. He made most of the rescued fliers, irrespective of rank, strip to their skivvies and throw their soiled clothes overboard. The chief didn't like Will's sandals either; he handed him a new pair and pitched his old sandals into the sea. By eight fifty-six p.m., *Hake* and the two guerrilla sailboats had parted company. Under the command of Lieutenant R. F. Heysinger, *Hake*'s communications officer, *Hake*'s machinists shifted the boat from battery power to engine propulsion, and *Hake*'s air-breathing diesel engines rumbled to life. Slowly accelerating on the surface to sixteen knots, *Hake* took up a course of 195 degrees and headed to her home away from home, the American submarine base at Fremantle, Australia, with her cargo of grateful airmen.

Belowdecks, *Hake* had the look and feel of a crowded subway car. Taking on the twenty-nine rescued airmen had increased her normal complement of eighty men by nearly 40 percent. The refugees queued up in the narrow passageways for cups of soup and for hot showers and shaves, and the submariners distributed clean clothing to all. Will was surprised to learn that the submarine uniform belowdecks for all hands under way in the tropics was boxer shorts and a T-shirt. The rescued men sat down in the enlisted men's mess area to eat in shifts, and the submariners' chow exceeded the airmen's wildest expectations. Cooks doled out generous portions of roast chicken, mashed potatoes, carrots and peas, gravy, olives, coffee, and, for dessert, pineapple ice cream. After dinner, *Hake*'s officer of the deck ordered, "Darken ship," and the submariners doused all white lights, bathing all hands in the bloody glow of red battle lanterns.

On departing Tablas Strait, *Hake* cruised east of Palawan Island and sailed down the center of the Sulu Sea. On December 7, 1944, the third anniversary of the Pearl Harbor attack, she navigated the shoal-obstructed waters of Tawi-Tawi Island and transited Sibutu Passage. In two days, she had traveled five hundred nautical miles from Panay, but she had two thousand more nautical miles to go.

The voyage to Fremantle was a military operation, not a pleasure cruise. Commander Haylor assigned the rescued airmen collateral duties and placed them on the watch schedule. Bill Shackelford became an assistant encoding and decoding officer and stood watch as an extra lookout on the bridge of the conning tower. But none of the airmen missed a meal or the chance to sleep. They ate in shifts and slept in shifts, "hot-bunking" in racks recently vacated by the submariners going on watch. When not eating or sleeping, the airmen loitered in nooks and passageways. They quizzed the crew about the boat's unfamiliar gauges, levers, switches, and valves. They played cards or dice, or squeezed themselves among the pipes and conduit to read books or magazines, or to write the letters they would mail home when they reached Fremantle.

As December 7 became December 8, *Hake* passed northwest of Celebes island and turned south into the Makassar Strait between Celebes and Borneo. At five forty a.m. on December 8, while running on the surface, *Hake* made landfall on Borneo, an island where Japan still possessed potent air and ground forces despite her recent military reverses in the Philippines. At about eight forty a.m. on December 8, *Hake*'s radar operator detected enemy aircraft closing rapidly from the direction of the island, which lay roughly forty-four miles to the west. *Hake*'s officer of the deck ordered an emergency dive and sounded general quarters. By eight forty-eight, *Hake* was running submerged at a depth of 150 feet.

Will had been asleep in his borrowed rack when *Hake*'s general quarters Klaxon sounded. The horn had jolted him awake. He had rolled out of his bed and dropped to the deck into a crowd of other sleepy, confused airmen. Shackelford had been in the officers' head shaving; his first impulse was to run, but there was no place to go. Submariners rushed fore and aft through the compartments, jostling past the startled airmen to reach their battle stations. With consternation and no little claustrophobia, Will watched the submariners shut the watertight hatches at each end of his compartment and dog the hatches. The air pressure rose slightly in Will's ears, confirming that he was now sealed within his space. Will stopped one of the submariners and asked whether this was a drill. Before the sailor could reply, Commander Haylor's voice crackled over the boat's 1MC and gave Will the unwelcome answer.

"Radar has detected multiple bogies approaching from Borneo," Haylor calmly reported. "The boat must dive and take evasive action." Haylor requested that his guests remain where they were and follow the instructions of the submariners in their compartments. "Please remain quiet, minimize movement about the boat to conserve oxygen, and find something solid you can hold on to," Haylor advised.

Will climbed back into his bunk, disbelieving. To die now by drowning aboard this submarine after all he had been through seemed the cruelest possible twist of fate.

Haylor's advice proved sound. At eight fifty a.m., a Mitsubishi F1M reconnaissance seaplane, known as a Pete, attacked *Hake* with bombs. The detonations were muffled at first, but they grew progressively louder as the Pete seemed to zero in on *Hake*'s position. Will lay on his back with his eyes closed, gripping the metal frame of his rack. He sensed *Hake* gently rolling from side to side as she changed course to confound her attacker. There was absolutely nothing Will could do. He was out of his element. Only luck mattered now. Even Commander Haylor had to guess from which direction the enemy airplane might attack next, and Haylor did not guess correctly every time. A bomb from a second aerial attack that developed at ten twelve a.m. erupted close by *Hake*, and the submarine shuddered. Will's metal rack swayed on its chains; the boat's battle lanterns flickered and her deckplates rattled. Will tensed for the next explosion. He expected to see the metal skin of *Hake*'s hull crack open above him and spring a high-pressure leak that would be impossible to contain. The spray of water would be the last thing he would see. But the bombing suddenly ceased, and Commander Haylor ordered his crew to secure from general quarters.

When the bombing stopped, the only perceptible sounds in Will's compartment were the hum of *Hake*'s machinery and the relieved murmurs of the other men nearby. The submarine had become suffocatingly hot. Soaked in sweat, Will rolled out of his bunk and stood weak-kneed in the passageway. One of the young submariners in the compartment grinned at him. "Bombing ain't too bad, sir," the submariner said reassuringly. "Airplanes can't stay overhead as long as ships. The bastards have flown off, I'll bet." Will was too drained of emotion to reply. In all his wartime experience, he had never been as frightened as he was in the rack that morning aboard *Hake*, not even during his terrifying final torpedo run on *Musashi*. That night, *Hake* surfaced, and the men took turns climbing to the conning tower bridge to inhale the fresh salt air. Will and Bill Shackelford were among them, glad to be alive.

By December 12, *Hake* had closed to within a few hundred miles of Darwin on the northern coast of Australia, and, for the balance of her run to Fremantle, the submarine sailed beneath the umbrella of Allied air cover. Tension eased aboard the boat, and *Hake*'s crew and passengers, like schoolchildren anticipating a holiday, looked forward to arriving in Fremantle. On December 15 at six twenty p.m., while running on the surface in the balmy light of a summer's evening— December is high summer in the southern latitudes—*Hake* exchanged recognition signals with an Australian Beaufighter, a long-range, twin-engine fighter occasionally used by the British as a torpedo bomber. On December 16 at six fifty-six a.m., *Hake* maneuvered carefully through the antisubmarine nets outside Perth Harbor and entered the estuary of the Swan River. There, she moored outboard of the submarine tender *Barbel* at Number Three Wharf, Fremantle.

Hake's executive officer, Lieutenant Commander J. C. Weatherwax, presented a certificate to each of the rescued airmen who filed off the boat in Fremantle. The certificate bore the signature of Commander Haylor and Weatherwax and read:

"Know ye that the above named 'ZOOMIE' did, on a certain date, in a certain area, while hedgehopping and flathatting about in the 'wild blue yonder,' in a flying machine, well knowing said machine to be of an unsafe and dangerous nature, allow himself to be most ignominiously and thoroughly shot down by the enemy, thus bathing in the ocean, being out of uniform the while; nor was it even yet Saturday night. . . . Be it recorded, however, that the above named 'FLY-FLY' did, though unwillingly, serve, after a fashion, on board a SUBMA-RINE of UNCLE SAMMY'S UNDERWATER FLEET, namely the U.S. HAKE (SS-256), in enemy controlled waters, from 5 December 1944 to 16 December inclusive, and did acquit himself well; that is as well as one might expect a clipped sparrow to acquit himself if forced to live in a sardine can immersed in a fishbowl."

Will walked off the *Hake* on December 16 weighing 120 pounds. He and the other rescued navy personnel, including Williams and his aircrew, Shackelford, Ritchie, and McAdams and his two crewmen, reported to the naval station for physical examinations and a round of intelligence debriefings. The officers were housed in the submariners' rest home, a large hotel-like facility with views of the sea and lush gardens of palms, banana trees, and bougainvillea. The men collected their back pay and fattened themselves on milk and ice cream while they awaited orders and transportation stateside. Will toured the city of Perth with Williams and the others but declined to buy one of the matching flowered shirts Williams had urged everyone to purchase as a souvenir of their time together at Libertad and on the *Hake*.

Will telegraphed his sisters that he was safe. He was a little disappointed to learn on his return to the United States that they didn't know he was missing. Apparently the chief of naval personnel had never sent a telegram to his next of kin informing them he was missing in action. The official telegram advising Will's sisters he had been "returned to United States Naval jurisdiction" and that "the Navy Department rejoices with you at this good news" did not arrive until January 26, 1945, after Will had returned home.

The rescued airmen spent the Christmas holidays in Perth. There were no Christmas trees for sale in Perth, so Will Fletcher and Bill Shackelford borrowed a car and harvested a fir tree from a city park. They hauled the tree back to the rest home, and the indulgent Australian matron who managed the home found bits of colored ribbon and other trinkets with which the boys decorated the tree. On Christmas Eve, 1944, Will attended a candlelight service of verses and carols in an Anglican church in a quiet section of the city. He sat in the pew among strangers and listened to the prophecies of hope and new beginnings, as he had as a child. When the sanctuary grew dark and the candles were lit, he joined the parishioners in singing "Silent Night." Holding a flickering candle in his left hand, Will clutched in his right the lock of his mother's hair that he had carried with him throughout his Pacific ordeal.

The navy did not attempt to convert Commander Coleman's battle-weary torpedo plane and dive-bomber pilots to Hellcat pilots. *Intrepid* weighed anchor at Ulithi on December 2 and set sail for Pearl Harbor, via Eniwetok, with VT-18 and VB-18 safely on board. The ship arrived at Pearl Harbor ten days later, and Commander Coleman announced to his air group that the crippled carrier could not be repaired in Hawaii and would be ordered home to Alameda. This news precipitated twenty-four-hour-a-day celebrations among the Carrier Clowns and Sunday Punchers. Air Group 18's pilots had taken their "liquor mess" with them when they left Hawaii in August; the liquor bottles were stored aboard the carrier in a steel locker, the door to which had been welded shut. With Commander Coleman's permission (and a stern warning that abuse would not be tolerated), the seal was broken and the whiskey flowed freely. The torpeckers were genuinely sorry for their VF-18 buddies still on the line aboard *Hancock*, but not sorry enough to curb their enthusiasm for going home. On December 20, *Intrepid* passed under the Golden Gate Bridge, and Kenny Barden made a final entry in his diary: "With Frisco in sight what more can be said."

EPILOGUE

★ ★ ★ ★ ★

The Japanese government was loath to admit the loss of *Musashi*. The survivors, approximately twelve hundred of them, were detained for a time at Corregidor. Ultimately, 150 of *Musashi*'s survivors volunteered for infantry duty in the Philippines as the "Kato Regiment"; at least 120 of these sailors died while fighting with the Japanese army in defense of Manila. The balance of *Musashi*'s survivors were shipped home to Japan, but their ordeal was not over. An American submarine torpedoed a Japanese freighter carrying about 420 *Musashi* survivors and sank it; only about 370 of these men were pulled from the water. When the remaining survivors finally reached their homeland, most were confined to islands in the Seto Inland Sea to prevent them from disclosing *Musashi*'s sinking.

In postwar analyses of the sinking of *Musashi*, U.S. Navy investigators concluded that torpedoes had inflicted the fatal damage, not bombs. They also concluded that the navy's standard hammer-and-anvil torpedo attack, in which torpedo bombers assaulted both flanks of the enemy warship, was not the most effective tactic. Torpedoing both flanks permitted damage-control engineers to counterflood more effectively and keep the ship upright. Based on the later sinking of *Yamato*, investigators recommended concentrating all torpedo attacks on one side of the target; attacking one side overcame the compensating effects of counterflooding and caused the ship to capsize more quickly.

Aerial torpedo attack, VT-18's specialty, did not last much longer. The Battle of Leyte Gulf, known at the time as the Second Battle of the Philippine Sea, was both the high-water mark and the final curtain of aerial torpedo attacks on capital ships (except for the sinking of *Musashi*'s sister ship, *Yamato*, on her one-way suicide mission to Okinawa in April 1945). Torpedo runs were extraordinarily hazardous, and a high number of hits was required to sink a well-armored warship. During the immediate postwar years, the U.S. Navy continued to build new versions of carrier-based warplanes capable of carrying torpedoes, such as the Martin AM Mauler, but none was used in naval combat. (In the Korean War, the U.S. Navy dropped torpedoes from propeller-driven AD Skyraiders in an effort to destroy a hydroelectric dam; this attack was an inspired use of torpedoes but not one for which the weapons had been designed.) The advent of jet-powered aircraft and missiles rendered torpedo-bombers obsolete.

Commander William E. Ellis rose to vice admiral, commanded the 6th Fleet in the Mediterranean during the 1964 confrontation between Greece and Turkey, and served as chief of staff to the Supreme Allied Commander, Atlantic. Ellis died in New York in 1982. Many of VT-18's pilots remained in the navy after the war, or continued to fly in the Naval Air Reserve. Lloyd Van Antwerp retired as a rear admiral after a thirty-year career, which included command of the naval air station at Roosevelt Roads, Puerto Rico. Bud Williams, who survived at least twenty carrier combat missions and a ditching at sea, was killed in an automobile accident in the 1950s. Ken Barden obtained a degree in aeronautical engineering from California Polytechnic Institute, retired as a commander, worked for Boeing Aircraft Company for a time, and later headed the science department at Louisiana State University. Ken and Margie raised a daughter and a son; the latter, Ken Jr., served as a marine sniper in Vietnam. Will Fletcher returned to Illinois intent on making the navy a career and married Faye Emily Frickenstein, the homecoming queen of Edwardsville High School, class of 1943, who seemed oblivious initially to Will's charms and his status as a war hero. Faye and Fletch raised three children, and Fletch retired from the navy as a captain, having last served as assistant chief of staff for the Naval Air Technical Training Command. He became the director of Memphis International Airport and was the rising chair of the Airport Operators Council International when he died in 1985. Ben St. John left the navy, but not before marrying a pretty navy

WAVE whom he had met while on active duty, and obtained a degree in electrical engineering from the University of Cincinnati. He worked as an engineer for Grumman Aircraft Engineering Corporation on various aircraft designs and weapons systems and retired to Long Island. Lloyd Karch left the navy and retired to California with his wife, Betty, after a career in the pharmaceutical industry. Bill Bates and Vernon Sistrunk made the navy a career, and Squatty Vaughn and Kurt Schonthaler flew in the Naval Reserve for a number of years after the war.

Of the twenty-eight pilots who put to sea with VT-18 aboard *Intrepid* in August 1944, fifteen were awarded Navy Crosses for their torpedo attacks against Japanese fleet units between October 24 and 26. The Navy Cross is the navy's highest award for valor in combat, second in precedence only to the Medal of Honor. I have listed VT-18's recipients of the Navy Cross in the appendix. The Navy Cross citations for VT-18's pilots speak of "extraordinary heroism," of "disregard for personal safety," of "outstanding airmanship and courage," and of "boldly flying through intense antiaircraft fire to press home the attack." Several pilots, such as Ken Barden and Ben St. John, also received Air Medals or Distinguished Flying Crosses for their exploits over Formosa and in the Visayas. Virtually all of the squadron's enlisted aircrew received Air Medals for exceptional performance in combat.

I have not calculated the total number of medals for bravery, or medals for bravery per capita, awarded to VT-18 as compared with other squadrons. I suspect my subjects would fare quite well in such statistical comparisons, but I also suspect they would disapprove of them. The men of VT-18 viewed themselves as ordinary people who simply did their job in the face of extraordinary danger, no more deserving than any other serviceman who diligently performed his duty within range of the enemy's guns. As with most men and women who have experienced combat, they were glad merely to have survived the ordeal. My father and Ben St. John, I know, regarded those who did not return as the real heroes.

But the pilots of VT-18—and their fellow carrier pilots in the Pacific and European theaters—were different from ordinary mortals, of course. They had learned how to fly a complex war machine. They accepted the day-to-day risks of carrier operations and willingly assailed the enemy in fair weather and foul, knowing that they might be shot out of the sky on any mission or fail to find the ship on their return. To hurtle low over the earth and pass through a blizzard of enemy fire to deliver your ordnance requires a special form of courage. It is the willingness of such men to sacrifice that continues to fascinate and inspire us. The men of VT-18—and of the other torpedo squadrons of the 3rd and 7th Fleets that tangled with the Imperial Japanese Navy off the Philippine Islands in the autumn of 1944—were a special breed of naval aviator, and they did their country a great service. Neither the words of their citations nor mine in this book can truly do their bravery justice.

—Greg Fletcher
Memphis, 2012

ACKNOWLEDGMENTS

★ ★ ★ ★ ★

Although writing is a monastic endeavor, publishing is a cooperative enterprise. I am very fortunate to have had a skilled team of professionals to help bring this narrative to life. I thank James D. Hornfischer, an award-winning naval historian and literary agent, for sensing potential in my submission and encouraging me to write the broader story of Torpedo 18; Brent Howard, my editor at Penguin, for his gentle criticisms and his patient guidance throughout the process; Tiffany Yates Martin, my copy editor, for her sharp eye and sensible questions; Lum Pennington for her well-executed maps and line drawings; and Barrett Tillman, perhaps the foremost authority on World War II naval aviation, for reviewing the manuscript and offering technical corrections and comments. They did their best; any errors that remain in this work are mine alone.

I extend special thanks to Ben St. John, Ken Barden Jr., Peggy Paulson, Bill Shackelford, Ed Auld, and Mildred Schonthaler for generously sharing their documents, photographs, memories, and anecdotes, materials that greatly humanized the historical record. For facilitating my access to the historical record, I thank the courteous and helpful staff of NARA at College Park, Maryland; NARA is an agency of which every American citizen can be proud. I thank David Dickson, a former colleague of the Memphis Bar and a recognized expert on the Imperial Japanese Navy, for sharing his personal collection of archive materials and directing me to various sources related to *Musashi* and *Yamato*, and Keith Schap, an author and former professor of English literature, for his review and comment on an early draft. Last, I thank again my wife, Carolyn, who suffered long stretches of quasi-widowhood as this book came together, but who was unfailingly committed to the story and my true partner in the process.

GGF

APPENDIX OF AWARDS

Torpedo Squadron 18 Roster and Awards

★ ★ ★ ★ ★

Of the twenty-eight VT-18 pilots who departed Hawaii in August 1944 aboard *Intrepid*, fifteen were awarded the Navy Cross, the navy's highest award for valor in combat. In the hierarchy of military awards for bravery, the Navy Cross is second only to the Medal of Honor. The Navy Crosses were all awarded for action against the Japanese fleet between October 24 and 26, 1944. In this appendix, those VT-18 officers who received the Navy Cross are identified by the notation "NC"; the date of the action for which each received the Navy Cross is in parentheses.

At least three other VT-18 pilots received a Silver Star, and five others received a Distinguished Flying Cross. At least two pilots, Joe Rubin and Ben St. John, received a Navy Cross *and* a Distinguished Flying Cross. Those VT-18 officers who received the Silver Star are identified with the notation "SS"; those who received the Distinguished Flying Cross are identified by the notation "DFC." (Some pilots may have received additional awards after the date of the 1945 letter that is the primary source for this appendix.)

More than forty-five of VT-18's aircrewmen, nearly the entire complement, received an Air Medal. This appendix lists those crewmen who were Air Medal recipients.

VT-18's roster changed over time, as is evident from this book. This appendix lists all officers who were assigned to VT-18 during the period July 1943 through November 1944, or for part of that period, and who served as pilots. Those officers killed in training are identified by the notation "KIT." Those officers who deployed with the squadron aboard *Intrepid* in August 1944 are identified by an asterisk. Those officers who replaced pilots lost after the squadron deployed aboard *Intrepid* in August 1944 are identified by the notation "RPL." Those officers killed in action are identified by the notation "KIA."

This appendix lists only those VT-18 enlisted personnel who were KIT or KIA, or who were Air Medal recipients; this is not a complete roster of all VT-18 enlisted personnel.

The sources for KIT and KIA are Torpedo 18's squadron history, and Carrier Air Group 18 aircraft-action reports. Sources for awards and citations are: Letter of July 6, 1945, commander, First Carrier Task Force, Pacific, to commander, Carrier Air Group 18, Awards; Navy Cross indexes and lists, World War II, www .homeofheros.com.

VT-18 Pilots

Lieutenant Junior Grade Kenneth P. Barden,* NC (10/25)

Lieutenant Junior Grade William C. Bates,* NC (10/25)

Lieutenant Junior Grade Robert Brisbin* (Disabled, 8/25/44)

Lieutenant Leo M. Christensen, KIT

Lieutenant Vernon A. Delaney*

Ensign Paul Dilgren, RPL (DFC)

Lieutenant Junior Grade Frank D. Doyle,* NC (10/25)

Lieutenant Junior Grade Stephen Dragan, KIT

Ensign Willard M. Fletcher,* NC (10/24)

Lieutenant Junior Grade Marvin Perry Horton, KIT

Lieutenant Junior Grade Lloyd E. Karch,* NC (10/24)

Ensign Daniel Laner,* KIA

Lieutenant Albert J. Long* (DFC)

Ensign Lyman A. Matthews, KIT

Lieutenant Junior Grade John T. McKee,* NC (10/26)

Lieutenant Junior Grade Donald W. Morris,* NC (10/24)

Ensign Ralph N. O'Donnell, RPL

Lieutenant Junior Grade Robert E. Olson,* NC (10/25)

Lieutenant Junior Grade Donald B. Pieper,* SS

Ensign Nicholas T. Redeye, RPL

Ensign Charles D. Relyea, RPL

Lieutenant George B. Riley,* NC (10/24)

Lieutenant John Lewis Robinson, KIT

Ensign Nicholas J. Roccaforte,* KIA

Lieutenant Junior Grade Joseph L. Rubin,* NC (10/25) DFC

Lieutenant Junior Grade John Joseph Savage,* KIA

Lieutenant Junior Grade Kurt W. Schonthaler,* (DFC)

Ensign Richard M. Schoubee, RPL

Ensign Vernon J. Sistrunk,* NC (10/26)

Lieutenant Junior Grade Raymond J. Skelly,* KIA

Lieutenant Junior Grade Thomas P. Spaulding,* (DFC)

Ensign Bernard J. St. John,* NC (10/24) DFC

Ensign Ralph R. Ursch,* SS

Lieutenant Commander Lloyd W. Van Antwerp,* NC (10/24)

Lieutenant Junior Grade Leon S. Vannais,* SS

Lieutenant Junior Grade Elmer B. Vaughn,* DFC

Ensign Donald E. Wallenback, RPL

Lieutenant John G. Williams,* NC (10/26)

Ensign Owen F. Williams,* NC (10/26)

Ensign Luther L. Zeigler, RPL

VT-18 Aircrew

AIR MEDAL RECIPIENTS (BY RATE)

ACOM W. M. Crenshaw

AOM1c J. Dixon

AOM1c R. C. Hoy

AOM1c L. L. Spain Jr.

AOM2c D. F. Brooks

AOM2c I. A. Dugas

AOM2c R. J. Hanzak

AOM2c D. S. Hudson

AOM2c M. W. Johnson

AOM2c R. W. Jones
AOM2c F. E. Kingsbury
AOM2c J. F. Knoop
AOM2c F. G. Krause
AOM2c W. T. Lalor
AOM2c H. E. McCollum
AOM2c A. A. Royce
AOM2c W. H. Russell
AOM2c J. J. Schmitz
AOM2c R. L. Wagner
AOM3c P. D. Jernigan
ARM1c I I. B. Erminger
ARM1c S. E. Garber
ARM2c C. A. Balascio
ARM2c F. Bellamy
ARM2c J. M. Cammarata
ARM2c A. M. Cepon
ARM2c H. E. McCoy
ARM2c C. M. McLerran
ARM2c R. L. Miller
ARM2c R. A. Stein
ARM2c W. H. Stephenson
ARM3c A. C. Aasgard
ARM3c J. C. Beeson
ARM3c G. T. Bonner
ARM3c C. W. Fort
ARM3c T. James
ARM3c G. G. Jesperson
ARM3c D. R. Koegler
ARM3c A. Okicich
ARM3c M. E. Pellish
ARM3c G. Schrier
ARM3c G. W. Wallace
AMM3c R. E. Huber
AEM1c E. J. Nink

VT-18 Aircrew Killed in Training and in Action

ARM3c F. V. McCann (KIT)

AOM3c J. S. Sirrine (KIT)

ARM3c E. J. Kwiatkowski (KIT)

ARM2c G. E. Siegrist (KIT)

AOM2c G. H. Stewart (KIT)

ARM2c W. P. Young (KIT)

AOM3c W. H. Besoain (KIT)

ARM2c A. P. Rybarczyk (KIA)

AOM2c O. A. Sharninghouse (KIA)

ARM2c A. B. Lankford (KIA)

AOM3c F. R. Krantz (KIA)

ARM3c B. G. Hunter (KIA)

ARM2c B. B. Galbreath (KIA)

AOM2c W. J. Telliard (KIA)

ARM3c R. G. Westmoreland (KIA)

AMM2c G. E. Christman (KIA)

ARM2c C. M. McLerran (KIA)

AOM2c R. W. Jones (KIA)

AMM3c H. H. Schnack (KIA in 11/25 kamikaze attack)

BIBLIOGRAPHY

★ ★ ★ ★ ★

Books

Baldwin, Hanson. *Sea Fights and Shipwrecks*. New York: Alfred A. Knopf, 1955.

"The Battle for Leyte Gulf," reprinted by permission, *Combat Pacific Theater*. New York: Dell, 1958.

Beasley, W. G. *The Japanese Experience*. London: University of California Press, 1999.

Bix, Herbert. *Hirohito and the Making of Modern Japan*. New York: Harper-Collins, 2000.

Cavendish, Marshall. *Encyclopedia of World Geography*. London: 1994.

Churchill, Winston S. *The Second World War, Vol. I and II*. New York: Time Incorporated, 1959.

Cray, Ed. *General of the Army: George C. Marshall, Soldier and Statesman*. New York: Cooper Square Press, 1990.

Cutter, Thomas J. *Battle of Leyte Gulf*. New York: HarperCollins, 1994.

Doll, T. E., and B. R. Jackson. *Grumman TBF/TBM Avenger*. Fallbrook, California: Aero Publishers, 1970.

Drendel, Lou. *Walk Around, TBM/TBF Avenger*. Carrollton, Texas: Squadron Signal Publications, 2001.

Drury, Bob and Tom Clavin. *Halsey's Typhoon*. New York: Grove Press, 2007.

Emerson, Bill, and Kathy Emerson, ed. *The Voices of Bombing Nineteen*. (August 1993), (Records of George T. Lewis III).

Foot, M. R. D., and I. C. B. Dear, ed. *The Oxford Companion to World War II*. New York: Oxford University Press, 1995.

Forsyth, John F. *Helldivers. U.S. Navy Dive Bombers at War*: Osceola, Florida: Motorbooks International, 1991.

Francillon, R. J. *Japanese Aircraft of the Pacific War*. New York: Funk & Wagnalls, 1970.

Friedman, Kenneth. *Afternoon of the Rising Sun*. Novato, California: Presidio Press, 2001.

Goodspeed, M. Hill, and Rick Burgess. *U.S. Naval Aviation*. Hong Kong: Hugh Lauter Levin Associates, 2001.

Hoffman, Jon T. *Chesty*. New York: Random House, 2001.

Hornfischer, James D. *The Last Stand of the Tin Can Sailors*. New York: Bantam Dell, 2004.

———. *Ship of Ghosts*. New York: Bantam Dell, 2007.

———. *Neptune's Inferno*. New York: Random House, 2011.

Hoyt, Edwin P. *Battle of Leyte Gulf*. New York: Weybright and Talley, 1972.

Hynes, Samuel. *Flights of Passage*. New York: Frederic C. Bile, 1988.

Inoguchi, Rikihei, Tadashi Nakajima, and Roger Pineau. *The Divine Wind*. Annapolis, Maryland: Naval Institute Press, 1958.

Ireland, Bernard. *Leyte Gulf 1944*. New York: Osprey Publishing, 2006.

Jackson, B. R. and T. E. Doll. *Grumman TBF/TBM Avenger*. Fallbrook: Aero Publishers, 1970.

Johnson, Francis. *U.S. Navy Pre-Flight School, Athens, Georgia*. Philadelphia: Campers Publishing, 1943 (Records of W. M. Fletcher).

Kenney, George C. *General Kenney Reports, a Personal History of the Pacific War*. New York: Duell, Sloan & Pierce, 1949.

Kinzey, Bert. *TBF & TBM Avenger*. Carrollton, Texas: Squadron/Signal Publications, 1997.

Lundstrom, John B. *The First Team*. Annapolis, Maryland: Naval Insitute Press, 1984.

MacArthur, Douglas. *Decisive Battles of World War II, Leyte Gulf*. Ed. Peter Young. New York: Gallery Books, 1989.

Manchester, William. *American Caesar*. New York: Little, Brown, 1978.

Matsumoto, Kitaro, and Mastaka Chihaya. *Design and Construction of the* Yamato *and* Musashi. Reprinted by permission from U.S. Naval Institute Proceedings, October 1953.

Miller, Nathan. *The U.S. Navy, An Illustrated History*. Annapolis, Maryland: Naval Institute Press, 1977.

Morison, Samuel E. *History of United States Naval Operations in World War II*, vols. XII, XIII, and XV. Boston: Little, Brown, 1958.

——. *The Two-Ocean War: A Short History of the United States Navy and the Second World War*. New York: Little, Brown, 1963.

Mrazek, Robert J. *A Dawn Like Thunder*. New York: Little, Brown, 2008.

Nelson, Craig. *The First Heroes*. New York: Penguin Group, 2002.

Nish, Ian. *A Short History of Japan*. New York: Frederick A. Praeger, 1968.

Nourse, Mary. *Kodo: The Way of the Emperor*. New York: Bobs-Merrill, 1940.

O'Hara, V. P., Dickson, W. D., Worth, Richard. *On Seas Contested*. Annapolis, Maryland: Naval Institute Press, 2010.

Okumiya, Masatake, Jiro Horikohi, and Martin Caidin. *Zero!* New York: Ballantine Books, 1957.

Phillips, Christopher. *Steichen at War*. New York: Harry N. Abrams, 1981.

Polmer, Norman. *Aircraft Carriers, A Graphic History of Carrier Aviation and Its Influence on World Events*. New York: Doubleday & Company, 1969.

Prange, Gordon W. *At Dawn We Slept*. New York: Penguin, 1982.

——. *Miracle at Midway*. New York: McGraw Hill, 1982.

Roberts, John. *The Aircraft Carrier Intrepid*. Annapolis, Maryland: Naval Institute Press, 1986.

Rottman, Gordon. *World War II Pacific Island Guide: A Geo-Military Study*. London: Greenwood Press, 2002.

Rowthorn, Chris. *Philippines*. Victoria, Canada: Lonely Planet, 2003.

Sheftall, M. G. *Blossoms in the Wind: Human Legacies of the Kamikaze*. New York: NAL Caliber, 2005.

Smith, Peter C. *Curtis SB2C Helldiver*. Ramsbury: Crowood Press Ltd., 2004.

Spector, Ronald H. *Eagle against the Sun*. New York: Free Press McMillan, 1985.

Stamp, L. Dudley. *Asia*. New York: E. P. Dutton & Company, Inc., 1938.

Stewart, Adrian. *Battle of Leyte Gulf*. New York: Charles Scribner's Sons, 1979.

Sumral, Robert. *U.S.S. Intrepid (CV-11)*. Missoula, Montana: Pictorial Histories Publishing Company, 1989.

Swanborough, Gordon, and Peter M. Bowers. *United States Navy Aircraft Since 1911*. England: Funk & Wagnalls, 1968.

Thomas, Evan. *Sea of Thunder*. New York: Simon & Schuster, 2006.

Tillman, Barrett. *Avenger at War*. Annapolis, Maryland: Naval Institute Press, 1980.

——. *Clash of the Carriers*. New York: NAL Caliber, 2006.

——. *Hellcat: The F6F in World War II*. Annapolis: Naval Institute Press, 1979.

Toland, John. *The Rising Sun: The Rise and Fall of the Japanese Empire*, vols. I and II. New York: Random House, 1970.

Willoughby, Charles A., and John Chamberlain. *MacArthur, 1941–1951*. New York: McGraw Hill, 1954.

Wolfert, Ira. *American Guerrilla in the Philippines*. New York: Simon & Schuster, 1945.

Woodward, C. Vann. *The Battle for Leyte Gulf*. New York: Skyhorse Publishing, 2007.

Yoshimura, Akira. *Battleship Musashi*. Tokyo: Kodansha International, 1991.

Zollo, Anthony F. *Day by Day: Accounts of the Carrier* Intrepid *in World War II*. Virginia Beach, Virginia: Donning Company, 2001.

——. *U.S.S. Intrepid*. Paducah, Kentucky: Turner Publishing, 1993.

Articles

Alameda Naval Air Museum. "NAS History." http://www.alamedanavalair museum.org/History/NAS.aspx.

Dickson, W. David. "IJN *Yamato*." *Warship International* 4, 1975, pp. 294–318.

"Edwardsville Flyer Home, Saved by Filipino Fighters." *Edwardsville Intelligencer*, February 20, 1945, p. 1C.

Hackett, Bob and Sander Kingsepp. "Tabular Records of Movement: *Atago, Chokai, Haruna, Kongo, Kumano, Musashi, Nagato, Noshiro, Tone, Suzuya, Yamato*." http//www.combinedfleet.com[Ship Name]

Hancock, Orville. "New Airport Director Aviation Gives Him a Full, Busy Life." *Memphis Press Scimitar*, September 16, 1975.

Mazza, Eugene. "USS *Growler* SS-215 Sixth War Patrol." Submarine Sailor Dot Com, June 2007, http://www.submarinesailor.com/boats/ss215growler/patrolno6/growlerpatrolno6.asp.

Murray State College. *College News*, January 1943.

National Museum of the United States Air Force. "U.S. Air Force Fact Sheet, Bliss-Leavitt Mark 13 Aerial Torpedo." http://www.nationalmuseum.af .mil/factsheets/factsheet_print.asp?fsid=1035&page=1

Obituary of William E. Ellis, *New York Times*, 1982. http://www.nytimes
.com/1982/09/30/obituaries/vice-adm-william-ellis-74-ex-chief-of-staff-in-
atlantic (retrieved May 30, 2009).

"Reunion Brings Memories of Philippine Adventures." *Gosport*. Naval Air Station, Pensacola, Florida, February 11, 1966.

Schubert, Mary. "Navy Veteran Tells about WWII." *Pasadena Star News*. May
29, 2000, pp. A1, A6.

USN/USMC Combat Loss Forms/Accident Reports: Lieutenant Junior Grade
Stephen Dragan, Ensign Daniel Laner, Ensign Willard M. Fletcher, Lieutenant Junior Grade James Ritchie, Lieutenant Junior Grade John J. Savage;
Lieutenant Junior Grade Raymond Skelly. http://www.accident-report
.com/navy/html, September 10, 2011.

Wood, Lewis. "U.S. Defeats Japanese Navy; All Foes Ships in One Fleet Hit;
Many Sunk; Battle Continues." *New York Times*. October 26, 1944, p. A1.

Primary Sources

Interview, Mr. Edward Auld (Friend of Lloyd E. Karch, VT-18)

Interview, Colonel Kenneth P. Barden Jr. (Son of Commander Kenneth P.
Barden, VT-18)

Interview, Mrs. Faye E. Fletcher (Wife of Captain Willard M. Fletcher, VT-18)

Interview, Captain Willard M. Fletcher, USNR (VT-18)

Interview, Mrs. Betty Karch (Wife of Lloyd E. Karch, VT-18)

Interview, Mr. John Kiselak (VT-10)

Interview, Mr. Robert McAdams (VT-19)

Interview, Mr. Daniel Nygaard (VF-18)

Interview, Mrs. Betty Jane Paul (Sister of Captain Willard M. Fletcher, VT-18)

Interview, Ms. Peggy Paulson (Daughter of Commander Kenneth P. Barden,
VT-18)

Interview, Mr. Wallace Russell (VT-18)

Interview, Mrs. Mildred Schonthaler (Wife of Kurt W. Schonthaler, VT-18)

Interviews and statement, Mr. William G. Shackelford (VF-28)

Interview, Mr. Steve Sistrunk (Son of Commander Vernon J. Sistrunk, VT-18)

Interviews and statement, Mr. Bernard J. St. John (VT-18)

Interview, Mr. Gerald Van Antwerp (Son of Rear Admiral Lloyd W. Van Antwerp, VT-18)

Letters of Cadet W. M. Fletcher to mother, Naomi Fletcher, November 21, 1942, through March 10, 1943 (Records of Betty Jane Paul and Faye E. Fletcher)

Diary of Lieutenant Junior Grade Kenneth P. Barden, VT-18, *Intrepid* (February 26, 1944, through December 20, 1944) (Records of Colonel Kenneth P. Barden Jr.)

Diary of Lieutenant Junior Grade George T. Lewis, VT-19 Intelligence Officer, *Lexington* (Excerpts, August 29, 1944, through November 20, 1944), (Records of George T. Lewis III)

Archival and Official Sources

Captain W. M. Fletcher, USNR Ret., Personnel Record Excerpts and Personal Papers:

Aviators Flight Logbook, Ensign W. M. Fletcher

"Short snorter" (a two-dollar bill on which, as was the custom, he recorded significant events and dates)

"The Slipstream, Mark IV, Ed." U.S. Naval Air Training Center, Corpus Christi: Aviation Cadet Regiment, 1944.

"History of USS *Intrepid* (CV-11)." Ship's Data Section, Public Information Division, Officer of Public Relations, Navy Department, February 1948 (Records of W. M. Fletcher).

Race, George. *Air Group Eighteen Combat History Aboard C.V. Intrepid, May to November 1944* (Unpublished history, including description of November 25, 1944, kamikaze attacks).

Johnson, Francis L. *United States Navy Pre-Flight School, Athens, Georgia.* Philadelphia: Campus Publishing Company, 1942–1943.

Department of the Navy, welcome-aboard brochure, USS *New Jersey* (BB-62), "Firepower for Freedom," 1990.

National Archives and Records Administration (College Park, Md.):

R.G. 24 Casualty Branch, missing-in-action reports, VT-18

R.G. 38 aircraft-action reports, Carrier Air Group 18

R.G. 38 deck log, U.S.S. *Hake*, SS-256, November 7, 1944, and December 5, 1944

R.G. 38 deck log, U.S.S. *Intrepid*, CV-11, August 1 through December 20, 1944

R.G. 80-G, photographic records of the United States Navy in World War II

Still Picture Branch Library, Aviation Training Division, Office of the Chief of Naval Operations, U.S. Navy. *Introduction to Naval Aviation*. OPNAV 33-NY-85, January 1946.

R.G. 313, records of Naval Operating Forces, commander, 2nd Carrier Task Force—administrative messages, operations plans, action reports, logs, board recommendations, 1944–1945

R.G. 407, G-1 Periodic Report No. 10, USAFFE 6th Mountain Division, October 1–31, 1944

R.G. 407, G-1 Periodic Report No. 11, USAFFE 6th Mountain Division, November 1–30, 1944

Allied Translator and Interpreter Section, Southwest Pacific Area, *Japanese Navy Operation Plans and Orders, 1941–1944, Sho Operations*. April 1945.

Commander Aircraft Battle Force. *Current Tactical Orders and Doctrine, U.S. Fleet Aircraft Vol. I. Carrier Aircraft USF 74*. Navy Department, March 1941

Headquarters of commander in chief, United States Fleet. *Current Tactical Orders and Doctrine U.S. Fleet USF 10A*. Navy Department, 1944.

U.S. naval technical mission to Japan, January 6, 1945:

Reports of damage to Japanese warships—*Yamato* (BB), *Musashi* (BB), *Taiho* (CV), *Shinano* (CV)

Japanese records of major warship losses

Japanese eighteen-inch gun mounts

Japanese projectiles—general types

National Museum of Naval Aviation, Emil Buehler Library, Pensacola. Florida, *Pilot's Handbook of Flight Operating Instructions, Navy Model TBM-3 Airplane*. Bureau of Aeronautics.

Papers of Lieutenant Commander Ernest Allen, Naval Historical Center

Race, George. *Air Group Eighteen Combat History Aboard C.V.* Intrepid, *May to November 1944* (Published history), (Records of Bernard J. St. John).

Silk Map, "Manila." Royal Australian Air Force Cartographic Section, September 1944 (Records of George T. Lewis III).

Roster of VT-18 officers, August to November 1944, with summaries of combat record and next of kin (Records of Bernard J. St. John and Lloyd E. Karch)

United States Naval Academy, *Lucky Bag*, class of 1930

United States Pacific Fleet Air Forces, Torpedo Squadron 18 history, July 1943–August 1944 (Records of Bernard J. St. John)

United States Pacific Fleet Air Forces, Torpedo Squadron 18, participation in the Second Battle of the Philippine Sea, October 24–26, 1944 (Records of Bernard J. St. John)

SOURCE NOTES

★ ★ ★ ★ ★

Ibegan this project too late, and for that I apologize to my subjects and the reader. By the time I decided to write the broader story of VT-18, I could locate only two surviving members of the squadron, Ben St. John and Wallace Russell, and only two of the twenty-nine airmen evacuated from Panay on *Hake*, William Shackelford and Robert McAdams. Regrettably, I missed talking with pilots Lloyd Karch and Vernon Sistrunk by only a few months (although Sistrunk's son, Steve, directed me to an Internet video of his father in which he describes his torpedo attack against *Musashi* during Strike 2 Baker). I was able to locate wives of squadron members, including Mildred Schonthaler and Betty Karch, and the children of squadron members, including Gerald Van Antwerp, Ken Barden Jr., and his sister, Peggy Paulson, all of whom generously shared their memories and photographs.

Ken Barden Jr. and Peggy Paulson furnished me with copies of their father's day-by-day wartime diary, which was an invaluable resource for better understanding the personalities and attitudes of many of the pilots in the squadron, as well as for fleshing out the events described laconically in the official aircraft action reports. Ed Auld, a teacher and close friend of the Karch family who has educated scores of California schoolchildren about Lloyd Karch's attack on *Musashi*, was unfailingly responsive to my requests for documents and other information about Karch's experiences. John Kiesalak, an Avenger radioman who served aboard *Intrepid* with VT-10 later in the war, happily described life in the "tunnel," and Dan Nygaard, a Hellcat pilot with VF-18, provided many details of life aboard the carrier. None of this primary research would have been possible without the patient assistance of my wife, Carolyn, whose Internet skills far exceed mine.

Will Fletcher, my father, died in 1985. As a child, I had become familiar with his heroics by reading newspaper accounts (preserved in a family scrapbook) of his attack on a Japanese battleship, his crash landing, his rescue by Filipino fishermen, his life among the Filipino guerrillas on Panay, and the sinking of the Japanese patrol boat. I had also seen his Navy Cross citation, which he had framed and hung in his study. But it was not until I became a naval aviator in 1971 that my father, in a late-night conversation while I was home on leave, disclosed to me the full story behind the yellowing newspaper articles and his Navy Cross citation, including the details of his attack on *Musashi* and his survival. He offered many details in that singular conversation: his last acey-deucey game with Ray Skelly, the spectacular gunfire coming from Center Force, the heavy antiaircraft fire on his final torpedo run against *Musashi*'s starboard side, the sense that he was attacking unsupported, the loss of Skelly, his thoughts of his mother, the explosion in his left wing, *Musashi*'s escorts shooting at his stricken airplane, the plumes of seawater erupting ahead of him, the terrifying fire in his cockpit, his crash landing, the left wing shearing away, his horror at discovering the headless Christman and the pain of being unable to do anything to save Westmoreland, his near drowning, flying gloves "slick as snot," his long swim to the uninhabited island, his fear of sharks, conceiving and building the bamboo raft, his uncertainty whether to shoot the Filipinos who discovered him adrift, the kind Filipino woman, the impaled bodies in the narra trees, his sailboat ride to Panay, Lieutenant Colonel Garcia's instructions to make him an infantry officer, the hastily organized ambush of the patrol boat and someone firing prematurely on the boat, the gathering up of survivors, the interrogation of the Japanese survivors and his violent pummeling of the Japanese sergeant, the tormenting of the burned prisoners by the villagers of Libertad, the beheading and shooting deaths of the other prisoners. These details were burned into my mind. Other details (such as sleeping in the narra tree on his first night on the islet because he was afraid of snakes and encountering the curious porpoises) are anecdotes my mother, Mrs. Faye E. Fletcher, recalled from her conversations with my father and related to me long afterward. My father usually responded to questions about the Battle of the Sibuyan Sea and his attack on *Musashi* by saying, "I zigged when I should have zagged," and he deflected inquiries about his experiences with the guerrillas by praising the Filipino people for their hospitality and generosity. Though he was a career naval officer with a distinguished combat record, and proud, he never wore his individual accomplishments on his sleeve, and he soundly criticized those who did. On more than one occasion, he silenced fatuous conversation about the romance of war by saying, "War is a terrible thing." His descriptions were vivid and compelling— delivered to me when he was about forty-eight years old—but, being a young man absorbed in my own life at the time, I did not write them down. He died suddenly and much sooner than anyone expected. I do not have a recording or a transcription of my conversations with him that I can cite.

Ben St. John was my primary source for how things worked or didn't work in VT-18, at least from the time he joined the squadron in August 1944 until *Intrepid* returned to Alameda in December 1944. Ben has a remarkable memory and is quite definite in his recollections of how events unfolded and how the Avenger performed in combat. We spent an entire day together at his home on Long Island and exchanged many telephone calls. He was kind enough to review and critique my descriptions of flying the Avenger, and, of course, he offered many details of his own combat experiences.

Wallace "Red" Russell provided an enlisted man's perspective on Ellis, Van Antwerp, Bud Williams, and many other VT-18 officers. Russell was no doubt fond of these men and believed that most of the squadron's pilots were good officers who cared for their crews. Red invited me into his home for a day, and we spoke frequently by telephone. Unfortunately, Red passed away before the manuscript was complete.

Bill Shackelford, the downed Hellcat pilot from *Monterey* who spent several months on Panay as a guest of the guerrillas and joined my father at Libertad, was my primary source for details about life in the guerrilla camps. He participated in the ambush of the patrol boat and confirmed the fate of the prisoners. Bill managed to leave the island with a trove of diverse historical treasures, including guerrilla currency, letters, orders, correspondence, bolo knives, and cigarette wrappers, and he had photographed the navy fliers rescued from

Panay as they recovered in the Submarine Rest Home in Australia. Like St. John, Shackelford has an excellent memory, and Bill recalls his time on Panay vividly. I visited personally with Bill and his son, Tom, on two occasions, and he gave me full access to his papers.

The most important archival sources for this narrative, and the abbreviations for each such source as used in the following endnotes, are:

a. Air Group 18 aircraft action reports (AAR);

b. USS *Intrepid* deck logs (IDL);

c. VT-18 squadron history (SH). This was probably written or edited by Lieutenant Commander Ernest Allen; what appears to be an original typewritten version of this history resides in his papers at the Naval Historical Center. This is a month-by-month narrative and ends when the squadron goes to sea in August 1944;

d. Air Group 18 history (AGH). This was written by Lieutenant George Race. There is a "published" and an unpublished version. A copy of an interlineated, unpublished version, including Race's description of the kamikaze attack of November 25, 1944, resides in my father's papers. The "published" version, which omits the kamikaze narrative and was probably edited by Commander Ellis, was circulated among squadron members and resides in the papers of Ben St. John, among others;

e. The diary of Lieutenant Junior Grade Kenneth P. Barden (KBD), of which there are also two versions. One version was, according to Peggy Paulson, slightly "sanitized" for reading by Barden's father; the other was Barden's "original." There are very few differences between versions; the sanitized version omits most references to drinking and partying;

f. *Introduction to Naval Aviation, 1945* (INA), cited in the bibliography;

g. U.S. Naval Technical Mission to Japan (TMJ), cited in the bibliography;

h. Statement by, and interviews with, Bernard J. St. John (BSJ);

i. Statement by, and interviews with, William Shackelford (WGS);

j. Interviews with Wallace Russell (WHR);

k. Interviews with Ken Barden Jr. (KBJ) and Peggy Paulson (PP);

l. Interviews with John Kiesalak (JK);

m. Interviews with Dan Nygaard (DN);

n. Interviews with Gerald Van Antwerp (GVA);

o.   Details I received from my father are noted as (WMF);

p.   Still Pictures Branch, National Archives and Record Administration (NARA), College Park, Maryland;

q.   For some descriptions of carrier life, I have drawn upon my own experiences in 1968 as a midshipman aboard *Hornet*, a sister ship of *Intrepid* (where I was privileged to observe from Vulture's Row a World War II–style deck launch of a squadron of propeller-driven Skyraider attack aircraft), and as a naval aviator who carrier-qualified aboard *Lexington*. In describing principles and sensations of flight, I have drawn on my experience as a flight instructor in the navy's Basic Jet Training Command, and as one who continues to fly.

Endnotes

CHAPTER ONE: IN THE PHILIPPINE SEA

Reveille at four o'clock, flight quarters at five: INA, 292; IDL, 10/24. Reveille bugle call in Officers Country: WGS. (NOTE: Post–World War II, the boatswain mate on duty usually sounded reveille in Officers Country with a pipe call, not a bugle, and by announcing over the 1MC, "Reveille, reveille. Now turn to and trice up. Now reveille.") Junior officers' bunk room referred to as "Boys Town": Emerson, *Voices of Bombing 19*, Ensign Don Engen, 24. Not scheduled to fly, passage to Barbers Point, WMF ("Short-Snorter"). *Intrepid* speed, position, T.G. 38.2 composition: IDL, 10/24.(Carriers *Hancock* and *Independence*, normally part of Task Group 38.2, had been detached on the morning of October 24.) Strategic support, AAR, 10/24 (See endnotes to chapter five for a description of information available in aircraft action reports). Leyte Gulf invasion: Morison, *History, Vol. XII*, 130–34; Ireland, *Leyte Gulf 1944*, 10–11, 34–35; Foot, Dear, *Oxford Companion*, 883. MacArthur retirement, field marshal, escape from Corregidor, promise to return: Manchester, *American Caesar*, 159–60, 173, 189–91, 258–71. MacArthur defense of Philippines, Bataan Death March: Foot, Dear, *Oxford Companion*, 114, 115, 880. Japanese troop strength, MacArthur's return, speech to Filipinos: Manchester, *American Caesar*, 374, 383–89. Third Fleet, Task Force 38, command structure: Morison, *History, Vol. XII*, App. I. English immigrants, tea bags: WMF. Background of Skelly, Barden, Williams, Ellis, and Van Antwerp: roster of VT-18 officers and next of kin, SH, records of Ben St. John and Lloyd Karch; GVI. Skelly relationship, acey-deucey: WMF. Barden schooling, athletics: KBJ. Barden as scheduling officer: KBD 8/12/44 (NOTE: I refer throughout to the "unsanitized" version of Ken Barden's diary). Search mission: AAR 10/24; Race, AGH, 21, 22 (NOTE: page citations to Race's air group history refer to the unpublished version). *Darter, Dace*: Morison, *The Two Ocean War*, 439; Friedman, *Afternoon of the Rising Sun*, 82–97. Air Group 18 composition: "Squadron Board" photographs, VT-18, VF-18, VB-18, Records of Ben St. John and Wallace Russell; Morison, *History Vol. XII*, App. I. Aware of a possible strike: BSJ; Forsyth, *Helldivers*, 10. *Intrepid* description and features, including island, flight and hangar decks, ready rooms, and barriers: Roberts, *The Aircraft Carrier Intrepid*, 30–37, 42–43; Zollo, Intrepid *50th Anniversary*, archive photographs at 24, 75; Zollo, *U.S. Intrepid CV-11, Day by Day*, archive photographs at 50, 251; author's experience as midshipman aboard *Hornet* and aviator aboard *Lexington*. Lieutenant Williams as one of the boys: KBD, 5/6/44; WHR. Williams called "Granny": BSJ, WHR. Allen background: Papers of Lieutenant Commander Ernest Allen. Strike 2 Able composition and *Cabot* contribution: AAR, 10/24; Morison, *History, Vol. XII*, 184. Torpedo attack, Mark III: INA, 223–24, 311–12; Drendel, *Walk Around TBF/TBM Avenger*, 39; *U.S. Air Force Fact Sheet, Bliss-Leavitt Mark XII Aerial Torpedo*. General quarters, material and readiness conditions: IDL 10/24; *Current Tactical Orders and Doctrine U.S. Fleet USF 10A, 1944*, 2-1, 2-2; *Current Tactical Orders Aircraft Carriers USF 74*, 2-412 through 2-414. Starboard up, port down rule: Zollo, Intrepid *50th Anniversary*, 95. First Avenger launch with torpedoes and drop tanks: KBD 10/26/44; BSJ; AAR 10/24. Sector Three report, Millar: AAR 10/24. Skelly reaction, "Every time . . . this shit happens": WMF. Flight gear, survival gear: Phillips, *Steichen at War*, Archive photographs, 116–17, 140–41; WJS; BSJ; WMF. Importance of halting Japanese Center Force relative to Leyte Landings: Baldwin, *The Battle for Leyte Gulf*, Special notes by Admiral Thomas C. Kinkaid, 350; Manchester, *American Caesar*, 391–92. Takeoff sequence, including Fox flags, black balls, at the dip, horn and whistle, verbal orders, and rendezvous procedure: INA 283–84; *Current Tactical Orders and Doctrine, USF 10A*, 3-10 through 3-11; *Current Tactical Orders Aircraft Carriers, USF-77*, 15. Flight deck description and functions of flight deck personnel: INA, 123–27. Aircraft side number and bureau number for Strike 2 Able aircraft flown by Fletcher: AAR, 10/24. Avenger dimensions and characteristics: *Pilot's Handbook of Operating Instructions*, 1–8. Air Group 18 aircraft paint scheme: NARA photographs; Sumral, *USS Intrepid (CV-11)*, 25; Drendel, *Walk Around TBF/TBM*, 4. Forsyth exchange with Skelly, "You torpedoes are going to get it today": Forsyth, *Helldivers*, 11. Halsey learns of Center Force position: Thomas, *Sea of Thunder*, 199. Halsey's order to attack and timing: Morison, *History, Vol. XII*, 175; Thomas, *Sea of Thunder*, 200. *Intrepid* launch course, timing, speed, weather: IDL 10/24. Avenger checklists, start, takeoff, climb, flap retraction, "Diddlewith Doakes": *Pilot's Handbook of Operating Instructions*, 21–35. Description of VT-18 overweight takeoff: BSJ. Strike 2 Able's path into Sibuyan Sea, Morison, *History, Vol. XII*, 185. Ellis insistence on radio silence: *Commander Carrier Air Group Eighteen, Comments and Recommendations King II Operation, 10–21 October 1944*, AAR. Aircraft formation structures and signals: *Current Tactical Orders and Doctrine, USF 74*, 1–48. "Point Option": BSJ; *Current Tactical Orders Aircraft Carriers, USF 77*, 26. Discovery of Center Force in Tablas Strait beneath the clouds, location, time over target: AAR 10/24; NARA photographs; Forsyth, *Helldivers*, 12–13. Composition of Center Force: Morison, *History, Vol. XII, App. 1*; Friedman, *Afternoon of the Rising Sun*, 122. Combat history of ships of Center Force listed: Hackett and Kingsepp, *Tabular Records of Movement*. Multicolor intense antiaircraft fire, all calibers, up to sixteen thousand feet, Ellis order to attack, split of VT-18's Avenger division six-two: AAR 10/24. Pilots remaining with Williams: AAR 10/24; WMF.

CHAPTER TWO: IN CALIFORNIA

Commissioning of VT-18, Lieutenant Al Long as temporary commander, few airplanes: SH 9/43. Alameda NAS: Alameda Naval Air Museum. Doolittle departure from Alameda: Nelson, *First Heroes*, 57–60. U.S. Navy and British carrier strength at outbreak of war, relative tonnage and aircraft complement, U.S. numbers late in war: Foot, Dear, *Oxford Companion*, 194; O'Hara, *On Seas Contested*, 233; Morison, *History, Vol. XV*, 29-33. Number of torpedo squadrons, number of aircraft assigned to VT-18: Jackson, Doll, *Grumman TBF/TBM Avenger (Supplement)*, 20–25. Van Antwerp assumes command: SH 8/43. Van Antwerp background: GVA. Van Antwerp talkative, chuckling manner of speech, approachable: BSJ, WHR. CIS Committee, Clear Lake, Robinson borrows OD car, confinement: SH 8/43. Ely demonstration, Veracruz flight as first military aviation combat mission in U.S. history, Admiral Moffette as father of naval aviation: Goodspeed, Burgess, *U.S. Naval Aviation*, 23, 25, 27–29. Ellyson, Veracruz, Admiral Fisk as father of the torpedo plane, Admiral Moffette as father of naval aviation, Billy Mitchell, airpower has "completely superceded sea power," Miller, *The U.S. Navy, An Illustrated History,* 251–52, 279, 281. DT-1 details, SC-1 details, T3M details, F8C details, BM-2 details, TBD-1 (Devastator) details, F2A details: Swanborough, Gordon and Bowers, *United States Navy Aircraft Since 1911,* 153–55, 118–19, 290–92, 294–95, 160–61, 67–68. SBD-3 (Dauntless) details: *Warbird Alley.* Taranto Raid, "balance of power decisively altered," Churchill, *The Second World War,* 164. Japanese torpedo experiments, "[T]he British strike encouraged Fuchida greatly," Prange, *At Dawn We Slept,* 158, 160–61, 320. VT-8 Devastator losses at Midway, Mrazek, *A Dawn Like Thunder,* 116–17, 141. Poor air group coordination at Midway and "exaggerated picture of the action's results," Prange, *Miracle at Midway,* 243–48. Lessons of Midway, poor coordination, TBM superiority, necessity for direct fighter escort: Lundstrom, *The First Team,* 430-434, 556, 558. Torpedo planes viewed as "flying coffins:" BSJ. VT-18 legatees of VT-8, WMF, BSJ. Air Group 18 organized, AGH, 1. Ellis background, traits, "winning personality": *Lucky Bag,* class of 1930. Ellis reserved, demanding: WHR, BSJ. Rumor of deployment, "make up their feeble minds," Monterey training, loss of Ensign Matthews and crew: SH 9/43. Standard torpedo run: *Current Tactical Orders and Fleet Doctrine, U.S. Fleet, USF 10A,* 311–12; Tillman, *Avenger at War,* 53–57. Dead reckoning, sea state charts: BSJ. Van Antwerp and tight formation flying: BSJ, WHR. "Stay on the bearing line . . . I want them to find your wreckage exactly forty-five degrees aft of mine": Author's experience. Parade formation over San Francisco, Point Reyes, loss of Lieutenant Junior Grade Horton, Lake Merritt Hotel Bar, movie incident, FCPL at Monterey NAS: SH, 10/43. Russell background, enlisted training, observing FCLP, reaction to Lieutenant Riley: WHR. TBM bombing angle limited to sixty degrees: *Pilot's Handbook of Operating Instructions,* 76. FCLP procedures, LSO: Forsyth, *Helldivers,* 53; Author's experience (NOTE: FCLP in jet aircraft is flown at higher altitudes.) Ensign Johnson's error, Carmel and Pine Inn, Van Antwerp and highway patrol incident, SH, 10/43. Instrument refresher, carrier qualifications aboard *Cohapee,* accidents, Bar at Hotel del Coronado, move to Hollister, "big night-flying syllabus," pool and softball, Van Antwerp and Vannais champions: SH, 11/43. "Flaming Hookers:" Author's experience. Night formation flying difficulty, rendezvousing on a "constellation": Forsyth, *Helldivers*, 105; author's experience. Vannais night crash: SH, 11/43. McWhorter family background, Barden and Margie McWhorter romance, Christmas at McWhorters', Joe Rubin and Dickie McWhorter romance, father's visit, Barden marriage: PP. Relationship among wives, picnics on ranch: Telephone interviews with Mildred Schonthaler and Betty Karch; Lieutenant Ernest Allen papers and photographs. Doyle accident, Barden accident, SH, 12/43. Ensign Dragan accident, Ensign Roccaforte arrival, new TBM-1C aircraft delivered to squadron, SH, 1/44; Jackson, Doll, *Grumman TBF/TBM Avenger (Supplement)*, 23. Orders to *Lexington*, "damp from alcohol not the weather," SH, 2/44. Vaughn "too much bourbon," passed under Golden Gate at two thirty p.m., Air Groups 18 and 19 aboard, Seebees as passengers, KBD 2/24/44. Van Antwerp disheveled on departure: WHR.

CHAPTER THREE: IN HAWAII

Voyage to Pearl Harbor, "Whatta ship," poker games, many ships at anchor in Pearl Harbor: KBD, 2/24, 2/26, 2/28/44. (NOTE: hereafter, all citations to Barden diary entries refer to 1944.) *Intrepid*'s tribute to sunken battleships on arriving at Pearl Harbor: Emerson, *Voices of Bombing 19*, Ensign Don Engen, 10. Transfer to Ford Island, to Hilo in a rainstorm: KBD 2/28, 2/29, SH, 2/44. Helldiver problems: Smith, *Curtis SB2C Helldiver*, 32–51; "Continuing malfunctioning, structural failures": Polmer, *Aircraft Carriers, A Graphic History*, 345. New "rocket guns," shopping, gunnery practice: KBD 3/4, 3/11, 3/13. Base bus to Hilo: KBD, 3/4; WHR. "Women lovely . . . liquor excellent": SH, 5/44. HVAR characteristics: R.G. 313, letter of 11/25/44, commander, Air Force Pacific Fleet, sight settings for five-inch HVAR. Torpedo exercises in Area Two Sugar North, instructions to "be on hand" during torpedo loading and make positive identification on target ship: R.G. 313, Letter of 4/3/44, commander, Air Force Pacific Fleet. Torpedo exercise procedures and restrictions and summaries of results: R.G. 313, letter of 5/22/45, commander, Air Force Pacific Fleet. VT-18 liquor ration, promotion party brawl, sold ration, rumor of assignment to *Bunker Hill*, KBD, 3/6, 3/8, 3/11, 3/13. Massed attacks: current tactical orders and doctrine, USF 74, 3–102. Group gropes "awesome to the enemy as well as to the participants": Emerson, *Voices of Bombing 19*, Ensign Don Engen, 19; KBD, 8/18, 8/19. "Group attack this morning a TARFU affair," and "Ellis still pulling his hair": KBD, 3/14. More training, mine-laying school at Barbers Point: KBD, 3/23, 4/18, 4/19; SH 5/44. Sand-filled bombs: Forsyth, *Helldivers*, 59. Bombing the "Rock" from Barbers Point: BSJ; KBD, 6/1. Navy lighter-than-air pilots called "Bag Pilots": WMF. Barbers Point mosquitoes, exchange of chaplain for Seagram's, April Fools' Day tow plane assignment, announcement of "nite [sic] low level" bombing: KBD, 4/19, 4/21, 3/27, 4/1, 4/3. Night radar bombing, three a.m. launch: KBD, 5/6, 5/10, 5/11. Night fighter units, Morison, *History, Vol. XII*, Appendix I. "Washing Machine Charlies": BSJ Wallace as bus driver, Hilo Hatties: WHR. Seaview Inn, Volcano House, Naniloa, Quarrells: KBD, 5/14, 5/2, 5/19, 4/7. Williams relieved as executive officer, resentment: KBD, 4/9. Gripe session, impatience for war, "will we never see action," word of transfer to Oahu, orders to Kaneohe, promised carrier qualifications aboard *Franklin*, celebratory farewell, Barden not unpacking, bumped from *Franklin*: KBD, 5/15, 5/25, 6/1, 5/23, 6/2, 6/4, 6/5, 6/6. Commander Ellis 6/23/44 letter to all hands: Papers of Lieutenant Commander Ernest Allen. Kaneohe, "beautiful base . . . excellent food," officers' club "a thing of beauty:" KBD 6/16, 6/8. Baseball, watching DiMaggio and Mize: KBD, 6/7. Naval Aviation Cadet Training Program curriculum: *College News*, Murray State College. Navy Preflight School curriculum; "most strenuous [program] ever undertaken" and "five thousand calories per day": Johnson, *U.S. Navy Pre-Flight School, Athens, Georgia*, 8, 23. "The awful-est thing happened last night": Letter of 3/7/43, Will Fletcher to Naomi Fletcher. Will Fletcher as a youth, frequent moves, alcoholic father: WMF, Interview with Betty Jane Paul. Yellow Peril flight: WMF pilot log; Author's experience. Transfers to Norman Oklahoma, Corpus Christi, Miami, and Barbers Point: WMF pilot log and "Short-Snorter." Corpus Christi curriculum, airfields named for aviators who died in action, Chase, Waldron, Cuddihy, Rodd, Cabaniss: *The Slipstream Mark IV, Ed.*, 40–45. War chronology, Schweinfurt, Regensburg, Tarawa: Foot, Dear, *Oxford Companion*, 1330–32, 983–84, 1103. Total hours of more experienced pilots: Karch pilot log. "Broken-down outfit," carrier qualification accidents on *Ommaney Bay*, Commander Ellis's warning to get better or face six more months of training, Lieutenant Riley and Lieutenant Christensen as division leaders: KBD, 6/14, 6/22, 6/26, 7/5. Loss of Christensen and search, Race provides whiskey: KBD, 7/9, SH, 7/44. Hellcat/Helldiver midair collision: Forsyth, *Helldiver*, 52; KBD, 4/8. History of USS *Intrepid*, "big potato chip," manning the rail for Roosevelt:

Ships Data Section, *History of USS Intrepid. Intrepid* at Pearl Harbor, berths, lines, and services from shore: IDL, 7/12, 7/25, 7/27, 7/29. *Intrepid* characteristics, fuel and gasoline capacities, dazzle camouflage: Roberts, *Aircraft Carrier* Intrepid, Table 2, 9, 10. Honolulu flyover, "now I know I'm voting for Dewey," KBD, 7/25; "Every plane . . . Dewey would win": SH, 7/44. "Get the Philippines Back," Manchester, *American Caesar*, 370. Transfer of ground personnel, *Intrepid*'s aborted sortie, "Decrepit, Queen of the Dry Docks": AGH, 1. Waiting at Kaneohe for repairs to *Intrepid*, more training, loss of Lieutenant Robinson: KBD, 8/1, 8/2; SH 8/44. Luau, Van Antwerp carves the pig and serves: WHR. Ben St. John background, ride to the carrier, impressed with tight formation: BSJ. Fletcher flies aboard, WMF pilot log. Task Group 19.11 designation, ships' speed: IDL 8/10. Carrier approach and landing, altitudes, procedures, LSO signals, danger of stack gas turbulence: *Current Tactical Orders, Aircraft Carriers, USF 77*, 401 through 405. "Okay pass": Author's experience. Avenger checklists, pitch changes: *Pilot's Handbook of Flight Operating Instructions*, 34, 36. Tension between air group and ship's company, "dislike whirr and clatter . . . operate without planes": AGH, 2. Air Group 20 regarded as "hot outfit": AGH. Will flies ASAP: WMF pilot log.

CHAPTER FOUR: IN LINGGA ROADS

Second Fleet at Lingga Roads in early August, *Atago* Vice Admiral Kurita's flagship: Thomas, *Sea of Thunder*, 138; Morison, *History, Vol. XII*, 69; Hackett and Kingsepp, *Tabular Movement*. Decisive battle: Morison, *History, Vol. XII*, 167-68. Pacific war chronology, General Archibald Wavell decamps to India, New Guinea campaign, Coral Sea Battle, Battle of Midway, Battle of Philippine Sea, Ichi-Go Operation: Foot, Dear, *Oxford Companion*, 855–63, 1322–33, 1267, 795–97, 271–72, 748–49, 884–85, 233. ABDACOM, Europe First strategy: Hornfischer, *Ship of Ghosts*, 33–37. Southwest Pacific Ocean Area and command divisions, New Guinea diseases: Manchester, *American Caesar*, 283–84, 298. Battle of Midway: Prange, *Miracle at Midway*. Guadalcanal sea battles: Hornfischer, *Neptune's Inferno*. "Our combined fleet in several engagements . . .": Combined Fleet, Ultrasecret Dispatch 041213, 5/4/44. Honolulu Conference: "Mindanao, Mr. President . . .": Manchester, *American Caesar*, 365, 368; Spector, *Eagle Against the Sun*, 417–20; Toland, *The Rising Sun*, 662. "Battle situation has become more serious . . .": Combined Fleet Task Force, Ultrasecret Serial 1003, 8/10/34, 37–38. *Musashi* gun batteries and armor: TMJ, *Reports of Damage to Musashi (BB)* and Japanese eighteen-inch gun data, gun mount, and turret weight; Dickson, "IJN *Yamato*," *Warship International. Iowa* class data: Department of the Navy, "Welcome Aboard, USS *New Jersey*" (BB-62). Design and construction of *Musashi*, dredging harbor, hemp blinds, cold sake, ultrasecrecy, launch, chalk used during construction, thirteen decks, elevator, fans, telephones, watertight compartments, kilowatts, gun tests and guinea pigs, named after Musashino Plain, typhoon off Palau, sortie to avoid air raid, return to Kure, *Tunny* attack, antiaircraft gun upgrade, *Musashi* song: Yoshimura, *Battleship* Musashi, *The Making and Sinking of the World's Biggest Battleship*, 20, 23, 29, 87, 44, 36, 47, 68, 113, 99, 119, 124, 77, 68, 127, 128–29, 143–45, 147, 150, 144. Construction caused shortages of rope: Matsumoto and Chihaya, "Design and Construction of the *Yamato* and *Musashi*," Naval Institute Press. *Musashi* and *Yamato* war record: Hackett and Kingsepp: *Tabular Record of Movement*. Underestimate of *Musashi* tonnage: TMJ.

CHAPTER FIVE: IN THE MIDDLE LATITUDES

(NOTE: Air Combat Intelligence officers (ACIs) in Air Group 18, such as Lieutenant Commander Allen and Lieutenant Race, prepared a joint aircraft action report (AAR) after most combat missions, which recorded data pertinent to the mission, including: date; strike identification (strikes were identified by letter and by the order in which they were launched, e.g., Able, Baker, Charlie, Dog, Echo, etc.); launch and recovery times in local time; carrier latitude and longitude at launch; number and type of aircraft launched and recovered (VF, VB, VT); target description; target location; tactical purpose of mission; ordnance carried by aircraft type; weather over target; bombing tactics used; enemy aircraft encountered; enemy aircraft destroyed; antiaircraft fire encountered, including type and intensity; results of bombing and torpedo attacks; length of mission, ordnance expended, and fuel consumed by each aircraft type; time of flight; aircraft destroyed or damaged by type, side number, and bureau number and probable cause; personnel lost or wounded and probable cause; a short narrative of each squadron's tactics (VF, VB, VT); and operational and tactical commentary. An AAR was typed up for each strike and occasionally supplemented with combat photographs and line drawings. Commander Ellis, each of his squadron commanders, and an ACI officer signed each AAR. Air Group 18's AAR are preserved in R.G. 38 at NARA.

The AARs do not contain a roster of every pilot or crewman who participated on each strike. Strike-by-strike rosters may exist for some carrier squadrons or air groups during this period of the war, but I was unable to locate such records for Air Group 18. Each AAR usually identifies the strike group leader for the mission and sometimes identifies the leaders of VF, VB, and VT divisions. Personnel lost or wounded on the strike are always identified. Lieutenant Race's air group history (AGH) describes the same missions that are reflected in the AARs but with less operational detail. Race's AGH, however, often discloses the names of pilots and crewmen who participated on a specific strike, and he offers much commentary. The roster of VT-18's officers, August to November 1944, with summaries of combat record and next of kin (roster), provides non-strike-specific information about each pilot's history (e.g., "Torpedo hit on Jap BB," or "Sunk Jap freighter off Subic Bay by torpedo attack"). Each pilot's log-book (maintained by a squadron yeoman) contains the date of each flight, the aircraft flown (identified by type and bureau number), the duration of flight, the nature of the mission by code ("G" indicated bombing; "H" indicated torpedo), the names of crewmen or passengers carried, and pilot remarks (usually entered well after the event). To reconstruct a relevant list of pilots who participated in each strike, I have used the following convention: (1) accept AAR names; (2) accept AGH names; (3) cross-check against pilot logbook, where available; (4) cross-check against Barden diary; (5) cross-check roster for type of mission; (6) cross-check against *Intrepid*'s deck log (which notes aircraft and crewmen lost by day). Ben St. John was able to recall some of the pilots who were with him on key missions (as was my father), and I also used other pieces of evidence, such as the Sistrunk interview and John Forsyth's *Helldivers*. As this description makes clear, my convention had many moving parts and, while I am confident the actions of the main characters are accurately depicted, I cannot represent that my microhistory has correctly identified all participants.)

"Flight operations . . . well handled," "If you have two . . . draw one," arrival at Eniwetok, "whiskey is Schenley's," "middle of Times Square surrounded by Jap spies," Brisbin/Sistrunk rocket mishaps, pass beneath Truk en route to Palau Islands, Padre's prayer book, "little of interest" over Palau, "regretfully sank three sampans," "neutralize Babelthuap," loss of Lieutenant Junior Grade John

Savage, Riley could "scarcely see the captain": AGH, 3, 4, 5, 6, 7. AAR, 8/18, 9/7, 9/8. Group grope composition, arrival at Eniwetok, Brisbin/Sistrunk rocket mishaps, learns Palau will be first target, "Mindanao, oh, God!" fighter sweep over Palau 9/6, loss of Savage: KBD, 8/6, 8/24, 8/25, 8/26, 8/16, 8/29, 9/6, 9/7, 9/8. "Carrier Clowns" emblem development, designer an aspiring Disney artist; patches not allowed in combat zone: WHR. Emblem design contest held, arrival at Eniwetok: Emerson, *Voices of Bombing 19*, 19, 22–23. VF-18 and VB-18 squadron nicknames: Squadron Board photographs; BSJ. Representative injuries aboard carrier, machine gun discharge in hangar bay, man overboard, Palau launch position, weather: IDL, various dates, 8/24, 9/1, 9/7. Savage and Fletcher friendship: inference from notation in WMF pilot log ("Best friend shot down Palau Is. Airfields"). "Playing carrier," best guess on cause of rocket mishap, pull emergency release as a backup, purchase of Savage's share in liquor mess: BSJ. Task Force 38 composition on 8/29, Palau Islands place names, Palau a "staging point," Morison, *History, Vol. XII*, 12–13, 31, 33. Palau history, topography: Rottman, *World War II Pacific Island Guide*, 348–49. Recognition training: Papers of Lieutenant Commander Ernest Allen. "Better dead than look bad": Author's experience. Fear of capture, knowledge of Japanese atrocities against aircrew: WMF. Glide bombing and dive-bombing attack procedures: *Pilot's Handbook of Flight Operating Instructions*, 71–77; *Current Tactical Orders and Doctrine, Carrier Aircraft, USF 74*, 2-212 through 2-214; BSJ; Forsyth, *Helldivers*, 13–15, 60, 106–07. WMF pilot log, 9/7, 9/8.

CHAPTER SIX: IN THE VISAYAS

Imperial rescript quotation: Bix, *Hirohito and the Making of Modern Japan*, 480. Reorganization of Japanese air forces in Philippines, damage inflicted by Task Force 38: Inoguchi, *Divine Wind*, 22–24. Japanese command structure in Philippines: Morison, *History, Vol. XII*, 67–70. Halsey quotation, "Kill Japs": Thomas, *Sea of Thunder*, 1. RAAF Map of Visayas distributed to pilots: Records of George T. Lewis III (Air Group 19). Order to avoid bombing residential areas, controversy over reconnaissance photographs, "Burn Davao," Commander Ellis reads fighter pilots "the riot act," "routine four-a-day . . . waste of power and bombs," Halsey comment "unbelievable and fantastic": AGH, 8, 10, 14. Barden credited with rocket hit, "Manila here we come," "success at last" over Fabrica, Halsey "well-done" and "Tokyo here we come," "Idea of entire [Luzon] operation is to draw out the Jap fleet for a showdown battle": KBD, 9/12, 9/13, 9/15, 9/11. Matina, Daliao, Davao, Negros, Fabrica, Peleliu, and Anguar air strikes, loss of Ensign Daniel Laner, camouflaged enemy aircraft, "general melee," "Fighter sweeps, unimpeded by escort duty, look like the answer," napalm problems: AAR, 9/9, 9/10, 913, 9/14, 9/17. WMF pilot log, 9/9, 9/10, 9/12, 9/14.

CHAPTER SEVEN: OVER LUZON

Slept through general quarters, receiving wife's letters "bigger thrill," lectures on Luzon, "10 gallons of gas remaining," "Skipper has the measles," recovery in foul weather, Coron Bay mission, *Intrepid*'s arrival at Saipan, typhoon at Ulithi and sortie, Okinawa "First attack on Jap homeland very successful," different air groups assigned different target areas, KBD, 9/20, 9/21, 9/22, 9/24, 9/27, 9/29, 10/3, 10/10. Clark Field, Subic Bay, Lingayen Gulf, Coron Bay, and Okinawa Ie Shima air strikes, Lieutenant Riley craters runway intersection, some bombing "far below standards," diagram of torpedo runs in Subic Bay attack: AAR, 9/21, 9/22, 9/24, 10/10. Torpedo drop procedures: *Pilot's Handbook of Flight Operating Instructions*, 74–77. Mark 13 gun sight normally not used on torpedo runs, flown caged: BSJ. Musical interludes in ready room: AGH, 20. Lloyd Karch sings "Wabash Cannonball": BSJ. "Best work in worst weather," Japanese prisoners on Saipan bathing in open, Riley goes ashore in search of "bore sight," "China weakening," Rear Admiral Bogan staff arrival at Ulithi, Coron Bay strike: AGH, 11, 14. "[T]he number of combat-ready planes had been cut in half by American striking forces, which threw heavy raids at Davao . . . Cebu . . . Legaspi . . . Tacloban . . . [and] the Manila area"; Admiral Onishi urges "body-slamming tactics" in August 1944: Inoguchi, *The Divine Wind*, 24, 25. Official acceptance of "body-crashing" tactics: Sheftall, *Blossoms in the Wind*, 27–29. Admiral Toshihira Inoguchi background, brother, son: Inoguchi, *The Divine Wind*, 65, 66. *Musashi* damage control drills, crew "exceptionally well-trained by Japanese standards": TMJ, 17. Coron Bay strike: Forsyth, *Helldivers*, 106–10. WMF pilot log: 9/21, 9/22, 9/27, 9/30, 10/9, 10/10. (NOTE: My father ascribed the remark, "No man who has the wit . . . chance of being drowned," to one of his buddies in the squadron who "had some college." My father found the remark amusing, and I have ascribed the remark in this narrative to Savage, although I cannot confirm it was he who said it. The original source is Samuel Johnson, quoted by James Boswell in *The Life of Sam-*

uel Johnson, London: Everyman's Library, 1973, 645. The actual quotation is, "No man will be a sailor who has contrivance enough to get himself in jail; for being in a ship is being in a jail, with a chance of being drowned.")

CHAPTER EIGHT: OVER FORMOSA

Formosa description, head-hunters, electrified fences: Stamp, *Asia*, 631–34. Japanese expansion, Korean incursion, Shimonoseki Treaty: Beasley, *The Japanese Experience*, 231–35. Formosa strikes: AAR, 10/12, 10/13. Mitscher warns that Formosa attacks will be "no surprise," launch conditions "black as the inside of your hat," Van Antwerp's tight formation flying and head-on turns into enemy fighters, flight into the clouds, steel cable wrapped around Bates's propeller shaft, sneaking onto flight deck to watch antiaircraft fire, float lights used to guide Japanese night attackers, Tokyo Rose quotation, Admiral Nimitz quotation, musical interlude after Formosa strikes, basketball on forward elevator: AGH 15, 16, 19, 20. Steak-and-eggs breakfast before first Formosa strike: WHR. Japanese yen and "talkie-points" distributed, survival advice: BSJ; Emerson, *Voices of Bombing 19*, Ensign Peck, 41. Loss of Lieutenant Commander Eslick over Formosa, separation of Van Antwerp's strike group in bad weather, Eslick's character, Forsyth "furious" at Lieutenant Junior Grade Eisengrein, loss of Lieutenant Junior Grade Eisengrein on October 13: Forsyth, *Helldivers*, 69–75. Ben St. John participation, attack on Van Antwerp's formation, separation from Lieutenant Junior Grade Joseph Rubin in the clouds, solo return to *Intrepid*, recognition procedures: BSJ. "Picnic is now over," group "flew until we saw the "China coast," Luzon missions "duck soup" by comparison, promised Leyte operation "too good to be true," Readiness Condition 11, "chilling" wait, "thank God we weren't launched," "uproar" over launching with drop tanks: KBD, 10/10, 10/15, 10/14, 10/13, 10/16. "Like so many eggs thrown . . .": Toland, *The Rising Sun*, 670. Japanese counterstrikes of October 13, initial Japanese reaction to Formosa air battles, Vice Admiral Shima's intentions: Morison, *History, Vol. XII*, 93–96, 108–09, 103; Spector, *Eagle Against the Sun*, 424–25. Order to destroy "remnants," Admiral Halsey "retiring at high speed" quotation: Thomas, *Sea of Thunder*, 164. Formosa remains a "serious obstacle, "window" dropped for first time over Formosa and details, "excellent effect on morale:" AAR 10/13 (ACA-1 supplement). Rest, refueling after Formosa, Ping-Pong prowess: KBD, 10/15; IDL, 10/15; WMF. "Peckerwood Fighting Funstes": Lieutenant Commander Ernest

Allen Personal Papers. Night attacks on *Intrepid*, course changes, antiaircraft counterfire, refueling: IDL 10/12, 10/15. WMF pilot log, 10/12, 10/13.

CHAPTER NINE: IN THE SIBUYAN SEA

General MacArthur's departure for Leyte Gulf, American seizure of Dulag and Tacloban airfields: Kenney, *General Kenney Reports, A Personal History*, 445, 450–57. "Sturdy hulls ploughed the water . . .": MacArthur, *Decisive Battles of World War II, Leyte Gulf*, 235. Leyte Gulf invasion preliminaries, Admiral Toyoda is alerted, Admiral Kurita sorties from Lingga Roads, movements of forces commanded by Vice Admiral Kurita, Vice Admiral Nishimura, and Vice Admiral Ozawa for the period of October 18 through 22, American reconnaissance submarines off Bungo Strait withdraw temporarily and fail to detect Vice Admiral Ozawa's sortie from Inland Sea, *Darter* and *Dace* encounter with Center Force: Morison, *History, Vol. XII*, 116–27, 166, 167–68, 169–72. V. Admiral Kurita background ["Takeo" means "great warrior," torpedo expertise, Etajima graduate, descendant of scholars, a "faithful old sea dog," battleship commander at Guadalcanal, discussion of Sho-1 plan aboard *Atago* at Brunei Bay, subordinates' objections, "miracles . . . glorious opportunity . . . what man can say . . . ," subordinates' banzai cry, rescue from sinking *Atago*], Imperial Navy operations officer's plea to "bloom as flowers of death": Thomas, *Sea of Thunder*, 74–76, 304, 75, 102, 186–87, 190–91, 142. Vice Admiral Kurita at Midway, "solid sheet of blinding . . .": Toland, *The Rising Sun*, 682, 675. Appari, Panay, and Negros strikes: AAR, 10/18, 10/19, 10/21. "No targets worthwhile" at Appari, low fuel return on return, "everything went wrong," drowning loss of Lieutenant Long's radioman Hunter, rest and relaxation overdue, played bridge: KBD 10/18, 10/21, 10/22, 10/23. VT-18 aircrew blame Long for Hunter's loss: BSJ. Inoguchi orders interior paint stripped from *Musashi*, objects at Brunei Bay conference to use of big guns against transports: Yoshimura, *Battleship Musashi, The Making and Sinking of the World's Biggest Battleship*, 164, 153. Inoguchi orders *Musashi*'s weather decks blackened with soot: Hackett and Kingsepp, *Tabular Records of Movement*.

CHAPTER TEN: ON STRIKE 2 ABLE

Vice Admiral Kurita anticipates air attacks, disposition of Force A: Inoguchi, *The Divine Wind* (Diagram), 5; Friedman, *Afternoon of the Rising Sun*

(Diagram), 122. Petty Officer Hosoya's duty station on *Musashi*: Toland, *The Rising Sun*, 687. Hachimaki headbands, *Musashi*'s crew go to battle stations, radar detects incoming American planes, effects of dive-bombing attack, near-misses, bomb strips armor plate: Yoshimura, *Battleship Musashi, The Making and Sinking of the World's Biggest Battleship*, 159–60; TMJ. "Anvil" torpedo tactics, VT-18 torpedo attack on *Musashi*: INA, 311; *Current Tactical Orders and Doctrine, Carrier Aircraft, USF 74*, Fig. 1-68, 127, 2-409 through 2-416. Weather, attack on starboard side, intense antiaircraft fire, division split, torpedo release altitudes, speeds, and distances (diagram), probable hits: AAR, 10/24; TMJ. Williams's division descent through the clouds, division split, Lieutenant Junior Grade Elmer Vaughn as section leader, section passes over destroyer, death of Lieutenant Junior Grade Skelly, *Musashi* a monster ship, antiaircraft fire beautiful, like Fourth of July, seeming futility of attack, concentrated, prayed to be reunited with mother, hit as turning away, huge burning hole, canopy carried away, no communication with crew, fire in the cockpit, smoldering shoe, escorts firing too far ahead, reached plumes as they subsided, left wingtip caught waves and wing sheared away, right wing like a sail, dazed, forgot to remove parachute and flying gloves, wet gloves were "slick as snot," Christman decapitated, Westmoreland likely dead, plane sank quickly, struggle to remove gear, nearly drowned, discharged one side of Mae West, came to surface, retched, shoulders rubbed raw, wounded in thigh, began to swim west toward clouds, nearest island: WMF; "Edwardsville Flyer Home, Saved by Filipino Fighters," *Edwardsville Intelligencer*. (NOTE: Relative range and bearing calls attributed to Westmoreland are not his in fact, but would be typical for any anvil torpedo run that began with a head-on approach to the target. INA, 311.) Descriptions of damage to *Musashi* in first strike, chief of number one machine gun squad killed: Toland, *The Rising Sun*, 687; Yoshimura, *Battleship Musashi*, 161; TMJ. "Guts and courage . . . unexcelled," Forsyth, *Helldivers*, 15.

CHAPTER ELEVEN: ON STRIKE 2 BAKER

Morning air battles of October 24, loss of *Princeton*, *Birmingham* casualties, Rear Admiral Oldendorf prepares for Vice Admiral Nishimura, Vice Admiral Ozawa's air strikes inflict little damage but alert Admiral Halsey to presence of enemy carriers: Morison, *History, Vol. XII*, 176, 198, 203, 192. (NOTE: Air Group 18's AAR for Strike 2 Baker on 10/24 is missing from the NARA file. My account of Strike 2 Baker is drawn from a description contained in a three-page document styled, "Participation in the Second Battle of the Philippine Sea, October 24–26, 1944," with the letterhead, "United States Pacific Air Forces, Torpedo Squadron Eighteen." This document is among Ben St. John's papers; it describes all three of VT-18's strikes in the Sibuyan Sea on October 24, the squadron's single strike against Ozawa's carrier task force off Cape Engano on October 25, and its strike against the retreating Center Force off Panay on October 26. This document specifically identifies Lieutenant Commander Van Antwerp as the leader of the torpedo division on Strike 2 Baker, October 24, and specifically discusses the participation of Lieutenant Riley and Lieutenant Junior Grade Morris; Riley's torpedo bomber, hit by antiaircraft fire, crash-landed, and Morris had a "possible" torpedo hit. VT-18's roster also indicates that Bates and Rubin made torpedo runs on the Japanese battleship task force (they normally flew as members of Van Antwerp's 1st Division), and Barden's diary, 10/24, reflects that he participated in Strike 2 Baker and took a shell through his right wing. That Sistrunk participated in Strike 2 Baker is apparent from his video interview; he refers to "the skipper" as leading the anvil attack.) "Formosa was a set-up compared to the AA I saw today," KBD, 10/24.

CHAPTER TWELVE: ON STRIKE 2 CHARLIE

Kurita requests for air cover: Thomas, *Sea of Thunder*, 204. Request to Rear Admiral Inoguchi to fire eighteen-inch guns, Inoguchi concerned about trim, Inoguchi relents, first firing of *Musashi*'s eighteen-inch guns in combat, Kurita message "in severe sea fight," sixth attack on *Musashi* and damage, Kurita temporary retirement, signal to *Musashi* "go forward and ground," Inoguchi wounded, Captain Kato takes charge, sinking of *Musashi*: Toland, *The Rising Sun*, 688–89, 689–94, 690, 691. Damage to *Musashi* in third, fourth, fifth, and sixth attacks: TMJ. Service life of eighteen-inch guns: TMJ. Damage to *Musashi* from second, third, fourth, fifth, and sixth attacks, "every man for himself," and sinking: Yoshimura, *Battleship Musashi*, 162–71. Few enemy aircraft encountered, shootdowns: AAR, 10/24. Attitude in VT-18 ready room before Strike 2 Charlie, Lieutenant Bud Williams's debrief: BSJ. Strike 2 Charlie torpedo runs, approach, altitudes, speeds: *AAR* 10/24 (diagram). Lieutenant Long fails to drop torpedo: BSJ, AAR, IDL. St. John furious at Long, morphine stolen from Karch's airplane: BSJ. Injury to Lieutenant Junior Grade Karch's gunner, "badly shot up," return flight to *Intrepid* in damaged Avenger, Dugas bleeding, terrified of sharks, Karch's assurances to Dugas: Schubert, "Navy Veteran Tells about WWII," *Pasadena Star News*. Admiral Halsey's decision to pursue Ozawa's carriers, options considered, order issued: Morison, *History, Vol. XII*, 193–97; Thomas, *Sea of Thunder*, 217–72. "[T]he destruction of the Japanese fleet was my paramount objective": Baldwin, *Sea Fights and Shipwrecks*, special notes by Fleet Admiral William F. Halsey, USN (Ret.), 360. Aftermath, grim mood in VT-18's ready room, "I am of the opinion . . . destroyed by intense enemy fire," "to say today was terrible," "roughest day . . . so far": missing-in-action reports; KBD, 10/24; AGH 23. Fletcher swam for six hours: WMF pilot log late entry. Floated across coral reef, cut shoe: WMF. Latitude, longitude of *Musashi* wreck: Hackett and Kingsepp: *Tabular Records of Movement*. (NOTE: According to Mr. Sander Kingsepp, other Japanese sources (the log of her escorts) place the sinking at twelve degrees, fifty minutes north, and 122 degrees and thirty-five minutes east. Mr. Kingsepp has accepted *Musashi*'s deck log position as authoritative, but acknowledges that the battleship's bridge was a shambles and that there could be lag or error in the deck log entry. E-mail exchange of August 31, 2011.)

CHAPTER THIRTEEN: OFF BANTON AND CAPE ENGANO

Fletcher lands on uninhabited island, no water, ate cherry tomatoes, drank coconut milk, slept in narra tree, built bamboo raft for escape, snakes on island, "snakes be damned," bamboo coolie hat and bamboo cups: WMF; "Edwardsville Flyer Home, Saved by Filipino Guerrillas," *Edwardsville Intelligencer*; Hancock, "New Airport Director, Aviation Gives Him Busy Life," *Memphis Press Scimtar*. Banton Island location, topography, RAAF map. Battle of Surigao Strait, transit of Center Force into Philippine Sea, Battle Off Samar: Morison, *History, Vol. XII*, 198–241, 196, 242–88; Woodward, *The Battle for Leyte Gulf*, 83–119; 153, 203. Sacrifice of *Hoel*, *Samuel B. Roberts*, and *Johnson* off Samar: Hornfischer, *The Last Stand of the Tin Can Sailors*. "Storm the center": Freidman, *Afternoon of the Rising Sun*, 148. "Trusting in divine guidance": Thomas, *Sea of Thunder*, 224. Strike 2 Able, October 25 (diagram of torpedo runs), "check all switches . . .": AAR, 10/25. Antiaircraft blew huge hole in Barden's fuselage, *Intrepid* heads south to intercept Japanese task force, 38.3 and 38.4 stay behind "to polish off . . . the cripples," "everyone P.O'd at the move," Doc Fish's whiskey welcome that night, "lost the coin toss" on 10/26, "a man lucky enough to fly through that AA three consecutive times," "our big beautiful battleships . . . haven't fired a damned shot": KBD, 10/25, 10/26; AAR, 10/26. Return flight on 10/26, scattered aircraft, "at the limit of endurance": AGH, 24, 25; KDB, 10/26. Tokyo Rose, Admiral Halsey dispatch, "honor to be your commander": AGH, 25.

CHAPTER FOURTEEN: OFF BANTON AND LUZON

Hornet, VT-11, aircraft shifted to *Intrepid*, "God only knows when it will be mailed," Long turns in wings, Karch requests transfer, "Things are so bad . . . ASP today," "No food, no bombs, no pilots . . . fought all alone . . . shoe clerk . . . expect a mutiny," Crowley's Tavern at Ulithi, replacement pilots "not half-way ready," pilots meet Commander Coleman, Delaney fight, rumors of bombing Tokyo, Commander Ellis promoted to air officer, Air Group 18's statistics compared to Fifth Fleet, "small wonder we were tired," "best news of the week . . . Fletch . . . is with our forces on Panay": KBD, 10/27, 10/28, 11/2, 11/3, 11/7, 11/9, 11/11, 11/12, 11/15, 11/14. Clark Field, Legaspi strikes, AAR, 10/29, 11/5. Air department running "slick as a whistle," less "inertia, red tape," Delaney knocks down obnoxious pilot from Air Group 19, "anyone else from nineteen?" first kamikaze hit on October 29, Clark Field an "unhealthy place": AGH, 29, 26. Kamikaze hit on October 29: Zollo, *Intrepid*, *Day by Day*, 131. Mass ditching of Lieutenant Bud Williams's division: AAR, 10/29; BSJ. Fletcher encounter with porpoises, encounter with Filipino fishermen, initial uncertainty regarding intentions of fishermen, "should I begin a small naval war right here," taken to Banton, angry natives ashore, old Filipino woman cares for him in hut, mayor's daughters sing "Let Me Call You Sweetheart," led to cave, first meeting with guerrillas, raid on village, bodies impaled in narra trees, sailboat ride to Panay, kept mostly in hold, meets Lieutenant Junior Grade James Ritchie, arrives on Panay near Kalibo: WMF; Hancock, "Aviation Gives Him a Full Life," *Memphis Press Scimitar*. Lieutenant Junior Grade Ritchie's ship, squadron, and date of forced landing: USN/USMC combat loss forms. (NOTE: My father spoke distinctly of being transported to Panay in a "hot, smelly" sail-powered fishing boat and of stopping to pick up another downed navy pilot en route. He spoke of being "crammed in the hold" with the other pilot. I have no independent evidence confirming that his companion was Ritchie. Jim Ritchie fits the profile because he was forced down at about the same time as my father, and because he was a fighter pilot who had no crewmen with him. With the exception of Bill Shackelford, the navy pilots who ended up in the Libertad camp were, according to Shackelford and U.S. Navy transportation records, torpedo-plane pilots with surviving crewmen. The *Gosport* article cited in the bibliography reports that Fletcher and Ritchie "made their way to Panay independently." This could be true, except perhaps for the final leg of the journey. On the other hand, the second pilot in the sailboat could have been someone else. There is no doubt Ritchie and Fletcher lived together among the guerrillas on Panay for nearly six weeks. Similarly, I have no independent corroboration of the atrocities perpetrated against the villagers on Banton. The Periodic Reports of the Sixth Mountain Division for October and November 1944 do not mention this incident. Although USAFFE records contain numerous reports of Japanese atrocities in the Philippines, the guerrilla accounts seem to be focused on incidents that occurred on the major islands or involved soldiers or political figures.) Downed pilots cautioned not to speak with natives when en route: WJS. Composition of 61st Infantry Combat Team, Third Lieutenant Ricardo Duremdes, M Company: R.G. 407, *G-1 Periodic Report No. 10, USAFFE Sixth Mountain Division.*

CHAPTER FIFTEEN: ON PANAY

Guerrilla organization in the Philippines, old Philippine constabulary, death of General Simeon de Jesus, Philippine Regional Section established, coordination and supply, coast watchers, some guerrilla units "communist tainted," Allied Intelligence Bureau, escape routes established, incorporated into USAFFE, radio broadcasts from station KAZ in Australia, Franco Vera Reyes as collaborator: Willoughby, Chamberlain, *MacArthur, 1941–1951*, 58–59, 214–15, 216, 230, 219. Guerrilla organization, "criminality and score-settling," Japanese landings on Panay: Foot, Dear, *Oxford Companion*, 879, 881. Panay geography and place names: RAAF silk map. Ati legend: Rowthorn, *Philippines*, 333–34. Death of Second Lieutenant Conrado Aguila, prisoner pen near Kalibo, downed Japanese aircraft near Kalibo, Patria and Libertad camp locations; Colonel Peralta background and character, Lieutenant Colonel Garcia background and character, Garcia suspected of corruption, "due to poor organization . . . for shipment," guerrilla general orders for camp life, "women of doubtful virtue," devalued currencies on Panay, native complaints against guerrillas, guerrilla pay levels and pay shortages, food shortages on Panay, educational level of guerrillas, conflict between Peralta and Tomas Confessor: R.G. 407, *G-1 Periodic Report No. 10, USAFFE Sixth Mountain Division*, and *G-1 Periodic Report No. 11, 1 October 1944 through 30 November 1944.* (NOTE: The latter report records: "On 24 Nov a motor boat that was anchored at Libertad, Pandan was also sank [sic] by men of 'M' Co.") Headquarters 61st Infantry, "General Orders, Nos. 1 and 4, 11 Oct. 44 and 5 Oct. 44"; R. K. Sutherland, general headquarters, G-2 Section, South Pacific Area, "Guerrilla Resistance Movements in the Philippines," March 31, 1945. "Staff Study on the Present Conflict Between the District Commander on One Hand and Mr. Tomas Confessor and His Political Faction on the Other, 18 Aug. 44"; Message to General MacArthur from Colonel Peralta, July 5, 1944, regarding dispute with Tomas Confessor. Will's clothing in camp, reddish beard, age range and appearance of guerrillas, some armed with spears: WMF. Shackelford background, circumstances of crash landing on Panay and rescue, life in camp with Lieutenant Colonel Chaves and wife, guerrilla ambush of Japanese staff car, guerrilla refusal to bury Japanese on Philippine soil; journey to Libertad, Second Lieutenant John Wilder and cigarettes, Chaves loan, two-hundred-peso fine for confiscating a chicken, Libertad village and schoolhouse description, "common goal [of Americans] to get fed enough," foraging for food with Fletcher, offer to fish for food declined, faux rice coffee, Japanese patrol boat description, made of wood, many antennae, machine gun in bow, burning of boat, beheading of Japanese sergeant, drinking sake afterward, standing watch on *Hake*, bombing attack on submarine, Shackelford shaving, submarine grew hot, Submarine Rest Home, poaching Christmas tree from city park, Lieutenant Colonel Garcia's letter of certification to Shackelford for participating in raid on Japanese motorboat November 24, 1944, off Libertad: WGS and WGS personal papers. Fletcher's overland trip from Kalibo to Patria camp, encounter with downed Japanese aircraft, Lieutenant Duremdes presents Japanese flag to Will, food in camp, guerrillas ate bat meat, monkey meat, "rooster killed in cockfight," ambush of Japanese patrol boat from bramble at water's edge, premature shot fired, rounding up of survivors, motorboat caught fire and burned, petty officer spits in Fletcher's face during interrogation, Fletcher pummels petty officer, beheading, treatment of burned Japanese prisoners, two prisoners tried to escape and were killed, Raczynski dives into surf to capture flag, bolo knife presented to Fletcher, white circles made of bamboo and covered with ladies' underwear; "didn't give a damn . . . in the next hut," gave pistol to Duremdes and knife to wounded Filipino boy, stripping before boarding *Hake*, chief petty officer provides new sandals, good food, crowded boat, bombing attack off Borneo and reaction, fear, Lieutenant Colonel Garcia's letter of certification to Fletcher for participating in raid on Japanese motorboat. (NOTE: The letter certifies participation "in the ambush of a Japanese motorboat by a platoon under Lieutenant Duremdes of "M" Co. 2nd. Bn. this regiment, on 24 November, 1944, off Libertad, Panay, resulting in the sinking of said boat and a casualty [sic] of an estimated twenty (20) Jap soldiers and crew.") WMF and WMF personal papers. Strikes on Clark and Nichols fields, "indulging in aerobatics": AAR 11/19. Relief message, ten more weeks at least: KBD, 11/19. Lieutenant John Wesley Williams of VT-29 embarked on *Cabot* shot down October 24: Friedman, *Afternoon of the Rising Sun*, 126–27. Williams as senior American officer in charge at Libertad: *Hake* deck log, 12/5/44; WGS. Lieutenant Junior Grade Robert K. McAdams of VT-19 background, crash, rescue: RKM. Raczynski served as Williams's turret gunner: missing-in-action reports. All *Hake* times, courses, depths, speeds, personnel during rescue and rendezvous with two sailboats: *Hake* deck log, 12/5/44. Loss of *Growler*: Mazza, "USS *Growler* SS-215 Sixth War Patrol." Passage to Australia, bombing attack off Borneo, exchanged signals with *Beaufighter*, berth at Perth: *Hake* deck log. Submarine certificate presented to Fletcher as rescued "Zoomie" by Lieutenant Commander J. C. Weatherwax and Commander F. E. Haylor: WMF personal papers. Thanksgiving feast on *Intrepid*: AGH, 36, KBD 11/21. Quiet "won't last": KBD, 11/21. Kamikaze attacks on *Intrepid* and damage, November 25, 1944: IDL, 11/25; AGH, 30–34. (NOTE: Lieutenant Race's graphic description of the kamikaze attacks, "Kamikaze Special Assault Corps," including his account of the death of Lieutenant Commander Jack "Doc" Fish, appears only in his unpublished version of the air group history.) Last launch before kamikaze attack, Ensign Vernon Sistrunk's close call, Ben St. John's sinking of minesweeper at Marinduque, strike group diversion to Tacloban airfield: BSJ; telephone interview with Steve Sistrunk. Lieutenant Joe Purdy was VB-18's ACI officer: Forsyth, *Helldivers*, 89. Air Group 18 rejoining *Intrepid* at Ulithi; Doc Fish "helleva swell fellow," rumor of Hellcat checkouts, VF-18 transferred to *Hancock*, "one big unhappy family," "parties in progress 24 hours a day," "what more can be said": KBD: 11/25 through 11/28, 11/29, 11/30, 12/14, 12/20.

EPILOGUE

Fate of *Musashi*'s crew: Yoshimura, *Battleship Musashi*, 176–77. Fatal damage done to *Musashi* by torpedoes, not bombs: TMJ. Commander Ellis's career: *New York Times* obituary. Ben St. John career, Williams's fate: BSJ. Karch career: interview with Ed Auld. Careers of other named pilots: interviews with next of kin. Awards, see appendix.

INDEX

A-Go Plan, 131, 143, 172, 196
Aasgard, ARM3c A. C., 376
ABDACOM, 125
Acey-deucey, 7, 22, 154
Admiralty Islands, 129, 235
Aegean Sea, 58
Aerobatics, 99
African American gunners, 311
Aguila, Second Lieutenant
    Conrado, 333
Air Group 18 (see Carrier Air
    Group 18)
Air Medal, 368, 373–76
Air-sea rescue, 146, 210, 220
Air-to-air gunnery practice,
    84–85, 94
Akagi (aircraft carrier), 127, 128
Alabama (battleship), 294
Alameda Island, 53
Alameda Naval Air Station
    (NAS), 53–57, 64–66, 69,
    106
Alicante Airfield, Negros Island,
    181
Allen, Lieutenant Commander
    Ernest, 7, 13, 14, 21, 22,
    24–26, 50, 87, 93, 152–55,
    170, 173, 174, 177, 178,
    194, 203, 210, 223, 267,
    289, 354
Allied Intelligence Bureau (AIB),
    327
Amerman, Lieutenant Junior
    Grade C. P., 192
Amphibious operations, 92
Anderson, Lieutenant Junior
    Grade M. A. "Andy,"
    157–58, 175
Angaur Island, 152, 160, 161,
    177, 183–84
Anitaquipan Point, Philippines,
    288
Antisubmarine patrol duty
    (ASP), 122, 199, 235, 321

Aparri, Philippines, 230–31
Approach circle, 113–14, 116
APX-2 IFF equipment, 113
Area Two Sugar North, Hawaii,
    86–87
Argus (aircraft carrier), 61
Arizona (battleship), 63, 110
Ark Royal (aircraft carrier), 62
Armor box, 136–37, 266
Arnold, General Henry, 125
Arresting gear cables, 30
Atago (cruiser), 123, 229, 233,
    235, 298
Ati people, 329, 331
Attu Island, 141
Australia, 125, 126, 152, 235,
    236, 360, 363
Avengers (see TBM1C Avengers)

B-17 bombers, 186
B-25 bombers, 54
B-29 bombers, 132
Babelthuap Island, Caroline
    Islands, 152, 156–69, 175,
    187
Balacaue Point, Panay Island,
    329
Balanacan Bay, Philippines, 354
Balascio, ARM2c C. A., 376
Ballale Island, 141
Baltimore (cruiser), 108
Banton Island, Philippines, 280,
    285, 294, 301, 302, 304–9,
    328, 349
Banzai charges, 200
Barden, Lieutenant Junior Grade
    Kenneth P. "Kenny," 8–11,
    14, 37, 70, 82, 83, 87, 107,
    108, 112, 192, 202, 219,
    223, 226, 235, 314, 323,
    340, 350, 368, 374
    background of, 7
    death of Christensen and,
    104–5

diary entries of, 81, 93, 145,
    154, 178, 179, 218, 224,
    233, 278, 294, 299, 321,
    322, 325, 355, 365
    as duty officer, 103
    as flight officer, 7, 23, 237, 277,
    321
    Formosa strikes and, 209, 214,
    218
    Margie and, 75–78, 185, 303,
    304, 367
    marriage of, 78
    Philippine strikes and, 175,
    178–80, 182, 192, 232, 233,
    260, 261, 289, 290, 299,
    310
    plane hit and damaged, 290
    promotion of, 85–86
    training accident and, 76–77
    training and, 89–95
Barden, Margaret "Margie"
    McWhorter, 75–78, 87,
    185, 303, 304, 367
Barrier area, 30, 31
Barth, Bruce, 184
Bataan Death March, 5
Bataan Peninsula, 5, 186, 326
Bates, Lieutenant Junior Grade
    William C. "Bill," 70, 78,
    82, 85–86, 111, 112, 209,
    212–14, 216, 232, 260, 299,
    310, 314, 368, 374
Beatley, Lieutenant Junior Grade
    R. C. "Beatle," 176, 206
Beaufort scale, 39
Beeson, ARM3c J. C., 376
Bellamy, ARM2c F., 291, 376
Belleau Wood (light carrier), 151
Besoian, AOM3c William
    Henry, 150, 377
Biak Island, 126, 143
Big Fleet Battle, 21–22
Big Island of Hawaii, 82
Biloxi (cruiser), 3

Biplanes, 60
Bird strikes, 69
Birmingham (cruiser), 259–60
Bismarck Sea, 129
Bismarck (pocket battleship), 62, 64
Boeing Aircraft Company, 100, 132
Bogan, Rear Admiral Gerald F., 13, 21, 23, 24, 26, 28, 37, 151, 154, 168, 194, 196, 201, 203, 209, 218, 222, 223, 231, 232, 236, 237, 278, 294, 311, 314, 353, 355
Bohol Island, Philippines, 286
Bolger, Captain Joseph P., 13–14, 110, 121, 145, 176, 183, 194, 200, 223, 312, 314, 355
Bombing Squadron 18 (VB-18), 8, 22, 27–29, 40, 51, 65, 84, 88, 113, 147, 178, 179, 365
SB2C3 Helldivers and, 9, 14, 16, 27, 31, 32, 39, 46, 68, 82–83, 105, 145, 154, 156–59, 161–62, 164–66, 174–76, 180, 186–88, 191, 193, 196–97, 204, 209, 211–14, 217, 219, 220, 243, 266, 268, 269, 289, 290, 297, 298, 309–12, 340, 355
Bonner, ARM3c G. T., 376
Borneo, 124, 125, 135, 143, 229–30, 232–35, 361
Bougainville Island, 129, 133, 141
Brewster Aeronautical Corporation, 61
Brisbin, Lieutenant Junior Grade Robert "Bris," 93, 150, 374
Brooks, AOM2c D. F., 375
Brunei, Borneo, 135
Brunei Bay, Borneo, 229–30, 232–35
BT-1 dive-bombers, 61
Bugasong, Panay Island, 329
Bunker Hill (aircraft carrier), 87, 150, 151, 191, 201, 209, 225, 231, 236, 268
Burma, 125

Cabot (light carrier), 3, 6, 23, 28, 37, 46, 150, 151, 203, 209, 236, 237, 260, 268, 269, 272, 343, 351
Calamian Group, Philippines, 197
California (battleship), 63, 263, 287

Camiguin Island, Philippines, 231
Cammarata, ARM2c J. M., 376
Canberra (cruiser), 221, 222, 237
Cape Engano, Philippines, 293, 294, 299
Cape Esperance, Battle of, 129
Capiz, Panay Island, 329, 331
Caroline Islands, 5, 106, 141, 152, 200–1
Carrier Air Group 8 (Air Group 8), 150, 191
Carrier Air Group 9 (Air Group 9), 340
Carrier Air Group 15 (Air Group 15), 265, 343
Carrier Air Group 18 (Air Group 18), 8, 154, (*see also* Bombing Squadron 18 [VB–18]; Fighting Squadron 18 [VF–18]; Torpedo Squadron 18 [VT–18])
aircraft, 9
commander of (*see* Ellis, Commander William E. "Wild Bill")
plane handlers, 10–11
scuttlebutt concerning assignments, 65, 77–78, 87
squadrons, 8
transfer to Oahu, 93–94
Carrier Air Group 19 (Air Group 19), 94, 106, 265, 289, 325
Carrier Air Group 20 (Air Group 20), 122, 145
Carrier Air Group 28 (Air Group 28), 341
Carrier Air Group 29 (Air Group 29), 26, 27, 51, 268, 271, 343
Carrier Air Service Unit (CASU), 69
Carrier Air Service Unit One (CASU-1), 95, 103, 111
Carrier landing pattern, 114–20
Catapult area, 30
Cebu Island, 173, 177–79, 187, 194, 197
Celebes Island, 124, 361
Central Visayas, 9, 172, 173, 177–78, 183, 203, 224, 232, 234, 341, 350
Cepon, ARM2c A. M., 376
Chaves, Lieutenant Colonel Jules P., 341–42, 344
Chiang Kaishek, 201
Chikuma (cruiser), 292, 298
Chinese airfields, 201, 227

Chinese Communists, 124
Chinese Nationalists, 124, 201
Chitose (aircraft carrier), 290, 299
Chiyoda (aircraft carrier), 299
Chokai (cruiser), 50, 292, 298
Christensen, Lieutenant Leo M. "Chris," 104–5, 111, 374
Christman, AMM2c George E., Jr., 24, 34–35, 41, 42, 48, 160, 166–67, 191, 245, 247, 249, 251, 253, 278, 285, 295–97, 349, 377
Churchill, Winston, 62
Clark Field, Philippines, 172–73, 186, 191–94, 303–4, 309–13, 322, 325, 340
Close air support, 92
Close unity doctrine, 312, 313
Cockpit escape procedures, 253, 254, 313
Cohapee (escort carrier), 73, 80
Colahan (destroyer), 158, 205
Coleman, Commander Wilson McConnell, 321, 325, 340, 350–53, 365
Confessor, Tomas, 328, 338
Copaghe, Carlos, 341
Coral Sea, Battle of the, 3, 126–27
Coron Bay, Philippines, 9, 196–97
Coronado Island, 74
Corregidor, Philippines, 5, 125, 366
Cowpens (light carrier), 151
Crenshaw, ACOM W. M., 375
Crossing the T tactic, 287
Cruising readiness condition, 16–17
Curtis, Glenn, 57
Curtiss Aircraft Company, 59, 61, 83
Cushing (destroyer), 299

Dace (submarine), 8, 13, 17, 20, 21, 235–36
Daliao, Mindanao, 175, 177
Dampier Strait, 126
Darter (submarine), 8, 13, 17, 20, 21, 235–36
Darwin, Australia, 363
Davao City, Mindanao, 173–77, 194
Davao Gulf, Mindanao, 174
Davison, Rear Admiral Ralph E., 151, 221, 236, 263, 266
DC-3 Skytrain, 58
De Jesus, Brigadier General Simeon, 327

Dead reckoning, 66–67, 102, 199, 216
Delaney, Lieutenant Junior Grade Vernon A. "Duke," 75, 90, 232, 267, 269, 299, 321, 325, 340, 374
Destroyer Squadron 53, 151, 203, 286–87
Dewey, Admiral George, 57, 108
Dilgren, Ensign Paul, 374
DiMaggio, Joe, 95
Dimarzo, Lieutenant D. D., 353
Dinagat Island, Philippines, 228, 229, 263, 286
Dingalan Bay, Philippines, 186
Distinguished Flying Cross, 368, 373
Division-vee formation, 213, 214
Dixon, AOM1c J., 375
Doolittle, Colonel James, 54
Douglas Aircraft Company, 58, 59, 61
Doyle, Ensign Frank D. "Doc," 70, 76, 91, 94, 187–89, 191, 223, 289–91, 374
Dragan, Lieutenant Junior Grade Stephen, 77, 78, 374
Drop tanks, 18, 19, 22, 28, 34, 40
DT-1 biplanes, 58–59
Dugas, AOM2c I. A., 375
Dugas, AOM2c Irving, 270–71
Dulag, Philippines, 4, 231, 232
Duremdes, Third Lieutenant Ricardo, 324, 331–35, 339, 340, 344–49, 356, 358
Dutch East India Company, 207
Dutch East Indies, 124, 125

East China Sea, 208
East Island, 127
Eastern Aircraft Corporation, 78
85th Imperial Rescript, 171
Eil Malk Island, 152
Eisengrein, Lieutenant Edward H., 211, 217, 219, 220
Ellis, Commander William E. "Wild Bill," 8, 11, 14–16, 19, 21, 23, 24, 26–29, 39–40, 46–48, 51, 88, 150, 176, 179, 223, 239, 343, 355
  assumes command of Carrier Air Group 18 (Air Group 18), 64–65
  Babelthuap strikes and, 157, 158
  birth of, 64
  death of, 367
  ferry flight to *Intrepid* and, 112, 116

Formosa strikes and, 209–11, 213
in Hawaii, 81–82, 89, 93, 94
nickname of, 89
Okinawa strikes and, 204–6
personality of, 64
Philippine strikes and, 174, 175, 177, 186, 231, 232, 237, 256, 268–70, 289, 297, 298, 309–10
physical appearance of, 64
promoted to *Intrepid* air officer, 321
training of pilots and, 89, 93, 94, 104, 111, 120, 121, 185
Ellyson, Lieutenant Theodore G., 57
Ely, Eugene, 57
Eniwetok Atoll, Marshall Islands, 106, 122, 129, 133, 146–48, 150, 151, 153
Enterprise (aircraft carrier), 63, 122, 127, 128, 145, 151, 263, 266, 268
Erminger, ARM1c H. B., 376
Eslick, Lieutenant Commander Mark, 180, 197, 209, 211, 212, 217, 220
Essex (aircraft carrier), 151, 259, 264–66, 268, 269
Essex-class aircraft carriers, 50, 79, 105, 108, 151
Europe first policy, 125
Evans, Lieutenant Junior Grade G. W., 359
Explosive D, 167

F2A Buffalo fighters, 61
F4F Wildcat fighters, 61, 231
F6F Hellcat fighters, 9, 14, 16, 26, 28, 31–32, 39–40, 46, 51, 91, 105, 145, 156, 157, 161–62, 164, 175, 180–82, 184, 186–88, 191–93, 197, 199, 204–6, 209, 212–16, 219, 221, 231, 232, 243, 246, 248, 264–68, 289, 297, 309–14, 341, 355
F8C Falcon biplanes, 59
Fabrica, Negros Island, 180, 182
Fanshaw Bay (escort carrier), 292
Field carrier landing practice (FCLP) procedures, 71–74, 94, 104, 112
Fighting Squadron 18 (VF-18), 8, 22, 27, 29, 65, 88, 113, 147, 158, 159, 163, 174, 178, 365
  F6F Hellcats, 9, 14, 16, 26, 28, 31–32, 39–40, 46, 51, 91,

105, 145, 156, 157, 161–62, 164, 175, 180–82, 184, 186–88, 191–93, 197, 199, 204–6, 209, 212–16, 219, 221, 231, 232, 243, 246, 248, 264–68, 289, 297, 309–14, 341, 355
Fighting Squadron 37 (VF-37), 323
Fish, Doc Jack, 192, 271, 294, 314, 340, 353–55
Fiske, Admiral Bradley A., 57–58
Flap retraction, 44
Fletcher, Betty, 97, 98, 155, 296, 364
Fletcher, Ensign Willard M., 1, 6, 8–12, 16, 22, 24, 147, 148, 267, 268, 374
  adrift and swimming in Sibuyan Sea, 256–58, 260–62, 273, 275, 279
  antisubmarine patrol duty (ASP) and, 122, 199
  as assistant maintenance officer, 197–99, 202
  in Australia, 364–65
  Avenger hit by antiaircraft fire, 249–51
  Babelthuap strikes and, 158–69
  on Banton Island, 314–20
  builds escape raft, 294–95, 301
  cadet training of, 95–102
  castaway on islet, 279–80, 283–86, 294–97, 301–2
  childhood of, 97–98
  commissioned, 101–2
  crash and sinking of Avenger and, 252–56, 262
  death of, 367
  death of mother and, 98, 155
  death of Savage and, 169–70
  ferry flight to *Intrepid* and, 112–20
  Filipino boat rescue of, 307–9
  with Filipino guerrillas on Panay, 314–20, 323–24, 331–37, 339–40, 343–50
  first landing on *Intrepid* by, 112–20
  first mission of, 158–68, 187
  flight training and, 102–4
  Formosa strikes and, 217, 221
  hometown of, 2
  journey to Banton Island by, 304–7
  journey to Panay by, 323, 324
  love of flying, 98–99
  marriage of, 367

mechanical bent of, 198
Musashi strike, 51, 240–48
and
news of survival of, 325
Okinawa strike and, 205
parents of, 97
Peleliu strikes and, 184
personality of, 3
Philippine strikes and, 25–26,
    39, 47–49, 51, 174–77, 179,
    187–93, 240–56
physical appearance of, 3, 308,
    340, 364
as ping-pong player, 223
preparation for mission and,
    23–25, 30, 33–39
presumed dead, 277, 278, 296
raft trip to Banton Island by,
    301–2
submarine rescue of, 357–64
takeoff from *Intrepid* by,
    41–44
transfer to *Intrepid* and, 107–8
transferred to CASU-1, 103
voyage to Hawaii and, 2
weapons and equipment issued
    to, 24–25
Fletcher, Faye Emily
    Frickenstein, 367
Fletcher, Gerry, 97, 98, 155, 296,
    364
Fletcher, Naomi, 96–98, 155,
    247, 296, 297, 306, 365
Fletcher, Norman, 96
Fletcher, Rear Admiral Frank
    Jack "Black Jack," 3, 127,
    128
Fletcher-class destroyers, 3
Flight deck, 30–33, 117, 119
Flight deck director (Fly 1),
    39–40, 42, 43
Flying Fish (submarine), 142
Ford Island, Hawaii, 81, 82, 107,
    110, 115, 121
Formation flying, 20, 28, 46, 68,
    74, 113, 159, 213, 214, 216
Formosa, 9, 20, 133–35, 200,
    201, 203, 206–24, 234,
    278, 325
Forrestal, Secretary of the Navy
    James, 222
Forsyth, Lieutenant Junior Grade
    John F., 34, 40, 212, 217,
    220, 256, 290
Fort, ARM3c C. W., 270, 376
Fouled deck, 114, 116, 118, 158
Fox Corpen, 36, 37, 39, 45
Franklin (aircraft carrier), 94,
    151, 221, 222, 263, 266,
    268, 269, 325, 351

Free deck launch, 31
Free Philippine government, 328,
    336–38
Fremantle, Australia, 360, 363
Fukudome, Vice Admiral
    Shigeru, 208–9, 218, 221,
    222
Fuso (battleship), 286, 287

Galbreath, ARM2c B. B., 377
Gambier Bay (destroyer escort),
    292, 300
Garber, ARM1c S. E., 376
Garcia, Lieutenant Colonel
    Cirillo, 324, 334–35, 338,
    340, 345, 350, 356, 358,
    359–60
Gato-class submarines, 356
Gay, Ensign George H., 63
General Motors Company, 78
General quarters, 15–16
Ghesquiere, Lieutenant
    Commander George D.,
    217, 219, 220
Ghormley, Admiral Robert L.,
    126, 128, 129
Gilbert Islands, 5, 63, 78, 101,
    122, 129
Glenn L. Martin Company, 59,
    60
Glide-bombing, 68, 162, 180,
    211, 221
Go-around, 114
Greater East Asia Co-Prosperity
    Sphere, 327, 329
Ground effect, 43
Ground personnel, 107, 109
Group breakup circle, 113
Growler (submarine), 356–57
Gruenewald, Lieutenant Junior
    Grade John W., 212
Grumman Aircraft Engineering
    Corporation, 19, 61
Guadalcanal, 50, 122, 128–30,
    133, 141, 151, 153, 228
Guam, 131–33, 152
Guerrilla movement, in
    Philippines, 314–20,
    323–24, 326–50, 331–37,
    339–40, 343–50, 357–60
Guimaras Island, Philippines,
    329

Hachimaki, 239
Haguro (cruiser), 292
Hake (submarine), 356–57,
    359–64
Halsey, Admiral William F., 6,
    37, 126, 129, 130, 134,
    150–52, 172, 173, 182–84,

    186, 194, 204, 221, 222,
    224, 234–36, 264, 272–73,
    278, 288, 293, 294, 297,
    300, 353
Halsey Powell (destroyer), 192,
    314
Hammer-and-anvil torpedo
    attack, 28, 51, 242, 260,
    265, 366
Hancock (aircraft carrier), 151,
    203, 209, 235, 268, 351,
    355, 365
Hanzak, AOM2c R. J., 375
Hardhead (submarine), 356–57
Harris, Lieutenant Cecil,
    180–82, 312
Haruna (battleship), 50, 234,
    238, 288
Haylor, Commander F. E.,
    356–57, 360–63
Heermann (destroyer), 292
Helena (cruiser), 63
Hellcats (*see* F6F Hellcat fighters)
Helldivers (*see* SB2C-3 Helldiver
    dive-bombers)
Heysinger, Lieutenant R. F.,
    360
High-velocity aircraft rockets
    (HVAR), 84, 85, 150
Hirohito, Emperor, 124, 141–42,
    153, 165, 171, 204, 208,
    222, 229, 230
Hiryu (aircraft carrier), 127, 128
Hiyo (aircraft carrier), 133
Hoel (destroyer), 292, 300
Homing and directional beacons,
    66
Hong Kong, 124
Honolulu Conference, 108–9,
    133–34
Horizontal bombing, 68
Hornet (aircraft carrier), 54, 63,
    127, 151, 303
Horton, Lieutenant Junior Grade
    Marvin Perry, Jr., 69, 374
Hosoya, Petty Officer Second
    Class Shiro, 239, 240, 248,
    274, 276–77
Houston (cruiser), 151, 203, 222,
    237
Hoy, AOM1c R. C., 375
Huber, ARM3c R. E., 376
Hudson, AOM2c D. S., 375
Huerta, Victoriano, 57
Hukbalahap (People's Anti-
    Japanese Army), 326, 328
Hunter, ARM3c Billy, 232–33,
    377
Hunters Point Naval Shipyard,
    San Francisco, 106

Ichi-Go offensive, 201
Ie Shima Island, 204–5
IFF identification channel, 216
Illustrious (aircraft carrier), 62
Iloilo, Panay Island, 329, 331
Incendiary bombs, 176, 178
Independence (light carrier), 122, 150, 151, 203, 209, 236, 237, 351
Indochina, 208
Inoguchi, Lieutenant Junior Grade Satoshi, 195
Inoguchi, Captain Rikihei, 195, 196
Inoguchi, Rear Admiral Toshihira, 195–96, 229, 233, 239, 252, 266–67, 271, 274, 275
International Date Line, 148
Intrepid (aircraft carrier), 93, 94, 153, 185, 236. (*see also* Carrier Air Group 18)
air attacks on, 218–19, 221
air department," 10–11
brain trust, 13–14, 17
carrier landing pattern, 114–20
commissioned, 105
discipline aboard, 183
ferry flight of VT-18 to, 112–20
flight deck, 30–33, 117, 119
flight deck personnel, 32
general quarters call, 15–16
hangar bay of, 10
hazards aboard, 147–48
junior officers' bunkroom, 1
kamikaze attacks on, 311, 321, 351–55
landing area, 30
in Marshall Islands, 105
primary flight control station "pri-fly," 31, 36
radio call sign of, 164
ready rooms, 11–13
repairs to, 106, 111
return to U.S., 365
in Saipan, 200
shakedown cruise, 109, 110, 113, 121
ship's company and air group personnel relations, 109–10, 121
size of, 107–8, 117, 120
songfest aboard, 223–24
supplies and equipment, 106–7, 109
transport duty and, 106
typhoons and, 9, 201–2, 322
at Ulithi, 200–3, 322–23, 325
war games and, 150

Iowa (battleship), 3, 203, 278, 294, 351, 354
Iowa-class battleships, 26, 50, 136, 137
Isuzu (cruiser), 357
Italian campaign, 101
Italian navy, 62

James, ARM3c T., 376
Japanese forces
1st Air Fleet, 172, 195
First Striking Force, 228–35
2nd Fleet, 50, 123, 124, 135, 143, 144
6th Base Air Force, 208
Fourteenth Army, 4
kamikaze (special tactics units), 195, 221–22, 293, 311, 351–55
Kawaguchi Brigade, 153
Mobile Fleet, 132–33, 143, 172, 224, 229, 230, 232, 299
Japanese prisoners, 332–33
Java Sea, 124, 125, 222, 228
Jernigan, AOM3c P. D., 376
Jesperson, ARM3c G. G., 376
Johnson, AOM2c M. W., 72–73, 375
Johnston (destroyer), 292, 300
Joint Chiefs of Staff (JCS), 125–26, 133, 227
Jones, AOM2c Rodger W., 311, 376, 377
Jones, Banton Island, Philippines, 294
Juneau (cruiser), 151

Kaga (aircraft carrier), 127, 128
Kagoshima Bay, Kyushu, 63
Kalibo, Panay Island, 323, 324, 329, 333
Kaneohe, Hawaii, 7
Karch, Lieutenant Junior Grade Lloyd E., 187, 188, 192, 223, 267, 269, 270, 314, 368, 374
Kaskaskia (tanker), 183
Kato, Captain Kenkichi, 251, 262, 266, 267, 271, 274–77
Kawaguchi Brigade, 153
Kawasaki fighters "Nicks," 212
Kawasaki fighters "Tonys," 191, 192, 213–15, 221, 332
Keelung, Formosa, 207
Kempeitai (Japanese secret police), 327
Kiirun Harbor, Formosa, 209–14, 217, 219, 220
King, Fleet Admiral Ernest J., 125, 133, 134, 300

Kingsbury, AOM2c F. E., 376
Kinkaid, Vice Admiral Thomas C., 227, 263, 288, 291, 293, 300
Kishinami (destroyer), 235
Kitkun Bay (escort carrier), 293
Kiyoshima (destroyer), 275
Knoop, AOM2c J. F., 376
Koegler, ARM3c D. R., 376
Kongo (battleship), 50, 228, 238
Kongo-class battleships, 50
Korea, 208
Korean War, 367
Koror Island, 152
Krantz, AOM3c Francis R., 181, 377
Krause, AOM2c F. G., 376
Krueger, Lieutenant General Walter, 227, 232
Kumano (cruiser), 50
Kure Naval Yard, 141–44
Kurita, Vice Admiral Takeo, 50, 123, 124, 134, 144, 228–31, 233–36, 238, 241, 252, 264–66, 269, 271–74, 277, 286, 291–94, 297
Kusaie Island, 152
Kwajalein, Marshall Islands, 106, 129, 133
Kwiatkowski, ARM3c Edward J., 69, 377

Lae, New Guinea, 126
Lalor, AOM2c W. T., 376
Lamon Bay, Philippines, 4, 269
Landing signal officer (LSO), 71
Laner, Ensign Daniel, 103, 181, 349, 374
Langley (aircraft carrier), 59, 61, 126, 151, 259, 264
Langley, Samuel P., 59
Lankford, ARM3c Alfred B., 181, 377
Law (destroyer), 169
Le Hug Airfield, Philippines, 178
League of Nations, 153
Leahy, Admiral William D., 125, 133
Legaspi Field, Philippines, 173, 194, 322
Lexington (aircraft carrier), 59, 78–82, 94, 106, 126, 127, 151, 232, 259, 264–66, 268, 269, 289, 325, 343
Leyte Gulf, Philippines, 3–6, 15, 17, 18, 26, 228, 231, 233, 236, 239, 262–64, 266, 272, 274, 277, 286–89, 291, 293, 355

Leyte Island, Philippines, 8, 133, 173, 177, 178, 197, 227, 231, 232, 234, 236, 263, 286, 354

Libertad, Philippines, 340, 342–50, 356–58, 364

Lindbergh, Charles, 98

Lingayen Gulf, Philippines, 4, 192, 193, 227

Lingga Roads, 124, 134, 135, 144, 196, 228–30, 235

Lipa Field, Philippines, 322, 350

Littorio (battleship), 62

Live-ordnance bombing exercises, 90

Long, Lieutenant Junior Grade Albert J. "Al," 53, 55, 205, 214, 216, 232–33, 267, 268–70, 313, 314, 321, 374

Long Lance torpedoes, 229

Los Negros Island, Admiralty Islands, 129

Louisville (cruiser), 287

Luzon, Philippines, 4, 5, 9, 17, 26, 47, 57, 131–33, 143, 172, 177, 185–94, 227, 230–31, 233, 234, 236, 264, 272, 278, 288, 291, 293, 320, 322, 326

MacArthur, General Douglas, 108–9, 133, 153, 172, 173, 186, 197, 203
 as commander in Southwest Pacific area, 125, 126, 128–30
 escape from Corregidor, 5, 125
 Philippine guerrilla movement and, 326–29, 338, 343
 Philippine invasion and, 4–6, 133–34, 197, 203, 227–28, 232

Mae Wests, 24–25, 255–58, 273, 301, 302, 306

Maestra de Campo, Philippines, 280

Maier, Lieutenant J. F., 359

Makassar Strait, 361

Makin Atoll, Gilbert Islands, 129

Malakal Harbor, Palau Islands, 142

Malay Peninsula, 125

Mallory, Lieutenant Junior Grade C. M., 192

Manchuria, 208

Manila, Philippines, 177, 188, 227

Manila Bay, Philippines, 5, 14

Manus Island, Admiralty Islands, 129, 235

Mariana Islands, 5, 26, 50, 124, 131, 132, 143, 152, 172, 196

Marinduque Island, Philippines, 343, 354

Mark IV inflatable life raft, 253

Mark 13 aerial torpedoes, 15, 18, 20, 46, 86, 187, 289

Marshall, General George, 125

Marshall Islands, 5, 63, 106, 122, 129

Martin AM Maulers, 367

Martin BM-2 dive-bombers, 60

Masbate Island, Philippines, 47

Massachusetts (battleship), 111, 294

Massed attacks, 88–89, 161

Matina Airfield, Philippines, 174–77

Matsuyama Airfield, Formosa, 217–19

Matthews, Ensign Lyman A., 66, 374

Maya (cruiser), 236, 298

McAdams, Ensign Robert K., 343–44, 364

McCain, Vice Admiral John Sidney, 151, 221, 235, 236

McCampbell, Commander, 293

McCann, ARM3c Fred, 66, 377

McCollum, AOM2c H. E., 376

McCoy, ARM2c H. E., 376

McKee, Lieutenant Junior Grade John T., 75, 374

McKee, Lieutenant Junior Grade Robert, 93

McLerran, ARM2c Carl M., 311, 376, 377

McWhorter, Dickie, 75–77

McWhorter, Herbert, 75, 76, 78

McWhorter, Honey, 75, 76, 78

McWhorter, Margaret (*see* Barden, Margaret "Margie" McWhorter)

Meiji, Emperor, 207–8

Metzger, Lieutenant Junior Grade A. R., 359

Miami (cruiser), 3, 151, 203, 351

Midway, Battle of, 3, 26, 50, 63, 64, 83, 122, 124, 127–28, 130, 141, 171, 228

Millar, Lieutenant Junior Grade W. H., 22

Miller, ARM2c R. L., 376

Milne Bay, Papua New Guinea, 128

Mindanao, Philippines, 5, 47, 133, 152, 154, 173–77, 183, 234, 288, 326

Mindanao Sea, Philippines, 262, 263, 286, 287

Mindoro Island, Philippines, 14, 21, 25, 48, 49, 227, 238, 239, 242, 258, 280, 296, 297

Mine laying, 90

Minimum release altitude, 169

Mitchell, General William "Billy," 58

Mitscher, Vice Admiral Marc A., 6, 28, 37, 151, 168, 174, 184, 204, 209, 224, 225, 236, 264, 271, 272, 289, 290, 299, 351

Mitsubishi
 A6M fighter (Zeke/Zero), 180–81, 193, 290, 310, 351–52
 F1M reconnaissance seaplanes "Petes," 362
 heavy bombers "Sallys," 193
 medium bombers "Bettys," 191–93
 reconnaissance airplanes "Dinahs," 193

Mize, Johnny, 95

Moffett, Rear Admiral William A., 58

Mogami (cruiser), 286, 287

Mogami-class cruisers, 50, 272

Monowing design, 60–61

Monterey (light carrier), 151, 341

Moot, Lieutenant R. N. "Dick," 114, 117–19

Morison, Samuel Eliot, 54

Morris, Ensign Don, 168

Morris, Lieutenant Junior Grade Donald W. "Moe," 217–18, 223, 260, 374

Mount Arayat, Philippines, 186

Mount Baca, Philippines, 280

Mount Halcon, Philippines, 280

Mount Ngerchelchuus, Babelthuap, 161, 165, 166

Mount Niitaka, Formosa, 207

Murphy, Lieutenant Commander E. J., 184, 310

Murray State Teachers College, Kentucky, 95

Musashi (battleship), 229, 233, 234, 238, 251–52, 256, 285, 288, 298, 299, 363
 armament of, 136, 140, 143, 144
 casualties onboard, 274, 275
 construction of, 135–38
 Hirohito's visit to, 141–42
 hull armor of, 137
 Inoguchi as commander of, 195–96
 launch of, 138

Musashi (battleship) *(cont.)*
  at Lingga Roads, 124
  name of, 136, 140, 143, 144
  Sanshikidan shells fired by, 267
  sinking of, 275–77, 282
  size of, 136
  submarine attack on, 142
  superstructure of, 139
  survivors of sinking of, 366
  Task Group 38.3 attacks on, 51, 240–48, 260–62, 265–66, 269–71
Mussolini, Benito, 62
Myoko (cruiser), 236, 250, 288, 298, 299

Nachi-class cruisers, 50, 51, 256
Nagato (battleship), 50, 136, 234, 240, 288, 293
Nagumo, Vice Admiral Chuichi, 50, 127
Nakajima, 172
  fighters "Irving," 212
  fighters "Oscar," 213–15, 309, 310
  fighters "Tojo," 214, 215
  heavy bombers "Helen," 192
Nansei Shoto, 204
Napalm bombs, 184
Nashville (cruiser), 227
Naval Air Auxiliary Air Station (NAAS)
  Hollister, California, 74–77, 91, 278
  Monterey, California, 70–73
Naval Air Station (NAS)
  Barbers Point, Hawaii, 2, 90, 93, 95, 115
  Bermuda, 102
  Hilo, Hawaii, 82–94
  Kaneohe, Hawaii, 94–95, 103–5, 107, 109–11, 115
  Key West, Florida, 102
  Maui, Hawaii, 92
  Miami, Florida, 102–3
  Norman, Oklahoma, 98
Naval Air Training Center, Corpus Christi, Texas, 100–2
Naval Air Training Command, 102
Naval Aviation Cadet Training Program, 95
Navy Cross, 368, 373
Near-vertical dive-bombing techniques, 59–60
Negros Island, Philippines, 47, 179–81, 209, 211, 232, 326

Neighbours, Lieutenant James B. "Jim," 181
Nevada (battleship), 63
New Britain, 126, 128, 133, 141
New Georgia, 133, 152
New Guinea, 5, 101, 125, 126, 128–30, 133, 203, 227
New Jersey (battleship), 3, 37, 152, 203, 218, 272, 278, 293, 294, 351, 353, 354
Nichols Field, Philippines, 340, 350
Night carrier operations, 90–92
Night flying training, 74–75, 91–92, 104
Nimitz, Admiral Chester, 108–9, 125–27, 134, 151, 153, 194, 222
Nink, AEM1c E. J., 376
Nishimura, Vice Admiral Shoji, 234, 263, 264, 271, 274, 277, 286–89, 293
North Africa, 62
North American Aircraft Company, 100
Northrup Corporation, 61
Noshiro (cruiser), 50, 250, 298

Oakland (cruiser), 151, 203
Oakley, Commander T. B., Jr., 356–57
O'Donnell, Ensign Ralph N., 374
Okicich, ARM3c A., 376
Okinawa, 9, 143, 200, 201, 203–6, 208, 224, 234, 367
Oklahoma (battleship), 63, 81
Oldendorf, Rear Admiral Jesse, 228, 229, 231, 263, 278, 286–89
Olongapo, Philippines, 186–87
Olsen, Lieutenant Junior Grade Robert "Ole," 93
Olson, Lieutenant Junior Grade Robert E., 374
Ommaney Bay (escort carrier), 103, 112, 117
Onishi, Vice Admiral Takijiro, 195, 259, 260, 293
Ormoc Bay, Philippines, 197
Ostfriesland (dreadnought), 58
Over-water navigation training, 67, 94
Overland navigation training, 67
Overweight carrier takeoffs, 18–20, 22–23, 28, 40–41, 45–46, 225

Ozawa, Vice Admiral Jisaburo, 50, 132–33, 143, 172, 224, 229, 230, 232–34, 264, 265, 272, 286, 288, 294

P-40s, 186
Pacific Ocean Area, 125–26
Padre, 154–55
Palau Islands, 9, 131, 132, 142, 152–70, 177, 182, 183, 224, 354
Palawan Island, 8, 14, 235, 288, 361
Palembang oil fields, Sumatra, 124, 144, 196
Panama Canal, 136
Panay Island, Philippines, 47, 48, 232, 238, 297, 318, 320, 323–24, 326, 328–50, 357
Pandan Bay, Panay Island, 329, 333, 335, 340, 343, 346, 358
Papua New Guinea, 126, 128, 129
Parachutes, 34–35
Passi, Ensign W. L., 193
Patuxent (fleet oiler), 303
Pearl Harbor, Hawaii, 81, 106, 108, 110–11
  Japanese attack on, 4, 50, 62–64, 81, 123, 124, 127, 147, 153, 263
Peleliu Island, 152, 156, 160, 161, 182–84, 355
Pellish, ARM3c M. E., 376
Pennsylvania (battleship), 228, 263
Pennsylvania (cruiser), 57
Peralta, Macario, 328–29, 331, 335, 338–39, 350
Philippine Army, 4, 326, 337
Philippine Constabulary, 327
Philippine Division, 4, 5
Philippine Insurrection, 331
Philippine Islands, 29, 57, 125, 153
  American invasion of, 3–6, 26, 133–34, 171–73, 197, 203, 227–32, 234, 316
  Bataan Death March, 5
  Cebu Island, 173, 177–79, 187, 194, 197
  Central Visayas, 9, 172, 173, 177–78, 183, 203, 224, 232, 234, 341, 350
  Coron Bay, 9, 196–97
  Corregidor, 5, 125, 366
  guerrilla movement in, 314–20, 323–24, 326–50, 331–37, 339, 340, 343–50, 357–60

Japanese seizure of, 124, 186, 208

Leyte, 8, 133, 173, 177, 178, 197, 227, 231, 232, 234, 236, 263, 286, 354

Luzon, 4, 5, 9, 17, 26, 47, 57, 131–33, 143, 172, 177, 185–94, 227, 230–31, 233, 234, 236, 264, 272, 278, 288, 291, 293, 320, 322, 326

map of area, 149

Mindanao, 5, 47, 133, 152, 154, 173–77, 183, 234, 288, 326

Mindoro, 14, 21, 25, 48, 49, 227, 238, 239, 242, 258, 280, 296, 297

topography of, 47

VT-18 strikes, 9, 14, 15, 17, 21–52, 173–82, 185–94, 196, 231–33, 237, 240–56, 260–61, 265–71, 289–91, 297, 298, 303, 304, 309–14, 322, 340, 351, 354, 355

Philippine Scouts, 324

Philippine Sea, 3, 26, 33, 50, 188, 194, 239, 277, 288

Philippine Sea, Battles of the, 50, 122, 131, 135, 143, 151–53, 171, 172, 208, 325, 367

Pieper, Lieutenant Junior Grade Donald B., 103, 375

Plane captains, 32–35, 38

Plane handlers, 10–11

Plank owners, 110

Point Reyes, California, 68, 69

Ponape Island, 152

Port Moresby, Papua New Guinea, 126–28

Post, Wiley, 98

Pratt & Whitney radial engines, 39

Preble, Commodore Edward, 105

President Quezon's Own Guerrillas, 328

Princeton (light carrier), 151, 259–60, 264, 272, 278, 293, 300

PT boats, 286

Pullout, 166

Pushover, 165

Qing Dynasty, 208

Quezon, Manuel, 4, 328, 338

Rabaul, New Britain, 126, 128, 133, 141

Race, Lieutenant George, 105, 121, 151, 156, 176, 193,

194, 219, 278, 311, 314, 321, 325, 352, 354

Raczynski, AEM1c Bronislaw, 348

Radar, 160, 199, 210, 241

Radio silence, 88, 114

Radio wave technology, 66

Raleigh (cruiser), 63

Ranger (aircraft carrier), 62

Ranger-class carriers, 60

Ready rooms, 11–13

Redeye, Ensign Nicholas T., 375

Regensburg, Germany, 101

Reggio di Calabria, Italy, 101

Relyea, Ensign Charles D., 375

Reno (cruiser), 221–22, 259

Reyes, Franco Vera, 329

Riley, Lieutenant Junior Grade George Benson "Ben," 72, 104, 105, 158–59, 161–69, 200, 204–5, 217, 260, 261, 277, 278, 375

Ritchie, Lieutenant Junior Grade James, 323–24, 331, 333, 334, 340, 343, 364

Robinson, Lieutenant Junior Grade John Lewis "Robbie," 56, 75, 90, 111, 375

Roccaforte, Ensign Nicholas J., 78, 93, 103, 192, 310, 311, 375

Rochefort, Commander Joseph, 127

Roi-Namur, Marshall Islands, 106

Romblon Island, Philippines, 47, 328, 343–44

Roosevelt, Franklin D., 4, 5, 300

at Honolulu Conference, 108–9, 133–34

Royce, AOM2c A. A., 376

Rubin, Lieutenant Junior Grade Joseph L., 70, 75–78, 82, 85–86, 105, 180, 181–82, 209, 213–15, 232, 260, 289, 310, 311, 321, 373, 375

Rubin, Louis, 77

Run-up area (barrier area), 30, 31

Rupertus, Major General William, 153, 183

Russell, AOM3c Wallace H. "Red," 69–70, 72, 79, 92, 147, 158, 209–10, 376

Rybarczyk, ARM2c Albert P., 169, 377

Ryukyu Islands, 203–4, 225

St. John, Ensign Bernard J. "Ben," 23, 40, 111–13, 170, 209, 213–16, 267, 269, 270,

313–14, 351, 354, 367–68, 373, 375

St. Lo (escort carrier), 293, 300

Saipan, Mariana Islands, 131–33, 143, 152, 199, 200

Salamaua, New Guinea, 126

Salerno, Italy, 101

Salinas River valley, California, 74

Samar Island, Philippines, 3, 46–48, 177, 178, 232, 234, 237, 264, 286, 288, 299–300, 323, 326

Samuel B. Roberts (destroyer escort), 292, 300

San Bernardino Strait, Philippines, 26, 37, 234, 236, 262, 264, 271, 274, 277, 288, 289, 293, 297

San Diego (cruiser), 151, 203

San Fernando Point, Philippines, 193

San Jacinto (light carrier), 151

San Jose, Antique, Panay Island, 329, 331

San Jose, Philippines, 4

San Pablo Airfield, Philippines, 178

San Pedro Bay, Philippines, 4

Sangamon (escort carrier), 323

Sanshikidan shells, 266–67

Santa Cruz, Battle of, 50, 228

Santee (escort carrier), 293

Sartwelle, Ensign William H., Jr., 197

Savage, Lieutenant Junior Grade John Joseph, 155–56, 158, 159, 162–63, 165, 166, 168–70, 199, 202, 349, 354, 375

Savo Island, Battle of, 50, 129

SB2C-1 Helldiver dive-bombers, 83

SB2C-3 Helldiver dive-bombers, 9, 14, 16, 27, 31, 32, 39, 46, 68, 82–83, 105, 145, 154, 156–59, 161–62, 164–66, 174–76, 180, 186–88, 191, 193, 196–97, 204, 209, 211–14, 217, 219, 220, 243, 266, 268, 269, 289, 290, 297, 298, 309–12, 340, 355

SBD Dauntless dive-bombers, 61, 82–83, 128

SC-1 torpedo bombers, 59

Schmitz, AOM2c J. J., 376

Schnack, AMM3c H. H., 377

Schonthaler, Lieutenant Junior Grade Kurt W., 73–74, 90, 93, 368, 375

Schoubee, Ensign Richard M., 375
Schrier, ARM3c G., 376
Schuykill (fleet oiler), 223
Schweinfurt, Germany, 101
Scrano, Lieutenant Frank, 13, 14, 94, 105, 111, 267, 277–78
Seabees, 79
"Set material condition Yoke," 16–17
"Set material condition Zebra," 15, 16
Shackelford, Ensign William G. "Shack," 341–46, 350, 361–64
Sharninghouse, AOM2c Ora H., 169, 377
Sherman, Rear Admiral Forrest, 236, 259, 260, 264, 265, 272, 300
Sherman, Rear Admiral Frederick C., 145, 151, 221
Shigure (destroyer), 287
Shima, Vice Admiral Kiyohide, 224–25, 234, 263, 287–89
Shimakaze (destroyer), 250, 275
Shimonoseki, Treaty of (1895), 208
Shinano (aircraft carrier), 140
Shinchiku Airfield, Formosa, 219–21
Sho-1 plan, 196, 225, 229, 230, 233, 263, 264
SHO operations, 134–35
Shokaku (aircraft carrier), 126–27, 133, 290
Shuttle-bombing, 11, 132
Sibutu Passage, Philippines, 361
Sibuyan Island, Philippines, 47, 269, 280, 328
Sibuyan Sea, Philippines, 8, 14–17, 21, 22, 26, 37, 44, 47, 48, 234, 237, 238, 254, 256, 261, 262, 265, 267, 269, 272, 273, 278, 280, 281, 286, 288, 289, 294, 297–99, 304, 316, 343, 350
Sicily, 101
Siegrist, ARM2c George E., 111, 377
Signalmen, 36
Silay Airfield, Negros Island, 180
Silver Star, 373
Simara Island, Philippines, 280, 294
Singapore, 124
Sirrine, AOM3c James S., 66, 377

Sistrunk, Ensign Vernon J., 103, 150, 260, 261, 351, 368, 375
Skate (submarine), 142
Skelly, Lieutenant Junior Grade Raymond J., 6–11, 17, 22, 23, 24, 34, 40, 44, 46, 51, 53, 70, 91, 94, 112, 242–47, 249, 256, 267, 268, 277, 278, 285, 349, 375
Smoke laying, 90, 92
SND Dauntless dive-bombers, 58
SNJ Texans, 72, 100
SNV-1 Vultee "Valiant," 100
Soho (light carrier), 126
Solomon Islands, 5, 125, 128, 129, 141, 153
Solomon Sea, 129
Soryu (aircraft carrier), 127, 128
South China Sea, 124, 125, 186, 201, 207, 235, 356
South Dakota (battleship), 294
Southwest Pacific Area, 125
Spain, AOM1c L. L., Jr., 375
Spanish-American War, 331
Spaulding, Lieutenant Junior Grade Thomas P., 85–86, 375
Sprague, Captain Thomas L., 106
Sprague, Rear Admiral Clifton A. F., 291–94
Sprague, Rear Admiral Thomas, 231, 234, 278
Spruance, Rear Admiral Raymond, 127–29, 132–33, 134, 152, 325
Stack gas turbulence, 118
Start position, 117
Stearman N2S-3 "Yellow Peril," 98–99
Stein, ARM2c R. A., 376
Stephenson, ARM2c W. H., 376
Stepped-down alignment, 45
Stewart, AOM2c George H., 111, 377
Straits of Gibraltar, 62
Subic Bay, 9, 23, 186, 188–91
Sullivans, The (destroyer), 151
Sulu Sea, Philippines, 143, 263, 361
Sumatra, 124
Surigao Strait, Philippines, 234, 262, 263, 272, 286, 287, 289, 293
Survival gear, 25, 34
Sutherland, Lieutenant General R. K., 335
Suwannee (escort carrier), 293

Suzuya (cruiser), 50, 298
Switchology, 84–85, 86, 89, 163
Swordfish torpedo bombers, 62

Tablas Island, Philippines, 48–49, 239, 241, 258, 260, 280, 328
Tablas Strait, Philippines, 17, 26, 37, 48–50, 238, 240, 242, 280, 286, 296, 297, 316, 319, 343, 359, 361
Tabung Point, Panay Island, 329
Tacloban, Philippines, 4, 5, 178, 194, 231, 232, 354, 355
Taffy groups, 288, 289, 291–93, 297, 299, 300
Taiho (aircraft carrier), 133
Tail dragger, 43–44
Tail hook, 116, 120
Taiwan, 207, 208
Takao (cruiser), 235, 236, 298
Takeoff area forward (catapult area), 30, 31
Tansui River, Formosa, 209, 211, 212, 216, 218
Tapei, Formosa, 209
Taranto, Italy, 62, 63
Tarawa, Gilbert Islands, 101, 129, 133
Task Force 16, 127
Task Force 17, 127
Task Force 38, 22, 37, 151–54, 156, 170, 173–74, 177–78, 182–84, 185–86, 194, 203–6, 209, 221, 225, 230–32, 234, 272–73, 286, 288, 292, 293
Task Force 58, 132, 143, 325
Task Group 12.3.2, 122
Task Group 19.11, 113, 120–21
Task Group 30.3, 222
Task Group 38.1, 151, 199, 235, 236, 260, 278, 303
Task Group 38.2, 3, 6, 9, 13, 22, 23, 37, 39, 151, 194, 201–4, 209–22, 224–25, 235–37, 278, 289, 293, 297, 303, 321–22, 325, 350, 355
Task Group 38.3, 26, 151, 221, 232, 236, 259, 260, 264, 265, 267, 268, 272, 278, 294
Task Group 38.4, 26, 151, 221, 236, 260, 263, 266, 268, 278, 294
Task Group 58.2, 105
Task Unit 12.3.2, 145, 148, 150
Tassafaronga Strait, Battle of, 129
Tawi-Tawi Island, 143, 361

Tayabas, Philippines, 335
TBD-1 Devastator torpedo
  bombers, 60, 61, 63, 64
TBF-1 Avengers, 54–55
TBM-1C Avengers, 9, 14, 15, 17,
  21, 63, 102, 145. (*see also*
  specific pilots)
  antisubmarine patrol (ASP),
    122, 199
  APX-2 IFF equipment, 113
  Babelthuap strikes, 158–69
  bird strikes, 69
  bombing techniques, 68–69
  carrier landing pattern,
    114–20
  cockpit equipment, 35
  cockpit escape procedures,
    253, 254, 313
  compared to Devastators, 64
  construction, 33–34
  engine, 33, 35, 38–39, 42–43
  flap retraction, 44
  flying by dead reckoning,
    66–67, 102, 199, 216
  Formosa strikes, 9, 209, 210,
    212–17, 219–21
  launch sequence, 36, 38
  machine guns, 85
  mechanical idiosyncracies,
    198–99
  Okinawa strikes, 9, 204–6
  overweight takeoffs, 18–20,
    22–23, 28, 40–41, 45–46,
    225
  paint color, 32
  Palau Island strikes, 152–70
  Peleliu strikes, 184
  Philippine strikes, 9, 14, 15,
    17, 21–52, 173–82, 185–94,
    196, 231–33, 237, 240–56,
    260–61, 265–71, 289–91,
    297, 298, 303, 304, 309–14,
    322, 340, 351, 354, 355
  prestart checklist, 35
  procedures of carrier
    departure, 27–28
  rendezvous after takeoff,
    44–46
  rocket guns, 84, 85
  survival equipment, 25, 34
  takeoff checklist, 42
  training, 66–77, 84–93
  turret gunner characteristics,
    69–70
  wings, 41
Telliard, AOM2c W. J., 377
Tennessee (battleship), 263
Teraoka, Vice Admiral Kimpei,
  172, 174, 194, 195
TG-2 torpedo bombers, 59

Thach Weave, 159
Thailand, 125
Thompson, Lieutenant William
  R., 312
Thvedt, Lieutenant John A.,
  217
Ticao Island, Philippines, 47
Tight-formation flying, 20
Tinian, 131–33, 152
T3M torpedo bombers, 59, 62
Tokyo, Doolittle raid on, 54
Tokyo Rose, 194, 222, 299, 300
Tone (cruiser), 50, 292, 293
Torp Cocktail, 187
Torpedo attack, history of, 57–58
Torpedo attack training, 86–87
Torpedo Squadron 1 (VT-1), 59,
  64
Torpedo Squadron 2 (VT-2), 59
Torpedo Squadron 3 (VT-3), 63,
  64
Torpedo Squadron 6 (VT-6), 63,
  64
Torpedo Squadron 8 (VT-8), 63,
  64
Torpedo Squadron 11 (VT-11),
  303
Torpedo Squadron 18 (VT-18).
  (*see also Intrepid*)
  aircraft of (*see* TBM-1C
    Avengers), 9
  antiaircraft fire against,
    174–75, 177, 181, 183, 189,
    210–12, 217, 220, 240–50,
    256, 260, 261, 267, 268,
    270, 277, 298, 299, 322
  antisubmarine patrol duty
    (ASP), 122, 199, 235, 321
  awards and roster, 368,
    373–77
  bad weather carrier landings,
    193–94
  baggage of, 109
  casualties and accidents, 66,
    69, 77, 104, 111, 150,
    168–70, 181, 193, 197, 204,
    206, 212, 216–18, 220,
    232–33, 253, 254, 285, 298,
    311, 312, 374
  CIS committee, 56, 73
  commanding officer of (see
    Van Antwerp, Lieutenant
    Commander Lloyd Wilbert
    "Van")
  commissioned, 6, 53
  competition with Air Group
    20, 145
  enemy fighters against,
    179–83, 191–92, 194,
    212–17, 309–11, 322

  first torpedo strike by, 187
  Fletcher assigned to, 7
  formation of, 53, 54
  in Hawaii, 81–95, 103–5,
    107–9
  Japanese cargo ships and,
    179
  message drops by, 146
  nickname of, 146–47
  nonflying officers, 12
  pilot dress, 11
  possibility of capture and,
    155–56, 173
  preparations for first strike by,
    154–55
  procedures of carrier
    departure, 27–28
  radio call sign of, 147
  ready room, 11–13
  requalification for carrier duty,
    103
  return to U.S., 365
  search-and-rescue missions by,
    146
  statistics on flying hours and
    sorties of, 325
  stress of combat operations
    and, 320–21
  strikes by (*see* TBM-1C
    Avengers)
  torpedo attack technique, 15
  training and, 20–21, 55–57,
    65–66, 67–77, 82–94,
    103–6, 111, 120–21
  transport to Hawaii, 78–81
  war games and, 150
Torpedo Squadron 19 (VT-19),
  79, 81
Torpedo Squadron 27 (VT-27),
  278
Torpex, 14
Toyoda, Admiral Soemu, 123,
  124, 130–32, 134, 143,
  144, 171, 172, 196, 208,
  222, 225, 228–30, 233,
  271, 277, 293
Truk Atoll, Caroline Islands,
  106, 126, 133, 141, 142,
  153
Tsushima Strait, Battle of, 123,
  228
Tunny (submarine), 142
Two-blocking, 36

Ulithi Island, Caroline Islands,
  9, 200–3, 222, 235, 236,
  260, 303, 320, 321–23, 325,
  355
Unbalanced vee formation, 28,
  46

United States forces. (*see also* Carrier Air Group 18 ; Torpedo Squadron 18)
  1st Marine Division, 153, 182–84
  3rd Fleet, 21, 37, 134, 150, 152, 173, 203, 209, 222, 224–25, 228, 234, 236, 264, 300, 320, 355
  5th Fleet, 134, 152
  Sixth Army, 4
  7th Fleet, 4, 6, 134, 203, 227, 236, 263, 288, 300, 327, 356
  8th Air Force, 101
  81st Infantry Division, 184
  Armed Forces East (USAFFE), 324, 326, 327, 329, 330
  Army Air Corps, 54, 101
  birth of naval aviation, 57
  Bureau of Aeronautics, 58–60, 78
  Marines, 92, 101, 128–29, 148, 153, 156, 182–84, 200
Ursch, Ensign Ralph R., 375
Urukthapel Island, 152

Van Antwerp, Lieutenant Commander Lloyd Wilbert "Van"
  background of, 55
  command of VT-18, 20–21, 54–56
  ferry flight to *Intrepid* and, 112–14, 116
  Formosa strikes and, 209–16, 218
  leadership approach of, 73
  Philippine strikes and, 197, 232, 237, 260, 289, 290, 298–99, 310–11
  physical appearance of, 55
  reshuffling of personnel by, 104
  retirement of, 367
  as temporary air group commander, 321
  training of pilots and, 67–68, 71, 74, 75, 90, 91, 93, 111, 169, 181

Van Dyke, Lieutenant R. D., 215
Vannais, Lieutenant Junior Grade Leon S., 74–75, 76, 107, 223, 375
Vaughn, ARM3c Louis D., 298
Vaughn, Lieutenant Junior Grade Elmer B. "Squatty," 24, 40, 46, 53, 70, 78–79, 82, 85–86, 91, 93, 112, 146, 174, 175, 179, 187–89, 191, 242–46, 256, 314, 368, 375
Vee of vees formation, 159
Vella Lavella, 133
Veracruz expedition, 57
Vincennes (cruiser), 3, 151, 203, 351
Visayan Sea, 179, 329
Vitiaz Strait, 126
VT-18 (*see* Torpedo Squadron 18)
Vulture's Row, 40, 41

Wagner, AOM2c R. L., 376
Wake Island, 142
Wallace, ARM3c G. W., 376
Wallenbeck, Ensign Donald E., 375
Washington (battleship), 294
Washington Naval Treaty, 137, 140
Wasp (aircraft carrier), 129, 151
Wave-off, 71, 114, 116, 118, 119
Wavell, General Archibald, 125
Weatherwax, Lieutenant Commander J. C., 363
Webster, Ensign Harry W., 216
West Virginia (battleship), 63, 263, 287
Western Pacific, map of, xii
Westmoreland, ARM3c Robert G., 24, 34–35, 41, 42, 48, 116, 160, 163–64, 190, 191, 199, 221, 241–47, 249, 251, 254, 285, 295–97, 349, 377
White phosphorus, 51
White Plains (escort carrier), 292, 293
Whitney, General Courtney, 327
Wilder, Second Lieutenant John M., 342–43

Williams, Ensign Owen F., 103, 157, 375
Williams, Lieutenant John G. "Bud," 7, 22, 23, 27–28, 40–41, 44, 46, 49–52, 53, 55, 70, 72, 78, 90, 91, 93, 94, 104, 105, 157, 169, 174–77, 179, 182, 187–89, 191, 217, 221, 240–44, 256, 267, 268, 270, 289, 290, 311–14, 354, 367, 375
Williams, Lieutenant John Wesley, 343, 344, 346, 356, 360, 364
Wilson, Woodrow, 57
Wind speed, 39
Window, 210–11, 220, 221
Winters, Commander T. H., 289–90
World War I, 57, 58, 153
Wright Cyclone R260020 engine, 33, 38–39, 41, 42

Yamamoto, Admiral Isoroku, 50, 141
Yamashiro (battleship), 286, 287
Yamato (battleship), 124, 135–37, 140–44, 172, 229, 230, 233, 234, 238, 241, 265, 273, 288, 293, 343, 366, 367
Yamato-class battleships, 26, 27, 37, 50, 51, 135–37, 139, 140, 142, 144, 241, 268, 272, 299
Yap Island, Caroline Islands, 131, 132
Yokosuka Naval Base, Japan, 141
Yontan Airfield, Okinawa, 205
Yorktown (aircraft carrier), 63, 87, 126–28
Yoshihito, Emperor, 153
Young, ARM2c William Patrick, 150, 377

Zeigler, Ensign Luther L., 375
Zuiho (aircraft carrier), 290, 299
Zuiho-class carriers, 290
Zuikaku (aircraft carrier), 126, 133, 141, 290, 299

ABOUT THE AUTHOR

Gregory G. Fletcher served as a naval aviator from 1969 to 1974, and he is now a practicing attorney. He is the son of USS *Intrepid* pilot Will Fletcher, who was awarded a Navy Cross of heroism for his actions in World War II.